Switched On

Also by Albert Glinsky
Theremin: Ether Music and Espionage

Switched On

Bob Moog and the Synthesizer Revolution

ALBERT GLINSKY

Foreword by Francis Ford Coppola

OXFORD
UNIVERSITY PRESS

Oxford University Press is a department of the University of Oxford. It furthers the University's objective of excellence in research, scholarship, and education by publishing worldwide. Oxford is a registered trade mark of Oxford University Press in the UK and certain other countries.

Published in the United States of America by Oxford University Press
198 Madison Avenue, New York, NY 10016, United States of America.

© Albert Glinsky 2022

All rights reserved. No part of this publication may be reproduced, stored in a retrieval system, or transmitted, in any form or by any means, without the prior permission in writing of Oxford University Press, or as expressly permitted by law, by license, or under terms agreed with the appropriate reproduction rights organization. Inquiries concerning reproduction outside the scope of the above should be sent to the Rights Department, Oxford University Press, at the address above.

You must not circulate this work in any other form
and you must impose this same condition on any acquirer.

Library of Congress Cataloging-in-Publication Data
Names: Glinsky, Albert, author.
Title: Switched on : Bob Moog and the synthesizer revolution / Albert Glinsky.
Description: [1.] | New York : Oxford University Press, 2022. |
Includes index.
Identifiers: LCCN 2022008555 (print) | LCCN 2022008556 (ebook) |
ISBN 9780197642078 (hardback) | ISBN 9780197642092 (epub)
Subjects: LCSH: Moog, Bob (Robert) | Electronic musical instrument makers—United States—Biography. | Synthesizer (Musical instrument)—History.
Classification: LCC ML424.M69 G55 2022 (print) | LCC ML424.M69 (ebook) |
DDC 786.7/419092 [B]—dc23
LC record available at https://lccn.loc.gov/2022008555
LC ebook record available at https://lccn.loc.gov/2022008556

DOI: 10.1093/oso/9780197642078.001.0001

3 5 7 9 8 6 4

Printed by Lakeside Book Company, United States of America

To Linda, Luka, and Allegra,
and
to Bob Moog,
wave maker supreme

Contents

Foreword ix
    Francis Ford Coppola
Prelude xi

PART I. THE FLUSHING GEEK

1. Depression's Child 3
2. Bronx Cheers 17
3. Our Guarantee 25
4. No Exit 37

PART II. SLIPPING BACKWARDS ON A BANANA PEEL

5. Transistor Man and the Crusaders 45
6. Do It Yourself 56
7. The Abominatron 66
8. A Eunuch in a Harem 80
9. A Few Thousand Screws 89

PART III. COSMIC SOUNDS

10. Hallucinations for Your Ear 101
11. The Star Collector 119
12. Long Live the Moog! 133
13. Hello, HAL 146
14. The Plastic Cow Goes Moooooog 163
15. Socket to Me, Baby! 175

PART IV. SHORT CIRCUITS

16. Panicsville	189
17. Mini and the Beast	201
18. A Palace Revolution	221
19. The Island of Electronicus	235
20. I Bought Bob Moog	248

PART V. AN APOCALYPSE NOW

21. The Gelatin Pit	263
22. Vexations	280
23. Genericide	292
24. Yankee Go Home	306
25. The Briar Patch	318

PART VI. THE GRAND POOBAH

26. Genius for Hire	331
27. Comes Now the Defendant	344
28. The Desperate Voyager	357
29. Patron Saint of Electrogeeks	367
30. The Show That Never Ends	381

Postlude	395
Acknowledgments	401
Notes	407
Index	451

Foreword
Francis Ford Coppola

Of all ironies, the gentle music of Claude Debussy was my entry point into the soundtrack for *Apocalypse Now*. I had heard Isao Tomita's 1974 album, *Snowflakes Are Dancing*, a reinterpretation of the French Impressionist composer's music on a Moog synthesizer. Debussy's familiar melodies and harmonies were present, and yet distant at the same time—recognizable, but heard through the new possibility of electronic sound manipulation. Somehow, that album planted the seeds for the soundtrack of *Apocalypse Now*.

To test the idea, I invited George Lucas and Walter Murch to my home—Walter would be the Director of Soundtrack for *Apocalypse Now*. I sat them down in my screening room, turned out the lights, and played them Tomita's quadrophonic record entirely in the dark. By the time we switched the lights back on, Walter had intuited what I was after. It was the key to building a soundtrack that could hold its own with the visual experience of *Apocalypse Now*.

The decision to go ahead with the Moog didn't obviate the need for a conventional score, of course. For that, I turned to my father, Carmine Coppola, a Juilliard-trained composer who had played solo flute in the NBC Symphony Orchestra under Arturo Toscanini. My father's passion was composition and he had already written music for my earlier *Godfather* films. When I approached him about the score for *Apocalypse Now*, I explained that this project would be handled somewhat differently. He would compose the music, but instead of orchestrating it for traditional instruments, I would personally hand it over to our team of synthesists who would realize it on the Moog and other type synthesizers.

When Carmine's score was completed, the synthesizer experts, now all legendary—Patrick Gleeson, Bernie Krause, Don Preston, and Nyle Steiner—went to work. Their job was daunting. It was my thought to orchestrate each line of Carmine's score not with orchestral instruments, but with the sounds of the jungle and warfare. The strings would be the wind, the bass would be the "wop wop" of helicopter blades. I had imagined the very sound of Vietnam warfare as a recurring motif. I wanted to capture the whine of bullets, the scream of jets, the whir of helicopters. The Moog gave us the ability to roll sound effects and music into one.

The drama of filming *Apocalypse Now* is well known. The cast and crew were hit with everything from typhoons to heart attacks. The synthesizer team had their own parallel drama, and the artistic disputes that broke out among them were heated. As Bob Moog once remarked, "many tempers were maimed, and egos battered" in the process. It could hardly have been otherwise, given that we'd assembled an ad hoc group of super-charged synthesists from the San Francisco area and tasked them with building this impossibly difficult, experimental soundtrack. Working practically around the clock, in uncharted territory, they struggled in tedious monophonic work, note by note. They could spend days on a single cue, only to have it wiped out altogether in favor of another idea.

The unique synthesized score broke even more ground when it debuted in theaters using a pioneering sound design scheme. *Apocalypse Now* was the first film to be released in what is called "5.1 format." During the production of the film, Walter Murch had worked with Dolby Laboratories to design a sound system that would deliver a more vivid experience to theater audiences. The result was an array of five speakers positioned around the theater: three in the front (left, center, and right), and two in the back (left and right). After *Apocalypse Now*, 5.1 surround sound became the industry standard for film and digital broadcast media. It remains so to this day.

In 2006, *Apocalypse Now* was re-released in a boxed set that included the original 1979 version along with a newer version, *Apocalypse Now Redux*. The set included several features documenting the making of the film. One of them, *The Music of Apocalypse Now*, concluded with a dedication to Bob Moog, who had passed away the year before. As we noted: "The instrument used in the film's score was the largest Moog synthesizer in existence at that time." That instrument gave us the ability to conceive the soundtrack to *Apocalypse Now* as an entity in itself—one that joined with the film, and was at least as important as the film.

Prelude

On a sticky summer night in 1969, under a full moon, 3,000 fans squeezed shoulder to shoulder, jockeying for any spot they could find. Latecomers perched on statues or dangled from trees. Through a haze of pot smoke they craned their necks to get a glimpse of the jazz combo's gear: not pianos, drums, or guitars, but *machines*. A truckload of black boxes, wires, amps, and speakers were plugged into a single electrical outlet—the only one in the Garden. Toward the end of the show, when the band tore into a high-energy improv, a woman stood up on the housing of the electrical socket for a better view. Slipping off, she accidentally kicked out the plug that fed every piece of equipment. The machines went dead, and the last of the deafening licks echoed into silence. For a heart-stopping moment the musicians froze. But the crowd, figuring the set was planned that way, erupted in cheers. Bob Moog, the young inventor of the machines, called the show.

A woman's foot had switched off the first-ever all-synthesizer concert, a much-buzzed-about event at the Sculpture Garden of New York's Museum of Modern Art. Reviewers had fun with the mishap—*Socket to Me, Baby!*—but the incident exposed the downside of the radical new technology: no juice, no sound. Yet beyond that, the crowd could see for itself what the future might look like: music without instruments, forged completely in towers of equipment, driven by electricity coursing through circuits.[1]

The Moog synthesizer could mimic any sound, from trumpets to rain to the rumbling of a helicopter. It could conjure sounds no one had ever heard before—anything you could dream up in the mind's ear. The very idea drove the musicians' union nuts. Was this the end for musicians? If you could synthesize a band or an orchestra, what was next? Gone would be the shimmying lead guitarist, or the self-absorbed drummer flailing wildly, or section violinists gliding their bows in unison in giant orchestras. Now, just a few players, hunched over electronic keyboards tethered to panels dripping with cords and dotted with knobs, could do the work of legions of musicians. There was something mildly alienating about a musical instrument that looked like the console of a spaceship. But many musicians were beginning to plug into the synthesizer revolution, and there was no turning back.

With its nearly infinite palette of new sounds, the Moog synthesizer arrived at the right moment. It was the perfect soundtrack for the technicolor '60s. For millions watching the televised coverage of the first moon landing, it painted the deep caverns of outer space. It was a mind-expanding aural backdrop for drug trips. As a space age techno-hallucinogenic toy, it was taken up by groups like the Beatles, the Doors, the Byrds, and the Monkees. It hit the big screen as an off-color underscore for movies featuring aberrant human behavior in classics like *Apocalypse Now* and *A Clockwork Orange*.

With *Switched-On Bach*, an LP that soared in the charts and won platinum status, the Moog inspired dozens of "switched-on" album arrangements of everything from country songs to Christmas carols. In the '70s, the Moog was a regular in Stevie Wonder's stable of instruments, and a defining sound in the "krautrock" genre with groups like Kraftwerk and Tangerine Dream. When disco adopted the Moog in Donna Summer's 1977 hit, "I Feel Love," the electronic dance music movement dawned, and led to electro, house, and other EDM styles. Even establishment-heavy Madison Avenue co-opted the Moog magic for a new subliminal voice in hundreds of TV ads and sound logos.

By the mid-'70s, the term "Moog synthesizer" had entered the dictionary along with recent inductees like "space capsule" and "miniskirt." The name, with its cool double-o in the middle, came to be spelled with a lower case "m," and used as a noun or a verb. It even became a generic term for synthesizers; a competitor showing his own synth once, had audience members asking, "Isn't that what is called the Moog Synthesizer?"[2]

Behind this revolutionary device was one man: Bob Moog himself inspired a mythology that bordered on the fanatical. At a festival once I witnessed a fan stagger toward him in disbelief: *"Wow! Bob Moog! I thought you'd be BEAMED DOWN . . ."* Bob's daughter Michelle remembered an admirer approaching him at a convention and kneeling down like he was saluting the Pope. Bob's image—with that memorably contoured face, deeply penetrating eyes, and wiry mane of Einstein hair—was lionized on psychedelic posters.

Yet up close, Robert Arthur Moog was an unlikely cult figure. He was a modest, 1950s geek who could never have envisioned his deification by 1960s acidheads. He preferred classical music and poring over circuit diagrams, and his sartorial style ran to shlumpy shirts and pocket protectors. Built like an overgrown teddy bear, he was big and padded, with a genial air. Poking through the gentle exterior was a humor that ran to the bawdy and scatological—a teddy bear with a potty mouth.

Bob was intense and complex, filled with contradictions. He was a techie through and through, with engineering degrees from the Ivy Leagues, but he was never the stereotypical a-religious scientist. His life passed from one spiritual tribe to another, from his roots in Judaism, on to Ethical Culture, Unitarianism, and back to Judaism, with stop-offs for Native American ritual and parapsychology. Toward the end of his life, he even felt ambivalent about his own achievements and the Pandora's box he'd opened up. Without asking for the job, he'd become a spokesman for a plug-it-in-and-switch-it-on musical culture, and he often had a nagging discomfort with its social outcomes.

Moog fans might be surprised to learn that Bob didn't always appreciate the over-the-top adulation of fans—it could make him downright irascible. Fundamentally he was an introvert who squinted uncomfortably in the spotlight. He habitually downplayed his celebrity; his own children, growing up, had little awareness of his iconic status. At school once, his daughter Renée happened upon his bio in the *Encyclopedia Britannica* when the class was leafing through one of the volumes. "Isn't that your dad?" another student asked.[3]

For all his hallowed status, Bob didn't invent the synthesizer. The first synth-like instrument was actually Thaddeus Cahill's behemoth 1897 Telharmonium that used huge, rotating electro-mechanical wheels to generate sounds that could be played from a keyboard, long before radio technology made the same results practical with the invention of the palm-sized vacuum tube. And the first devices widely referred to as "synthesizers" preceded Bob's work by about 10 years: the RCA Mark I and Mark II were one-off monsters, each capable of sophisticated sound synthesis, but impossibly difficult to operate, immovable from the large rooms they occupied, and valued in the $25,000 range in the 1950s.

While the RCA leviathans were being developed, Bob was still a nerdy college student tinkering with hobbyist projects in a home basement workshop with his dad. Together, the two made original models of the strange, 1920s-era theremin, the electronic musical instrument played by waving the hands near its two antennas, without ever touching it. In 1963, while slogging through a Ph.D. program in engineering physics at Cornell, Bob still had no idea what direction his life would take. A chance meeting with a Long Island music professor led to some audio experiments, just for fun, and out of those sessions, Bob's first synthesizer prototype was born: a rudimentary collection of "modules" that could perform various sound functions more effectively than earlier attempts at carving music out of electronic sound.

Over the next few years, Bob refined his system, adding new modules requested by musicians, until his celebrated "voltage controlled analog modular synthesizer" emerged. The device offered a brilliant and efficient method of electronically generating, controlling, and shaping sounds, packaged, for the first time, in an accessible system. It opened up electronic music to musicians outside the walls of academia and the avant-garde, and eventually to musicians of every stripe, who scattered seeds of the new sounds throughout the culture, where they blossomed into our modern musical soundscape.

As the founder of the synth industry, Bob enjoyed a few early years of unrivaled dominance. But once the winds he'd set in motion had drifted into the culture, storm clouds of imitators moved in. It wasn't long before his instruments were swept up in the tempest of the digital revolution and blown away by Japanese competition in the '80s. Quickly bumped off their pioneering pedestal, they were exiled to the outskirts of the field in less than 20 years. Then, in the late '90s, they came thundering back to a treasured spot as "vintage" classics. It turned out that many musicians found the clean sound of digital synths *too* clean—sanitized—lacking the character of the "dirtier" analog tone, the elusive primal sound that defined the first synths. It's the sound that Moogs are still coveted for today.

Bob's storied career as "father of the synthesizer" was nothing he'd planned for, and he often joked about his accidental success. Part of the reason for that success was the classic fate of "being at the right place at the right time." Conditions were favorable in 1964, and his work plugged easily into the Zeitgeist. He himself acknowledged that if his synth had debuted 10 years earlier, people might not have known what to do with it. But in the 1960s, his instrument was like striking a match in a dry forest—it made the whole place catch fire.

No sooner had Bob's original prototype come off the workbench than customers began lining up to buy more of the systems. Ready or not, Bob was suddenly in business. But manufacturing synthesizers, he quickly learned, was a logistical nightmare. It wasn't like making T-shirts. It meant stocking thousands of parts, and the instruments were all built by hand. It was a new, untested industry and he was the first one out in the field, plowing a path through unknown terrain. The sudden demand for his work took him by surprise.

Running a business was always anathema to Bob. He was a dreamer who loved to linger in the warm bath of ideas, uninterested in stamping out mass-produced units. He was much more interested in hewing to the scientific spirit of pursuing an idea wherever it might lead, regardless of deadlines, success, or money. And he'd never abandoned the hobbyist ethos of his youth—the unwritten law of giving away ideas, of sharing everything with the brotherhood of tinkerers—happily publishing recipes for his discoveries in prominent electronics magazines.

Bob's passion for fine wood cabinetry, dating back to the days in his dad's basement workshop, carried over into his instruments, which he approached with the love of a luthier sculpting priceless violins and guitars. He considered himself a "toolmaker" at the service of individual musicians, listening to their needs and tweaking his designs to taste. And he was easily distracted by forays down rabbit holes to explore one-off custom projects. His mind was usually a million miles away from his factory. His friend and sales distributor, Walter Sear, once remarked, "Sometimes Bob forgot he *had* a business."[4]

Still, to the outside world Bob Moog looked like the prototypical American success story—a corporate titan sitting atop a company like IBM or AT&T. Musicians naturally took advantage of that perception, trying to wangle free equipment or strike some sort of a deal in exchange for taking a synth on tour or featuring one on a record. Keith Emerson, of Emerson, Lake, and Palmer, one of Bob's heartiest advocates, made a bid for a complimentary instrument, but—no deal. Ditto for Frank Zappa, and many others.

And here, *I* have to take a number and get on line, too. In 2000, my biography of Leon Theremin, inventor of the electronic musical instrument that bears his name, was published with a foreword written by Bob. At lectures and book signings I was hoping to have a brand-new Moog theremin to take along, and I called Bob to ask if I could have a freebie—the instrument listed for $369. I assured him I'd give his theremin, and his company, plenty of exposure. There was dead silence on the line. I thought we'd been disconnected. I waited a few beats longer, and then my answer came: "That'll be $369." It was OK. I was happy to pay, and I promptly forgot about it.

A decade later, I recalled that exchange as I went through Bob's archives—poring over yellowed documents stashed in cardboard boxes in his basement—and I suddenly put two and two together. I was gobsmacked when I realized what had really been going on during our phone conversation. At the moment I'd asked Bob for a free theremin his company was on life support. Few of us outside the firm had any idea. But on the inside, every dollar counted. Bob wasn't being stingy or mean—he simply needed every bit of the $369.

As I dug further, I realized this wasn't an anomaly. It was the story of Bob's life and every single company he'd ever run. He could never seem to parlay his professional triumphs into any financial stability. Everyone else seemed to be profiting from his synthesizer but him. While Keith Emerson played to a crowd of 600,000 at the Isle of Wight, firing cannons from the stage and thrashing around in "freak-outs" with his "Monster Moog," Bob was desperately scrambling to build the hip new gear, working from his rough-and-ready little factory in the provincial village of Trumansburg, New York. The composer Mort Garson earned $20,000 for a commercial in which he literally played one note on the Moog, while Bob himself struggled to pay for his daughter's dance lessons. As his company ate up greater and greater portions of the family's assets, he continued foraging for any way to feed the business. I still recall how friends were slack-jawed when I told them that Bob was nearly broke most of his professional life. "How could that be?" they wondered. I understood their perception: the impact of Bob's contribution remains indelible in the public consciousness, and we typically assume fortune follows fame.

As a scientist working the rungs of the corporate world, Bob wrestled with shifting technologies, ruthless competition, global markets, and fickle consumers, all to deliver a beloved product for a grateful but unsuspecting public. Ultimately, the success of his synthesizers can't be measured in simple sales numbers. His classic instrument, the Minimoog—the first fully integrated compact synthesizer, which set the standard for most small electronic keyboards to follow—sold its complete run of about 12,000 units in just over 10 years. To put that into perspective, Yamaha sold the same number of its digital DX-7s in less than three months. Moog synthesizers existed in smaller numbers, but they exerted an outsized cultural influence. In the end, that legacy is what mattered most to Bob.

Beyond the arc of his career, and his turmoil-ridden personal life, Bob's story is also a microcosm of enduring questions we continue to grapple with: the complete electrification of our lives, business ethics, and the personal price of entrepreneurial risk.

In 2002, the publication of *Analog Days: The Invention and Impact of the Moog Synthesizer*, by Trevor Pinch and Frank Trocco, marked the first traversal of Bob's career and the cultural influence of his synthesizer up to 1972. The present book spans the entire personal and professional sweep of Bob's 71 years until his death in 2005, and is the first to be able to draw on an exceptional resource: Bob's personal archive. That vast storehouse of documents, which Bob's family generously put at my exclusive disposal, unraveled the mysteries and myths of his career, and revealed a more intimate view of the man and his circumstances than had ever been seen before.

Another essential resource I drew upon was the series of new interviews I conducted which added much color and nuance—even if, at times, an individual's recall of events from decades earlier wasn't always accurate. In trying to pin down the truth, descriptions of events often needed to be corroborated by other interviewees, and solid documentary evidence. In any showdown between oral testimony and written documentation, the written evidence has been my lodestar. With the infusion of these numerous new resources, Moog aficionados will find many of the commonly accepted stories and claims overturned here, or told in a different way.

∾∾∾

It's customary to eulogize people by saying that they "live on in their work," and we all understand that phrase to be meant figuratively. With Bob, I take that expression literally. More than once, he spoke in almost mystical terms of how he "connected" with his instruments, and could actually sense what was going on inside the circuits. He had a strong bond with them, and—yes—he felt that they retained a "memory" of him.

If there's a vestige of Bob to be found in his instruments, it's not a stretch to say that there's a vestige of him in the pages of this book as well. Bob was a spectacular writer—funny, disarming, and honest. He should have written an autobiography. Absent that possibility, I've tried to let him speak for himself as much as possible. His personality comes through so palpably in his writings and interviews that I couldn't deprive the reader of the chance to exclaim, "Oh, that's classic Bob!" when recognizing one of his typically laugh-out-loud or pithy turns of phrase.

When word got out in 2005 that Bob was dying, his son set up a CaringBridge webpage to offer friends a way to communicate their thoughts. The family was stunned when the page mushroomed into an outpouring of international grief: in slightly over one month, 80,000 people signed on to leave comments and tributes, 20,000 alone on the day Bob died. "Thank you for the sounds," they said. And, "You truly changed the world." For better or worse—he wasn't always sure which—Bob Moog helped create the musical universe we live in today.

PART I
THE FLUSHING GEEK

1
Depression's Child

Mr. Moog fathered a child out of wedlock. The mother was happy enough to raise the baby by herself, but she wanted nothing more to do with the father. In fact, she took him to court, and won. It was a rare victory for a single woman. Moog was ordered to sign over all his possessions to her, including property he owned, "along with all future earnings, inheritances, and fortunes that might come his way."[1] Then she drove him out of town.

The mother raised her child alone, but she died when the boy was nineteen. With no remaining family, he determined to seek his future abroad. On the shores of his adopted country, along with his baggage, he would unload the full weight of his family karma. Through his bloodline, fortunes would be won and lost, marriages would be consummated and torn apart, and vast legal wars would drag on, ending in smug victories and humiliating defeats.

Georg Conrad Moog arrived at the Castle Garden immigration station in New York City on August 6, 1869, the survivor of a traumatic childhood. He'd never known his father, Jacob Moog, and he and his mother, Juliane Becker (who herself had been born out of wedlock), had been shamed and ostracized in the small German town of Wenkbach, where Georg was born in 1849. Coming to America, he escaped with his skin, ducking out of the draft on the eve of the Franco-Prussian War.

By 1876 Georg was a successful New York restaurateur, opening Die Post-Keller in Manhattan at 229 Broadway, on the future site of the Woolworth Building. Die Post-Keller was an elegant restaurant with fine wines, liquors, and cigars. Georg took great pride in his work and was celebrated in the food business. But he drove himself too hard and developed heart trouble. After he turned the day-to-day operations over to others, a business partner absconded with the profits. At age 47 he succumbed to a sudden heart attack and was buried in a Lutheran cemetery in Queens. His widow and three children tried without luck to run the restaurant, and were forced to sell it.

Flushing, Queens. Fall 1934.

A woman pushed a stroller. Her baby boy had bright blue eyes and little platinum blond curls. His name was Robert, but she liked to call him Robbie. She considered him her "prized possession." She went out of her way to walk the half-mile from her home to the supermarket to show him off, hoping everyone would notice what a "handsome couple" they made.[2]

Robert Arthur Moog came into the world on the morning of May 23, 1934, at Flushing Hospital. Two-and-a-half hours later the infamous outlaws Bonnie and Clyde were gunned down in a hail of bullets in Louisiana. It was the middle of the Great Depression, with a gutted economy. The serial rampage of bank heists prompted the FBI that year to take down other notorious gangsters as well: John Dillinger ("Public Enemy No. 1"), Baby Face Nelson, and Pretty Boy Floyd. But American popular culture pressed on. Along with Robbie, 1934 saw the debut of Donald Duck, Shirley Temple, the Three Stooges, and the Flash Gordon comic strip.

Robbie might have been named "George," following the ancestral line of Georges who came before him: his father was George Conrad; his grandfather was George Alfred; and his great grandfather, the restaurateur, was Georg Conrad. But his parents broke with the family tradition. His last name—originally of Dutch origin—was pronounced "Mogue" in Germany. But in the United States, the family surrendered to the Americanized pronunciation, "Mooog."

***

The restaurateur's son, George Alfred, had married another German émigré, Freda Ott. The couple had two children: George Conrad (Robbie's dad), born November 10, 1904, and a daughter, Florence Emma, born January 24, 1915. At the age of 46, George Alfred committed suicide—an act that would haunt his children for the rest of their lives. Suddenly, at age 20, George Conrad was the breadwinner for his mother, Freda, and his 10-year-old sister, Florence.

George took work as an electrician and spent his evenings in night school studying electrical engineering. He also volunteered with a National Guard unit of the Coast Artillery Regiment that provided harbor defense for southern New York and New Jersey. George was intrepid and resourceful, but painfully shy. His college yearbook noted that he always needed his "pal" to speak up for him as a surrogate in social situations.

Contrasting Robbie's full German ancestors on the Moog side, his maternal grandparents were Polish Jews. Max Szymanski, 22, and his 18-year-old wife, Rebecca, emigrated to America in 1906 so Max could avoid conscription, changing their last name to "Jacobs" to match a cousin already in the United States. Their first child, Shirley (Robbie's mom), was born in Elizabeth, New Jersey, on July 7, 1907, followed soon after by two other girls. The family moved to Canada in 1910 where two more sisters were born.

Max Jacobs was an artist who supported his family by painting murals on the walls and ceilings of Toronto theaters. He was vain—in one self-portrait he cast himself as a dapper Errol Flynn type, sporting a cigarette. Max was a philanderer who hid spare cash from his wife in the ceiling moldings to spend on lady friends. With five daughters he was hell-bent on a son, and, defying the doctor's advice ("your wife will not survive another child"),[3] he pushed Rebecca into a sixth pregnancy. At 38 she died in childbirth along with their stillborn boy. One sister remembered hanging clothes in the backyard and seeing the vision of an angel overhead as her dying mother screamed over the dead baby. Max buried his wife the next day and remarried less than three months later. His new wife was the classic stepmother, driving 18-year-old Shirley and two of her sisters to flee to New York City to find jobs. The adolescent siblings left Canada illegally, at great risk.

One day, on an outing to Coney Island, George Moog and his "pal" came upon the Jacobs sisters. Through the awkwardness of introductions, his friend managed to interpret George's interest in Shirley and the shy engineer began dating the Jewish girl from Toronto. George eventually proposed. But there was a problem.

For Shirley, to marry outside the faith was more than unthinkable. It was a disgrace, a *shanda*. If someone in the family married a non-Jew, relatives would "sit shiva," observing the Jewish mourning ritual for the death of a loved one. Shirley demanded the only possible solution: George would have to convert. But she required a full commitment, beyond simply studying Torah. As one relative put it, it was "the very most painful way a man could convert—he must have really loved her."[4] An army doctor needed assurance that George was serious about the circumcision: "Well, I'll do it, son, but are you sure you wouldn't rather *wear* it off?"[5] Following his healing period, George married Shirley on September 7, 1930, and the couple moved into an apartment in the Flatbush area of Brooklyn.

Shirley was 23, and had been working as a restaurant cashier, struggling to stay afloat in New York. Her marriage to George released her from the grip of the Depression. George earned his electrical engineering degree from the Polytechnic Institute of Brooklyn in 1932 and went to work for the Consolidated Gas Company (soon to become the Consolidated Edison Company of New York). From his office in the Con Ed building at Irving Place in Manhattan—a stylish Neoclassical skyscraper—he supervised electrical repairs around the city for the giant public utility.

George was lucky to have a secure job. Out West, record heat waves and drought had turned arable land into the "dust bowl," bankrupting farmers and creating a population of itinerant poor. Hundreds of thousands of Americans had lost their homes and were living in slums, and President Franklin Roosevelt's New Deal was promoting the creation of public housing. But George and Shirley were an anomaly in Depression-era America. They could afford to move to Flushing, Queens, a suburban enclave within New York. George's Con Ed bragged that its 37,000 employees enjoyed a higher standard of living than other workers, and his circumstances fell right in line with the claim: by 1939 his salary of $3,500 was nearly twice the American average.

George and Shirley bought their first house in 1936, shortly before Robbie's second birthday. Located in East Flushing, at 51-09 Parsons Boulevard, it was a modest, single-story Cape Cod that sat on a 60 × 100-foot lot. They could live a bucolic life there, with a small garden behind the house, and a block-and-a-half stroll to the sprawling Kissena Park, a 234-acre stretch with a lake, tennis courts, picnic areas, and many varieties of exotic trees. Shirley grew lettuce, carrots, peas, tomatoes, cabbage, and kohlrabi in the backyard, where a trellis gateway dripped with flowers. Lilacs and irises bloomed around the periphery, and there was a built-in brick fireplace for cookouts.

This was an exceptional American Dream in the midst of the Great Depression. Shirley had landed an engineer husband with a college degree, a house in the suburbs, and nice furniture. George had a relaxing haven at the end of his day and a woodworking shop in the basement. Their young son had a room of his own and a yard to play in. It was a Norman Rockwell vision with happily-ever-after potential.

But from his earliest memories, Robbie sensed a strange family chemistry. Relatives recalled the dynamic: "Everyone, including the father, lived in fear of Mrs. Moog. She was a very dominating personality. The only thing she did in the house was cook; the father washed the dishes and cleaned the house and went to work." "Shirley told George what to do and George did it: 'George, you schmuck, you didn't polish the floor enough. Go back and get that! George, what a schmuck you are, you're such a schmuck.' It was all one word: 'you're-such-a-schmuck!'" "George smoked and he had to go down to the workshop or outside to smoke." "We'd often find him outside smoking, lost in his own thoughts. He would always say, 'I'm the shlepper.'" "There was one dominant personality, and the other personality was resigned to his place."[6]

Shirley lavished her affections on Robbie, fussing over their stroller outings and riding him around in the most stylish outfits as an accessory to her own vanity, even starching his white shoelaces so the little bows stood up. "She was always a very well put together woman," one relative recalled. "Her hair was always perfectly coiffed and she was always relatively dressed up. Her wardrobe was one vivid color or another—high quality, no wrinkles, and sharp dress shoes that she wore with hose."[7] Shirley kept up appearances, but underneath she struggled with depressive episodes, leaving the radio on all night because she couldn't sleep.

∿∿∿

Flushing was a bedroom community to the cosmopolitan Manhattan, only a subway ride away. It was a place of quaint comforts; in the early years of Robbie's childhood, milk was still being delivered in a horse-drawn wagon. But everything would soon change. A massive landfill project converted the Flushing Meadows ash dump into a site where the world community would stage the most ambitious international exposition of the century.

The Fair was intended as a blueprint for a new world order—a balm for a population staggering out of the Depression. In a city built from scratch on 1,200 acres, 200 buildings went up, 10,000 trees were planted, and pavilions for 58 nations and 33 American states were erected. There were over 300 eating places and more than 1,300 exhibitors. On opening day, April 30, 1939, President Roosevelt delivered the first-ever televised address, seen live by the 200 or so households around the metropolitan area that were lucky enough to have a television set. Albert Einstein gave a speech about cosmic rays, followed by the ceremonial lighting of the entire fairgrounds to "a symphonic spectacle of fire, water, light, color and sound"—a symbolic bow to the Big Bang.[8] The 1939 New York World's Fair, dubbed, "The World of Tomorrow," was born in Robbie's backyard.

Towering over the grounds, the monumental geometric symbols of the World of Tomorrow formed the Fair's architectural epicenter: the 180-foot-wide Perisphere, the "largest globe ever made by man"[9] and the 610-foot

Trylon, a slender three-sided obelisk rising beside it. Every hour nearly 8,000 spectators ascended into the belly of the Perisphere on giant escalators, to witness a utopian vision of the year 2039. From revolving observation platforms they looked down on "Democracity," a "panoramic prophecy of the city of the future."[10]

The Trylon and Perisphere were the tallest structures in Queens and could be seen from miles around. In distant Manhattan they suggested a golf ball next to a vertical white dagger, rising from flatland, like some science fiction city on another planet. The massive symbols were visible from Robbie's house, which stood only four-fifths of a mile from the Fair's entrance gates.

The World of Tomorrow was a five-year-old's dream carnival. There, Robbie and his dad could bond over science—especially electricity, a major theme of the Fair, hawked as the force that would engineer a harmonious new world. Con Ed's pavilion, in fact, showcased the infrastructure George Moog managed every day. Its feature attraction, "The world's largest diorama," was a city-block-long, three-story-high replica of Manhattan—a 12-minute show with moving cars and subways, a thunderstorm, and the magic of lights popping on in thousands of windows at nightfall.[11] At the General Electric building, spectators thrilled to bolts of manmade lightning shooting 30 feet in the air.

Electricity in the service of sound and music was on display too. The AT&T pavilion unveiled a speech synthesizer that could electronically simulate the sound of the human voice. The Voder (or "voice operation demonstrator") used the same circuits Robbie would one day employ for the heart of his own work: oscillators, filters, and amplifiers. A specially trained team of women operated the Voder using a keyboard and a set of foot pedals to make the machine speak in complete sentences, sing a song with words, and imitate the sound of a grunting pig, a bleating sheep, or a chugging locomotive.

Two musical instruments debuted at the Fair. The Storytone, the world's first commercially available electric piano, was demonstrated at the RCA pavilion. The Hammond Novachord—an electronic keyboard instrument that could simulate the sound of the piano, harpsichord, organ, trumpet, strings, woodwinds, and Hawaiian guitar, and could create unique tone colors—was unveiled at the Ford pavilion. These instruments were part of a growing trend to marry music to electricity. The iconic Hammond organ, the future electrical sound signature of churches, ballparks, jazz, and rock'n' roll, had been patented only five years earlier. The very month Robbie was born, *Radio-Craft* magazine featured a column on the "Polytone," an organ-style keyboard evolved from the earlier "Radio Organ of a Trillion Tones."[12] The Polytone purportedly allowed living room amateurs "to command an orchestra to play what you will . . . or tone colors which you yourself may invent on the spur of the moment."[13] Several months later, *Radio-Craft* offered a story on the "Syntronic Organ," described as using "sound synthesis" to create "a universal musical instrument," one that could produce "its own unique tone characteristics" and "tones of other well known instruments."[14]

With all the wonders at the Fair, Robbie was still only five, and his fondest memory was not an exhibit, but an attraction in the Amusement Area: the Ferris wheel. He remembered it especially at night, with its revolving lights. He wasn't much interested in riding on it, but he was fascinated by how it worked.

In spite of the Fair's noble ideals, the fantasy city ended up being a brief Camelot between the dark decade of the Depression and the approaching cataclysm of the Second World War. Four months after President Roosevelt's opening day speech, Hitler invaded Poland, and many of the nations with neighboring pavilions were suddenly at war with each other. The motto in the Japanese pavilion, "Dedicated to Eternal Peace and Friendship between America and Japan," evaporated soon after with the attack on Pearl Harbor. In 1940, The World's Fair Corporation declared bankruptcy and the gates closed for good that October. Most of the buildings were leveled to the ground, and ghostly avenues and boulevards became aimless paths to nowhere. A desolate circle of flat earth marked the spot where the great Trylon and Perisphere once stood. The grounds were mostly abandoned and would languish in decay for the foreseeable future.

Flushing returned to normal. For all Robbie knew, the Fair could have been some odd 1939 *Wizard of Oz* dream. When he woke up, his mother had arranged piano lessons for him with a neighborhood teacher. Shirley had taken lessons as a child at her father's insistence. Like many Poles, Max idolized the piano virtuoso, Ignace Paderewski, a Polish national hero, venerated along with Chopin. Max had gotten it into his head that his daughter would be a piano prodigy, but he ended her lessons after he concluded she had no talent. Years later, Shirley was still smarting over her childhood failure and determined that Robbie would carry the torch and become the next Paderewski, whether he liked it or not.

He did not. "It wasn't my idea to play the piano," he insisted. "I was never particularly good at it."[15] Shirley made Robbie sit at the instrument two hours a day, and hovered over his practice sessions. She kept him away from sports to protect his hands—though she didn't hesitate to whack him on the knuckles with a wooden spoon every time he hit a wrong note. Oddly, other than the enforced regimen at the keyboard, there was little music in the Moog home that Robbie recalled: "My mother would sit down and play 'The Glow-Worm' once in a while. My father was completely unmusical. He had taken violin as a kid. Once in a while he would get out the violin. He and my mother would squeak some pop tunes. That was about it."[16] For all Shirley's grand musical plans, the family never attended concerts and there was no phonograph in the house.

Just the same, Shirley continued pushing her Paderewski mission, raising the stakes and dragging Robbie into Manhattan to cut souvenir acetate records as bragging gifts for relatives. Anyone off the street could pay for one of these 78 r.p.m. sessions, but they were a high-wire act requiring nerves of steel—just one take, straight through, with no second chances. For Robbie it was always an ordeal: "My parents ceremoniously marched me to the recording studio once every six months or so. Once there, I was placed at a monstrous concert grand. The engineer came in to adjust the microphone, then disappeared to put a virgin black disk on the cutting lathe. When the light went from green (standby) to red (record), every single sound that came out of that piano,- wrong notes, sloppy timing, and uneven dynamics included,- went onto the disk for all of posterity to hear. . . . it was a no-win situation."[17] Two days after his seventh birthday Robbie made one of his first records at the Federal Recorder Company in New York—a run-through of Albert Ellmenreich's hackneyed "Spinning Song."

At six, Robbie started first grade at P.S. 24, a typical rough-and-tumble neighborhood school, seven blocks from his home. "It was lower-class Catholic," he remembered. "The kids were forever fighting and beating each other up. I couldn't relate to it. I was a chicken."[18] One of Robbie's favorite childhood books, *Ferdinand the Bull*, perfectly embodied his outlook: "Ferdinand liked to sit peacefully under a big cork tree and smell the flowers," he explained to an interviewer years later. "His handlers overestimated his ferocity and sent him to the city to be in a bullfight. Once in the ring, Ferdinand sat down and smelled the ladies' flowers, so there was no bullfight. They took him back to his cork tree where he lived out his life in peace."[19]

Thinking back on the futility of P.S. 24, Robbie admitted, "I knew I was smarter than they were, so they felt compelled to beat me up periodically to keep me in my place."[20] But physical violence was also part of the classroom.

Robbie remembered the corporal discipline used to enforce rote learning in a third grade phonics lesson: "Mrs. Logan, who must have been 98 years old, with her unceasing scowl, wrapped in her inevitable black-grey silk print dress, backed up by several white window shades on which were written AB EB IB OB UB, was bloodying some poor soul's knuckles with her ten-pound ruler."[21]

In the spring of Robbie's fourth grade year, Shirley upped the ante on piano again, enrolling him in lessons at the Manhattan School of Music Preparatory Division. Now his Saturdays would be given over to the conservatory pre-college program where parents vied to show off their young geniuses, and students re-auditioned every year to remain in the program. After his piano lesson, Robbie was compelled to stay on for classes in ear training and sight singing. "I could play the likes of Beethoven, Chopin, and Rachmaninoff. But I never liked it. I was always much happier hanging out with my father in his hobby shop."[22]

The basement of the Moog home was George's domain, with a wood shop and a place to tinker with electronics. "My mother had the rest of the house," Robbie later joked.[23] The house was small, and with few places for Robbie to escape to when his frustrations boiled over, going downstairs offered a retreat. For George, who never played sports—and Robbie, who wasn't allowed to—the basement was their refuge. "Solace. You know, when I was in my mother's presence I had to worry about, was I practicing the piano enough. My father didn't make those demands on me."[24]

In the basement, Robbie got a taste of his father's off-hours talents. George was an accomplished woodworker. Most of the end tables, bookshelves, and cabinets in the house were his handiwork. Shirley would go through a catalog, point something out, and ask George to build it from scratch, which he unfailingly did. Downstairs, he and Robbie made small constructions—birdhouses or little shelters for pet turtles—but the main projects were electronic. "As a lot of people at Con Edison were wont to do," Robbie remembered, "he 'liberated' a lot of stuff . . . all sorts of tools from Con Edison that I suppose Con Edison never missed, but he'd go broke trying to buy them in a local hardware store."[25]

George could amuse himself for hours repairing radios and fiddling with circuits. As a pastime he subscribed to hobbyist magazines that published plans for simple electronic devices. He taught Robbie to read schematic diagrams, and solder, and together they assembled simple electronics projects in their subterranean lair. Robbie recalled building a one-tube battery-operated radio—just a detector and an amp circuit—and a two-tube radio that developed enough volume to drive a loudspeaker. Eventually he and his dad made one-tube organs even before Robbie graduated from elementary school. For George, these projects were a way of connecting with his son. Doing something together—in a household where neither parent was emotive or open with their feelings—gave the two a sense of closeness.

For Robbie, his parents were an emotional conundrum. In some ways he admired his mother for being the strong person she was, but at the same time he resented her, on his own behalf, and on behalf of his father, whom he saw as ground down. In the basement, George talked to Robbie about his marriage to Shirley, because there was no one else he could confide in. If Robbie had to choose, the stronger alliance was with his father.

At home, he was still "Robbie," but at school his teachers called him "Robert," and his classmates knew him as "Bob." He hardly made time for friends, with one exception: Nathaniel Nord. "Nat," who'd known him since kindergarten, was the only peer to witness his world closely enough to appreciate who he really was. Nat was more of a tagalong buddy, mostly in awe of his friend. "I was just happy to be where he was," Nat recalled. "He was the brains of the school, and resident musical celebrity; one just couldn't compete with the kid intellectually. Everybody was average except for Bob Moog. While I struggled for 70s on exams, he eased into 90s and 100s without an eye blink."[26] In the classroom, Bob occasionally took advantage of his status out of boredom or impatience. One time he cornered his fifth grade teacher on something, correcting her in front of the class. She snapped, "Robert, do you think you know *everything*?" "Yes," he replied.[27] The incident was duly noted on his report card: "More control over lips."[28]

Still, Bob's teachers were quick to acknowledge him as a standout, intellectually and musically. He was typed as *the* musician of P.S. 24, asked to play the processional at every assembly, and sometimes a solo piece. Whenever the school mounted a small musical, Bob was enlisted as the piano accompanist, carrying the whole show by himself as the only player in the pit. For Nat and most of the school, who viewed his talent through a provincial lens, Bob was considered the best musician in all of Flushing. "For us he was a child prodigy," Nat recalled. "No question."[29]

For all Bob's stardom at the keyboard, Shirley's strategy to shield her son's piano hands with a permanent moratorium on sports reverberated in his social life at school. The very topic of sports, the lingua franca of American boys, left Bob out to sea. "The kind of conversations schoolmates got into in those days, at that age," Nat recalled, "were mostly revolving around batting averages, win-loss records, that kind of stuff. And Bob couldn't have cared less about that."[30] The first person to show Bob how to hold a baseball bat, in fact, was his sixth grade teacher, Miss Griffin. Team sports were a lost cause for him; he preferred solitary activities: swimming and hiking—what he called "the non-strenuous sports."[31]

∿∿∿

Caught between the upstairs and downstairs outposts of his parents, Bob also wrestled with the duality of his religious heritage. "My mother was Jewish; my father was born Gentile, so I never had a clear sense of belonging. I was sort of halfway between."[32]

Shirley's Judaism was a pervasive part of the Moog household. She'd attended a Yiddish school in her childhood and could speak, read, and write Yiddish fluently. She and her sisters spoke Yiddish to each other, and Bob picked up a lot of colorful expressions. When the relatives came over for Jewish holidays, she toted out all the traditional dishes: matzo ball soup, stuffed cabbage, brisket, and the sweet, baked pudding of eggs, noodles, and fat, called kugel. George, even though he'd converted under the knife, could never quite adjust his palette to the new regime. He tolerated the weekly kasha varnishkes—noodles and kasha—though he dubbed it, "varnished kishkes" ("kishkes" being Yiddish for "guts").[33]

As soon as the Moogs left their front door, the penalty for being Jewish in Flushing was a daily fact of life. Stepping around the inescapable bias had been a long-established tradition. In 1926 the Jewish Men's Swim Club was established in Flushing because Jews were not welcome at the YMCA, or at golf courses or country clubs. A Jewish boy who had his heart set on joining the Boy Scouts of America would likely have signed up with a Jewish troop. In the same year Flushing established its Jewish Swim Club, the National Jewish Committee on Scouting was formed, mandating Hebrew and Yiddish as qualifiers for language merit badges, and offering a new honor for Jewish scouts: the Ner Tamid Eternal Light Award.

When Bob joined the Cub Scouts in fifth grade, his religious identity followed along. Later, as a Boy Scout, he and his buddy Nat became members of Troop 159 in Flushing, a Jewish troop that met weekly at Nat's synagogue, Temple Gates of Prayer. Troop 159, and its scoutmaster, Adrian Silberman, did all the usual Boy Scout activities, using nearby Kissena Park for recreation. Typically, when the rest of the troop built toy racing cars, Bob created an electronic measuring device for timing them.

When faced with the overwhelmingly Christian culture of 1940s Flushing, even Shirley had to invent workarounds. As much as she tried to keep a Jewish household, it was often easier to surrender to conformity rather than face the anti-Semitism of the community. Keeping in step with the neighbors, she always made a fuss over Christmas. Christmastime was an especially problematic season for Jewish families. It was not uncommon for them to assume the outward commercial trappings of Christmas—putting up a tree and exchanging gifts—in a bid to blend in. A relative recalled, "Particularly after the war, there was this collective traumatization after the Holocaust, and everybody wanted to disappear into the woodwork—that was when Judaism got to be its most Protestant. It took about 50 years to assimilate the shock of the Holocaust."[34]

Inside the Moog home, Shirley's Yuletide celebrations could twist the holiday to her own inexplicably diabolical ends. One Christmas morning, in particular, was seared into Bob's psyche for the rest of his life. He'd dashed into the living room with heart-pounding anticipation, expecting a pile of gifts around the tree. But the room appeared as it always did—no tree, and no gifts. After an awkward silence his mother handed him a large wrapped present—and told him to bring it to the boy next door. It seemed bizarre. But Bob brought the package over as she'd asked. When he returned, a tree was set up with gifts under it. Some sort of mind game was in progress, a relative recalled: "And then of course she would laugh: she had this wild, cackling kind of laugh. But the kid didn't know what was going on or why she did it, and I'm sure he didn't think it was real funny."[35]

When it came time for Bob's ritual initiation into manhood, his bar mitzvah, Shirley took the matter of religious ritual seriously. She signed the family up at the Free Synagogue of Flushing, a liberal Reform congregation, so Bob could attend Sunday school there and prepare for the milestone celebration that coincided with his thirteenth birthday. George was dragged to High Holy Days services at the synagogue, and went along without objecting, though as one relative put it, "I'm sure he wasn't *allowed* to object."[36]

Bob learned just enough Hebrew to weather the bar mitzvah ceremony. But he knew the spiritual significance was mostly beside the point. For the Moog family, the main event was the afterparty. To prepare for it, George had walled off his workshop and remodeled the rest of the basement into a social area. He installed a pinball machine and an electronic baseball game that lit up and made bell sounds—both salvaged from an amusement arcade. He disabled the money slots so the kids could enjoy endless play. The party was Shirley's moment—an excuse to show her relatives how a successful engineer's wife does it, with a sumptuous spread served from a newly remodeled basement in a posh neighborhood. But the whole thing backfired. A cultural faux pas over an Italian neighbor's spumoni that lay untouched put an awkward pall over the proceedings and quickly cleared out the crowd. Bob fled to his room with friends to pass the rest of the evening adult-free.

In Bob's final year at P.S. 24 he'd become "Mooogie," and Nat had become "Nord." His eighth grade class had remained together as a group since kindergarten, and were flailing now in a pool of post-pubescent hormones: "I clearly remember that John beat the shit out of me for saying that he smelled like a barn, Joe beat the shit out of me for tattling on him, Gloria roughing me up because I made some crack about her 'knobs'. . . . Gertrude getting my watery sap really rising when she sang Nature Boy in one of the Assemblies . . . that kissing party at Gloria's house, when the lights were turned out and we all lined up in front of the girls like Friday afternoon at the bank, and Margerita somehow landed up on the floor with her feet in the air." And another girl he remembered: "she was tall, even stately, pretty, smart, and had access to incredibly vivid pornography."[37]

Bob's sights were set on ninth grade now. Not the local high school and the specter of this unruly pack for four more years, but a specialized school far away in the Bronx with very selective citywide admissions. His application was strong: an "A" average, an eleventh grade reading level, and a 142+ I.Q. from the Pintner Intermediate test. Piano inevitably headed up his list of extracurriculars—Shirley had made sure he'd never slacked off. "My mother gave me piano lessons like you give somebody an enema," he complained.[38] He'd just made another obligatory platter cutting of Rachmaninoff's *Prelude in C-Sharp Minor* and Chopin's "Minute Waltz" at the G. Schirmer studios in New York, and had given a recital performance of Edward MacDowell's challenging *Rigaudon* at the Manhattan School.

Bob's activities list also noted a recent pastime: photography—a bug he'd caught from his mother, who spent hours around the house poised behind still cameras, or shooting footage with her 8 mm home movie camera. Out in public, when she was on one of her filming jags, she'd always hand her purse to long-suffering George, who had to walk around with it while she indulged her fancy.

On graduation day, Bob stood at the top of his class, again—this time pretty conspicuously. At the commencement he was called to the stage for Scholarship and Commendation medals. "My mother took movies," he recalled, "and the guy in back of my father said aloud that he would walk out if that kid (me) got any more medals."[39]

Then there was the requisite black-and-white class picture: 33 half-smiling, blank-faced, and sullen 14-year-olds posed in dark suits and white dresses, arranged in four ascending tiers against a huge American flag and the brick exterior of the school, all surrounding their stern-faced teacher and principal seated in the middle. "As I remember it," Bob mused, "I am there with a face like a young Bugs Bunny, and Norman looks like he's trying to figure out how to steal the photographer's wallet."[40]

At last, it was over. Soon Bob would be joining an elite company of students handpicked from all five boroughs—each of them a class brain like himself. He couldn't wait to fit in.

2
Bronx Cheers

"He was completely terrified by all those brilliant Jewish girls there," a relative recalled. "They were really Jewish. And he didn't really feel Jewish."[1]

At the Bronx High School of Science, intellect was taken for granted. What counted was social status, and Bob learned he didn't have much of that. "Here are all these super-vain, loquacious Jews," he recalled. "All these people had fathers who were lawyers, they were businessmen; they talked smoothly and urbanely and I never saw my father talk that way. My mother, she was Jewish but she wasn't educated. So I was out of it at Bronx Science too."[2]

To make matters worse, Bob's mother insisted on shopping for all his clothes, calibrating his wardrobe to turn off his female counterparts. At a school presentation once, his aunt was shocked to see him in knickers, high socks, and a button-down sweater, looking like "a little old man."[3] Shirley's plan succeeded, and Bob never dated in high school.

But he got back at his mother in another way. There was little time to practice the piano now. With a four-hour round-trip commute on the subway between Flushing and the Bronx, his heavy academic workload forced him to do his homework on the jiggling train. When his piano teacher at the Manhattan School confirmed the obvious—that he'd never be a concert pianist—he happily broke free and shelved his mother's dream. "I was not a piano practicer or musician at heart," he insisted. "I never saw myself as a pianist; I saw myself as a technical person who had to do this because his mother wanted him to."[4]

For companionship Bob hung out at the Temple Social Club of the Free Synagogue of Flushing, and at camporees with his scout troop. Scouting was an especially transformative experience for him that engendered a lifelong rapture for nature. At Ten Mile River, a month-long camping experience he did for four summers in a row in the foothills of the Catskill Mountains, he earned the Order of the Arrow and rose to Senior Patrol Leader. He came into his element there, living in a lean-to, cooking outdoors, exploring the wilderness and lakes, and hiking the Appalachian Trail.

∿∿∿

On George's side of the family, Bob had found a kindred spirit—an erudite adult unlike either of his parents. In her sophistication she was more like the parents of his Bronx Science classmates. And she happened to be a friend of the school's founder and principal, Morris Meister. Jotted in Bob's permanent record at the school was a casual reference to her: "Aunt, Professor at Washington University—researcher."[5]

Bob's Aunt Florence, George's younger sister, had weathered her father's suicide three days before her tenth birthday in 1925. After George and Shirley's wedding in 1930, she was left alone to care for her widowed mother, Freda. Florence never married and lived with her mother for the rest of her life until Freda's death.

As a woman in the 1940s, Florence had bucked the trend and had carved out a life for herself in a male-dominated technical field, managing to garner respect from professional peers. She'd earned a Ph.D. from Columbia and started out as a research associate in zoology in 1942 at Washington University in St. Louis, where she'd remain on the faculty for the rest of her life. She'd logged many professional honors, and in 1948 published an article in *Scientific American* on the properties of living tissue and the extension of human life span, a piece that won her a Westinghouse Award for excellence in science writing.

Florence adored Bob, and in many ways was the mother he never had. She valued his range of interests—especially his scientific bent. "He always felt that Aunt Florence had much more warmth and understanding of him than his mother," a relative remembered. "His mother really wasn't into warmth and understanding."[6] Florence doted on Bob in his childhood, keeping him supplied with educational gifts like a microscope kit and books on invention. "My earliest memories of Florence," he recalled, "were of an ambassador from the adult world who, unlike most other adults, went the extra mile to ask me questions, and to listen to my answers. To Florence I was a person, an individual. I had my own interests; I heard my own drummer. While other adults kept me in line, and told me what was so and what was good for me, Florence lifted the curtains, turned on the lights, and listened."[7]

Florence was nontraditional and nonconformist in every way. Given to pragmatism and atheism, she never hesitated to share weighty existential matters with her nephew. She made sure he understood "the difference between knowledge and faith," and he remembered vividly, "those early conversations on what was known and what was unknown."[8] Her political leanings were also an influence. His father's views were strictly right-wing, but Florence swung the other way. "George was 'Management,'" a relative observed, "and he thought like Management. Management's Republican. Union is Democrat."[9] Florence subscribed to *The Progressive*, the monthly magazine known for its anti-war and anti-corporate platforms, and its agenda on human rights and labor. Following her example, Bob began reading *The Progressive* and became a subscriber. His move to the left skewed his relationship with his father, and more and more it was impossible for the two to discuss politics.

Florence was the person Bob most identified with. She would remain his lifelong mentor, advisor, sounding board, confidante, and spiritual and intellectual beacon through dark times. Her campus career in St. Louis kept their communications long distance, but through the medium of her letters—a correspondence Bob would treasure his whole life—she exerted more influence on him than his own parents, and she became a greater science role model than his father.

Politics aside, Bob and George could still build projects together in the basement—electronics as usual. The do-it-yourself culture of the 1940s, when Bob came of age, was a mindset he inherited from his father that would run through all his future work. Ham radio, a pastime of George's, was one way the two could connect. As a "radio amateur," George chatted with other ham enthusiasts over available frequency bands using his personal call letters. The kick of talking to random strangers across private airwaves on devices you rigged up yourself was a popular hobby. Copying his father, Bob assembled his own ham radio equipment in his bedroom and registered his own call letters. "Back then it was the electronic equivalent of hot-rodding your car," Bob recalled. "You very often wound up building your own equipment because you couldn't buy everything you needed."[10]

On weekends, Bob and his father roamed the quarter in lower Manhattan where tubes and parts were plentiful and cheap. Like a strange dream where every shop in the neighborhood was a radio store, Radio Row was a six-square-block carnival of all things electronic. The district began in 1921 with City Radio, a single dealer on Cortlandt Street that served the new craze of broadcasting and do-it-yourself tinkering. A competitor moved in across the street, a few more speculators set up down the block, and in a couple years radio shops multiplied in all directions, inhabiting nearly every storefront in the area. There was Metro Radio, North Radio, Leonard Radio, Cantor the Cabinet King, Radio Ham Shack, Terminal Radio, Leotone Radio (Bob's favorite), and so on. Every one of them was a delicatessen of tubes, knobs, antenna kits, and wires. Some were only a shallow aisle off the street, piled floor to ceiling with shelves and electrical parts, the excess spilling out onto the sidewalk with buckets of condensers and surplus junk. Inside, crushes of customers gestured and yelled at harried merchants who dashed around behind counters grabbing parts or poking inside broken radios for an on-the-spot fix.

George and Bob would return from Radio Row with the day's catch of parts and set to work on some new project in the basement. Using George's industrial-sized metal-working machines, big drill presses, a big lathe, and a sizable workbench, they fashioned an electronic organ that Bob brought to school for a Science Congress in the spring of his freshman year, together with a homemade Geiger counter made from war surplus radio parts. Both contraptions won Bob the school's Fred Z. Kean Memorial Award. Gradually, though, as the equipment became more sophisticated, Bob could see the limits of his father's knowledge, and he took to working by himself, scouring issues of *Radio News* or *Popular Electronics* for a solo challenge.

Flipping through the October 1949 issue of *Radio and Television News*, one article caught his eye: "A Simple Electronic Musical Instrument: The Theremin."[11] The photo illustration pictured a four-tube chassis with two antennas lying next to it. The author's byline—typical of these magazines—included his ham radio call letters: Ernest J. Schultz W2MUU. The finished product, for anyone who could build it from the instructions, sounded too weird to be believed: *The Theremin is played with the hands, although no physical contact is made with the instrument.* The design was deceptively simple: a box with two antennas sticking out of it at right angles. The musical sound came from waving the hands near the antennas—one antenna for notes, the other for volume. At the heart of the device was the box, its electronic innards producing electromagnetic fields around the antennas which interacted with the player's own natural body electricity.

The idea of a musical instrument you could play without touching seemed like science fiction. Bob knew nothing more about it than what Schultz had written in his article. And he had no idea that back when his mother was wheeling him around in his stroller, a milestone performance on this instrument was taking place in Manhattan, just across the East River, that would set his entire career in motion decades later:

Halloween eve, 1934.

A woman stood on the stage of Town Hall, erect, trance-like, surrounded by an electromagnetic field. Gypsy-chic and sultry, she wore a white floor-length sleeveless gown that hugged her figure. Her halo of dark hair was parted in the center and drawn back in a tight bun. Rigid and immobile, she fixated on some distant world. Her right hand extended out at eye level, trembling occasionally. The curled fingers—with nails painted in polished crimson to match her lipstick—darted out and back, sometimes rippling forward and retreating. Her left hand seemed to be pumping an invisible yo-yo up and down. She touched nothing. But her electrically charged body caused two antennas on the wooden box before her to send out amplified melodies that sang like a wordless soprano.

Fifteen hundred elegant patrons packed the hall to witness Clara's séance of disembodied sound, watching her massage the air, sculpting the melodies of Bach, Tchaikovsky, and Rachmaninoff, to the accompaniment of a pianist. Electricity could do just about anything these days, so maybe it was ready to take on music. Could this be the future? Could a machine like this replace musical instruments? Nobody was sure. But critics weighed in the next morning: "From her deft and dainty fingers . . . over the ghostly box, came dulcet and lovely sounds"; "a prophetic indication of a future not too distant."[12]

Clara Rockmore was a 23-year-old Russian émigré, the new darling of New York's cultural elite. The "ether wave" instrument she played was the invention of her compatriot, Lev Sergeyevich Termen, known outside Russia by his Gallicized name, Leon Theremin. He'd invented it in 1920, and by 1927 he was barnstorming through Europe with his electrical marvel, leaving a trail of headlines and press hysteria—"the greatest musical wonder of our time."[13] Theremin sailed for New York later that year, mesmerizing capacity audiences who thought he was a magician, conjuring music from the air with nothing but his hands. At the same time, the strange electrical voice was unlike anything people had ever heard.

The instrument came to be known simply as "the theremin," and a handful of musicians—amateur and professional—took it up seriously. It was "monophonic," meaning it could only play one note at a time, but it was still a complete bear to play; most people couldn't coordinate their left and right hands enough to pull anything resembling a melody out of it. Clara, however, with a background as a violin prodigy, was the undisputed queen of the instrument. Her theremin debut that night would launch a career of plugged-in performances and position her as an ambassador for the coming age of electrical music.

∿∿

Bob continued on in Schultz's article. The author warned that the instrument was hard to tame: *While capable of beautiful effects when in the hands of an experienced player, the instrument emits horrifying wails and ear-piercing shrieks when first approached by a novice. For those experimenters interested in breaking leases or becoming musicians, the "Theremin" is a natural when backed up by a good sound system capable of delivering several watts output.*[14]

For a 15-year-old, the whole thing had a mischievous appeal. Bob was sold. The theremin project spoke to him the way the piano never had. Here, finally, was the ideal outlet for his talents—something combining technical ingenuity with music, a project he could get lost in. As far as he knew, it was just a collection of wires and tubes, something the author had probably come up with. He knew nothing about the instrument's storied past. He didn't know about Clara Rockmore and her Town Hall debut. He had no idea she was still performing—just recently before a crowd of 4,500 in Manhattan's Lewisohn Stadium. And he didn't know the inventor was alive and living in Russia after fleeing New York as a Soviet spy a decade earlier. He just knew he had to build this thing.

Bob and George managed a fair replication of Schultz's plans, but after powering it up, Bob recalled, "it didn't work worth a hoot."[15] He brought it to Bronx Science, and with some help he got it working enough to pass his hands over the antennas and make a few sounds. But the results were a letdown. Apparently, Schultz's claim that his theremin could "mimic many instruments and even approximate the sound of a choir" was just a shot of snake oil—the device emitted a siren-like howl that could set the teeth on edge. It was nothing like a choir or an acoustic instrument.

But having walked through basic theremin circuitry, Bob decided to try again, using Schultz's design as a template, hoping to make a more sophisticated original model that might sound better. He was inspired to go whole hog with musical circuits now, sending away for service manuals to study, and reading up on the work of pioneers like Laurens Hammond, inventor of the Hammond organ, and Winston Kock, creator of the Baldwin Organ.

Through all his reading and research, however, Bob likely missed a prophetic article that appeared in the *New York Times* in 1946: "'Tone

Synthesizer' Amazes Scientists." The *Times* explained that the machine, "built about five years ago but kept secret during the war, has an almost infinite number of tones . . . so that not only every kind of tone ever produced (including the human voice) can be reproduced accurately by measurement but also millions of tones that no present musical instrument is able to make."[16]

The "Tone Synthesizer" was the work of a Bell Labs physicist and was demonstrated at Columbia University before 700 scientists who heard approximations of a piano, organ, cello, "the deep diapason of the organ, so richly vibrant it shook the walls," and "the ringing tones of a great bell." No particular purpose was prophesied for the device other than the novelty of measuring different musical instrument qualities and reconstituting them electronically. But the *Times* ventured that "the new synthesizer is expected eventually to have an artistic usefulness by producing innumerable tones and shadings that have so far escaped the music makers."[17]

By the spring of his junior year at Bronx Science, Bob had made an original theremin model worthy of bringing to school. When he demonstrated it at an assembly, he extracted a compliment from his grumpy physics teacher: "Moog, that was *damn* good!"[18]

He also showed off a series of homemade electronic organs he called, "Moogatrons." After he played on one with the Bronx Science orchestra, the guidance office noted: "These instruments were the result of two and a half years of careful testing . . . entirely unaided."[19]

With graduation approaching, every senior at Bronx Science was sweating over college applications. Like most of his peers, Bob had applied to top-tier schools: Yale, Cornell, Princeton, Columbia, and M.I.T. Some people considered Bronx Science to be the nation's most academically distinguished high school, and its students were bright and high-powered. But the college odds were stacked against them. Inside the Ivy Leagues, an alarm had been sounding since the 1920s over "the Jewish problem," as some called it. With greater numbers of immigrant Jews qualifying to fill freshman classes, the fear of "WASP flight" and the erosion of these schools' reputations as strongholds of the moneyed elite took hold. The impact on Bronx Science was severe: between 1950 and 1952—exactly as Bob was applying—only seven students from his largely Jewish high school entered Yale, compared with over 275 from the mostly WASP Andover Academy boarding school.[20]

Bob threw everything he had at his applications, and the guidance office added a glowing imprimatur: "It is rare to find an individual who is so well balanced in all directions. . . . He is a gentleman in the best sense of the word."[21] In his admissions essay, Bob wrote, "I devote most of my spare time to music and electronics research. I consider myself somewhat of an introvert, but I am not anti-social. My vocational goal is that of electronic engineer."[22] He was careful not to mention his Jewish background or his synagogue activities.

"I remember feeling good on graduation day," he mused about his Bronx Science commencement, "just sitting anonymously, even though it was 97 degrees and I had a blue serge suit."[23]

3

Our Guarantee

It was called "the Harvard of the proletariat." New York City's visionary municipal college system famously opened its doors to immigrants and Jews left behind by Ivy League discrimination.[1] At $7.25 a term, plus books, Queens College, a school in the City system, was a bargain for Bob. He lived at home, and the walk to campus was only about 20 minutes.

At Queens he found a new peer group: "I got in with a bunch of guys who were basically overgrown boy scouts." He'd discovered the perfect fraternity to fit his personality: no hazing, no frat houses, no dares or dangerous pranks. Just a gang of do-gooders with lofty ideals. Alpha Phi Omega was founded by Boy Scouts, and if you'd been a Scout, you were in, no questions asked. You even got a little Greek letter pin. And APO didn't discriminate against Jews like most other fraternities. "I sort of began life as a human being there," Bob recalled.[2]

Bob was a physics major at Queens, but there was more. He'd also been accepted to Columbia University for engineering. He'd earn degrees in the "Combined Plan for Engineers"—a partnership program with three years at Queens for a B.S. in physics, and two additional years at Columbia to add a B.S. in electrical engineering. He'd cracked the Ivies after all. He was one of the few—one of "the chosen."

But there were still worries that fall. The Korean War had been raging for two years and Bob was eligible for military service. He'd be safe from the draft for two years by committing to the Reserve Officer Training Corps Course at Queens, and he decided to wager his luck with the Air Force ROTC. His official draft status was changed on October 27, 1952, from "1A" ("available to serve"), to "1D" ("deferment for a member of a reserve unit").

Living at home and still not dating, Bob spent his evenings with his father in the basement working on electronics. George was scrambling now to keep up with his son's expertise in tabletop hobby projects. As a power engineer at Con Ed, his brand of electronics was different: he painted with a broad brush, working with the heaviest machinery—massive generator rotors and transformers—in a huge maintenance building in Astoria, Queens, that he

Switched On. Albert Glinsky, Oxford University Press. © Albert Glinsky 2022.
DOI: 10.1093/oso/9780197642078.003.0003

helped design, right down to the steelwork. He supervised 250 employees and drove around town in a company car, monitoring onsite repairs. He was proud to say that he could get anywhere in the city without a map.

In December 1953 George enjoyed two-and-a-half minutes of fame when his work was highlighted in a newsreel feature for WPIX-TV. The human-interest spot aired at 11 p.m. on television sets around the city. The story focused on a segment of Con Ed's street work that most New Yorkers probably passed by every day without noticing. In the scripted interview, announcer John Tillman introduced his guest as, "George Mooog, Assistant General Superintendent of Con Edison's Shops Bureau." George's homegrown Brooklyn accent was on full display when Tillman asked him what Con Ed does with all the cable it pulls out of the streets:

Much of it is salvaged. It is inspected, and cleaned, foot by foot. Mine-uh damage to the sheath is repaired. Finally, the ends uh sealed, and it's retoined to stock fuh future use. George told Tillman that cables were rerouted, *to make way fuh civic improvements such as the U.N. building at Foist Avenue and Fawty-Foist Street....*[3]

In the basement shop, Bob and George had developed a new synergy. Their latest foray was a completely original theremin design. Bob took the lead in wiring the fine circuitry, and his father wrapped it in a swift-looking cabinet. The new theremin was conceived as a true musical instrument, deserving of being enrobed in polished wood, the hallmark of the master instrument builder. George crafted an elegant plywood and Masonite housing for it, adorned with a hand-cut rose hole carved into the front speaker panel in the tradition of the elegant floral sound holes on Renaissance lutes. The aesthetic stuck with Bob, who would pay homage to the classic wooden body of acoustic instruments in almost all his future designs.

For the first time, a Moog instrument emerging from the basement was christened with a model number: "201." That sounded about right. But then there'd have to be a company name standing behind it: "RAMCO, Flushing, NY" seemed catchy. RAMCO was short for the "Robert Arthur Moog Company"—pure fiction. A schematic diagram, dated November 1953, rendered to look professional, was initialed by two "employees": GC and SJ. Bob later admitted it was "just bullshit. 'GC' were my father's initials and 'SJ' were my mother's initials."[4]

Taking the fantasy this far, the inevitable wasn't far behind. Could they actually make a go of this? To test the waters, Bob and George decided to unveil the Model 201 publicly. Bob's name would appear in print for the first time. It would be his publishing debut, at the age of 19.

In the generous spirit of sharing original electronic recipes for other hobbyists to cook up, Bob burst onto the scene in the January 1954 issue of *Radio and Television News*, the same magazine he'd discovered Schultz's theremin project in five years earlier. Like Schultz, he proudly displayed his ham radio call letters next to his byline: Robert Moog, K2AMH. "By popular request," the teaser promised, "another Theremin article. This new design incorporates many refinements that provide greater operational stability—it is easy to build."[5]

Bob began his article with a bit of theremin history, informing readers that the instrument hadn't been built commercially for 25 years. RCA had, in fact, manufactured a run of 500 theremins in 1929, making the company the first outfit to mass-produce an electronic musical instrument. But its theremin turned out to be a white elephant—pricey, bulky, heavy, and nearly impossible to play. There were no theremin method books, teachers, or film tutorials for buyers, and the instruction manual didn't help. Only a single page was devoted to playing the instrument—just six photos of a woman holding various arm positions in front of it. Two shots—the only clues on how to play a melody—had the captions: "Right-hand position for High Pitch Tones," and "Right-hand position for Low Pitch Tones."[6] That was it, essentially sending the message, "you're on your own." The notion that anyone could learn to master the theremin—a fiendishly impossible instrument to tame—by studying six pictures was like learning to fly an airplane by looking at photos of a cockpit. Most RCA theremins were banished to granny's attic or consigned to antique shops.

Less than a year after RCA introduced its theremin, with the Depression going full tilt, the company halted production of the units. In the decades that followed, no one else had made theremins—not that there would have been much demand.

The theremin Bob described in his article was based on his Model 201. One of its promised "refinements" was the addition of two switches toggling the character of the basic sound between a cello-like tone and an oboe or English horn timbre. The detailed instructions, like Schultz's, were aimed at the true tinkerer who could build the instrument from scratch. But for the less technically equipped, Bob and George had solutions. The simple hobby article was really a pitch for their services. Calling themselves the "R. A. Moog Company" now, they took out a small ad in the same issue with no hint that they were a son-and-pop operation running out of a suburban basement. "My father and I thought we'd just do a sort of garage business," Bob recalled.[7]

The ad offered three options: advanced hobbyists could buy a few components, like pre-wound coils; intermediate-level builders could send away for a complete, ready-to-assemble kit for $59.95; and for the reader who couldn't be bothered fiddling with circuits and wires, the R. A. Moog Company could provide a "completely assembled and tested Theremin housed in a beautiful hand polished mahogany cabinet. 16 lbs. OUR PRICE $87.95. ONE YEAR UNCONDITIONAL GUARANTEE. . . . We refund overpayments."[8]

There was only one catch. "The instruments were terrible," Bob conceded. "Any professional would have said they were terrible, but, of course, I had no way of judging that at the time." Still, Bob was in a good position: "Anybody who wanted a theremin at that time would have had to come to me."[9] All in all, he figured they'd built and sold about 10 or 15 complete theremins.

Buoyed by the orders, Bob and George took the plunge and put the R. A. Moog Company on the books. In mid-1954 they set up shop as a legal entity—a sole proprietorship—and got to work on their next generation of theremins: instruments they called the "Model 305" and the "Model 351."

To bestow an aura of legitimacy on the operation, Bob asked his Queens College art professor to lay out a glossy, eight-page "company" brochure, stapled through the spine, with photos and specs on the new instruments. The pamphlet bolstered the corporate façade, but it still betrayed a homegrown look: page 2 featured a picture of Aunt Estelle, Shirley's youngest sister, standing in the Parsons Boulevard living room in front of the Model 351, arms outstretched and hands poised as though she were playing it. The brochure announced with bravado, and a good amount of chutzpah: "the first truly modern adaptation of Leon Theremin's original instrument . . . completely revised, using the most modern circuits and components known to the electronics industry."[10]

The back cover displayed a smart logo: a zigzag sound wave running across a musical staff to a vacuum tube, symbolizing "music made with electronics." Arced confidently over the top, in block letters, was the name: R. A. MOOG. On top, a promotional spiel lent the impression of a modern plant with a bustling assembly line:

All R. A. Moog instruments are fabricated from high quality, conservatively rated components, and assembled by skilled craftsmen. . . . all instruments undergo more than forty hours of exhaustive tests and adjustments to achieve uniform and optimum performance. Because of advanced design, quality control, and thoroughness the musician can own the R. A. Moog theremin with pride and play it with confidence.[11]

Beneath all the hype, Bob and George had actually engineered a good bit of sophistication into their instruments. Both models were smaller than the original RCA, with compact mahogany cabinets and black front grilles; they had removable antennas fashioned of polished aluminum, and the volume antenna was a plate, replacing the larger loop of the RCA. The 351 was the deluxe model, offering two additional features: an "Overtone Selector" (for slightly varied tone colors), "not found in any other musical instrument" and "made possible by the advanced design developed by the R. A. Moog Co."; and a "Synthetic Format" switch to choose one of four varied timbres, giving the player "the ability to select a tone quality suitable to his need."[12]

As if theremins weren't enough, Bob and George got in over their heads when they decided to go the distance and offer an original accessory: the "Model 400" amplifier with a "chassis and heavy-duty loudspeaker" housed in "an attractive mahogany cabinet."[13] Like all R. A. Moog Co. products, it was backed by a pledge: "All instruments are guaranteed for a period of one year from date of purchase against improper operation arising from defects in material or workmanship."[14]

Looking at the raw numbers, the basement operation appeared to do an impressive business in its first few months: the gross earnings for R. A. Moog in 1954 were $6,750.00. Considering that the average annual salary at the time was below $4,000, a typical new car could be had for under $2,000, and a new house went for less than $20,000, this was remarkable.

But it wasn't the end of the story. In their giddiness, Bob and George apparently forgot to factor in the cost of supplies, not to mention their time. Expenses added up quickly, and when all was said and done, their tax return revealed that they pulled in a loss of $302.25 for 1954. In essence, they wound up paying for the privilege of building new theremins for their customers.

But typical of Bob, profit wasn't at the top of his list. "I liked building stuff," he explained. "It's as if you like knitting sweaters, and you decide to knit sweaters for a living, and you enjoy it because it's the same thing as your hobby but you're getting paid for it."[15] Material considerations were secondary; his first love was the joy of invention itself. He could even be sanguine about his dormant love life: "There I was, a college kid, living with my parents, doing what I liked to do at night."[16]

The following year things picked up slightly. Gross receipts for the R. A. Moog Company in 1955 totaled $4,010.00 for roughly 18 units sold. After expenses and deductions, Bob and George eked out a profit of $232.

∿∿∿

In the fall of 1955, Bob's physics study at Queens was complete and he'd started his two-year Columbia program in engineering. He was 21, and still relying on return visits to Queens College for a social life that orbited around his APO buddies. Here and there he ventured a few tentative steps toward dating. "I know he went out with at least two girls who went to Queens College," a relative recalled. "Kind of tough gals. They were from the Bronx. I remember them both being kind of vulgar and being able to tell you in many colorful ways where to go." But Mrs. Moog was always lurking in the wings. The relative remembered, "His mother's idea was that Robert would live at home until he was 40 and spend all his engineer's money on her. So I don't think she encouraged anything."[17]

During his last year at Columbia, in the fall of 1956, Bob returned to Queens on November 16 for a jointly sponsored party thrown by APO and the Gamma Sigma Sigma sorority. The sorority sisters were rehearsing a follies for their March of Dimes fundraiser, and Bob recalled, "There was this girl sitting there. She looked like it'd be worthwhile to go over to talk to her so I did. And I guess she thought the same of me."[18] The girl later recalled: "I was wearing a red dress and an arty ring. I had very long dark hair severely pulled back and braided down the back of my head. Very close to the end of the party, when we were practicing, Robert came in and he apparently eyeballed me. When I was done and I went to sit down, he came over and sat next to me and immediately remarked on my ring. That was a conversation starter."[19]

Bob was intrigued—in spite of her name. "My two friends came over," she recalled, "and said, '*Shirley*, you said we were going to leave early,' and I looked up and I said 'um, I don't think so.' And that was the first encounter."[20]

∿∿∿

By the time Bob met the Sigma Sigma sorority girl, he was a twice-published writer. *Audiocraft* magazine had run his latest article, "Music from Electrons," in its June 1956 issue.[21] It was another do-it-yourself giveaway, this time for the Model 351 theremin. "It is profusely illustrated," Bob bragged to Aunt Florence, "with oscillograms, schematic diagrams, and even a couple pictures of me."[22]

For his readers, Bob got to the heart of how electronic sounds are shaped into music. He analyzed properties of acoustic instruments, describing what accounts for each instrument's unique sound—why the average person can hear the difference, say, between a violin and a flute. Then he explained how the circuits in electronic musical instruments "synthesize" approximations, or illusions, of acoustic instruments. In the Model 351, circuits and filters were controlled by the "Synthetic Format" switch that could simulate four different tone colors: woodwind, horn, strings, or a basic sound. Bob was awed by the theremin's simple engineering—elegant and economical—and it offered him a perfect sonic environment to play with different waveforms, learning about them as building blocks for more complex electronic sounds he'd use later on.

Since his last article, Bob had unearthed more theremin history and he tried to bring his readers up to speed. He'd learned about Clara Rockmore, but the instrument's inventor remained shrouded in mystery. "I knew very little about Theremin when I first started," he admitted. "The Cold War between the United States and the Soviet Union was going full blast back then and it was extremely difficult for anybody in this country to get information on people like Theremin." What he *did* manage to get his hands on was an RCA theremin schematic. It was eye-opening: "That was the beginning of my real understanding of what a genius Theremin was."[23]

But Bob had no idea that the very same "genius" behind the musical instrument was also behind all sorts of nefarious ends. At a recent summer job, Bob had worked for two physicist brothers who'd assisted in the Manhattan Project development of the first atomic bomb. One of the brothers even remembered feeling the heat on his face in the New Mexico desert during a test detonation. But while the brothers were working for the American war effort, Theremin's mentor, Soviet physicist Abram Ioffe, was reporting to Stalin with information leeched from the Manhattan Project, espionage that helped the Russians birth their own atomic bomb by 1949—an effort Theremin was likely involved in. Bob had no clue that Theremin had concocted elaborate bugging devices to spy on Western powers, or that he was still working for the other side in the Cold War, deeply entrenched in Soviet intelligence organizations.

After Bob's *Audiocraft* article appeared, the Moogs got a call out of the blue from a national broadcast celebrity. Raymond Scott was the bandleader on NBC's popular TV show *Your Hit Parade*, a countdown of the week's top songs, sponsored by Lucky Strike cigarettes. Scott was a quirky genius. As a composer, his manic, jazzy tunes were especially familiar to children as the underscore for Looney Tunes and Merrie Melodies cartoons. As a bandleader, he was a feared taskmaster who demanded an impossible precision from his players. Out of frustration he began assembling a collection of machinery he hoped might compose, reproduce, and record music to his perfectionist standards, without the expense or nuisance of human performers. Gradually he withdrew from public life, planning to make commercials by himself in his basement.

Bob and George were invited—ordered, really—to Scott's Manhasset, Long Island, estate. "My father and I had never seen anything like that place," Bob remembered. Scott led the Moogs on a tour of his massive four-story European-style mansion with 32 rooms, an elevator, and a screening room. They walked through the recording studio on the main floor and descended to the inner sanctum of Scott's strange world. Bob's eyes popped out: "The whole basement was like a wet dream for a handyman. . . . You can't imagine all the shit he had. . . . I mean, it was a football field down there—half a dozen BIG rooms in his basement, impeccably set up. The floors were painted, like some high class industrial laboratory. . . . There my father and I were, with our mouths hanging open."[24]

The Moogs were led into a large room filled with high-quality machine tools, then passed through a woodworking shop, an electronics assembly room, and a stockroom with electronics parts. The largest room was a laboratory where Bob remembered rack upon rack of relays, rotating motors, steppers, electronic circuits, and all sorts of patch cords and switches. For Bob, Scott was "larger than life. He had all this goddamn money, and he'd spend it on this playground."[25] At the end of the evening it was clear why Bob and George had been summoned there. Scott placed an order for a Model 305 theremin.

Several months later, Scott phoned again. Bob and George were to come out to Long Island immediately—he had something to show them. "Off in one corner of his electronics workshop," Bob recalled, "was our theremin that we had sold to him, with the pitch antenna cut off! In place of the pitch antenna there were wires going off to an assembly of parts in the back of a keyboard."[26] Mad scientist Scott had cannibalized the Model 305 for his latest creation, an instrument he called the "Clavivox." It was Scott's reimagining of the theremin as a keyboard instrument. The idea was to make the characteristic theremin sound—the siren-like glide from note to note—by playing on the black and white keys, rather than through the fluid, imprecise waving of hands in the air near an antenna.

Scott had allowed Bob and George to see the Clavivox prototype, he explained, because he was planning a commercial product based on it. A couple of months later, in February 1957, the Raymond Scott Office sent the R. A. Moog Company an "agreement" letter laying out draconian terms. Bob was asked to grant Scott full rights to the ideas behind the Model 305, and, if any of it was patentable, he'd agree to assign the patent rights to Scott for free. But the letter was a ruse: Scott had already applied for a patent on the Clavivox, with Bob's circuit built into it; he was simply covering his bases. Whatever his plans, though, his obsessive paranoia over others filching his ideas made him hoard his work, keeping it close to his chest, unlikely to be released into the world for manufacture.

∿∿∿

Soon after Bob met the sorority girl from Queens, the two began dating. Shirley—that was indeed her name—was wholly unprepared for the ire of Mrs. Moog. From the start, Bob's mother didn't like the sound of this new girl, who recalled her first encounter with Mrs. Moog's prejudices: "She thought I was Chinese because my name was Shirley May Leigh. She thought he was going with someone who was Oriental, and she had me over right fast to visit, and then she could see I wasn't Oriental."[27]

It was only the start. Face to face, Shirley subjected Shirley to the third degree: "There was almost nothing she didn't ask me. She was also looking to see if I had any health imperfections. She just wanted to make sure he was getting a perfect model. I think Mrs. Moog really wanted Robert to marry a very rich, decent looking—but not beautiful—girl, so that Mrs. Moog, who was not that beautiful, but felt she was, would have the upper hand; not any one who could outdo her in any way."[28] Bob's mother, in her tireless vanity, insisted that her own long hair as a young woman was some sort of subliminal trigger for Bob's infatuation with his new girlfriend. The morning following the grilling, Mrs. Moog delivered her verdict. Signaling Bob from behind her newspaper in the living room, she rattled the pages, muttering, "I don't approve. I don't approve."[29]

Shirley May Leigh was Bob's junior by two years. At Queens she was majoring in education, with a minor in psychology. Her parents were Romanian Jews. Her father, Ben, had come to America after his family watched their house and shop, and their entire village, burned to the ground in a pogrom. When the family settled in Manhattan, Ben's father stayed home full-time to study Torah, sending his children out to work to support the household. Shirley's mother, Lillian, was a second-generation American of some means who grew up with fur coats—stone marten wraps and the like—courtesy of her father's furrier business.

When Ben married Lillian, he opened a men's clothing store on Second Avenue in Manhattan called Benley Haberdasher & Hatter—a contraction of "Ben Leigh" that disguised his Jewish surname of Liebowitz with an Anglo-Saxon mask. When Shirley was four, the Depression claimed the business and the family moved to a house in Queens.

Shirley was raised in Flushing, about a mile from Bob's house, just across the street from the old World's Fair grounds. Her Jewish family, like his, was a minority in a mostly working-class Irish, German, and Italian neighborhood rife with anti-Semitism; she was one of only three Jewish kids in her elementary school. "Some people told me I couldn't walk on the sidewalk because I was Jewish," she remembered, and she recalled being chased home after school by gangs of kids shouting racial epithets and hurling stones at her. "I was this chubby little kid holding onto my underpants for all I was worth, and running home."[30]

Shirley's family changed their name legally from "Liebowitz" to "Leigh" when the United States entered World War II, to help her older brother camouflage his heritage—Jews, they'd heard, were being sent overseas first. During the War, a younger brother, Matthew, was born, but his life was defined by illness. After a bout with the mumps, he contracted nephritis and nephrosis of both kidneys and doctors were stumped. He was routinely in and out of the hospital, and died when he was 10, during Shirley's senior year of high school.

Bob and Shirley lived only a mile apart in Flushing, but they rarely met in person, likely due to Mrs. Moog. Their courtship was conducted mainly by mail. In an early letter, Bob ventured, "You are an awfully sweet kid, and I'm very anxious to see you again," signing it playfully, "Sincerely, Boob."[31] In January 1957, over Mrs. Moog's objections, the two were "pinned"—the 1950s ritual sign of a couple "going steady." Shirley placed Bob's APO fraternity pin on "the most pointed part" of her left breast. "I wore it all the time like it was a part of me," she recalled.[32]

For Shirley's mother, who was completely enamored of Bob, the pin wasn't enough. When Bob came to call one night, the Leighs cornered him and demanded a private conference while their daughter waited outside. Bob emerged dazed, explaining that her parents tried to offer him money to buy an engagement ring, but he'd refused. Contrary to the Leighs' breathless enthusiasm, Mrs. Moog's strategy was to erect every roadblock. Bob wasn't allowed to use the family car for dates, and the phone was often placed "off limits."

"I ripped open the envelope," Bob wrote Florence, "and scanned the enclosed sheet like a pickpocket in a crowded elevator scans the mob." He'd just been accepted to Cornell University's College of Engineering for an M.S. degree, and eventually, a Ph.D. On top of it, he'd been awarded the prestigious RCA Fellowship in Engineering Physics: a full-tuition ride of $1,100 for one year, plus a cash stipend of $2,100. He crowed to Florence, "For this much I'll be able to live in style for eight months. The gelt is enough to make anyone happy.... I call it one big streak of old-fashioned luck."[33]

Luck definitely had a lot to do with it. Bob's Columbia grades had slipped since he'd been dating Shirley. In his senior year he couldn't repeat his Dean's List standing from the year before, and by his June 4th graduation—where his B.S. in Electrical Engineering was conferred—his transcript showed a "D" in Mechanical Engineering, and three "Cs" in Electrical Engineering classes. It hadn't helped that he constantly had to duck the crossfire between the two Shirleys. He had no control over his mother's agenda, and he'd found an equally headstrong mirror image of her in his girlfriend. Shirley had no difficulty matching Mrs. Moog's manipulative maneuvers. After she began smoking to lose weight, Bob asked her to quit. "And I just looked at him," she remembered, "and I said, 'You don't own me.' And I took the pin off and I gave it back to him. And then he started to tremble and shake."[34]

When it became obvious to Mrs. Moog that an engagement was imminent, Bob's decision to go away to Cornell gave her an opening. She encouraged him to put a freeze on the relationship until he had a chance to size up other options on campus—something he was willing to consider until the younger Shirley swiftly put the kibosh on it. When Mrs. Moog saw she was licked, she adapted her strategy, jockeying to seize control of what now appeared inevitable. After she went out and bought a cheap, ostentatious ring for Bob to present, he rejected it and bought one he picked out himself.

All that remained now was the proposal. But it would be orchestrated by Mrs. Moog. On September 7, one week before Bob was due on the Cornell campus, he and Shirley sealed the deal at a location chosen by his mother. The occasion was a sideshow to the main event: Bob's parents' own wedding anniversary celebration. The couples went away to a hotel where an unceremonious proposal could be staged on cue from Bob's mother. "I knew it was coming," Shirley recalled, "which took away a lot of the surprise. It was in front of his parents—after the champagne toast to *them*.... He said, 'Shirley, I want you to marry me' and I said 'yes,' and he put the ring on my finger, and that was that."[35]

Knowing all this was going to happen, Bob and Shirley had announcements printed up in advance, which they addressed and sent out from the hotel: *Shirley Leigh and Robert Moog Take Pleasure in Announcing Their Engagement*. It was Shirley's ploy to show her parents she'd secured the engagement on her own terms, without their interference. But the plan backfired. She'd forgotten that people get their mail at different times of day. "So the result," she admitted, "was that other people got them before my mother did, and called her up to congratulate her about my engagement, and she didn't know about it. And my mother called up my sister weeping: 'And this is what Shirley has done! Isn't this horrible?' And then my sister came in and told me I was a Communist. My sister was jealous. She had married what every good Jewish girl was supposed to marry: a dentist. A dentist, a doctor, or a lawyer. And I was marrying this esoteric guy who was going to be an engineer, and get his doctorate. And that was taken as direct one-upmanship."[36]

4
No Exit

"Mother is 100% opposed to the marriage, is convinced that nothing but bad will come of it, and is hoping for nothing more than a speedy divorce." Bob was writing Aunt Florence from his new Cornell dorm room. "Contrary to what you may think," he continued, "Dad was the one who came out with the prize. He said that Shirley wasn't good-looking enough."[1] Bob wasn't telling Florence anything she didn't already know. "As you can guess," she divulged, "I have been thoroughly briefed on their numerous objections to the whole thing."[2]

Bob was on his own for the first time, relishing his independence. He was free to stir around his values and ideals now until they coalesced into a solid adult worldview. The catalyst in this coming of age was Aunt Florence, the one person he could trust as the custodian of his innermost thoughts. Next to his own conscience, she was the sole repository for the unedited impulses of his id. "It's a relief to know that I have one close relative who has some perspective," he confided, "and who would not consider my ideas cynical, communist, or just plain crazy."[3] The rewards of their epistolary relationship went both ways. Florence assured him: "It's a great pleasure to me to know that I have one relative with whom one can discuss serious matters in an intelligent fashion."[4]

Bob's other regular correspondent was Shirley. It was their year of forced separation, and they traded letters daily, sometimes twice a day. He signed them "Boob"; she was "Shirl," "Shirlareenio," and "Your Chinese girlfriend." In multi-page missives, they commiserated over tests and textbook readings and bantered about the weather, movies, plays, food, and sex. In one, Shirley slipped in a newspaper ad for bedroom "help" products like pillows embroidered with the word "YES" or "NO," and an "ingenious Snore Ball to check snoring."[5]

In a return letter, Bob couldn't resist riffing on the ad with a few of his own ribald drawings of imaginary bedroom aids. He proposed "speed pajamas" with zippers down the arms, legs, and torso to avoid "fumbling in the dark." He sketched giant wedges for tipping partners into the middle of the mattress, for marriages "on the rocks." But his pièce de résistance was the "Electronic Intensi-gasm"—"Guaranteed to put a kick into any marriage." His sketch of a detailed chassis was complete with meters, wires, and electrode cuffs to be hooked up to the couple in bed. The caption read: "Dual heart beat detectors sense when things are slowing down. When things slow down to below a pre-set level, a jolt of juice is shot through the bed springs, shocking partners into closer cooperation. Works from sixteen automobile storage batteries. Safe for adults under 60."[6]

On the Cornell campus, Bob was delirious over the many country club perks: two swimming pools, a golf course, riding stables, and a ski lift. He wrote Shirley that his private room in Cascadilla Hall was "perfect," and he'd found a warm camaraderie with other students on his floor. The future wedding ceremony was not especially in the foreground of his thoughts.

Back in Flushing, though, Shirley and her parents were gathered in a tight huddle, planning every detail of a lavish wedding. They'd set the date (June 15, 1958), booked the venue (the Riviera restaurant and yacht club on Manhasset Bay in Port Washington, Long Island), and hired the Buddy Brooks band to entertain. Ben Leigh would be footing the bill—but everyone else, bride and groom included, would be paying the price for his largesse. For Ben it wasn't really about the matrimonial ceremony; it was an excuse to throw a huge party to show off to his friends and relatives, and he wanted everything to be just the way he wanted it. One of the things he wanted was a traditional Jewish wedding with a rabbi officiating.

He wasn't prepared for his daughter's pushback. "I had unpleasant experiences being Jewish and being discriminated against," Shirley argued. "My mother lit candles on Friday nights, and we did a Seder, but it was totally irrelevant to me. It had very little to do with who I was."[7] Bob was equally adamant, and told Florence, "I'm trying to arrange not to have a Jewish wedding."[8]

Bob continued wrestling with his faith and turned to Florence, his oracle: "Some people just won't talk about religion, while others, like me, subject it to the same scrutiny that they subject any other branch of knowledge, if religion can be considered a branch of knowledge."[9] She replied with typical candor: "I am completely a-religious. . . . It is the ethical aspect of religion that alone seems to me to be worth serious attention. What I am most opposed to is the modern hypocrisy that makes church-going a substitute for ethics. . . . The synagogues and the churches have equally degenerated to the rank of social clubs devoted to mutual admiration among their members."[10] Bob understood: "I agree with your views. . . . I have found the most positive type of religion in the Ethical Culture Society. Here theology is neglected completely, with the main emphasis placed on the means of improving man's lot."[11]

Before they'd met, Bob and Shirley had each tuned in regularly to the Ethical Culture Society radio broadcasts, and later they'd started a tradition of Sunday morning dates at the Society's meetings in Manhattan. The idea of an Ethical Culture wedding appealed to them and they floated the idea with Ben, but he shot it down. The issue escalated into all-out war until a happy revelation secured a truce: the Ethical Culturist who agreed to marry them turned out to be Jewish. Ies Spetter, of Dutch ancestry, was a Holocaust survivor. With Spetter, the Leighs could be happy.

∿∿∿

Through all the distractions over the wedding, it was hard for Bob to stay focused on his Cornell program. And lately he'd been unsettled by an alarming international event that rocked the University's scientific community. In a campus lecture on the U.S. Missile Program, a prominent authority calmly speculated on plans for launching the first American satellite into orbit within a year. "Dr. Green asked for questions," Bob wrote Florence. "One member of the audience stuck up his hand. Asked he: 'Dr. Green, could you tell us how the competition is doing?' No, Dr. Green could not. All he could say was that at the last international meeting on the subject, the Russian delegates would only say that they would let us know when they successfully launched a satellite. Another member of the audience stuck up his hand: 'Dr. Green, have you heard tonight's news report?' 'No.' 'They just let us know.' Dr. Green's face dropped about six inches, and he said nothing for nearly ten seconds."[12]

Bob's gallows humor betrayed the enormous existential import of the Soviet Sputnik launch, a threat he tried to convey to Shirley in a letter: "The fact that the Russians have fired a satellite automatically means that they can make an ICBM anytime they want. This means that they can bomb us off the earth just by pushing a few buttons. A rather sobering thought, eh?"[13] Shirley, wielding her minor in psychology, responded with a numbingly repetitive four-page bromide packed with truisms and numbered points, counseling him to embrace his life and relax.

Aunt Florence had a different take: "My own view is that the Russians have done us a great favor in shaking this country out of its insufferable complacency and delusions of superiority. Maybe now American society will start being more polite to us eggheads who can't do anything but think."[14] But Bob wasn't sure the eggheads could be trusted. "Understand," he argued, "that it is 'intelligence' which is responsible for blowing the world apart."[15]

※

As much as he tried, Bob couldn't stem the unrelenting flow of wedding minutiae spewing from Shirley's letters, and even communications from her mother, who entreated him in one note, "Take good care of yourself, because you belong to Shirley."[16] The comments rankled, and his discomfort metastasized along with the wedding plans. Shirley persisted, badgering him over wedding rehearsals. "Rehearsals?" he snorted. "I don't see that a rehearsal should take more than ten minutes, unless you plan to include the Rockettes, the Corps de Ballet, the All Male Chorus, and Raymond Paige leading the symphony orchestra on the sinking platform as part of the ceremony."[17] In one letter he exploded, "Call off the Riviera wedding and we'll serve cheese and crackers, because I don't want to be indebted to your Father any more than to the other guests."[18]

Shirley nagged him to weigh in about silverware, furniture, closet sizes, and even fitted sheets, and pages of their letters devolved into petty scraps exposing conflicting priorities and basic incompatibilities. As their sparring continued, Bob insisted, "We HAVE to eliminate every suspicion of the existence of negative attitudes toward each other before the Ides of June rolls around."[19]

The engagement was beginning to feel like the military sort. In letter after letter, Bob's rage boiled over. "As your future husband, I am telling you to quit that job. I can't beat you or have you arrested if you don't. But there is not a single reason in the world for not obeying me."[20] In another letter he railed, "don't ever give me the 'hurting your Mother when she doesn't deserve it' routine. I can't think of profanity strong enough to describe the falsehood of this thought."[21] Shirley dug in her heels: "This doesn't leave much room for individual taste, does it, if one wants to meet with your approval." Then she flashed him a disingenuous smile: "Hurry home, darling and leave your sword in Ithaca—You won't need it. Love n kisses, Shirl a may."[22]

Perhaps neither Bob nor Shirley saw the irony—and the reflection of themselves—in a casual discussion of Jean-Paul Sartre's existentialist play, *No Exit*, that came up in a letter. Sartre's play about three strangers—two women and a man—locked into a room together for eternity in a modern conception of hell, follows their tortured encounters, mind games, and failed dalliances as they grapple with each other. Sartre's iconic line in the play was, "Hell is other people." "I don't know how you took 'No Exit,'" Bob wrote Shirley. "To me it is the only believable and intellectually appealing concept of Hell. I don't see how anyone could fall for the traditional concept of a load of burning sulfur with little red men with tridents poking you in the tuchus.... Sartre says the same thing.... 'Hell is other people.'... If there is going to be a picture of Hell, the worst possible punishment for a human soul, I think it should be Sartre's picture: people refusing to cooperate with each other for the benefit of the other person."[23]

In the run-up to the wedding, Aunt Florence informed Bob that she and her mother wouldn't be attending. The only relative coming from the Moog side of the family would be Great Aunt Emma, Florence's Aunt. "I pity her, - she'll be all alone," Bob wrote Florence. "I hope for her sake that she tanks up with a few good cocktails right at the beginning, to ease the 'pain.' Needless to say, I'm looking forward to June as the beginning of a new something or other. So much for the wedding. It'll be over in just about a week, thank goodness."[24]

That week, Shirley graduated with her Education degree from Queens College and wrote Bob about the wedding: "And then there's Sunday—Mm! Boy! Honest—I'm looking forward to it—Everyone's in such a good humor—it should be a ball!!"[25]

The Leighs had lost the battle for a Jewish wedding. But they got an Ethical Culture ceremony with a kosher meal. The Riviera had its resident *Mashgiach* vet all the food to ensure everything was ritually pure. Ben paid for 97 guests and a generous repast. There were whiskeys, scotch, punch, and a Napa rosé with the entrée. It was a stretch for the Leighs, who didn't even own a car and got their groceries by sending Shirley to the supermarket on her bike. It would cost Ben half a year's salary.

After months of preparation, the "extravaganza" didn't quite come off as planned. For starters, the wedding party attire was pretty much improvised. Instead of a formal wedding gown, Shirley wore a less expensive mid-calf white dress with a full nylon skirt. The maid of honor, Cora—her best friend since elementary school—outclassed her with an elegant dress from

Bloomingdales. Bob settled on the same blue serge suit he'd baked in at his high school graduation, but the best man—his cousin Ray—looked more like a groom in his newly purchased formal white jacket.

As everyone lined up to process, Shirley's sister Mildred—the one who'd called her a Communist—refused to come into the room for the ceremony. The pianist from the band was late, and one of Bob's musician friends from Queens College was pressed into service to play the wedding march. The Leighs made sure there was a chuppah, the traditional canopy Jewish couples exchange vows under, and Ben walked his daughter down the aisle toward it—a welcoming arch of ferns embedded with white peonies and ribbon runners. But the officiating Ethical Culturist, Ies Spetter, had pushed the podium out from under it—consigning it to mere decoration and robbing it of its religious symbolism—and his blessings for the couple made no reference to God. Cora recalled that Bob and Shirley wanted it that way. "They didn't even practice Ethical Culture that much but they found it at least viable. They didn't want any part of organized religion of any kind."[26]

After the ceremony people lined up to shake hands with the best man—cousin Ray—mistaking him in his elegant white jacket for the groom. In the June heat, Bob's mother made sure she kept her $950.00 Cerulean Mink stole—her "battle jacket," as George called it—wrapped around her shoulders, a trophy purchased especially for the wedding. Ben Leigh barged up to her with a blunt, "They'll do fine if you don't ruin it!"[27] As the guests trickled into dinner, Bob pleaded with Shirley for a swift exit, but she insisted on dancing. The Kosher food didn't appeal to her, and she danced through the rest of the dinner, fueled only by a cup of coffee from breakfast and the requisite bite of wedding cake the couple fed each other. Instead of champagne, sparkling burgundy was poured for the toast, but no one knew what it was and it sat untouched. After everyone left, the newlyweds each took a side of the room and sloshed down glass after glass of it at the empty place settings.

"We drove up the freeway for a bit," Shirley recalled, "and we got off in Kingston and pulled into a motel—we had no reservations. I was starving because I had nothing but a cup of coffee and we went to a steakhouse. I had a 7-course fish dinner and Robert looked at me and said, 'you'll never finish it,' and I said, 'Sit there and watch me.' I finished it. Every drop. I mean, I would have eaten the tablecloth. So that was our first night."[28]

PART II
SLIPPING BACKWARDS ON A BANANA PEEL

5
Transistor Man and the Crusaders

They'd landed in the middle of God's Country. The two Queens kids who'd just orchestrated their wedding to shut out organized religion were suddenly living in its heartland. In this rural Christian community, it was not a matter of whether you would join a church, but only which one you would join. Every clergyman in the area was in hot pursuit of the new folks from New York City.

Bethel Grove was only four miles from the Cornell campus, but culturally it was on a different planet. Somehow, Bob and Shirley managed to dodge the church dilemma by sticking with Ethical Culture as members-at-large of the American Ethical Union—a casual, long-distance affiliation.

The couple's new address lay along a country road. The rental—a three-room attic apartment—was a steep climb up a staircase outside the triple-story house. Deer grazed on the front lawn and raccoons raided the garbage pails at night. The newlyweds had the run of the 40-acre property, with a picnic area, a stream, and maple trees with running sap. They were allotted a garden patch where they could grow corn and strawberries. The Boy Scout in Bob found country living alluring, and Shirley happily embraced the rural lifestyle. "She was very domestic," her friend Cora remembered. "She was looking forward to cooking and canning, and she was very excited about being a housewife."[1]

Bob had a half-time assistantship at Cornell to research gases in a vacuum—nothing to do with music or electronics, but it paid well. Shirley found a full-time job teaching first and second graders at the Bethel Grove School, a two-room schoolhouse she could walk to across a field, over a log in a stream, and up a hill. Half the students were farmers' kids, the rest were children of Cornell professors.

Starting with their honeymoon at the Bit 'n' Bridle dude ranch in Stony Creek, New York, Bob and Shirley had made a sudden break with urban life. The isolation wasn't only about a change of scenery, though. "We were both real happy to get away from our mothers," Shirley recalled.[2] But Mrs. Moog was indomitable. From 250 miles away, she insisted on picking out and mailing Bob his shirts, ties, jackets, and even underwear. Shirley had had enough, and to force a separation—if only a psychological one—she resorted to a symbolic gesture. By slicing off the l-e-y from the end of her name and replacing it with l-e-i-g-h, she could keep her maiden name and distance her identity from Bob's mother. Her signature was now "Shirleigh" Moog.

Another change to her name—and the future of the Moog brand itself—came about after an incident at the two-room schoolhouse. The farm children in her classroom got out of hand one day in a free-for-all chorus of cow mooing: *Mrs. MOOOOG! Mrs. MOOOOG!* She appealed to Bob: "There's got to be a way out of this. And he said, 'well, half of the family says Mogue,' and I said, 'Oh really?' And that's when it became 'Mogue.' He didn't care until I objected to being called Mrs. Moooog."[3] For Bob's parents, it would remain Moooog, but for Bob, it would be "Mogue" from then on.

The future of his theremin business was uncertain. During his first year at Cornell, Bob had filled a few orders when he was home for the holidays, but that was it. Now he'd have to handle everything without his father's help. Back in January, he'd alerted Shirleigh that he planned to take "the corpse of the R. A. Moog Co." with them to Ithaca. "I've pretty well decided to rent a small hole somewhere to deposit it," he told her. "If everything works out, then the R. A. Moog Co. will continue to exist. If not, not."[4] The small hole turned out to be a rented space in the basement of their landlord's house—a 10 × 11-foot furnace room. The plan now was to develop a new line of instruments: theremins called the "Vanguard" and "Professional."

Every night the drill was the same: Bob would disappear into his basement shop, leaving Shirleigh to clear the dinner dishes and fill her evenings alone. She found it a disturbing behavior, all too reminiscent of his basement escape routines at Parson's Avenue to flee his mother. She also suspected that he was spending his time daydreaming and dabbling. One night she asked if he'd gotten a lot accomplished. He admitted that he hadn't. "Well, what did you do down there all this time?" she demanded. "I watched a spider build a web," he told her.[5]

While Bob was sequestered in the basement with his theremins, his physics colleagues spent their evenings in campus labs advancing their thesis projects. Shirleigh couldn't understand why he remained in the doctoral program; his heart didn't seem to be in it. Part of it was pressure from Aunt Florence. With her academic bias, she expected her brilliant nephew to complete his engineering physics degree and slip handily into a position at Bell Labs or I.B.M., or distinguish himself with a university teaching post. In his usually candid relationship with her, he now had to temper his comments, afraid of displeasing her. He was careful to avoid any mention of the R. A. Moog company or his theremin work, keenly aware of her judgment. He knew she'd disapprove of any distraction from his Ph.D. He valued her approval more than that of his parents, and he began downplaying his real passion—music and electronics.

There was also the issue of money hanging over their relationship. Pitying the poor graduate student getting by on an assistantship, Florence sent Bob and Shirleigh money at holidays, and his great aunt Emma mailed them a $100 monthly allowance. If either Florence or Emma got wind that he was running a company, it might seem like he and Shirleigh didn't need the money. It was better to stay mum.

Bob kept up the charade, letting his aunt down slowly, hoping she'd pick up on his disillusionment with the doctoral program. "I didn't do so hot last term," he confessed. "I don't think I'm cut out to be a 'true scientist.'" If he completed his thesis in the future, he told her defiantly, "After that, who knows? . . . I don't expect to develop an interest in working for a living for a good many years yet."[6]

The new Vanguard model was in production by 1959—"production" meaning that Bob made each instrument by hand, one at a time, which took about 20 to 25 hours a unit. All the handiwork was his, except for the cabinetry—a woodworking contractor in Ithaca stood in for George's skills. Bob borrowed the name "Vanguard" from hip '50s lingo to suggest a cool, cutting-edge, off-beat instrument. The name was even embodied in the model's appearance: a 20-inch-high wedge-shaped cabinet of "hand-rubbed solid mahogany," sprouting anodized aluminum antennas for a space-age modernism; the volume antenna was just a sickle-shaped wisp off to the left. The instrument's aura anticipated the industrial design minimalism of the 1960s.[7]

None of this work, of course, could get back to Florence. In November he wrote her, "This year will be spent building and trying out the apparatus."[8] The "apparatus" in this case was a device to measure the attenuation of ultrasonic waves in solids—part of his thesis research.

The R. A. Moog one-man show in the furnace room was a remarkable feat. If no one had suspected the original "company" was just two men in a basement, it was unimaginable now as a solo operation. Yet the "little man behind the curtain" would pull all the design, production, owner's manual, shipping, and advertising levers by himself. And all this while taking two physics courses at Cornell and working a research assistantship.

Despite its forward-looking name and appearance, the Vanguard was running on 40-year-old vacuum tube technology, the same technology Bob had known since he was a kid and had used in every instrument he'd ever built. The vacuum tube was to electronics what flour is to bread—the base ingredient of all electronics technology. It dated back to the birth of radio. When it was discovered that the vacuum tube placed in a feedback circuit—with its output looped back into its own input—vibrated wildly or "oscillated," musical tones could be generated, and electronic instruments like the theremin were born. The "oscillator" became their electronic vocal cords.

Now the vacuum tube itself was about to be shoved aside in a seismic shift to a new technology: the transistor. The vacuum tube was about the size of a pickle, but the transistor took miniaturization a step further: it was barely larger than the tip of a shoelace—a hundred fit neatly in the palm of the hand. It was more durable, and it pulled as little as one-hundred-thousandth the power of a vacuum tube. *Fortune* magazine declared 1953 "the year of the transistor" and predicted the "pea-sized time bomb" would, "almost certainly stimulate greater changes in commerce and industry than . . . atomic energy."[9] The transistor was an American innovation, developed at Bell Labs in New Jersey, and some placed it next to the atomic bomb as the most important invention of the twentieth century.

Bob remembered his first close-up look at transistors. It was right before his senior year at Columbia, when he took a summer job in 1956 at Sperry-Rand, the huge defense contractor on Long Island. He recalled a technician taking 30 of the earliest silicon junction transistors out of a box. They weren't cheap: at $30 apiece, the box was worth the same as a good used car. At Sperry-Rand, Bob was allowed to do creative circuit design with transistors, and he beamed to Florence, "Working with them gives one a little pioneering feeling."[10] But within a year, transistors were a $100 million industry, with 30 million units manufactured.

By 1959, while Bob was selling the Vanguard, the unit price of transistors fell to about a dollar, and he knew it was time to jettison vacuum tubes for the industry's new paradigm. As a companion instrument to the Vanguard, he designed a fully transistorized theremin he called the "Professional." The instrument had a version of his earlier Synthetic Format switch to offer subtle tone colors for the discerning ear. The name "Professional" implied that there were customers who were serious musicians hoping to take up the theremin on a "professional" level. But with few people coming forward with that goal, the market he was imagining would have to be created.

The first step was a slick catalog with up-to-date Madison Avenue polish. A swirling motto on the cover announced, *The R. A. Moog Theremins—music's most modern instrument.*[11] Above it, a black-and-white pen-and-wash illustration took its cue from Lord & Taylor newspaper fashion ads—a graphic artist's sweeping sketch of an ingénue wearing nothing but a wraparound white toga, her ponytail flying backward, lithe arms outstretched toward the Professional model. Little glimmering cross-hatch stars in cloud smears ran around the periphery. It was as "now" as the latest issue of *Vogue*—pure fab '50s style and free-wheeling caprice. It also exploited the male advertising bias of using the image of a young woman as product bait. But a photo inside undid the luxe glamour on the cover: it was Shirleigh, standing before the Professional like a stern schoolteacher in her no-nonsense black calf-length dress and heels, hanging her outstretched arms dutifully before the antennas—a sequel to Aunt Estelle's living room pose for the 1954 catalog.

Bob's brochure heralded the Vanguard as "a modern adaptation of Leon Theremin's original instrument," and claimed, "the Professional Model Theremin has been designed to meet every need of the accomplished Thereminist." Hoping to find such a person out there, he closed with a swaggering pledge: "No effort has been spared to produce an instrument of as high quality as the state of the art of electronic instrument manufacture permits. . . . the Professional Model proudly takes its place in the foreground among modern musical instruments."[12]

The first customers to line up for the new theremins weren't quite what Bob was expecting. Arnold Carl Westphal started the buzz among his colleagues about the new products. "He was an itinerant preacher," Bob explained. "He and his wife played things like glasses and all these novelty instruments. They went from church to church, putting on services and passing the hat, and the theremin was one thing he played. And he played it very badly. But that was apparently fine for his audiences, because in addition to using our instruments, he sold a couple of dozen Vanguards to other people like him."[13]

Rev. Westphal was known as "the Children's Shepherd" for the children's sermons he preached. His book, *Visual Surprise Sermonettes*, offered a scissors and string game to fashion a tug-of-war between sin and Jesus. In his full congregational shows he performed on his "Miracle Sleigh Bells," with "chemical novelties, mechanical devices," and his "Singing Heart"—a theremin disguised behind a huge heart-shaped shield that appeared to have two rabbit-ear antennas protruding from it, a "V" framing his face as he played. Westphal's contacts—all men of the cloth and their families who brought the Word to host churches around the country—became Bob's main customers.

Typical was Rev. Curt Emmons, his wife, and their daughter, Ethelee—the Curt Emmons Crusaders—who hailed from Winona Lake, Indiana, and traveled the country as an evangelistic team, doing church residencies for up to two weeks at a time in a single parish. Billing themselves as "the old fashioned word in a new fashioned way: revival sermons and bible prophecy," they performed on musical glasses, whiskey bottles, cowbells, sleigh bells, singing saw, marimba, hand bells, saxophones, Hammond organ, piano, and their "Instrument of Mystery," the theremin. Following each performance, Rev. Emmons switched to the pulpit to "bring the message."[14]

Even if Bob refused to attend a church, he seemed fated to deliver the Word by default. Shirleigh even remembered a custom theremin he built from white translucent plastic, shaped like a heart, and bearing the inscription: "Beautiful because Yielded." A friend of Westphal's once testified to Bob: "I definitely feel led to buy a theremin for the main purpose of bringing people to church to hear the instrument for the first time, which gives us the opportunity to tell them about Christ's love and salvation. . . . We're determined to bring young people into the church and that's where the theremin comes in."[15]

For a while, Westphal and his circle of evangelists kept the R. A. Moog Company afloat, though just barely. In spite of the ambitious brochure, the R. A. Moog Company was still operating like a hobby. Bob's tax returns told the real story: his occupation was listed as "student," while Shirleigh's was listed as, "teacher." Company receipts for 1959 totaled $1,798.00.

As the price of transistors tumbled, overseas corporations, especially in Japan, began licensing the technology, and the floodgates flew open. Japan's dominance in consumer electronics, in fact—a force that would reverberate through American companies, including Bob's, for decades—happened because of the transistor, and an ironic twist of fate. Following Japan's defeat in World War II, American occupying forces supervised everything in the country from the food supply to the economy, and even weighed in on the new Japanese Constitution, demanding a specific clause that renounced war and the production of anything with "war potential." The restrictions had an immediate effect on industry, with Japanese companies scrambling to figure out what kinds of products would be acceptable to make. American occupiers proposed one patronizing suggestion after another, steering the Japanese toward simple consumer products like silk pajamas and shirts, or cocktail napkins.

At the same time, Japanese scientists were routinely invited to tour American plants and research labs, and allowed to take unlimited pictures. No one saw them as threats, either technologically or commercially. Quite the opposite: as potential licensees, Japanese execs were courted for their purchasing power.

In late 1953, Akio Morita, a former lieutenant in the Imperial Japanese Navy and the cofounder of Tokyo Tsushin Kogyo (the future Sony Corporation), secured a transistor license from Western Electric. In 1955, Morita's company released the first product bearing the Sony name: the TR-55 transistor radio. Before long, transistor radios accounted for 77% of Japan's electronics exports. By 1958, Japanese research into transistors for televisions led two years later to the first transistorized TV sets.

American hubris had backfired. The irony of the limitations the U.S. had imposed on Japanese manufacturing was plain: while postwar American industry focused strongly on defense, wooing its best engineers into military work, Japan's top scientific minds quietly went about growing their country's consumer electronics industry into a force of tidal wave proportions. The U.S. had won the battle over military might, but ultimately lost the economic war for world dominance of the electronics market.

By 1959, Japanese corporations had even found a way to sell Americans their own technology back to them in the form of the transistor radio—at an enormous profit. In that year alone, Japanese firms sold 6 million transistor radios in America. It was a prime example of Japanese ingenuity: every American household already owned a radio, but the "transistor radio" opened up a whole new market. For the first time, Americans could listen to music or sports broadcasts out on the street and even at the beach. With its personal earphone, the palm-sized radio caught on with teenagers as the latest must-have fashion appendage. And the best part: it was cheap.

Now it was Bob's turn to take a page from the Japanese playbook. He'd already made the first steps toward transistor technology—his upscale Professional model was the first transistorized theremin. But its external shell was still big and heavy like Leon Theremin's 1920s instruments. To capitalize on the rage for smaller transistorized devices, he'd need a cheap, portable instrument. His idea was to develop a transistorized theremin *kit*. He figured he could sell a few of those to his hobbyist network.

With this new enterprise on the horizon, it was more important than ever to throw Florence off the scent. In August 1960 he informed her, "We have no plans for the future, absolutely none. One reason is that we don't know when 'the future' will begin. Second reason is that I don't really know what I am interested in.... My grades have been very average and I have done absolutely nothing original or distinguished.... I don't intend to enter the academic world; I have neither the intelligence nor the drive nor the disposition to." But he left one door open: "I am beginning to think that my disposition and peculiar set of abilities may be safest from abuse if I were to be in engineering."[16] It was a temporary bone to throw in Florence's direction to silence her. In his own mind, "engineering" was something more akin to the kit project that now occupied most of his waking hours.

But that fall, the "future" made an abrupt entrance when Shirleigh learned she was pregnant. Now she'd have to take a leave from her teaching job in the spring to wait for the baby. Bob was in his last course at Cornell, and the kit project suddenly took on new urgency as a source of income. His plan was to resurrect the tried-and-true strategy: another hobbyist article for constructing a theremin from scratch. Just as in the past, the real intention would be to sell kits and finished instruments.

Bob christened his new model the "Melodia." The completed prototype had a walnut-finished hardwood cabinet and gold-anodized solid aluminum antennas. Its five-octave range spanned the lowest note on the cello to the top notes on a violin. He'd offer it as a kit for $49.95, or as a fully assembled instrument for $75.00.

He lucked out when his "Build Your Own Transistorized Theremin" was chosen as the cover feature for the January 1961 issue of *Electronics World* magazine (the former *Radio and Television News*).[17] Splashed across the cover in living color was the Melodia, its top slid back to expose the compact chassis inside with miniaturized components and a 6-volt battery to power everything. The rectangular light wood cabinet appeared like a long, flattened-out shoebox. It was pure early '60s utilitarian simplicity, and fit in perfectly with the shrinking dimensions of new transistorized gear.

A photo insert on the cover showed a polished male model in suit and tie, arms outstretched before the instrument, ready to play, looking suave and confident. But operating the instrument wasn't simple. In his article, Bob touched on the inexact science of how hobbyists might actually *play* the instrument once they'd built it. With no teachers, method books, or performer role models, theremin technique remained a self-taught art. The tricky separation of hands was an exasperating trial of coordination, akin to patting the head and rubbing the belly at the same time. One hand had to move toward and away from the body in a horizontal plane near the pitch antenna, while the other had to dip and rise in a vertical motion over the volume antenna. Without a sophisticated finger technique like the one that Clara Rockmore had developed for herself, gesturing with the right hand alone in front of the pitch antenna would simply smear the melody notes into a molasses-like whining. The left hand required precise pats and jabs over the volume antenna to help slice the whine into discreet notes. But Bob blithely glossed over the volume issue and encouraged his prospective customers anyway: "Even if you never take the time to become an accomplished Thereminist, the instrument will provide you and your friends with hours of entertainment."[18]

Oddly, the theremin was still unfamiliar after years of public exposure. Most people didn't know they'd already heard one in film soundtracks like Miklos Rozsa's 1945 score to the Hitchcock thriller *Spellbound*, which used the instrument's muffled wail as a cue for the onset of Gregory Peck's psychotic episodes. By the 1950s, the theremin was a regular in sci-fi soundtracks like *The Day the Earth Stood Still*, where viewers shivered to its buzzing tremolo while the robot, Gort, emerged menacingly from his flying saucer to stand down a terrified U.S. Army. Electronic music was still an alien medium, so the instrument was ideal for painting dark or deviant emotions. As the main public ambassador for electronic music, it only reinforced the associations of electronic music with strange phenomena each time it made a cinematic cameo. *Time* magazine wagered that "the Theremin is now the industry's most fashionable musical device."[19]

The thereminist behind those Hollywood scores was a bit strange himself. Dr. Samuel Hoffman was a foot doctor by day who transmogrified into a musician after dark. Starting in 1947, with *Music Out of the Moon*, he racked up hits with commercial recordings in the new "lounge music" genre, tapping the theremin for its soothing qualities to calm postwar nerves with sweet tunes—like hummed lullabies—over a light popular orchestra and choir. In the 1950s, Hoffman was a regular guest on radio and television, playing his theremin and joshing with its looney interface in gags on nationally syndicated shows like *You Asked for It*, *Truth or Consequences*, *The Mickey Mouse*

Club, and *The Johnny Carson Show*. Yet in spite of all the exposure he gave it, the theremin never seemed to gain traction as a household word. As late as 1959, with a decade of television guest spots behind him, Hoffman's appearance on a show with George Jessel drove hundreds of irate viewers to call the network, convinced they'd witnessed a hoax.

Bob's kit, even as a cover feature, would hardly be expected to generate a consumer stampede. It would be a waiting game now to see if the new transistorized model could strike a broader nerve.

A month after the article ran, Shirleigh took a leave from her spring semester's teaching to stay home, preparing to give birth in May. Bob's coursework was finished, and except for his assistantship, they could look forward to a quiet spring anticipating the arrival.

Then it happened. Orders started rolling in—not one or two at a time, but hundreds, mostly for kits. At $50.00, the kit had found a robust market. This time it wasn't traveling preachers, but electronics hobbyists, an almost exclusively male demographic ranging from teenage nerds-in-training to college professors and businessmen. The R. A. Moog Company had never known this sort of demand. Bob had no experience filling so many orders by himself, and it would be a full-time job to rush units out the door as new requests flooded in. Shirleigh was recruited to assist with assembly, but after ruining some soldering joints she was demoted to packing. Each kit took 45 minutes to wrap for shipping. To serve a clientele beyond the preachers would require a loaves-and-fishes miracle of productivity.

To clear out the hours for the sudden manufacturing boom, Bob took a six-month leave from his Cornell assistantship, making sure not to mention it to Aunt Florence. Instead, he concocted a line about devoting himself to his dissertation: "I intend to put in a good many 60-hour weeks toward launching my thesis before Junior (or Junioress) sees the light of day."[20]

When he wrote Florence on May 3, "You'll receive our product report soon now," it was a wry reference to the impending birth. "'D-Day' is but a week or two away," he added. "An atmosphere of impatience, tinged with anxiety fills our otherwise airy and carefree home. We're all equipped with the standard regalia—bassinet, bathinet, baby clothes, and half a cubic light-year of diapers."[21]

Three days later, on May 6, 1961, Laura Moog was born at Tompkins County Memorial Hospital in Ithaca. When they'd decided on Laura as a girl's name, Shirleigh recalled, Bob leapt to the theremin and played the well-known song, "Laura," from the 1944 movie of the same name. The birth announcement was a whimsical homemade sketch by Bob: two wine bottles labeled, "Vino Roberto, 1934," and "Vin du Shirley, 1936," and a sign above reading, "OUR FIRST VINTAGE." On the flip side Bob drew a scroll with a coat of arms, a champagne bottle popping its cork, and doodles of bassinets and wailing babies decorating the corners.

As the living room assembly line of kits rattled along at a dizzying pace, Bob resorted to full-on doublespeak with Florence. In June he told her evasively, "The 'major effort' at Cornell is continuing." Referring to his thesis, he reported, "for the next couple of weeks I will be polishing the brass knobs and plaques on my apparatus, and honing my poor brain so I can make intelligent conversation with the experts."[22] The real apparatus, of course, was the Melodia theremin, and the "experts" were his customers.

Knee deep in kits and diapers, Bob managed to slip away to Hi-Fi shows in New York and Philadelphia, where crowds pressed around his Melodia demonstrations. By December, orders for nearly 500 assembled kits and finished instruments brought in more than $26,000—over six times what Shirleigh would have made that year if she'd taught. "That was a lot of money, a lot more than we needed," Bob remembered. "I couldn't get the idea out of my head that maybe I could be a kit manufacturer. If that was all there was to making a lot of money, well fine. But here I was getting a Ph.D. in Engineering Physics and thinking of going into kit manufacturing. Somehow the two didn't seem to go together, but Shirleigh encouraged me. She said, 'with a Ph.D. we'll never starve. Get your Ph.D., and get the kit business out of your system.'"[23]

6
Do It Yourself

"I thought I had found the goose that laid the golden egg."[1] Bob was intoxicated with his kit success after harvesting another $9,000 in 1962. It seemed like the sure path to his future. Now he was thinking beyond theremin kits, envisioning a whole line of products for the do-it-yourself culture. Since the 1940s, the Heathkit company had done well with its popular ham radio and oscilloscope kits, and lately, an amplifier kit with vacuum tubes. The trick for Bob was simply to figure out what his theremin kit clientele wanted next.

To find out, he sent his hobbyist network an "in-house newsletter" from the R. A. Moog Company. The maiden issue of *Moog Music—A newsletter of sundry topics on electronic musical instruments* (Fall–Winter 1962), was an eight-page masterpiece of artifice covering all the wonderful goings-on at the R. A. Moog Company. Bob was a one-man masthead: founder, publisher, editor, and writer.[2]

A tear-off ballot on the back page—*Cast Your Vote for What You Want*—looked like an innocent customer survey, but it was really an attempt to divine the whole future course of Bob's company. Every choice was a kit. The first was an open-ended suggestion: *simple electronic instruments other than the theremin, designed to work in conjunction with a home audio system, and to be easy to play*. Bob himself probably wasn't completely sure what he meant by that. The other two options were more traditional: *an amp kit for guitars and accordions*, and *a combo amplifier-loudspeaker kit* that would be "portable," "high fidelity," and powered by "rechargeable batteries."

The poll results trickled in, and the winning pick was clear: the portable hi-fi amp. Hi-fi sets were all the rage in living rooms, and the new amp would have an added advantage: like the transistor radio, it could go to the beach or be put on a boat. The survey thumbs-up was all the encouragement Bob needed. The portable amp would be the next big product from the R. A. Moog Company. But the project would have to be worked around the family's new domestic reality: just as Laura turned one in May, Shirleigh found out she was pregnant again. Space was tight, and the family rented a seven-room house in the fall.

Switched On. Albert Glinsky, Oxford University Press. © Albert Glinsky 2022.
DOI: 10.1093/oso/9780197642078.003.0006

That autumn, Bob wrote Florence one of the most significant letters of his life. He hadn't leveled with her yet, but he needed to keep her updated. It was still too soon to intimate that his business might turn into his career, but at least he could begin easing her into an understanding of his motivations.

Instinctively, he outlined for her—and for himself—the idea of melding the two defining paths of his life: "I have found my interests repeatedly drawn into that no-man's land between 'science' and music. In recent years, this area has attracted a number of workers, and I can foresee exciting developments in the coming years. So I am planning to enter this field. My initial work will probably be in developing new musical instruments (most likely electronic). Later on, I will try to do some fundamental investigations in the relationships existing between music and the listener. This is my present plan, and I am firmly convinced that at least my initial efforts stand a chance of being successful."[3]

His aims were a moonshot, and he couldn't fill in the details yet. He sensed there was more he wanted to do with electronic music than the theremin, and presciently, he was beginning to form notions of some kind of composition and performance device. In his newsletter he was more specific than what he had dared let on to Florence. For his readers, he talked about "electronic musical instruments that will offer the composer the musical resources of electronic technology, while at the same time offering the musician a convenient way of controlling these resources while performing." He declared grandly, "In its own research work, the R. A. Moog Co. is working toward this goal."[4] He didn't have a name for any specific apparatus yet, but as early as 1962 he had staked the company flag in the ground over the notion.

While Americans spent 1962 rocking out to the Four Seasons and Dion, Bob immersed himself in music completely outside the cultural mainstream. In his newsletter he explained that avant-gardists of the electronic music scene composed their music directly on sound equipment—usually a tape recorder—playing it back through speakers. No musicians were needed for the "performance" of this music.

A concert without musicians was an alien notion for most people, but Bob compared it to "a painter, who 'composes' a painting at his leisure and in private, then puts his completed work on display for the public to view and experience."[5] The avant-garde electronic music Bob described was the stuff of classical composers from academic ivory towers, or engineers at radio stations who had access to state-of-the-art equipment. Far from stuffy, their electronic music experiments were wild and unpredictable. Bob introduced his readers to the two leading schools of electronic music: *musique concrète* in France, and *Elektronische Musik* in Germany.

Musique concrète composers like Pierre Schaeffer at Radiodiffusion Francaise in Paris recorded ambient noises on magnetic tape—real world sounds like locomotives, saucepans, canal boats, percussion instruments, and spoken and sung words. These "sound objects" were then manipulated and distorted by cutting, splicing, and reordering pieces of the tape, running the tapes backward or at different speeds, applying effects like reverb and filtering, and mixing them into a recorded sound collage that became a finished piece of music.

By contrast, the *Elektronische Musik* composers like Karlheinz Stockhausen, based at Radio Cologne, generated music through strictly electronic means, using oscillators and control circuits. The German composers were adamant that only authentically forged electronic sounds were acceptable raw materials. A rivalry existed between the two schools—the Germans scorning the French for using live sounds, the French detesting the Germans for their electronics-only dogma.

Regardless of where the sounds came from, the average listener found the results a bit screwball. The music seemed to evoke aliens one minute and digestive noises the next. In the absence of melodies and harmonies, traditional listeners wondered if this was even music at all. A 1956 *Time* magazine article, "Music of the Future," described Stockhausen's work as "vague rumbles, whooshes and thunders," and quoted the composer's own admission that his works had "little appeal."[6]

In the United States, the same sort of experiments were going on, and Bob made sure to tell his readers about the first American electronic music studio, started in 1951 by two Columbia University music professors, Otto Luening and Vladimir Ussachevsky. Both were unaware of the French and German attempts, and Ussachevsky was busy reinventing the wheel with an Ampex 400 tape recorder, playing back taped piano sounds in reverse and at varying speeds. Like Schaeffer, Ussachevsky was an inveterate collector of any and all sounds as raw material. One Sunday he visited Pottery Barn, knocking and recording every piece of pottery and glass he could get his hands on.

The first concert of "tape recorder music" in the United States was held at New York's Museum of Modern Art in 1952 and featured three pieces by Luening, along with Ussachevsky's *Sonic Contours*. *Time* magazine ran a story, "Music: The Tapesichordists," calling the tape recorder the musical instrument of the twentieth century.[7] The *New York Herald Tribune* proclaimed, "music and the machine are now finally wed."[8]

Understandably, there was a sense of estrangement at early tape recorder concerts. *New York Times* critic Harold Schonberg observed the spooky atmosphere at a Columbia electronic music concert in 1961: "there was nothing on stage 'cept us loudspeakers. And those speakers produced sounds that were unknown, for all practical purposes, twenty years ago. . . . It gives the feeling of something antiseptic, untouched by human hands."[9] Even concert etiquette made no sense anymore: Should audiences just sit and stare at an empty stage? Should they applaud the loudspeakers at the end?

And if musicians had to share the stage with electronics, they usually weren't happy about it, either. When Ussachevsky and Luening were commissioned by the famed Louisville Orchestra to write a jointly composed concerto for tape recorder and orchestra in 1954, Ussachevsky never forgot the conductor's lament that "you can't look a tape recorder in the eye."[10]

In 1960, Leonard Bernstein commissioned Ussachevsky and Luening to write another concerto for tape recorder and orchestra to be performed at a Young People's Concert broadcast on CBS television, and on the regular New York Philharmonic season at Carnegie Hall. Ussachevsky was listed as the tape recorder soloist, but the tape recorder wasn't considered a legitimate instrument, and a dispute broke out among the stagehands' union, the electricians' union, and the CBS union over who would be allowed to operate it. The stagehands won, but Ussachevsky had to step in when the appointed union man lost control of the machine and mangled the tape.

In his newsletter, it was evident Bob had done his homework. *Moog Music* finished off with a bibliography of books and journals—including one on how to make *musique concrète* at home—and a recommended listening list of recent LPs by Stockhausen, Luening, Ussachevsky, and others.

∿∿∿

Bob continued to keep Florence in the loop over his middling performance in the Ph.D. program, hoping she might intuit his real career passions. Following a rocky comprehensive exam he reported, "When the oral part was over, I couldn't see how they could pass me. The only explanation is that my examiners know much more than I do, one of the things being how to pass a student who has just made a complete ass of himself." The outlook for his thesis wasn't much better. He'd missed the latest submission deadline, and he strung Florence along feebly: "I believe I am at the point where I can coax some useful data from my apparatus."[11]

But as the calendar flipped to 1963, Bob couldn't stand the equivocation anymore and finally came clean with Florence: "Now hold on to your hat! I am going to set up my own business. According to my present plan, my business activities will be divided into two parts,- some bread-and-butter development and manufacturing of 'commercial' musical instruments to provide an income, and long-range research and development. This may seem like a half-wit scheme to you, but I have thought quite a bit about it, and now I give myself a 2/3 chance of succeeding."[12]

∽∽∽

The Moogs' second daughter was born on January 26, at Tompkins Community Hospital. She was named Renée, after Bob and Shirleigh's friend Renee Brandt, who, with her husband, Richard, had hosted their first dinner date back in 1956. With two children to care for now, Shirleigh began to fray. The household was becoming her whole world. The teaching door had closed to her after the maternity leave she'd taken for Laura left her short of the required time to earn tenure in the Ithaca school system. Lately she'd started adding long postscripts to Bob's letters to Florence, complaining in one, "I am finding little time for self-expression or leisure activities. Any time of the day or night there are clothes to be folded or mended or washed. I guess this is my housewifey time of life."[13]

But Shirleigh also brought extra work on herself. As a compulsive gardener, she grew mounds of flowers and vegetables, enlisting Bob's hands for planting. The owner of the house they were renting would return to find an acre of his land populated with flowers, asparagus, Jerusalem artichokes, 25 raspberry plants, rhubarb, tomatoes, peppers, corn, squash, and melons. Bob was supposed to be launching a new product, but he was investing a lot of time in backyard farming. Overall, though, the full burden and boredom of domestic work fell to Shirleigh, and the loneliness was suffocating.

∽∽∽

With theremin sales beginning to dwindle, everything rested on the amp project now. Bob and Shirleigh figured the pile of money they were sitting on from the kit bonanza would tide them over until the amp was ready. With that cushion, Bob decided to take the leap and establish a brick-and-mortar factory—a true professional space—no more basements or furnace rooms. He'd hire a staff, and the "we" in R. A. Moog would no longer be a subterfuge.

To get the venture going, he and Shirleigh began scouting for a business location. The Village of Trumansburg was several miles north of the Perry City house they were renting, and it seemed like a convenient location. Trumansburg was a former mill town—an unhurried little hamlet barely larger than a square mile. The Village was bisected by Main Street, a single east-west strip of storefront properties running through an otherwise rural community. The population of 1,700, like the children in Shirleigh's two-room schoolhouse, reflected the odd mix of long-time locals and Cornell families. One resident described the town as "a place with five churches and five bars . . . everybody knows everybody out there."[14] Despite its isolation, Trumansburg was just 11 miles northwest of Ithaca on the west side of the picturesque Cayuga Lake, near Taughannock Falls State Park.

Bob found an airy 3,000-square-foot commercial space in Trumansburg at 41 East Main Street, the former location of the Baldwin Furniture Store. Baldwin's had been a local institution for 25 years, owned and operated by Karle J. "Baldy" Baldwin, a life resident of Trumansburg. The exterior of the storefront ran a good distance along the sidewalk, with six towering display windows. In its heyday, the ample interior, with a lofty ceiling and endless floor space, had been a showroom for sofas and bedroom sets. A full second floor and basement were included in the lease. Just through the back door, the Trumansburg Creek ran its course, emptying into Cayuga Lake several miles to the east.

In late July 1963, the R. A. Moog Company officially took occupancy of the Main Street storefront. Bob set up a desk near the front entrance, preparing to take on the role of "boss." He hired a cabinetmaker who could also handle metal fabrication, and a technician who could act as a tester and do design work. Bob would oversee business matters. The skeleton staff was filled out by Shirleigh as the unpaid bookkeeper.

The move was disastrously premature. The only products shipping from the cavernous storefront were the last stragglers of the Melodia kits, and a few units of a high-end Melodia model—the Troubador—that shipped fully assembled. The hi-fi amp existed only on the drawing board. It would be months before it could go into production, much less earn any income for the company.

But there was no turning back. When Bob wrote Florence in October, he took a defiant tone: "Let me stress that whatever is done in the next couple of years will be done for my own edification and satisfaction, which is the best justification I can come up with for choosing a line of work."[15] The only argument he could muster was one his aunt probably dismissed as frivolous: he enjoyed it. Since his childhood he loved being cocooned in his own thoughts, safely removed from the world, and absorbed in problem-solving. It wasn't "work" in the traditional sense, but it was the "work" he wanted to do.

Aunt Florence was still not on board with Bob's ideas, and she'd made her skepticism clear in a letter where she enclosed a hostile editorial on electronic music from the Washington University campus newspaper. Bob's reaction was blunt: "I'm keeping it as a textbook example of the cultural inertia inherent in the art of music. . . . If you think that the composition of Electronic Music is more dehumanized and automated than the performance of conventional music, you are probably wrong."[16] But Florence knew enough not to be offended. She was Bob's sparring partner and she kept him honest. For her birthday, Bob and Shirleigh had sent her a recording of Bach organ music. "This is one of our favorites," he told her, "and we hope you will enjoy it too. (It's a far cry from electronic music.)"[17]

In the summer, the family had followed the company up to Trumansburg, renting a duplex on King Street. Bob and Shirleigh insisted on planting another sizable flower and vegetable garden—a huge drain on their time—and by October they were exhausted. Bob took a leave of absence from Cornell, assuring his advisor on the excuse form, "will write thesis away from campus."[18] But the thesis would have to take a back seat to the business. The amplifier kit still wasn't ready after three months of development, and in the meantime, the whole operation—rent, salaries, inventory, and loan payments—teetered on the wobbly back of the little Melodia.

With no advertising to speak of, Bob still relied on word-of-mouth salesmen like his preachers. In his 1962 newsletter he'd boasted about the "stringent requirements" for anyone wanting to be a Moog sales agent. But like everything else, behind the façade, the reality was more humble. The newsletter carried the bios of the two current Moog salesmen. Charles Gregory had a Vanguard model and traveled the Midwest with it. "He was an entertainer," Bob recalled. "He put on shows. He would play things like a vacuum cleaner, and he had an RCA theremin that wasn't holding up for him and he desperately needed something he could travel with, so we built him some instruments. He might have been responsible for a couple of orders."[19]

Walter Sear, Bob's other salesman, by contrast, was a professional musician with an eye and ear for quality. Sear was a tuba player with a background in chemical engineering. He'd attended the celebrated Curtis Institute of Music, played with the Philadelphia Orchestra, earned a master's degree in music from Catholic University, and had joined the Air Force Band during the Korean War.

Sear played tuba with the Radio City Music Hall orchestra, doing four shows a day. When his instrument wore out, he began a business in New York City designing and making tubas from parts he ordered from abroad. Eventually he sold about 2,000 of the instruments.

In the 1950s, Sear had built a rudimentary theremin from scratch and moonlighted with it on commercial jobs, including television appearances on *Captain Kangaroo*, and a giveaway show where the theremin was the prize for anyone who could identify what it was. In 1961 he was the soundtrack thereminist on a short-lived CBS mystery series, *Way Out*. When he learned about the R. A. Moog Company, he bought a Vanguard model. In 1962 he wrote to Bob about purchasing theremins that he could resell, and was promptly made an official sales rep for R. A. Moog.

Sear began adding theremins to his tuba line, and invited Bob to split the cost of a booth at the annual conference of the New York State School Music Association (NYSSMA). It would mark a turning point in Bob's life. The conference was a gathering of 1,500 music teachers from around the state, held at the Eastman School of Music in Rochester, New York, from December 4 to 7, 1963. Sear was tickled that the howling theremin demonstrations at their booth drew crowds to his tubas. The two men made a polished-looking team: Sear with his tightly swept dark hair and black pencil mustache; Bob, slim and distinguished in his six-foot frame, with prematurely graying salt-and-pepper hair.

One of the attendees at the conference was a young music professor and composer from Long Island's Hofstra University, Herbert Deutsch. The year before, he'd ordered and built a Melodia kit, and at NYSSMA he was wandering the booths with random curiosity. "I walked into a large display—mostly tubas, and theremins on stands," he recalled. "And there was one man there—I remember him as very tall, very shy." Deutsch noticed the R. A. Moog sign and assumed the man was a regional salesman for the company. "I walked over and said, 'what are you showing here?' And he said, 'well, these are the Melodia theremins,' and I said, 'Oh, well I built one of those,' and he said, 'Oh! My name is Bob Moog.' And I said, 'Oh, that's fantastic!' And we started talking."[20]

Deutsch explained how he'd been experimenting with the theremin in his college classroom as an ear-training tool—though it hadn't worked out very well. Then he mentioned that he was a tape composer in the avant-garde tradition of people like Ussachevsky. "When I met Herb," Bob explained, "he asked me if I knew about electronic music and I said, 'Sure, I know all about that.'"[21] Having Bob's ear, Herb launched into his frustrations over composing electronic music. He described his slow and painstaking process. Like Schaeffer and Ussachevsky, he recorded ambient sounds and distorted them on tape. He bought test oscillators from a radio repair store to generate various waveforms, learned to control their pitch by changing their frequency, and made sounds any way he could. Between recording and re-recording, mixing and splicing, magnetic tape was a hassle.

Bob was taking it all in. Standing at the booth, trading comments—musician and engineer—the two started floating ideas about how to streamline Herb's process. On his way out, Herb invited Bob to a concert the following month in Manhattan: "I told him I was having some electronic music on it. It was my own stuff, with an oscillator from the radio store, and people singing, and the main performer was a percussionist."[22] When Bob returned to Trumansburg he wrote Deutsch, "I was delighted to meet you in Rochester, - I considered that alone to justify my attending the convention. Naturally, I am looking forward to meeting you again at the concert."[23]

Deutsch's performance was hosted by his Hofstra colleague, sculptor Jason Seley, at the artist's ground floor loft studio at 428 East 13th Street in Manhattan, on January 10, 1964. Bob and Shirleigh arrived to find an elite crowd of 200 invitation-only guests, along with reviewers from the *New York Daily News* and *The New Yorker* who were tipped off that something groundbreaking was about to happen. The audience gathered in a clutter of folding chairs facing an improvised stage platform with a grand piano and enough room for a handful of musicians: a percussionist, flutist, oboist, cellist, and singer, all students from Hofstra.

The program was titled, "A Concert of Compositions and Improvisations by Herbert A. Deutsch, assisted by the sculpture of Jason Seley." Not the *sculptor* Jason Seley—the *sculpture* of Jason Seley. Fifteen of the artist's towering abstract works loomed over either side of the stage like menacing intruders. The monsters were constructed from chrome car bumpers welded together with a blowtorch—Seley's trademark medium—and had hollow areas that rang with an assortment of resonant sounds when struck. At 8:45 Seley lowered the lights and the music began.

Herb played several of his pieces with the musicians, sometimes improvising, occasionally rising to hammer away manually on the strings inside the piano. Just before intermission he offered his tour de force: a work he called *Contours and Improvisations for sculpture, percussion, and tape mix*, a mélange of *musique concrète* sounds played through a speaker, with live improvisation by the percussionist Steven Elmer playing on Seley's sculptures.

The *Daily News* did its best to characterize Deutsch's tape track, calling it, "eerie disembodied voices, city noises, and bursts of melody."[24] The *New Yorker* reviewer got carried away with the percussionist: "Amid rising expectations, Elmer took the stage, solo, and laid out brushes, sticks, and two wooden mallets. He started softly, with brushes, against a background of Deutsch's tape mix. Changing to mallets, he addressed one of the gleaming bumper constructions and let fly. A sculptural medley with echoes of the auto-repair shop! Another sculpture took voice, and another. Louder and louder rang the bumpers. Faster and faster beat Elmer. At the end, there was frenzied applause, with shouts of 'Bravo!' "[25]

The sculptor and composer were natural collaborators, as Seley told the *Daily News*: "We're at about the same stage of what you call far-outness."[26] But like the work coming out of Paris, Cologne, and Columbia, this wasn't yet music for the broader public. "Do people like this kinda stuff?" the piano tuner quizzed Seley before the concert. The sculptor said that some people do. "Well," the tuner replied, "thank goodness after all these years we still have Guy Lombardo and Lawrence Welk!"[27]

But Bob was sold: "It was absolutely the most exciting musical performance I had ever seen up till then."[28] After the concert, he and Shirleigh joined Herb and his wife at an Italian restaurant in Greenwich Village. "We talked about the concert," Herb recalled, "but more important, Bob and I definitely got into talking about, when are we going to get together and what can we do? It was some sort of an electronic device that we could use to explore electronic music. Bob wasn't sure what to call it."[29]

7
The Abominatron

It was a mismatch made in heaven. The Trumansburg Rotary Club invited Bob to make his formal introduction to the community in April 1964 to help locals understand the curious new business at the former Baldwin Furniture Store. Bob gave a talk on the history of electronic music and played the Rotarians recorded examples of his favorite *musique concrète*—tape music by Stockhausen, Ussachevsky, and Luening. "It cannot be said that the effects were pleasant to the ear," the *Ithaca Journal* reported. It was a tough sell, but Bob was persistent. The chastened reporter from the paper noted, "Moog said that little of the music we now like achieved any success in its original rendition. In due time the popular ear adapts itself to newer artistic effects with the same enthusiasm as it did to Beethoven and Mozart."[1]

The *Journal* described Bob as "a quiet, unassuming and scholarly young man," and assured its readers that R. A. Moog's esoteric research projects for "non-conventional clientele" would be financed by the more practical amplifier kits. Unfortunately, the conventional clientele were still waiting, while the portable amp kit lingered on the workbench and the family bank account financed everything.

Trumansburgers, like most Americans, were transfixed by another kind of music capturing the nation. The Beatles' debut album, released in the U.S. on January 10, 1964—the same day Bob sat spellbound in Seley's studio—had set off the "British Invasion." "I Want to Hold Your Hand" soared to number one on the U.S. singles charts, and a month later, on February 9, the "Fab Four" made their American debut on *The Ed Sullivan Show*, a must-see event watched by a record 73 million television viewers. But Bob remained immune to the "Beatlemania" epidemic sweeping the country. On February 11 he'd invited Herb to visit Trumansburg that June: "I am thoroughly excited about our plan to work together this summer. I should have a good assemblage of 'studio equipment' in a few months."[2]

The kind of puzzlement the reporter from the *Ithaca Journal* displayed over the knotty strains of Ussachevsky's music tended to be the rule, not the exception, for this rarely played music. Support for research in electronic music was virtually unheard of in the 1960s; no one saw a market for it. "Electronic music was still an absolute fringe activity," Bob remembered. "Nobody knew about it. The electronic musicians of the world, except the ones that were financed by the big European radio stations, were working in the basement with whatever junk they could get from physics departments and war surplus houses."[3]

No university would expect a biology lab to be housed in a professor's home, but electronic music labs were a different story. Ussachevsky remembered the early years of shuttling Columbia's electronic music equipment around: "Two years at my apartment, and six months in Luening's apartment, and one year in a house."[4] Electronic music literally became an underground activity at Columbia when the studio finally found a home in the basement of the McMillan Theatre on campus during Bob's time there. "While I was going to Columbia," he admitted years later, "I heard vague mention of this weird musician Ussachevsky who was doing something in the basement somewhere on campus but I never went to hear him and I never pursued it. The person who told me about it was my lab instructor, Peter Mauzey, who I didn't realize at the time was also the technical advisor to Ussachevsky. That's all I knew.[5] . . . It would have been a walk across campus, but I never did it."[6] Mauzey remembered Bob only as an engineering student who, "asked more questions in class than the other students."[7]

Bringing sophisticated electrically forged music out of the basement and into the wider culture meant simplifying the process and automating it in some way—an advancement requiring a financial commitment that institutions like Columbia weren't willing to make. The obvious solution would be the investment of a large corporation, but that scenario had already played out over 50 years earlier, with disappointing results.

Back in 1897, the American inventor Thaddeus Cahill patented a giant music-synthesizing machine, the Telharmonium, and formed a company to build it and disseminate its music. Cahill hoped to prove that his device was capable of producing scientifically perfect tones that could be manipulated with mathematical precision, correcting the "imperfections" of acoustic instruments, which would be assigned to the junk heap forever. Unfortunately for Cahill, the technology of the time wasn't up to the level of his hubris.

The Telharmonium was installed in New York City in 1906. It wasn't a single, self-contained musical instrument, but a vast 200-ton complex of equipment the size of a power plant. Each of its massive, electro-mechanical rotors—giant tone wheels—spun around to generate a sine wave (the basic building block of sound), along with other sine waves above it of a higher frequency. The idea was to simulate the physics that determine the distinct tone colors of different acoustic instruments, each note of these instruments being a fundamental sine wave tone, with overtones on top of it that give it its special character. Stacking up sine waves to build sounds of distinct timbres is the principle of "additive synthesis," and Cahill, in his patent, anticipated the term "synthesizer" when he explained that, out of these "elemental electrical vibrations . . . I synthesize composite electrical vibrations answering to the different notes and chords required."[8]

A player sitting at the Telharmonium's master console with its touch-sensitive keyboards could trigger the device's network of whirling rotors, generating electrical currents that corresponded to the notes being played. The currents were sent through telephone wires to "broadcast" the music to hotels, restaurants, and private homes as a subscription service. The sound quality was limited because amplification and electrically driven dynamic loudspeakers hadn't been invented yet. The Telharmonium's music was piped through what were essentially telephone receivers acoustically boosted with large megaphone horns—some as long as six feet—or channeled through carbon arc lamps that could oscillate with the electronic signal.

No recordings of the Telharmonium exist, but those who heard it, even through the feeble speakers, were reportedly charmed by the fidelity of its orchestral sounds in transmissions of classical favorites, like Rossini overtures, and popular music. Restaurants and hotels, smitten with this early form of Muzak, were happy to dismiss entire resident orchestras for the simple subscription cost of the canned music. When Mark Twain encountered the Telharmonium, he quipped that he'd have to postpone his own death to see how it developed. Telharmonic Hall, a dedicated venue, was established in New York for regular live Telharmonium concerts, and the device appeared to be on track to dominate the American musical landscape.

Then everything fell apart. The Telharmonium's transmissions began interfering with telephone conversations, and new inventions like the player piano were encroaching on the novelty of automated music. The final nail in the coffin was the little glass vacuum tube that made amplification and wireless broadcasting feasible; the tube rendered the Telharmonium's earthbound broadcasts, involving miles of telephone wires and huge power requirements, impractical, and marked the machine's mechanics as cumbersome and outdated. After Cahill's company had sunk hundreds of thousands of dollars into the operation, subscribers began to flee in droves. By 1914 Cahill declared bankruptcy, and all three Telharmoniums his company had built were eventually scrapped.

In the decades that followed, the quest for the perfect electrical alchemy of music continued. An endless parade of ingenious, but dizzyingly complex contraptions were made by inventors attempting to bend the limited technologies of their time to the purpose of music.[9]

Forty years after the failure of the Telharmonium, it took an industry giant like the Radio Corporation of America to gamble once again on the commercial potential of intricate electronics and music. But the aim wasn't to help composers like Ussachevsky and Luening untangle their laboratory methods. The purpose was brazenly mercantile: to replace professional musicians with a machine that could play, mix, and record commercial music all in one. After two years of secret development, RCA unveiled its Electronic Music Synthesizer—dubbed the Mark I—to reporters in a private demonstration at RCA's David Sarnoff Research Center in Princeton, New Jersey, on January 31, 1955. The *New York Times* reported on February 1, "Electronic Device Can Duplicate Every Sound; Synthesizer Also Can Produce New Ones, R.C.A. Reports."[10]

After sinking $25,000 into its development, RCA bragged that its machine could imitate "the notes of a piano, the many tones of hillbilly and jazz bands, the pealing of an electric organ," and could "conjure up all sounds in nature."[11] It could even evoke the human voice, a prospect that prompted one *New York Times* commentator to fret that it might be used as a weapon in psychological warfare, to synthesize the voice of a great leader: "Sir Winston Churchill might be made to make a synthetic speech in which he urged his people to lay down their arms."[12] The prototype instrument remained under lock and key at the Sarnoff Research Center.

Two years later, a second-generation version, the Mark II, was built, with expanded features. Like the earlier model, it had no keyboard and couldn't be played live, but the aim of the Mark II was the same: to cut out musicians. Sounds were programmed in from a typewriter-style key-punch that poked holes along a sheet of paper, like an old player-piano roll. When the sheet was read back, sounds became audible through a system of tuning forks and vacuum tube oscillators. The output was sent to a tape recorder or a disk-cutting turntable. Every facet of sound could be specified, up to 32 changes a second, but it took hours to program a short passage of music. The machine was enormous: a three-ton installation made up of seven tall, rectangular units, seven feet high, that stood shoulder-to-shoulder like a line of lockers along a wall.

To publicize the Mark II, RCA released a demo record with cheesy, synthesized instrumental arrangements of popular tunes like "Blue Skies" and "Nola," along with a Bach Fugue. Bach's music was a natural choice to show off the Synthesizer because of its tendency to sound good no matter what it's played on. But the demo record failed to impress the music industry, and with no commercial takers, the Synthesizer was mothballed in New Jersey.

Ironically, the people who came to its rescue were a couple of underfunded academics: Ussachevsky and Princeton University composer and professor Milton Babbitt. In 1959, Columbia University formally established the Columbia-Princeton Electronic Music Center through a Rockefeller Foundation grant as a permanent site for Ussachevsky's and Luening's itinerant equipment. After RCA gave up on the Mark II, the Center approached the company about leasing it. Ussachevsky and Babbitt had no commercial aims and simply wanted the instrument as a tool for their avant-garde compositions. RCA agreed to lease the Mark II to the Center for a dollar a year and finally gave up and just donated it to the University. In its new home, it streamlined the electronic composition process, but its complexity called for an engineer more than a musician. In the end, only Babbitt and a few other composers wrote music on it.

The RCA Mark II arrived at Columbia when Bob was already at Cornell, several years after he'd graduated with his master's and had left the New York campus. But the massive instrument wasn't a model for what he had in mind for Herb anyway. He was starting to zero in on the essential problem with most electronic music systems: they overwhelmed the composer. The very act of dealing with the machinery was a distraction. Composers shouldn't have to think about circuits and voltages—that was *his* job. An electronic music system should be intuitive. It should let composers do what they do best: compose.

After the loft concert, Bob became fixated on building his "assemblage of studio equipment." He recalled, "Having seen Herb's concert, heard his music, I had an idea of what he was trying to do. . . . All these things Herb heard in his mind, and tried to describe to me . . . I was able to understand what it was that he was after and come up with circuits that did these things."[13]

To devise the circuits, Bob thought back to an article he'd read in the December 1961 issue of *Electronics* magazine, written by Harald Bode, a German émigré known for his invention of electronic musical instruments.

The article described Bode's latest experimental device, the "System Synthesizer," an apparatus that fit on a table and functioned like a miniature *musique concrète*–making machine. Acoustic instruments, the human voice, or electronic signals could be picked up by a microphone, then routed through processing circuits and recorded onto tape.

What really grabbed Bob's attention was the so-called modular design of Bode's Synthesizer. It was a series of self-contained circuits, or "modules," that separately performed one function, and one function only, each putting its stamp on a sound and passing it on to the next, until the final customized sound was output to a speaker. "From that I learned what a modular system was," Bob recalled.[14]

But Bode's Synthesizer had more to offer: his amplifier module was "voltage controlled." The idea dated back to the 1930s and had driven several musical devices in the past. It was a concept that resided in Bob's subconscious. "During those first months of 1964," he recalled, "when I was thinking of what to put together for Herb, the idea of voltage control suggested itself. . . . I knew about voltage control. Voltage control was a technique that was just becoming practical because of the properties of these new silicon transistors that were coming out."[15] The new transistors—now only 25 cents apiece—had a unique characteristic: an exponential relationship between voltage and current that aligned perfectly with the exponential relationships in music.[16]

In one inspirational flash, Bob's musical training and his electronics background converged. "I'm not sure at which point I saw this clearly, but musical parameters are exponentials. Pitch, you know—one octave is a factor of two. All musical intervals are ratios."[17] The same thing held for volume. He saw that the engineering could mirror the music.

Building on that insight, Bob created a one-volt-per-octave setup, meaning that a one-volt increase in the control input boosted the output pitch by one octave. Now an oscillator could be swept through its full frequency range—from sounds too low for human perception to dog whistle sounds and higher, way above audible range—by simply turning up the voltage. In the same way, the amplifier could be swept through the full spectrum of volume by boosting the voltage.

Voltage control was also ideal for a layout where modules continually perform lightning-quick electrical operations on each other, back and forth, something that could never be done manually with knobs or switches. "If I had to do that with my hand, I couldn't possibly, because my hand can't move that fast," Bob explained. "But electronics can move that fast."[18] Voltage control was like an unseen robotic hand, calibrating and altering sound properties of frequency, volume, and timbre in real time. Now the pieces began to fall into place: Bob would build a system with modular design, driven by voltage control.

∿∿∿

In June, Herb arrived in Trumansburg with his wife Peggy and their two-year-old daughter. Hofstra University had given him a $200 grant to support the project, and the family rented a cabin in Taughannock Falls State Park so the trip could double as a vacation.

The first morning, Herb and Bob met at the Main Street storefront and went down to the basement. On a little bench, the skeleton of the studio equipment lay in sections, connected by wires. Bob had attached a cannibalized electronic organ keyboard to the setup. The system was laid out on "breadboards"—circuit boards that were out in the open, Bob explained, "like a hot rod without any body on."[19] That way, if any components had to be soldered on, or changed, it would be easy. There were two oscillator boards to produce musical tones—called "VCOs," for "voltage-controlled oscillators"—and an amplifier board—called a "VCA," for "voltage-controlled amplifier." That was it.

Herb sat at the keyboard and played the first thing that came to mind—Bach's *Two-part Invention in C Major*—picking out the opening bars with just his right hand. Even though it was a standard keyboard, Bob had made it monophonic, so Herb could only play one note at a time. The tone was familiar, like the test oscillators Herb had used for his tape pieces. The only difference was that they could be turned on with the keyboard.

Herb was disappointed. But Bob was about to demonstrate that this tangle of wires and transistors was not a finite instrument, but a matrix of possibilities for new types of sounds. He showed Herb that the breadboard oscillators could produce a tone in three different waveforms—square, triangle, or sawtooth—each with its own distinctive quality. It was like the "Synthetic Format" option on the Model 351. Bob's theremin work, in fact, had sharpened his ears to the connection between tone colors and waveforms, something he'd once described to his *Audiocraft* readers in 1956: "A square-wave tone is hollow and woody, like that of a clarinet."[20] As a teenager he'd already intuited these relationships, adjusting circuits by listening carefully, watching his voltmeter, and following the visual squiggles of waveforms on his oscilloscope. "By the time I graduated from high school, I was a virtuoso operator of my oscilloscope and interpreter of its patterns," he recalled. "I knew that stuff cold. . . . I knew what sound changes happened when you did certain technical things."[21]

Bob showed Herb that with the modular setup, the two oscillators could be connected to make the electrical signal from one act on—or "modulate"—the electrical signal of the other. If one oscillator was operating below the range of human hearing, for instance, its slow, up-and-down waveform motion could modulate the audible tone of the second oscillator, making it waver with a vibrato. Likewise, if the amplifier were modulated by that same low frequency oscillator, the *volume* would rise and fall between loud and soft, loud and soft, at the same rate as the slow, modulating wave. Inputs and outputs from the three breadboard modules could be mixed and matched in endlessly interactive ways.

"Everything was designed to work together," Bob explained, "rather than as an incongruous bunch of parts. All of a sudden you didn't have to understand electricity, you just had to think of sound in its component parts. The whole idea of patching one part to another began to make musical sense."[22]

Herb was ecstatic, Bob recalled: "'Boy, I've been trying to get that sound for five years. Boy, great.' And then he went right to work."[23] Herb had brought along his Sony reel-to-reel tape recorder to lay down trial tracks. He worked for a good 8 hours daily, starting at 9:00 a.m., learning the equipment, improvising, and splashing in a pool of sounds. "That was one of the most exciting times in my life," Herb recalled, "to be able to sit there and be within fingertip control of what were really new sounds at that time."[24]

After working for several days, though, the novelty of the "new sounds" was wearing off. They began to strike Herb as mechanical. He summoned Bob downstairs and described the problem: when a key was pressed, a sound started, and stayed on until the key was released. On. Off. On. Off. What was missing was the effect musicians call "articulation"—the initial attack of a sound that allows the ear to immediately recognize the difference between sounds like the "plink" of a high piano key and the punctuated blast of a trumpet's note. And there was no control over the shape of a sound. Acoustic sounds don't merely stop—they have a natural "decay," like the volume fade after a piano key is held down for a few seconds. Herb wondered if there was any way to make these modular sounds seem more natural.

Bob took out a legal pad and began jotting notes. Herb recalled, "Bob said, 'I'll need a trigger device. Do me a favor, go across the street to the hardware store and pick up a doorbell button.' And I went over and picked up a doorbell button. I paid 35 cents for it. By the time I got back, he had already sketched out some things on a piece of yellow paper. Within an hour he wired the doorbell button into a little breadboard, and he said, 'O.K., now when you play a note on the keyboard, press the button at the same time.' And so I would play a note and press the button, and the note would be articulated."[25] A few days later Bob rigged up a second keyboard with two switches built into each note. One took care of pitch, and the other—taking the place of the doorbell button—triggered the articulation. For added subtlety, Bob installed two potentiometer knobs—"pots," for short—one for attack time, and one for decay time, to dial in gradations of articulation.

What Herb had asked for was the concept musicians call a "sound envelope"—the contour of a note from its beginning ("attack") through its fall off ("decay") to its end ("release"). Bob had essentially built an early "envelope generator," a controller for molding the shape of a note through those three stages.[26]

After the doorbell fix, Herb recorded a line from the Bach *Invention*, played it back over a speaker, and added the second part live from the keyboard. The Bach could be played with more expression now, but the unfamiliar sounds of the device were starting to inspire completely new types of musical ideas, and he began work on an original piece: *Jazz Images: A Worksong and Blues*. As a foundation track for the composition, he recorded a library of sounds: pitches and noises running the spectrum from outer space bleeps and squeals to scratchy white noise blasts and hisses, imitation jazz-bass pizzicato beats, and bluesy melodies with electronic-organ-type tones. Back at home he'd add his own trumpet and piano playing into the final recorded mix.

Upstairs, with no air conditioning, the doors to the sidewalk lay open and the sounds wafted out to the street. Bob remembered how Trumansburgers passing by were startled and perplexed by "all this weird shit coming out of the basement."[27] But history was being made: the first-ever piece written on the new device.

Bob had never heard a full composition made with his modules before. On the bench, the sounds hadn't sounded musical to him, but when they were assembled musically on tape the effect was different: "That blew my mind. All of a sudden it became a piece of music. That was totally amazing," he remembered.[28] "What really drew me was the idea of what musicians would be able to do with it."[29]

But there was another puzzle to be solved: What sort of interface would be used to control the device? Bob just happened to hook up a standard keyboard, but he saw Herb's first reaction when he sat down at it—he played Bach. The black-and-white keyboard was associated with Western music—the scales, melodies, and harmonies signifying centuries of musical thought. But electronic music implied something altogether different. A composer who wanted the sound of rainfall had no use for a keyboard; rainfall couldn't even be notated on a musical staff. A keyboard might lead composers to think in less creative ways. The modules' different sounds could be set off by push buttons, joysticks, or even a theremin antenna. Any of those "controllers" would work.

Since interaction with any machine has a profound influence on how it's used, the best interface would be one that wouldn't call attention to itself, something like the steering wheel of an automobile, an interface so intuitive no one gives it a second thought; an alternative would be hard to imagine. Bob and Herb tossed around possibilities.

Bob phoned Vladimir Ussachevsky to ask his advice. Predictably, Ussachevsky, with his history of working with tape recorders and the RCA Mark II, voted for no keyboard. "He was afraid of how people's keyboard technique would come through on material that really shouldn't be organized according to pitch," Bob remembered.[30] But Herb recalled Ussachevsky's biggest objection: "Vladimir said it's going to put it in the hands of the pop musicians and they're just going to do junk with it."[31]

Herb argued in favor of a keyboard: it wasn't the interface that mattered as much as the sounds themselves, and the sounds suggested new musical ideas, different from what might be written for traditional instruments. Besides, a keyboard was practical, he felt: "More people are going to want to use it, and it's going to really become something people will know about."[32] In the end, the keyboard won out. At the time it seemed like just another design feature that could be useful; Bob and Herb couldn't have known what a momentous decision it would turn out to be.

At this stage, the device was just another extension of Bob's hobbyist ethos; it gave him that personal rush that he got from fiddling and problem-solving. "There was no end result in store," he remembered. "It was just that I always enjoyed building electronic instruments for musicians, and I guess that's how my musical training figured in is that I had some sense of what the needs of a musician were and I could talk the language of a musician," he remembered.[33]

"Herb and I had no vision of a complete musical instrument and certainly of no commercial aspects coming out of our venture."[34]

Unfortunately, there were no commercial aspects coming out of the R. A. Moog storefront venture, either. When Herb left for home, Bob tumbled out of the clouds and back to his amplifier prototype. But there was a tough reality to face: in less than a year the company had burned through most of the family's savings. As the unpaid bookkeeper, Shirleigh fretted over the numbers. Bob could retreat to the world of his ideas and inventions, but doing the books was sobering and left her exhausted. They'd have to borrow money now—the most expensive path forward—but it was the only way they could hope to roll out the amplifier. Together they applied to the Small Business Administration for a $17,000 loan. The SBA application was approved, Shirleigh recalled, only because Bob had a friend at the bank.

Every further step into debt set the two of them at each other's throats. Shirleigh had always tallied the books on paper, adding the columns by hand with no way to double-check her accuracy, and she pleaded now for an adding machine, but Bob pleaded poverty. "I said, 'Anything, Robert,'" she recalled, "even a hand-crank, you know, with just the paper that I could check things.'—'No, we couldn't do that.' A month or two later he bought a $200 punch press, which somehow we could afford, but $10 for a hand-crank adding machine we couldn't afford."[35]

∿∿∿

That August, Bob invited Herb up again for a week. Since their last session, he'd rebuilt the device in preparation for giving it to Herb. There were now two VCAs, to go with the two VCOs; he'd gathered the exposed breadboards into modules with aluminum panels, added input and output jacks for patch cords, attached knobs, marked everything with paper labels, and enclosed it all in two handmade portable walnut cabinets. The keyboard remained a separate unit.

The apparatus was still a best-kept secret, but on a lark, Bob and Herb decided to solicit outside feedback. The University of Toronto Electronic Music Studio (UTEMS) was only a four-hour drive from Trumansburg and was known for its cutting-edge work in electronic music. When Bob contacted the Studio he was invited to bring up his modules, but, cryptically, he was told to leave the keyboard behind.

Bob tossed the prototype into his VW bug. It was a squeeze—Herb and Bob in the front, the modules tucked into the back seat. At the Rainbow Bridge border checkpoint in Niagara Falls, it was evident their cargo didn't fit anyone's notion of a musical instrument, and Canadian customs officials eyed it with suspicion. Without its keyboard it could have been a homemade bomb. Bob and Herb were escorted inside for questioning. "*Bob* tried to explain it," Herb recalled. "*I* tried to explain it. Neither of us could talk them into it. Then a young, French-speaking customs official suddenly entered and was standing there listening to the argument. He looked at the back of these things and he said, 'Is this like *musique concrète*?' And I said, 'Absolutely! You know about *musique concrète*?' and he said, 'Oh yes! *Musique concrète— musique électronique—je comprende!*' He signed our customs slip and we were off."[36]

Walking into UTEMS with their homemade modules, Bob and Herb knew instantly they were out of their league. Bob remembered, "That was the first electronic music studio I had ever been in. . . . my first introduction to the electronic music establishment."[37] UTEMS had a sophisticated lineup of equipment funded by the Canadian government. The studio was founded in 1959 by the musicologist and composer, Myron Schaeffer, and was equipped by the Canadian physicist, engineer, and composer Hugh Le Caine, who'd already had experience with voltage control from building his monophonic Electronic Sackbut in the 1940s. The jaw-dropping array of instruments Le Caine had installed at UTEMS included an oscillator bank with multiple waveforms that used a touch-sensitive keyboard, and various voltage-controlled components.

Myron Schaeffer met Bob and Herb and introduced his colleagues, the composers Gustav Ciamaga and Anthony Gnazzo. It was Schaeffer who'd told Bob to leave the keyboard behind, and now it was clear why. The UTEMS team wanted to see if they could output a digital version of the same Bach *Two-Part Invention* Herb had played in Bob's basement. They programmed the studio's room-sized mainframe computer, feeding it with cards, then hooked up Bob's prototype. Through a digital-to-analog converter, Bob's modules "played" the Bach. The Canadians were impressed. Before the visit ended, Ciamaga offered Bob a tip: he should consider adding a voltage controlled filter module to the prototype. Ciamaga knew filters from the ones he used at the UTEMS studio, and suggested they could add clarity and color to the sounds.

The UTEMS composers, with their state-of-the-art facility, recognized immediately that Bob's small contraption was revolutionary, that its electronic legerdemain could outperform their roomful of equipment with easy, sonic somersaults. The UTEMS studio components, with all their aural sophistication, were like Bode's System Synthesizer: each element could process a sound and hand it off to the next—oscillators to filter, filter to amplifier, amplifier to final output, all in one direction. Everything was linear.

Bob's modules, though, were open-ended and interactive: they could speak among themselves and perform changes back and forth on each other before their processed sound went to the final output. In other words, each module had many potential functions. An oscillator could be a sound source, but it could also control the volume of the amplifier, replacing a human hand turning the volume up and down with a knob. An oscillator could also be used to control the panning of a sound back and forth between speakers, or to control the opening and closing of a filter. A filter could feed back on itself and act like an oscillator. An oscillator could control an amplifier that controlled a filter that controlled another oscillator, and so on. There were virtually no limits to the combinations.

Bob's voltage controlled scheme was also unique in the way it used a keyboard. A UTEMS keyboard might be voltage controlled, but its voltage was used to play notes. The control voltages on Bob's keyboard could also trigger notes, but the keys could be programmed to trigger anything: gradations of volume, levels of filtering to make a sound brighter or darker, or any sound parameter. Bob didn't invent voltage control, but he invented a way to manipulate it that made it possible for anyone to use it. His system automated labor-intensive processes and opened up worlds of new sounds. His modules were small, inexpensive compared with the cost of a full electronic music studio, and powerful.

∿∿∿

Back in Trumansburg, Bob was prepping his modules to send to Herb when a thought occurred to him: maybe he could make the device polyphonic so Herb could play chords from the keyboard instead of just one note at a time. He overhauled the circuitry to experiment with the scheme, and afterward wanted to get Herb's reaction. In an audio letter, he taped short passages of music and talked through the functions of the apparatus, now christened with a sarcastic moniker: "Before I begin to show you the modular components that I'm gonna send you, Herb, I thought I'd play a little bit on the 'Abominatron' here. Doesn't sound like much when I play it. Maybe someone with more musicianship and imagination can get some good things out of it."[38]

Dusting off his piano skills, Bob ran scales and arpeggios and showed how a chord could glide up and down like a siren. Then he played different effects—vibrato and pulsing sounds. But he wondered whether the polyphonic setup was really an advantage. The tone complexity of each note was so rich that piling up additional notes just muddied up the sound. The polyphonic scheme didn't seem to justify itself. He ended with a casual sign-off to Herb: "Well, I'd appreciate your comments—what you think the potential of a contraption like this is."

The following day Bob got a surprise call from Jacqueline Harvey, director of the commercial exhibits at the Audio Engineering Society (AES) convention in New York City. Gustav Ciamaga at UTEMS had alerted her to Bob's work. It turned out that CBS had canceled its AES exhibit—the company's product wouldn't be ready in time—so Harvey offered Bob the vacant booth. Normally it would cost $200, but he could have it for free. "Don't tell anybody we're doing this," she cautioned him, "but we think it'd be good to have somebody who's doing something interesting."[39]

When Harvey called, the "Abominatron" was less than three months old. Bob had slapped it together with scrounged parts; it was the first time he'd put together circuitry in that way. Now he'd be sitting at the booth where everyone would be expecting to find CBS, an industry titan with an army of researchers; he'd be exhibiting alongside the likes of Ampex and Scully. In less than two months he'd need to switch the device back to a monophonic system and ready it for display. "It's sort of a two-faced deal," he told Herb. "It's a tremendous opportunity to get this stuff going sooner than I had thought; but on the other hand it's a tremendous opportunity for me to make an ass of myself."[40]

8
A Eunuch in a Harem

The cabin of Bob's VW bug barely fit the family and their luggage. On the way to the AES convention, the modules were packed into a large black box that was lashed to the roof and looked like a coffin. People in passing cars stared, and Shirleigh remembered Bob's devilish fun in staring back, pointing to the roof, and mouthing the word, "Mother."

Mom, in fact, had been unloading to Florence, who was having her own mischievous fun refereeing gossip between families. "I was somewhat surprised to hear that Ma & Pa Moog are disappointed in Jr.," Shirleigh volleyed back to Florence. "They have never hinted at disappointment—surprise-yes. They both had visions of Rob in a suit & tie each day, going neatly to a huge lab & earning many money; Nice—Neat—Secure Paternal Nouveau Rich Waste-Maker Type (otherwise known as Successful Jew)."[1]

In spite of her vexations over Bob, Shirleigh was always the first to defend him and she tried to make his case to Florence: "Since working is a means to live in this world, isn't it the ideal solution to be able to do something you enjoy for a living? So isn't Rob entitled to give it a whack? I grant you that the kooks are the first ones attracted, with the evangelists running second, but I do believe that electronic music is the next step and some of it is music!!" While she was at it, Shirleigh went ahead and spilled the whole story to Florence: "Did you know that Rob has had this business going on a kiddish, more part-time scale, since he was 18??? Or that prior to Laura's birth he wrote an article for an R. A. Moog theremin kit that sold more than 1,000 kits?" She pressed Florence to make the pilgrimage to Trumansburg to see Bob's work for herself. Maybe then she'd understand: "It would be a joy to see such a superlative Aunt (even if you don't completely approve of us)." But with the storefront business operating on fumes, Shirleigh's anxiety leaked out: "Praying that the R. A. Moog Co. makes it thru October."[2]

The 1964 AES convention in Manhattan ran from October 12 to 16 at the Barbizon-Plaza Hotel. "I'd never seen anything like it in my life. These incredible professional audio exhibits. I was sort of disoriented," Bob recalled.[3]

"I knew nothing about conventions in New York. I knew nothing about the audio industry.... It was still just a hobby."[4]

Bob located his booth and set out his wares. There was no disguising the improvised feel of his display: a card table draped with one of Shirleigh's Indian print bedspreads. He had four handmade modules in two handmade wooden cases, with paper labels stuck on with rubber cement. "The panels were constructed from sheet aluminum that I got out of the student shop at Cornell and sprayed with paint. And there I stood."[5] All Bob had were two VCOs, two VCAs, and a keyboard.[6] "I was surrounded on all sides by these highly professional New York exhibits—Ampex and 3M, Scully with their huge machines that were incomprehensible complexity and class....[7] I felt just like a eunuch in a harem."[8]

Armed with a pair of headphones so the alien bleeps and squawks from his modules wouldn't intrude on the corporate decorum, Bob waited for passersby to notice his table. Two technicians from the Columbia-Princeton Electronic Music Center came over: his old lab professor, Peter Mauzey, and James Seawright, a sculptor. "God, that's fascinating," Mauzey quipped. "So what else are you going to do for a living?"[9] Seawright was intrigued and went to find someone he thought would be interested: his friend and occasional collaborator, Alwin Nikolais, the internationally celebrated choreographer.

Nikolais had pioneered a genre of multimedia modern dance where every element was under his control—movement, lighting, costumes, and music he composed himself. His first scores used percussion, but he quickly migrated to *musique concrète*. Like Ussachevsky, any noise was raw material for him. "If you give me a Schnauzer, two Armenian chastity belts, and a 19th century dishpan," he claimed, "I would attempt to create something with it. I had an old Ford gas tank that was a marvelous instrument. I called it my Cambodian water drum."[10]

Lately Nikolais had been assisted in creating his scores by Seawright, whose own works included transistorized sculptures with electronic sounds and flashing lights that were interactive and changed according to environmental stimuli. Early in 1963, Seawright and Nikolais had used the RCA Mark II synthesizer to compose an electronic score for Nikolais' work *Imago (The City Curious)*.

"Alwin Nikolais came running in," Bob remembered, "and said, 'Say, Jimmy Seawright just told me you have something fantastic. Let me see. Wow. Great. I'd like a couple of these and a couple of these.'... I didn't know I was going to be selling anything.'"[11] Suddenly, Bob was in business.

Next up at the booth was Eric Siday, a pioneering jingle writer. "He was Mr. Big in commercial sound logos at the time . . . he was single-handedly establishing sound logos as an advertising gestalt," Bob recalled,[12] ". . . the five seconds of sound that will identify a corporation or a product on radio and TV. . . . He was a genius at it."[13] Siday's Maxwell House percolating coffee theme played in most Americans' heads every day, along with his other earworms like "You can be sure if it's Westinghouse," "You're ahead in a Ford," and the ABC-TV sound signature. Siday was out front in the industry with the electronic sounds he used in his ads, but like Nikolais, he depended on *musique concrète* techniques. He was the very sort of client RCA had hoped to woo with its Mark II. At Bob's display he liked what he saw and set up a visit to Trumansburg.

A leading figure of the academic avant-garde approached Bob's table next. Lejaren Hiller had a rare mix of talents—chemist and composer. He was the founder of the Experimental Music Studios at the University of Illinois in 1958, the second campus electronic music lab in the U.S. after Columbia's. Hiller was the first person to teach a computer to compose music. Using statistical mechanics, he found a way to program the University's room-sized ILLIAC I computer to write a composition that was printed out on sheet music and premiered by a live string quartet in 1957. Hiller once jokingly threatened to eliminate rock music by programming a computer to create all possible rock songs, copywriting them, and refusing to allow anyone to perform them. Looking over Bob's modules he considered an order for the Illinois studio.

At a mid-week AES conference session—"Music and Electronics"— Bob introduced his Abominatron with a paper, "Voltage-Controlled Electronic Music Modules." It was an intimidating crowd. Harald Bode chaired the session of speakers—all heavies in the electronic music establishment: Hugh Le Caine, Lejaren Hiller, a rep from the Brandeis University Electronic Music Studio, and David Luce, an M.I.T. research engineer who would cross paths with Bob in a big way a decade later. In an afternoon session, Harry F. Olson and Herbert Belar, the inventors of the RCA Mark I and II synthesizers, delivered papers.

Two weeks after the AES, Eric Siday and his technician arrived in Trumansburg to order a smorgasbord of modules—the most ambitious collection of circuits Bob had ever built. Bob calculated the total price at around $1,700—what he thought was fair. The order was a godsend. Writing to Siday, he betrayed the hand-to-mouth reality of the storefront: "I must thank you sincerely for your most considerate advance payment which will enable us to purchase the necessary materials in economical quantities."[14]

On the home front, things were chaotic. The family was moving again—the new address in Trumansburg on Cayuga Street was another duplex rental with plenty of land for a vegetable garden. From the back door it was only 800 feet across a wooded area to the rear of the Main Street shop. In the midst of it all, Shirleigh was busy putting up 100 quarts of preserves and 60 jars of jam while taking care of the girls. She was also juggling the company bookkeeping, and in December she summed up the precarious situation to Florence: "The business is at the exciting point now of being on the verge of 1) being discovered by all who count & 2) almost bankrupt. If we can only hang on for a couple of months we'll be o.k."[15]

Bob, with a staff of four now (including Shirleigh and himself), plus a handful of orders after the AES conference, was emboldened and pulled out all the stops in a tenth anniversary Fall–Winter company newsletter. It was another faux corporate spin on recent happenings: *During this past year we have greatly expanded our research and production facilities and are now embarked on a program of development of electronic instruments for the musician.*[16]

The newsletter, and a fancy new product catalog, announced the big news: the unveiling of the portable amp kit, the new PMS-15. After he'd spent nearly two years developing it, Bob hit prospective customers over the head with every possible reason to buy it, ensuring that no detail was spared in a sales pitch cribbed from the likes of Ampex or Scully:

The PMS-15 is . . . capable of clean, accurate reproduction, yet completely portable and self-powered. . . . take it into the back yard for patio parties and barbeques, to the beach or remote vacation spots, wherever you go. . . . It's brown leather-like case fits into any décor. . . . The outer shell is vacuum-molded Royalite, the same material used in the finest luggage. . . . A rugged, yet attractive, rattle-free handle mounted on top of the cabinet completes the effect of functional elegance.[17]

The technical specs were a telling and painful record of the time and sweat Bob had poured into the project. The newsletter explained how he'd researched construction and design standards in modern hi-fi equipment, devised unconventional circuitry, and studied advances in the field of foam plastics for a speaker enclosure to ensure quality sound. He offered the PMS-15 as a kit with a "profusely illustrated, step-by-step assembly manual," or as a completely built unit that was "factory assembled and tested."[18]

Unable to leave well enough alone, Bob followed the idea to another level. For the creative whims of his hobbyist brethren he offered the XP-2 "experimenter's kit" for serious tinkerers who might want to customize the amp. The documentation was head-spinning: The XP-2 came with a "textbook-style instruction booklet," loaded with data on how to design and build the cabinet and chassis, and wire the circuit boards from scratch.[19]

For the launch of the PMS-15, Shirleigh remembered, "Robert said to me, 'What's the least we could sell?' I said, 'I don't know'—big market expert here, with two kids—'Um, a hundred?' So Robert tooled up for a hundred of these things, and he sent out notices." After two years of anticipation, the response was devastating: "We got an order for three . . . and it was like . . . Lordy-Lordy, what do we do now?"[20]

"As successful as the theremin kit was, that's how big a bomb the musical instrument amplifier kit was," Bob remembered.[21] "Nobody was going to buy this kit because it was an ill-conceived product."[22] He realized it was overpriced and conceded, "It was becoming obvious to me that I was not going to necessarily make it in the kit business."[23]

There was one bright side to the ill-fated PMS-15: it was the first of Bob's products to display what would become the indelible R. A. Moog logo—a circle enclosing an abstract musical note—designed by a customer in exchange for a Melodia theremin.

At year's end, Bob was in the hole for advertising, salaries, materials, rent, and a host of other operating costs, totaling a business loss of over $28,000. Two days before Christmas, Shirleigh wrote Florence, "Thank you so much for the gift for the girls. It would be a plump untruth if I said we didn't especially appreciate it now. I'm bushed from about 6 batches of baked goods for Rob. It's his only gift this sparse year."[24]

Florence responded a week later with a $5,000 gift from her mother's estate. Freda had died a few months earlier, and Florence rationalized it as a grandson's inheritance that should have been left to Bob anyway. Setting aside her reservations, she wrote, "I gather from what I have been hearing lately that times are a bit tough up your way. I wouldn't want your venture to fail for want of help that I can easily give, and so I am sending the enclosed check. I hope it is enough to make a real difference to you. I was very much impressed by the list of customers Shirleigh mentioned."[25]

Bob wrote back, "Your letter and gift were expected less than anything you can imagine.... I am just beginning to realize that making money is an important requisite to staying in business and, with a little luck, I will remain solvent long enough to apply this new bit of knowledge."[26]

The new year, 1965, kicked off with the delivery of Bob's first modular sale, installed at Alwin Nikolais' home studio in New York City. The choreographer was anxious to have the system so he could compose an electronic score for a March concert of his Alwin Nikolais Dance Company, his resident troupe at the Henry Street Playhouse on Manhattan's Lower East Side. The system had two VCOs, two VCAs, a bandpass filter, a white sound source, a ribbon controller to shape sounds by sliding a finger along a strip, a keyboard, and a power supply. The order was late, setting in motion a pattern that would repeat throughout Bob's career. As a stopgap, Bob had to deliver a set of loaner modules to Nikolais so the choreographer could meet his deadline.

A few weeks later, the instrument Eric Siday had ordered for his commercial jingle work was installed at his apartment in New York. Siday was "a very urbane English-trained violinist," Bob recalled. Siday's wife Edith was a Jewish blues singer and dancer, and the couple lived lavishly off the fat of Eric's lucrative career. Their 10-room apartment in Manhattan's tony Apthorp, an Italian Renaissance Revival building on the Upper West Side, was a cluttered repository for Eric's equipment. "He had completely taken over the living room and the maid's bedroom for his studio work," Bob recalled. "They lived in the dining room. The kitchen was a complete disaster.... That was their environment."[27]

Bob had loaded Siday's equipment into two hefty cardboard boxes and chaperoned it from Trumansburg on an all-night Greyhound bus. In New York he wrestled it into a taxi and arrived strung out at the Apthorp: "I got the thing up on the tenth floor," he recalled, "pushed the boxes out, rang the doorbell and there was Eric in his shorts or something, and he let me in.... It was an incredible load of stuff we made. We worked months and months and sweated it out." Siday's order was huge: five oscillators, two amplifiers, a white noise source, a mixer-amplifier-filter, a keyboard, and a ribbon controller. Bob also included a "rolling equipment table" he'd offered to make from walnut, to match the rest of the cabinetry.

"It was eight o'clock in the morning," Bob recalled, "and Edith's watching this like a shy child. She's watching this from one of the doorways. I put one of the boxes down and take the lid off and take all the packing out and spread it on the hall floor. Take one of the instruments out and set it up. Begin to unpack the next box and I didn't realize this but Edith is slowly losing control of herself.... All of a sudden she screams out 'Eric, more shit in this house! All you ever do is bring shit in this house! One piece of shit after the other!' She broke down into a complete ball of blubber and somehow I got the instrument set up, and got out of there that day."[28]

With the sales to high-profile buyers, Bob was ready to make a serious go of his modular systems. In the January 1965 *AES Journal* he placed an ad: *R. A. MOOG announces the availability of ELECTRONIC INSTRUMENTS FOR THE COMPOSITION AND PERFORMANCE OF CONTEMPORARY MUSIC.*

But constructing these large, custom machines entailed laying out more cash than he'd planned, and like his original 201 theremin project a decade earlier, he always wound up on the losing end. The modular systems he'd made had already eaten up Florence's gift money from her mother's estate. The thesis remained on the back burner, and Bob was taking on odd jobs at Cornell for quick cash. One project was a machine to count apple cells for the pomology department. "Wondering if each month is the last," Shirleigh wrote Florence in March. "If we can hold the line until September I think we're in."[29]

Meanwhile, in the land of aesthetes and the well-heeled, Bob's modules made their sonic debut before a live audience. On March 19, a sophisticated crowd at the Henry Street Playhouse heard Alwin Nikolais' Moog-composed "sound score" in his new choreographic piece, *Galaxy*, a "dance theater trilogy," that was beginning a five-week run. The full-evening work was the first public hearing of one of Bob's "Electronic Instruments for the Composition and Performance of Contemporary Music." Nikolais had a nickname for his new toy: he called it his "Moogaphone."[30]

Nikolais' surround-sound score was projected from speakers placed at the four corners of the theater. On stage, the multimedia work indulged in surreal, kaleidoscopic effects. The dancers' faces and props were covered in fluorescent paint illuminated by ultraviolet light. Dancing against a black backdrop, only heads and objects appeared to move about in ghostly, shifting patterns. The *New York Times* described the "fluorescent bands of elastic attached to the waists, thighs, knees and ankles of dancers linked in chains. The effect is that of a white rail fence stretching and contracting and changing position." Nikolais' Moog score, the paper ventured, "is itself colorful and excellent for the various kinds of dancing."[31]

By April, Bob was desperate and down to counting pennies. He'd gone to Texas to the convention of the Music Teachers National Association—the MTNA—hoping to make some sales, and his situation, as he wrote to Shirleigh from Dallas, was dire: "Want to know what I've eaten today so far? Breakfast: 3 coconut patties and 4 mint patties from a candy manufacturer's exhibit. Lunch: a skinny chopped egg sandwich, coffee, and more candy." George and Shirley had sent him money for the trip and he confessed, "I'm trying like all hell not to bite into my parents' check, but I doubt that I'll be able to make it. Happy Hour has just ended in my room—I've finished a can of beer. Now is the lonely time of the day, - intensified, of course, by everybody else's getting dressed to kill and going out to live it up."[32]

But at the booth next to his, Bob met an exhibitor of like mind—someone who would one day shine a life-altering beacon on his career path. George Kelischek was an instrument builder from Witten, Germany, who'd emigrated to Atlanta, Georgia, in the 1950s. Kelischek single-handedly built impeccable copies of historical instruments ranging from medieval hurdy-gurdies to Renaissance lutes, viols, crumhorns, Baroque violins and recorders, and folk instruments like hammer dulcimers and penny whistles.

Kelischek remembered setting up his display booth at the convention one morning: "Just as I laid various instruments on the table I grabbed one of my crumhorns and played a few notes. A couple minutes later, at the next booth—divided from mine with a little curtain—I heard some funny noises that sounded similar to my crumhorn. And then the curtain was pushed aside and a smiling Moog said, 'did it sound alright?' and I said, 'yeah, how did you make it?' and he said, 'I used my synthesizer to create that sound.' And that's how we met."[33]

Kelischek's success, even though he dealt in an esoteric market of specialized instruments, showed that it was possible to prosper as a small, independent instrument builder. Bob sensed an immediate spiritual kinship with him. Here was a virtuoso woodcrafter of one-off instruments—a true luthier, fellow connoisseur of classical music, and a self-made businessman—who was supportive and encouraging. Bob confessed his anxieties over the way forward, but Kelischek counseled him not to surrender to despair; he predicted that with patience Bob would reap the fruits of his efforts in two or three years.

There were other hopeful signs. "I haven't taken official count yet," Bob wrote Shirleigh, "but it seems that nearly fifty colleges and conservatories' teachers have left their names, and at least a dozen, from Rhode Island to Colorado, have said that they were fixing to set up studios. If half of these materialize within the next year, we'll be in great shape—IF we make it to September."[34]

9
A Few Thousand Screws

"At the depths of depression (mid-March), Rob accepted a job making cheap amplifiers," Shirleigh confided to Florence. "Junk amplifiers as we call 'em."[1]

It was a bitter irony. Bob's high-end amp kit lay stillborn, and he'd completely missed the obvious: while his head was in the highbrow clouds, the Beatles and Rolling Stones had burst onto the scene in 1964 and touched off a stampede of teen fans toward cheap electric guitars and low-end amps. The very glitches Bob had spent two years ironing out of his deluxe amplifier—distortion and noise—were just what the kids wanted now. Cheap amps were doing a runaway business.

Bob's newfound prestige, and his "non-conventional clientele" like Nikolais and Siday, weren't paying the bills. The only hope was an emergency "bread and butter" product. A massive influx of electric guitars to serve the new youth market was pouring in from Japan, and it opened up an opportunity: every guitar needed an amp, but the amps were too bulky and expensive to ship from overseas. Walter Sear, trying to help Bob out, brokered a deal with several Manhattan music dealers for R. A. Moog to knock out hundreds of cheap vacuum tube amps to meet the new demand. Speed was everything in this business and quality mattered little—the opposite of Bob's credo—but a job was a job.

To get an assembly line going, Bob placed want ads in the *Ithaca Journal*. The applicants, he remembered, were "farm wives, town wives, and they just wanted money to buy curtains for their house, a couple of new dresses every now and then."[2] Sear recalled, "they'd been knitting all these years—they still had some manual dexterity, so they were the wirers and solderers."[3]

Sear's first order—for 100 amps—was on the table in May 1965. It was a shaky tightrope walk between the slim profit margin for Bob and Sear, and the skinflint New York wholesalers who insisted on paying bottom dollar. "Every penny is going to count on this deal," Sear cautioned Bob. "Otherwise, we go broke."[4] The whole operation had a shady feel. By June, the Main Street shop ladies were cranking out units and slapping on cabinet labels for made-up brands—"Amper" and "Segova"—scrambling to do the work of an industrial assembly line. The constant correspondence between Sear in New York and Bob in Trumansburg left a bloody record:

SEAR: *Trying to figure out a way to get these amplifiers down to a price where I can make a profit and I haven't been too successful. . . . assumes that a unit can be put together in 11 minutes (I doubt it) . . . .*
BOB: *Let's plan to visit U.S. Musical Monday Morning. . . . I will explain how much money I have lost and then let you do the rest of the talking. . . . we also desperately need at least some of the money that is tied up in this stuff. . . . I think you should do battle with Davidoff and soak him as much as you like . . . .*
SEAR: *Davidoff wouldn't advance any money—said that he was tight. . . . I am looking forward to the day when we are all so well capitalized that a few thousand screws in inventory won't upset the bank balance. . . . we are not making anything on the Davidoff stuff—*
BOB: *I am not making any money either.*[5]

In the thick of the amp project, Bob got a cryptic request from a research scientist working with missile trajectories and artificial intelligence. The complex, custom order, from a Mr. David Rothenberg of the New York Research Group, was slated for a psychological study by the Air Force. The device, if Bob could make it, would be used to measure test subjects' recognition of patterns in musical scales from non-Western countries. The purpose of the experiments wasn't made clear, but there was some sort of application to decoding spoken language. Rothenberg's nearly impenetrable order involved "a microtonal polyphonic performance instrument" with "thirty-one independent oscillators per octave, seven octaves, and a special two-dimensional keyboard with 479 keys."[6] The project tossed Bob into the deep end of his research—a brain challenge he thrived on, but a Gordian knot that would consume his time and drain his meager resources, all for a $2,500 fee dangled at the end of the project.

Hemorrhaging money on the amplifier mill and laying out more capital for the Rothenberg project, Bob piled on yet another one-off to generate cash flow. Walter Sear, trying to throw Bob more work, used his connections to secure a specialized commission in the stratospheric echelons of New York's music circles—a chance for Bob to hitch his star to the world-famous avant-garde composer, John Cage, for a high-profile concert at Lincoln Center.

Cage was the musical renegade who famously kicked down the wall between music and noise. All sounds could be music for him. Cage pioneered a method of composing with "chance operations," tossing coins and consulting the ancient Chinese *I Ching* book of divination to determine which notes and rhythms to write down. In what he called "indeterminacy," many of his works left compositional choices to performers, inviting them to interpret a score freely, in the moment, lending it a fresh identity at each hearing. His *Imaginary Landscape No. 4* for 12 radios called on performers (the radio operators) to twiddle dials, capturing live broadcasts in a random cacophony of talk radio, sermons, music, ads, and white noise between stations.

Cage's "chance" world of spontaneity belonged to what New Yorkers called "downtown music," a freewheeling performance art– based aesthetic that grew up in the bohemian spaces of Manhattan's Tribeca district. "Uptown music," its philosophical opposite, was considered more structured and classically rooted, identified with the Columbia-Princeton center and the chin-pinching earnestness of academic composers.

Cage titled his book of ruminations on music, *Silence*, a tag that aptly described his signature work, which he called 4′33″. In the score—consisting entirely of one paragraph of instructions—players were told to sit with their instruments on stage, in silence, for exactly 4 minutes and 33 seconds. The random ambient noises, along with coughs, titters, and whispers contained in that time span, became the composition at any particular performance.

When Cage wrote specific sounds into his music, they were often achieved by unconventional methods; his "prepared piano" pieces called for an assortment of screws, nuts, bolts, and objects like weather stripping, cardboard, and bamboo to be placed around the strings of a conventional piano to turn it into a thumping, clanging percussion ensemble.

Cage sometimes dabbled in *musique concrète*, and the project Bob was recruited for magnified that technique to gargantuan proportions and added chance elements. *Variations V*, a multimedia work, involved dance, film projections, and a massive conglomeration of electronic gear. Bob's part was to furnish one element in the daunting mechanical infrastructure that Cage required to realize his vision. "We built a set of antennas that were sensitive to dancers' movements," Bob explained, "and they were just rods about five feet long and 3/8″ in diameter and they sat in platforms around the dance area. When a dancer got within a few feet of them they would respond electrically."[7] It was a theremin concept—antennas reacting to body capacitance—but designed only to trigger sounds in other electronic devices provided by Cage.

Bob had a crew of 8 to 10 people working overtime on the project, but things weren't going well. With the job already behind schedule, the phone rang one night at 9 p.m. Henri Sack, Bob's thesis advisor, was on the line. Shirleigh recalled, "He said, 'Moog, how's the doctorate?' And Rob said, 'I'm working on it,' and Sack said, 'What isn't on my desk by this Friday won't be in your dissertation.' So Robert finished whatever he could and went to give the dissertation in."[8]

Sack's office was on the sixth floor of Cornell's new physics building, Clark Hall. Bob rode the elevator up to drop off his thesis, *Ultrasonic Absorption in Sodium Chloride*—a last-minute draft thrown together hastily. The moment was a fitting climax to an eight-year tussle with the degree. As the elevator ascended, Bob's mind strayed from solid-state physics to the physics of sound. Something about the natural resonance of the elevator caught his attention and he started jumping up and down to test it out. The car stalled between floors, he rang the bell, and people peeked in. By the time he was finally rescued, Sack had left, and Bob shoved the dissertation onto his desk. The incident made the rounds the next day and Sack reportedly had a laugh over it. Shirleigh recalled, "Robert got poor marks and incompletes all the way through because he was building theremins. He squeaked out of there with his Ph.D."[9]

After years of hand-wringing over the degree, Bob inserted an unceremonious little aside in the middle of a letter to Florence: "I suspect you have heard that my thesis is finished, through that thorny branch of the grapevine that runs through my parents' house. The final exam is over, and the thesis is being printed up as a report to the Atomic Energy Commission, the outfit that supported my research."[10]

When Bob arrived with his antennas at Lincoln Center's Philharmonic Hall for Cage's dress rehearsal, he found the *Variations V* team scrambling over the stage in a labyrinth of technology. He'd joined a lofty clique of avant-garde glitterati and engineering heavyweights: Max Mathews, the famed Bell Labs engineer who in 1957 had written the first digital computer program to synthesize music; Nam June Paik, the celebrated "father of video art"; David Tudor, pianist, composer, and darling of the avant-garde who'd premiered

Cage's *4′33″*; Merce Cunningham, the innovative modern dancer and choreographer who was Cage's lifelong partner; plus a technical support team and six dancers from the Merce Cunningham Dance Company.

Bob and his workers struggled to hold up their end. R. A. Moog hadn't yet advanced to the point of making printed circuits, so all the wiring was done by hand, and a batch of plated metal soldering lugs failed when the plating flaked off. "We had an awful time," Bob recalled. "We had to rebuild all of those, right up to the minute the concert began. We were in way over our head."[11]

The premiere of *Variations V* took place on July 23, 1965, as part of the New York Philharmonic's French-American Festival. The work took up the entire second half of the evening, after intermission.

Nothing could have prepared the audience for what they witnessed: a 40-minute din of blaring *musique concrète* noises with the chaos of dancers leaping and dashing around Bob's antennas, all beneath a giant screen with a flickering collage of distorted TV images and rehearsal video of the dancers. The jungle of equipment networked together to make it all happen was stupefying: when dancers' motions set off any of Bob's 12 antennas, or interrupted beams from 12 photocell sensors sitting at the base of each antenna, they activated a dizzying array of short-wave radios and tape recorders with pre-recorded sounds, all controlled by three assisting composers on a platform at the back of the stage. One composer alone handled 12 tape recorders and 12 radios by himself.

Other sounds came from contact microphones embedded in the dancers' props. At one point, a dancer stood on her head wearing a hidden microphone in her headdress while her partner rocked her back and forth to pick up floor sounds. A total of 96 audio sources were routed through a dense carpet of patch cords to a 50-channel mixer designed and manned by Max Mathews, and sent out to six loudspeakers spread around Philharmonic Hall.

Variations V was an interlocking anarchy where each participant could influence the work, but no one person could control it. The piece used dancers as co-composers, with their movements shaping the work's musical identity as it progressed. Critical reaction was mixed, but mostly positive. The *New York Times* reviewer, Allen Hughes, wrote of Merce Cunningham, "At the very end, he put a potted plant in the basket of the bicycle he just happened to have with him and rode merrily through the maze of spears to achieve, I suppose, the kind of bravura closing one usually associates with Rossini scores . . . a fascinating, if extremely primitive, glimpse into an extraordinary theater of the future." The review garnered Bob his first mention in the *New York Times* when Hughes noted briefly that Cage was "aided by Robert A. Moog, an electronics expert."[12]

For Bob, the fleeting celebrity was satisfying, but the experience, much less so: "I know that disorder is a very important part of Cage's aesthetic," he conceded, but "it takes a certain amount of order even to connect that stuff up." He vented to Florence, "Purpose of all this? There is no purpose!"[13]

Bob's parents had arrived at the performance swaggering over his Philharmonic Hall debut but left a bit bewildered. George made the best of it in a letter to Florence: "Last Friday nite was the big nite at Lincoln Center for Robbie's electronics. The entire program was ultra modernistic and the last half featuring his instruments was ultra-ultra. . . . We hope this will open things up a little for Robbie."[14]

∼∼∼

Back in the shop, Bob's crew of ladies continued needling away at the junk amps with solder splattering on the creaky wooden floors and its stench spewing into the air. Still, despite its humble ambience, the Main Street shop was becoming a destination for the musical aristocracy. Siday, Cage, and Tudor had been up, and the latest dignitary to make the pilgrimage was Vladimir Ussachevsky, coming to order equipment for the Columbia-Princeton Center. The Pottery Barn forager had commissioned Bob to make an envelope generator module to shape sounds in four discreet stages—what he called, "attack," "decay," "sustain," and "release," or ADSR. Ussachevsky had no clue that his idea would someday become the industry standard; at the moment he simply figured it was the most efficient way to plot the contour of a sound. With Ussachevsky's aversion to keyboards, he made sure to set up Bob's ADSR modules at the Columbia-Princeton studios with push-button switches.

The chasm between the elite clientele Bob was hosting in Trumansburg and his mercantile rat race for a buck was growing wider. Looking to spread the word about his modules so he could jettison the day job, he brainstormed with Herb. The two cooked up a plan to host a three-week seminar at the storefront for serious electronic music composers, especially professors from big-budget universities. The "Summer 1965 Workshop and Seminar in Electronic Music Composition" would take place from August 9 to 28. It could accommodate a maximum of 12 participants. The hidden agenda would be to hook the composers on the equipment and send them back to their campuses clutching purchase orders.

"Big Bob has informed me that he expects a picnic a week," Shirleigh complained to Florence. "Ay de mi! Where I get $ for food—I don't know."[15] Bob assigned her to set up lodging in the homes of local residents for the workshop participants and their families. The attendees were a varied lot, from a 19-year-old student from Michigan State University to a 73-year-old Dean Emeritus from the University of New Mexico. There were two math professors from the University of Illinois and a violinist in the Atlanta Symphony.

Bob expected Shirleigh to fill the attendees' downtime with tours of Ithaca and visits to the Moog house. Trumansburg, Shirleigh found, wasn't quite ready for the freewheeling communal familiarity of it all. She remembered how her neighbors across the street were convinced the business was prospering because she was "putting out" for the men coming and going at all hours. "I can remember one woman staying at somebody's house," she recalled, "and the gossip was that Robert put her up there and was going over and servicing her. God bless small minds."[16]

The Workshop participants studied electronic music terminology and techniques with Bob and Herb, and worked in teams on three modular setups in cordoned-off spaces. The final day featured an in-house concert of music composed at the workshop. The closing piece, *A Little Night Music-1965*, by Herb Deutsch, was a collage of *concrète* sounds made on Bob's modules with a spoken track of random quotes from the August 6, 1965, issue of the *Ithaca Journal*, recorded by seminar participants. The random quotes, Herb explained, ranged "from 1965 being a year of terrible racial problems in California, to the Vietnam War, comic strips, and comments on the prizewinning dog in a dog show."[17] Herb couldn't resist dropping in a reference to the dog ("bitch, bitch, bitch") that sorely offended Bob's soldering ladies upstairs.

At the seminar, participants also tried to come up with a name for Bob's system. Somehow, *Electronic Instruments for the Composition and Performance of Contemporary Music*—the wording in the January AES ad—didn't roll trippingly off the tongue. Nikolais' "Moogaphone" wasn't much better. The best the participants could come up with was "Goombars"—a jumbling of the letters of R. A. Moog with the "b" from Bob—but it was voted down.

The modules—still nameless—were showcased for the first time as a live performance instrument on September 25, played by Herb with the New York Improvisation Quartet at Town Hall. The primitive-looking contraption was powered on stage by two car batteries. A WNCN Radio reviewer did his best to give it a name: "Some very startling sounds emanated from the electronic console which was played by Mr. Deutsch."[18]

By October, when Bob released his first price list of modules, he was still referring to them as "Electronic Music Composition Instruments." With no name for the full system, he'd already made sure to christen each module with its own number—starting with the first deliveries to Nikolais and Siday—adding a ring of professionalism in the tradition of the model 305 and 351 theremins. All the modules were assigned numbers in the "900" range. Rather than asking for a garden variety VCO, customers could order the *901 VOLTAGE-CONTROLLED OSCILLATOR*, or the *902 VOLTAGE-CONTROLLED AMPLIFIER*.

A viable R. A. Moog Company was materializing. "I got into the electronic musical instrument business like slipping backwards on a banana peel," Bob was fond of saying.[19] "Out of that AES show, which I got to attend purely by accident, if CBS hadn't canceled I might have been working for IBM or Bell Labs. I don't know. At the end of that show, I was in business. I had orders and I just had to fill them."[20]

But the direction forward still remained uncertain. College installations and systems for private clients were prestigious, but they were sporadic one-offs and expensive to produce. It wasn't clear how you could sustain a business with high-end specialized equipment in a niche market, especially one that was on the cutting edge and still untested in the larger world.

༺༻

In and around the amp lunacy, Bob tried to finish the New York Research Group project but fell short. In December he wrote Rothenberg, "It is reasonable to expect that you will lose all confidence in me. All the evidence (that is, all of my unkept delivery promises) do in fact suggest this. You may wish to cancel the purchase order and request that we return all advance payments to you. . . . The instrument which I am building for you is extremely complex and sophisticated, and it is probably impossible for anyone to build something like it in the times that we originally promised . . . I sincerely hope that this won't have a disastrous effect upon your relations with the Air Force."[21]

Coming in late on delivery was getting to be Bob's default mode. In a letter to Florence, Shirleigh called him "Procrastination Q. Cornpone." But she fretted over his health: "I am beginning to think he will never rest. He goes on uncomplaining and dedicated, catching sleep where he can but still I pray for a wee amount of rest for him. I shall welcome a little $ucce$$ though—this scrimping has begun to lose its novelty. But we are slowly crawling out of debt and I even buy olives once in a while."[22]

Bob's staff, business partners, and customers were barely aware of the silent partner who held his world together. Shirleigh tirelessly answered every call to duty, from packing theremin kits or feeding 30 seminar participants on a $35-a-month food budget, to balancing the company books. She managed every household and mothering duty—cleaning, canning, cooking, baking, laundry, naptime, trips to the library, bedtime stories—and stole a few spare moments for herself to read a magazine. Her cycle of chores ran in a never-ending loop. Her situation, whether she realized it or not, typified the plight of most American women of her generation. Betty Friedan, in her era-defining book, *The Feminine Mystique*, published two years earlier in 1963, called it "the problem that has no name." Shirleigh was clearly a poster child for the "mystique."[23]

Friedan laid out a compelling case about the postwar migration of college-educated women from jobs they'd held while the men were away in the war, right back to the home after the GIs returned. Women, she argued, were made to feel that their biology was their fate, and their identity. They were told they had a maternal obligation to bear and raise children, perpetuating the species and supporting the male half of society, whose job it was to advance civilization through the workplace. The "mystique," she claimed, was a concerted effort by educators, sociologists, psychologists, and even women's magazines, to advance that cause. Women, she felt, had been taught to glory in their role as women, and they "wrote proudly on the census blank: 'Occupation: housewife.'"[24]

"Experts," Friedan explained, "told them how to catch a man and keep him, how to breastfeed children and handle their toilet training, how to cope with sibling rivalry and adolescent rebellion; how to buy a dishwasher, bake bread, cook gourmet snails."[25] In one interview Friedan conducted, the mother bore a chilling resemblance to Shirleigh: "I love the kids and Bob and my home.... But I'm desperate. I begin to feel I have no personality. I'm a server of food and a putter-on of pants and a bedmaker, somebody who can be called on when you want something. But who am I?"[26]

During the summer workshop, Shirleigh had labored along in the "mystique." "I didn't have a dishwasher," she recalled. "I was washing dishes from lunch and getting ready for dinner. My hands were really in water 70% of the day." When the seminar ended, she asked Bob for a dishwasher, but it was the adding machine tug-of-war all over again: he told her she could have one if she paid for it herself. "So I substitute taught at the elementary school a couple of times," she remembered, "and that gave me enough money to buy a dishwasher."[27]

After Laura's birth, Shirleigh's identity on the annual household tax form read, "Occupation: Housewife." As the year wrapped up, she wrote Florence, "Needless to say things here are bustling; presents to wrap and doll clothes yet unmade, pie to bake, tree to cut & decorate and an office party to whip up. . . . Laura wants to make cut out cookies with me. . . . What some women do to keep a man!"[28]

PART III
COSMIC SOUNDS

10
Hallucinations for Your Ear

The Maytag washing machine was rumbling and shaking. Filled with rocks and tethered to a long extension cord, it was wheeled down the main corridor of the San Francisco Conservatory of Music, rolling noisily behind a dancer. The audience wandered out of rooms filled with ambient tape music and followed the dancer and the washing machine down the hall as strolling participants in a multimedia "happening" of electronic music, improvisational theater, dance, and whatever else was going on at the moment.

The theatricality was straight out of John Cage and the "downtown" credo of art in the moment; but the electronic sounds belonged to the "uptown" ideology of finished compositions piped through speakers. On the West Coast the "downtown" and "uptown" had married in a happy alliance of technology and loopy artistic stunts. And the union was often consummated with psychotropic drugs.

The *washing machine action-event* was the brainchild of two composition students at the San Francisco Conservatory, Ramon Sender and Pauline Oliveros. The happening was the finale to their 1961–'62 "Sonics" concert series at the Conservatory. Sender and Oliveros each dabbled in *musique concrète*, despite a paucity of resources. Oliveros took to recording sounds using cardboard tubes as filters, and her bathtub as a reverberation chamber. Another of their colleagues, the clarinetist Morton Subotnick, made tape compositions by recording himself dashing through his garage hitting automobile parts and the guts of an old piano hanging from the rafters.

By the summer of 1962, Sender and Subotnick decided to put an institutional roof over their heads and assemble a real studio. In an old Victorian house on Jones Street in the Russian Hill district, they formed the San Francisco Tape Music Center. The site was a laboratory hangout for musicians to toy with electronics, and doubled as a community space to host experimental concerts. Despite the uptown-sounding name, the Center excelled primarily in downtown-influenced work. Oliveros, who joined Sender and Subotnick there, did one piece bobbing on a seesaw fixed on a rotating platform under a chattering mynah bird, and ended another work with a performer shooting a pistol with blanks into a piano.

The Center pushed the spirit of these performance art events to new levels with a happening by Sender and two collaborators in 1963 that used the entire city of San Francisco as its performance space. *City Scale* shuttled the audience around in two trucks to witness a light show projected on the Wells Fargo building, a "car ballet" in North Beach with colored headlight gels and coordinated headlight blinking to the popping of firecrackers, and funhouse moments like a trombone player in the Broadway Tunnel, a woman in a store window singing Debussy in a bathrobe, and two dancers in a broken-down convertible pretending to argue as husband and wife over a driving lesson. The evening ended at 2 a.m. with participants running and screaming across a park toward four 17-foot weather balloons Sender had inflated, inadvertently scattering two teenage gangs gathered there for a rumble.

City Scale questioned the line between art and reality and put the Tape Music Center at the hub of the nascent San Francisco counterculture. But the blurring of lines sometimes backfired. When Sender accidentally burned down the Jones Street house by short-circuiting a fuse, fans of the Center rushed over to see the "big fire on Russian Hill" they'd heard about on the radio, figuring it was another happening: "Wow, great event!" one of them told Sender excitedly.[1]

By the spring of 1963, the Tape Music Center had found a new home on Divisidero Street at the border of Haight-Ashbury. The "Haight," boasting the first head shop in town—the Magic Theater for Madmen Only—would quickly become the epicenter of hippie culture as the unintentional host to an infusion of disenchanted youth swarming in from around the country. The radical transformation of the district affected the Tape Music Center. As the local temple of experimental arts, it began to draw adherents of a new genre: "psychedelic rock," a style that began as an underground San Francisco movement in a few clubs and grew to define '60s counterculture. The music was a patchwork of folk, jazz, blues, and Indian raga, with bits of Cage and *musique concrète*. Artists who lived in the neighborhood—Janis Joplin, members of the Warlocks (soon to be the Grateful Dead), Big Brother and the Holding Company, and Grace Slick, future member of Jefferson Airplane—were showing up at Tape Center concerts.

Sender and Subotnick pressed on in the studio, assembling their *concrète* pieces through the same tedious splicing and processing drills they'd always used, grappling with the hodgepodge of equipment at the Center that they'd cobbled together from military surplus, junkyards, scientific laboratories, telephone companies, and even an insurance company liquidation from an electronics store fire. None of it was originally designed for making music. With their limited technical knowledge, they needed someone with the engineering know-how and musical background to streamline the process for them.

An audience regular at the Tape Center was Donald Buchla, a composer of sorts, with a background in physics and electronics. When he found out the Center had a three-track tape recorder, he talked Subotnick into granting him studio time to edit his *concrète* music (one of his pieces used recorded insect sounds). Buchla was a native Californian, born in 1937. Like Bob, he'd studied piano and tinkered with ham radio as a child. He earned a physics degree from the University of California at Berkeley in 1959 and stayed on for graduate studies, joining in jobs there for NASA and the Lawrence Radiation Laboratory, where much of the atom bomb development had gone on in the early 1940s. He joined the Berkeley Free Speech Movement which ignited on campus in October 1964, and found that his loyalties as a government-commissioned scientist were tested. When he signed on to the student civil disobedience acts that set the stage for American campus protests in the '60s, he was marked as anti-establishment and couldn't continue working with his physics colleagues. He dropped out of Berkeley soon after.

When Buchla first arrived at the Tape Center, in early 1965, he was tapped for his technical skills and handed an informal title: "member engineer." His first contribution was a ring modulator—a device that outputs the sum and difference of two frequencies fed into it—built to supplement the Center's random collection of equipment. Hoping to further grow the studio, Sender and Subotnick applied to the Rockefeller Foundation for support. In their May 20, 1965, application they listed the Tape Music Center's existing equipment—everything from "22 oscillators" to a "reverberation system," a "tape transport chain," a "variable equalizer," a "ring modulator," and the three-channel tape recorder.[2] There was still no system in place to get around the annoying tape splicing Sender and Subotnick struggled with, and they hoped Buchla, with his engineer's imagination and the incentive of some underwriting, might see them out of the rut.

A small grant of $15,000 from the Rockefeller Foundation was awarded to the Tape Center on July 1, 1965, "to further its experimental work in the performing and visual arts."[3] Sender and Subotnick peeled off $500 for Buchla to create some kind of composition-based circuitry. Buchla had no prior experience designing electronic musical devices, but he'd made an apparatus for blind students he worked with at Berkeley. His "ORB" ("optical ranging for the blind") helped the students navigate physical spaces with its LED light beam that measured the relative proximity of objects and set off musical tones that corresponded to the varying distances.

Buchla's experience with optical technology seemed like a good starting point for a musical system at the Center, and he began with a light-sensing scheme. "The first thing I built there," Buchla explained, "was a device that analyzed the shape of a hand to create a wave shape—so that as you moved your hand in an optical path and spread your fingers, you'd get a harmonically rich wave shape, but if you kept your fingers together, you'd get a sine wave. And you could vary the pitch with a foot pedal."[4] The system worked, but it seemed like the wrong direction to follow.

Through the summer and fall of 1965—while Bob's Trumansburg seminar rolled along, as Siday and Nikolais composed with their new Moog modules, as university labs in Illinois, Toronto, and Columbia assimilated Bob's equipment, and Herb Deutsch played a modular system at Town Hall—Buchla, Sender, and Subotnick plugged away to find their own solution. Seemingly, none of them was aware of Bob's system. Had they known about it, their work could have started out several levels higher. "There were a lot of meetings and talk about what we needed," Subotnick recalled. "We wanted to be able to control amplitude and frequency. . . . For the next few months, the three of us began a theoretical journey with pencils."[5]

That July, Bob had gone public for the first time with the circuitry behind his modular scheme, publishing the details of his October 1964 AES talk, in the *Journal of the Audio Engineering Society*, in an essay titled "Voltage-Controlled Electronic Music Modules," a revelation that reverberated through the electronic music community.[6]

In the end, in the fall of 1965, Buchla decided to configure his system as a series of voltage controlled interactive modules with oscillators, amplifiers, and envelope generators; his scheme also added a ring modulator. Unlike Bob's modular system, Buchla's configuration didn't include a filter, and it wasn't set up with Bob's one-volt-per-octave arrangement because, along with Sender and Subotnick, he wasn't interested in creating traditional melodic and harmonic music.

The same conversation came up about the keyboard-versus-no-keyboard conundrum that Bob and Herb had had a year earlier. Sender, a pianist, wanted a standard black-and-white keyboard as a controller. Subotnick and

Buchla argued for a different approach. Earlier, Buchla had built a small unit with 10 pressure-sensitive copper touch plates. Each plate or "key" triggered one of the Center's 10 tape loop machines that ran *musique concrète* sounds. Buchla added this interface to his modules as a controller.

Buchla's crowning touch—something Bob didn't have—was a device called a "sequencer," his pioneering controller that repeated a series of events in a continuous cycle, like a person counting to 10 over and over. Bob remembered how Raymond Scott had once used the idea with his carnival of contraptions: "He had rack upon rack of stepping relays that were used by the telephone company. The relay would step through all positions when dialed. . . . It was a huge, electro-mechanical sequencer! And he had it programmed to produce all sorts of rhythmic patterns. The whole room would go 'clack—clack—clack,' and the sounds would come out all over the place!"[7] Scott's system used his Clavivox—with Bob's theremin circuitry—as one of many sound sources it could tap to cycle through a series of notes.[8]

For Buchla, the sequencer idea started as a simple labor-saving device: "You wouldn't have to splice 16 pieces of tape together if you wanted a sequence of 16 notes," he explained.[9] But Buchla's voltage-controlled analog sequencer could step through more than just a group of notes; it could repeat a set of almost anything, like sounds, timbres, or volume levels.

Sender and Subotnick wanted the system mainly for composing, but Buchla was looking more at live performance. He liked the Cage aesthetic of random sound patterns unfolding in real time, and a brilliant feature of his setup was how three sequencers could interact with each other. By coupling them and setting them to unequal numbers of stages, they could create a complex set of constantly shifting patterns over time, like a robot let loose to improvise on its own.

Buchla delivered a partly finished modular prototype to the Tape Music Center in November 1965 and demonstrated it in the concert hall. He christened it the "Modular Electronic Music System," or MEMS. Two small cabinets housed the modules, and everything interacted with patch cords. Bill Maginnis, the Tape Center's technician, sat up all night in the studio and played with it until 4 a.m., writing the first-ever composition on it—a piece he called *Flight*. "I was feeling so good about what was now beginning to happen," Maginnis recalled, "that I played a little joke on Pauline Oliveros, who was to start working that morning around 9 or 10 A.M. I programmed the sequencer to play the first eight notes of 'Yankee Doodle' over and over again as soon as the main power was turned on. This plan backfired; the joke was on me. Pauline called at 8:30 A.M., woke me out of a sound sleep, and I had to go back to the center and stop it."[10]

∿∿∿

The psychedelic scene in San Francisco was heating up under the influence of LSD. The drug's hallucinogenic effects were known as early as the 1940s, and by the '50s its consciousness-altering properties were explored by the Central Intelligence Agency as a possible tool for interrogations. The CIA ran top-secret trials on human subjects—willing and unwilling—and in 1959, a San Francisco area writer, Ken Kesey, signed up as a paid guinea pig. Several years later, Kesey published his popular novel, *One Flew Over the Cuckoo's Nest*, and started taking LSD recreationally; he called it "acid"—short for its chemical name, lysergic acid diethylamide.

Kesey lived in a log house on a six-acre property in La Honda, 45 miles south of San Francisco. A sign outside the entrance warned, "No Left Turn Unstoned." Living communally on the property were a band of nonconformist rogues calling themselves the Merry Pranksters for their sadistic pleasure at throwing others into confounding situations. They indulged in LSD parties called Acid Tests that stretched over days, and once invited the whole San Francisco chapter of the Hell's Angels, who took easily to the pleasures of turning on.

In the fall of 1965, Kesey met Augustus Owsley Stanley III—better known as Owsley—an audio engineer and chemist who made LSD from his Berkeley home and had just produced nearly 300,000 doses in three months. When he started distributing it in San Francisco, his tabs set the standard—suddenly everyone wanted "genuine Owsley," prompting Kesey to move his Acid parties into the community as public events. "Can *You* Pass the Acid Test?" the slogan on flyers goaded. For a one-dollar admission fee, takers could party all night in a bash of lights, music, and new dimensional vistas playing out in their heads.

Building on the momentum of the Acid Tests, the San Francisco avant-garde joined forces with the counterculture to mount an ambitious multi-day show they called the Trips Festival—a sort of "electronic art happening." The mix of Tape Center people like Ramon Sender, Bill Maginnis, and Don Buchla with rockers like the Grateful Dead and Big Brother and the Holding Company showed how thin the boundaries had become between these worlds. The acts hyped for the Festival could have come from an acid trip: "nude projections, 'the god box,' the endless explosion, the congress of wonders, liquid projections, the jazz mice, hell's angels, ron boise & his electric thunder sculpture, & the unexpectable."[11] The festival was billed as a non-drug event, but Saturday's show was scheduled to include "Ken Kesey & The Acid Test," with "the Merry Pranksters & their psychedelic symphony."

The Trips Festival ran during the weekend of January 21–23, 1966, at San Francisco's Longshoremen's Hall. In the center of the space, a lofty scaffolding supported a load of multimedia gear. Don Buchla sat perched up above the crowd, working a "sound-light console" and his PA system that the Pranksters had nailed to the ceiling, switching the bands on and off and working the complex of lights. The Grateful Dead never missed an Acid Test, and played, along with Big Brother and the Holding Company, who were making their public debut. During downtimes between acts, Buchla debuted his now-completed voltage controlled modular system, filling the hall with strange new electronic sounds that he improvised as solo interludes.

The Trips Festival was sheer sensory overload, powered by electricity. The Tape Center projected films; ecstatic dancing on the floor pulsed with flashes of Day-Glo paint fluorescing under ultraviolet lights; a trampoline artist in a ski mask dove off a balcony, executing midair tricks in the flickering freeze frames of a strobe. Kesey, on the run after two recent marijuana busts, showed up disguised in a silver space suit with a visor over his face and flashed strange messages on the wall from the overhead projector: "Anybody who knows he is God go up onstage." At Saturday night's Acid Test there was plenty of LSD punch to go around; inside the throbbing din and the high-pitched anarchy, the Pranksters announced, "Can you die to your corpses?" "Can you metamorphose? Can you pass the twentieth century?"

Bob had his first whiff of interest from a rock group that summer. The Beach Boys had just released their groundbreaking *Pet Sounds* album with a theremin-like sound on the song, "I Just Wasn't Made for These Times." The effect came from an "electro-theremin," a device constructed by an LA session musician, Paul O. W. Tanner, as a shortcut to the tricky theremin interface. The instrument used a hands-on workaround with a sliding knob controlling an oscillator, and a rotating dial for volume. Tanner was recording another electro-theremin track for the song "Good Vibrations," slated for release as a single that fall, and the group asked him to join them on tour. Tanner refused, so a substitute for the electro-theremin had to be found.

Walter Sear remembered the Beach Boys trying out a standard theremin in his studio: "I demonstrated it and they tried to play it, and they said, 'No, no, this is impossible.' I said, 'Well a musical instrument does take a few years to learn to play it.' They said, 'Oh, no, we're guitarists. Can you do anything like a fret board?'"[12] Sear bounced the question over to Bob, who came up with a solution based on the ribbon controller like the ones he'd made for Siday and Nikolais—what he sometimes called a "stringer," a "slide-wire," or a "linear controller"—a resistance strip that allowed continuous, siren-like sweeps of pitch as a finger was slid along its surface. The variation he designed for the Beach Boys—he called it a "Melsinar"—was packaged in a two-foot-long walnut box with the ribbon controller running along the top. Sear remembered marking the location of the notes with a grease pencil along the strip to make it easier to play. For the Beach Boys' Mike Love, it was a hassle-free solution on tour and would become a signature part of the band's gear.

Most of the time Bob was still "scratching for loot," as Sear once described his own situation.[13] The junk amp business seemed more and more like a contraband operation when Bob learned in February that the celebrated classical guitarist Andrés Segovia had threatened to sue over the "Segova" nameplate on the amps. From now on, the plates would swap out a single letter for a revised bogus name: "Sekova." "I think the bit with Andrés Segovia is a gasser," Bob wrote Sear. "I laughed so hard that people began to wonder what was wrong with me. Sekova is an awful name but we will do it."[14]

Hauling in cash seemed much easier for those who simply *used* Moog equipment. *Time* magazine ran a one-page feature in November on Eric Siday and his jingle business, calling him "one of the highest-paid and most frequently played composers in the world," explaining, "No day goes by, in fact, that roughly 80% of the U.S. population does not hear at least one of his compositions."[15] There was no mention of Bob's name, but it was clear Siday was getting a good return on his modules. According to the article, his sound signatures—all of them under seven seconds—earned him an average of $5,000 a second.

For the man who *made* the oscillators, it was a different story: as 1966 closed out, R. A. Moog reported a business loss of $4,333, and Bob and Shirleigh claimed a personal income loss of $3,581.

The type of clients Bob kept company with were at least partly to blame. His pet customers were still university studios and avant-garde composers in the Herb Deutsch mold. He walked comfortably among academic musicians because they were like him: always examining their discipline under a microscope and reporting their findings in journals and at conferences. That was the crowd he wanted to be in with. To keep current with them, Bob unveiled a new scholarly publication in January 1967. *Electronic Music Review* was a magazine-format quarterly with articles by composers, music engineers, and electronic music historians. His co-editor was Reynold Weidenaar, the junior member among the composer participants at the Summer '65 Seminar. The mission of *Electronic Music Review* was to bridge the gap between scientists and musicians, offer hands-on advice to composers working in the electronic medium, and make new research in the field available. At 64 pages, including ads, the first issue had articles by Harald Bode, Karlheinz Stockhausen, Gustav Ciamaga, Bob, and several others.

The academic emphasis was fine by Florence, who finally came around after a pilgrimage to Trumansburg. "Now I think I really understand what Robert is doing," she wrote Shirleigh, "and (what is still more useful!) I can explain it to other people. From my experience I would say that the layman should get some insight into the process before he tries to judge electronic music in terms of the end result."[16]

The New Year 1967 brought a mix of emotions over the way forward. The February issue of *Electronics World* featured Bob's article, "Electronic Music—Its Composition & Performance," and he told Sear, "in my own modest opinion, I am the leading expert in electronic music equipment at the present time." In the same letter, he spoke about punting the amp business back to Sear. The bottom had fallen out of the market and he was selling off surplus parts at a loss. He suggested Sear set up a sound recording studio in his Manhattan office that would double as a "dandy showroom" for Moog equipment. The idea was based on a hunch that popular culture was about to seize on music technology. "From my vantage point high on the hills of Trumansburg," he ventured, "I see a full blown fad in pop electronic music about to erupt."[17]

High on the hills of San Francisco, from another vantage point, Don Buchla was making the rounds with his modules at Acid Tests after the Trips Festival. "I just showed up at the places with my instruments, took some acid, played some music," he recalled.[18] At the "Awareness Festival" in October

1966—just five days before LSD was made illegal in California—Buchla added doomsday noises from his modules to a mock apocalypse where stoned participants were informed that a Russian atomic warhead was about to strike, followed by a countdown, a blackout, and an explosive shower of flashbulbs. Other times, Buchla worked with Owsley on a state-of-the-art audio system for the Grateful Dead, and ran sound for the band's concerts, sprinkling in effects from his modules. Sometimes he hung out with the Hell's Angels and made recordings with them for his electronic compositions.

Buchla was left out on his own when the Tape Music Center relocated to Mills College in the summer of 1966 on a $200,000 Rockefeller Foundation grant. The new Mills Tape Music Center added equipment and evolved into a "classical studio," the label for an electronic music lab in the mold of Columbia-Princeton. For Oliveros, the new director, and Subotnick, who left for New York City, the old ragtag countercultural spirit of Divisidero Street was lost in the move. By then, Ramon Sender had resigned, abandoned the group, and retreated to the Morning Star Ranch commune in Sonoma County to change directions.

Even though Buchla wasn't a regular presence anymore, the new Mills Tape Music Center seamlessly integrated his MEMS into its studio equipment. In September 1966, a visiting reporter from the *Oakland Tribune* called the system "an electronic monster that could, in theory, drive the pianos and the orchestral instruments right out of the market."[19] The article never mentioned Buchla's name, but noted that the MEMS carried a "list price" of $3,420. Buchla had, in fact, set up business in a tiny storefront in Berkeley to sell more of his modular systems—now called the "Buchla Box"—under the name Buchla and Associates. "I wouldn't call it a factory," he remembered. "We would lay our equipment out on the sidewalk to have enough space to work."[20]

∿∿∿

Bob's April 1967 catalog was a breakout moment. With its banner—*Electronic Music Composition–Performance Equipment*—the word "performance" in the title encouraged people to think of the modules as real-time, live instruments, not simply studio gear.[21] Another linguistic milestone appeared on the interior pages, a generic name to wrap all the disparate audio equipment in: *Synthesizer*. Until now, Bob had been hesitant to adopt the name because of its association with the behemoth RCA Mark II. And there was a common perception that the word itself suggested something artificial, like plastic flowers. Buchla refused to call his modular systems "synthesizers" for that reason, citing the connection people made with rayon as a "synthetic" substitute for silk. But Bob was adamant: "Our instruments are called synthesizers because they are used to assemble musical sounds from their component parts. That is what 'to synthesize' means. The name of the instrument should not imply that the sounds that are produced are fake or imitation. They are real electronic sounds that may at times simulate acoustic instruments but generally have a distinct character of their own."[22] The catalog now called the individual modules "instruments" which could be combined into a complete synthesizer.

After three years of scrambling to please every client with a different custom setup, there were now three standard systems offered—hopefully simplifying life at the Main Street factory. Each came with a full complement of modules, from the entry-level Synthesizer I with 12 modules to the higher-end Synthesizers II and III with extra modules and functions. They ranged in price from $2,835 to $6,190, and customers could order any of the 27 "Single Function" modules separately. The catalog also announced an in-house recording studio at the rear of the Main Street shop—the Independent Electronic Music Center—left over from the Summer '65 Seminar. The call went out to "interested composers."

But the lavishly illustrated, 25-page catalog was still aimed at a customer base of classically trained musicians at universities. It was a problem, because Bob had already equipped nearly 40 schools and it was easy to see that the college market could quickly dry up. And with orders coming in fits and starts, long-range planning was nearly impossible. "Without a reserve of cash and good management," he recalled, "we were always running out of money. We had too much of one thing on the shelf and not enough of another. . . . We were wondering whether we could stay in business because we weren't making any money, and nobody understood our products. . . . We thought seriously of giving the whole thing up and my going out and cashing in my Ph.D. somewhere."[23]

As it happened, Bob was contacted out of the blue by a Los Angeles–based musician and owner of an instrument rental business, Paul Beaver, who wanted to represent R. A. Moog as the company's West Coast dealer. The timing was fortuitous. Bob was headed to LA in April for the AES convention and he'd just taken an order from a California customer, Ralph Swickard—his first sale west of the Rockies. Paul Beaver would arrange for Bob to have a booth at the convention to test the waters. "We'd see if there's any interest on the West Coast," Bob explained, "enough business to make it worthwhile for us to stay in this sort of business." For him and for Shirleigh, the LA trip would be the final verdict. They'd give it one last shot; if it didn't work out, they agreed to shut the company down and Bob would, as he put it, "get an honest job."[24]

Bob arrived in LA with Swickard's synth checked as excess baggage. He recalled trying to find Paul Beaver: "We missed each other at the Los Angeles airport because he was waiting at the first class ramp. He just assumed we were rolling in pure creamery butter."[25] The 1967 LA convention—from April 24 to 27—took place at the Hollywood Roosevelt Hotel, across the street from the famed Grauman's Chinese Theatre. Wrapped in his academic mantle, Bob was conference chairman of the session on Music and Electronics—the first time this category was offered at a West Coast AES. Eric Siday was presenting a paper on "Electronic Music and Communications," and Bob and Harald Bode were giving a joint talk on ring modulator designs.

The day before the convention, Swickard's Synthesizer III was brought to the display area at the hotel so Bob could make his West Coast debut. In the East-West room, at booth number 34, it was hooked up to a pair of headphones. "Once Paul Beaver saw that it worked," Bob recalled, "'cause he'd never seen one before, he says, 'uh, I need to call some of my friends about this.' . . . He was the sort of guy who instantly understood how to use it."[26]

"Well the exhibit opened, and people came pouring in. . . . They'd put the phones on and I'd start in, you know, 'turn this, put this in here,' they'd say, 'Oh, wow! Oh, man! OH MAN! OH WOW!' And then you leave them alone for 10 or 15 minutes, or maybe half an hour. And then the next guy would start. . . . Emil Richards who is a very well known studio percussionist out there . . . had his earphones on and played the keyboard, turning the knobs and saying, 'Oh man! Oh man! Oh man! There goes my Jaguar!' . . . . And guys were blown away. . . . They told their friends, and on the second day we had a line—four people were waiting at a time to hear this thing. It was unbelievable. . . . And they were coming from 50 miles away. The word was going up into the hills outside of Los Angeles. Paul was calling all of his customers who had rented instruments from him. All around they were pouring in and Paul took orders."[27]

Paul Beaver carried a lot of clout with the LA freelance musicians. A gentle soul with a generous spirit, he was revered for his talents on many instruments and for his wizardly technical skills. He was single, and a bit of a loner; at 41, he had a slender frame and a boyish, full-cheeked face, capped by a mop of dark hair that curled over his ears. He preferred dark suits, white shirts and thin ties, and his trademark Republican elephant pin blazoned on his lapel. He lived alone and didn't cook for himself, surviving mainly on fast food and burgers. Originally from Ohio, he came to California in 1947 after serving in Okinawa during World War II. In 1950 he earned a B.A. in psychology from UCLA. He'd played the piano since the age of five, and organ since he was 12; after college he began gigging as a jazz keyboard player in lounges. On his resume he claimed, "approximately two thousand favorite standard numbers memorized."[28]

Paul had quirky preoccupations. He was captivated by UFOs and dabbled in psychic phenomena, claiming he'd proved that "thoughts may be transmitted to anyone asleep and within three feet." He talked of having "other people's dreams."[29] During a bout of internal bleeding that nearly killed him, he focused his willpower and remained conscious, crediting his survival to L. Ron Hubbard's book, *Dianetics*, an experience that led him to study with Hubbard and join the Church of Scientology. As a "Founding Scientologist," he kept diplomas that marked his progress—from "The State of Clear," to "Operating Thetan, fourth level."

All through the 1950s, Paul tinkered with test tone generators, feedback, and rudimentary electronics. Beginning with the sci-fi flick *The Magnetic Monster* in 1953, he assisted Hollywood composers like Jerry Goldsmith, Maurice Jarre, and Johnny Mandel, sprinkling their film scores with electronic seasonings from his homemade contraptions—bits and pieces of acoustic instruments and objects that he hooked up to microphones or electrical components. In 1960 he acquired an old, one-story warehouse at 2825 Hyans Street near downtown LA, where he amassed a stable of electronic instruments to rent out for film studio sessions: Hammond B-3 organs, Novachords, and even an RCA theremin. Sometimes he rented himself out with his instruments, to play or program them. Over the years he racked up a long list of Hollywood contracts with classics like *Doctor Zhivago*. Out in the community he was known mainly for his occasional organ recitals. Beaver lived in the back of his shop, and kept a prized rosebush outside the front entrance—the only bit of life amid the vast concrete landscape.

During the AES conference, Beaver was doing an LA recording gig for an album called *The Zodiac Cosmic Sounds*. For the sessions, he was playing his regular electronic instruments and it dawned on him that the Moog might add some never-before-heard effects to the tracks. With Bob's blessing, he arranged for Swickard's synth to be spirited out overnight to the studio between the final two days of the conference.

The Zodiac Cosmic Sounds was the brainchild of Jac Holzman, the tough guy founder and CEO of Elektra Records, who signed acts like the Doors and Judy Collins. Holzman had an eye and ear for the unusual; he trusted his gut instincts and wasn't afraid to take chances. The Doors' keyboardist, Ray Manzarek, remembered, "He was an intellectual, the cowboy from New York. He was like Gary Cooper riding into town, but with brains."[30] Holzman sensed the temperature of the times and envisioned a new sort of album celebrating the countercultural vogue for psychedelia and mystical worlds. "That was a time when you would meet people in a bar," he recalled, "and they'd say, 'Oh, what's your sign?'"[31] His concept album extended the astrology idea to 12 tracks, each depicting a sign of the zodiac. The music was by Mort Garson, a seasoned music industry composer, songwriter, and arranger who'd worked with artists like Doris Day and Mel Tormé; the poetry, narrated by Cyrus Faryar, was supplied by the writer Jacques Wilson.

Track titles mirrored hippie culture: "Libra—The Flower Child," or "Cancer—The Moon Child"; the spoken lyrics were straight out of a hallucinogenic journey: *Incendiary diamonds scorch the earth. . . . Sleep is burning, dreams are charcoal. . . . Pisces playing the pipes of peace, painting people with promise, pouring the world out of a Moonstone.* The instrumental tracks alternated repetitive, high-energy acid rock licks with more dissonant, outer space–like stretches of languid music. Exotic instruments surfaced and disappeared everywhere in the textures: an electronic harpsichord, or a seductive flute line weaving through an Indian tabla and sitar.

The night the Moog arrived at the studio, Bob came along to observe. The small ensemble represented some of LA's top regulars: Emil Richards on the "exotic percussion," Bud Shank on bass flute, Hal Blaine on drums, Carol Kaye on bass guitar, and Mike Melvoin on keyboards. Beaver was ready at the Synthesizer III to pepper in some newly patched effects.

As it turned out, the very first sound that would be heard on the album was added as a long, air raid siren glissando—10 simultaneous frequencies—rising from the Moog and cross-fading with a driving guitar lick. That opening—the "Aries" track—kicked off a historic moment. *The Zodiac Cosmic Sounds* album would mark two milestones: the first time a Moog synthesizer was used on the West Coast, and the first commercial recording with a Moog synthesizer.

Bob was awestruck by the sheer technical sophistication of the equipment. "I'd never heard anything like this before in my life," he recalled. "And I'd never been in a studio. There were these gorgeous big speakers and big fat sounds and all the gadgets to manipulate the sounds from the musicians."[32] But on playback, he wasn't sure about the *Zodiac* album itself: "The narrator comes on. He had a voice as deep as crude oil, and he said, 'Nine times the color red explodes like heated blood. The battle's on.' . . . It seemed so funny, so corny."[33]

As the evening wore on, the cultural divide between Bob and the production crew became clearer and clearer. "All these LA types," he remembered, "they were like people from a foreign country for a New York boy. You know, these grown men with suntans and they didn't believe in undershirts. All these people were going around with a big, mother-fucking amulet . . . these huge, gold amulets, probably a couple thousand dollars around their neck all the time, and elaborate hairdos . . . and their potbellies sticking out. And they're talking to each other about how great it is to be on dope. You know, they were all this kind of LSD over that kind and the experiences they had—it was just bullshit. And they got through a couple of takes and they listened to it and it sounded pretty good. And these guys were dancing around the control room, literally dancing, saying, 'oh, this is great head music. . . . Every head in the country is gonna have to have this!' Congratulating themselves that this was such a big seller record because it was so IN. They were convinced that this was going to be a quantum leap in commercial pop music. . . . But I thought that was such a crock of shit, you know. I didn't know if I wanted to have my synthesizer associated with that."[34]

Bob began to put the pieces together: "It was the very beginning of the wave of head records," he recalled. "That was just when LSD was becoming hip and the Beatles were going from wearing suits and ties to something a little more far out."[35] But he had to admit, "I hardly knew who the Beatles were; I didn't know who the Grateful Dead were. . . . I just didn't sit around listening to music. I was working. I had a family. . . . I wasn't a participant in the culture. I didn't wear long hair. I didn't have beads. I didn't walk around with platform shoes or bellbottoms. . . . I didn't do dope. No LSD, for sure. God knows, no coke. I was a social toker for a while, and all that happened is I fell asleep. I'd rather get drunk, tastes better. . . . And, on the other hand, I didn't pass judgment on it. . . . I'm too old to have been a part of that. You know, I went through college in the fifties, where you had short hair and you went out and you got a good paying job."[36]

Less than a month after the AES convention, on May 20, Elektra released *The Zodiac Cosmic Sounds* album. "Astrology has become a religious force in our time," the ad proclaimed. "This is the love sound of the future." The cover art fairly defined the psychedelic era: zodiac signs swirling through colorful paisley patterns under a wavy, cartoonish title. On the back, a message in purple declared, "MUST BE PLAYED IN THE DARK."

With the recording debut of the Moog synthesizer, whether Bob condoned it or not, he and his instrument were ceremoniously inducted into head culture. The momentum was unstoppable. On June 3, two weeks after the *Zodiac* album's debut, Hal Blaine released his own Moog-infused tracks on the first-ever 45 r.p.m. single to feature the synth—two relentlessly driving percussion instrumentals with Paul Beaver riding through the textures on his modules. Both tunes—"Wiggy (November)," and "Love-In (December)"—were from Blaine's forthcoming LP, *Psychedelic Percussion*, a 12-part cycle based on the months of the year, that would employ Beaver and the Moog on every track. Not to be outdone, Emil Richards released a concept album the same month—another 12-part series, this one based on the birthstones—called *New Sound Element: "Stones,"* with the Moog programmed by Beaver, and Richards playing on it for every track. It was the first time a Moog synthesizer was credited by name on an album.

In the weeks following, Paul Beaver could see that his hunch about working as Bob's West Coast rep was on the money. California was fertile ground for the technology. Buchla had already scattered seeds in the San Francisco Bay area, and the new albums were taking hold and spreading the sounds through the hipster grapevine. Now Paul needed to exploit the titillation he saw in the musicians, producers, and control room techies at the *Zodiac* session by hawking the synth at a public venue.

~~~

Ever since the Trips Festival, hippie culture had been gathering momentum at a dizzying rate. By the spring of '67, nearly 100,000 young people from around the country had converged on the Haight-Ashbury neighborhood to explore alternative lifestyles. To assist with anticipated needs like clinics, housing, sanitation, and food, a sympathetic alliance of local theater, social, and underground newspaper groups was formed under the name Council for the Summer of Love. The expression caught on as the enduring motto for that particular nexus of time and place.

A landmark event in the "Summer of Love" was the Monterey International Pop Music Festival, a three-day concert held from June 16 to 18 at the Monterey County Fairgrounds, 100 miles south of San Francisco. The Monterey Pop Festival would later be hailed as the template for all future multi-day rock festivals showcasing a mixed lineup of bands. The headliners were heavies and included the Grateful Dead, Jefferson Airplane, the Mamas & the Papas, the Byrds, and Simon & Garfunkel; the Festival hosted the first major American appearances by the Who, Ravi Shankar, and the Jimi Hendrix Experience—with Hendrix memorably setting his guitar aflame at the end of his set—and the first large-scale public performances of Janis Joplin and Otis Redding. Stretched across the front of the stage, a banner read, "Music, Love and Flowers."

Over the three days, an estimated 30,000 people spilled out of the 7,200-seat arena onto the festival grounds. Attendees could gorge on Owsley's latest LSD treats—"Monterey Purple," cooked up for the occasion—or stroll freely with marijuana joints, courtesy of a rare pact with the police. One festival-goer recalled, "We would take uppers . . . and make love beads for three days. Either you were high on pot or you had dropped acid or mushrooms. We might have been a little paranoid, but we were all on the same spaceship."[37] Scattered around the grounds, some 40 shops and booths sold groovy paraphernalia: paper dresses, pins, earrings, buttons, amulets, posters, balloons, sandals, macrobiotic food, and flowers. Banners decorated with astrology signs undulated in the breeze.

Across from the arena and the main midway, inside the Hunt Club building, Paul Beaver was set up at a Moog booth with a Synthesizer III and a pair of headphones. Only seven weeks after he'd seen the instrument for the first time, he was armed with sales literature Bob had sent along. His display, like the others around the room, was cordoned off with pipe and drape into a small 8 × 10 cubicle. Opposite Paul's booth, to the right of the entranceway, there were displays for Jordan Amplifiers and Guild Guitars. Ken Lopez, a USC music professor, remembered: "As you walked up the stairway and in the doors, the first thing you saw when you walked in on your left was the Moog booth—and I stopped there first. I walked up and said, 'what the hell is this?'" Paul explained, "'Well you know, we've got these oscillators and wave shapers. We can patch things together.' So I said, 'oh cool!' And we experimented with patching different modules together in different sequences. I had fun making whizzy, bloopy noises, and said, 'cool—well that's really neat'—and I made a mental note about the name of the company."[38]

The Festival was rare for its open atmosphere where rock superstars mingled easily with concertgoers and vendors throughout the grounds. Brian Jones of the Rolling Stones showed up even though his band wasn't on the roster and strolled around the Festival site all weekend in a wispy pink cape. Lopez recalled a memorable encounter just after he left the Moog booth: "I wandered over to the people at Guild and we started playing guitars. And we'd started up an informal jam and just minutes after we started, Al Kooper came in and said, 'Let's jam!' So we did. We started this jam with Al Kooper, myself on guitar, another friend of mine on guitar, and a friend of mine playing drums. So we started doing some Chicago blues. Bob Weir from the Grateful Dead, came in and started playing; Paul Simon was standing behind us with maracas, singing harmonies."[39]

At that point another player edged up to Lopez. "He said, 'Hey, can I sit in?' and I said 'yeah!' I didn't know who he was—a Black guy with an afro and he had his own guitar. He and I stood literally shoulder-to-shoulder, with guitar necks crossing, 'cause I'm right-handed and he's left-handed. And we were just playing Chicago blues and having a lot of fun. And at the end he says, 'hey, that was a lot of fun—Jimi.' And he sticks his hand out. And I said, 'Ken. Cool. Great to meet you.' I played with him for well over a half hour—it was Hendrix! There was a crowd of a couple hundred people there, jam-packed like sardines."[40]

Paul Beaver sat at his booth, working with anyone who came in, sometimes without using the earphones. "There was eerie music in the Fine Arts Building," the *Monterey Herald* reported, "coming from electronic equipment mysteriously labeled 'Moog Synthesizer,' and a tiny Chihuahua dog beat a hasty retreat from its high pitched sounds."[41] For Paul, the weekend was worth it—several rock icons or their managers showed interest or placed orders. Roger McGuinn of the Byrds recalled, "I found Paul Beaver, the Moog guy, who was demonstrating the instrument inside a tent in the fairgrounds, and I flipped out on it. Later I went back to Los Angeles and bought one from him for $9,000."[42] Micky Dolenz, of the Monkees, was walking around in his flashy Native American feathered headdress. Dolenz, who would soon order a system from Paul, remembered: "I can vividly recall seeing the Moog exhibit. It was more than a booth. That was the future. It was like hallucinations for your ear."[43]

11
The Star Collector

"I just prevented a sale of Buchla equipment," Walter Sear scribbled to Bob on an invoice. "I think I have the guy switched to yours." Sear had signed on as the exclusive Moog rep east of the Rockies and made sure to warn Bob of every near miss. "Just got a call from Gershon K," he reported, "screaming about October delivery and that he was going to buy Buchla equipment etc. I cooled him by pointing out that Buchla wouldn't hop in a cab when he was in trouble and change a fuse for him. These bastards never appreciate a favor."[1]

Bob's incursion into West Coast "head" territory was being mirrored on the East Coast now by the Buchla box's arrival in New York and the inroads it was making into the sphere of Bob's clientele. Ussachevsky had just purchased three complete Buchla modular systems for the Columbia-Princeton Center; Bob's handful of modules already there—two ADSR envelope generators, two VCAs, and two envelope followers—seemed to be all the Moog equipment Ussachevsky cared to have.

More of Buchla's systems were migrating east via Morton Subotnick, who'd moved to New York in 1966. Months before the *Zodiac Cosmic Sounds* recording, Jac Holzman had conceived an idea for an entire album featuring a solo synthesizer. In the fall of 1966, he'd handed Subotnick a $1,000 commission to realize the concept on his Buchla Box. Holzman saw it as a landmark: the first-ever commission of a piece to be created for the medium of home stereo. He would issue it on his Elektra subsidiary label, Nonesuch—a budget line of recordings designed for listeners game to gamble on an album for the price of a cheap paperback book. "It intrigued me," Subotnick recalled, "that it would go from living room to living room and that someone listening would recreate my experience for $1.69."[2]

Subotnick composed the piece, *Silver Apples of the Moon*, working 18 hours a day, 6 days a week, for months, teaching himself to use the Buchla while wrestling with the intricacies of his soundscape. *Silver Apples* was basically uptown music—an atonal, spacey environment of tinkly textures, sliding whines, and white noise spurts. But there were also stretches with

Switched On. Albert Glinsky, Oxford University Press. © Albert Glinsky 2022.
DOI: 10.1093/oso/9780197642078.003.0011

syncopated, foot-tapping patterns that were cumulative and increasingly frenetic.

Before *Silver Apples* was released, Subotnick was approached by two rock promoters planning a sensory-immersive discothèque in New York—something on the order of an East Coast Trips Festival reimagined as a nightclub. Subotnick was hired as artistic director, and Don Buchla was imported as sound designer to integrate the Buchla Box into voltage control modules that could synchronize the music and lighting. The Electric Circus would occupy an old three-story building at 23 St. Mark's Place in Manhattan's East Village, an area of tenements, panhandlers, and a recent influx of hippies.

On opening night, June 27, 1967, a festive throng of New York literati, political icons, and beautiful people, together with the local hippie crowd—1,500 strong—pushed into the Electric Circus for a gala benefit to aid underprivileged children, sponsored by Senator Robert F. Kennedy and his family. The writers George Plimpton, Tom Wolfe, and the historian Arthur Schlesinger Jr. filed in. Tuxes and party dresses mixed with the freaky attire of the bohemian set adorned with painted faces, tattoos, and strange garb like backless, sideless metal dresses—everyone ready to turn on all their senses at once. "We've duplicated the LSD experience with no drugs," the producers boasted. "It's a trip."[3] No alcohol was sold on the premises, but many showed up stoned anyway. Inside the cavernous space, an ecstatic sound-and-light show throbbed away amidst a lineup of acts—mimes, flame-throwing jugglers, clowns, tumblers, overhead aerialists, puppeteers, and a dizzying wash of liquid projections, deflecting mirrors, movies, and flashing lights.

Buchla and Subotnick sat at the controls, sliding levers and patching cables, orchestrating the sound mix and choreographing the projections. In the midst of it all, Subotnick debuted his not-yet-released *Silver Apples of the Moon*. To his surprise, he saw members of the Kennedy family and the manic crowd gyrating to the infectious beats, now ramped up to thundering levels through the sound system. The Buchla's sequencer had inadvertently forged a new kind of electronic dance beat.

The Electric Circus was primarily a rock club with acts like the Grateful Dead and Sly and the Family Stone, but through Subotnick's influence, some of the San Francisco-style cross-pollination of the academic avant-garde with the psychedelic head culture surfaced as well. Here and there, shows were set aside for Subotnick's "Electric Ear" series that hosted "serious" evenings of highbrow electronic music. Pauline Oliveros performed, along with composers like Lejaren Hiller and his University of Illinois colleague,

Salvatore Martirano, who took advantage of the venue's multimedia capabilities to augment their scores with films, modern dance, and projections.

In September, Nonesuch released *Silver Apples of the Moon* to positive reviews. *High Fidelity* called it "a beauty" and "sensational." The album sold well, and found a niche with a certain type of hip audience plugged in to both Stockhausen and acid rock.

∿∿∿

Despite the sudden initiation of Bob's synth into the pop fraternity in California, and the opportunities it might open up for wider sales, he was still focused on his avant-garde clients. The one-offs he crafted for them engaged his mind, and even though his 1967 catalog was aimed at steering buyers toward standardized models, he could never seem to turn down requests for specialized systems. That had been the case even with his first customer, Alwin Nikolais—the choreographer hadn't bought what Bob displayed at AES, instead ordering a custom setup.

Bob's latest apparatus was his oddest yet. The device was built for the composer Richard Teitelbaum, who, along with two other young, rebel avant-gardist Americans—the composers Frederic Rzewski and Alvin Curran—had formed a group they called Musica Elettronica Viva, based in Rome, where they were living.

Teitelbaum had been experimenting with harnessing the brain's alpha wave activity using scalp electrodes to trigger a series of oscillators. By adding contact microphones to the scheme, he could also pick up sounds from the body's vital functions. Altogether he had the makings of a music driven directly by the central nervous system. His idea was to "orchestrate" the physiological rhythms of the human body—heart, breath, skin, muscle, and brain. After Bob loaned him a used Moog synthesizer, Teitelbaum asked for a biofeedback amplifier for a brain-to-synthesizer interface to allow the body's electrical signals to work through the modules. Bob designed him a high-gain differential amplifier.

Armed with the first Moog synthesizer to land in Europe, and Bob's custom brain amp, Musica Elettronica Viva set off on a tour of the Continent in the fall of 1967. In a featured work they called *Spacecraft*, five musicians interacted in a network of body sensors and electronic gear using the neurological and physiological signals from their own bodies as musical materials. "Here we were these long-haired, mad-eyed, stoned-out hippies," Curran recalled, "you know, grungy clothes, but coming and suddenly making a music that no one had ever heard." At Berlin's conservative Akademie der Künste, he remembered, "People attacked us. They jumped on the stage and tried to stop us. This wasn't the only time."[4]

Bob happily sailed back into history with another pet project that had him communing with 1920s electronic music pioneers from Germany's Weimar Republic. In late 1965 he'd been approached by Max Brand, an Austrian émigré composer of avant-garde music. Brand had run afoul of Hitler for his Jewish heritage and communist leanings, but earlier he'd had great success in Germany with machine music and mechanical sounds, especially his 1929 proletarian factory opera, *Maschinist Hopkins*. Forced to flee Germany, he eventually settled in Queens, New York, and by the late 1950s he was composing tape music in a home studio.

Brand's proposal to Bob wasn't simple: he wanted an updated model of the Trautonium, an early electronic musical instrument introduced in Berlin in 1930 by its inventor, Friedrich Trautwein. The Trautonium was a monophonic instrument with no keyboard and a ribbon-controller type interface. An updated version, the Mixtur-Trautonium, was introduced in 1952 by the composer Oskar Sala, who performed on it and used it to compose the electronic soundtrack for Alfred Hitchcock's 1963 film, *The Birds*.

Using Brand's detailed specifications, Bob began work on his own version of the Mixtur-Trautonium—what he and Brand called the "Moogtonium"—early in 1966. Before it was through, Bob had built a humongous hybrid assemblage with two keyboards, two ribbon controllers, foot pedals, subharmonic oscillators, an oscilloscope, and two tape recorders. Bob's estimated time frame was two months, but, predictably, delivery stretched to two years, with Bob fussing over every detail as Brand made relentless demands to tweak this and that.

On Bob's workbench, waiting beside Brand's instrument, was yet another custom job: a polyphonic system for the pop pianist Peter Nero. As if the hurdles of designing an original one-off weren't enough, Bob even promised to first build a prototype for Nero's approval. Two synths for the price of one.

By tending to so many pots on the stove at the same time, something was always boiling over or burning. As the Moogtonium job was wrapping up, Bob received a threatening letter from a New York Research Group lawyer with an ultimatum: he had three weeks to complete the Rothenberg project or he'd face a suit for recovery of everything he'd been paid, plus damages. His breach of agreement for failing to deliver, he was told, had a serious adverse effect on what was now called the "Department of Defense" research project. "I have certainly acted in good faith over the past months," Bob huffed, "by spending two, three, or four days nearly every weekend on the premises of the New York Research Group. These frequent trips have involved much inconvenience, expense, and discomfort on my part. I will continue to act in good faith by spending a significant portion of my time in working on the instrument until it is completed to Mr. Rothenberg's satisfaction. More than that I cannot do."[5]

With huge amounts of time and resources devoted to side projects, Bob continued to be strapped for cash. He was supporting a staff of two technicians, a cabinet maker, a draftsman, four assemblers, and a secretary. In an exchange resembling a vaudeville routine, Sear sent him a $700 check from a sale, then turned around and billed him for the same amount. "Easy come, easy go!" Bob replied. "I am enclosing a check to you for $700.00. I assure you that I am just as 'up tight' financially as you are."[6]

Creditors were lining up to collect outstanding bills, and the pile on Bob's desk was overwhelming. To see him out of the predicament, he hired Rubin Gorewitz as company treasurer. Gorewitz was a designer-label accountant to cultural luminaries like Merce Cunningham and modern dance legend Martha Graham. He'd earned a reputation for helping artists erect complex tax shelters, but years later the *New York Times* would report that he pled guilty to federal conspiracy and tax-fraud charges. Apparently the best Gorewitz could come up with for Bob was a scheme to beg Moog's creditors for extensions, holding all of them off at once by tossing each of them installment payments. Most of the companies balked at the proposal.

Adding to the tumult, Shirleigh was expecting again. "When we found out I was pregnant," she recalled, "we had an extra bedroom, and Robert said, 'Nature abhors a vacuum'—which was very funny for him. It wasn't so funny for me. The babies were *my* responsibility."[7]

∿∿∿

In Los Angeles, Beaver was running from gig to gig with the Moog. A month after AES, the instrument was suddenly the new sonic flavor coveted by rock bands, TV producers, movie directors, film composers, and jingle houses. No industry professional needed convincing—everyone was lining up to use the new machine as soon as they heard it.

Beaver was hired with a Moog for the first film soundtrack to use a synthesizer—a head culture romp called *The Trip*—a simulated LSD experience brimming with visual and musical effects. Coming off the Summer of Love, the production was more than a clinical look at a hallucinogenic experience—it broke the fourth wall, crossing into real life when director Roger Corman and his cast and crew took LSD before filming. The movie starred Dennis Hopper, Susan Strasberg, Bruce Dern, and Peter Fonda in the role of a disillusioned TV commercial producer, Paul, who's coaxed into dropping acid by a friend offering to guide him through his psychic journey.

Paul's trip is larded with flowers, beads, body paint, and free love, and is portrayed through a psychedelic wash of spinning images, double exposures, split-screens, abstract kaleidoscopic bursts, and zebra patterns flickering and sweeping over nude bodies. Paul encounters the word "groovy" dozens of times, experiences paranoia, wanders into surrealistic landscapes with a gothic castle, a witch, a dwarf, black-hooded, caped figures on horses, and finally ends up witnessing his own trial and death. Corman intended the film as an objective, nonjudgmental look at the LSD experience, but the film company, worried about backlash over the illegal drug, added a disclaimer at the beginning, calling the movie "a shocking commentary on a prevalent trend of our time and one that must be of great concern to all." Over Corman's objections, the company superimposed broken-glass spider web lines across the final freeze-frame of Paul's face, to drive the point home. Nevertheless, *The Trip* helped open the way two years later for the blockbuster *Easy Rider*, which again paired Dennis Hopper—this time as director—and Fonda as another countercultural nomad on a sex- and drug-driven odyssey.

The soundtrack for *The Trip* was written by a new band, the Electric Flag—fronted by former Butterfield Blues Band guitarist, Mike Bloomfield. The group was the first rock band to integrate a mix of musical genres, the first to include brass instruments, and the first to use a Moog synthesizer. The musical scope of *The Trip* was broad—tracks inspired variously by R&B, country, bluegrass, rock, folk, electric blues, soul, pop rock, jazz, Indian raga, classical idioms, and even Dixieland. The Electric Flag, days before its official debut at the Monterey Pop Festival, had laid down tracks for *The Trip* over a 10-day period in an LA recording studio. Paul Beaver helped develop the musical cues for the movie using the Moog in elaborate improvisations with a core group of three musicians from the band. In the final edit of the film, the music figured heavily, and underscored every scene.

The soundtrack album for *The Trip* was released on September 9, 1967, just weeks after the film itself. It was the Electric Flag's first commercial release, and the first appearance of the Moog synthesizer on a rock album. All but one of the 18 tracks were instrumental. The Moog was showcased on many cuts, notably in "Fine Jung Thing," and "Flash, Bam, Pow," where Paul's synth broke new ground in pop music, both in the intro, with a squealing, frenetic improvisation over drums, recalling the cacophony of free jazz, and in the ending—an emphatic duet of drum/cymbal slams with rhythmic shots of static and wheezes from the Moog.

A week after *The Trip* opened in theaters in August, Paul Beaver was heard again on the soundtrack of another film release, *Point Blank*, a neo-noir crime thriller starring Lee Marvin and Angie Dickinson. Here the Moog was tapped to intensify the terror and mystery of Johnny Mandel's dark score, with sound effects and eerie melodic strains.

On September 14 the Moog made its television soundtrack debut on the premiere episode of *Ironside*, a crime drama starring Raymond Burr as a wheelchair-bound detective for the San Francisco Police Department. The music was by Quincy Jones, who was new to the synth, and recalled, "Paul Beaver played on that session, and we used it for the siren. And I went back to Paul and I said, 'what else have you got?' He said, 'I just gave you a synthesizer.' I said, 'we used that already.' He said, 'idiot, you don't get it.' He said, 'That thing's got the sounds that's infinity. . . . It's just an electrical signal that comes out that's straight, and you have to sculpt it into whatever sound you want.'"[8]

Beaver's chain of Moog studio dates and the buzz he started at the Monterey Pop booth were rewarded in September by a formal contract to represent R. A. Moog exclusively on the West Coast. The terms, arranged by Gorewitz, included a 30% commission. But the agreement rested on a rather outrageous expectation: Beaver's annual renewal was contingent upon $100,000 of sales the first year, $175,000 the second year, and $250,000 each year following. It was a misguided maneuver. R. A. Moog was in no position to justify Gorewitz's premature muscle flexing, a tactic that could only risk biting the one hand feeding the company west of the Rockies.

In his studio dates, Beaver's work wasn't easy—sometimes akin to a used car salesman exhausted after multiple test drives with the same customer. The endless menu of Moog sounds was especially confounding to musicians accustomed to working with typical instruments. A studio session for the Doors' new album, *Strange Days*, a sequel to their blockbuster gold debut album from January, was typical. The Doors' keyboardist, Ray Manzarek, recalled the session:

"Paul Beaver brought his huge modular Moog system into the studio and began plugging a bewildering array of patch cords into the equally bewildering panels of each module. He'd hit the keyboard and outer space, bizarre, Karlheinz Stockhausen-like sounds would emerge. He would then turn a mystifying array of knobs placed in rows around the patch cord receptacles and more and different space would emerge. He did this for about a half hour and we sat as if at an electronic music concert by some mad German composer. Who knew what he was doing? And then he turned to us, all huddled in the control room, and said, 'If you hear anything you want to use, just stop me.'" The producer, Paul Rothchild, spoke up, Manzarek recalled: "'Actually, that sound you had about three sounds back was very usable. Could you go back to that?' 'Which sound was that?' said Paul Beaver.'" Jim Morrison jumped in: "'That crystalline sound . . . I liked the sound of broken glass falling from the void into creation.' 'Which sound was that?' said the Beaver. . . . "Just go back to where you were," said Rothchild.

"And Paul Beaver began to unplug and replug patch cords, and twist little knobs, and strike the keyboard, which emitted strange and arcane and unearthly tones . . . . None of the sounds he was creating sounded pure and crystalline. And then we realized . . . he couldn't *get* back. He couldn't get back because he had no idea where he had been. He could only go forward, on to the next patch. Ever new, ever forward. You had to stop him as soon as you heard something you liked. He *was* a mad scientist. . . . The possibilities were endless. The permutations were infinite. And the Beaver seemed as if he were going to try them all, as we watched, going slowly insane."[9]

In the end, the Doors used the Moog for two songs. "Strange Days" had an effect modulating Morrison's vocal, recalled by session engineer, Bruce Botnick: "We created an envelope where we could feed Jim's track into the Moog so that he could play any note on the keyboard and it would process his voice."[10] "Spanish Caravan," released on the Doors' next album, used an electronic wind sound Beaver had created. Overall, Morrison was impressed with the Moog; two years later in an interview with *Rolling Stone* he called it "a keyboard with the complexity and richness of a whole orchestra."[11]

The *Strange Days* album was released in October 1967 and shot up the *Billboard* charts to No. 3 by November 18, sitting just below the Beatles' *Sgt. Pepper's Lonely Hearts Club Band*. Immediately, Beaver was on call again, this time for a new Monkees album.

After Monterey Pop, Micky Dolenz had made good on his Moog infatuation and bought a model IIIp from Paul Beaver on September 15—the first rock musician to own one of Bob's instruments. The "p" stood for "portable"—a more mobile version of the standard III model, enclosed in three separate rectangular cabinets designed to stand on a table behind the keyboard. Micky viewed the instrument as his contribution to an updated sound for the band, inspired by the sonic breakthroughs on the Beatles' *Sgt. Pepper*. For the Monkees' fourth album, *Pisces, Aquarius, Capricorn & Jones Ltd.*, he kept Beaver in the studio to help him with his new toy.

The Monkees were an odd pop phenomenon—a boy band, assembled through national auditions to form a fictional TV group for a sitcom called *The Monkees*. Engineered to be teen idols, their weekly TV episodes featured the group in fantasy plots with Marx Brothers–like antics in situations where they might be stranded in a ghost town, or mixed up with a spy ring or a mad scientist. Their songs played in the background, and each episode included a music video. The first season of *The Monkees* earned two Emmy Awards, and by the end of their first year, in the spring of 1967, the group became the biggest grossing musical act in the U.S. The four were sometimes derided as television actors pretending to be a rock band because most of their songs were written by professional songwriters and were accompanied by session musicians, but their records sold in the millions, and like the Beatles, they were routinely mobbed by female fans. Their status in the rock stratosphere, in fact, found them hanging out with the Fab Four, partying and jamming together in England.

Two songs on the *Pisces* album used the Moog: "Star Collector," written by Gerry Goffin and Carole King, was an up-tempo pop number about an obsessive groupie: "She's a star collector (collector of stars), She only seems to please young celebrities."[12] The song featured Beaver's Moog dancing a jaunty melodic solo in a synthetic twang, with a coda of fluttering percussive sounds. "Daily Nightly," written by the band's own Mike Nesmith, dealt with the recent Sunset Strip "hippie riots" protesting police curfews. The lyrics sparkled with the latest hallucinogenic images: "Passioned pastel neon lights, Light up the jeweled traveler, Who, lost in scenes of smoke-filled dreams, Find questions, but no answers."[13] Micky Dolenz took the lead vocal and sat in the driver's seat of his new synth. At strategic points in the moderate-tempo rock ballad, a Moog oscillator interjects with swooping squeals and manic trills, adding a space age gloss to the trippy words.

The *Pisces* album hit the *Billboard* charts on November 25 and jumped to No. 1 a week later, besting the Beatles' *Sgt. Pepper*, the Door's *Strange Days*, and a greatest hits album by Diana Ross & the Supremes, remaining in the top position until January.

From November 1967 to February 1968, three episodes of the Monkees' TV series showcased a video of "Star Collector." The "Daily Nightly" video, showing Dolenz at the Moog, was a landmark moment, offering the broader public its first glimpse of a synthesizer. In the black-and-white feature, which ran on the January 8 and March 11, 1968, episodes, a full-screen close-up of the Moog modules pans out to reveal Dolenz sweeping his hands up and down the keyboard as he mimes the synth part and lip-syncs the song; behind him, his band mates—minus their instruments—sit air drumming and gesturing to the music. As the clip ends, Peter Tork blithely plasters a hookah pipe to his lips and Dolenz, peering quizzically up at the viewer from his keyboard, mutters, "psychedelic!"

January 1968 saw more Moog synthesizer on vinyl. The release of the latest album by the Byrds, for Columbia Records, *The Notorious Byrd Brothers*, signaled the band's turn toward a more electronically processed, futuristic sound. Paul Beaver sat in on the Moog for "Natural Harmony," and Roger McGuinn, who'd been smitten by the Moog at Monterey Pop, took turns at the instrument with producer Gary Usher for the album's closing track, "Space Odyssey."

McGuinn also recorded an instrumental solo, "Moog Raga," using the synth by itself in a 3½-minute homage to Indian classical music. The sounds were an imitation of a tambura, a tabla, and a *sarangi*—the traditional string instrument used to intone a whining melody. To mimic the sarangi's gliding quality between notes, McGuinn used a ribbon controller. In the end, he felt the separately recorded tracks sounded out of tune with each other, and the piece was cut from the record; it was later released on a Byrds CD compilation.

In March, the Electric Flag released their debut album, *A Long Time Comin'*, with Paul Beaver on the Moog again. *Billboard* called the all-star group effort "a musical grab-bag that covers rock, blues, soul, country or whatever possesses them at the moment."[14]

On March 31, Shirleigh gave birth to a 7½-pound baby at Tompkins County Hospital. "It's a girl—our specialty," she announced to Florence.[15] Baby Michelle came home to a farmhouse the family had rented in late July 1967. The Moogs couldn't afford a down payment for a mortgage, but they hoped to be able to buy the property in another year.

The place was an isolated country haven, just a mile southeast of the Main Street storefront. With three bedrooms and an additional rental apartment, it sat on 52 acres, with woods climbing up a steep hill out back, and a vast stretch of untilled farmland beyond. There was a five-stall horse barn with a loft and a 100-foot frontage out to Taughannock Park Road. Running parallel on the other side of the two-lane route, the majestic Taughannock Creek rolled and spilled over glistening flat boulders on its way to Taughannock Falls State Park, one mile to the northwest. Back behind the house, blackberries, rhubarb, and asparagus grew wild. Blue jays, chickadees, and woodpeckers decorated the lazy silences with song.

The idyllic life was alluring, but it was a lot of work. Bob and Shirleigh spent hours planting willow, locust, and birch trees around the property, and they started an apple orchard out front. Shirleigh, even with her bad back, sometimes mowed the two acres of lawn by herself.

Bob's isolation in Trumansburg—far from the East and West Coast cultural meccas—left him an obscure figure. His equipment was everywhere—even the antennas he'd made for John Cage were traveling across Europe and the U.S. in a 29-performance tour of *Variations V*—but as a personality he remained in the shadows. Sensing it was time to put a face to his name, he hired Jacqueline Harvey, the AES exhibits director who'd facilitated his Abominatron unveiling at the 1964 convention, as his publicity rep. Harvey wasted no time in prospecting for feature articles.

In March, *Electronics Review* carried a pointedly promotional story that gave Bob the floor to brag how his company had grossed $150,000 in sales the previous year. An accompanying photo captured him in the new pose that was calculated to highlight the technology: as he sat in determined profile before a towering modular with patch bays and dripping cords, his right hand caressed the lower keyboard, his left reached up to man the futuristic control panel, twisting a dial. The studied posture would appear again and again with different subjects at the modules. The caption read: "Music man. Inventor Robert Moog is setting the tone for a new kind of music with his sound synthesizer."[16]

A second feature appeared in March in the inaugural issue of *Eye Magazine*, a short-lived Hearst publication aimed at the youth market. Jacqueline Harvey's new motto for Bob, "Moog rhymes with vogue," was planted strategically in the first paragraph. Walter Sear was interviewed for the story, and wrote Bob, "I haven't seen a copy yet to see how misquoted I was."[17] He found out quickly enough: the column noted that Bob was "described by one friend as 'not realistic... something of a dreamer.'"[18]

To establish Bob's visage as instantly recognizable and iconic, he'd need targeted photo ops, and he asked Harvey set up a shoot with the psychedelic folk-rock band, Lothar and the Hand People. The group had lately joined the pantheon of rock heavies, sharing the bill at festivals and club dates with the Byrds and the Grateful Dead. "Lothar" was the band's mascot: a Moog theremin used since their formation in 1965. Bob figured the group's endorsement could boost sales of his Troubador theremins that he'd begun making again—he'd recently shown them at the 1967 National Association of Music Merchandisers convention in Chicago (the NAMM show).

The notion to hitch his star to the Hand People came when he read a *New York Times* feature on teeny-boppers that profiled the Lothar band as archetypical idols of a new underground youth culture. It was a Faustian bargain: a chance to promote his brand and his theremins, but yet another tiptoe into the rock culture he remained skittish about, and an implicit endorsement of that culture as the real home to his instruments.

The *Times* exposé that Bob had read stressed the galvanizing power of rock and musical electronics among teeny-boppers—14- to 19-year-olds who streamed into Greenwich Village from New Jersey and New York's outer boroughs every Saturday night, fleeing the suburban banality of their lives to try on a mild version of hippie life. The feature traced their ritual wanderings through the MacDougal Street neighborhood in miniskirts, bellbottoms, and paisley tops, toking cigarettes and joints, sometimes dallying with casual sex, and popping into clubs like the Café Wha? for fixes of loud rock—a major draw in the teeny-bopper scene. Without mentioning Bob's name, his role in the new high-decibel, psychedelic sound was unmistakable in the article's reference to John Emelin, the 21-year-old founder, vocalist, and thereminist of Lothar and the Hand People: "John Emelin, whose own group's theremin is one of the loudest electronic creations of them all, argues... 'It makes you peak out emotionally.'"[19]

Electronic music was invading the popular mainstream at such a rate that even doyens of the classical music establishment were getting on board. The

New York Times' inveterate classical music critic, Harold Schonberg, in a January 1968 opinion piece titled, "The New Age Is Coming," mused, "For the first time, electronic music is breaking away from the professors and pedants. The kids are beginning to use it in a loose manner, far from the carefully serialized blips and boops and appalling sterility that have been only too prevalent up to recently. . . . I can only cheer."[20] Shirleigh was warming to the trend too, telling Florence, "Right now big record companies are interested in buying synthesizers which *may be* grand monetarily for us (we have orders from Columbia, R.C.A. & Motown). Right now the 'serious' people are getting stereotyped & much more exciting stuff is being done on the 'pop' front."[21]

Bob was hearing the message from everyone. The March profile on him in *Electronics Review* began with the wager, "It's doubtful the Beatles will be replaced by the Moog," but the article predicted, presciently, "before long they may be using one."[22] At home, the Trumansburg Teen Council—likely the children of the Rotarians who'd snoozed through Bob's *musique concrète* lecture—thought he was the coolest thing with his connection to the Monkees and the Beach Boys. At a concert by the local Southshore Road Band, they made him the honored guest.

The identity of electronic music, its future role in the culture, and how the synthesizer fit in, were nagging questions. Two decades of the classical studio had defined the art in terms of *musique concrète*, pigeonholing it as a highbrow indulgence of a cultural fringe. For purists like Ussachevsky, who lived by razor blades and piles of tape strands, synthesizers seemed like a cheating shortcut. He complained in a May 1967 *Newsweek* article, "The new equipment makes it too easy to diddle around. Never before in history has everybody been able to play the most elementary exercises and pass them off as compositions."[23]

Still, for Bob, the growing rapture over his synth by the pop recording industry and its counterculture clientele appeared to hold the clue to his success. But it put him at a crossroads: his synthesizer had come into its own and slipped off into the culture, breaking free of his influence; he wasn't entirely sure he approved of its new identity, or the crowd it was hanging with.

But it was only a matter of time before he was forced to take a position. By the spring of 1968, the handwriting was on the wall. However reluctantly, he began adding his voice to the chorus hailing electronics as the shining path forward for popular music. At the annual meeting of the Acoustical Society of America in Ottawa, Canada, from May 21 to 24, he presented a paper,

"The Role of Electronics in Rock-and-Roll, or Popular Music Will Never be the Same Again."

Only months earlier, he'd been recruited to aid in the trend himself. In December 1967 he was hired for a recording session of Simon & Garfunkel's *Bookends* album, asked to help John Simon, an assistant producer for the project, patch a Moog synthesizer for its cameo role on the record: a part in the song, "Save the Life of My Child." It was a jolting experience. Bob suddenly witnessed the collateral damage his synth could inflict as a stand-in for traditional instruments.

He recalled the *Bookends* session: "At that point I could get sounds pretty fast. I knew the equipment. But one sound I remember distinctly was a plucked string, like a bass sound. Bump, bump, bump. Bump, baahhh. Then it would slide down—it was something you could not do on an acoustic bass or an electric bass. And John finally did it with a pedal. And I can remember, while John was fooling around and getting this sound . . . a couple of session musicians came through. One guy was playing a bass and he stops and he listens, and listens. He turned white as a sheet."[24]

After Bob's Ottawa talk, the issue of how musicians would fare in a synthesizer world caught him off guard. A network television reporter, interviewing participants coming out of the conference, sat him down, established who he was, and leaned into his face. The reporter, he remembered, "shined his lights on me and asked, 'Tell me, Mr. Moog, don't you feel guilty about what you've done?'" Bob recalled that he "shit a brick," and realized, "People were afraid that we would replace conventional instruments."[25]

Shirleigh recalled, "He was so furious that I remember we left the conference and got in the car, and Robert wanted to head out of town and go home—and he drove around the block three times before he could orient himself. Steam was coming out of his ears."[26]

12

Long Live the Moog!

A rock band, a medieval ensemble, and a synthesizer player walked into Carnegie Hall. It could've been the setup for a joke. The Electric Circus had taken over Manhattan's historic concert venue on two evenings in December 1967 for a multimedia show. *An Electric Christmas* offered an improbable lineup: low-decibel Renaissance lutes, viols, and sweet voices from the stately New York Pro Musica, alternated with the ear-splitting rock energy of the band Circus Maximus, tied together by film and light projections and interludes of live electronic sounds from Morton Subotnick. It was a bold experiment, daring to cross lines of genre, period, and style in the belief that a single audience could merge it all into a happy aesthetic experience.

The *New York Times* critic Donal Henahan described a typical moment in the 80-minute show: "A Gregorian chant would give way to a rock number, then both would be overlaid with electronic sounds while kaleidoscopic sugarplums were made to dance on the walls of Carnegie Hall."[1] The two performances drew sold-out crowds of mostly young people who proved they could tune into the old and the new with equal enthusiasm.

Critics looked at the mashup as a harbinger. Henahan saw it as a breaking down of the walls separating the hallowed experience of "high art" and the plebian sport of "entertainment," and found there was no longer any distinction between the two. "Like it or not," he chided, "1967 could not care less." The *Times*' Harold Schonberg praised the show as a healthy reconciling of modern currents: "All techniques are being synthesized. The Beatles had something to do with it, and John Cage, and the Columbia-Princeton Electronic Music Studio, and the jazz boys, and some of the movie composers, and some television commercials, and Viet Nam, and the psychedelics."[2] Bob himself took note and reprinted Schonberg's column in the January 1968 issue of the *Electronic Music Review*, his noble effort that would cease publication later that year with the July edition, after only seven issues.

The critics had astutely put their finger on the busy intersection of movement across artistic borderlines. Henahan coined a term for composers of the "Electric Ear" series down at the Electric Circus; they were jumping from

Switched On. Albert Glinsky, Oxford University Press. © Albert Glinsky 2022.
DOI: 10.1093/oso/9780197642078.003.0012

the academic avant-garde to the "avant-groove," he claimed.[3] Classical music audiences were opening their ears to pop groups, and rock listeners were turning on to sophisticated classical works.

The growing complexity of rock music and its use of electronics had suddenly opened the door to academic music. Jac Holzman told the *New York Times*, "We would have had no success with 'Silver Apples' without the Beatles."[4] Younger listeners were hearing the old *concrète* composers now as so off-the-wall they were hip. Stockhausen was a particular hero, and his photo peered out of the celebrity crowd on the cover of the Beatles' *Sgt. Pepper* album. Big record labels even started gambling on academic music. In late 1967, RCA released a group of LPs featuring composers like Stockhausen, and in November, Columbia Masterworks issued 17 avant-garde classical titles, many of electronic music, selling the lot out in a month. Even Ussachevsky and Luening were riding the wave with their esoteric CRI label's top seller—a disk recorded back in 1958.

As part of the trend, Nonesuch released its second all-synthesizer album in July 1968, a follow up to *Silver Apples*. This time it was a showcase for the Moog. Bob had recommended composer Andrew Rudin as the commission recipient for the project. Rudin was a recent University of Pennsylvania graduate and the impetus behind the School's purchase of a Moog studio in 1965. When he first began exploring the new Penn instrument, he composed a 15-minute work, *Il Giuoco*, in 1966 that was likely the first extended composition ever written on a Moog.

For the new Nonesuch album, Rudin composed a 37-minute work, *Tragoedia*, a composition in four movements exploring four "conditions" of Greek tragedy. *Tragoedia* stood as the first commercial recording spotlighting a Moog synthesizer by itself. The avant-garde work proved a hit with the psychedelic crowd. Rudin recalled, "There were kids who apparently bought my album and used it when they were turning on—doing LSD or mushrooms. There were always people who could not believe that I had made the music that I made if I hadn't done drugs."[5]

At the other end of the historical spectrum, Baroque, medieval, and Renaissance music on Nonesuch was notching hefty sales at college bookstores—centuries-old masterworks unearthed like exotic finds. To make these archaeological artifacts more palatable to the youth market, the music was sometimes recast with a pop attitude. Elektra's 1965 *The Baroque Beatles Book* borrowed Lennon and McCartney tunes for brilliant arrangements by composer Joshua Rifkin that sounded exactly like the music of Handel, Bach, and Telemann—often indistinguishable from authentic eighteenth-century music. On the cover, the briskly selling album bridged the pop-classical divide with humor: painted caricatures of the Baroque masters—Bach wearing an "I Like the Beatles" T-shirt and Handel surveying a manuscript of "I Want to Hold Your Hand." The tracks had titles like *Cantata for the Third Saturday after Shea Stadium*.

Serving up classical music to the public with full-out comedy was the shtick of composer and humorist Peter Schickele, who used his fictitious P.D.Q. Bach character to parody the conventions of Baroque music in sold-out shows at Town Hall and Carnegie Hall, and on LPs popular with the college set. Schickele's headshot as the clownish P.D.Q. Bach was plastered on his album covers, staring out in mock deadpan with a full period wig.

Here and there classical music was reworked as popular music. The Swingle Singers, a vocal jazz octet, crooned the instrumental music of Bach and other Baroque composers in an up-tempo scat style (bob-uh-dob-uh-DUM) over a brisk trap set and a gentle, sprinting bass line. Starting in 1963, their albums earned several Grammys and a broad following. The British progressive rock band the Nice, with keyboardist Keith Emerson, stitched Bach's music into a song on their 1968 debut album, *The Thoughts of Emerlist Davjack*.

All these unlikely marriages of tastes would finally shove Bob's synthesizer out of the shadows and into the public spotlight. In a defining moment of serendipity, it would happen through the artistry of one of Bob's earliest customers—someone named "Walter Carlos."

Carlos was born in Pawtucket, Rhode Island, in 1939 and struggled with gender dysphoria. Unequivocally she identified as Wendy, not as her birth name, Walter. Carlos's upbringing paralleled Bob's childhood in many ways: piano lessons starting at age six refereed by a ruler across the knuckles, and audio hobbyist projects. At 14 she won a Westinghouse Science Fair scholarship for two home-built computers.

Carlos thrived on outlier sounds. When she learned how to tune her parents' piano, she tried non-standard tunings on it. She wrote her first composition at age 10, and in high school she made electronic music with a home-built studio in her parents' basement, experimenting with every homegrown workaround of the time: test tone oscillators, shower stall echo chambers, white noise static from off-air radio stations, and photocell devices she invented to trigger percussive sounds. Stockhausen was a big influence.

Carlos earned a bachelor's degree in music with a minor in physics from Brown University. At the Columbia-Princeton Electronic Music Center she joined the graduate program in 1962 to study with Ussachevsky and Luening. Granted the graveyard shift in the lab, her solitary access to the equipment each night until dawn yielded pieces for acoustic instruments and tape like *Dialogues for Piano and Two Loudspeakers,* and in a satirical relief from Columbia's deadly serious avant-garde program, her sarcastically titled *Pomposities for Narrator and Tape.*

Graduating with her master's from Columbia in 1965, Carlos began work at New York's Gotham Recording Studios as a mastering engineer, tape editor, and disc cutter. Ussachevsky introduced her to Bob, and by 1966 she began ordering modules. At Gotham she hitched her small Moog synthesizer to the studio's sophisticated gear to make sound effects and jingles for television ads.

Carlos, with her technical background in music, could scrutinize Bob's equipment with an analytical eye and ear much more than Bob's other customers. The two often brainstormed over coffee shop lunches about improvements in the synthesizer's functions. "She really understood instinctively what I was doing right and wrong," Bob recalled.[6] "In my entire lifetime I'd only seen a very few people who took so naturally to an instrument.... It was just a God-given gift."[7]

At Bob's invitation, Carlos produced the first R. A. Moog demo recording, a 10-inch vinyl giveaway disk called *Moog 900 Series Electronic Music Systems* that debuted at the fall 1967 AES convention. The nine-minute sampler featured a polished narrator extolling the benefits of voltage control and capped off with Carlos's sonic examples of effects suggesting distant gunshots in a driving rainstorm, and catfight yowls, and ended with a pop instrumental arrangement.

When Carlos's friend, jazz singer Rachel Elkind, heard an electronic realization of Bach's *Two-Part Invention in F Major* that Carlos had created in her last year at the Columbia-Princeton studio, Elkind encouraged her to try a Bach realization on her Moog. A few months later, Carlos came up with a fully synthesized version of the first movement of Bach's *Brandenburg Concerto No. 3* and Elkind suggested the idea of an entire album of Bach's music on the Moog. The timing was ideal: CBS, the parent company of Elkind's former employer, Columbia Records, was launching a "Bach to Rock" campaign, and through a contact at the company she submitted a master tape of the *Brandenburg* arrangement. CBS execs were lukewarm, but they needed some actual Bach to fit their campaign slogan, so Carlos and Elkind were offered a $2,500 advance and the artistic license to produce an album.

During the spring and early summer of 1968 the entire production—soup to nuts—was created in the cozy studio area tucked into a corner of Carlos's one-room apartment at 410 West End Avenue on Manhattan's Upper West Side. With her Moog, a mixing board, and an Ampex 8-track recorder, Carlos hoped to place the intricate sounds of the synth in a familiar, tonal setting that might appeal to a broad spectrum of listeners. Her purpose was "to demonstrate to the world that electronic music did not equate with a stereotypically weird and unapproachable collection of disjunct bleeps and boops lacking anything one might call musical expression and performance values." That perception, she claimed, resulted from "the tightly circumscribed world of academic music out of which most electronic music had originated."[8] She explained, "I was never into the avant-garde. . . . I didn't go for that type of non-rhythmic, non-melodic, non-harmonic music."[9]

Carlos and Elkind set up a production company for the new album, Trans-Electronic Music Productions, Incorporated, or TEMPI, and invited Benjamin Folkman, a musician and musicologist, to join them on the creative team. Carlos handled the musical and technical tasks, Elkind acted as producer and sounding board for musical decisions, and Folkman was the historical authenticity police, vetting Bach's standards of musical ornamentation, tempos, tone color choices, and other fine points. The three set out to prove that electronics wouldn't dehumanize Bach's music, but would instead offer a fresh perspective on it through an unfamiliar sound palette.

Tone colors on the synth were developed to suggest the flavor of Baroque instruments without specifically replicating the sounds of the originals. Here, the envelope generator was essential—adjusting the attack, decay, sustain, and release times of notes so a harpsichord-like sound had a shorter decay time, and a sustained, organ-like sound would decay more slowly.

But the process of creating the album was painstaking. Because the Moog was monophonic, recording the totality of instrumental lines in the intricate web of Bach's counterpoint meant inputting each part one at a time. The separate tracks then had to be stacked up and synchronized to play simultaneously in order to achieve the full ensemble effect. Carlos compared it to a Disney animator working frame by frame to create the eventual illusion of motion. The procedure became still more challenging when, after a few notes of a melody were recorded, the Moog's oscillators would drift out of tune and have to be recalibrated again before another small set of notes could be recorded. The snippets of recorded music were sometimes as short as five seconds.

In order to achieve any kind of musical expressivity, Carlos was constantly fighting what she felt were the deficiencies of the Moog. Bob took her criticisms seriously, and her suggestions and requests yielded two technical additions he developed for her.

One hurdle was the keyboard touch. Carlos remembered her "constant whining to Bob that some kind of pressure and velocity sensing was missing, and dearly needed. Bob realized it, too, and wanted to find a way to add this to the current instruments. . . . The first prototype was disappointing. I tinkered with it, found some constructive criticism. I returned it to him, with my meddlings. He came up with another variation. I hated parts of the response, and rebuilt parts of it. He was good natured about the way I'd messed with it, and made yet another version, and it went around for several months."[10] The new keyboard was an improvement, but Carlos still found it "clunky with all those touch-sensing mechanical gadgets in it." Bob then added two custom envelope modules that responded to touch sensors in the keyboard. "Suddenly," Carlos recalled, "I could perform without losing all human nuance," and she credited the new modules with allowing the Bach project to sound as musical as it did.[11]

Carlos also asked for a polyphonic keyboard to play the Baroque "continuo" chord patterns in the Bach works. Bob responded by building her a "polyphonic generator," an oscillator bank that sat in a long box behind the keyboards and allowed Carlos to chain a series of oscillators together to play the chords.

In the final audio mix of the master recording, every dimension was finessed in intricate detail, including the stereo panning of sounds at different locations across a nearly 180-degree plane in front of the listener. The distribution helped to distinguish different lines and timbres within the overall network of counterpoint. Folkman explained, "no combination of live instruments could achieve the clarity of texture of this recording."[12]

For Bob, a dose of Bach on his instrument was refreshing. His background in classical music, despite his exasperating childhood piano lessons, was broader than most people realized. In his Cornell dorm he'd spent leisure hours with an opera fanatic buddy, indulging in Verdi's *Othello* and listening to Wagner's massive music drama, *Die Götterdämmerung*, with the full orchestral score—"turned on a big light for me," he told Shirleigh.[13] In the first summers after they were married, he and Shirleigh scheduled camping trips around Boston Symphony Orchestra concerts at the Tanglewood Music Festival; on one trip they attended a full weekend of Bach performances.

By late summer 1968, Carlos's master tape was ready to deliver to Columbia; now it was just a matter of the title. Carlos suggested *The Electronic Bach*, but John Berg, CBS's art director, had another idea: *Switched-On Bach*. It could be abbreviated as *S-OB*. "They had horrible names they wanted to call it," Carlos remembered, "and we stopped laughing and we thought, 'well SOB might be better than *The Electronic Bach*. To me, the project had a smile around the corners of the mouth. I never considered *Switched-On Bach* to be pompous and awesome. It was good fun. I had fun doing it and expected people to smile when they heard it."[14] The album was scheduled for release in the fall.

∿∿∿

On July 1 the Main Street operation took a giant leap. The R. A. Moog Company—a Sole Proprietorship since Bob and George first opened their basement doors for business in 1954—was now the R. A. Moog Company, *Incorporated*. Bob had chosen to go it alone, having all 200,000 shares of common stock issued in his name. But it had little impact on the fiscal equation. By August, Sear's commissions on sales had reached $10,000 and he hadn't seen any of the money. "I could use some cash," he wrote Bob. "If you are plush, send some on down."[15]

Sear continued to broker sales of modulars in good faith, but it was frustrating work. He was habitually nagged for spontaneous demos, griping that 90 percent of the time he was beset by "time wasters, young children, stray dogs, and indigent composers."[16] But when he did make a sale, he ran up against another hurdle: there had never been a viable users' manual for Moog equipment. Once he sold a system, his work was only beginning. Many customers barely knew how to turn it on, and he wound up going to their places for free three-hour lessons in synthesizer technique.

And beyond the mechanical puzzle, for users who didn't have the ears of a Carlos or a Beaver, there was still the quandary over the Moog's endless supply of sounds. Composers of acoustic music who scored for a violin or a trumpet knew exactly what sound they'd be getting. But in electronic music there were no similar ready-made synthesizer sounds to select. Even if you had a specific sound in mind, it was impossible to know what sort of tangled cat's cradle of patch cords could make it for you. With ad agencies, Sear complained that he often had to give patching advice over the phone: "A lot of people, especially the music houses would call up at 2 in the morning and say, 'I need a thirst sound, for this commercial.' I mean, I had to program it. I programmed over the phone at all hours."[17]

Once again, Jac Holzman put his weight behind a novel solution by bringing Paul Beaver together with another musician. Beaver had begun offering informal classes out of his LA studio for anyone interested in the Moog. The sessions drew a cross-section of movie composers, teachers, and future synthesists. Among the group was Bernie Krause, a musician doing consultancies for Nonesuch. Holzman had introduced him to Paul, hoping the two might click as an artistic team.

Bernie and Paul shared a passion for electronic music, but ideologically they were polar opposites: politically, Bernie sat far to the left of Paul's Republican leanings. Bernie was a guitarist who'd been a late replacement member of the Weavers, the legendary folk ensemble known for their advocacy of labor unions, civil rights, and anti-militaristic causes—positions that got them blacklisted during the McCarthy era in the 1950s and banned from radio and TV. Bernie had joined the players in 1963 in the "Pete Seeger chair," performing in the group's Reunion concert at Carnegie Hall, and on tour, until they disbanded in 1964.

After he left the folk scene, Bernie worked briefly for Motown Records and then moved to San Francisco, enrolling at Mills College in the fall of 1966 to study the Buchla with Pauline Oliveros. Disillusioned with the avant-garde scene at Mills, he stumbled on the November 1966 *Time* magazine profile of Eric Siday. When he read about the composer's $5,000-a-second pay scale, he instantly knew his future lay in the commercial music business.

Late in 1967 Bernie was learning about the Moog in Paul's class.[18] He took copious notes and taped the sessions on a cassette recorder. As the concepts came together, he thought about the idea of chronicling the principles and techniques behind synthesis in some sort of recorded, published form, to offer Paul's lucid explanations to a wider audience. Maybe it was also possible to find a way to retrieve an earlier patch—what Paul couldn't do with the Doors—if sound samples could be named and catalogued. He took the idea to Holzman, who remembered, "Bernie Krause broached it. He said, 'If you believe in electronic music, let's document it, let's show what can be done.'"[19] Holzman put his blessing on the concept and approved Bernie's working title, *The Nonesuch Guide to Electronic Music*.

For Holzman, the notion of a whole recording of sound samples was familiar; he'd actually pioneered the idea back in 1961 with his lucrative *Authentic Sound Effects* LP series. While watching TV one night, he'd hatched the idea of a library of sound effects for commercial media producers. By 1964 he'd released 13 albums with hundreds of aural snapshots—everything from a jet taking off to a skidding car, a thunderstorm, a woman's terrorized scream, or a body tumbling down a staircase. The LPs were snatched up by producers in advertising, film, and TV, and quickly became a cash cow for Elektra. "It was one of the biggest financial stabilizers of the company," Holzman remembered. "We sold close to a million albums and we had no royalties to pay—no copyright, no Musicians' Trust Fund, no nothin'. And that gave us the money to fund Nonesuch and Nonesuch gave us the money to further fund Elektra."[20]

Holzman offered Bernie and Paul a $2,000 commission to create *The Nonesuch Guide to Electronic Music*. By March 1968, Beaver had bought his own Moog synthesizer and all the sounds were recorded at his LA warehouse studio. Meanwhile, back in San Francisco, Bernie worked feverishly at his kitchen table writing the text for the album booklet—listening, rewinding, and listening again to the tapes of Paul's seminars, poring over his pages of notes, and transcribing everything into a smooth flow of ideas.

The 16-page guide was the first attempt to create a recipe book of sounds for synth users, and an inside peek at the mysteries of what made electronic music tick. The booklet was co-dedicated to Bob. In his introduction, Bernie laid out the common dilemma: "Responsible critics often refer to the new taped sounds as 'drips, bird whistles, squiggles, burps, coughs, and other sorts of effects,' not knowing, perhaps, that . . . there is an emerging vocabulary that accurately describes the electronic musical genre."[21] Paul and Bernie's mission was to help users isolate generic synth sounds, learn to recreate each one from a formula, and have an identifying name for it. Together, the examples were a catalog of aural wallpaper samples, tabbed into sections by category, and labeled for easy reference.

The accompanying two-record set had 68 sound samples. The average cut was only 30 seconds long; the shortest was just 5. The track titles didn't exactly have that top 40 ring: "Triangular Waveform: Slow-motion audible example," "3 Square waves at different frequencies," or "White Sound—with fixed filters selected 3rd octave." The only complete composition on the set was a 3-minute jazz-like work called "Peace Three" that began and ended the album.

The Nonesuch Guide was released in late April 1968, and Holzman remembered, "My art director, when he heard the album, said, 'are you kidding?'

And I said, 'it's not being sold as *entertainment*, it's being offered for the curious.' We put the thing out and we were astonished with how well it did."[22] The album was a surprise hit, and remained on *Billboard's* bestselling classical charts for 22 weeks, peaking at number 17. The surge of sales wasn't on the order of Holzman's sound effects records, but it revealed a broad fascination with the synthesizer. As the first real lexicon of electronic sounds and techniques, it was invaluable for industry professionals. "The Nonesuch recording was a smart move," one USC music professor recalled, "because advertising guys would literally walk into a room with the album and say, 'This is the sound I want.'"[23]

Bob never forgot the sensation he made at the October AES convention in New York. After presenting his technical paper, "Recent Trends in Electronic Music Studio Design"—basically a look at Carlos's home studio—he ended by previewing the last movement of Bach's *Brandenburg Concerto No. 3* from the *Switched-On Bach* album just weeks before its release. "I walked off the stage," he recalled, "and went to the back of the auditorium while people were listening, and I could feel it in the air. They were jumping out of their skins. These technical people were involved in so much flim-flam, so much shoddy, opportunistic stuff, and here was something that was just impeccably done and had obvious musical content and was totally innovative."[24] Carlos, who was present, received a standing ovation.

The jacket cover for *Switched-On Bach* showed that classical people could poke fun at themselves. It took its cue from the campy humor of *The Baroque Beatles Book* and Peter Schickele's P.D.Q. Bach. The image was a staged color photo of a portly eighteenth-century composer seated with pen and manuscript, dressed in a blue frockcoat, white knickers and stockings, buckle shoes, a lace jabot around his neck, and a powdered wig—his puffy face mugging incredulously with bugged-out eyes, his earphones connected to a Moog synthesizer IIIp on a table behind him. Beneath the main title, the cover copy announced, "Virtuoso Electronic Performances . . . Performed on the Moog Synthesizer." Carlos's name appeared only on the back cover in small type—as "Walter Carlos"—credited with "Electronic Realizations and Performances . . . with the assistance of Benjamin Folkman." The liner notes ended with a salute from Bob: "This album is the most stunning breakthrough in electronic music to date."

The Columbia Masterworks' release party for its "Bach to Rock" campaign kicked off on December 4 at 9 p.m. in the 30th street studio of CBS, in Manhattan. "Dark suit," Jacqueline Harvey advised Bob. Along with *Switched-On Bach*, two other albums would be launched that night: *Rock and Other Four Letter Words*, and *Terry Riley In C*.

"CBS had no idea what they had in *Switched-On Bach*," Bob recalled. "When it came out, they lumped it in at a studio press party for Terry Riley's *In C* and an abysmal record called *Rock and Other Four Letter Words*. Carlos was so pissed off, she refused to come."[25]

Terry Riley was a pioneer of minimalism, a style that emerged in the early 1960s as a pushback against the dissonant, calculated, complex music of the "uptown" avant-garde. Minimalist music—a "downtown" phenomenon—drew its inspiration from the driving energy of rock, together with non-Western genres like African drumming. Minimalism stressed the repetitive, hypnotic pulsing of simple harmonies that shifted gradually over time. Riley's *In C*—which had its premiere at the San Francisco Tape Music Center in 1964 with Pauline Oliveros and Morton Subotnick among the 13 musicians—was an open-ended romp for any number of performers. The score instructed players to advance their way through 53 short, notated licks based in the key of C major, each player moving to the next unit at will until the full ensemble met at the end. The piece was utterly unpredictable, with the collective energy of the musicians at any given performance determining its length. The new Columbia recording clocked in at 43 minutes. *In C* was revolutionary in the classical genre because of its crossover into improvisation and the mesmerizing effect of its continuous C major wash.

Rock and Other Four Letter Words was an auditory extension of a book by the same name written by J. Marks, with photographs by Linda Eastman (soon to be the wife of Beatle, Paul McCartney). Marks and his collaborator, filmmaker Shipen Lebzelter, created the album with Columbia's John McClure as producer. The 13 tracks were an aural grab bag of snippets from Marks's interviews with rock stars mixed with excerpted recordings of rock bands, the Gregg Smith Singers, the Greater Abyssinian Baptist Choir, and electronic sounds. The text on the album jacket was mostly hip snark or impenetrable jumbles of interview outtakes. Judy Collins was quoted as saying, "Ta'a-nita'nit Exifit's-if' it's-of-ahah-if' it's-ah," to which J. Marks replied, "Yeahof' of' of' of.'" The tracks were generally chaotic sound collages with titles like, "Greatest Hits—Love Your Navel," "Baked Beans," and "Poop for Sopranos and Orchestra." The liner notes included a message: "This album is dedicated to Karlheinz Stockausen, who destroyed our ears so we could hear." Willy-nilly, Bob was in the mix too. The record jacket noted: "All electronic compositions on the album created by Marks and Lebzelter on the Moog III at CBS, New York."

Bob was out of his element at the party. "I remember there was a nice big bowl of joints on top of the mixing console," he recalled.[26] J. Marks—with amulets strung down his exposed chest—performed a theater work with his troupe. *Record World* reported, "Guests were treated to a 'total environment' program. . . . Terry Riley . . . performed a number of his works aided by a barrage of tape recorders, electronic equipment, keyboards and lightworks . . . and guests danced to the music of a rock band playing on various levels of a scaffold that rose to the high beamed ceiling of the studio."[27] With Riley and J. Marks out in force to represent their albums, and John McClure mingling in his full white suit, Carlos's absence was conspicuous. "So CBS, frantic to have some representation," Bob recalled, "asked me to demonstrate the synthesizer."[28] A photo op from the party showed a smiling CBS president Clive Davis posing with Bob, blank-faced, and visibly peeved.

In his press release for *Switched-On Bach*, John McClure wrote, "Synthesizers are suddenly good dinner conversation. The word is becoming as popular in musical circles as charisma is in political ones."[29]

The three "Bach to Rock" albums were announced in *Billboard* (two with comical typos: "witched On Bach," and "Terry Riley INC."), and by November 30, just after its release, *Switched-On Bach* had jumped onto *Billboard*'s classical charts at No. 24, only three slots below *The Nonesuch Guide*. There was stiff competition—Columbia's recent disk of music from *2001: A Space Odyssey* featured classical chestnuts like *The Blue Danube*, and *Also sprach Zarathustra*, played by the New York Philharmonic and the Philadelphia Orchestra, enhanced with a unique twist advertised prominently on the jacket cover: "Added Electronic Effects by Morton Subotnick." Columbia, in its push to integrate electronics into classical music, hoped to ramp up the market for the already popular *2001* soundtrack scores with new connecting interludes from Subotnick and his Buchla.

By December 7, in its second week on the charts, *Switched-On Bach* was biting at the heels of Columbia's *2001* disk, sitting just below it, at No. 8; by December 28 it had climbed to No. 2, leaving the *2001* album in the dust at No. 22.

The sudden spike in *Switched-On Bach*'s sales wasn't accidental. The mainstream press, which typically treated electronic music with a mix of curiosity, polite respect, and a dash of cautious praise, went all-out in its enthusiasm.

Donal Henahan was the first to weigh in. In a multi-column review for the Sunday *New York Times* on November 3, he called the LP "an astonishing experience, and possibly one of the year's most significant records." Weighing the larger impact, he wagered, "here, almost at one leap, is the much-promised revolution: not only can traditional sounds be imitated, but new sounds found that prove to be musically valid." Still, he was skeptical about electrified Bach, worrying that, "esthetically, we are being plunged into deep waters." But he admitted, "the essence of Bach's musical thought is retained in this recording—his structural design, his élan, his grandeur."[30]

At the same time, Henahan betrayed a misunderstanding of how *Switched-On Bach* was put together. The album notes certainly hadn't made it clear. The cover described the recording as "Virtuoso Electronic Performances," suggesting that Carlos sat at the Moog keyboard and played the music in real time with dazzling dexterity. In his album liner notes, Benjamin Folkman gave no hint of the laborious frame-by-frame method creating the illusion of a live performance. His notes, in fact, even compounded the problem, explaining, "Often two pairs of hands and several feet are needed to take advantage of all that the Moog Synthesizer can do." The reference was likely an allusion to the "pedal-and-keyboard-triggered switches" Carlos used to control the musical phrasing—devices she might have asked Elkind and Folkman to operate while her hands were busy with other tasks.[31] But Henahan told his readers: "Since two pairs of hands and feet are needed to play the synthesizer, it may fairly be compared to a great organ (an assistant to pull stops for a busy organist is allowed even in the most virtuosic circles), or to a piano being played four-hands."

Gene Lees, in *Hi Fidelity*, wrote that Carlos "has humanized synthetic music, and thereby parted company with Ussachevsky.... Carlos has opened the floodgate that held electronic music, and nothing is going to stop it now."[32]

Bob finally made his celebrity debut in the *New York Times*—his public anointing as the official poster boy for the synthesizer. In a December 11 follow-up article in the paper, Henahan talked about synthesizers—Bob's and Buchla's—and pronounced the demise of the RCA Mark II. A front-and-center photo was planted at the top of the article: Bob, handsome, smiling at the camera in a white shirt and tie, seated against the backdrop of his patch cord-strung modules. It was a branding moment—a face, finally, to go with the name. But the best part was Henahan's title: "Mark II is Dead, Long Live the Moog!"[33]

13
Hello, HAL

"If it were not a conflict of interest, I would run around grabbing up all the Moog stock I could get my hands on," Harold Schonberg declared in the *New York Times*.[1] "A Merry Time With the Moog?" was the paper's second major profile of Bob's work. In the February 1969 feature, Schonberg echoed Henahan's applause: "As an indication of what can be done with the Moog Synthesizer, 'Switched-On Bach' is breathtaking. . . . This is where the future of music probably lies." Bob was tickled at the recent flurry of attention. "When you see yourself looking out at you from the *New York Times* you begin to suspect you've done something important."[2]

The buzz was spreading through wire service stories and regional news features. The *Syracuse Herald-American* ran a typical curiosity piece: "Electronic synthesizer; Produces unlimited sounds." The alien technology was an irresistible scoop for the press: "the synthesizer looks like the operational panel of an atom smasher with a keyboard incongruously attached in front."[3]

The column revealed R. A. Moog's rising sales figures, but picked up on Bob's vibe: "Moog doesn't seem overly happy at the success. His great love is not money but the synthesizer and the music it can make." Bob wasn't searching for stockholders; he was looking for composers to experiment in the back room of his factory. "The only time he really gets excited," the reporter explained, "is when he talks of the new work coming out of the studio."

The story featured a photo of Bob at his modules feigning the classic pose, left hand reaching for a knob, right hand poised over the keyboard. Behind him, a dark-haired young man in horn-rimmed glasses stood casually in chinos and turtleneck, sleeves rolled to the elbows, observing with a half-smile of intrigue. The caption read: "R. A. Moog demonstrates his Synthesizer to Composer Jonathan Weiss at the inventor's laboratory."[4]

Jon Weiss was Bob's latest hire. Weiss had studied composition and violin at Antioch College and had originally come to Trumansburg for a three-month work-study term as composer-in-residence in August 1968. When the position expired he was granted a second three-month stint and soon realized he

Switched On. Albert Glinsky, Oxford University Press. © Albert Glinsky 2022.
DOI: 10.1093/oso/9780197642078.003.0013

was inseparable from the company. He never returned to Antioch. Jon had no electronics experience when he was hired. Growing up in Colorado, he'd known about electronic music—Stockhausen in particular—but he was just now beginning to write his own tape pieces. He proved a quick learn on the synthesizer and his first creations surprised Bob, who called him a "major talent" in a *National Observer* interview.[5]

The composer-in-residence position was a two-way street: Jon had access to the modules, plus a salary, and Bob had a musician guinea pig at hand to advise him on artistic hurdles with the equipment. Bob liked to call himself a "toolmaker" to musicians—someone who listened to their concerns and tweaked his instruments to fit their needs. Weiss's intuitive ease with the modules also made him invaluable as a techie, and Bob began sending him around to assist customers like Eric Siday and Peter Nero, and used him as a demonstrator and teacher in the shop studio.

On September 3, 1968, an order came in from the Rolling Stones for a Synthesizer IIIp. Mick Jagger was behind the request, and his agent, Allen Klein, expected Bob to fly to London to set up the instrument. Bob refused, and drafted Weiss to go in his place. With no user's manual for the systems, a purchaser had the choice of coming to Trumansburg for lessons or importing an onsite tutor. Weiss had found he could often explain modular concepts to musicians even better than Bob—musician to musician, with less engineering lingo.

When Jon landed in London with the Stones' synth he was detained for three hours; Jagger's address on the odd cargo sent customs agents rifling through the packing crates looking for drugs. Eventually the instrument was delivered to Mick's house, where Weiss would be staying. Jon found Jagger to be warm and friendly, devoid of the posturing bravura of his stage persona, and he was blown away by Mick's record collection—American Blues, avant-garde electronic albums, and even classical music. He found himself welcomed into the Stones' inner circle, riding in Keith Richards' Bentley, meeting Paul McCartney, and swept into the high-flyers' party scene with the "beautiful people." What was to be a stay of a few days turned into a month.

Weiss wasn't sure how the synthesizer would fit into the music the Stones were doing. It seemed they were more fascinated by the concept than anything else. He stood by as the group hovered about the exotic toy trying to figure out what it could do, and what it could do for *them*. At one point Keith Richards tried patching his guitar through it for live processing, but the results were disappointing. Jon spent a few sessions working one-on-one with Mick, reviewing the function of each module and tracing signal paths to patch a few sounds. "He was really quick learning that machine," Jon recalled, "one of the quickest studies of anybody I ever showed it to."[6]

As the other Stones gradually lost interest in the synth, Mick's sessions with Jon had to be scheduled around a competing project: Jagger was doing a shoot for a bizarre crime-sex-psychedelia film, *Performance*, where he played a reclusive rock star harboring a gangster in his West London townhouse. *Performance* coursed through episodes of graphic violence, sadism, nudity, hallucinogenic journeys on mushrooms, a ménage à trois, and liaisons that spilled over into reality with Jagger in sex scenes with Anita Pallenberg, the Stones' romantic muse and the real-life partner of Keith Richards (and formerly of Brian Jones). With the Moog lying around Mick's house as another expensive gadget that nobody knew what to do with, the idea came up to use it as a space-age prop in the movie. The IIIp was delivered to the set and Weiss remembered the workers' bewilderment: "Agh, it's a fabulous sanitizer and what does it do? Play us a tune."[7]

The instrument wound up in a two-minute cameo sequence late in the drama—the first visual shot of a Moog in a feature film. Mick, as the crazed rocker, Turner, sits on a pillow over an oriental rug, with the keyboard and synth in front of him, the modules framed by brilliant white fluorescent tubes. With tape reels revolving at one side, he plugs in a patch cord, then rises to wield one of the tubes, using it like a lightsaber, swinging and jabbing it in a menacing dance. Through the whole freak-out scene the Moog lies mute—futuristic techno furniture—while the song, "Poor White Hound Dog" by the soul and gospel singer Merry Clayton, throbs underneath.

The soundtrack for *Performance* was added later, back in the U.S., as a potpourri of music by composer Jack Nitzsche, and songs by Ry Cooder, Buffy Sainte-Marie, and other artists. Five songs, including the title theme, "Performance," featured a Moog played by Bernie Krause, who was now gigging on the instrument along with Paul Beaver.

With the Moog relegated to a set design accessory for the film, there was little more for Weiss to do, and he returned to Trumansburg. In the end, the Stones never used their Moog live, or on any of their albums. *Performance* finished filming in 1968, but Warner Bros. delayed its release until 1970 while bits of the most controversial content were snipped onto the editing room floor.

In November, Beaver and Krause got a call for an LA session being produced by Beatle George Harrison. Harrison was overseeing the debut album of British rocker Jackie Lomax for the Beatles' newly formed Apple label. The LP was being recorded at several locations: in California, and in London, at the E.M.I. and Trident Studios, with a backup roster of stellar musicians that included Eric Clapton, Paul McCartney, Ringo Starr, and Harrison himself. The album, *Is This What You Want?*, would use the Moog on several tracks. Lomax remembered how Bernie "set it all up in the studio and then we pushed him off it and started playing with it ourselves. Cheeky boys from Liverpool."[8]

In the early morning hours of November 11, after the last LA session wrapped at Sound Recorder Studios, Harrison asked Bernie to stay behind and show him the Moog—the setups used on the session, and other possibilities. "It was already quite late," Bernie remembered, "around 3:00 a.m., and I had flown in from San Francisco early the previous day. In my exhausted state, I didn't notice that he had ordered the engineer to keep a tape machine rolling."[9] Bernie went through the usual paces—white noise gunshots, whistling oscillators scooping up and down, random buzzing melodies, howling wind in an echo chamber, cascading sirens, dissonant bleepy improvisations, crickets, reverberant chirps, gurgling squiggles of sound, high pulsing car alarm effects, metallic swarming insects, and the like. Harrison was impressed and asked about buying a Moog.

George was already keen on sounds outside the standard instrumental timbres. He'd studied the sitar with Indian master Ravi Shankar, and played the instrument in the Beatles' song "Norwegian Wood" on their 1965 *Rubber Soul* album, blending the instrument into rock for the first time. On the band's *Revolver* album, the following year, his song "Love You To" had full-out influences of Indian classical music with a sitar, a tabla, and a tambura. During the Lomax sessions, Harrison put out the Apple label's debut release—and the first solo album by a Beatle—a film soundtrack called *Wonderwall Music*, heavily steeped in the Indian classical sound world. For his second solo album, he was considering the Moog.

On January 15, 1969, Harrison placed an order through the Beatles for a model IIIp from Paul Beaver. Bernie was now partnering with Paul in sales transactions from time to time, and, following Jon Weiss, he would be the second human user's manual summoned to England. When he and his wife arrived in London they were detained, but not for suspicion of drugs this time. He recalled the scene:

"From customs' perspective, the synthesizer was still an uncategorized or miscellaneous electronic device. The import duty would therefore be some outrageous sum of 60 or 70 percent. However, if it was an electronic organ, the duty fell below 10 percent—an enormous savings. . . . The agent allowed me to unpack the synthesizer and demonstrate it to him. I plugged it into the amplifier, patched a few oscillators, quickly synthesized a Hammond B-3 organ sound, and proceeded to play a couple of musical lines. Satisfied that it was only an electronic organ, he allowed Apple to pay the requisite tax and let the instrument into the country."[10]

When Bernie arrived at Kinfauns, Harrison's bungalow home in the London suburb of Esher, the IIIp was already set up in the living room opposite two tape recorders. As Bernie talked through the ways of the modules, George scrawled detailed notes on a yellow-lined pad. At one point, George interjected, "I want to play something for you that I did on a synthesizer. Apple will release it in the next few months."[11] Bernie was puzzled—George had just taken delivery of his Moog the day before. Harrison hit the "play" button on the tape recorder. Bernie was certain he'd heard the material somewhere. It sounded eerily like what he'd demonstrated to George after the Lomax session. George didn't deny the connection, but explained that he'd edited Bernie's sounds into his own composition. For the 25-minute piece, he'd taken the original isolated sound samples and woven them into a layered, multi-track interplay, bouncing them off each other and combining them into a progression of shifting textures. George explained that the track would be issued on Apple's new subsidiary label, Zapple.

Bernie was irate: "George, this is my stuff, we need to talk about how we're going to split this, how we're going to share this . . . I don't like it very much, but if you want to put it out, we've got to work something out."[12]

The question of where to draw the line was a tough one. Was a simple tutorial, recorded for later reference, equivalent to pirated intellectual property? Were Bernie's sonic elements free to be sculpted into a finished work, or was co-opting them in any way outright plagiarism? How different were Bernie's brief LA demos from the excerpts commercial producers used from *The Nonesuch Guide*'s formulas? Were synthesists in a recording studio—a new breed in 1968—there to serve as engineers, or were they musicians in their own right who owned any material they spontaneously demonstrated? These were fuzzy areas. Beaver and Krause, in fact, were credited on the Jackie Lomax album, together with two sound technicians, under "special effects."

Bernie recalled George's rejoinder: "Don't worry. I've edited it and if it sells, I'll send you a couple of quid. . . . Trust me, I'm a Beatle!"[13] As Bernie was leaving, George asked a favor: Could he set up a patch to sound like a bagpipe?

On May 9, 1969, the disputed track was released on the Zapple label as one side of George's LP, *Electronic Sound*. He called the cut "No Time or Space," after an expression he used for his practice of Transcendental Meditation. Side two contained another single-track work: an 18-minute piece he'd written on his Moog in the living room after Bernie left. He called it "Under the Mersey Wall," a reference to "Over the Mersey Wall," a newspaper column in the *Liverpool Echo* by an unrelated journalist, George Harrison. Later he admitted that his process of composing it was improvisational and arbitrary: "All I did was get the . . . Moog synthesizer, with the big patch unit and the keyboards that you could never tune, and I put a microphone into a tape machine. I recorded whatever came out."[14]

"Over the Mersey Wall" begins with George testing out the bagpipe sound—jabbing it repeatedly high and low, sometimes sustaining it like a distant truck horn, with spacey noises coming and going in the background. After that, random events stream along as if the listener were on a porch with sporadic traffic rushing by—sometimes a roaring motorcycle panning left to right, followed by quieter periods dotted with random machine and environmental sounds, or distant sirens; here and there, doodled melodic fragments pop in unannounced. The last six minutes drift along with hollow outer space tones overlapping gently into a fadeout.

On the record sleeve, the credits for "Under the Mersey Wall" read, "Recorded at Esher in Merrie England; with the assistance of Rupert and Jostick, The Siamese Twins: February 1969." The bow to George's Siamese cats was apparently a thank you for their musical contribution in trotting across the Moog keyboard as the recording was in progress.

The album artwork, front and back, looked like a child's color drawing in its naive simplicity, but it was actually George's own painting—a comment on recent events in his life. The back cover depicts a room with windows, furniture, and wall hangings, and specific people who Harrison later identified: Derek Taylor, the Beatles' press officer is shown sitting in a chair, "flying an angry kite," symbolizing, as George put it, "holding onto all of Apple's aggravation and problems that are looming over everyone."[15] "Grapple with it," George painted in one corner. Neil Aspinall, director of the Beatles' umbrella company, Apple Corps., is portrayed as a frowning face on the chair, and Mal Evans, the Beatles' friend and assistant, is a smiling face on the chair. Eric Clapton is pictured with a guitar, and George himself is shown "making the tea."

But pride of place was reserved for Bernie Krause, the focus of the front cover. George painted him as a mad scientist with a green cartoonish face in "bowtie and pocket square," sitting behind a psychedelic mixing board patched to George's IIIp. Behind him, the synth cabinets are caricatured as four boxes with even rows of polka dot holes (three boxes for the synth itself, and the fourth for George's "Sequencer Complement"). Attached to one side of the mixer an exhaust pipe spews vibrantly colored squiggles of sound. In the lower right-hand corner, Jostick the cat is a small, green devil-like figure.

The Zapple label was set up by Apple in February 1969 as a conduit for avant-garde experiments and spoken word recordings, but it was shut down in June by the Beatles' new manager, Allen Klein, after only four months. Harrison's *Electronic Sound* album and John Lennon and Yoko Ono's *Unfinished Music No. 2: Life with the Lions*—both released concurrently in May—were the only two Zapple issues before the label folded. The Lennon/Ono record had one side containing a live concert with John's distorted guitar feedback under Yoko's wailing, bleating vocalizations, and on side two, the couple taking turns chanting newspaper articles about themselves, long tracks of a baby's heartbeat, two minutes of silence, and radio stations flipped through with a dial as John makes a phone call in the background.

Neither record charted in the UK. In the U.S., *Unfinished Music No. 2* reached No. 174, and *Electronic Sound*, No. 191. Critical reaction to Harrison's album was harsh. *Rolling Stone* called the textures "mundane" and found the pieces lacked any cohesiveness. Roger McGuinn, who'd recently bought his own Moog, commented "as a Moog musician," saying that George's album "was something you do the first day you get it home and you try it out if you put the tape recorder on and let it roll. He went into a bunch of white noise riffs, a bunch of oscillator warble riffs—things that are very simple and really just show off the novelty gadget. . . . It wasn't musical."

Electronic Sound, with its meager sales and tepid reception, would likely have earned few "quid" for Bernie anyway. But some credit was duly given where credit was due: George, after enshrining Bernie's image on the cover, added an acknowledgement for "No Time or Space" on the disk sleeve: *Recorded in California: November 1968 with the assistance of Bernie Krause.*

Switched-On Bach hit a historic milestone on January 18 when it burst through the roof of the classical charts to join the ranks of *Billboard*'s coveted Top 200, mingling with giants like Bob Dylan and Sammy Davis Jr. At No. 194, it was the lone classical LP on the list. A week later, *Saturday Review* reported that 50,000 copies had been sold, and nine days after that, *Newsweek* logged the number at 75,000.

The tornado of interest in *Switched-On Bach* put Bob instantly in the media spotlight. On the frigid morning of February 5, 1969, he showed up at the NBC studios in New York for his national television debut on *The Today Show* with Hugh Downs. It would be the Moog synthesizer's broadcast unveiling, and Bob was joined by Carlos for the appearance. When they arrived at 5:00 a.m. to rehearse, they walked into the middle of a dispute: members of the musicians' union and the electricians' union were arguing over who was authorized to plug in the synthesizer.

Carlos was agitated for another reason. Public appearances now meant masquerading as the "Walter" listed on the *S-OB* album—dressing as a man, although she'd regularly been taking female hormones. Years later, in an interview with *Playboy*, she described the "brouhaha that erupted backstage": "Rachel heard a couple argue: 'Well, come on, that's a girl.' 'No it isn't. It's a boy.' 'No it's a girl pretending to be a boy.'"[16]

At 8:38 a.m. the feature spot began with a 15-second excerpt of Bach's Chorale Prelude, "Sleeper's Awake," from the *S-OB* album. Hugh Downs strolled over to the Moog on stage and addressed the camera: "Harold Schonberg, the music critic of *The New York Times*, wrote last December that what he wanted most of all for Christmas was a Moog Synthesizer. And a Christmas present of another kind did come to a lot of people in the music business. It was a record called 'Switched-On Bach,' in which some of the great Bach's mightiest compositions were realized on this astonishing machine. . . . the Synthesizer may indeed be a musical instrument that might one day be as important as the violin. 'Switched-On Bach' is the fastest-selling Bach album in history. . . . I'd like you to meet Dr. Robert Moog, the developer of this astonishing instrument."[17]

Bob answered questions and Carlos demonstrated compositional techniques on the instrument. To close the 14-minute segment, Downs played the *S-OB* track of the *Third Brandenburg Concerto*, last movement, flooded visually with psychedelic projections from the Joshua Light Show, a liquid light montage by another guest on the program, Joshua White, known for his spectacles at the Fillmore East in shows by artists like Janis Joplin and Jimi Hendrix.

154   COSMIC SOUNDS

Three days later, on February 8, a Moog appeared on the stage of Philharmonic Hall at Lincoln Center, the space where Bob's antennas had stood four years earlier in Cage's *Variations V*. It was a Young People's Concert with Leonard Bernstein and the New York Philharmonic. A capacity house bustled with kids swinging their legs and staring in open-mouthed puzzlement at the maestro. Bernstein challenged them with a sophisticated proposition: "Bach Transmogrified." He hoped to show them that Bach's music was so versatile it could survive transcription to any medium, including rock, with a live band he had on hand for the concert. He began with the *Little Fugue in G Minor*, played first by an organist, then the full orchestra, and then, in what he called a "much more kooky version, for the newly famous Moog synthesizer."[18] Carlos had been scheduled to appear, but at the last minute she opted out and Walter Sear came on in her place, bringing along a tape of his own synthesized version of the Bach fugue he'd hastily assembled.

Bernstein introduced the instrument as "the much talked about and written about Moog synthesizer." He gestured stage right: "And here it comes now." Sear and three other men ceremoniously wheeled the stacked modules on stage. The Synthesizer III appeared even taller with the addition of a Sequencer Complement cabinet and a lofty tape deck perched precariously at the top. The whole contraption, on its table legs, was spewing clusters of patch cords and sporting two keyboards like rows of teeth, all of it piled up to suggest a robot with an instrument panel body. "Hello HAL," Bernstein joked as a wink to the kids—(some brief laughter). It was an intentional cheap shot to win their attention with a reference to the talking computer from the recent *2001: A Space Odyssey*.

The presentation treated the synth in a half-mocking, "what-do-we-know-about-this-crazy-futuristic-technology?" parody as a way to connect the children with what they were about to hear. "It can do anything but stand up and take a bow," Bernstein explained (more laughter). "It can produce almost any kind of variation on pure sound. Including some sounds never heard before—on this earth, at least."

Walter Sear stood to the left of the machine as Bernstein talked about the "bizarre version of the Bach fugue it's about to play for us." The audience would be listening to Sear's recording and would have to imagine its connection to the instrument sitting on stage as a prop. "Now are you ready?" Bernstein asked. "Prepare decompression chambers. Force field operative" (an embarrassed smile from Sear). "All systems go." Bernstein reached up to switch on the sequencer's left-to-right sweep of blinking lights for the full automation effect. "And . . . blast . . . off." He clicked the "play" button on the tape recorder and sat on the side of the stage letting the metallic Moog sounds stream out to the audience.

Carlos saw the segment as comic relief for the program and felt sorry for Sear. She thought it was common in some classical music circles to dismiss her work, and the synth, with a smirk, or at best, as something trendy or campy. The *New York Times* reported, "The Moog Synthesizer had a restless audience and only respectful applause, as did the rock group."[19] On April 27, a tape of the concert ran nationally as a CBS televised broadcast that was syndicated to 40 countries.

Switched-On Bach began scaling the tallest peak on March 1, reaching *Billboard's* Top 40 at No. 39—a ridiculously impossible feat for a classical album. On March 7, *Time* magazine tallied nearly 150,000 copies sold, and by the 21st the *St. Louis Post-Dispatch* reported sales had passed the 200,000 mark and were showing no signs of slowing down. The album reached its final record altitude on April 26, slotting at No. 10, just beneath a collection of mammoth releases—the original cast recording of *Hair*, at No. 1, followed by Blood, Sweat & Tears, Glen Campbell, Donovan, the Temptations, Tom Jones, Glen Campbell again, Iron Butterfly, and in the ninth slot, Creedence Clearwater Revival. *S-OB* would stay in the Top 40 until the end of June.

In the pop world, middle-aged composers and arrangers were latching onto the Moog to don its hip sonic garb and sneak in on the *au courant* youth culture. Mort Garson followed up his *Zodiac Cosmic Sounds* with a take on *The Wizard of Oz*—a parody he called *The Wozard of Iz (An Electronic Odyssey)*— that recast the tale in the hippie world where Dorothy tries to discover "where it's at." Garson's score was written entirely for the Moog, with Bernie Krause on the instrument. Jacques Wilson wrote and narrated the story, with dialogue and songs performed by six actors.

In March 1969, Dick Hyman released the first Moog LP by a jazz musician: *MOOG: The Electric Eclectics of Dick Hyman*. Walter Sear programmed the instrument for Hyman, who filled the album with mostly original pieces, playing the Moog as a live studio instrument combined with guitars, drums, piano, and Lowrey organ. Hyman recalled, "I'd say to Walter Sear, 'Surprise me with some sounds.' And he'd patch in something and I'd start to play whatever it suggested."[20] The album notes proclaimed: "Dick Hyman's electronic themes . . . may soon make every kind of music we have known seem obsolete. . . . Dick Hyman, Command Records and the Moog synthesizer play it not like it is, but like it will be."

When Hyman promised to "play it like it will be," he was channeling the youth argot of the "now" culture, and "telling it like it is," just like Dorothy in *The Wozard of Iz*, who wanted to find "where it's at." Electronic music had become a portal to this hip domain. Even pop fluff had been recast in the new modish electronic sound, right down to the title. *The In Sound from Way Out (Electronic Pop Music of the Future)* was a 1966 LP by Gershon Kingsley and Jean Jacques Perrey (Kingsley, in his German accent, called it *zee EEN sound from vay OWD?*). The album—made before the pair discovered the Moog—was a cartoonish collection of instrumental pop ditties that used electronic bleeps and quacks to play bluesy, bossa nova, and light classical-influenced numbers, accompanied by studio musicians. The tracks had titles like "Barnyard in Orbit," "Electronic Can-Can," and "Jungle Blues from Jupiter."

The kitschy effects on *The In Sound* were achieved with elaborate tape loops, clavinet, and Perrey playing his pet instrument, the ondioline, a portable monophonic keyboard with vacuum tubes—invented in 1941—which could mimic standard instruments and play sounds of its own. From Perrey and Kingsley's standpoint, their liner notes told it like it was: "Here is the electronic 'Au Go Go' that might be heard soon from the juke boxes at the interplanetary way stations where space ships make their rest stops." For a parting thumb in the eye to people like Ussachevsky, they taunted, "As for that avant-garde wing, we say more power to it. But there are other things in the future, such as pleasure."

In early 1968 Perrey and Kingsley released a follow up LP, *Kaleidoscopic Vibrations (Electronic Pop Music from Way Out)*, this time adding a Moog. Later that year Perrey issued a solo record, *The Amazing New Electronic Pop Sound of Jean Jacques Perrey*, his first lone foray with a Moog. The end result might have been "Amazing," but Perrey, without Kingsley at his side, struggled with the synth. Sear complained to Bob, "Jean Jacques doesn't know how to even plug it in."[21]

Gershon Kingsley—soon to become one of the Moog's biggest champions—was an American success story. He was born Goetz Gustav Ksinski in 1922 and grew up in Berlin in a Jewish family. His main musical education came from playing in synagogues. As a 15-year-old he fled the Nazis and arrived in Palestine by himself in 1938. In the 1950s he came to the United States and found his calling on Broadway as a conductor and arranger—he was nominated for a Tony Award in 1958—and went to work as a staff arranger for Vanguard Records.

When Kingsley saw Eric Siday's studio he was bowled over by the pop potential of electronic music. In 1967 he visited Bob in Trumansburg and, encouraged by his wife, cleaned out their joint bank account to purchase a Moog for $3,500. "About three weeks later I had my first commercial with the Moog synthesizer," he recalled. "It was for a hairdryer. And I got $3,500 for it. So I got my money back after about three weeks."[22] Kingsley set up his own studio for radio and TV ads—the New Music Factory—and began writing commercial jingles for accounts like AT&T, Chevrolet, Coca-Cola, and General Foods.

In his more serious compositions, Kingsley found a new audience for the "way out" sound: Jewish youth who didn't mind rocking out to the Sabbath service. In April 1969, *Variety* reported, "The unlikely combination of electronics, psychedelic lights, rock and religion blended perfectly in 'Shabbat '69,' a special musical service at Temple Rodeph Sholom on New York's upper west side Friday evening. Gershon Kingsley orchestrated the event and sat in on Moog Synthesizer. . . . Kingsley played extraterrestrial music while the lights dramatically focused on the Holy Ark containing the Scriptures. . . . young people can identify with religion if allowed to express their feelings in familiar terms."[23]

Kingsley's folk-rock service—he sometimes called it "Shabbat for Today" or "Shabbat Now"—was commissioned by the Temple Sharey Tefilo in East Orange, New Jersey, and debuted there on May 10, 1968. "Since its premiere," *The Jewish News* reported in April 1969, "the 'Shabbat Now' has been performed at 63 synagogues in Cleveland and Los Angeles and most recently in New York."[24]

In May 1969 Kingsley turned Bob's name into a sexual verb with the release of *Music to Moog By*. The suggestive title was clear in the album cover art (flowers with nipple centers) and the jacket back (a photo of a mattress branded with a woman's parted lips and a backboard made of stacked Moog modules). The LP was a collection of Kingsley's original tunes, arrangements, and covers of two Lennon-McCartney songs—everything assembled from a plethora of Moog sounds. "Pop Corn," a track inspired by a Jewish folk tune—Kingsley claimed the melody came to him in less than a minute—got its title from an engineer on the session who suggested it was "pop" and "corny."[25] Another Kingsley track was a shout out to Bob: "Trumansburg Whistle."

Back on Main Street, the company operation was expanding. In the fall of 1968, Bob had a staff of over 20 and he put out the call for a string of new positions in the $4,000 to $8,000 range—generous compensation for the time; by March 1969 he had a staff of 33. Besides Bob, there was only one other engineer: Eugene Zumchak. The story of his hiring was typical of Bob's casual, instinctual method of bringing people on at the spur of the moment. Gene recalled his interview for a summer job in 1967: "I went up there and saw Moog and he says, 'What do you know?' I says, 'Not much.' He says, 'Know anything about digital stuff?' I says, 'Yup, it's analog stuff I don't know much about.' He says, 'Don't worry—I know all about analog.'"[26]

Bob assigned Gene to develop the 960 Sequencer module as his summer's work. "It was a pretty straightforward digital project," Gene remembered. "I didn't have to invent any of the functionality of it; Bob defined the functionality and I simply implemented it in digital silicon. He didn't really know that much about the technology that went into it, and he trusted me and I whipped it out and built it." Once Bob assigned a project to an engineer, Gene recalled, "it was out of his hands and he just didn't want to even look at it or talk about it. He didn't want to look over your shoulder and say, 'What'd you do today, Gene? How's it coming? Is it working the way we expected it to? Any problems?' Nothing. *He* either did the job or *you* did the job, and there was nothing in between."[27]

In early 1968 Gene returned to R. A. Moog full time after finishing his electrical engineering master's at Cornell, and finding out, to his relief, that he'd been rejected for service in Vietnam because of flat feet.

By the spring of '69, Bob needed a second staff engineer. Bill Hemsath had a degree in engineering from Case Institute of Technology and was assisting the composer Donald Erb in the electronic music studio at the Cleveland Institute of Music. He'd passed through Trumansburg a number of times since 1965 to borrow equipment from Bob for concerts, and on one visit to Bob's back-room studio with Erb to edit a recording, Hemsath recalled, "Bob called me off to the side and said, 'say, would you like to work here?' and I said, 'yes please.' So that was it. And in the middle of '69 I started work at the Trumansburg factory."[28]

Bob was a loyal boss who kept staff members on as long he could. Dick Ritter, the product manager, was Bob's first-ever employee, present at the birth in 1963 when he started as a wiring and testing technician. Ray Hemming, the general manager, had a background in livestock, but knew nothing about electronics.

Bob was also doing his best to support the local citizenry. Challenge Industries, a social service organization in Ithaca, asked companies to farm out work to their clientele—people with physical and mental disabilities. "In one section," the *Ithaca Journal* reported, "a man and a woman are working on electronic assembly for R. A. Moog, Inc. of Trumansburg. Eleanor is cutting and then dipping into liquid solder hundreds of spaghetti-like wires which will become jacks for the Moog Synthesizer. . . . Eleanor is confined to a wheelchair as a result of a neurological injury. Lester operates a drill press, putting graduated holes into strips of plexiglass which will also go into Moog assemblies. Lester has been a resident of state institutions for 35 years and travels weekdays from Sampson State Hospital at Willard to operate the drill press. . . . As his skill improves, his self-image grows."[29]

In the rear studio, Jon Weiss wasn't the only composer now. David Borden, a very different personality, would make a unique contribution by proving that a mishap can be the mother of invention.

Born in 1938, Borden possessed a host of impressive credentials: bachelor's and master's degrees from the Eastman School of Music, a second master's in music from Harvard, and a Fulbright year at the Hochschule für Musik in Berlin. In 1966 he was one of only 11 composers in the U.S. to land a Ford Foundation composer-in-residence position with a school district. His placement at the Ithaca junior and senior high schools came with a $5,500-a-year salary and no teaching obligations; his only mandate was to write works for the schools' vocal and instrumental groups, and to act as a community ambassador for contemporary music. Most nights he could be seen in a lit-up room on the roof of the darkened DeWitt Junior High School, composing in his little fire-hazard-condemned studio.

The Ithaca schools already had a strong commitment to contemporary music—the high school concert band had commissioned 15 new works—but Borden reveled in shaking things up as a renegade, anti-establishment role model and pushing the envelope as far as he could. His first big composition for the Ithaca High School concert band, *All-American Teenage Lovesongs*, opened with claps and whistles ("in case nobody claps at the end," he deadpanned), followed by a cacophony of 34 jumbled pop tunes ("they were embedded in the piece because I didn't want to be sued"), ending with a cue for the players to put their instruments in their laps and turn on their own transistor radios for a noisy, Cage-inspired coda.[30] The following year his new piece for the concert band was entitled, *VARIATIONS ON AMERICA BY CHARLES IVES AS HEARD ON THE JINGLE JANGLE MORNING IN*

EMERSON PLAYGROUND BY YOU AND THE SIGNERS OF THE UNITED STATES CONSTITUTION (AND WHO KNOWS, MAYBE THE F.B.I.)—for band and electronic tape.

Borden volunteered to teach all levels of the junior high music classes for several weeks, as an experiment, playing examples of his music and challenging the kids with his countercultural values. At the conclusion, he solicited their anonymous comments, which ran the gamut: "David Borden's music gives me *no* feeling at all"; "I wish it were all over with"; "I like Mr. Borden's music, but I don't think it's really music"; "He feels nobody should have a boss, and I agree"; "He doesn't sell his music. If he did sell it for a living, the buyers would 'control' him"; "I believe he's taking up space. Prancing around the school building with his greasy beard and blue jeans with the paint on them"; "actually he makes quite a lot of good sense! HE'S THE GREATEST"; "If I were he I'd shave off that kooky beard and get a job and compose after business hours."

Borden wasted no time in using the comments as a text for a new piece written for the ninth-grade choir. DeWitt's principal narrated some of the lines and some were projected on a screen. Everything was accompanied by plastic flutes, bicycle horns, police whistles, party horns, transistor radios, balloons, plastic machine guns, and cap pistols.

In the fall of 1968, after his two-year school residency ended, Borden was hired as a composer and pianist for the Cornell dance program. When someone told him that "this guy" in Trumansburg had an electronic music studio and wanted composers to come and experiment, he located the R. A Moog Company in the phone book and made an appointment. "It looked like a dilapidated, crummy place," he remembered. "Everything on the inside and the outside of this building was very funky."[31] Just through the front door and up a flight of stairs he found the company secretary, Leah Carpenter, who ushered him into Bob's office in the adjoining room. Bob was sitting behind his desk, and Borden remembered the nameplate—not "Robert," or "Moog," just three words: "Rhymes with Vogue."

Downstairs in the studio, Borden recalled how Bob sat at a modular and talked him through the functions: "He went module by module and showed me how they interacted and how you hooked them up. But he wouldn't use any musical terms, he would be using engineering terms which I didn't understand. Every once in a while he would say, 'you following me?' And I guess I really was a jerk, because I should have said, 'No, I can't understand what the fuck you're talking about.' He would have liked that. But I said, 'oh sure!'

So he spent between an hour and two hours with me. And it was getting toward closing time and he said, 'why don't you just come back tomorrow and see what you can do?' "[32]

The next day, Borden sat in the studio by himself staring at a stack of modules, two keyboards, a couple Scully 2-track tape decks, a Scully 4-track, and a turntable. No matter what he did, he couldn't manage to hear anything from the speakers. Bill Hemsath recalled, "Dave Borden was working for half an hour trying to get the thing patched up, and he couldn't get any sound out of it. I went down and turned on the power switch." Borden recalled, "Bill looked at me and said, 'That helps a lot.'"[33]

"I think it was after less than 3 weeks," Borden remembered, "I ruined my first module. You could smell the burn in the studio. There were dozens of patch cords hanging from various things that you could use. I knew where the oscillators were. Outside of that I was a little hazy. I hooked up the controllers to control something that shouldn't be controlled and I hooked something into the controller that was feeding back—none of it should have been there—and I was going, 'that's funny. It smells funny. I should call Bill again. It smells funny in here. And it doesn't sound right.' So he came down, he looked at it, and he could tell right away that none of the connections made sense once you got past the oscillator. He went, 'hmmm.'" Hemsath called another person down. "'Ooooh, uh-oh. We gotta call Bob.'"

"And then Bob came down and he took one look at it and said, 'Holy shit.' And I thought, 'that's it, I'm outta here.' I started getting my coat to go and I said, 'I'm very sorry, I didn't mean to. . . .' And Bob came right over to me—and he's not a huggy guy, you know?—and he put his arm around my shoulders and he said, 'Don't worry, don't worry.' I kept going, 'Oh I'm so. . . .' 'Don't worry.' He said, 'We'll go upstairs and Leah will give you a key and you come in at night, anytime. But when you leave, *leave it set up.*'"[34]

Borden began opening the shop with his key each night at 7:30 or 8:00, staying until midnight by himself back in the studio under the fluorescent lights in the day's stench of cigarette smoke. By the end of the first week, Shirleigh got a call from the police about someone in the factory at night. "Is there a blue VW outside?" she asked. "Yes." "Then that's ok." Borden remembered, "Apparently I burned out other modules because I could tell the smell was back, and I would leave a note—'I think something burned out.'"

"After about a month, Bob came to me and said, 'well I can tell that you know what you're doing. 'Cause for the past few weeks everything has been hooked up correctly.' He said, 'I must tell you, here's what we've done. We've redesigned almost every module. So no matter how you hook it up it will not impede it in any way or, you know, destroy it or anything like that. So you've been invaluable really as kind of an idiot-proofer.' And he *thanked* me. It was interesting for him to watch the process. They didn't ever tell me, 'you can't do this, you can't do that.'"[35] Hemsath recalled, "Bob really liked that, because David was sort of the most naïve user we had—so David could break it and we wanted to find out why. David was very valuable to us there."[36]

14
The Plastic Cow Goes Mooooooog

The Moog seemed to be everywhere in the summer of '69. Mort Garson's daughter, Day, recalled her excitement on July 20: "They started to televise them landing on the moon, and walking around and putting the flag down. And yes, all of that was a great big deal. But the big deal for my family was that my dad's music was playing in the background . . . and that he had used the Moog synthesizer, which was perfect for that because that was an out-of-this-world experience."[1]

Garson's Moog soundtrack, heard by millions fixated on the Apollo 11 moon landing, was the underscore for a 6½-minute film CBS-TV aired at recurring intervals during the July 1969 mission—footage from earlier NASA flights showing a blastoff, separation of the stages, close-up shots of the moon, earthrise, and astronauts playing inside the ship. "The only sounds that go along with space travel are electronic ones," Garson told the *Los Angeles Times*, explaining that the music "has to echo the sound of the blastoff and even the static you hear on the astronauts' report from space. . . . So I used a big, symphonic sound for the blastoff, some jazzy things for the zero-G game of catch . . . and a pretty melody for the moon."[2]

Electronic space-inspired music went to the moon, literally, with the Apollo 11 astronauts. Neil Armstrong was a fan of Samuel Hoffman's *Music Out of the Moon* album, and brought a cassette tape of it along to play in quiet times throughout the mission. During the return journey to earth, Houston suddenly heard the gentle strains of Hoffman's lounge music theremin singing "Radar Blues" inside the space capsule in a raspy transmission. Armstrong and Buzz Aldrin went back and forth with Charlie Duke at Mission Control:

> Armstrong: Did you copy our music down there?
> Duke: Rog. We sure did. We're wondering who made your selections?
> Armstrong: That's an old favorite of mine. It's an album made about 20 years ago, called Music Out of the Moon.

Switched On. Albert Glinsky, Oxford University Press. © Albert Glinsky 2022.
DOI: 10.1093/oso/9780197642078.003.0014

Duke: Roger. It sounded a little scratchy to us, Neil . . .
Aldrin: It's supposed to sound that way.[3]

Two weeks later, on August 6, the Moog synthesizer was about to have its official unveiling in the Ithaca community. The event would feature yet another mishap, courtesy of David Borden. The free outdoor concert was part of the "music-by-the-lake" series at the Stewart Park pavilion. Three hundred onshore listeners, plus locals in 30 boats moored at the edge of Cayuga Lake, ogled the assemblage of gear on the pavilion porch stage. Seated among the audience was J. J. Johnson, the great jazz trombonist and composer who'd come to Trumansburg for a crash course on a synth he was hoping to use for jingles. "Half the world of new musicians had come to Moog's Trumansburg door," the *Ithaca Journal* admitted, before "his neighbors 15 minutes away finally found him."[4]

Bob was a regional legend, but not many had met him or seen his instrument up close, and a group lined up to get his autograph on the *Switched-On Bach* album. *The Free Press* of Trumansburg conceded, "Now that Bob Moog has arrived, we can swallow our crow in great lumps and realize that this mysterious man has offered our village a great opportunity in its advancement."[5]

Area residents were excited for the concert, aware that Trumansburg had landed on the map because of Bob. Starting with the Beach Boys, who'd stopped off before a show at Ithaca College in November 1966 to thank him for their melsinar, celebrity visitors were becoming common. Residents often did a double take over these icons passing through their little town. And the visitors were often shocked to learn that this was the habitat of the hallowed Bob Moog. The backwoods nature of the place was always on display to his guests. In January 1967, Raymond Scott—who'd ordered a few custom circuits from Bob over the years—blew into town on a trip, desperate for a magistrate to marry him to his third wife, Mitzi. Bob arranged for the Trumansburg justice of the peace, a chicken farmer, to perform the ceremony.

David Borden got a kick out of the provincialism two doors down from R. A. Moog on Main Street at Kostrub's Luncheonette—BREAKFAST-LUNCH-DINNER-SODAS. Kostrub's was the default greasy spoon for Moog employees. Mrs. Kostrub, her son, and teenage daughter worked the soda fountain and waited tables. "They had these Coca-Cola ads hanging on the walls," Borden recalled, "probably from the '30s. And the youngest woman who worked there must have been 16." One Moog employee, he recalled, "fell totally in love with her. She looked like she could have been in one of those Coke ads. Her hairdo was 1930s. The whole town looked like a western—like a guy would walk out and shoot you, you know?"[6]

At the same time, the lure of Bob's esteemed operation was irresistible, and for one New York City musician, a jaunt to Trumansburg convinced him to make it his new home. In the spring of '69, Chris Swansen, a composer, showed up on Bob's doorstep. Swansen was born in Milwaukee in 1939, and his resumé, like David Borden's, was impressive: a bachelor's degree in music from Dartmouth, training at the Berklee College of Music, and study with the composer Aaron Copland. He'd performed as a jazz trombonist in New York with giants like trumpeter Randy Brecker and saxophonist Joe Henderson, and had done stints in the big bands of Stan Kenton and Maynard Ferguson. Through a musician colleague in New York he'd learned about Bob and the synthesizer. When he came to Trumansburg with his wife Meg, Bob gave him a quick tour of the modules and turned him loose.

Chris had never seen a synthesizer before in his life, but he took a jazz chart, and with sounds he'd just figured out how to make, he laid down over a dozen individual parts on tape, mixing them into a finished piece the same day. "Moog was just blown away," Meg remembered. "He'd never witnessed anything like that, to have someone take to a synthesizer like a duck to water."[7] Bob offered Chris a composer-in-residence position on the spot, and on April 15 Swansen began working in the studio, four to six hours a day, five days a week. Jon Weiss stayed on, and David Borden kept his evening schedule.

Swansen and his family were now Trumansburg residents, and Meg recalled how the townspeople took a while to warm up to them: "I was one of the hippies. I wore full-length dresses and had long hair, and my husband had long hair and a ponytail—we were definitely suspect."[8] Bob and Shirleigh, on the other hand, had acclimated fully to domestic life in the town. In August, Shirleigh divulged casually in the middle of a letter to Florence, "I guess I should let you know that Moog #4 is in the works for an early March delivery. The 9 mos. of carrying are concerning me right now—back and varicose veins being a problem."[9]

On July 18, as the astronauts were on their way to the moon, Americans were distracted by the news that Senator Ted Kennedy's car had veered off a bridge into a pond on Chappaquiddick Island near Martha's Vineyard, killing his passenger, 28-year-old Mary Jo Kopechne. On the 25th, Kennedy made a solemn, contrite statement before the nation over live television. David Borden was experimenting with his home tape deck, using a trick for taping sound directly from his TV, and recorded the broadcast.

Twelve days later, at the open-air concert at Stewart Park pavilion, Borden's music was scheduled to be featured, along with the compositions of Bob's back-room studio composers, Jon Weiss and Chris Swansen. Borden's contribution involved a pre-recorded tape of Moog sounds he'd prepared as a background to live sounds he'd create with another Moog, randomly, on the spot, in the spirit of Cage. "I was in a terrible hurry to make it to the venue on time," he recalled. "I grabbed a tape. . . . When the tape started playing I immediately realized that I had grabbed the wrong one." Borden instantly recognized it as the recording he'd made of Ted Kennedy's grave testimony to the nation. "So, in the spirit of chance and indeterminacy," he remembered, "I proceeded, live, with my plan anyway."[10]

"Some squirmed," the *Ithaca Journal* critic reported. Trying to understand Borden's intent, she strained to imagine Kennedy's panic and his passenger's suffocating death in the live electronics: "You could hear the choking, and the conscience voices, and the pre-dawn sweat. And all of it, except the Kennedy statement, was made by the vibrations of the machine."[11]

Borden recalled that Bob received a letter from someone who'd been in the audience that day: "It amounted to a long hate letter about my music, condemning the invention of such a musically destructive piece of trash and that he should destroy all of the synthesizers that he had made before more damage could be done. He absolutely loved this letter and every time he thought of it he would start laughing very loudly. He hung it up on his wall in the office."[12]

∿∿∿

Thousands of cabbage white butterflies liberated from cardboard boxes fluttered over the heads of fans thronged at the Rolling Stones free concert in London's Hyde Park on July 5. In the heat, many of the nearly dead insects rained down on the gathered faithful of more than 250,000. It was a tribute to Brian Jones, who'd died two days earlier. Mick Jagger, in a laced white poet's blouse that appeared like a little girl's dress over white pants, stepped forward—the romantic dandy—to read a poem by Shelly. A pack of self-styled British Hell's Angels the Stones had hired for security snaked through the crowd in black leather jackets, helmets, and swastikas. The concert ended with an 18-minute version of the Stones' new song, "Sympathy for the Devil."

Kenneth Anger, an American underground filmmaker, strolled around the event shooting footage for a new film, *Invocation of My Demon Brother*. Anger was a friend of Jagger and his circle, and his work was inspired by the British occultist Aleister Crowley, a self-styled prophet and founder of the religion of Thelema and the practice of "Magick."

Anger finished *Invocation* later in July, assembling the 11-minute short from clips of the Hyde Park concert and scenes shot at two interior locations in San Francisco. Anger himself played the role of Magus, a Zoroastrian priest; Anton LeVey, the real-life founder of the Church of Satan, was cast as His Satanic Majesty. For the role of Lucifer, Anger recruited Bobby Beausoleil, a 21-year-old musician and drifter mixed up in the sex-and-drug trade. Beausoleil was known by a series of aliases—Cupid, Bummer Bob, Snofox, and sometimes, Tophat, because of his trademark hat. *Invocation of My Demon Brother* was a string of sped-up, shaky shots and double exposures with no dialogue or sound effects. Like a silent home movie, the film flickered along in satanic, ritualistic vignettes: people smoking from a skull pipe, a cat's funeral, nude boys wrestling, blazing fires, a midnight Black Mass, and at the end, a hand-lettered sign, "ZAP YOU'RE PREGNANT THAT'S WITCHCRAFT."

Anger had installed Bobby Beausoleil in an 11-piece rock group, the Magick Powerhouse of Oz, to play lead guitar and sitar, hoping to use the band as background music for an earlier film, *Lucifer Rising*. When the plan failed, Jagger was recruited to write the soundtrack instead, but the music wound up as the underscore for *Invocation*. "He was great," Anger recalled of Jagger's effort. "He did it for me in one night; we just climbed on the same wavelength."[13]

Jagger's secret was simple: he used his Moog synthesizer with a sound still patched on it from Jon Weiss's demo in the fall of 1968. Weiss later recognized it as a sample he'd put together for Jagger. A repeating rhythmic lick on one note, with barely perceptible variations, ran hypnotically in three-second cycles through the full length of *Invocation*. Here and there Jagger threw in some white noise static and low frequency rumbles. The movie debuted on the underground film circuit in August, and showed up at New York's Elgin Theatre, where it soon became an art-house cult classic.

That summer Bobby Beausoleil took something of his role as Lucifer out into the world. Lately he'd signed on as a member of Charles Manson's "Family," the criminal cult surrounding the messianic leader at his California commune. On July 27, at Manson's direction, Beausoleil inflicted the fatal knife wounds on musician Gary Hinman, as the climax to a grisly, torture killing over a money dispute, setting off the serial killing spree of actress Sharon Tate and six others by the Manson gang two weeks later. Beausoleil finished the Hinman deed with the words "political piggy" smeared on the wall in the victim's blood—an attempt to implicate the Black Panthers in the murder—while other Manson followers looked on. The words referenced Manson's obsession over an imminent apocalyptic race war, and the personal anthem he chose to associate with it: the Beatles' song, "Helter Skelter."

The Beatles, at that moment, were at the EMI Recording Studios on Abbey Road in London working on their final album as a group. Back on January 30 they'd made their last live appearance, a 42-minute concert filmed on the roof of the Apple Corps building.

After the release of *Electronic Sound*, George Harrison had tried out his Moog again, playing it on a record he produced for Apple—Billy Preston's *That's the Way God Planned It*—to be issued later in August. In the final weeks of the Abbey Road sessions, George hauled it into room 43 of the studio to decorate the last mixes of the songs. Alan Parsons, an assistant engineer, remembered, "Everybody was fascinated by it. We were all crowding around to have a look."[14] John had actually seen one already. "I threw a party for John Lennon one night," Micky Dolenz remembered, "and he sat there at the Moog for four hours making flying saucer sounds. It was great for flying saucer sounds."[15]

George was still finding his way around the synth, and Mike Vickers, formerly of the British band Manfred Mann, was brought in to program it. "It was one thing having one, and another trying to make it work," George groused. "There wasn't an instruction manual, and even if there had been it would probably have been a couple of thousand pages long. I don't think even Mr. Moog knew how to get music out of it."[16]

On August 5, the first Moog tracks were laid down. In John Lennon's song "Because," George played the synth part, doubling the guitar with a brassy solo in the middle section, and flying a hollow, fluty melody over the harmonized vocals near the end.

On August 6, as David Borden performed his unplanned Chappaquiddick piece on the shore of Cayuga Lake, Bobby Beausoleil was taken into custody after he nodded off at the side of the road in Hinman's Fiat. The murder weapon—a bowie knife—was found in the car. At the EMI Studios that same day, Paul McCartney was laying down Moog tracks on "Maxwell's Silver Hammer": "Bang, bang, Maxwell's silver hammer came down upon his head, Bang, Bang, Maxwell's silver hammer made sure that he was dead." "I spent three days on 'Maxwell's Silver Hammer,'" Paul explained. "It was the early-days Moog work and it did take a bit of time. (Although nowadays, three days is just for switching the machine on!)."[17] In the mix, Paul added a melodic Moog solo to link the first chorus to the beginning of the second verse, and played a howling theremin-like sound with the ribbon controller for a counter melody on the second verse and after the third chorus, to the end.

On August 8, John was at the Moog. "That machine can do all sounds and all ranges of sounds," he recalled, "so if you're a dog, you could hear a lot more. It's like a robot. George can work it a bit, but it would take you all your life to learn the variations on it."[18] For "I Want You (She's So Heavy)," John used the white noise generator to add a rushing wind sound over the last two minutes of the song. "He actually had Ringo supplement it," engineer Geoff Emerick remembered, "by spinning the wind machine secreted in the Studio Two percussion cupboard." Emerick recalled John's compulsiveness: "As we sat in the control room mixing the track, he started becoming almost obsessed with the sound. 'Louder! Louder!!' he kept imploring me. 'I want the track to build and build and build,' he explained, 'and then I want the white noise to completely take over and blot out the music altogether.'"[19] In a final defiant touch, Lennon ordered Emerick to physically slice off the tape during the repeating vamp in the outro, causing the song to stop abruptly, mid-phrase, with no warning.

On August 19, at the last playing sessions for the *Abbey Road* album, the final Moog tracks were laced in as George finished the mix of his song "Here Comes the Sun." He later said he'd conceived the song in a few minutes as he was unwinding among the trees at Eric Clapton's house after a trying day. "The song came right out," he remembered. George played the Moog on the repeat of the opening melody, joining it to the guitar line with a gentle howl that finished with a downward slide, and then added it in the same role in the second verse. In the middle section, "Sun, sun, sun, here it comes," he bolstered the accompanying melody with a fat Moog buzz. "When you listen to the sounds on songs like 'Here Comes the Sun,'" he later reflected about the Moog, "it does do some good things, but they're all very kind of infant sounds."[20]

The final mix and running-order session for *Abbey Road* on August 20 was the last time the Beatles gathered in a recording studio as a group. But it wouldn't be the last time members of the group used a Moog. Both George and Paul would find places for Bob's instruments on future albums.

∿∿∿

Billboard reported that *Switched-On Bach* had passed the 300,000 sales mark on July 26, and on August 14 the album earned Gold status from the Recording Association Institute of America (RIAA) for sales in excess of $1 million. John McClure at Columbia, still riding high on *S-OB*, followed up with *Switched On Rock—The Moog Machine*, and Moog LPs were sprouting up everywhere. *Billboard* headlined a story, "Moog the Medium as Companies Get Electronic Message." July's new crop of entries included *Moog Groove, Moog Rock, Moog Power, Exotic Moog*, and *Switched-On Bacharach*. In August there was the tongue-twisting, *Genuine Electric Latin Love Machine*, and an eye-roller from producers who apparently never got the memo: *The Plastic Cow Goes Mooooog*. August also saw another Dick Hyman album—mostly covers this time—*The Age of Electronicus*—and a Beaver and Krause collaboration, *Ragnarök*. In a back cover endorsement on Paul and Bernie's album, Beatles' producer George Martin wrote, "The invention and development of the Moog synthesizer is like a dream come true."[21] In September, Martin bought a Moog of his own.

Bob wasn't happy. He found the latest rash of recordings faddish and opportunistic—seizing the Moog name for a quick buck—and he was embarrassed to be associated with them. "There are a couple of records I've heard that make me feel like a Frankenstein," he told the *National Observer*.[22] One album, *Moog España*, particularly stuck in his craw. "Musically ... it was dreadful," he griped to an interviewer.[23] But the press, still joyriding on the runaway Moog train, didn't agree. *Record World* raved about the LP: "Another stand-out Moog album is here."[24] *Billboard* concurred: "From the world of thingamabobs and gismos, comes some really fascinating—and not all that esoteric—music keying on the Moog Synthesizer. . . . the result is highly effective."[25]

The titles kept rolling: *Moog Plays the Beatles, Spaced Out*, and Walter Sear threw his hat in the ring on the Command label with *The Copper Plated Integrated Circuit: Plugged In Pop*, a collection of his original instrumentals with titles like "Circuit Breaker," and "Feedback Circuit," and covers of two

Beatles songs. Sear had recorded everything in his studio on two Moogs, an electric harpsichord, a Novachord, and a modified electric organ. *Record World* was upbeat: "Walter Sear, well-known electronic music wizard, is the guiding light behind this collection of switched-on pieces. . . . it's all interesting and filled with new sounds."[26] *Billboard* agreed: "Command Records enters the moog sweepstakes and they should fare very well with the initial entry."[27]

While the record companies were making a killing, Bob complained to Florence, "We see no royalties or other tangible reward from the successful records. 'FAME' is not an altogether welcome by-product of my work. My mail is choked with 'please-send-me-all-information' letters from report-writing sixth graders on one hand, and 'Congratulations-now-how-about-paying-us' letters from our flock of creditors on the other hand."[28]

For an August 24 *New York Times* feature, "Is Everybody Going to the Moog?" Donal Henahan interviewed Bob over a beer at a midtown Manhattan steak house. The reviewer noted Bob's habit of suspending people in long, uncomfortable silences before answering a question. "He weighs out his words with the caution of a State Department press officer. . . . His habitually pursed lips allowed themselves a small smile as he contemplated the heady vision of a world in which every living room had its baby-grand Moog." Bob, Henahan explained, "wouldn't mind at all going down in history as the Adolphe Sax of electronic music, or even the Stradivari. And it could happen. The Moog music synthesizer . . . is coming to stand in the public's mind for all music synthesizers."[29]

But Henahan was puzzled. Bob, he felt, "sounded slightly bitter for a man whose name is becoming a generic term." Bob got right to the point: "Sure, I like the idea of my name becoming a generic term for the synthesizer. But I don't like the fact that cruddy records are being put out with my name attached."[30] He refrained from naming names, but many were damned by omission. He made only one exception, an odd one: "Of the pop people," Henahan divulged, "he regards Gershon Kingsley, the Broadway composer, as probably the most proficient ("Music to Moog By"). Moog contends that most of what is produced is inferior stuff, principally because 'there are maybe 25 people in the world who have the necessary competence in both physics and music to exploit the Moog's potential."[31] What a physics background had to do with artistic excellence on the synth wasn't clear.

Sear was livid over the article and wrote Ray Hemming at the company: "I do not believe that Bob is qualified to set himself up as a music critic. He has been doing this quite consistently and often incorrectly. He is in a position to help with sales of records which I have made which IN TURN help me to sell synthesizers.... In the case of the Command 'Moog' album which Bob apparently didn't like on a musical basis, it has been on all of the charts (pop and otherwise) for 21 weeks now.... it would help me with future sales if Bob would mention these things whenever he gets free press coverage. The Sunday Times article is a good example of what I mean. I hope that it will not be said again what I heard from one of my customers who called me about the article today—that Bob forgets his friends once he doesn't need them."[32]

Sear was working overtime to promote the Moog. The *Electric Eclectics* album by Dick Hyman—one of his good friends—was a project he'd helped bring about. "I notice that Dick Hyman's record is doing fairly well," Bob wrote Sear. "I am pleased for his sake, but still think that it will do no good for our products in the long run because of its flip and gimmicky quality. That, obviously, is my own opinion."[33]

By mid-July, though, *Electric Eclectics* had reached No. 30 on the *Billboard 200*—trouncing *Switched-On Bach* at No. 67—and had sold over 125,000 copies. "Minotaur," a single from the album, had logged over 130,000 sales. Sear was helping Command Records endorse its three recent releases—the Hyman LP, his own *Copper Plated Integrated Circuit* album, and the *Electric Latin Love* record of Richard Hayman. The three were grouped together as the label's "Electronic Pop Music" series, and the company even invested in a 10-page brochure with testimonial articles by Hyman, Sear, and Hayman, to push the three LPs.

While Bob was disparaging the *way* his instrument was being used, the very use of it at all was coming into question by the musicians' union in New York. In January, Sear had alerted Bob, "I saw my lawyer about the Union—he doesn't think that we have any trouble—I hope he is right."[34] But by April, *Rolling Stone* reported, "The officers of the American Federation of Musicians (AFM), meeting here to set contracts for the coming year, very nearly wrote the Moog synthesizer out of recorded music in this country. Early reports had it the musicians' union leadership had approved a clause which said 'Moog synthesizers and similar devices shall not be used to replace instrumentalists,' and would effectively have made it economically unfeasible to record with them."[35]

A West Coast AFM official, in fact, remembered that the LA union insisted a synth player would have to be paid the equivalent of the combined fees of all the musicians replaced on any session—a tactic to discourage use of synthesizers in the first place. For the time being, Sear managed to keep the New York union at bay with the old ruse Bernie Krause had pulled. Bob recalled: "He took one of the modular systems down to the union, and he convened all the experts. He set the oscillators a little bit out of tune—and a very dull tone—and he played it, and he said, 'you see, it just sounds like a bad Hammond organ. There's nothing to get excited about.' "[36] *Rolling Stone* reported, "Following a demonstration of the synthesizer by a Moog representative, the anti-synthesizer restrictions were apparently tabled."[37]

But the fears were not unfounded. Nearly every article featuring Bob and his work made clear that his synth had talents at impersonating acoustic instruments. A rave review of *Switched-On Bach* in *Life* magazine claimed, "the synthesizer is diabolically clever at imitating genuinely baroque trumpets, oboes, and harpsichords."[38] A UPI story explained, "The electronic marvel called the Moog, can come close to doing the work of a whole symphony orchestra with a single musician at the keyboard."[39] In July, Bob had claimed defensively to the *National Observer*, "My objective . . . is not to reproduce old sounds but to make new ones. That the machine can sound like a violin or a flute is merely a byproduct. If a composer wants flute music, he can hire a flutist."[40]

But in his interview with Henahan, Bob appeared to be talking out of both sides of his mouth, making Sear's appeal to the union even harder. Bob happily explained to Henahan ("perhaps a trifle smugly," the reviewer noted) that one of Chris Swansen's synthesized jazz-pop tapes had tricked Vladimir Ussachevsky into believing he'd heard an acoustic ensemble. Speaking about the RCA Mark II, Bob told Henahan, "RCA meant it to do what 20 live musicians could do." That never succeeded, he explained, and then declared, "but the Moog, which was designed for no traditional purpose, turns out to be suitable for that."[41]

In his tirade to Henahan, Bob complained: "For a while last year the union banned the Moog and similar instruments, such as the Buchla, in recording studios and advertising agencies. Nobody was to use them without union permission. . . . The union refused to let the case be tested in court and dropped the whole matter. I thought it was a big joke, myself."[42]

Sear, still fuming, shot off a second letter to Hemming: "I am beginning to get flak about the Times article from the Union. I spent over $200.00 as well as 2 days during the Union negotiations to make sure that we would not be banned. . . . Not a radio station, TV, Agency, or record company can use a Synthesizer if the union bans it and to have Bob say what he said in that article can undo what Paul Beaver and I spent 2 weeks to do. I cannot emphasize enough that if Bob wants to go on making antagonistic and incorrect cracks about the Union, it will get to the point where they will put him out of business AND THEY CAN. . . . For God's sake, tell him to cool it about the Union."[43]

Sear understood the union's concerns through personal experience. As a Moog dealer, he knew what customers typically wanted: "There were people who were buying the instrument with the age old quest of replacing musicians, and more often than not they would say 'give me a violin' and I would say 'well, hire one.' So most people didn't think of it in terms of creating new sounds."[44]

But Sear admitted he'd also been complicit in the problem. *Midnight Cowboy* had recently been released in movie theaters in May, and as a Moog programmer and keyboardist for the soundtrack, he remembered his encounter with the composer. "John Barry came around to hear what I could do on the Moog, so I played a few things. He was so impressed he asked to use my phone, called the studio where he was working on the score, and sent the musicians home. It was the beginning of the end."[45]

15

Socket to Me, Baby!

The power of the 1906 San Francisco earthquake returned with a roar to that city in April 1969, shaking 10,000 of its residents. It was only Bernie Krause re-enacting the low-frequency gut churner on a Moog synthesizer for the city's commemorative "celebration" of the cataclysm. A few months later, a Moog sat atop San Francisco's Twin Peaks, playing the score for a car ballet in the streets below, staged with searchlights and building illuminations. It was composer Robert Moran's happening, *Thirty-Nine Minutes for Thirty-Nine Autos*.

A Moog synthesizer played live was still a rare sight in 1969, even two years after the R. A. Moog catalog advertised "real time performance" with "voltage control." Richard Teitelbaum, of course, had strapped his players up to a Moog for biofeedback improvisations in Europe; Gershon Kingsley had played a Moog at his mod Shabbat services; and lately, Lothar and the Hand People were the first rock band to tour with the instrument. In July 1969, the pianist and harpsichordist Rosalyn Tureck would play the music of Bach—her specialty—on a Moog at a concert at Lincoln Center. But the main obstacle to live performance was the incessant plugging and unplugging of patches to make every new sound, an almost impossible task while a player was in the heat of battle before an audience.

In the spring of '69, New York's Museum of Modern Art approached Bob with an offer to host a live performance by an ensemble of Moogs. The event would be groundbreaking: synthesizers alone carrying an entire concert. The August 28 presentation was scheduled as the conclusion to MoMA's Jazz in the Garden summer series. The billing of artists for the other dates in the series was based on the name recognition and cachet of the musicians, but for this concert, Bob recalled, "They weren't concerned about the performers. They just wanted synthesizers to be performed on."[1]

Bob was offered—and quietly accepted—a nominal fee of $300 to stage the event, a token honorarium that barely made a dent in the costly outlay the undertaking called for. New modules with preset capability had to be designed

Switched On. Albert Glinsky, Oxford University Press. © Albert Glinsky 2022.
DOI: 10.1093/oso/9780197642078.003.0015

for changing patches on the fly; two headliner performers, Herb Deutsch and Chris Swansen, would be recruited, each with his own combo of additional players; equipment and musicians would be transported to New York and installed in a hotel for rehearsals; and a support crew for setup and teardown was needed. R. A. Moog would shoulder the cost, but Bob was sanguine: "We decided it would be good publicity, it'd be good experience, fun to do."[2]

Bill Hemsath was charged with retrofitting modulars so performers could switch patches instantly. In the system he devised, they could simply press a button on one of seven preset boxes and a light inside the box would illuminate photocells controlling trimpots that were calibrated to preset voltages. Only one sound could be selected at a time, but the sound each preset box controlled could be set or altered ahead of time by configuring the trimpots with a screwdriver. Bob called the preset boxes "1CAs" for "computer aided" because they technically had memory and could "remember" different patches.

Everything was still coalescing in New York the night before the concert because Bob and his engineers had had just a few months to customize and outfit the modulars. Bits and pieces of equipment were arriving in stages with staggered flights from Ithaca. "The musicians were just freaking," Shirleigh recalled.[3] With everyone huddled in a single hotel room, performers vied for practice time on the assemblages that Bob's engineers were still picking over. "The rehearsals were pretty dreadful," Herb recalled. "We were playing things that never existed to these people before. I had a drummer playing on an instrument that was controlled by a keyboard."[4]

Ed Bland, the Jazz in the Garden director, clearly had little concept of what was involved in mounting this never-before-attempted technical extravaganza with its arsenal of gear about to be hefted into his outdoor venue. In a confirmation letter he "strongly suggested" that Bob come by the Museum at 4 p.m. on the day of the concert to confer with the MoMA sound technician in case "any amplified instruments" were being used.[5] When Bob and his crew arrived, they found that amplification, in fact, wasn't a priority in the Garden: there was only one electrical outlet. The synths, amplifiers, and the whole network of hardware would rely on tributaries of extension cords running into the single socket receptacle.

Walter Sear, who was lending a hand with the setup, recalled how it had rained earlier that afternoon: "It was very wet out there, and here I'm stringing these power cables all over the place. We were standing on wet cement, and Bob wasn't big on safety grounds. The whole thing was jerry-rigged. I could see the headlines in the *Times*, you know, 'twenty musicians electrocuted in Garden.' It would be very hard to sell synthesizers after that."[6]

In the afternoon, the crew scuttled around, testing circuits, patching and re-patching, while a gaggle of reporters trailed along, ambling through the Garden for a sneak peek; television cameras zoomed in to eavesdrop on private consultations.

Advance ticket sales were heartier than for other events in the series, and by 6 p.m. a large crowd was lined up on 53rd Street, eager to pay the $2.25 admission. Many late arrivals were turned away. Doors swung open at 7, an hour-and-a-half before starting time, letting patrons into the Garden to mill around and sip beer and soft drinks, and nibble on sandwiches from the restaurant. In plain view, Bob and the engineers hovered around the equipment with the urgency of stagehands arranging props behind a closed curtain—turning potentiometers, flicking switches, every sound shielded from the audience through the privacy of their earphones. *DownBeat* magazine described the scene: "the sculpture garden of the Museum of Modern Art, one of New York City's few havens of pastoral and aesthetic beauty, the busy tumult of the city muffled by high walls and the branches of overhanging trees. And sitting in the middle of all this bucolic simplicity: four devices of modern technology, covered with jumbles of complicated wire connections, mysteriously blinking lights, rows of switches, keyboards and cables."[7]

A hundred or so V.I.P. chairs were set up, and Bob's parents were sitting proudly in the front for what George called "the Museum of Modern Art deal." "He didn't understand any of it at all," Bob recalled. "Neither did my mother, but the one thing my mother understood is that she could hold up all these Moog records to her friends and neighbors. . . . It was their son up there, big event, famous. You know, the Yiddish word is they were getting *naches*."[8]

Behind the rows of chairs it was a free-for-all, with an overflow headcount threatening to burst the cloistering walls of the Garden. The *New York Times* reported, "people sitting, standing, perched on statues and steps, swinging in trees, lying under bushes or doing whatever else they could to obtain a bit of space in the garden."[9] Bob recalled, "At some point a couple of people climbed up into the tree that was near where my mother was sitting. And after a while it looked to me like there was a little fire inside the tree, you could see smoke coming out of it. . . . I more or less knew what was going on, you know. . . . And after about a half an hour or so my mother says, 'Robert, what is that wonderful smell?'"[10]

Right up to starting time, Bob and his engineers were still puttering around the equipment with soldering irons. At 8:30 Bob strode to a reflecting pool, bent over to wash his hands, ran his dripping palms over his cheeks, and bolted up with a smile to address the audience. The capacity crowd, *Variety* reported, "warmly received inventor-emcee Robert Moog who explained the 'Moog Quartet' setup and stressed that the recent popularity of synthesizers and electronics owed as much to musicians as it did to the designers."[11]

Because the music would be jazz, and the four modular synthesizers would be carrying the whole concert without any reinforcement from traditional instruments, the idea was to emulate a typical combo: a lead synth for melody; a polyphonic synth for harmony; a bass synth; and a drum synth. Bob introduced the first group: Herb's ensemble, billing themselves as the Electric Jazz Quartet. The combo featured Herb at the lead synth on the melody line, Hank Jones, the jazz pianist, at the polyphonic synth to "comp" the harmony, Artie Doolittle manning the bass synth, and Jim Pirone working the percussion synthesizer that used a keyboard and foot pedals to trigger sounds like snare drum, bass drum, and cymbals. Jon Weiss ran sound from the mixing board.

"Following a few preparatory bleeps, hoots, and grunts," *Audio* reported, "the musicians swung into a pleasantly melodic four-movement suite that seemed strong on treble-bass contrasts but was somewhat lacking in emphatic mid-range voices."[12] Herb had written numbers called "Stage One," "Space Walk," "Blues for Lunar Landscape," and "Peace," in what he considered a bebop style. For the *Audio* reviewer, the sounds were "reminiscent of trumpet, flute, saxophone, harpsichord, accordion, and several varieties of drum."

On the second half, Swansen's group took their places at the four instruments—Chris at the lead synth; the jazz pianist Hal Galper on the polyphonic keyboard; the drummer Bob Moses on the percussion instrument; and English guitarist John McLaughlin—later of Mahavishnu Orchestra fame—on bass synthesizer. The group began with a tune in a contemporary jazz-rock-pop style. "Ooh Baby," *Variety* wrote, "featured 15 minutes of freakout pandemonium. . . . guitarist John McLaughlin supplied steady patterns on the bass unit while Swansen spewed forth chirps, gurgles and whistles that sounded like a fox let loose in a chicken shack."[13]

Suddenly the lone power outlet blew a fuse. The musicians strolled around the audience while it was being replaced, returned to their instruments, and leaned into a free improv, only to have a second blackout mute the gear again.

Bob stood up to call the show but the crowd protested and Chris's group started in for one more round. "They got to wailing," Bob recalled, "just making huge waves of sound and it got raunchier and louder and more dissonant. It just built up and built up and built up, and the crowd was going nuts, and somebody who was standing next to this electrical outlet decided to stand on the box that the outlet was in, so she could see better. She stood up on it, she slipped off the box, knocked the power cord out of the socket, and everything went dead very abruptly."[14] A final, unplanned chord rang into silence, and Herb remembered, "the audience went crazy. They thought it was the greatest ending that you could imagine. So that was the concert... they simply ended the concert."[15]

"Shortly before 10 o'clock last night," the *New York Times* reported, "Robert A. Moog declared that the first concert utilizing Moog synthesizers in the live performance of jazz had been a success."[16] Any success, some reviewers concluded, only proved the synthesizers' debt to the almighty electrical outlet. The *New York Post* bannered its review, "Moog Music Blows Fuses At Museum."[17] *Variety*'s headline, playing off the popular television show *Rowan & Martin's Laugh-In* and its trademark line, "Sock it to me!," and Aretha Franklin's hit song "Respect" ("sock it to me, sock it to me, sock it to me, sock it to me"), summed it up: "'Socket to Me, Baby' Is Theme of Moog's Synthesizer Concert."[18]

Bob had cautioned the audience, "Electronic music is at its awkward growing stage, its young adult period."[19] The *Audio* reviewer agreed, calling the concert, "less than a total musical success."[20] Allen Hughes in the *New York Times* was more blunt: "Actually, not too much happened that really held the attention. Much of the time, the music sounded like a rather clumsy imitation of jazz. The generally buzzy sounds were not unpleasant and not too loud, but they were not very arresting either."[21] Still, Herb could tell that none of it mattered to the audience: "You gotta understand that there was a good deal of pot wafting around the air that night. And everybody was having a wonderful time, so how good and bad the music was—it was not particularly great—any reviews all give kind of reference to that."[22]

DownBeat went further, delivering a gut punch: "Quite simply, it was a musical disaster." Don Heckman, in his cover story, "The Moogs' Coming-Out Party," refused to cut Herb a break, and griped, "As a hedge, he apparently had written out his 'improvisations' ahead of time, and they might well be memorialized as classic examples of mediocrity on the wing. Poor Hank Jones... was relegated to comping.... On the one or two occasions when he got the opportunity to solo, Jones provided the evening's only indication of the synthesizers' true musical potential."[23]

But if turnout was any barometer, the concert was a success, setting a Sculpture Garden record. The Museum's final attendance tally was 3,175—three times the average for the seven other events in the Garden series that summer.

~~~

With live performance on synths still a rare occurrence, Sear was right when he claimed that Moog recordings were the primary stimulant for sales of the instrument and its visibility on the cultural radar. Dick Hyman's latest, *The Age of Electronicus*, hit No. 110 on the *Billboard* 200 on October 25, above *Switched-On Bach* at No. 143, although *S-OB* remained at No. 1 on the Classical charts after 48 weeks. The Moog was only a bit player on the Beatles' *Abbey Road* album, but its very presence on four songs was the heaviest imprimatur yet. The LP had been released on September 26, and by November 1 it went to No. 1 in the U.S.—a position it would hold for 11 weeks.

That fall, record labels kept spinning out Moog platters: *The Happy Moog*, *Switched-On Nashville: Country Moog*, *The Electric Zodiac*, and *Electric Love*. The Christmas season saw *A Very Merry Electric Christmas To You!*, *Switched On Santa!*, and *Christmas Becomes Electric*—another Columbia offering from the Moog Machine, with synthesized Christmas carols and pictures of angels playing Moog synthesizers on the cover.

In a move to woo the *Switched-On Bach* audience, RCA issued *The Moog Strikes Bach*, a lame copycat effort to go Carlos one better with music of Bach, Chopin, Mozart, and other classical composers, arranged and played on a solo Moog by the organist Hans Wurman. Wurman's treacly arrangements could sometimes make the Moog sound like a broken organ. Mort Garson, eager to keep riding out the wave, took the sequel idea to a new level after *Zodiac Cosmic Sounds*. In a seven-week flurry, he conceived and mastered 12 albums for the A&M label—each LP dedicated to a single sign of the zodiac—all of it scored for solo Moog synthesizer and three narrators. On another A&M release, called *Electronic Hair Pieces*, Garson cranked out instrumental Moog arrangements of songs from the musical *Hair*.

"No matter how you cut it," *Rolling Stone* pronounced in May, "the Moog Synthesizer is going to be The Next Thing."[24] *Billboard* reckoned in July, "The Moog has become the pop music industry's new fair-haired boy."[25] An

August UPI story called the instrument "the biggest thing since the invention of the piano 260 years ago."[26] In September the *St. Louis Post-Dispatch* declared, "The Moog has made the breakthrough that electronic music has been waiting for all these years."[27] Gershon Kingsley, talking to a UPI reporter, said he was offering a course on the Moog at Manhattan's New School for Social Research and found he had to turn people away.

The Moog was now so hip that it became an entry in the countercultural directory, the *Whole Earth Catalog*. Stewart Brand, co-producer of the Trips Festival, published the *Catalog* as a sort of paper website resource before there were personal computers or an internet. The publication promoted books and products for personal empowerment beyond the "establishment" sphere, or what Brand called "government, big business, formal education, and church."[28] "Every kind of tool is listed," the *San Francisco Examiner* explained. "It recommends the best sleeping bags and a miraculous paint you can use to make a water-tight, plywood bathtub and a Moog synthesizer to make electronic music with."[29]

Bob's star was rising in the professional engineering community, too. In April, the AES had honored him with the status of "Fellow," and on October 28 he hit a milestone with the awarding of U.S. patent 3,475,623 for his "Electronic High-Pass and Low-Pass Filters Employing the Base-to-Emitter Diode Resistance of Bipolar Transistors"—what he called his "ladder filter." The module—his first ever patent, that he'd filed for three years earlier—was the source of the trademark "fat Moog sound" so many had come to prize.

The R. A. Moog Company was thriving. Simon & Garfunkel and Jimi Hendrix had ordered Moogs, and the territory of Moog distributors had expanded to cover the northern Midwest and Canada. An October 1969 company brochure advised, "HOW TO DO BUSINESS WITH THE MOOG MEN," and disclosed that "more than 250 Moog Synthesizers have been installed in educational, commercial and individual studios throughout the world."[30]

The town of Trumansburg was eager to get behind the flourishing company. The *Ithaca Journal* reported in September that R. A. Moog had plans to break ground for a new manufacturing plant. The 15,000–16,000-square-foot, one-story, steel building would be erected on 12 acres of land at a cost of $200,000 to $300,000, and was slated to be underwritten by a collective of investors. Bob's workforce was projected to grow from the current 35 employees to 100. Lest anyone think he was dropping his creative experimentation for high-volume manufacturing, however, Bob clarified to the

Journal, "Ours is an innovative, technological business, and our work is to come up with new things in the world of music. We are definitely not a mass production organization."[31]

With the ascendancy of the Moog synthesizer, many artists figured Bob was loaded and happy to set them up with loaner synths to test drive for extended periods. Jazz pianist Paul Bley and his wife, the singer, pianist, and composer Annette Peacock, were typical. The couple learned about the Moog from *DownBeat*'s Don Heckman and journeyed to Trumansburg, scheming to wangle a free model. Before the day was over, they'd enlisted Bob's help in loading an instrument into their station wagon on a vague promise to remit the rental bill sometime in the future. On November 8, they presented a Town Hall concert with Peacock singing her own compositions with an electric bass player, a drummer, and Bley at the Moog. Peacock distorted her voice through the modules, morphing from traditional jazz styling into robotic gargling tones and swoops, weaving her sound in and around Bley's licks of melody and noise effects on the synth.

For anyone who missed the concert, the headline from the *New York Times* review was sure to capture the eye: "2 Concert Novelties: Moog and Topless." "As though the Moog synthesizer were still not enough of a novelty in concert," the critic wrote, "Paul Bley also added a topless vocalist . . . . when she returned for the second half, her costume was a black skirt from waist to ankle and a pair of black pasties, adding a welcome, flesh-and-blood, human quality to the mass of electronic equipment scattered about the stage."[32] Walter Sear was in the audience and told Bob's new Marketing and Sales Manager, Al Padorr: "His Town Hall concert was really bad—disorganized, bleeps and bloops—most of the audience walked out but at $6 a ticket, he must have done very well."[33]

On December 6, Wendy Carlos appeared with the St. Louis Symphony. It was the first time a Moog synthesizer was played live with an orchestra. The event was trumpeted in the program booklet: "Tonight the St. Louis Symphony Orchestra is playing perhaps the most unusual program of its ninety year history." *Switched-On Bach* had crossed over to pop consumers, and Carlos had just released a follow-up album, *The Well-Tempered Synthesizer*—music of Bach, Handel, Scarlatti, and synthesized choral sounds in a work by Monteverdi—and Columbia was pushing an album tour to capitalize on the novelty of the synthesizer. The St. Louis program featured music from Carlos's new album played by the orchestra alone, and with Carlos added as Moog soloist.

Carlos, though, faced the same dilemma as the Beatles after *Sgt. Pepper*: it was impossible to take complex studio-engineered music and recreate it live. At best, Carlos could play a one-handed melodic line on the Moog over pre-recorded tracks or live acoustic instruments. Bernstein had avoided the issue altogether by playing his audience a recording. But now, by trying to dazzle listeners with the live virtuosity of the Moog, the curtain was pulled back and it was clear that the intricate, stratified layers of Carlos's recordings couldn't be replicated in real time. The instrument wasn't a great organ after all.

But technical hurdles were the least of Carlos's problems. Her deeper futility with these live situations was her struggle to inhabit the wrong pronoun to match her album covers. In St. Louis the charade was exacerbated in the program notes: "The featured artist is the brilliant, young physicist-musician Walter Carlos at the keyboard of his specially built Moog Synthesizer." Carlos had been living permanently as Wendy since the previous May, only dressing as Walter for a few scattered appearances, including a spot on the nationally syndicated Mike Douglas TV talk show in October, guest-hosted by comedian George Carlin. She recalled the trauma of the St. Louis trip:

"I insisted to Rachel that I would not fly to St. Louis dressed as a man, and didn't. I went dressed as I normally would have, as a woman. We checked into the Holiday Inn, and they didn't know who the hell this woman was. When we got into the suite, I ceased being a woman and suddenly became this Walter Carlos person. And I began crying hysterically. I couldn't do it. Rachel cajoled me. Eventually, I pasted on my sideburns and put on a wig to hide my hair, which was pretty long at that time and streaky. I filled my pores with dirt from an eyebrow pencil to simulate five-o'clock shadow. I tried to lower my voice as bottom-heavy as it could get. Tried to be macho. It couldn't have mattered less. When I went down to eat that night, some hotel guests thought they recognized me. A timid person said he had seen my sister earlier."[34] Carlos's St. Louis appearance would be among her last live promotions for her records—a huge disappointment for her, and for Columbia Masterworks.

In honor of Wendy's latest album, Donal Henahan had written a *New York Times* feature in October entitled, "A Tale of a Man and a Moog." The unfortunate headline obfuscated what was an otherwise intelligent analysis showing he'd finally begun to fathom the subtleties and complexities that set Carlos's work apart. "Each instrumental track must be recorded separately," he explained, "and the music grows by accretion like a crystal. Layer by layer . . . until finally it is complete in all its geological striations."[35] In the end, whether or not the public could see the mysterious figure behind the switched-on albums for who she truly was, Wendy's work was a major contributor to Bob's reputation, and his ascent in 1969 and beyond.

∿∿∿

The same night Carlos played in St. Louis, another Moog sat on stage at the Altamont Speedway just west of San Francisco. It was the final concert of the Rolling Stones' American tour, advertised as a free outdoor event with an all-star lineup of bands. Doug McKechnie, a musician, and his friend Bruce Hatch were among a volunteer team enlisted to assemble the massive infrastructure for the event—erecting the stage and towers, stringing cables, and installing the sound system. In exchange for his help, McKechnie was promised a cameo performance during the concert on Hatch's Moog synthesizer. McKechnie was a regular at light shows around the San Francisco area, improvising on the synth, and sometimes harnessing its envelope generators as voltage triggers for lighting sequences.

After working all night with the crew, McKechnie set the Moog up on a hill near the stage and played the sunrise, improvising for the gathering crowd and the bleary-eyed stalwarts who'd camped out overnight on the grounds. Conjuring his favorite technique, he got the sequencer going in a jogging bass line and added a free melody from the keyboard over the top, constantly shifting filter settings to morph the sound through different tone colors. McKechnie played for over an hour as nearly 300,000 people filled in every remaining space on the fields, collecting farther and farther back from the stage. Roads were choked for 10 miles, and access was limited to foot traffic, motorcycles, or helicopters.

The Altamont Free Concert was billed as a sequel to the Woodstock Festival just four months earlier—another revelry of countercultural peace, love, and music. But as the crowd gathered, a foreboding vibe hung in the air: too much acid, DMT, mescaline, and alcohol were being passed around. Stepping off his helicopter with the Stones, Mick Jagger had already been punched in the face by a crazed fan. There was no police presence, and Jagger had paid the Oakland chapter of the Hell's Angels $500—in beer—in exchange for guarding the stage and providing security.

The concert got underway at 11:50 a.m. as the Stones' tour manager, Sam Cutler, took the stage to announce, "This can be the greatest party of 1969 that we've had!"[36] Santana was the first band up, and the air was already thick with tension. The Angels were saturated with beer and began beating back stoned audience members with sawed-off pool cues and motorcycle chains as the crowd pressed forward, many trying to clamber onto the stage. When Jefferson Airplane came on for their set, band member Marty Balin was knocked unconscious in a scuffle with an Angel. The Flying Burrito Brothers took the third slot and managed to spread a temporary calm during their set.

In the late afternoon, Doug McKechnie sat at stage right with his Moog and launched into his promised solo—an interlude just before the entrance of Crosby, Stills, Nash & Young. The seven-minute improv pulsed out over the throng with throaty wah-wahs under chirps that evolved into bleeps, sliding up in a long siren to hold on a high squeal to the cheers of the crowd, then plummeted to an ominous drone—hallucinogenic audio for a tripped-out mob. A long melodic middle section brought back McKechnie's sunrise style with a bopping sequencer bass fluctuating in filtered mutations under fluty and siren-like melodies on top. For the ending, white noise hissing cymbals, howling winds, and shot blasts worked up to the planned climax.

Owsley Stanley was running sound that night, and McKechnie remembered, "For whatever reason, he was the engineer in the tower out in the middle of a hundred thousand people, up three stories. So, I knew what I thought I would try. I'll just start with a low frequency and I'll just run it all the way up this ramp wave, you know, to siren and off into space. It'll blow everybody's mind, right? So, I start this with the controller and the keyboard and start going slowly up frequency, and I don't have any VU meters in front of me since it's all going into a box and off into the control where Owsley is. And he watches his needles and can't really hear anything yet, and as the sound is starting to pin his needles he goes, "What the fuck is this?" and shuts me off. Period. Wouldn't turn me back on."[37]

McKechnie's finish, like the Jazz in the Garden finale, was an unplanned silence—in this case, Owsley's reflexive move to stem a blow-out of the whole sound system when he couldn't signal the performer remotely.

After sundown, the Stones came on to close the concert. Mick Jagger, still in Lucifer mode, wore a Bobby Beausoleil-inspired top hat decorated in an Uncle Sam style, and a T-shirt with the Greek letter omega emblazoned on the front, signifying "the end." In the middle of "Sympathy for the Devil" a skirmish broke out in the crowd and the song had to be stopped. When the music resumed, fights continued erupting around the stage area. The Grateful Dead had planned to do a set, but when their helicopter landed and they got word of the violence they balked and lifted off again.

During the Stones' "Under My Thumb," a scuffle broke out between the Hell's Angels and a tall, Black teenager in a lime green suit, named Meredith Hunter, who was high on meth. When Hunter brandished a gun he was stabbed, brutally beaten, and stomped to death by the Angels. Hardly aware of what was happening, the Stones continued on with eight more songs, finishing with "Street Fighting Man." When it was over the band rushed offstage, piled into their helicopter, and tilted off into the night above the swirling, out-of-control horde.

The day-long concert left behind a detritus of horror that littered the Altamont landscape: Meredith Hunter's murder, two hit-and-run deaths, an irrigation canal drowning, injuries from stabbings and beatings, property damage, stolen cars, and hundreds of bad acid trips. *Rolling Stone* called it "perhaps rock and roll's all-time worst day."[38] Many saw it as the apocalyptic end to the sixties: flower children left to their own devices in a dark orgy of drugs and violence—Woodstock's Antichrist.

∿∿∿

From the perspective of the final hours of the 1960s, the *New York Times* ran an article on December 30, looking back on the decade and second-guessing the currents of the 1970s about to kick off in two days. "Arts in the 60's: Coming to Terms With Society and Its Woes" was a roundtable of *Times* arts critics tossing questions out to each other. The film reviewer Vincent Canby remarked, "Almost anybody can now buy an 8 mm sound camera. This is producing a whole new horizon, a whole new future for films." Harold Schonberg jumped in: "Same thing's happening in music." Canby retorted, "Well, everybody can always play a piano." Schonberg disagreed, "No, no, forget about piano. That's ancient. Buy yourself a Moog Synthesizer—a series of electronic things. You don't even have to know how to read music. And a lot of the kids are doing that."[39]

PART IV
SHORT CIRCUITS

16

Panicsville

"I get the impression that Bob just isn't around anymore," Sear told Beaver. "He is running all over the country being a 'star' and as a result, things back in Trumansburg are not getting done."[1]

Bob was on a high at the start of the new decade: *Billboard* magazine feted him with a 1970 Trendsetter Award; Jim Henson, the legendary Muppets creator, was using a Moog in his *Sesame Street* TV show; and Bob sat for a *Vogue* magazine portrait arranged by Jacqueline Harvey to hammer home the "Moog rhymes with vogue" campaign.

At the 1970 Grammy Awards in New York on March 11, Bob was honored with a "Special Merit Award," the NARAS Trustees Award, presented to "individuals who, during their careers in music, have made significant contributions to the field of recording." Bob's instrument also figured in several categories. *Moog Groove*, by the Electronic Concept Orchestra, was a nominee for *Best Engineered Recording*, and the Beatles' *Abbey Road* won the category.

Switched-On Bach picked up three awards. For *Album of the Year—Classical*, Carlos and Elkind beat out heavies like the Cleveland Orchestra, the Los Angeles and New York Philharmonic orchestras, and the BBC Symphony. For *Best Engineered Recording—Classical*, Carlos was recognized as the engineer. Her third award was oddly ironic: *Best Classical Performance—Instrumental Soloist or Soloists*. In this category *S-OB* had bested international virtuosi like violinist Henryk Szeryng, even though it hadn't been "performed" in real time.

It was a fair assumption that *Switched-On Bach* had knighted the Moog synthesizer as the hot new commodity—an investor's dream—but things weren't what they seemed. In truth, if Harold Schonberg had grabbed up all the Moog stock he'd dreamed about, he would have regretted it. Behind the glittering public image, the Trumansburg operation was stumbling badly.

By early 1970, R. A. Moog couldn't build instruments fast enough to meet the rising demand. The company had become a victim of its own success. The Trumansburg shop was run like an old-fashioned musical instrument *atelier*. Each synthesizer was assembled as a custom job, with a typical delivery time of 12–15 weeks after an order was placed. When Walter Sear closed a sale, he'd frequently have to lend out his own equipment as a stopgap because Bob's deliveries were late. The lag time frustrated buyers and made it hard to bring in enough cash to keep the business operating.

Quality control was handled on a shoestring. Before a synthesizer shipped, its final health check was executed by a "drop test": each side of the instrument was lifted six inches off a table and released to slam back down. If it still worked, it was ready to go. In rare cases, a more radical "crash test" was performed from a greater height, a practice that became urban legend. A May 1969 *Rolling Stone* article explained, "The Synthesizers are built slowly with a great deal of care, and before each one goes out it is left on for a week and then dropped on the floor."[2]

Bob's production line was erected on a house of cards. He wrote Sear at one point, "Panicsville here right now. Ritter's ulcer started bleeding over the weekend and he was out for two days. I've been having to fill in on the test bench, doing the work that Dick has heretofore reserved for himself."[3] The threadbare nature of the operation was obvious to Sear. When Bob left a tool behind once, Sear couldn't resist ribbing him about it: "You left your soldering iron & solder. . . . Hope that it doesn't put you out of production."[4]

Pricing was another conundrum. In November 1969, Al Padorr had hiked up stickers, insisting that many items were "grossly underpriced or given away."[5] But Paul Beaver was outraged and shot back a missive arguing that quality had to improve first: the filters made too much noise; he'd wrestled with the oscillators; and a 910 Power Supply blew up right after he got it. The company had sold over 250 synthesizers, but the lack of a user's manual, he complained, was an egregious lapse. He cautioned, rather presciently, that hefty prices, coupled with only a single patent on Bob's work—his ladder filter—could spark competitors to clone his equipment at lower prices. "Only one approach seems reasonable to me in the case of this highly probable eventuality," he advised. "Be and remain the 'Rolls Royce' of the field."[6] In response, Padorr backpedaled and suggested *lowering* prices—a strategy the company could scarcely afford.

In late 1969, optimistic after a healthy year of sales, Bob had taken on additional employees. But the drain on the budget began to exacerbate the downturn. Ray Hemming had been fired in September, replaced by a new general manager, John Huzar, who came with a manufacturing background. But in Bob's typical generosity, Huzar's terms of employment were ridiculously out of proportion with the modest means of the small company: a handsome salary, a $50,000 life insurance policy, health insurance, three weeks paid vacation, a stock option, a 5% annual bonus, and moving expenses.

Additionally, Bob had brought on another engineer in September in one of his spur-of-the-moment hires, although the new team member would prove invaluable to the company. Jim Scott was a recent electrical engineering graduate from UC Berkeley who'd written Bob about a job. Scott remembered his awkward interview at the Los Angeles AES meeting: "We finally got aside in the lobby and we didn't say anything for a while. Then he said, 'how about $8,000 a year?' I said, 'Yes!' And that was the whole interview!"[7]

Brimming with youthful idealism over working for the legendary R. A. Moog, Scott soon got a dose of reality. In Trumansburg he met with the usual jolt of small-town culture shock: his beard immediately earned him the nickname "Abraham Lincoln," a pairing with Chris Swansen, whose long hair and ponytail had cast him with the sobriquet "George Washington." Scott became a regular at Camel's bar, a local watering hole. "In the morning it was a farmer's bar," he recalled. "All the farmers came in and talked about the weather and the price of corn and hog jowls."[8]

When Scott started at the company, assemblers were frantically putting together modulars, but he was puzzled by the tasks the engineers occupied themselves with: "Bob was taking on all kinds of one-of-a-kind special projects. Some of them advanced the state of electronic music, and a lot of them cost the company a lot of money—and they didn't have much."[9] Bill Hemsath was working on an ambitious high-end studio mixing board that Scott thought was "overly complex." Another engineer, Chad Hunt, was charged with hot-rodding a MacDonald Recording Systems tape deck to transform it into a sophisticated, hybrid multi-track recorder, the Moog-MRS—employees called it "Mrs. Moog." "That was a highly advanced tape recorder for its time," Scott recalled, "but they tried to do way too much way too soon. I don't know that we ever sold one of those." Scott was assigned a one-off vocoder for the State University of New York at Buffalo. "I'm sure we lost money on it—just on materials, let alone my time put into it."[10]

Hemsath remembered how Bob indulged the engineers in a freewheeling shop atmosphere: "He allowed us to do our own thing. I could invent and build stuff and try stuff and he was not against that. Most of the engineers would try things and Bob actually encouraged that. A lot of it didn't come to anything."[11]

The folksy quality of the shop sometimes drained the engineers' time shoring up problems with off-the-wall solutions. Scott remembered how musicians complained about the Moog 905 Reverberation Unit in the rear studio: "It sounded kind of clangy and funky—very poor quality. And the musicians asked for a good reverb unit." The fix was an ingenious, budget-conscious workaround with a little engineering mischievousness thrown in. Up in the second floor "attic," a reverberant space where the administrative and engineering offices were, Hemsath set up a loudspeaker at one end and a microphone at the other. "*That* was our reverb chamber," Scott recalled. Musicians working in the studio below were unaware of the ruse. All they saw was a panel on the synthesizer with input and output jacks that said "Reverb." "So the sound went in one jack," Scott explained, "upstairs, out the loudspeaker, across the room, into the microphone, and down to another amplifier, and back to the other jack on the synthesizer. The reverberation of all the sound around that big room produced a pretty good reverb."[12]

Once, the improvised scheme backfired. Scott remembered the musicians complaining about a lot of spurious noises ruining their work—"these clanks, and thunks and thuds. Well, we found out the Red squirrels were taking up residence and they were rolling acorns or something all around up there in our Reverb Chamber. And so the cure—without telling the musicians—was to take the loudest blast of 'booooo!' and blast it up to Reverb for a minute and all the squirrels left. And it was fine."[13]

By mid-1970, the financial status of the company, reported to Bob by his accountants, Ernst & Ernst, was hard to process. R. A. Moog's sales ending June 30, 1970, were close to $700,000. That was the good news. The bad news was that net income was $12,235. It didn't make sense—sales were up from the previous year. But a closer look at the figures revealed what had happened: in 1969 the profit margin was 11.29%; by 1970 it had plummeted to 1.76%. Sales were growing, but profits were slipping. At its peak in late 1969, R. A. Moog had 42 employees. Many had to be laid off in the new year.

The 1970 numbers didn't just expose the weak business skills at R. A. Moog. They questioned the very viability of the industry itself. Was building synths even feasible? If Bob couldn't make it in this business—with his illustrious name, a head start over competitors, and a product everyone wanted—who could? Behind every synth were hours of assembly and a multitude of parts; and many instruments were lovingly sheathed in real walnut. With operating expenses, salaries, and everything else it took to produce a Moog, the cost of building a synth was catastrophically high. Each one was essentially a gift to the customer. Bob admitted to an *AP News Features* writer, "There are a lot of expenses in developing them. I haven't been able to see how to get wealthy."[14]

Others, however, clearly saw how to get wealthy from the Moog. Commercial musicians were cleaning up with their modulars. Dick Lavsky, head of Music House Incorporated in Manhattan, bragged to *Billboard* about his latest Moog-dominated ads for Elizabeth Arden and AT&T. Members of Lothar and the Hand People were using their Moog in commercials for General Tire, Gillette, and Pepto-Bismol. The prize for the easiest haul was Mort Garson, who told an interviewer, "I was making so much money with this instrument. There were four guys that came down to my studio. They wanted a five second commercial.... The boss man of these guys said, 'look: just *one* note.' And I was getting, I think, $20,000 for this commercial. So I went to the Moog and I pressed one note down—*Diiiiing*—it was a C. He says, 'that's *it!*' And that's what they used! It's a funny business."[15]

The *Long Island Press* quipped that Kingsley, with five Moogs in his tiny 55th Street Manhattan studio, had "enough electronic equipment to launch an Apollo spacecraft."[16] Kingsley was creating sound logos for ABC and CBS TV, and music for the Kodak Exhibit at the 1970 World's Fair in Japan. A newswire article described his Moog score for a movie short, *Market In Motion*: "It's not Fellini's latest. It's the new film from the New York Stock Exchange."[17] But the writer wasn't far off. Fellini's *Satyricon*, recently released in theaters, used an excerpt from Andrew Rudin's all-Moog *Tragoedia* LP for the soundtrack of one scene, though without the composer's knowledge or permission.

Bob's Trumansburg staff was becoming concerned. It seemed foolhardy to keep going with long-shot research projects and custom jobs, especially when orders for modulars weren't paying the bills either. Moving away from studio jobs and into the live performance and consumer markets meant smaller, simpler systems—the practical way forward, they felt.

At a staff meeting the year before, Gene Zumchak had suggested a compact synth in a single cabinet—something easier and less expensive to produce that could be sold for about $1,000. But the boss shut it down. Zumchak remembered Bob's knee-jerk retort: "Moog said, 'We're not going to do anything like that. We make Cadillacs. That's all we make.' In other words, he was not interested in any sort of mass production and making any kind of numbers. He was making one-of-a-kinds, mostly for universities. Moog was the only person that thought that way."[18] Zumchak knew the university market was limited and could bottom out, and he saw that the other engineers shared his enthusiasm over compact instruments.

In the spirit of the free invention that Bob encouraged, Zumchak went ahead and explored his one-cabinet synth idea anyway, gathering an assembly of 900 Series modular components into a single unit that could be played from a regular 951 keyboard. He called it the Model 10 Synthesizer.

Zumchak remembered that Hemsath, in particular, was motivated to explore the idea of a marketable synth. Portability had always been an issue. But there was another: simplicity. Hemsath observed how musicians gravitated toward the same types of patches over and over. He saw that users were usually happy enough with a small palette of sounds, especially if it got them up and running faster. With that in mind, and with Zumchak's Synthesizer 10 for inspiration, he willy-nilly put together a prototype in his spare time that would ultimately rescue the company and evolve into the firm's signature product.

In the fall of 1969, on a lark, Hemsath began rummaging through a pile of rejected parts up on the second floor—a dumping bin the staff referred to as the "graveyard." Finding a discarded five-octave keyboard, he grabbed the bottom three octaves that were still intact and hacksawed a case down to match its length. He carted the remnants back to his office and began assembling a small, rudimentary synthesizer, piece by piece, during his lunch hours. "I'd sit down at my desk and take an apple out of one drawer and a module out of the other," he recalled.[19]

Hemsath collected just enough parts to build an instrument with the modules he always used in demonstrations, interconnected in the way he typically did. There was one new 901A oscillator, but everything else came from salvaged parts. No patch cords were needed; everything was hardwired inside. There were two oscillators, and Hemsath recalled, "you could either have one or two oscillators playing, so that might be two patches, but that's it. Then into the filter. There was a voltage-controlled amplifier and two envelope generators, and that was all there was."[20] The front surface panel of modules consisted mainly of knobs. Paper labels—like the ones on Bob's first prototype—were slapped on to distinguish the functions. A hole in the left cheek of the old keyboard case Hemsath had cannibalized once housed a portamento control, and he used it as the inspiration for a new feature. To fill the gap, he inserted a slide pot for pitch bending.

The little instrument measured about 2 feet wide, 14 inches tall, and a foot deep. Hemsath christened his miniature Moog the "Min." Sitting tidily on his desk, with its boxy contours, it looked like a Lilliputian upright piano without legs. The fine wood scraps from Bob's original cabinetry, bolted together for the case, gave it the look of an authentic Moog instrument.

The Min materialized in less than three weeks and was completed around Thanksgiving 1969. It wasn't a secret—all the parts were lying around on Hemsath's bench—but he never discussed it with anyone. "It was something I did on a whim just because I felt like it," he recalled. "It was entirely my own idea of how I thought the thing should be put together. The idea was, it was always operational; all you had to do was just twist some knobs and off you go. So it was simplicity first. And one part of building it all into one box was the portability."[21]

The concept was Hemsath's, but everyone agreed that the elements still came from Bob's original engineering. "Bob's most important contribution was the invention of the synthesizer in the first place," Hemsath explained, "in particular, the Moog filter and his invention of the one-octave-per-volt pitch control system that made the synthesizer practical. The Min was made entirely of his original modular parts including the case. I just rearranged the modules, wired it up a bit differently, and fastened the keyboard to the box."[22]

Hemsath recalled the big moment: "I voiced the thing to sound like a Baroque pipe organ and I played Bach's little *Prelude No. 1 in C major* for Bob, and that was the first he heard of it. He liked it—I wasn't chastised or anything—he just said, 'Yeah, that's nice.' That was about it."[23] Bob recalled, "Hemsath was always doing shit like that. And so was I. You know, we were always putting stuff together. Nothing unusual about it. And on top of that, things are really crazy, money going in, money going out. I was a rotten manager, we had no controls. I didn't have too much time to think about doing stuff like that. I had to worry about was the IRS guy going to come."[24]

A month or so later, Hemsath was still thinking about the Min, and he recalled, "The voice came to me and said, 'put this into production.' That was what spurred me on—divine guidance." Using his first model as a prototype—calling it the "Min A"—Hemsath ruminated on a second-generation version he'd call the "Min B." For the A model Hemsath had simply placed the modules shoulder-to-shoulder and screwed them into a cabinet. For the B version, the original setup was replaced with a one-piece length of black sheet metal as a unified faceplate. "I took a notepad one morning before I got out of bed," he remembered, "and drew the whole front panel. When I got into work I gave it to a draftsman and he made the artwork. Later that week I had the case, control panel, and all the parts. Everything went together and worked on the first try."[25]

Now a user could visualize how a synthesizer worked in a way that wasn't possible with a modular setup. "Basically it flows from left to right," Hemsath explained. "It looks like a picture, a schematic." All the stages of signal processing were laid out, in order, across the front.

Hemsath topped off the B model with a few enhancements—an extra five keys at the top, and again, thinking of the user, a more tipped-back front panel for easy viewing. And because it would be portable, he designed a matching wooden lid with a carrying handle that clamped seamlessly over the keyboard and front panel. "A portable sewing machine came to mind," he recalled. "When it's in place you have a little suitcase."[26]

Bob liked the instrument enough to order a second, exact copy, from production. But he balked at any thought of manufacturing it. Everyone else at the company, especially John Huzar, saw the B as the lifeline they'd been praying for to save their jobs. With persistence, Huzar got Bob to pay lip service to a production sometime in the future. Huzar didn't like Hemsath's name, "Min," and argued for "Mini." Scott recalled that the two "had quite a contest of wills over this," but Huzar prevailed.[27]

A January 24, 1970, story in *Billboard*, "Mini-Moog to Be Unveiled," offered Bob a chance to talk up the new model, but he remained guarded in his comments.[28] The new Mini was not at the top of his list. Hemsath would have to wait to do anything more with the project.

∽∽∽

Back in February 1969, two investors—William Waytena and Vernon Siegel—had approached Bob with an offer to buy into his company with cash and management expertise. The offer was tempting, but Bob decided to pass. After R. A. Moog recorded over $260,000 in sales the second quarter of 1969 alone—the largest amount for any quarter in the company's history—he felt vindicated in his decision. But by 1970 the company's fortunes were sinking in inverse proportion to the rise of its synthesizer's fame.

In December 1969, the two investors approached Bob again. They'd seen Hemsath's Min A prototype and it had redoubled their interest. Like Bob's staff, they were convinced the company's pricey "professional models" had tapped out the universities and recording studios. The new miniature instrument seemed like the ticket to success; consumer and educational markets would be the way to go.

It wasn't a message Bob wanted to hear. Building stripped-down synths for high schools or retail sales didn't appeal to him. And every month seemed to bring him new awards and honors. He had prestige to burn. But the investors had money to burn, and as negotiations wore on, the speculators poked Bob in his weak spot: panic over his debt. More than anything, he just wanted his business to keep going.

It was Gene Zumchak who'd connected Bob with Bill Waytena, a Buffalo, New York, venture capitalist, and his business partner, Vernon Siegel, an engineer. Gene's Uncle John was married to Waytena's sister, and Gene envisioned a win-win situation: an investment opportunity for his relative, and a chance for Bob's company to grow.

Gene had known Waytena all his life. Bill had a degree in electrical engineering and had developed the first commercially available radar detector for cars, founding Radatron Inc. in North Tonawanda, NY, to market it. The battery-operated Radar Sentry was featured on the cover of *Popular Electronics* in September 1961, and written up in national newspapers and magazines. The company claimed it had sold 25,000 Sentries in six months.

Radatron was just one of Waytena's business ventures. Currently he was a director and vice president of Kistler Instruments Corporation, a company that had contracts with NASA. But Waytena had a gift for speculation and was always trawling for new investment opportunities.

In the year since Bob waived off Waytena and Siegel, he'd descended into near bankruptcy and was resigned to ceding a bit of control. Maybe these business partners could prove their worth if they could exploit his name for everyone's profit. On February 16, 1970, the two investors put their terms on the table, and on the 19th Bob wrote his accountant that he was "on the verge of what looks like an extremely attractive agreement."[29]

The next evening Shirleigh's water broke on the sofa while she was eating a bowl of maple walnut ice cream. Her bags were already packed for the hospital and she got up to walk to the car. When she reached the porch she felt the baby coming and yelled to Bob that she wouldn't make it to the hospital. "Robert's standing there in shock," she recalled. In the ice cold February air, Shirleigh opened the car door and lay across the front bench seat of their 1965 Ford Falcon station wagon, her head under the steering wheel and her legs sticking out the passenger door. Bob ran inside to phone the doctor and told her not to push. "It had nothing to do with pushing," she recalled. "That baby just *came*."[30]

The newborn popped his bloody head out, dragging a six-foot umbilical cord as he slithered off the end of the seat onto bits of dirt and gravel on the car floor. Shirleigh was afraid to get up and look, screaming for Bob, who remained frozen and dazed. "I said, '*The baby is on the floor!*' And he just stared at me and did nothing. I said, '*Robert, pick up the baby!*' And he just stared at me. So I finally said it slow enough for him to pick up the baby and give it to me." Shirleigh swaddled the infant in her Persian lamb coat, pulled her legs in, and implored Bob to drive to the hospital. "They got me into a wheelchair and took the umbilical cord and sort of draped it back over my dress," she recalled. "And we went to the E.R. entrance and one guy said, 'There's a do-it-yourself job!' "[31]

Shirleigh was installed in a room while the baby was placed in an incubator overnight to raise his body temperature. He was named Matthew in honor of Shirleigh's little brother who'd died of nephritis and nephrosis of the kidneys. That night, Jon Weiss was crashing at the Moog house on a break from the University of Pennsylvania. When the draft board noticed his free year in Trumansburg he'd rushed in the fall of '69 to reinstate his student deferment from Vietnam. Shirleigh recalled, "Robert came home after they had me safely ensconced in a bed and Jon sat him down with a bunch of brandy and just calmed him down. He was apparently still in shock."[32]

The next day, Shirleigh was nursing the baby when Bob dropped by her room to dump a sheaf of papers on her lap. "Robert came in with the payroll for me to do in the hospital," she recalled. "And there I was, and I just had a child, and I stayed a little bit extra because I had my tubes tied."[33] She got the payroll done. Besides her usefulness in balancing the books, Shirleigh was also a phantom figurehead at R. A. Moog. On a recent SBA loan application she was listed as company "Vice President, Secretary, and Director," but her salary was indicated as "--." Even though she had four kids to take care of now, Bob expected her to stay on top of the bookkeeping.

Bob and Shirleigh never expected to have such a large family, and they'd floated the idea of sterilization—a tubal ligation for her or a vasectomy for him. The two procedures were vastly different and carried a double standard. Women in the early 1970s still faced enormous societal barriers to voluntary sterilization. Ordering up a tubal ligation wasn't easy, even though there were no laws barring doctors from performing it. Women were often given the third degree by their physicians over the ethics of abbreviating their childbearing years, and they continually came up against the "120 rule," a widely accepted protocol used by doctors and hospitals: a woman's age, multiplied by the number of children she had, needed to equal or exceed 120 before she qualified for a tubal ligation. If she eventually prevailed, the operation usually involved a three- to five-day hospital recovery period.[34]

A vasectomy for a man, on the other hand, was a 15-minute in-office procedure with a quick recovery time, and it typically didn't involve any ethical stigmas or mathematical formulas. Doctors often performed it on request with no concern over how many children a man had. Bob could have had the procedure at any point during the marriage. "I asked Robert if he would have a vasectomy," Shirleigh recalled, "and he said, 'Oh, no, what if you should die, and I marry someone who wanted children?' And I just looked at him and I thought, 'Okay, Robert, I'll handle it myself.'" During her pregnancy with Matthew she remembered the doctor calculating her odds: "'Well, you're this-many-years old, and you've got varicose veins, and you've got three children, expecting a fourth—so you can have your tubes tied.' And I had my tubes tied."[35]

The whole issue was retired until Florence brought it up in a letter where she hammered away on one of her pet causes—population control—directing a pointed slight at the size of the Moog family. Annoyed, and a bit defensive, Bob volleyed back: "Shirleigh's doctor categorically refused to perform a surgical sterilization until she had four children. Once Matthew was born, her doctor performed the sterilization." Then he added, "Much advice regarding a vasectomy that we received pointed to possible psychological harm to me. Silly? Perhaps. Shoot me!"[36]

Florence wasn't buying it. "So this is dot schmart nephew?" she retorted. "This fragile male ego that would be shattered by a vasectomy? Oi, weh! Of course I'm familiar with this kind of schmaltz, but somewhere I'd got the impression that you had the kind of intelligence and independence that could see through the absurdities of the masculine mystique.... I'll content myself with expressing my satisfaction that it is the female in the family who has the strength to stand up to premature loss of reproductive activity."[37]

Typically, there were never any hard feelings among Bob, Shirleigh, and Florence after these eruptions. Florence continued blithely on with her next subject: "Well, anyway, I'm glad you liked that sheet of music I sent you. Can you sing it?"[38]

Bob was preparing for a March 26 closing on the agreement with Waytena and Siegel. When he opened his books all the way, though, the full extent of his catastrophe emerged. His own accountants, Ernst & Ernst, couldn't make heads or tails of the company's numbers for the past fiscal year. Worse, a toxic liability had been dumped into the mix: Rothenberg had suffered one too many delays and technical snafus, and Bob was named as the defendant in a lawsuit by New York Research Group. Judgment was demanded in the amount of $25,000.

R. A. Moog had been tumbling like an avalanche. "I didn't know what the hell I was doing and it was a fast moving, frenetic marketplace," Bob recalled.[39] "Basic management functions that you're supposed to have in a business just didn't exist. I didn't know what they were. When I didn't do them and paid the result, I learned what they were."[40]

Waytena and Siegel failed to show up for the March 26 closing, and for the next few weeks they kept Bob dangling, jerking him around with new promises, retracting them, tempting him with different ideas, then rebuffing him again. Bob was getting increasingly desperate, and by May, Waytena stopped answering his phone calls altogether.

Ironically, that same month, the New York State Small Business Administration contacted Bob to let him know he'd been named the SBA Small Businessman of the Year for New York State. The honor was awarded based on the company's astounding growth, culminating in $526,000 in sales at the close of fiscal year 1969. When Bob accepted the framed certificate on May 26, the SBA never noticed that his operation was being propped up by its own loan—a liability he was now hard pressed to pay off.

It was a whiff of déjà vu. From its earliest days, R. A. Moog was a Potemkin Village—a two-man operation burnishing an image of slick production lines and solid guarantees, yet still managing to pull in a loss. Bob's priorities were always the products, not the profits. Now that syndrome had been writ large. His company had moved from the basement to the world stage, but few suspected it was still pulling in a loss.

In June, Waytena and Siegel remained incommunicado as Bob clung to hopes of a deal. In July, he heard back from Waytena. The deal was off. The SBA may have been fooled, but Waytena wasn't.

R. A. Moog would have to go it alone now. And there were no guarantees.

17

Mini and the Beast

David Van Koevering was a Swiss Bell ringer and a crusader, and he was on a mission to find salvation for Bob's company. He offered an ambitious barter: in exchange for some free equipment, he'd bring the world to R. A. Moog's doorstep. It was a peculiar bargain, but Van Koevering had special powers and he was ready to deliver. Unlike Bob's original crusader salesmen who logged a few orders by word of mouth, Van Koevering was a holy roller of commerce—an evangelist huckster on steroids. "Watch out!" a Moog employee warned. "He'll sell you your own shoes."[1]

Van Koevering was born into a musical evangelist family in Grand Rapids, Michigan, in 1940. He spent his childhood on the road with his mom, dad, sister, and brother, crisscrossing the U.S. and Canada in a small truck towing a house trailer. The family performed at churches and Christian conferences for freewill offerings, playing on a hodgepodge of "novelty instruments" and singing in gospel quartets. In place of sermons, David's father used song lyrics to expound on the Word.

At five, Van Koevering was known as "Little David," playing a ukulele on stage in a tux. He claimed to have mastered 27 instruments by the age of 12, including accordion, piano, Hammond organ, trumpet (or "anything with valves"), musical glasses, and a gallery of percussion. He'd sometimes tune up pans, whiskey bottles, stones, rocks, and flowerpots. The family's "Music, Magic, and Monkey Show" included a trained monkey and a trick act using a horse "with two degrees in math" who kicked a tub a given number of times in response to arithmetic questions from the audience.[2]

At a preacher's "Youth for Christ" camp meeting in Florida, Van Koevering fell in love with the preacher's 14-year-old daughter, Becky, after she stood up in her pigtails and played "Holy City" on the accordion. The two were engaged when she was 16, and married when she turned 17. At 18 she gave birth to their first child. Van Koevering pursued church ministry and hosted his own religious radio and TV shows. But he loved life on the road and in 1965 he began touring the Midwest, Northeast, and Southeast with two 45-minute educational programs—*The Science of Sound* and *The History of*

Music. He worked three and four schools a day, 36 weeks a year, playing on 15–20 instruments, with an ending flourish performed on an RCA theremin.

Van Koevering first learned of Bob in 1961 when he built a Melodia theremin kit. After he heard *Switched-On Bach* he was bowled over by the synthesizer and soon after discovered an R. A. Moog magazine ad inviting composers to try out the rear studio ("visit . . . and use all of the Moog instruments").[3] He thought the Moog synthesizer might make an ideal modern-day finale for his school shows after years of closing with the 1920s-era theremin. In November 1969 he visited Trumansburg while Bob was away in Europe. "I parked on Main Street," he recalled. "It looked like a little cowpoke town out in Kansas someplace. They had a room that was that magic room—the back room where Chris Swansen could produce Oz. I heard him playing some of his stuff, layering the sixth or seventh track, and I was hooked."[4]

Van Koevering was impressed, but he advocated for a small, compact, affordable synth. He could see that the engineers agreed. "Jim Scott understood the need for under $1,000 for magic retail," he recalled. "He seemed to get it. He'd talked to enough musicians, that he knew they had to get rid of the cost on that instrument."[5] Van Koevering was shown Zumchak's new Synthesizer 10, contained in a single cabinet. If that was the most compact system he could buy, he was in.

In January 1970, Van Koevering wrote to Bob to unveil his plan: in exchange for two theremins and a Synthesizer 10, he'd buy a second model 10 and embark on his Moog crusade. He'd spotlight the Moog synthesizer under his professional alias of VAKO Productions Inc. for four years in 450 shows a season—and another 450 with his "second unit" (his Dad)—plus guarantee an additional 100 exposures annually on TV and radio. He would blazon the Moog logo on his VAKO vans and in news releases and brochures. Slipped into his proposal was a freehand sketch suggesting how the equipment would appear on stage. He'd stack everything—modules, keyboard, oscilloscope, R. A. Moog banner, and carrying cases—in the image of the cross. Bob was open to the idea. But first he'd need to see Van Koevering in action.

∿∿∿

Gershon Kingsley knew how to pull in an audience, too. He was set on making a splash with multiple Moogs in a major venue and approached Sol Hurok, the famous impresario. Hurok was willing to entertain the idea but wanted to hear the Moog for himself first. Kingsley auditioned the synth for Hurok, running it through "all the crazy sounds." Then Hurok asked if the machine could play a melody. Kingsley was ready with the ideal lure: "I know he's a Russian Jew and I had prepared, in case, on the ribbon controller—I played him this famous Yiddish tune, 'A Yiddishe Moma.'" Hurok devoured the bait, Kingsley recalled: "He said, 'Get me your telephone.' He called the office and said, 'Reba, what do we have open in January 1970? Ok, thank you. Kingsley, you have a concert in Carnegie Hall in January 1970.'"[6]

Kingsley next persuaded the Audio Fidelity label to pay him $35,000 for the privilege of recording the event for later LP release, and used the money to buy four new synthesizers from Bob. He hyped the event as the "First Moog Quartet," hoping that four live synthesizers would create a pioneering spectacle. After the Jazz in the Garden concert five months earlier, of course, it was no longer precedent-setting, and the novelty was diluted by the addition of traditional instruments and a vocal quartet.

The day of the concert—January 30—Bob hopped an afternoon train to Long Island, unannounced, to observe Van Koevering in one of his *Science of Sound* high school presentations. On stage, Van Koevering was tall, commanding, and congenial, sporting a dark, Elvis-like quiff hairstyle that swept back from his forehead, sideburns to his jawbone, a goatee, and glasses. At the end of the show Bob came backstage to meet Van Koevering, who recalled their conversation: "He said, 'I agree with you, that a Moog synthesizer would fit your show perfectly.' I was thrilled. Bob Moog is closing the sale! And he slapped me on the shoulder and said, 'What is your supper plan, what are you doing tonight?'"[7] Bob extended a spur-of-the-moment invitation to the Carnegie Hall concert, and dinner beforehand with his parents and his mother's sister, Aunt Dorothy.

"You could tell where Bob got his enthusiasm," Van Koevering recalled. "It came from Aunt Dorothy. Aunt Dorothy was a noisy lady; she was a laughing lady. She was a verbally skilled, silver-tongued, word machine. She talked about Bob's childhood and that he played with radios and could fix anything."[8]

At Carnegie Hall the group seated themselves in a row near the stage. In the program booklet, Kingsley's bio made it clear that he was reaping enormous profits from Bob's work: "Kingsley, one of the first musicians to recognize the Moog's potential, created over 125 commercials for radio and television with the instrument and was awarded two 'Clios,' the advertising industry's highest award."[9] One breathless newspaper preview of Kingsley's

Moog work called him, "the man behind one of the sweetest cash-register ringers in years."[10]

At center stage the four "moogists" sat with their backs to the audience so the modular panels were visible. On a platform to the right, a vocal quartet stood at microphones; on the left, a drummer and double bass player were perched on a podium behind an electric guitarist. At the extreme left, a grand piano filled out the ensemble. A huge rectangular screen loomed over the stage. The house was packed. Kingsley strode on stage in a blue shirt and red bowtie to emcee and conduct the concert—facing the audience. A melodramatic synth prelude, called *In the Beginning*, opened with a low, primal Moog tone under tongue-clicking pops and rapid-fire squealing note flourishes, accelerating into a wall of white noise and gusting wind that crossfaded with a steady distant thunder rumble, disappearing into silence.

The concert was a potluck of music spanning five centuries: arrangements of Renaissance instrumental works, a Bach fugue, a piece by Rossini, Paul Simon's "The Sound of Silence," the Beatles' "Eleanor Rigby," Kingsley's "Pop Corn" and a few of his other tunes, and music by the four Moog musicians. In one number, the vocalists recited children's poems from around the world in histrionic whining, chanting, whispering, and shouting, accompanied by outer space effects on the Moog. A few songs were reminiscent of the theatrical jazz-pop style of musicals like *Hair*. In an awkward moment of token exoticism, the African American jazz percussionist Danny Barrajanos came on bare-chested to play a conga drum solo entitled "Ritmo Primitivo." Films, cartoons, images of the musicians, and slides of paintings by Kingsley's wife, Sheila, flashed on the screen above in an attempt at multimedia—everything an echo of the Electric Christmas concert in the same hall more than two years earlier.

At the end, Kingsley expressed his gratitude—not to Bob, but to "the god of electricity for giving us clear circuits for two hours."[11] As the 2,800-seat crowd was clearing out, Aunt Dorothy realized no one had acknowledged Bob himself. Van Koevering remembered she was irate and stood up and shouted, "This is Bob Moog; this wouldn't have happened if it wasn't for my nephew Bob Moog! Bob, take a bow." Van Koevering recalled, "Bob stood up very embarrassed and very humble, and they gave him applause."[12]

On the whole, New York's major critics went to town on Kingsley, sparing no invective. Winthrop Sargeant reported in *The New Yorker*, "Mr. Kingsley, a short, tousle-haired figure, agonized in a manner that would have embarrassed Leonard Bernstein, and did this facing the audience, so that no grimace or soul-shattering look of orgiastic horror could be missed. As a demonstration of the possibilities of electronic sound, the evening was totally lacking in interest. The Moogs, like the original Theremin, are apt to get out of tune. Altogether, Mr. Kingsley's show is an elongated nightclub act."[13]

In the *New York Times*, Peter G. Davis wrote, "The whole production seemed to focus on Mr. Kingsley himself, who conducted the proceedings from center stage as though immersed in the angst of a Mahler symphony.... When they were audible, the four Moogs sounded rather like calliopes on a merry-go-round. Occasionally there was a bit of white noise or a touch of percussion and saw-tooth, but on the whole the potential of the instrument was smothered by the pretentious special effects."[14]

Van Koevering had just seen four Synthesizer 10s in action, each with preset patch boxes like the ones used at MoMA, and he liked them. It would be a month before he could have one, Bob explained, but he could come back to Trumansburg now for the weekend, sleep on the couch, and spend time at the factory learning the ins and outs of the instrument ahead of time. Van Koevering was headed to Chicago for school shows and Bob asked to hitch a ride back to Trumansburg. They'd have a chance to talk about the equipment.

For the night drive back, Bob sat in the passenger seat and the conversation strayed into the abstract. "Bob went into the theories of what he learned at Cornell," Van Koevering recalled, "that nothing is above the speed of light—until there are experiences that you have that you can't explain with any terms that are lower than the speed of light. What about some of the feelings you have, the insights you have?"[15]

Deep in the night, in the monotony of engine drone and the endless white lines shooting into the headlight beams from the dark, they drifted off into philosophical realms. "Where do ideas come from?" Bob asked. Van Koevering was intrigued: "Now we're talking about the synthesis of creativity. Is it all *from* you, or is it *through* you? And Bob said, 'it's *through* you, it's not *from* you.' And the spiritual world lit up for me concerning technology. That every good idea I have for a musical riff or a marketing idea or a way to teach an audience—I didn't have to learn it all. Bob confirmed in me that it came *through* him, it didn't all come *from* him ... something you have yet to see but you're getting glimpses. That part of creativity, Bob understood. And I'm sure he understood it because he could tap it on demand."[16]

Then the discussion shifted to the practical. Van Koevering wanted Bob on board with school shows because he saw a market there. "I deal with hundreds of high schools each season," he explained. "I'm going to get a sponsor. And my sponsor is going to pay the bill because some schools can't afford me." He could see synthesizers as a teaching tool and predicted they'd be in every school in America. Bob wasn't convinced; so far his customers had chiefly been professionals, not educators or consumers. Van Koevering persisted: "I said, 'I will change that.' And for me, that was an assignment, that was a destiny. I'm writing my own future. I'm saying, 'I will go there!' "[17]

A week after Kingsley's concert, Keith Emerson debuted a Moog modular onstage in London with the Nice. Like many, Keith had discovered the instrument by accident. In a London music store he'd heard *Switched-On Bach* and was puzzled. He recognized the Bach *Brandenburg Concerto No. 3* track because the Nice had featured an excerpt of it on their own *Ars Longa Vita Brevis* album, released the same month as *S-OB*. But the Moog was a sound he'd never heard before. It sounded to him "almost comical, like a load of elephants farting counterpoint with whoopee cushions in accompaniment."[18] But he was intrigued and put his manager, Tony Stratton-Smith, on the case to track down the device used on Carlos's album.

Stratton-Smith located Mike Vickers, who owned one of the few Moogs in London. Vickers invited Emerson to his apartment to have a go of it. Emerson was a talented pianist and couldn't understand why the "new beast of hardware," as he called it, could only play one note at a time. "But yet," he remembered, "the extraordinary sounds it made far outweighed its idiosyncrasies and imperfections."[19] Keith asked if he could borrow it for an upcoming concert. Vickers was uneasy, warning that he couldn't predict how it would behave in live performance, but he offered to stand by onstage to keep it in check.[20]

In the meantime, Keith tried to finagle a free synth out of Bob by leveraging his celebrity status, and asked Stratton-Smith to contact the Moog people. Walter Sear responded on behalf of the company, all too familiar with these types of well-intentioned pitches: "We have never offered instruments to groups for promotional use, first because of the cost of the unit and secondly, because of the small size of our company. It would also be quite unfair to the groups (such as the Beatles, Stones, etc.) in England who have purchased the equipment."[21] As always, he hastened to mention that some training was necessary before the instrument could utter anything at all.

The more Keith diddled around on Vickers' Moog, the more he saw it as his new playground. Having a ready spectrum of sound effects and tone colors under his fingers was central to his position in the band because the Nice was unique in having the keyboardist stand in for the role of the lead guitarist. He'd already tried every trick with speakers, amplifiers, and an electric organ, jamming, rigging, and forcing things to squeeze out new sonic colors with distortion. But nothing was reliable or easy to repeat. As the lead member of the group, he hogged the spotlight, ramping up the volume and the exhibitionism. His onstage antics were legendary. He routinely abused his trademark Hammond organ in "freak outs," manhandling it or stabbing it with his Hitler Youth dagger—to the horror of the Hammond people, who refused to service it. He recalled their disgust: "They said 'Oh no, we're not touching your stuff any more. . . . You don't respect your instrument, so go someplace else and have it done.'"[22]

For two back-to-back shows on February 7 at London's Royal Festival Hall, Mike Vickers loaned Keith his Moog. The 2,900-seat hall was packed. Keith commissioned a silver lurex space suit to wear so he'd match the Moog and its "space-age technology and flight deck layout," as he described it.[23] For safety, Mike Vickers crouched behind the instrument the whole evening to make sure it kept working. He would "jump up from time to time like a jack-in-the-box to change the array of patch cords," Keith remembered.[24] "He was there giving me the thumbs up or the thumbs down, and I could play."[25]

The *New Musical Express* reported, "The Moog was introduced for the first time on a British stage during 'She Belongs To Me.'"[26] The Bob Dylan song was followed by other covers, and a jazz-rock variation of a classical work—a hybrid style the band specialized in—the "Karelia Suite" by the Finnish composer Jean Sibelius.

The group's style was on view again—along with Keith in his silver space suit—when the Nice joined the Royal Philharmonic Orchestra and the Ambrosian Singers at Royal Festival Hall on March 6. Keith recalled his Moog performance in excerpts from the classical soundtrack to *2001: A Space Odyssey*—Ligeti's *Atmosphères*: "White noise swirling left and right, oscillators swooping with the aid of *portamento*, the audience were in a state of shock, not seeming to associate the weird sounds with the box of tricks erected behind the Hammond organ."[27] When the orchestra left the stage at the end, fans screamed for an encore. Shouts of "America" brought on a 20-minute, high-octane cover of Bernstein's "America" from *West Side Story*, with Keith on the Moog, flailing and gyrating in classic style.

Not long after the Nice played with the Royal Philharmonic Orchestra, Emerson announced he was breaking up the band. He felt it had run its course artistically, and he wanted to move on. Together with Greg Lake, the guitarist from the band King Crimson, and 20-year-old drummer Carl Palmer from the group Atomic Rooster, he formed a new band—Emerson, Lake, and Palmer—announced in the *New Musical Express* on May 30. Rehearsals to evolve a signature sound and build a stable of original songs began in June. For source material, Keith nudged the group toward the classical influences he'd used with the Nice. He assembled an epic suite based on Mussorgsky's virtuoso piano work, *Pictures at an Exhibition*, and a driving instrumental adapted from a piece he played on the piano: Béla Bartók's *Allegro Barbaro*.

Emerson, Lake, and Palmer—ELP—booked London's Advision Studios in July to record their first album ahead of their planned live debut in August. Keith remembered "spotting what I assumed to be the resident Moog Synthesizer in the studio's ante room.... The instrument had sat there so long everybody was afraid to touch it."[28] Without Mike Vickers around, Keith and Eddie Offord, the session recording engineer, gamely set about trying to get some sound out of it: "'I think if I stick this jack-plug in this hole and this jack-plug in this hole we should get some sort of a noise,' said Eddie. I tapped the keyboard hopefully and was rewarded with a rather bland tone. 'Try doing the same patch again with the other oscillator,' I suggested. Eddie complied and I tapped the keyboard again. This time it sounded a little more hopeful after fiddling with the oscillator's tuning. One oscillator left, we patched that the same way."[29]

ELP's first recorded use of the Moog was in "Tank," an instrumental by Emerson and Palmer with a long coda of Keith's Moog squealing out a jazzy, manic solo over a driving vamp.

Another song recorded in the early album sessions was the only other cut using the Moog. It would turn out to be one of the most memorable uses of the modular ever, yet it came together in a spontaneous, unplanned way. It happened when Keith arrived at the studio one afternoon and found Greg Lake strumming an unfamiliar folksy tune on an acoustic guitar, something that seemed out of character with the group's other songs. Lake called it "just a bit of fun," and asked Palmer to lay down some drum tracks underneath it.[30] Lake confessed he'd written the song on his first acoustic guitar when he was 12 years old, and when he'd tried to push it with King Crimson the year before, the band rejected it. He called it "a simplistic little medieval fantasy."[31]

"Lucky Man" was the story of a gentleman with "white horses" and "ladies by the score," who went to battle for honor and glory, was killed, and in the end, "No money could save him." "Oooh, what a lucky man he was," the chorus crooned. The tracks Lake and Palmer set down made a song of 3 minutes and 10 seconds, with a tacked-on outro of guitar strumming, repeated harmony "ahhs," and a drum fill. Everyone agreed the outro sounded a little barren and that a synth solo might round out the mix. Keith was happy to give it a sporting try, but he was still a greenhorn, wandering his way around the modules.

Keith puttered with the Moog, quickly figuring out a few things he could try. "The portamento knob seemed to be a load of fun during the level check," he recalled. "You could 'slur' notes. I made a mental note to use the effect when they ran the tape. . . . There seemed to be a never-ending wealth of 'licks' to be played over the simple modal outro." Keith got the signal and ran a first take. "When I'd finished," he recalled, "I looked up to see two happy faces in the control room." In Keith's offhanded first try, he'd nailed something his band mates were completely happy with. But Keith was completely unhappy. The oscillators were drifting out of tune and he was just fooling around. He pleaded for another take, but the others had decided it was a wrap. "I was not convinced," he recalled, "I thought it was the most mediocre solo I'd ever played."[32]

Keith couldn't have guessed that his one minute and 25-second ad lib—about to be engraved in the album's grooves forever—would become the gold standard for future synth solos and would wake pop listeners up to the synthesizer itself. Rather than blending into the mix, it flaunted everything a synthesizer was, and an acoustic instrument wasn't. "There's no real point in it if you can't tell if that's a guitar playing or a Moog," Emerson explained. "With me you say, 'That is definitely a Moog.'"[33] In its brief span, the "Lucky Man" solo managed to embody many of the characteristic Moog sounds: the theremin-like glides between notes; low to high sweeps; the classic "fat" sound; and the buzzing and morphing filter effects. The single take was a tribute to Keith's musicianship—a snapshot of instinct at work as he roamed the music the first time out, shaping phrases on an instrument he was just getting to know.

"Lucky Man" at first seemed like the awkward child of the album, but it would come to be the LP's most prominent ambassador. It also became, along with Pink Floyd's *Dark Side of the Moon*, a favorite way of testing the fine points of stereo systems. In the final mix, the instrument was bounced gently back and forth between left and right pans, and Lake pointed out, "The Moog at the end goes down to twenty-one cycles which is lower than most ordinary speakers can go. If you listen to it in a bass speaker it really makes your stomach rumble."[34]

Keith finally ordered (and paid for) his own Moog. It was a used model—the modular Herb Deutsch and Chris Swansen had played at the Jazz in the Garden concert. The Trumansburg crew figured its preset boxes would be a quick-change solution for Keith to use on the fly in performance.

"I excitedly broke into the box and there it was—my own Moog Synthesizer," Keith recalled. "I was living in a pretty small flat at the time, and The Beast didn't leave much living space. . . . I pulled it all out and began setting it up but it proved more complicated as there was no accompanying manual. . . . all I wanted to do was play it, but I didn't even know how to F'ing plug it in! . . . After an hour, I found out how to switch it on, but that was all. . . . I think I got a couple of lights to blink once, but that was about it."[35] ELP's first gig was only weeks away, and Keith wanted the Moog to play a major part in the debut. Vickers came to the rescue again, revving up the system and plugging together a few patches for Keith to use.

In late August, Keith brought his new Moog out before an estimated crowd of 600,000 at the 1970 Isle of Wight Festival. The event was hyped as another Woodstock communitarian utopia of "love and peace," despite the specter of the recent Altamont catastrophe. Fans from all over Europe and America amassed on the small island off the south coast of England for a five-day musical orgy of wall-to-wall artists and bands. Perturbed locals watched as legions of "hippies" and "freaks"—six times the resident population—piled onto their island, days in advance of the Festival, to settle over the concert site at Afton Down, camping on the hillside in tents or in the open air.

The lineup of acts promised another toke of '60s idealism, with a few Woodstock veterans on the bill like Richie Havens, Joan Baez, the Who, and Ten Years After. Two stellar figures would glow in one of their last sets before flaming out with the fire of the past decade: Jimi Hendrix would be dead in three weeks before having the chance to use his new Moog synthesizer, and Jim Morrison—who would perform the iconic "Light my Fire" with the Doors—would be gone within a year. But Emerson, Lake, and Palmer, the new progressive group, here for its second public appearance as a band, would begin to define the next decade with a few pyrotechnics of its own.

ELP had made its formal debut a week earlier, on August 23, at the Guildhall in the English city of Plymouth, choosing the intimate 800-seat theater as a low-pressure venue to work out any kinks before facing the throngs at the Isle of Wight. Now, at the huge Festival, their newly minted version of *Pictures at an Exhibition* would form the centerpiece of their set, and Keith wanted it to be a defining moment in the stage persona of the group. "'Pictures at an Exhibition,'" he recalled, "not only demanded theatrics, it yelled 'SHOWTIME' from the first 'Promenade' to the last 'Great Gates of Kiev.' Like everyone else who wanted to make an electric impression . . . our intention was to blow every other band off the stage with eccentricity."[36]

Keith meant his threat almost literally: ELP had located two antique cannons which they planned to use on stage. To test them out, they hauled the artillery onto an old truck along with a generous cache of gunpowder and headed to the only place loud enough to drown out experiments involving thundering detonations: the flight approach field at London's Heathrow Airport. Trial runs were carried out with the assistance of Rocky Morley, the group's loyal roadie. Using bits of wire, a battery, and a Jetex fuse, Rocky wired the chargers to the fuses, and to gauge the amount of gunpowder they needed, the group set off test firings from behind a low ridge. "Rocky put two wires together completing the circuit," Keith recalled, "but the result was disappointing, just a small bang and a puff of smoke. 'I think we can double the charge, don't you?' said Rocky. And with that, we tried again. This time there was an audible crack but, as we loaded the cannons back on the truck, I told Rocky that I thought it would be safe enough to triple the charge for showtime."[37]

The Isle of Wight Festival opened on August 26. Outside the protective fences rimming a hillside blanketed with paying audience members, bands of agitators began collecting, alarming police and security personnel. Five thousand squatters had already claimed the high ground and planted tents to hear the concert for free, stigmatizing the area as "Desolation Hill." Drugs moved around freely, and the ramshackle community was quickly dominated by roaming fringe groups—French and Algerian anarchists, a radical American organization calling themselves the White Panthers, and anti-Vietnam protesters.

Up on the Hill, a mob of 200 repeatedly rushed the fences trying to gate-crash the Festival. The White Panthers issued a demand for 12,000 tickets and free food for 10,000 people. Hell's Angels stormed the grounds and joined the rebel element to rip down barriers, setting fire to concessions and tents, starting fights, and chasing away guards who retreated to protect the stage area and the equipment. Singer-songwriter Kris Kristofferson recalled,

"They booed us, Joni Mitchell, Joan Baez, Sly Stone; they threw shit at Jimi Hendrix.... Peace and love it was not."[38] By the fourth day, security had lost control and the festival organizers—who'd ironically named their firm "Fiery Creations"—threw up their hands. Damage was estimated at £20,000. Fearing a riot, and having no choice, they declared the remainder of the Festival a free event.

On August 29, the fourth day of the Festival—now in the throes of Armageddon—ELP went on stage with no sound check. Keith recalled, "From the moment ELP started playing to that huge open field filled with a sea of bodies, I felt disconnected. The sound we were making left the stage and kept going. There was no ambiance and no feedback from an audience that appeared to be having one huge picnic breaking down the perimeter fences.... The radical fringe's attempts to force it into becoming a free event... were a constant peripheral obbligato to what went on in the main enclosures."[39]

Then came the big moment: *Pictures at an Exhibition*. Keith was still wrestling with the Moog's basic functions. The group struggled through the challenging 36-minute suite; there were tuning problems and the Moog interjected a few unplanned sounds here and there. Keith had reminded Greg Lake about the footswitch that would fire one of the cannons on cue during the grand finale of *Pictures*—"The Great Gates of Kiev." "An Italian photographer," he recalled, "intent on getting a picture of me positioned himself right over the barrel of my cannon. I looked across at Greg who had a barrage of photographers in front of his cannon, too. We both had foot-switches and flaming torches to fire our cannons individually and now that we neared the end, I could sense that if Rocky had done his job right most of Europe's paparazzi would be blown like charred confetti across the front rows.

"'There's no end, to my life, no beginning...' sang Greg as I contemplated the end of the Italian photographers. With both hands engaged with keyboards either side, my only way of signaling 'DANGER' was by shouting and nodding furiously, hoping that someone in the wings would get the message. My action was only misinterpreted as a true rock star in the throes of some orgasmic, triumphant conclusion to something. 'Life is death...' sang Greg majestically. I noted a brief clearance. After hearing the immortal, 'Death is life...' I stomped on the foot switch. KERBOOM! Five hundred pounds of wrought iron rose defiantly into the air, the shock waves sending a couple of photographers into the pit and I briefly noted a look of horror on Greg's face.

For a moment, I thought he'd wimped out of igniting his cannon, but he did it anyway... KERBOOM!"[40]

ELP had succeeded in blowing a couple of photographers off the stage, if not their goal of "every other band," and after a mostly instrumental 53-minute set, the crowd wouldn't let them leave without another 10 minutes of encores.

Reviews were mixed. John Peel, BBC Radio 1 DJ, called the ELP set "a tragic waste of time, talent, and electricity," but some top critics had good things to say.[41] Geoffrey Cannon, assessing the five-day Isle of Wight lineup, wrote in *The Guardian,* "The most spectacular act was Emerson, Lake and Palmer, whose colossal performance matched that of Pink Floyd at Bath.... Emerson's manic performance at his Moog synthesizer was astonishingly talented. By himself, he amplified Mussorgski's music, past the range of an orchestra.... Emerson played the 'Kremlin Bells' on the Moog and two helpers walked to the front of the stage with flaming torches, to touch off the two cannon placed there. As they went off, with staggering explosions, Emerson proved himself—with Pink Floyd, The Who, and Frank Zappa—as one of the most successfully ambitious showmen of rock."[42]

ELP had blasted off.

∿∿∿

Gershon Kingsley was out dazzling audiences with the modular Moog in his own way. In May, after the commercial LP release of his Carnegie Hall concert, he took the Moog Quartet on the road. Guest appearances with the Boston Pops orchestra and conductor Arthur Fiedler featured the group in the world premiere of *Concerto Moogo,* a work influenced by folk, country, and rock, that Kingsley claimed he'd composed in only three weeks. He'd embarked now on a mission to take electronic music to the masses and prove it wasn't the rarefied art of the avant-garde.

For R. A. Moog, the extravaganzas that Keith and Kingsley mounted helped spread the word about synthesizers, but the shows did little for the company's bottom line. Modulars remained pricy, specialized tools for select professionals. To crack the consumer and educational markets—where the *real* money was—another type of instrument was essential. If Van Koevering's dream of a Moog in every school were to come true, the synths would have to be smaller, cheaper, and simpler to operate.

Around the time Kingsley was staging his Carnegie Hall concert, David Borden had eyed the Min A sitting on Hemsath's desk and asked if he could take it out for a road test. Hemsath obliged, but it was an act of faith to loan out his one and only Min A to the man notorious for frying up modules. Borden was the first to try it out, and he'd wind up making history with it.

Borden was intrigued with the idea of a smaller Moog after grappling, like everyone else, with the intricacies of the large modular. The year before, in 1969, he and two other musicians, Steve Drews and Linda Fisher, had formed a contemporary music ensemble called "Mother Mallard's Portable Masterpiece Company," performing on modular Moogs. The three were borrowing the equipment and paying it off in installments to Bob, who refused to charge them interest. Despite its quirky name, the group couldn't stop venues from billing them simply as "The Moog Synthesizer," both for the unique music and the circus juggling act of knobs and patch cords the players went through to reconfigure sounds for each piece. Between selections they'd taken to darkening the stage and distracting the audience with classic 1930s Disney cartoon shorts while they frantically yanked and shoved cords in the glow of infrared flashlights. Each new pattern of patches was committed to memory, and rehearsed separately from the music with disciplined military-style drills. "We timed ourselves," Borden explained. "We got ourselves down from 10 or 12 minutes to 3 or 2½."

Just before Easter 1970, Borden had finished a new work and didn't know what to call it, so he simply named it *Easter*. It was pure coincidence that he premiered it on Easter Sunday at Cornell's Sage Chapel as a last-minute addition to a religious service. The piece was written for prerecorded tape, plus an accompaniment by Borden on the chapel organ, and Steve Drews on the Moog Synthesizer 10.

Borden repeated the work on a Cornell Dance Group concert on April 10—this time with the choreography it had been intended for. He and Drews were again the performers, but Borden used the Min A to substitute for the organ part. The concert, at Willard Straight Theatre, was the first-ever live performance of a mini synthesizer, and the debut of the first Mini Moog prototype instrument. On June 30, Borden and Drews encored *Easter* at Manhattan's historic Trinity Church on a series called "Praise the Lord with a Groovy Sound," with Borden on the Min A again.

A week after the April dance premiere of *Easter*, the Min A was back on the Cornell campus for a three-day social justice rally that clogged the University grounds with young people from as far away as Los Angeles and Toronto.

"America Is Hard To Find" was a peace, music, and political gathering in support of Daniel Berrigan, the well-known Jesuit priest, Cornell chaplain, and recent fugitive from federal authorities. Berrigan was a convicted member of the "Catonsville Nine," a radical group of Catholic protesters accused of burning 378 draft files at the Catonsville, Maryland, draft board with homemade napalm. Berrigan was on the run after he failed to report for his three-year prison sentence the week before.

Cornell's grounds were throbbing with spontaneous festivity: Hare Krishnas danced with flutes and cymbals; a young woman sat under a tree draped with brightly colored tie-dye shirts she was selling; a man was assembling a geodesic parachute dome in the makeshift tent city along the Arts Quad.

On Friday night, inside the massive Barton Hall—that normally held 4,800—a throng of 15,000 watched as Berrigan made a surprise appearance on stage, ripping off his motorcycle helmet disguise to don a black bandit hat and shades. In an anti-establishment rant, he stirred up the crowd: "This evening belongs to this community, it doesn't belong to the FBI."[43] Afterward, in plain view of planted FBI agents wearing hippie garb, he engineered a stealthy exit, shrouded in the costume of a 10-foot high Bread and Puppet Theater puppet, absconding as quickly as he came.

The folksinger Phil Ochs sang, and other fugitive firebrands spoke, including a member of the Black Panther Party, and the "Chicago Eight" defendant David Dellinger who was interrupted by a young man burning his draft card, triggering another dozen in the audience to follow suit. Dellinger bellowed, "Violence against property is not violence against people. . . . Right on—see you in the courts, the streets and the jails."[44]

On Saturday, John Cage performed in the morning, and by evening, the earnest political outrage was quickly forgotten in the euphoria of a bacchanal. Inside Barton Hall, rock groups roared as lines of snake dancers jostled through the crowd. Strawberry incense wafted to cover up pot smoke; wine jugs were passed around, and used paper plates from pay-what-you-can rice dinners were flung like frisbees into the rafters.

Chris Swansen came on stage to play a set, squinting out over a double keyboard at the endless carpet of humans bathed in blinding lights. The audience sat transfixed as he wailed on the monophonic Synth I with its preset box, and the Min A, over prerecorded tape tracks, playing his own compositions and a few pop tunes. Several errant dogs trotted through the packed crowd, and the *Ithaca Journal* reported, "A couple embracing, rocked and rocked and rocked, like mother and infant, to the music.[45] ... The crush of photographers around Swansen on stage became so great that marshals had to hustle everyone off the stage while he played."[46] Bob was present, and at the end, the *Journal* reported that Chris "called up the shy Trumansburg inventor to take credit for the music machine."[47]

∼∼∼

The public debut of Hemsath's other compact synthesizer prototype, the Mini B, like Borden's *Easter* performance on the Min A, wasn't anything Hemsath had asked for, and something Bob never would have imagined. It came about in a spontaneous moment of serendipity.

In the early summer of 1970, the brilliant African-American jazz artist Sun Ra made a pilgrimage to Trumansburg with his band. The pageantry of their entrance was unlike anything the town had ever seen. Ra called his group the "Arkestra," after the Ark of the Covenant, and members adopted his personal fashion styles—Egyptian headdresses, African robes, Mardi Gras beads, and outer space–inspired costumes. Bob remembered their ceremonial arrival in a motorcade of big, 20-year-old Cadillac limousines: "It was fourteen or fifteen people and they came up in... three or four cars... It was a happening."[48]

Sun Ra's biographer, John F. Szwed, described how Ra and his musicians always traveled in full regalia: "They spread out across every city they visited and in their costumes they were as conspicuous as Shriners.... You might find the whole band glittering and shining at breakfast in the middle of the night at Denny's."[49] As they stepped out of their cars on Main Street, Jon Weiss ushered the band of robed, bedecked visitors into Kostrub's for ice cream, turning many local heads.

Sun Ra was born Herman Poole Blount in Birmingham, Alabama in 1914, and went by the nickname "Sonny." He showed a talent for piano and composition, and as an African-American child growing up in Birmingham, he withdrew into deep introspection, burying himself in writings of ancient cultures, biblical scripture, occult works, science, and literature. The whole of society appeared out of balance to him, and he dedicated his life to proselytizing for a harmonious world through the voice of music.

Blount was active in the Chicago jazz scene of the 1940s. By the early '50s he'd evolved from his roots in big band swing toward a signature "cosmic jazz" style, a mixture of big band artists like Duke Ellington, with influences of ragtime, bebop, and free jazz styles. Sometimes melodic, the music was often wildly dissonant and unruly.

When Blount changed his name legally to "Le Sony'r Ra"—shortened to Sun Ra—he was channeling Ra, the Egyptian god of the sun. Renouncing his biological lineage, he assumed the identity of an interplanetary traveler bearing a message of peace from the universe—space as a sanctuary for the world's oppressed peoples. Music—jazz specifically—was his medium of travel through the galaxies, and the language of salvation for humankind. It was a metaphor for the African-American community's hopes to reverse the weight of history through a futuristic vision.

Sun Ra was respected in both hip and highbrow cultural spheres; his picture was featured on an April 1969 cover of *Rolling Stone*, and, with his fixation on space travel, *Esquire* magazine invited him to contribute to its July 1969 issue on the coming Apollo 11 moon landing.

In November 1969 Sun Ra had booked a session at Kingsley's studio to record his LP, *My Brother the Wind*. An element of his space philosophy involved electronic music—a futuristic medium for jazz—and he'd been an early performer on electronic keyboard instruments like the Clavinet (which he dubbed the "Solar Sound Instrument"), and the Farfisa organ (which he called his "Intergalactic Organ"). But his discovery of the Moog was a revelation. In the recording session at Kingsley's, Ra used two Moog modulars in an abstract free jazz mix with sax, woodwinds, and percussion. He told *DownBeat*, "The Moog Synthesizer in its potential and application to and for the future is tremendous in scope."[50] Ra saw it as a psychic vehicle to traverse the cosmos, and his talisman in a spiritual quest for civil rights.

At Trumansburg, Sun Ra and his entourage packed into the rear studio for a demo by Jon Weiss. When the Mini B was brought out, Ra fiddled around on it and someone started running tape. The session turned into an impromptu recording, with Ra doodling a series of fluent improvisations. His free flight would become the last five tracks on his next LP, *My Brother the Wind, Volume II*. With only two Mini Bs in existence, Bob was anxious to see how musicians might use them in the field. He was impressed with the jazzman's handling of the instrument, and as Ra was leaving, Bob lent him one of the Mini Bs.

A few weeks later, Ra and his Arkestra appeared at the Red Garter in New York's Greenwich Village for a three-day stint, from July 11 to 13. The West 4th Street venue advertised itself as a "unique beer palace-night club deluxe." A few years later, it would become New York's trendy club, The

Bottom Line. With no formal fanfare or announcements, the performances, willy nilly, marked the public debut of the Mini B, and Ra incorporated it into his ensemble of gear as seamlessly as though he'd been playing it for years.

Jon Weiss happened to be in New York and Bob asked him to drop by the club to see how Ra was handling the Mini B. Weiss was astounded. He could tell the instrument had been subjected to some sort of tinkering or abuse, but he found the results fit exactly with Ra's "out-of-this-world" aesthetic— something the engineers never anticipated. "He made sounds like you had never heard in your life," Weiss recalled. "I mean, just total inharmonic distortion all over the place, oscillators weren't oscillating any more, nothing was working but it was fabulous." Weiss found that the way Sun Ra was using the Mini B was just a more exaggerated version of the unpredictable quality of Moogs in general: "There were characteristics of the Moog synthesizer that existed only because of certain inaccuracies in the equipment that resulted in wonderful and bizarre events. . . . it was an instrument, it wasn't a machine. A machine would have created no inaccuracies."[51]

Photographer Lee Santa, who'd befriended Sun Ra, remembered coming to all three Red Garter shows that weekend. At the close of one show, Santa went up and spoke with Ra, who let him in on a secret about the albums, *My Brother the Wind*, volumes I and II. "He kept using that expression, 'my brother, the wind,'" Santa recalled. "I think he could see that I didn't understand what he was talking about. And then he let it drop that he was talking about the Moog synthesizer. That's what he would call it. He would use metaphors a lot."[52]

Ra held onto the Mini B longer, endowing it with more and more symbolism for his mission. In scenes from his forthcoming film, *Space Is the Place*, the instrument played a central role. The plot of the science fiction feature revolved around Ra's return journey to earth and his plan to spirit away members of the American Black community to colonize a utopian planet of their own. When his spaceship touches down in the desert before a small, fidgety crowd of reporters, Ra ceremoniously steps through a sliding door, his head adorned with a striped pharaoh's headdress supporting a towering crown of golden cow horns surrounding a sun disk. Then he seats himself at the Mini B for a ritual introduction to the earthlings.

A torrent of random white noise, grating squeals, and robotic diddling becomes the soundtrack as Ra's fingers stroke the Mini's keyboard. A reporter asks, "What is the power of your machine?" Ra answers, "Music," and continues, "This music is all a part of another tomorrow. Another kind of language. Speaking things of nature, naturalness. The way it should be."

In a final concert before his departure, Sun Ra sits on stage plinking an abstract solo on the Mini B, swaying his head in a silver chainmail headdress. The film's drama intensifies as a hailstorm of free jazz percussion crossfades with the Mini B intoning hoarse, distorted screeches, like the sounds Jon Weiss heard at the Red Garter. In a frenzied mix of dissonant jazz, the instrument remains in the underscore as Sun Ra bids farewell to the earthlings and his spaceship releases from the bonds of gravity, rising back into the stars.

Three weeks after his Red Garter shows, Sun Ra brought the Mini B overseas for its European debut. On the French Riviera he played a three-day engagement with 18 Arkestra musicians and dancers, from August 3 to 5, 1970, at the Fondation Maeght, a modern art museum in Saint-Paul-de-Vence. The longest number on the set list was "The Cosmic Explorer," a Ra solo featuring the Mini B croaking and shrieking for 20 minutes in a manic barrage of sound. Microphones were present, and the shows were immortalized in two later LP releases: *Nuits de la Fondation Maeght*, volumes I and II.

∿∿∿

Dick Hyman borrowed the second Mini B for a more traditional outing on August 6 at the Eastman School of Music in Rochester, New York. *Arranger's Holiday '70—An Extravaganza of Jazz* showcased Hyman playing the Mini over prerecorded tapes in two of his compositions: "The Minotaur, and *Dialogue for Piano and Moog Synthesizer*.

When Sun Ra gave the first public performance of the Mini B at the Red Garter on July 11, the date had clearly slipped under the radar at *Billboard* which ran a story the same day, "Mini-Moog to Be Unveiled at Museum Concert." The magazine reported, "The mini-Moog—'a synthesizer the size of an electric office typewriter,' invented by Dr. Robert Moog, will be unveiled Aug. 20 at a concert in the Museum of Modern Art."[53] The advertised event— part of the Jazz in the Garden series—was quite late to the party, coming after Sun Ra's American and European unveilings and Hyman's own Rochester appearance. But none of that seemed to matter to Bob, who was so uninterested in the Mini he neglected to tell his top salesman about it. In the lead-up to the MoMA event, Walter Sear wrote to him, "What is the story on the $1500 machine the size of a typewriter mentioned in Billboard? Shouldn't I be the first to know??? What about the unit for Dick Hyman? I will be helping him at the MOMA Concert. Polyphonic Keyboard??? Write the news."[54]

The MoMA performance had little of the hoopla surrounding the Moog event in the same Garden space a year earlier. Billed as "A Different Moog," it featured Hyman with a jazz trio calling themselves "Children of All Ages"—saxophonist Arnie Lawrence, bassist Richard Davis, and drummer Ed Shaughnessy—with three of Lawrence's children as guests playing a battery of instruments like slide-whistle, kazoo, trumpet, and percussion, and interjecting vocalizations from time to time. The showcase number for the Mini's "unveiling" was Hyman's "Minotaur," from his 1969 *Electric Eclectics* album. The piece had charted as the first top 40 Moog single, and its original recording used a Maestro drum machine, a tamboura-like drone, and a bass line to support a fleet melodic solo on the modular Moog. But it was the siren-like slides between the notes that shouted, "this is a synth." "That was really the point of the Minotaur—that effect," Hyman explained.[55]

For the MoMA concert, Hyman played the solo line on the Mini B while his trio covered the other tracks. MoMA's press release had mistakenly described the monophonic Mini B as "a portable synthesizer that can play melody and chords together for a live performance," and John S. Wilson, the *New York Times* reviewer, echoed the misunderstanding in his review. Explaining to readers that the original "Minotaur" recording needed accompanying instruments, he concluded, "The essential merit of the minisynthesizer" was Hyman's ability to produce the same result, "unassisted and as simply as though he were playing a piano or organ."[56]

In the main portion of the program, Hyman's group indulged in what he called a "free-form happening," adding in the children's contributions. "The happening ... lasted for 55 minutes," Wilson reported, "which was more than a large part of the audience did. Before it was half over, listeners were seeking shelter inside the museum and by the time it eventually stopped large areas of the garden had been cleared."[57]

The outings of the Min A and the Mini B, in the hands of Borden, Swansen, Sun Ra, and Hyman, were hints of a new era to come. The instruments were Davids to the Goliath of the Moog modular—the "beast" that had been the mascot of the first synthesizer revolution. But the beast was starting to lose its leadership role to the Mini, in what would be the second, and in some ways, greater, revolution. The shift—almost a crossfade—would allow the synthesizer to shrink down and join the familiar family of instruments. But the transition wouldn't be easy.

18
A Palace Revolution

Everyone seemed to believe in the Mini Moog except Bob. As far as he was concerned, the big modular was still his calling card. If recordings were any barometer, the "beast" was certainly alive and well. In a July 1970 promotional flyer, Bob proudly listed 42 LPs that used the instrument, even some he preferred not to talk about, like *Moog España*. Many were recent releases: *Moogie Woogie*, *Switched-On-Country*, *Electric Hair*, *The Electric Symphony*, *Cinemoog*, *Nashville Gold—Switched On Moog*, and one by Jean Jacques Perrey who should have known that his title, *Moog Indigo*, didn't rhyme with its reference to Duke Ellington's song, "Mood Indigo."

And there were new releases that hadn't made it onto Bob's list yet: *Switched On Blues*, *More Switched On Bacharach*, *Big Band Moog*, *The Electric Lucifer*, and *A Moog Mass*. One was simply titled *Moog!* Kingsley offered *Switched-On Gershwin*; Hans Wurman came back with *Chopin à la Moog*; Beaver and Krause issued *In a Wild Sanctuary*, and composer John Donald Robb, who'd been at Bob's summer 1965 Trumansburg seminar, came out with an avant-garde sampler with the forbidding title, *Electronic Music from Razor Blades to Moog*.

Bob's modular was also helping to define a new genre that would come to be known as "krautrock." On an album by the German band Popul Vuh, band member Florian Fricke used his Moog as the group's signature sound on its debut album, *Affenstunde*, in combination with percussion and tabla. The LP redefined the idea of a rock band in German terms, part of a national movement to reject the heavy beat and blues-influenced roots of American and British rock for a more abstract, ambient music—a sound based in synthesizers, electronic and acoustic instruments, and percussion, with influences from minimalism, *musique concrète*, world music, and jazz.

The Moog modular was starring in role after role, but the glamour still didn't translate into any royalties, or even steady sales, for the R. A. Moog Company. The very day Keith was running his Moog space effects with the orchestra at Royal Festival Hall, Bob was setting up a display at the Music Educators National Conference in Chicago's Conrad Hilton Hotel, hoping to attract a new type of clientele. The MENC event from March 6 to 10 was a testing ground for Van Koevering's hunch that synthesizers had a place in the classroom, but Bob was about to realize what he was up against.

MENC was the first time he was confronted with an up-close view of his competitors vying for a piece of the pie. For starters, CBS showed up with a surprise instrument: the Buchla. In 1969, Don Buchla had licensed his designs to the corporation. Its musical instruments division was looking to bring synthesizers into the fold, beginning with the manufacture of the Buchla 100. But more threatening to Bob was a recent Johnny-come-lately at the conference: a small, unassuming British synthesizer called the VCS3. The mastermind behind the new contender had an unusual story.

Peter Zinovieff had come to manufacture synthesizers through a circuitous route. Born in London in 1933 to Russian aristocrats who'd fled the Russian Revolution, Zinovieff earned a Ph.D. in geology from Oxford, did a brief stint as a mathematician, and stopped working altogether when he married a 17-year-old London beauty, Victoria Heber-Percy, whose fabulous wealth supported both of them in style. Zinovieff indulged his interest in *musique concrète* and built a state-of-the-art home studio beyond the reach of most individuals—more elaborate even than the BBC's legendary Radiophonic Workshop. For the crowning touch, Victoria sold her pearl and turquoise tiara so her husband could buy the most advanced digital minicomputer used in business and industry: the DEC PDP-8. At the time, in 1967, it cost roughly the price of a small house.

"The first concert in Britain given by a computer," the BBC announced in January 1968, when Zinovieff's PDP-8 made its stage debut.[1] A capacity audience at Queen Elizabeth Hall heard Zinovieff's *Partita for Unattended Computer*, a composition he'd programmed to allow the computer a "choice" at different points. The PDP-8 stood alone in the middle of the stage like a babbling robot, a sort of proto-artificial intelligence machine. The phenomenon was so unsettling, Zinovieff recalled, that anxious guards in the hall stood ready with fire extinguishers.

Zinovieff was a pioneer in this technology by using a computer, but he wasn't alone in experimenting with machines that could think up and perform music by themselves. Don Buchla, from the start, had designed random functions into his voltage controlled instrument for live performance situations—something that had never been a priority for Bob. Buchla's latest model, the Buchla 200, added two new modules for that purpose: the "Multiple Arbitrary Function Generator" (MARF), and one he called "Source

1. Two-year-old Robbie with parents, George and Shirley Moog, 1936.
Gertrude Herman, Moog Family Archives.

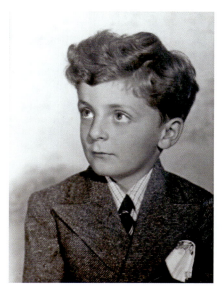

2. First Grade—P.S. 24 in Queens.
Moog Family Archives.

3. Florence Moog, Bob's aunt, "turned on the lights, and listened."
Sidney Ashen-Brenner Jr./Courtesy Ileana Grams-Moog.

4. Bob's childhood home at 51-09 Parsons Boulevard. Two worlds: upstairs and downstairs.
Shirley Jacobs Moog/Courtesy Ileana Grams-Moog.

5. Bob built a theremin in high school. "Moog, that was *damn* good."
Shirley Jacobs Moog/Bob Moog Foundation.

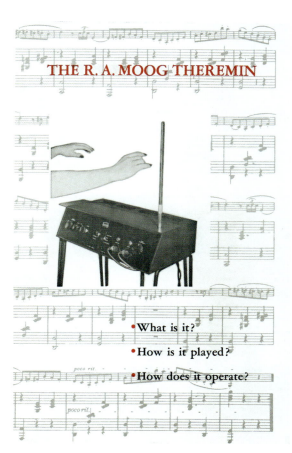

6. First R. A. Moog catalog, 1954. "We refund overpayments."
Courtesy Ileana Grams-Moog.

7. Aunt Estelle is the model for the 1954 theremin brochure. "All R. A. Moog instruments . . . are assembled by skilled craftsmen."
Courtesy Ileana Grams-Moog.

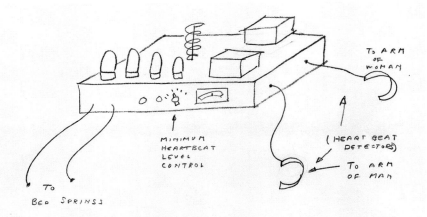

8. The Electronic Intensi-gasm. An early Moog circuit shocks partners into closer cooperation.
Courtesy Ileana Grams-Moog.

9. Wedding Day: Robert Arthur Moog and Shirley May Leigh, June 15, 1958. An Ethical Culture ceremony with a kosher meal.
Shirley Jacobs Moog/Moog Family Archives.

10. Composer Herb Deutsch at the Moog synthesizer prototype. "Fingertip control" of new sounds.
Bob Moog Foundation.

11. The Trumansburg studio of the R. A. Moog Company, where composers were in residence.
Courtesy Ileana Grams-Moog.

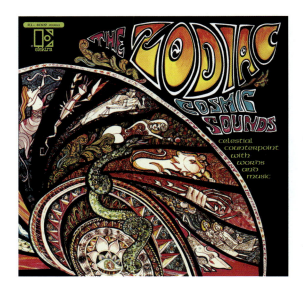

12. The *Zodiac Cosmic Sounds* album cover. "Must be played in the dark."
Rhino Entertainment Company.

13. The song, *Daily Nightly*, on the TV show *The Monkees*, gave many people their first view of a Moog synth in action. "Like hallucinations for your ear."
Michael Ochs Archives/Getty Images.

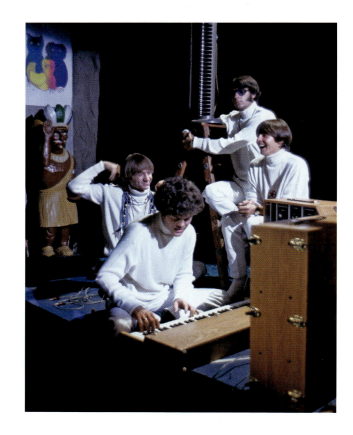

14. *The Trip*, 1967: the Moog becomes the first synthesizer in a film soundtrack. *Flash, Bam, Pow.*
Courtesy of MGM Media Licensing.

15. Bernie Krause, "with bowtie and pocket square," commanding the Moog, as painted by George Harrison on the cover of Harrison's album, *Electronic Sound*, 1969.

George Harrison/Courtesy G.H. Estate Limited.

16. Harrison's painting on the back cover of *Electronic Sound*. "Making the tea" for his friends.

George Harrison/Courtesy G.H. Estate Limited.

17. Paul McCartney exploring the Moog at EMI Studios, Abbey Road, 1969. "Three days is just for switching the machine on!" Center background: George Harrison and Mike Vickers.
© Apple Corps Limited.

18. John Lennon with the Moog at EMI Studios, Abbey Road, 1969. His first encounter with the Moog was "four hours making flying saucer sounds." Mike Vickers watches on the left.
© Apple Corps Limited.

19. Jazz in the Garden, Museum of Modern Art, 1969. "Ooh Baby, Socket to Me!"
Peter Moore/The Museum of Modern Art Archives.

20. Holy Moog—Gershon Kingsley used a modular for Shabbat services. His eighth album was entitled, *God Is a Moog*.
Courtesy Gershon Kingsley.

21. Mort Garson patches his modular Moog. "*Diiiiing*—it was a C." Garson family Christmas card.
Courtesy Day Darmet.

22. The Min A prototype—the portable answer.
David Kean/Audities Foundation.

23. Sun Ra with the Minimoog B, at the Red Garter, July 1970. "My brother, the wind."
Lee Santa.

24. Mother Mallard's Portable Masterpiece Company. L to R: Steve Drews, David Borden, Linda Fisher.
Peter Scheer.

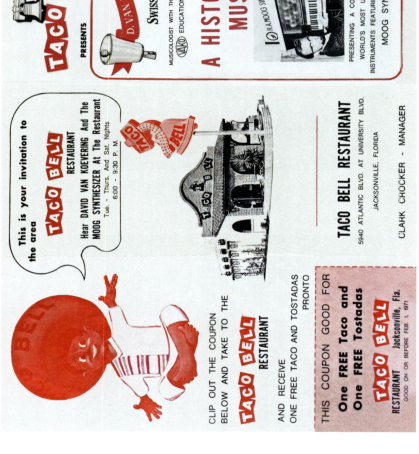

25. Free Taco and a Moog: the brainchild of David Van Koevering. Courtesy David Van Koevering.

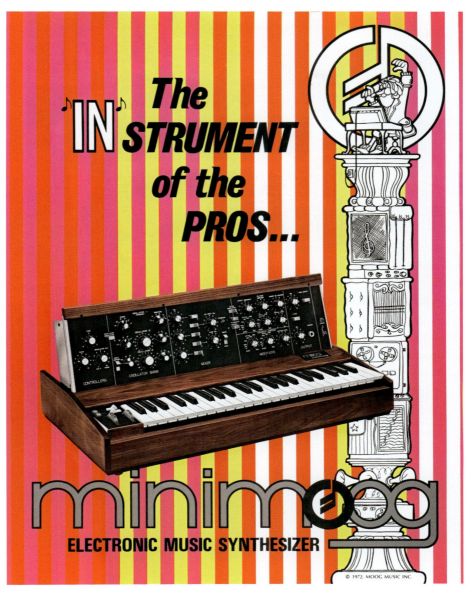

26. Norlin hypes its biggest seller, with "Maestro Moog" (upper right-hand corner). Courtesy Ileana Grams-Moog.

27. The first apple of the season, Trumansburg, 1970. Bob and Shirleigh at home with their own Minimoogs: baby Matthew, Laura (pointing), Michelle (holding up apple), and Renée. Karlheinz, the family German Shepherd, is behind Bob.
Moog Family Archives

28. Bob Moog, luthier: building a guitar in George Kelischek's workshop.
George Kelischek.

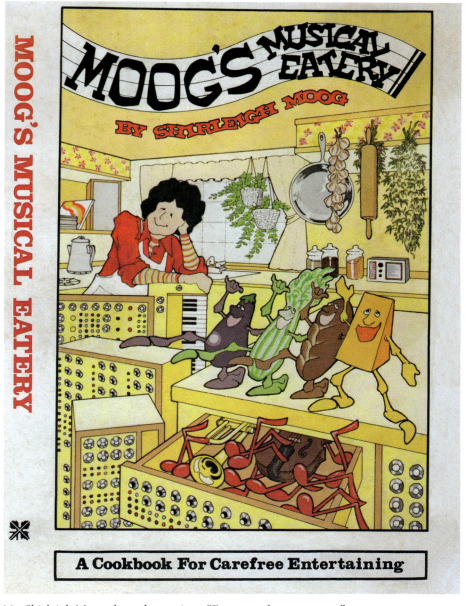

29. Shirleigh Moog shares her recipes. "Every meal, a sacrament."
Tom Parker.

30. Keith Emerson with his "Lucky Man," backstage at Rich Stadium, Buffalo, New York, 1974.
Mark Hockman/Bob Moog Foundation.

31. Rick Wakeman onstage with multiple Minimoogs: *King Arthur on Ice*, 1975.
Michael Putland/Getty Images.

32. The Minimoog unleashes a tidal wave of new songs.
Jim Siergey illustration from *Imoogination*, 1976.

33. Norlin exploits Bob in Japan as a cartoon character.
Courtesy Steve Smith.

34. The synthesizer as an existential question for musicians.
Michael Griffin/Smithsonian Magazine, March 1973

35. Solid gold record awarded to Bob for $1 million in sales of Alice Cooper's *Killer*, recorded with Minimoog and Sonic VI (shown), 1972. L to R: Warner Bros.' Carroll Hardy, David Van Koevering, and Bob.
Courtesy David Van Koevering.

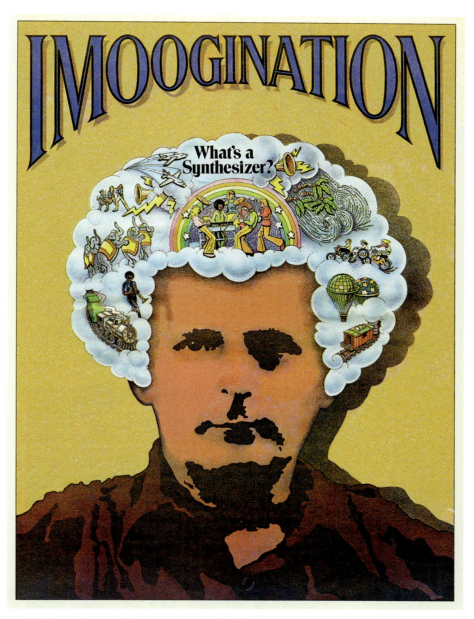

36. Norlin exploits Bob's image as a psychedelic musical guru on the cover of its promotional booklet.
Courtesy Steve Smith.

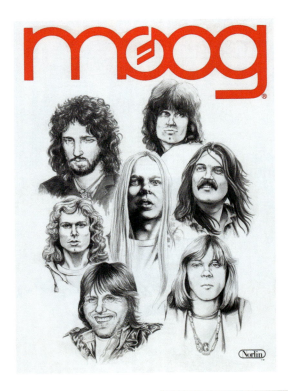

37. The cover of Norlin's 1978 Moog Music product catalog. Clockwise from top: Patrick Moraz, Jon Lord, Klaus Schulze, Keith Emerson, Tony Banks, Duncan Mackay. Center: Rick Wakeman.
Courtesy Ileana Grams-Moog.

38. By the early 1980s, Norlin boasted some of the biggest names in music.
Courtesy Ileana Grams-Moog.

39. Donna Summer and Giorgio Moroder: the Moog modular kicks off the genre of electronic dance music.
Echoes/Getty Images.

40. Composer Carmine Coppola with his score for *Apocalypse Now* that was about to be translated into synthesized sound.
Jon Sievert/Courtesy Wendy Sievert.

41. The Moog home at Big Briar Cove, Buncombe County, North Carolina, near Asheville: a custom-built round house on 89 acres.
Albert Glinsky.

42. Big Briar company headquarters: a metal building behind Bob's house.
Rudi Linhard.

43. Christmas 1989. L to R: Renée, Matthew, Michelle, and Laura (seated).
Moog Family Archives.

44. Moog enters the mainstream.
Reproduced with permission of Punch Ltd.

45. Honored on Hollywood's RockWalk on Sunset Boulevard.
Robert Knight Archive/Getty Images.

46. Bob shows Clara Rockmore his Series 91 theremin (model B), an homage to Leon Theremin's U-shaped design.
© 1993, Steve J. Sherman/Nadia Reisenberg & Clara Rockmore Foundation.

47. Bob with his hero, Leon Theremin, Stanford University, 1991.
Renée Moog/Global Village Photography.

48. Big Briar Series 91 theremin models. L to R: 91A (cabinet design inspired by the RCA theremin), 91C, 91B.
Bob Moog Foundation.

49. Smudging the new Big Briar facility with an eagle wing and a seashell of burning herbs, 1994.
Renée Moog/Global Village Photography.

50. Ileana, Miranda, and Bob, 1994.
Courtesy Ileana Grams-Moog.

51. Bob among the brotherhood: *Spirit in Fight: A Spring Gathering of Men*, May 1997. Facing camera on right: Rick Krebs.
John Waterhouse/Courtesy Ileana Grams-Moog.

52. Back to the Future: Moog Cookbook. Brian Kehew and Roger Manning.
Vicki Berndt.

53. The *moogerfooger* analog effects pedal.
Courtesy Moog Music, Inc.

54. The author with Bob, 1997.
Linda Kobler.

55. The inventor of the Moog Synthesizer is fascinated by an earlier groundbreaking keyboard—the Baroque clavichord—at the home of the author, 2000.
Albert Glinsky.

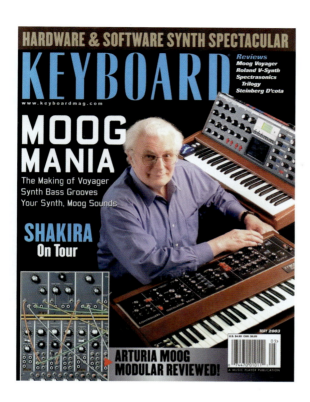

56. May 2003: Celebrating the release of the Voyager.
Courtesy Keyboard Magazine.

57. With Mike Adams, president of Moog Music, Inc.
John Warner/Courtesy Moog Music, Inc.

58. Bob Moog at his last public appearance, 2005. "Where do ideas come from?"
Courtesy University of Alaska, Anchorage.

of Uncertainty"—both programmable so the modules could be turned loose to do their own thing.

Composer Suzanne Ciani, who would go on to become the most active player and promoter of Buchla instruments—using them in classic commercials for major brands like Coca-Cola—also became known for her enthralling live, interactive performances on them. Working with the random controls in a sort of spontaneous dance with the instrument's interfaces, she created collaborative improvisational works before the very eyes of the audience. And sometimes she used the random functions to put the Buchla in the spotlight alone: "It can produce an ongoing composition just by interacting with itself," she explained. "The piece will actually generate itself and be interesting and ongoing and never the same and always musical. I did an installation at the University of California, Berkeley, Art Museum, where I put the Buchla in the museum and had it play for weeks."[2]

Bob's modules could also be rigged for the same, spontaneous kind of music. On the East Coast, the composer and professor Joel Chadabe, at the State University of New York at Albany, installed a huge array of Moog modules in 1969 which he called the CEMS (Coordinated Electronic Music Studio). Along with standard modules, Chadabe used a digital clock and a bank of eight customized Moog 960 sequencers built by Gene Zumchak that could run in any combination. Using CEMS in one of his compositions, Chadabe recalled, "I was able to program a pseudo-random process sufficiently complex to automate an entire composition. . . . I simply listened while the system was producing sound and while it was deciding what sounds to produce."[3] In another work, he himself collaborated with the system, like Ciani, using a joystick to control the modules and several sequencers, while the sequencers were randomly controlling the same modules: "Because I was sharing control of the music with the sequencers, I was only partially controlling the music, and the music, consequently, contained surprising as well as predictable elements. . . . I was, in effect, conversing with a musical instrument that seemed to have its own interesting personality."[4]

The question of who was in charge could become an aesthetic one. When Morton Subotnick released his second solo Buchla album, *The Wild Bull*, in 1968, the composer Tod Dockstader, reviewing the LP in *The Musical Quarterly*, wrote, "The Buchla has a sequencer at its center, and this device can be set up to produce complex, automatic rhythms, like a syncopated motor you start up and let run. . . . This is a case of the machine influencing the music—a continuing problem in electronic music, which depends so heavily on machinery for its composition and performance... the only thing that bothers me about this work: how much is the Machine, how much is the Man?"[5]

After Zinovieff unveiled his PDP-8 on stage, Victoria lost patience and insisted Peter find a way to bankroll his research. His solution was to found Electronic Music Studios, Ltd. (EMS) in 1969 to support his experiments, enlisting David Cockerell, an engineer, and Tristram Cary, a composer, as business partners. Merely as a practical way to raise cash for research, the three sketched out specs for a commercial synth—something small, compact, and cheap that might appeal to schools as a teaching tool. Zinovieff specified the functions, and after a few attempts, Cockerell designed the "VCS3"—"Voltage Controlled Studio no. 3," a fully portable modular synthesizer in a small L-shaped wooden cabinet.

The VCS3 owed much to Bob's ideas. Cockerell admitted that the voltage controlled oscillators and filters he'd already made for Zinovieff's studio were based on Bob's 1967 article in *Electronics World*, and he'd also learned about the concept of exponential control from Bob through the same generously detailed feature. Cockerell confessed that even his VCS3 filter was based on Bob's original ladder filter design that Bob had outlined precisely in a 1965 AES talk—before he'd applied for a patent—and again in his 1967 *Electronics World* article. Cockerell's ladder filter used diodes instead of transistors, though, saving money and conveniently circumventing Bob's patented design.

Everything about the VCS3 was miniaturized, so instead of patch cords, Cockerell designed a small matrix of 256 holes to insert pins that marked junctions where inputs and outputs met. The instrument had another unique feature: a built-in amplifier and speakers.

The VCS3 came dangerously close to preempting Van Koevering's plans for the educational market, and the hopes Bob's engineers had for a portable synth. Priced to help Brits avoid the steep cost of a Moog or a Buchla—with even heftier numbers after British import duties—Zinovieff and his partners offered their tabletop synth for £330 (about $794 in 1970), close to Van Koevering's "magic retail." The instrument didn't come with a keyboard—there was an optional one that could sit alongside it—and its oscillators tended to drift out of tune. Yet with its attractive price, the VCS3 took off in England. For a product intended only to fund research, the popularity of the instrument surprised its creators. After its debut, the instrument began appearing on rock LPs, starting with the November 1969 release of the Moody Blues' *To Our Children's Children*.

By the time Bob encountered the VCS3 at MENC in Chicago, it had easily penetrated the educational market—about 90% were sold to schools. The U.S. import price came to about $1,200 without a keyboard, but it was still the cheapest synth on the market. In America, the instrument was nicknamed the "Putney," for the South West London district where Zinovieff had his home studio.

A *Chicago Tribune* music critic who saw the Putney at MENC borrowed one for a test run, calling it "the English mini-car synthesizer line."[6] He described how he and his 13-year-old son easily got it up and playing on their dining room table for hours of fun, making sounds simulating fog horns, jets, industrial noises, and chirping birds. For Bob, the critic's use of the prefix "mini" was a telling brush with the lurking competition that augured trouble for the Mini Moog if its debut were delayed any longer.

Bob's engineers in Trumansburg were restless. "We'd saturated the world with modular synthesizers," Hemsath recalled, "and sales were just pitiful."[7] Scott remembered, "We were operating as if we were in bankruptcy. We had no credit to purchase materials."[8] Summit Distributors of Buffalo, in fact, was the only supplier willing to sell to R. A. Moog. Terms: 150% in advance. Things were so desperate that Scott remembered the staff pulling discarded transistors out of the wide cracks in the floor to build new products. "So we were sitting around in an engineering meeting and wondering, 'what are we going to do next?'" Hemsath recalled. "And one of the other engineers looked over at my workbench and pointed to the Min A and said, 'Well, why don't we manufacture his toy?'"[9] Bob's skepticism remained the only impediment. Now time was running out, with the VCS3 already situated in the educational market.

It was easy enough for the staff to cheer for a portable synth. *Their* money wasn't on the line. The risk fell on Bob and Shirleigh because they'd personally guaranteed a large chunk of the business. Any new project—particularly a speculative one—would add another layer of liability. But without a solid product to carry the company into the future, there would *be* no future. In July, Scott recalled, "Somewhat reluctantly, Bob relented and allowed development to start."[10]

The change of heart came just in time. Bob could see his competitors gaining on him in his peripheral vision, nearly neck and neck. Most of them were slated to make presentations at the October AES conference. The AES had always been Bob's brotherhood—his tribe—but suddenly a pack of interlopers was crashing the party. It was crucial that he bring something new and daring to the conference. AES would be the deadline for completing the next generation Mini-Moog "C" prototype. In his desk notebook, Bob scribbled target dates: *September 11—finalize block diagram; October 2—finalize vectorboard; October 6—finalize mechanical package.*[11] The engineering team—Bob, Scott, Hemsath, and Hunt—set to work, using the B model as a template.

Readers who happened upon the July *Billboard* column about the development of a "mini-Moog" the size of a typewriter might have pictured the company as a polished team of scientists in white lab coats with pocket-protectors, hunched over their multimillion-dollar equipment. The pocket-protector image was spot-on, but the rest would have been fantasy. The denim-clad crew—three of the four were still in their twenties—put the C together with the spontaneity of a scrappy start-up. Yet in spite of it all, they'd wind up engineering a synth that would be prized for its sound—a quality owing a lot to the spit-and-chewing-gum grit of its origins.

"It happened the way it did," Scott recalled, "because we were in a hurry on a shoestring budget."[12] The work was exacting, everything hand-wired on vector boards. Each of the engineers took a portion of the circuitry to work on, streamlining Bob's original modular designs, simplifying them to their essence. Hemsath did the power supply, Hunt, the modulation circuitry, Scott, the filter, amplifier, and envelope generators, and Bob, the oscillators. Everything was made in-house, including the front panel that was laid out by the resident draftsman and etched and punched in the metal shop.

For the Mini C to stand out as a consumer synth, it would need curb appeal in display windows and on store shelves. A slick package was something only an outside design group could dream up, and in July, Bob hired the New Jersey–based furniture and industrial design consultants Warren-Friedman Associates to come up with conceptual sketches for the Mini-Moog case. The timing wasn't ideal: the agreement would sink the company a further $1,000 into debt.

Warren-Friedman's drawings were mostly futuristic: "White sculptured plastic cabinets that suggested computer terminals," Bob recalled, "gleaming multicolored panels, and strikingly shaped controls."[13] As Hemsath remembered, "Stuff that looked like it came off of space ships."[14] The renderings were passed around the company and shown to customers for feedback. One of the drawings was different, as Hemsath explained. It was "just this little wooden box with sort of slope-up electronics. And everybody without question said, 'yep, that little wooden box over there in the corner, that's it.'"[15]

In the end, the consensus wouldn't have mattered anyway since the company couldn't afford the slick, space age designs that required expensive injection molds. But the little wooden box could be made in-house from the same stock of walnut Bob had used for years in his modulars—a cache he'd acquired from a farmer and stockpiled in his barn. One Saturday morning, he and Hemsath met at the company shop with the Warren-Friedman sketch, took a rough guess at the dimensions, and glued up the first Model C case in a few hours. The base was plywood, the sides and top, solid walnut.

∼∼∼

The night before the AES conference turned out to be a repeat of the Jazz in the Garden frenzy as Bob scrambled to complete the Mini C prototype in his Manhattan hotel room. The October 12 to 19 event at the Hotel New Yorker would begin the next day, when he was on the line to pull the cloth off the Mini and deliver a paper with Hemsath: "Compact Performance Synthesizer Design Considerations." "Bob got enough of it working," Scott recalled, "to give a credible demo to a critical audience of audio engineering professionals."[16]

At the 2:00 session in the Terrace Room, a gaggle of newly anointed synth moguls stalked around smugly, itching for a turn on the podium to hawk their latest voltage controlled contenders, remotely aware of the man in the same room who'd laid the groundwork for their success.

"The Putney: A New Generation of Synthesizers," was presented by Alfred Mayer, the company rep for Ionic Industries, the US distributor for the VCS3. The blurb for his talk shamelessly bypassed Bob's legacy: "After a period of thirty years, the Putney Synthesizer arrives on the scene to make electronic music a broader-based field."[17] His paper pushed the instrument as a solution for schools.

Another contender in the school market was Electronic Music Laboratories, Inc. EML had been involved in education since 1967 as part of Project PEP (the Pilot Electronic Project in Music Education), a Connecticut-based program teaching students to compose music using voltage-controlled modules. Project PEP was funded by a U.S. Office of Education grant. When the government required a 200-pound minimum weight for the rudimentary modules in the program, to ensure students didn't make off with the units, the engineers simply loaded them down with cinderblocks. The instruments were a big classroom hit, and by 1970 EML had refined the systems into the first ElectroComp, a small, entry-level modular selling on the consumer market for $1,300. At the AES session, EML proved its bonafides with student compositions made on the ElectroComp.

Yet another presenter was an Ohio University research engineer who offered "A Low Cost Educational Music Synthesizer Concept," explaining how music students with no electrical engineering background had learned to fabricate a voltage control device that purportedly allowed digital control of frequency, modulation, filtering, and envelopes, and offered a cheaper alternative to what he called "expensive studio hardware"—hardware Bob's entire career had been erected on.[18]

For Bob, the deepest cut of all came from the newest intruder on the modular scene: ARP Synthesizers, by Tonus, Inc., a firm from Newton Highlands, Massachusetts, outside Boston. The company's presence at AES was particularly galling because ARP had been formed as a direct challenge to Bob's synthesizers.

ARP was named for the initials of its founder, Alan Robert Pearlman, an engineer with an audio electronics background, but no experience in the music business. Pearlman was born in Manhattan in 1925, and like Bob he'd had piano lessons and a ham radio hobby as a child. His senior engineering thesis at Worcester Polytechnic Institute in 1948 was a device that could trace the sound envelope of acoustic instruments. He thought of it strictly as a novelty, but he predicted that a serious marriage of music and electronics was coming.

Pearlman started his career outside of music, building solid-state analog circuits and doing contract work for NASA's Apollo and Gemini space programs with a company he cofounded in 1960, Nexus Research Laboratory, Inc. Unlike Bob, Pearlman was a savvy businessman and grew Nexus to an annual revenue of $4 million before selling it in 1967. While he was sniffing around for another venture, he heard *Switched-On Bach* and his dormant interest in electronic music was reawakened.

To gauge the state of synthesizer technology, Pearlman consulted Gerald Shapiro, a Brown University composer and professor. Shapiro showed him the University's Moog modules and described the painstaking process Carlos had relied on to assemble *S-OB*, scrap by scrap. Pearlman saw the tuning glitch in the Brown University Moog (he'd already heard it in Buchla instruments), and concluded that neither brand had the stamina for live performance. He disliked the Moog's tangle of patch cords and the Buchla's lack of a keyboard; he saw them as impediments to the performer, and vowed on the spot to devise something better.

Pearlman founded Tonus in 1969, figuring his Nexus work had positioned him to take on the synthesizer field. It would be much easier now: Moog and Buchla had done the grunt work of laying the technical and cultural paths for the synthesizer. All he had to do was move the starting line and sprint off from the latest technology, deftly investing his startup capital in simple "improvements." Bob, meanwhile, was mired in the debts of his own legacy, trying to dig out and get back in the race.

Pearlman recruited David Friend, a 21-year-old Yale music and engineering graduate who was so eager to get in on the ground floor that he walked away from his Ph.D. program at Princeton. By January 1970 the two were constructing a prototype.

That March, Pearlman attempted a wily maneuver: claiming Bob had infringed on one of his Nexus-era patents, he tried to leverage a deal. "Apparently Pearlman is very anxious to get a license to use our voltage controlled filter patent," Bob wrote Verne Siegel. "I think he is trying to bluff us by suggesting that he has a case against us." Pearlman insisted that his "Antilogarithmic Function Generator" was an element in Bob's VCO circuit. "He claims that the two circuits are equivalent because it all depends what you regard as ground," Bob wrote. "I say bullshit."[19] A patent attorney, he told Siegel, assured him that Pearlman had no case.

On April 11, *Billboard* announced the debut of the "ARP Synthesizer." The company called it a "second generation" instrument and claimed it incorporated "all the separate design advances in synthesizers over the last five years."[20] The synth soon became known as the ARP 2500. The instrument was a well-engineered modular system with many of Pearlman's promised improvements.

For the 2500, Pearlman threw out the patch cord jungle altogether and substituted it with a clean system of slider switches he called "matrix patching." He also cleared the hurdle of the tuning issue. "Even just turning on a light bulb in the room," David Friend pointed out, "could warm up a component in a synthesizer by a few hundredths of a degree, and that's enough to make it go out of tune." Thermal issues like spotlights on stages made the newer stable oscillators a must for live performance. Kingsley's Moog Quartet, in fact, often desperately resorted to nudging the calliope sound back into focus with a ribbon controller while they played. Pearlman's oscillator-stabilizing secret was a circuit he'd invented at Nexus—his "Temperature Compensated Logarithmic Amplifier." "So that overcame one huge issue with synthesizers," Friend recalled.[21]

Keith Emerson would have called the 2500 another "beast": its mammoth cabinet was over 3½ feet long and nearly 2 feet tall, and housed an entire system of 15 modules with an option of wing cabinets containing 8 additional modules each on either side. Up to two keyboards could be attached. The 2500's sound had a clear, distinctive quality and its network of possibilities rivaled Bob's best modulars in its creative potential. But it had its flaws: its bulk and weight made it difficult to move around, and at $20,000 for a full set of modules with all the trimmings—or an entry-level model starting at $8,000—it made Bob's most generously loaded systems look like a bargain.

Despite its drawbacks, though, the 2500 began making incursions into the university market. Within a year ARP had major academic clients. Gerald Shapiro called the synth "unquestionably the finest studio instrument that I have seen."[22] Recording studios began queuing up for the 2500 with early clients like Jimi Hendrix's Electric Lady Studios in Greenwich Village. A September 4, 1970, *New York Daily News* feature, in fact, mentioned that Hendrix's new ARP was waiting "on call" in the studio alongside his Moog.[23] Sadly, he'd never have the chance to use either one; in exactly two weeks he'd be dead.

If Pearlman's instrument was a challenge to Bob, his advertising hit R. A. Moog below the belt. The ads elevated the ARP to revolutionary status while bashing Moogs as outdated and inferior. In a full-page ad in the April AES journal, ARP declared: "If you would like to spend your time creatively, actively producing new music and sound, rather than fighting your way through a nest of cords... you'll find the ARP uniquely efficient.

P.S. The oscillators stay in tune."[24]

ARP advanced a second frontal assault on Moog in the October *AES Journal* released just ahead of the fall convention, striking Bob in another sensitive area he hadn't explored: digital control of analog synths, an inevitable paradigm shift about to transform the music industry. The ad proposed: WHEN YOUR COMPUTER LEARNS TO WRITE MUSIC, LET IT PERFORM ON THE CONCERT GRAND OF SYNTHESIZERS—THE ARP. The ad revealed that Paul Conly, one of Bob's old Lothar buddies, had programmed a digital computer at Harvard to compose music that was played back on the university's new ARP. The copy finished off with an appeal to songwriters, recording engineers, filmmakers, professors, composers, rock musicians, and, of course, "computers," and suggested, "You could use an ARP very soon."

On the last page of the same issue, R. A. Moog fought back feebly. An understated ad—just white block lettering against a black background, the words moving vertically down the page in shrinking font sizes—had a simple message: "THE MINI-MOOG IS HERE; THE CLASSROOM SYNTHESIZER IS COMING." Of course, the Mini-Moog wasn't "here" yet. It was still just a prototype, and the classroom synth was a daydream. The simple message in stark black and white assumed that the heft of the Moog brand would still carry the day—what more need be said? But the veracity of that assumption was about to be tested in a suddenly crowded field.

One week after his AES presentation, Bob was in London for an audio fair at the Olympia exhibition center with the Mini C under his arm. In Europe, the Moog name was famous and revered, especially in the UK. "When synthesizers are mentioned," a reporter for *Beat Instrumental* wrote, "the name of Moog is almost a definition."[25] Bob's host in London was Dag Fellner, cofounder of Feldon Recording, Ltd., R. A. Moog's new exclusive European distributor. At the Olympia Fair, Bob offered modular demos and gave two formal presentations. He couldn't afford to miss this trip for all the publicity it would offer. But he couldn't afford it, either. After Fellner took him to dinner at an Indian restaurant, he wrote Shirleigh, "That was the first solid meal I've had since Saturday nite." He admitted he'd been subsisting on a cheap local beer. "I've been living pretty much on Red Barrel, which is easy to do."[26]

In the Putney district, Bob got a first-hand look at the high-flying lifestyle of Peter Zinovieff, whose stately home sat on the bank of the River Thames, with a patio area that extended right up to the river's edge. A large white garden shed housed the famous EMS boutique studio. Immaculately arranged equipment, including two PDP-8 computers, ringed the room, with an oriental rug in the center. Bob scratched in his notepad, *Zinovieff—bright, energetic, scatterbrained guy in his early 30's. Wife is loaded.*[27]

While in England, Bob was introduced to Keith Emerson by Fellner during ELP's fall European tour, and the two hit it off. Afterward, Keith sent a test pressing of the group's soon-to-be-released debut album to Bob's hotel room. ELP was soaring after their Isle of Wight launch, with a September *Melody Maker* poll that voted them "Brightest Hope International."[28]

Before leaving for England, Bob had ordered his shop to make three more Mini Cs to lend out to musicians. The instruments went over well, but Scott remembered, "There weren't enough of them to stimulate a worthwhile demand. We needed to get more units into the hands of musicians and onto the stage to make potential customers aware of the Minimoog's existence."[29]

By November, just back from Europe, Bob was still extremely cautious about going into production, and unable to see the urgency despite the relentless advance of the competition. On his way out again for another trip, he authorized the engineers to make 10 more Mini C models as loaners.

But the moment he was through the door, the engineers conferred. Hemsath remembered the discussion: "The three of us thought, 'ten more?' Come on, now.' We decided, 'look guys, if we don't get this thing into production in a month we're all going to be out of a job—it doesn't make any difference what Bob says—I mean he could fire us, we're still out of a job.'" Scott figured Bob couldn't fire all of them. "It was the decision of the three of us back in the factory that, enough of the Cs—we're done," Hemsath explained. "Now we're going into production with the D. And we did. Independently of what Bob wanted."[30]

Bob had ordered 10 more perf board models, but the staff disobeyed and made printed circuit board versions of the circuits so the new model could finally be mass produced. It was easy because the circuit boards could be made in the company photo shop upstairs.

Except for the new boards, the D model was basically identical to the C, with a single addition—one that would set the standard for most portable electronic keyboards in the future. Hemsath remembered it as another "divine inspiration."

The idea came about because the first completed model D prototype, like the C before it, had two slide pots on the left keyboard cheek for modulation and pitch bending. Hemsath felt the slide pots were too sticky to wiggle a good vibrato with, and he looked for something better. For a solution he turned to one of his early inventions at the company: the two-axis 959 X-Y Controller that was an option in Bob's catalog. An aluminum rod, about the size of a cigarette, it was like a model airplane joystick, and could control two different parameters of sound at once. By using only one axis, Hemsath reasoned, the rest was simple: "Replace the joystick with a plastic wheel. That was the birth of the wheel-type pitch bender. Another ten-minute invention from start to finish."[31]

The final design elements of the pitch and modulation wheels were a spur-of-the-moment contribution from Bob's purchasing agent, Don Pakkala, a former tool and die maker. Pakkala machined the first wheels out of plexiglass and added a finger notch on top and a spring mechanism that returned the wheel to center position after it was released. "The wheel most honestly can be said to be an invention of Don and me together," Hemsath explained.[32]

While the Mini D construction party was roaring on in Trumansburg, Bob was in New York City tracking the scent of big money. "We tried to get big corporations to buy the business out," Shirleigh recalled. "We had, like, $240,000 of personal debt, 'cause all the business debt was ours. And no business, big or small, was interested in taking that, paying it off, and then starting at ground zero."[33] Bob and Shirleigh also owed over $11,000 in personal income taxes, and Shirleigh remembered that the IRS was threatening to repossess their house and car, and garnish wages.

"One thing that I never did learn," Bob admitted, "is how to present myself as an entrepreneur to people with money. And towards the end I tried desperately to raise money and everybody shook their head and said, 'I don't see the potential, I don't see where it's going.' Other people that I know were able to just paint this incredible rosy picture with the sun coming up in the east, and peoples' wallets jump out of their pockets, you know, and they throw the money at you. I was just the opposite—I just could not do that. I was put in touch with some pretty high-powered people. One of them was George Barrie."[34]

George Barrie was the owner and CEO of the perfume and cosmetics firm Fabergé, and had contacted Bob about borrowing a Mini C—"extremely interested," Bob noted in his desk pad.[35] Barrie had bought Fabergé in 1964 for $26 million and later added the Brut men's cologne line, which he'd turned into an international bestseller. Barrie hung out with movie stars, lavished money and perks on celebrity endorsers, and started his own subsidiary film production company. He had a background in music and played several instruments, occasionally coauthoring songs with the celebrated songwriter Sammy Cahn. When he wasn't mixing his own perfume scents for the fun of it, he got together with a coterie of musicians for improv sessions. He was said to keep an electric piano on his private jet.

Bob came to Barrie's business office in New York for an audience with the CEO, hoping to make his case. "It was at one of these damn brownstones in midtown Manhattan," he recalled. "I arrived on the appointed day and 'Mr. Barrie will see you now,' and they took me upstairs to the second floor. And here's this huge room . . . and the room's got a desk in one corner and the entire rest of it is musical instruments. This guy, you know, when he felt like it, he'd just invite his friends in and they'd jam. . . . He shook his head, no, I don't think so, he said."[36]

Returning to Trumansburg, Bob entered the Main Street shop expecting to see the 10 Mini C models he'd ordered. "What we had produced were the first 10 D models," Scott recalled. "He was really opposed to it in the first place. He was upset that we had a palace revolution. He called us into a meeting, absolutely furious at us, pounding his desk, *'who the hell do you . . . you know nothin'* . . . . using language he had not learned from his mother. . . . demanding to know who the fuck made the decision to build the PC boards." Hemsath recalled, "We were just sitting there, looking at our fingernails, looking at the ceiling."[37] Nobody said a word.

19
The Island of Electronicus

"The synthesizer business has dropped off," Bob wrote Florence in March 1971. "The news media have strip-mined the area, the commercial musicians have burned up (and out) the layer of novelty, and our competitors (there are now eight) are battling us in prospecting for the next 'strike.' It's a grubby business now. I haven't done any engineering for four months." Then he turned his typically mordant sense of humor on himself: "It reminds me of a joke my Father-in-law tells:

JAKE: *A fine friend you are! You see me for the first time in five years, and you're not even interested in how I'm doing!*
SAM: *Geez, Jake, I'm sorry. How's business?*
JAKE: *Oy! Don't ask!*"[1]

When the smoke cleared after Bob blew up at his engineers, "he got over it," Hemsath recalled. "He realized that even though it was not *his* decision, it was still a *good* decision to produce these puppies."[2] "Production," of course, was a relative word. Bob was still gripping the reins tightly and hanging on to his skepticism: "I remember thinking, and saying to a lot of people, we're going to make a hundred of these and then we'll stop and see where we are."[3]

Beyond the financial risk, the whole affair was a conundrum for Bob—a philosophical crossroads that cut to the heart of who he was, and why he was even in this business. Jim Scott understood the dilemma: "Bob really wanted to advance music. His heart was in combining meaningful expression for artists so they could get effects that had never been produced before. He wasn't all that interested in making thousands of the same thing—ca-chunk, ca-chunk, ca-chunk. It was a strength because all these ideas came out of him; it was a weakness because you have to meet payroll."[4]

Bob was convinced that the Mini D was going into production before its time—it was really just a C prototype with printed circuits and two modulation wheels. He'd hoped the final production instrument would be a Model E, one with a touch-sensitive keyboard. But it was going to be what it was, and the D, despite everything, began to look like a classic in the making.

There was a kind of serendipity of mistakes that contributed to its distinctive sound. The instrument had no integrated circuits because Bob and his engineers didn't know how to design with them. But Scott explained that the discrete transistors in the Mini D allowed the circuitry to be driven hard with what he called "a fortuitous gentle distortion which enlivened the sound."[5] Hemsath agreed: "If you look at, say, an ARP synth, it was crisp and clean, and it was beautiful and sounded like water. Our instrument had punch to it, because we inadvertently overdrove the filter like crazy. Nobody knew that until a month or two before we started production, and then everyone said to leave it alone."[6]

The instrument was now officially called the Minimoog. Production of the first units began at a snail's pace, not enough to keep the company afloat. The first Minimoog, serial #1001, shipped to Walter Sear on November 20, 1970—poetic justice that he received the first production model synth, "the size of a typewriter," after he'd been kept in the dark about it.

But the Minimoog would be up against more competition than Bob had realized. Beyond ARP, Putney, and ElectroComp, a new "battling" competitor turned out to be someone who'd defected from his own ranks. One of his engineers was conspicuously missing from the Minimoog team. Gene Zumchak had clashed on and off with Bob over the 960 sequencer he'd built for the company, a standard module that was sold to countless customers over the years. Borden remembered that Hemsath would complain to Bob about the circuitry, Bob would confront Zumchak, and Zumchak would become defensive. "Over a period of time," Borden recalled, "Bob and Gene developed a very contentious relationship."[7] And Zumchak had hardly endeared himself to Bob after he'd taken it upon himself to construct the Synthesizer 10, along with being the loudest staff voice agitating for a portable synth, a perennial hot button issue with Bob. In the spring of 1970, Zumchak was fired.

For Bob, the timing of Zumchak's termination was unfortunate, given Gene's familial connection to Bill Waytena and his inside knowledge of Bob's work. Before Zumchak left, in fact, he'd taken a key souvenir with him: a Moog synthesizer he'd purchased with cash. He recalled, "Waytena says to me, 'Can't you build one of these things? I've got engineers in Buffalo; we don't need Moog. We can make our own. Just come to Buffalo.'" Gene admitted, "I knew what Moog did. I had all his schematics and stuff. I had his circuits. So we could steal what he was doing. So eventually I said, 'ok, I'll come.' "[8]

Waytena's manufacturing plant in Williamsville, New York—a village on the outskirts of Buffalo—was the site of his latest project, a business incubator he called Venture Technology, Inc. He'd started it with an assistant—a young engineer named Tom Gullo, whose sunny disposition was the perfect foil to Waytena's irascible nature. Gullo worked under Waytena at Kistler for seven years as an electronics packager and circuit designer. Waytena kept Gullo around to do his bidding in everything from engineering assignments to moving equipment.

Waytena began Venture Technology with no resident companies or employees, just a rented property on Academy Street in Williamsville that he outfitted like a party no one would show up to. With Gullo's help he furnished an empty building with 25 used desks, workbenches, lathes, and machines, and bought a government auction station wagon as the "company car." In mid-1970, Venture's first project began with Pro-Tek, a company Waytena started to make safety curtains for punch presses. When Zumchak arrived, Waytena added a second company under the same roof to make inexpensive classroom and consumer synths.

Back in May, while Waytena was giving Bob the runaround, he'd brazenly gone ahead and registered the name "Moog Electronic Music, Inc." But now he couldn't use any name connected with the Moog brand, and on October 1, 1970, he amended the Certificate of Incorporation to change the company name to "Musonics, Inc."

Musonics and Pro-Tek were bare bones operations, just four people rattling around in the huge Academy Street facility: Waytena, Zumchak, Gullo, and a machinist named Arkansas, who everyone called "Arky." Waytena found every chance to cut costs. None of the staff was being paid, and once when Zumchak protested, Waytena told him to sign up for unemployment. The skeleton workforce was subsisting purely on promises. "I was a young, junior guy there," Gullo recalled, "and Zumchak was a relative of Waytena, so, you know— 'we're gonna start a company, it's gonna be bigger than General Motors, and we're all gonna be rich.'"[9]

In September 1970, after holding out for over a year, Zumchak finally had the chance to design the synthesizer he'd dreamed of. Gullo would assist him. But the whole project reeked of hubris on Waytena's part, to think that his little squad could suddenly compete on the same playing field as Bob Moog.

The new instrument was analog, but Waytena knew Zumchak's expertise was in digital and he imported a former Kistler engineer, Fred Reinagel, as an analog coach to stand over Gene and advise him. "I learned about analog, not from working for Bob Moog for a couple years," Gene recalled, "but working for Fred Reinagel for a couple months."[10] Gullo laid out the circuit boards for the synth, packaged the electronics, and designed the case.

Zumchak hoped to get the credit for the instrument, right down to what it would be called. In the tradition of naming a synth for its inventor—like the Buchla and the Moog—the new instrument was slated to be dubbed the "Zummy." But when Waytena heard his kids call Zumchak "crummy Zummy," Gullo recalled, "he said, 'Well, they're gonna call this instrument the Crummy Zummy.' So that was the end of it."[11] Instead, the synth was christened the "Sonic Five," designated with the Roman numeral V. There were no previous models I through IV, but "Sonic V" had a certain ring.

Cosmetically, the Sonic V looked strikingly like the Mini B, with a walnut cabinet Gullo designed that slanted back. It shared many functions with the B, and Zumchak loaded it with extra features like built-in speakers, and a "duophonic" keyboard that allowed two notes to be played simultaneously. Zumchak also tackled the matter of oscillator drift with a fixed-temperature heated chip—the UA726—instead of the transistor scheme Bob had always relied on. The matched transistor pair chip would wind up as a standard component in a couple of Moog models in the future. All around, the Sonic V was poised to give the Minimoog a run for its money.

～～～

Back in Trumansburg, with every penny needed to keep Minimoog production up and running, the company continued to be plagued by spongers and schemers who ate up resources and time. Eric Siday—with his luxury suite of rooms in Manhattan—let unpaid bills linger for months. Bob had to swallow the sales tax and work out a system of monthly installments just to induce him to cough up what he owed. "We do have to borrow money on unpaid invoices like yours," Leah Carpenter admonished Siday, "and it is very costly."[12]

Paul Bley still hadn't paid a cent on the rental equipment he and Peacock had hauled away in Trumansburg over a year earlier, even after his Town Hall concert, and a second 1969 event at Philharmonic Hall. He'd also used the modules in recording sessions with Annette Peacock for their LP, *Revenge: "The Bigger*

The Love The Greater The Hate." The two were happy enough to pontificate in a July 1970 *DownBeat* interview on how they were seasoned experts on the Moog, but Bley refused to come to the door when Walter Sear finally showed up at his place to impound the instrument. "Bob Moog picked up a dead-beat," Sear groused to a lawyer. "This guy is a real operator."[13] Bley finally surrendered the instrument, but he wasted no time in moving on. A November 1970 *Billboard* notice reported that the "Paul Bley Synthesizer Show" was finishing an extensive European tour, and noted, "Bley uses the ARP synthesizer."[14] The jazzman had figured out a fresh angle. In December, *Billboard* revealed that he was now the "General Manager" of Synthesizers Inc., a new exclusive ARP distributor for the New York tri-state area.[15]

Sear, in the midst of helping Bob recover the modules from Bley, felt like he and the other sales reps were being taken for granted. While Moog management persisted in kowtowing to scofflaws, Sear, who'd been working faithfully with Bob for years without a formal contract, was owed more than $19,000 in commissions and had only seen $1,000 of it in two years.

With little cash flowing in, and not enough to pay out the company's obligations, Bob's anxiety escalated in January 1971 when Herb Deutsch threatened him with a lawsuit. The dispute was over an ambitious educational plan Bob had concocted the year before to impress Waytena—a pilot electronic music program for schools called Project Pulse. Herb, assuming, perhaps as everyone did, that R. A. Moog had deep pockets, had extracted a promise from Bob for specially designed equipment and a hefty fee for himself to stake out "exclusive regional rights" as the educational consultant for Project Pulse in schools from Maine to Ohio.[16]

Bob soon realized he had no time for the undertaking, and his nearly empty coffers couldn't have supported it anyway. Herb found himself out in the cold, even with Bob's signature on a binding contract. Unlike ElectroComp's Project PEP, with its generous government funding, Project Pulse was just another noble idea, lacking a pulse, destined to drive Bob's operation into further penury. "In lieu of suit by me," Herb wrote Bob, "it is necessary for the relationship between R. A. Moog, Inc. and Herbert A. Deutsch to be redefined."[17] In an uncharacteristically detached tone, he laid down his intentions and demanded restitution with an itemized list that included modular equipment, a Minimoog, and monthly installments of cash—all with specified dates of delivery.

Despite a modest blip in sales from small batches of Minimoogs inching out the door, it was looking like the end of the line for R. A. Moog. Things were at an impasse. "We were unable to reduce our debt," Bob recalled, "and we were unable to raise capital."[18]

Bob started grasping at straws. In a desperate move in late January, he assembled a resume for a teaching position. He detested the idea of teaching, but he'd been able to supplement his income in the past with a course he taught at Cornell called "Electronics and Music," during the 1969–'70 academic year. It only paid $2,500 for the full-year course, but at the time he couldn't afford to turn down the money. In his newest feeler, he argued his case in an earnest appeal to academics: "The problems of circuit design are of particular interest to me. My own professional activities in this area have been extremely fruitful, and I believe I can offer students the benefits of my experience and insight in a 'circuits' course."[19]

Professionally, Bob was backed up against a wall. "It was very tempting then to pack it all up," he recalled. "In fact, not only pack it all up but throw it in the garbage and declare bankruptcy—but we didn't."[20]

In early February, Bob picked up the phone. "He came to Waytena," Gene Zumchak remembered, "and said, 'I give up. I can't exist without money.'"[21] For Bob it wasn't just a sellout of his company; it felt like a personal sellout. But there were no other alternatives and it was worth one last try.

The timing was fortuitous: Waytena had been on the march in the school market with the first 100 Sonic Vs, but he'd found the synth had no traction with educators. Tom Gullo had taken the instrument to the NYSSMA conference and didn't have much luck: "I remember approaching some 55-year-old school teacher to explain what this instrument was and you could just read on her face, she wanted to scream and run away."[22] Part of the problem was that nobody recognized the Musonics name. In the end, the Moog trademark was worth more than Waytena had given it credit for, and now he was willing to come back to the table with Bob a third time. Despite both men's antipathy toward each other, each needed the other if they were to keep going in the synth business. There was no question, however, that Waytena had the upper hand.

Waytena proposed to bail out R. A. Moog to the tune of $250,000. It wasn't an injection of new capital to grow the company; it was just enough to pay off Bob's debts. In return, Waytena would extract a heavy price from Bob. In a preliminary agreement on March 6, 1971, Bob would have to sell his controlling interest in the company, turn over all his shares of Moog stock to Musonics, and become Waytena's employee.

Waytena wasn't reaching into his own pockets to pull this off. His plan was to raise the money by selling shares. Bob recalled, "He had his group of investors—doctors and lawyers, various businessmen and accountants, and would make them part of every deal he did. You know, get five thousand from this one, five thousand from that one, get a quarter million dollars to go into something, and in two years it would double and these people were happy as clams."[23]

The new agreement allowed Waytena 12 weeks lead time to see if he could line up investors before he'd be willing to commit to the deal—another delay that would keep Bob in limbo.

The day after Bob put his hand to the preliminary agreement, he was at Caesar's Palace in Las Vegas fulfilling a long-standing invitation to speak at the Twenty-first Annual University for Presidents. The man who was about to sign away the presidency of his own business would be addressing a gathering of young, successful presidents. The event was run by the Young Presidents' Organization, an elite international society for CEOs who'd headed their companies before the age of 40. Bob was out of his depths: he'd never achieved the minimum YPO membership criterion of annual sales over $1.5 million. His talk, "Sounds of the 70s," was illustrated with audio examples. Two weeks later he was in Los Angeles for a follow-up YPO conference on the theme "Mergers and Acquisitions." This time he wasn't lecturing; he was taking studious notes at a seminar entitled, "How it Feels to be Acquired."

~~~

Dave Van Koevering was raking in more money from his school shows than he knew what to do with. The Synthesizer 10 had boosted his audiences' enthusiasm, and, as he'd predicted on the night ride to Trumansburg, he'd found a major sponsor to underwrite everything. He was partnering with Glen Bell, owner of the Taco Bell fast food chain.

Bell was looking to boost traffic at his franchises, and hoped to tap Van Koevering's built-in audience of school kids. For Van Koevering, the perennial dealmaker, the proposition was music to his ears. He could name the number of school shows he wanted to do per day, and Bell would pay him generously for all of them—money was no object. Van Koevering's job would be to display the Taco Bell name on his trailer, and on stage, and to hand out flyers at the end of every show with clip-out coupons for a free taco. Bell owned nearly 200 restaurants across the country and expected Van Koevering to shower kids with coupons. Along with school shows, Bell asked Van Koevering to set up the Moog three nights a week at one of the restaurants and do a live performance to keep the coupon-wielding kids and their parents lingering for a second round of tacos.

On October 19, 1970, Van Koevering embarked on his odyssey. The *St. Petersburg Times* ran a human interest story: "Van Koevering will open in Fort Myers (for two weeks), go as far west as Los Angeles, north to Columbus, Ohio, and east to Greensboro, N.C."[24] The feature waxed laudatory over Van Koevering and Bell and their noble intentions of bringing music to schoolchildren everywhere. There was no mention of the coupons.

The restaurant gigs proved a big draw. "Man, the stores were flooded," Van Koevering recalled. "Their parking lot wasn't big enough, the store didn't have enough seats in it. I had to have a place near the garbage can and set my Moog up in the corner. And every kid that's in a rock band, they're all in there wanting to talk to me about buying a synthesizer." But Van Koevering found that many of the kids didn't care about exotic sounds. Typically, they'd tell him, "We don't have a flugelhorn in our high school band—could this play a flugelhorn? We don't have enough violins in our violin section."[25] It was the musicians' union nightmare all over again.

Still, Van Koevering made out like a bandit. "Glen's paying me $2,500 a week," he recalled. "And you gotta remember, this is in 1970—you could buy a new Cadillac for $6,000. I'm living in a brand new home that's custom built, for $9,000. And I'm driving a Cadillac! I'm saving $1,500 a week!"[26]

Van Koevering was helping sell tacos, but he soon tired of putting synthesizer medicine down with Mexican food. He just wanted to sell instruments. But it wouldn't be easy. For the synth to become a consumer item, the public would have to view it as a performer-friendly device sold in music stores, like other instruments.

When Van Koevering heard that the Moog company had just released something called a 'Minimoog,' he ordered one, sight unseen—the sixteenth instrument off the assembly line in Trumansburg. It shipped on February 1, 1971. When he showed it to Les Trubey, the owner of a major Tampa/St. Petersburg retail store, Trubey could hardly contain his excitement. His outlet, Central Music, sold pianos, Wurlitzer organs, and Martin and Gibson guitars, and he was certain the Minimoog was destined to be in every school, every Radio Shack store, and sold as a kit. Trubey was game to take the leap, but Van Koevering, a veteran salesman, knew he'd need to create a demand for the unknown instrument before there was any point in stocking units at Trubey's store. He'd have to show musicians and the general public that it was the next big thing in music, a must-have tool that would also fit their pocketbooks.

To get out the word, he'd have to proselytize—not a problem—and he needed a grand venue as his pulpit. Glen Bell had a suggestion. The Taco Bell magnate had recently taken an option on a property—the Tierra Verde Shopping Center—located on the small island of Tierra Verde, by the entrance of Tampa Bay, off St. Petersburg. The 43,000-square-foot complex had three main buildings, small shops, and parking facilities. One of the buildings lay empty, and Bell offered it on a short-term lease to Van Koevering to produce Moog shows for the general public. Van Koevering was in.

Tierra Verde had been in decline for several years. In its glamorous past, bandleader Guy Lombardo's Port-o-Call resort there had hosted legends like Frank Sinatra, Marlene Dietrich, and Mel Tormé. In recent years, there was a push to jump-start development on the island. Van Koevering figured that Tierra Verde, with its total landmass of little more than a square mile, was an ideal exotic location to hype the Moog as mystical and futuristic. The building he'd be leasing was a squat, one-story hexagonal structure with plate glass windows, somewhat like a car dealership. A few token palm trees and scattered bushes were studded around the outside amid an asphalt landscape.

Inside the 6,000-square-foot space, a vaulted ceiling of wooden beams arced high over a showroom floor, suggesting a contemporary church-in-the-round. Van Koevering built a small stage, like an altar, along one wall, with four white panels rising in back as projection screens. Speakers were hung from each of the 20-odd beams and connected to a high-octane sound system. "The amplifiers were like 500 or 600 watts per channel," he remembered, "and we ganged those up, a stack of them approaching 10,000 watts. And we could create 100 decibels at the front of the stage and 80 to 90 decibels at the back of the room. Your ears would bleed at 105. That was pure audio; there was no distortion."[27]

Van Koevering's imagination knew no bounds. His plan was to merge a mega-church spectacle with a psychedelic head experience. He called it "The Island of Electronicus." For a cover charge of $3.00, patrons could drive across the toll bridge for a clean-living re-enactment of a mind-expanding trip—a sound and light extravaganza driven by Moogs, with no drugs or alcohol. "It was a night club for teenagers, high school kids," he explained, "without the booze. We wanted parents to know it was safe for their kids to come; they're not going to be in a beer fight."[28]

Van Koevering promoted the show with 40 radio spots a day during drive time. The ads featured a deep-voiced narrator beckoning like a radio evangelist: *The Moog synthesizer . . . will play with your mind, with your body and heighten the horizons of your soul. . . . The Moog synthesizer is NOW! . . . . Come out to the Island of Electronicus . . . and share in this vast creative force. . . . It's here to stimulate your feelings, thoughts, and your love for your fellow man.*[29]

A poster in pink and magenta peddled the show with shades of the Trips Festival, promising, in warped psychedelic lettering, SWITCHED ON SOUNDS MOOG-NIFISANT and revealing Van Koevering and his stage partner as legends in their own minds: *Starring synthesists David Van Koevering and Tom Donovan, stars of television and international concert stage; three different live electronic shows each evening; buffet dinner; rap sessions; light and projection display—audience controlled; continuous Moog music from 7:00 p. m. until 11:00 p.m.*

Doors opened to the public on February 26, 1971. Inside—Van Koevering called it the "Moog Rotunda"—hundreds of beanbag pillows were scattered across the floor for the audience to sit on. Plastic chairs and nightclub tables arranged around the periphery welcomed the older and less adventurous; flickering candles on the tables cast green, red, and golden shadows. Van Koevering had no food license, so the advertised "buffet dinner" was a table stacked with free catered sandwiches, chips, and soft drinks that often ran out before the evening's last show.

On the left side of the stage, Van Koevering commandeered two Minimoogs—one for each hand—mirrored on the right side by his assistant, Tom Donovan, manning two additional Minis. Three more Minimoogs lined the front of the stage for patrons to diddle on at intervals during the program. Cabinetry in the center was stacked with a Synthesizer 10, a keyboard, a sequencer module with all its lights blinking, and three tape recorders, all capped by a small R. A. Moog banner. Two painted panels with psychedelic imagery framed either side of the stage.

The show began in pitch blackness. Van Koevering was the celebrant, and the Moog synthesizer the object of veneration—and, of course, the commodity for sale. His voice boomed: *You may never be the same again after hearing this music . . . we are approaching the dawn of a new musical experience. . . . All the sounds you've ever heard are like a second. The Moog is an eternity . . . Tonight we witness the dawn of a new enlightenment . . . seclude yourself now and let the music sweep you away and into the dawn. Seek to become newly aware of yourself, the world of nature around you, the people near you.*[30]

Van Koevering had written an original overture called *Sunrise* that started in the dark, with coordinated lighting cues that progressed with the music. "We gave them the experience of the sound of night," he recalled, "the cool, cold wind. . . . the night sounds of the animals and crickets, a coyote way in the distance. . . . then this 3-toned chord would begin, then it became a 5-, an 8-, a 12-, then a 20-note chord. It would crescendo up to the brilliance and brightness of sunrise. By the time it got to the crescendo, and the lights came on, everybody had their mouth open. It was almost like a worship. We'd have five minutes of applause."[31]

Before intermission, Van Koevering rolled out his tour de force: "We could do a motorcycle going left to right around the room," he recalled. "That's two Minimoogs. It was across 25 speakers or whatever the number of beams were. . . . You'd hear that motorcycle go around the room. We'd start a four-cylinder sports car up, an MG, and it would go the other way. It would squeal the wheels through four speeds as it shifted gears and we'd do that with another two Minimoogs. . . . Now you have two Minimoogs doing the sports car and two doing the motorcycle going the other way. And you'd pick up the speed—we had foot pedals for volume controls. You'd hear eeeeeeeerroooooommmm. . . . And around the room they'd go. And you'd hear this terrible screech of brakes and this horrendous crash—and a hubcap would roll out in the middle of the room . . . It'd go blub-blub-blub-blub . . . . blub . . . . blub . . . . .blub . . . and it would stop. And then you'd hear steam and dripping water."[32]

To hook audience members on the synth drug, Van Koevering involved them as performers in the show. He'd put Beatles songs or other hits on the house system and coax patrons down to play along on one of the Minimoogs at the front of the stage. All three instruments were often in use at the same time. Van Koevering listened through earphones and if he liked what someone was doing, he'd shine a spotlight on them and pump their instrument through the house PA system. "And I didn't care what they did," he admitted, "but if they came back a second night, they'd already learned something. And at the end of 3 or 4 nights, I'm going to ask them to buy this thing.

The purpose is to sell every musician that gets there a Moog. So we explain through the show what it is we're doing—all of these effects, we can explain them—and the kid gets the idea 'this is simple.' "[33]

Van Koevering placed cardboard overlays around the switches and knobs on the Minimoogs, with marks indicating settings for sound effects or specific instrumental clones like flute or saxophone. By lining up the controls with the labeled positions, players trying the instrument could adjust waveforms or change the filter settings instantly. "So the overlays made the guy perceive that he could do this," Van Koevering explained. "Whether he did it or couldn't do it wasn't the point. If you get him touching it, he will fall in love quickly, because he's never heard the power of this room, with him playing the synthesizer along with some song of the Beatles he already knows."[34]

While all this was going on, other patrons were busy concocting their own light shows. Colored fluids could be dropped into trays of oil on tables and mixed to make patterns. Hitting a switch set the table vibrating in sync with the music that was coming from a 15-inch speaker bolted to the bottom of the table. The jiggling images in the trays were beamed onto the wall panels above the stage with an overhead projector in a rudimentary light show of psychedelic patterns. The Trips Festival it was not.

Tuesdays through Saturdays, three shows daily drew up to 800 people a night. For those who showed up again and again, Van Koevering sold a special one-month pass that came with an honorary "staff badge," drafting the bearer as an unpaid vigilante to keep an eye out for trouble. But the one-monthers often made some trouble of their own. Van Koevering remembered a stunt where they repeatedly tossed a kid into the ceiling rafters with a stretched parachute, like a trampoline. "I don't know what my insurance claim would be if I had an insurance man look at it," he recalled, "but the kids were having a ball."[35] The *St. Petersburg Times* reported a typical attendee's reaction to the show: "You can get high on that thing but there are no after-effects and you want more."[36]

The after-effects of the Island of Electronicus didn't leave everyone on a sonic high. A practitioner of alternative medicine in Florida sent Bob a panicked letter about one of his patients, a certain Mrs. Billings, after she'd returned from the Moog Rotunda. Mrs. Billings, a yoga teacher and psychic, had apparently suffered interference in her "nerve-force fields," and required energy therapy to cure the pain and realign the electrical balances in her body. The practitioner theorized that her problems were caused by the purity of the synthetic waveforms in the electronic instruments—unlike natural acoustic instrument waveforms—creating a conflict with the waveforms in the plexuses of her body. He warned that the synthesizer, although it could be a "marvelous healing instrument," could also be a "potent weapon," and he cautioned Bob against continuing to sell it.[37]

20
I Bought Bob Moog

Sex was on everyone's mind. A January 1970 headline in the *Detroit Free Press* advised, "Getting Your Kicks in the 70s: Sex, The Moog and The Tube."[1] Bob's instrument was a prime stimulant in the New Age consciousness.

Two 1971 LPs linked it with the new sexual freedom. Mort Garson's *Music for Sensuous Lovers, By "Z"* was inspired by Joan Garrity's 1969 runaway bestseller, *The Sensuous Woman, By "J"*—a women's guide to the sexual revolution. Garson's album cover was even a takeoff of Garrity's waggish book jacket graphics. His light Moog pop score with percussive, dancey beats accompanied an undertone track Bob could never forget: "They got some guy who, in the record business, had put a microphone near his bed when he and his girlfriend, or wife, were fucking . . . and all her vocal sounds are recorded."[2] The 14 minutes of side 1 were titled, "Climax One," and the 12 minutes of side 2, "Climax Two."

David Reuben's 1969 international bestseller, *Everything You Always Wanted to Know about Sex*. . . . *but Were Afraid to Ask*—a manual for the sexual revolution—begat *Everything You Always Wanted to Hear on the Moog* . . . *but Were Afraid to Ask for*, a Columbia Records album by producers Andrew Kazdin and Thomas Z. Shepard. The LP of classical favorites sold 12,000 copies the week it was released in July 1971, and shot to No. 5 on *Billboard*'s classical charts by December, just below the indomitable *S-OB*, still parked at No. 1 after three years.

The Moog mystique was untouchable. No ARP, Putney, or ElectroComp could topple those four hip letters from their lofty pedestal, or disturb the instrument's status as a contemporary icon—a sonic mascot of radical '60s change. Even with modular sales slowing, Moog recordings were as current as ever. Anyone browsing the record racks would have thought R. A. Moog was a blue-chip company. The stream of LPs kept coming in 1971: *Gandharva* by Beaver and Krause; Popol Vuh's *In den Gärten Pharaos*; ELP's *Pictures at an Exhibition*; *Switched-On Buck* (Moog arrangements of country hits by Buck Owens); Sun Ra's *The Solar-Myth Approach, volumes I & II*; *Short Circuits*

Switched On. Albert Glinsky, Oxford University Press. © Albert Glinsky 2022.
DOI: 10.1093/oso/9780197642078.003.0020

(Moog settings of classical works by the American synthesizer pioneer Ruth White); and Mort Garson's *Black Mass Lucifer*.

Dave Van Koevering was still holding forth five nights a week at the Moog Rotunda on the Island of Electronicus. He'd sold 24 Minimoogs—all he could get ahold of from the pokey Trumansburg plant that was pumping them out at a crawl. But the sales got the attention of Bill Waytena, encouraging him to get going and finalize his option to buy R. A. Moog. It was really clear to him now that the only way he'd succeed in the synth business was to attach his company brand to the magic Moog name. On May 25 he filed an amendment to the Certificate of Incorporation for Musonics, Inc., registering a new name: Moog Musonics, Inc.

Three days later, at Waytena's lawyers' offices in Buffalo, the parties gathered around the table for the closing: Bob and Shirleigh, John Huzar, Waytena, two of his lawyers, and Bill Kohler, the new CEO and chairman of the board of Moog Musonics. Kohler had a music background from Oberlin College and management experience from industry. The first order of business was official resignations, a process that laid bare the mom-and-pop armature that was propping up R. A. Moog: Bob resigned as treasurer and director; Shirleigh resigned as vice president, director, and secretary; and John Huzar resigned as director.

Waytena's agreement laid out the new normal. In exchange for the promised $250,000 to rescue the company, Bob was now an "Employee," and Moog Musonics was the "Employer." Bob was granted a three-year contract at an annual salary of $25,000, a steep tumble from the $42,000 he was currently paying himself. He'd also have to sign over to the Employer his only patent—his classic filter—for no compensation, and anything he'd invent or patent during his employment would belong to the company. Waytena also dropped in a non-compete clause: for one year after leaving the company, Bob couldn't develop or produce any inventions that would compete with Waytena's business.[3]

"Moog Company Is Sold," the *Ithaca Journal* announced in a headline on June 17.[4] The paper reported that the Trumansburg factory would continue to produce the Minimoog and modular equipment with its 20 employees, and the Sonic V would be marketed from the Williamsville plant with its 15 employees. Bob's new title would be "director of research and development."

Waytena's bailout didn't guarantee Bob's success, however. The Minimoog—Waytena's great hope—had been on display at the April 1971

AES convention, but it was facing a new rival: ARP's portable alternative to its hefty 2500, the ARP 2600. The analog, voltage-controlled 2600 was aimed at an all-purpose market: education, home, live performance, and professional studios. It wasn't quite the integrated compact instrument the Minimoog was, but it was still formidable. As a "semi-modular," it had both internal hardwiring connections and jacks for additional patch cord modifications. It consisted of a main unit and a separate keyboard, each with its own suitcase— together, slightly larger than the Minimoog. The 2600 boasted extras like two built-in speakers, a four-octave keyboard, a ring modulator, and spring reverb. It retailed for roughly $1,000 more than the $1,495 Minimoog.

Buchla's latest instrument was also on hand at the AES, but it was orphaned now after CBS Musical Instruments bowed out. Following an initial production run of the model 100 modulars, the company had opted to pass on Don Buchla's long-range goals and retreated to its safer, traditional fare like the Fender guitar line. The inventor was cast adrift now to produce his own instruments under the Buchla and Associates banner.

It was probably just as well—Don Buchla had little in common with the corporate polish of a CBS. To the contrary, as Suzanne Ciani observed, "Don always claimed that he was designing these instruments for himself, and he kind of begrudged, on some level, that he had to sell them to other people . . . he never popularized his instrument." Ciani, after graduating with a master's degree in music composition from UC Berkeley, had started working for Buchla and recalled, "I was proselytized by Buchla because I took on his vision very quickly, working there. And that vision was very different from what was happening on the East Coast with Moog. I rejected the Moog and adopted Don's vision of these instruments. The problem with the Moog was that it spoke to popular culture very quickly because of the addition of the keyboard. But it meant that the potential of this instrument was lost."[5]

Buchla's new studio shop in Oakland, like Bob's Main Street operation, had a homegrown ambience, but his unorthodox style carried over into his workforce. "There were maybe 12 of us at most," Ciani remembered. "They were a very alternative group—not people who were hired because they had a lot of technical expertise in engineering. They were people that Don liked. There was a girl who was an Indian dancer; there was a guy who was a Buddhist. I remember talking to him and saying 'You know what I really want? I want a Buchla! I can't wait till I get my hands on a Buchla.' And he looked at me and says, 'You know, you shouldn't have any *wants*. You're not supposed to have attachments; you're not supposed to covet anything.' "[6]

An adjoining room was a large, dark, cavernous space filled with blinking lights and continuous music made by Buchla's automatically running instruments. "There were speakers all over the place," Ciani recalled. "Part of Don's vision had to do with the spatial movement of sound, and there was a swing in there, big ropes coming down, with a big wooden seat. *You* moved through the space and you heard the music while in motion. It was a wonderful spatial, sonic experience. People got stoned and they did funny things."[7] Buchla was having fun. With no skin in the game now, he could be his own man.

But back east, in June, barely over the shock of selling his company, Bob was abruptly flung into the dog-eat-dog arena of music retailing when Waytena handed him his first assignment: he was to attend the 1971 Chicago NAMM show to hawk the Minimoog. Waytena's new vision for the company would force Bob to leave behind his theoretical and academic heart for the mercantile necessities of staying afloat in a crowded sea of synth competitors. It wasn't Bob's style, but he admitted that Waytena had a point: "As crass and unmusical as he was . . . he was probably able to look at it and see where it was going in two or three years."[8]

At the NAMM Music Expo in the gigantic McCormick Place convention center, Bob found himself in the midst of a fast-paced merchandisers' carnival of familiar, ready-to-play instruments. On display was ARP's newest offspring: the Soloist. Alan Pearlman had raced out ahead of his rivals with a small, cheap instrument for consumers who wanted to feel they were playing a "synthesizer," but needed something with a "just add water" simplicity. The ARP Soloist had none of the sophistication of the Minimoog—technically it wasn't even a synthesizer. It consisted entirely of 18 preset "instrumental voices"—ready at the flick of a switch—that mimicked instruments like flute, bassoon, trumpet, violin, tuba, saxophone, banjo, and harpsichord. But in the context of the NAMM show, it was perfectly sufficient—even intriguing. All that mattered was its instant appeal for home, church, or live performance settings.

The Soloist was a little take-it-home-in-a-shopping-bag instrument housed in a single flat rectangular case, slightly smaller and lighter than the Minimoog. The keyboard and controls were seamlessly integrated into the one-piece design—a forward-looking innovation with no moving parts, unlike the Minimoog's angled front panel that had to be folded up into position. Better than the Minimoog, the three-octave keyboard had touch sensitive functions like a finger pitch bend to make a sound "wail" or, with more pressure, make it "growl." The sounds could be adjusted for "bright" or "muted." The unit came with a smoked plexiglass music rack, an owner's guide, and the "*Soloist Solos*" *Songbook*. It retailed for around $1,000.

The Soloist was monophonic and designed to be placed on top of an electric organ so it could be played with the right hand while an accompanying harmony was played on the organ with the left hand. ARP called it a "One-Hand Band." The liner notes on its sample demo record ended with the snarky claim, "We are witnessing the coming of age of an exciting new era in music, the age of the synthesizer. Does anyone want to buy a used tuba?"[9] It was enough to make Bob's blood boil: the implication that the Soloist was a real synthesizer—which it wasn't—and at the same time, the bald-faced attempt to promote the replacement of musicians.

But the ARP people had pegged the NAMM crowd perfectly. They'd put together a slick demonstration of the Soloist, playing its single voice together with an organ—a sleight-of-hand to give passersby the illusion that the instrument could do it all. Bob dismissed it as "cornball, everyday, pop music."[10] But ARP had figured out how to give customers a good time, and Bob was blindsided by how well-thought-out the presentation was.

The music trade was still a fairly traditional industry, especially when it came to a genuine synthesizer like the Minimoog. Bob recalled that none of the musical instrument retailers knew what a synthesizer was. "Most of the dealers didn't know what to make of an instrument with words like 'oscillator bank' and 'filter' on the front panel. Retailers would pass our booth and ask . . . 'What's that?' . . . 'You expect me to sell that in my store?'[11] . . . 'How do you expect musicians to deal with something so technical, with all those knobs? Musicians don't do knobs!'"[12]

While ARP was busy entertaining people, the Moog booth seemed like rocket science by comparison. "What *we* did," Bob recalled, "was we showed them, 'This is the low pass filter here, and this is an envelope generator.' You know, these poor retailers would say, 'What do you do with this?' And we couldn't show them."[13]

The ARP Soloist was a symbol of how far the synthesizer's identity had strayed from Bob's modular building blocks—a sign that commercial interests were moving in on the last vestiges of the "new sounds" market with cheap, portable, dumbed-down, mass-produced devices under the hallowed name of the "synthesizer." The Soloist was little more than a miniature electronic keyboard with 18 synthetic instrumental sounds and some user-selectable effects. If this was where consumer synths were headed, and the course Waytena planned to follow, it would be a crisis of conscience for Bob. NAMM was more than just another trade show; it was the portal Bob was shoved through to the next phase of his professional life.

〰〰

Bob briefly returned to his roots when Van Koevering brought him down to the Island of Electronicus for a special event in his honor, a demo—almost a game show—that proved what a true synth like the Minimoog could do. "We started doing these requests from the audience," Van Koevering recalled. "We'd let them challenge us with any sound: How would you create a windshield being broken with a sledge-hammer? Or a horse running down a dirt road crossing a hard top. And you'd hear him run down the dirt road . . . then we'd change the filter and the timing. Then you'd hear the shorter sound as he went across the hard top. People would give us other things. The sound of a sewing machine or the sound of an animal."[14] Van Koevering arranged for the event to be broadcast live around the world for U.S. Armed Services personnel through American Forces Network radio.

Not long after, Van Koevering finally decided to call an end to his Rotunda shows, signing off with characteristic pomp: "I wish to announce that you've just witnessed the last concert, the last presentation, of the Island of Electronicus. I intend to shut the island down tonight. Tomorrow, we will pack the equipment, and I will take the MiniMoog to music stores worldwide."[15] Trubey had already taken the plunge back on March 3 and put a Minimoog on view at Central Music, likely the first appearance of a Minimoog, or any synth, in a musical instrument retail store. Van Koevering had convinced him now, in the spring, to form a partnership between VAKO and Central Music to stock Minimoogs for resale to a network of music dealers. Van Koevering would go on the road and scatter his seed widely, hoping to root the instrument with as many dealers as he could.

Until then, nobody had thought of a synthesizer as an off-the-shelf musical instrument—least of all, music dealers. The Minimoog was compact, but it still didn't look like anything you'd see in a retail music shop. Customers couldn't just turn it on and casually patter over the keyboard to try it out; the instrument would be mute until a salesperson walked them through all the stages of sound production to hear something they could make sense of. And the instrument wasn't cheap: for a keyboard that only played one note at a time, it could be difficult to convince people they were getting their money's worth.

As soon as school let out, Van Koevering, Becky, their two children, and the family poodle, Fifi, piled into Dave's big Cadillac Fleetwood Brougham and set out across the country for a three-month adventure. They'd be hitting every city where a music dealer might be talked into stocking a Minimoog or two. For each destination the drill would be the same: the family would move into a Holiday Inn where the kids could splash in the pool, watch TV, or go sightseeing with Becky, while Dave prowled the city for music stores.

Van Koevering's goal was to stay in a city until he snared a dealer. His sales tactics were finely tuned. He could play any angle on the spot, like a chess master with endless variations up his sleeve. But his game plan always began the same way: he'd browse the Yellow Pages, finger a particular store, drive over, and pop in. He'd start by wandering around, gradually engaging the owner in talk about the merchandise. He'd find out what kinds of customers the place served, and how receptive the manager would be to new products.

Once he had the dealer's ear he got right to the point: he was a musician who used a Moog in his show, and he knew Bob personally. Then he'd put the owner in a psychological headlock: "I'd give them the pitch that the Moog is going to put $50,000 in some dealer's profit next year, because he could sell a Moog a month—or two Moogs a month—and he could make $500 on a Moog. He's gonna make $50,000 next year if he says yes. If he says no, somebody else in his city is gonna get that $50,000 and I'm telling him that up front. I'm not gonna leave town until I have a dealer."[16]

Van Koevering baited managers by sowing anxiety: If others were signing on to this new wonder, how would it feel to be left behind? He'd tell them, "I got dealers in *this* city, *this* city, *this* city, *this* city . . . and I want YOU." The manager was being anointed. "I'm choosing *you*. All you gotta do is give me a little bit of support." The dealer was usually skeptical—where would he find a customer? But Van Koevering had an answer: *he'd* find the customer himself. "When I bring a kid in here," he'd insist, "I'm gonna have a deal, ready for you to close."[17]

Van Koevering knew just where he could harvest a customer. Every city had nightclubs and hotels with musicians; even the Holiday Inns where the family stayed had lounges with guest bands performing after hours. He'd scope out a nightspot to see if there was a good set of drums, a Hammond organ, a Fender-Rhodes piano, or a clavinet, and show up an hour before the sound check with a Minimoog to tempt the keyboard player. There was no time to explain oscillators and filters, but his shortcut worked like a charm: "I carried tape in my pockets with scissors and I'd put red tabs on a sound, green tabs on a sound, yellow tabs on a sound, and then the kid could start playing a song."[18]

Van Koevering got the keyboardist psyched up over the Mini and had him gleefully playing it on the evening's first set as if it were his brand-new axe. Between sets, Van Koevering would slip out—he often worked two hotels at once—and he'd drop his standard line: "I'd say, 'I'll be back for your second set but I'm working with a kid over here in the Ramada Inn and I got to go over there.' Then I'd pull the slow-blow fuse out of the Mini and tell him, 'I'm just going to take the fuse out because I don't want you to have a problem that you can't fix when I'm gone.' Now he can't play his Minimoog, and I've left the building, and the second set comes on. On the back of the Moog I put M-O-O-G with house number lettering like you put on a mailbox; it had this day glow stuff on it that the bright lights would pick up so everybody in the audience knew what it was. And somebody in the audience tells the waitress, 'bring me another beer—and tell the kid to play the MOOOG.' And the kid couldn't play it. When I get back he's upset. *Now* the kid knew—and the owner knew—that the kid needed to own a Minimoog."[19]

The next move in Van Koevering's hotel-music store dance was the triumphal return to the dealer: "I'd go back and I'd bring the customer with me and close the sale. And we would always lay the Minimoog on top of a combo-organ, or a piano, or an electric piano. And I'd tell the dealer, 'That guy's going to buy a synthesizer out of my Cadillac right now, or he's going to buy it from you. And all you got to do is sell that one—and *order one more*.' I didn't have to use closing technique; I didn't have to use pressure, because he's got his customer standing there." Van Koevering made sure to add in a carrying case and extras that brought the total to around $2,500. The only question now was where a kid playing at a Holiday Inn for chump change would find that kind of money.

Van Koevering's endgame was his pièce de résistance. When a customer balked, he persisted: "'If the owner of the nightclub doesn't recognize he's going to have to advance you the money, we recommend that your girlfriend request it from her mother.' The kid is always proud of that, you know, 'the girlfriend's mom really loves me!' He's got the long hair, and he's a bit macho, and he's a star. He's gonna buy this synthesizer and it's so complex—it doesn't have *one* musical term on it, it's all technical: modulation-this, and filter-that. And this wizard is dating her daughter! He's just Number One!" Van

Koevering was always ready with a credit application he'd picked up beforehand from a local company: "I wanted the dealer to know that this kid knows what he needs to do. And I would have an application for a $2,500 loan given to that girlfriend and let her go get the money—Mom will co-sign that thing! All you need is her signature. And that sold probably 1 out of 5 Minimoogs."[20]

Before he left a city, Van Koevering made sure the store had someone on the floor who could demo and sell the Minimoog. He'd stay two days, or two weeks, it didn't matter; he just had to be confident that he'd set something in motion that would continue. The first store he landed was in Gainesville, Florida: Lipham Music. Then it was on to Tallahassee, Montgomery, Jackson, New Orleans, Atlanta. He was obsessed. He could not fail. He remembered leaving Omaha once without having closed a deal: "I'm driving 70 miles an hour, headed for Lincoln—it might have been 2 o'clock, 2:30 in the morning—and I made a U-turn through the grass and went back into town, checked back into the motel and the next morning went back to the club. And I had to find a different kid, a different band, and I found the dealer that I already chose, and I went back and stayed until we had that dealer."[21]

As Van Koevering was writing up orders for Minimoogs, he was unaware that Bob's Main Street operation was in the midst of an upheaval. On August 31, the *Ithaca Journal* announced, "Last Month in Trumansburg; Moog Plant Is Moving to Buffalo Area."[22] Van Koevering didn't know about Waytena, or the sale of the company, and he didn't know Waytena was consolidating all Moog Musonics work at the Williamsville plant. The Trumansburg facility would be closed effective October 1. The decision to relocate, Leah Carpenter told the *Ithaca Journal*, was made because the Williamsville plant was more suitable for manufacturing and closer to good shipping facilities.

Van Koevering was caught off guard in Texas in the midst of his hotel-dealer dance. "I get a message from Les Trubey saying I needed to return a call to somebody named Bill Waytena. He says it's the man who bought the Moog Company. Les gave me a heads up that he's an S.O.B. because he was cursing at Les on the phone. Waytena thought he'd find me in an office, but I didn't have an office; my office was the front seat of a Cadillac and a fancy briefcase. So I get to a pay phone and call from the office of a dealer. Waytena says, 'You need to meet me at the airport in Atlanta in the morning.'"[23]

Van Koevering objected, but Waytena insisted: "You'll meet me in the morning at the airport or you'll never get another Minimoog." Van Koevering was stunned: "'Tell me why I can't get any more Minimoogs. My deal's with Bob Moog.' He said, '*I bought Bob Moog.* Bob is *my* man and he's going to do what *I* tell him to do because I am his money. And I'm going to tell *you* what *you're* going to do because I build the Minimoogs that you want. If you ever get another one you're going to meet me tomorrow morning at the airport.' And the bastard hung up on me!

"So I call Bob and he tells me the rest of the story. He said, 'We would not be able to fill your orders if I hadn't sold the company. We were out of cash.' And he's close to tears. So I drive from Dallas to Atlanta and I meet Waytena with his big cigar in a motel at the airport. He's obnoxious, he's arrogant, he's uninformed. He somehow thinks that if you go into a music store and put this thing in the store that people will come and buy it. He doesn't know that they don't want it, they don't understand it, and he doesn't know they can't play it. He said, 'I want to hire you.' I said, 'I'm not for sale; I'm not available. I have a company, I have a partner.' He says, 'You're out of business. Your company is S-H-I-T. You're nothing. Your partner is nothing! I understand he's your money. Now *I'm* your money.'"[24]

Van Koevering had to decide if selling Minimoogs and continuing to work with Bob was worth stomaching Waytena. It was the worst time to have his hands tied because David Friend was just one step behind him, placing ARP instruments with dealers in the same territories he'd just secured. By the middle of August, a music store in Orlando was already advertising an ARP demo.

ARP had also pulled off a marketing coup at several major New York City music stores. Sam Ash, the venerated music dealership, located on Manhattan's famous "music row"—the West 48th Street block between 6th and 7th Avenues—was mecca for the music business, and *the* big prize for any instrument manufacturer. Having your equipment stocked there was a sign your brand had arrived. The store was carrying the Minimoog, but it was the only retailer Moog Musonics had set up outside of Van Koevering's leads. Not long after the Chicago NAMM show, Bob paid a sobering visit to the store. In the window display he caught sight of an ARP 2600 sharing space with a Minimoog and a Sonic V. Next door, at the highly coveted Manny's Music, he noticed a Putney in the window, and another ARP 2600.

ARP's ascendance worried Bob. "They're pushing like hell," he warned Kohler, "and we will lose the professional market entirely if we don't watch out!"[25] The Sam Ash rep had leveled with Bob: orders were pouring in for the ARP Soloist, and customers loved the touch-sensitive keyboard. The Minimoog, he thought, was overpriced. He urged Bob to come out with a presettable organ-attachment instrument as quickly as possible, and explained that the really big market now would be for $400 synthesizers.

∿∿∿

After four short years at the farmhouse, the Moogs were about to be uprooted from their 52-acre paradise. It was particularly hard on Shirleigh. She and Bob had just started putting their mark on the property: the kitchen was remodeled, the orchard in the front yard was yielding its first fruit, the pond behind the house had been dug and equipped for swimming, and Bob had etched a heart into a concrete slab on the front walkway with his and Shirleigh's initials. The two loved to unwind in long country walks with the four children—"the Minimoogs," as Shirleigh often called them, or sometimes, "the First Moog Quartet"—and she'd started a crafts fair in her barn, an event that looked like it could be an annual tradition. Their pets—Karlheinz, the German Shepherd, named for Karlheinz Stockhausen, and Smokey the cat, who lived in the barn and had frequent litters—would have to find new homes.

Bob's staff was taken by surprise. Most of them opted to remain in Trumansburg and find other jobs, rather than follow the company the 150 miles to Williamsville. While everything was being packed up at the Main Street factory, one surprise box came in. Sun Ra had returned the Mini B without any warning or fanfare. "He took it to the Mohawk Airlines terminal in New York City," Bill Hemsath recalled, "and bought it a ticket to send it back to Ithaca as luggage. No box. Just the wooden case that looked like a suitcase. When it arrived at the Ithaca airport, they turned the case over and found a label that said, 'R. A. Moog Company, Trumansburg, NY.' They called us and we said, 'Yep. It's ours. Send it up.'"[26]

Things were coming down off Bob's factory walls, many telling the story of the do-it-yourself place where Jim Scott could hammer up a board if he needed a shelf, or engineers could toss carcasses of failed prototypes into the "graveyard" upstairs—the ashes the Minimoog had risen from. On the second floor, by Leah Carpenter's reception area, David Borden's arch sense of humor graced the walls with his taped-up cartoons. In one, Borden had the speech balloon over Bob's head saying, *SAVE MONEY. BUY A GAS SYNTHESIZER.*

As his cartoons were peeled off the wall, Borden saw the easy sense of humor that bounced freely around the factory slipping away under the new management. He remembered an endearing moment when Bob's trademark explosive laugh surfaced in a relaxed social setting: "We all went to my house and drank cheap Gallo wine for hours, and he became totally drunk. He and Steve Drews would talk about the meaning of life and music and stuff, and it sounded so ridiculous to me. And after a while I would interject—I would say, 'that's some pretty deep shit!' And he would get hysterical. And every time they would talk about something serious I would say that, and he would get hysterical again."[27] Bob recalled the evening: "After a while, all of us would get the giggles for about five or ten minutes, and then we'd bite our lips and then somebody would say, 'pretty deep shit!' Then we'd start giggling again, and we did that the whole night."[28]

The expression became a running joke, so much so, that Borden immortalized it in one of his cartoons on the Main Street factory wall. As the sketch came down on the eve of the move to Williamsville, its silly humor portended something weightier: in the drawing, a lone hand reaches up from under a quicksand pool . . . *GLUG GLUG GLUG GLUG* . . . A little man passing by declares, *THAT'S SOME PRETTY DEEP SHIT!*

PART V
AN APOCALYPSE NOW

21
The Gelatin Pit

"They used to get rid of bodies by throwin' them in the pits out there." It was a rumor Jim Scott heard from one of Waytena's associates: "Waytena hung out with some rather unsavory characters," Scott recalled. "They looked like retired Mafia hit-men and probably were."[1]

Bob's new workplace was a nightmare. Waytena's Academy Street facility, where Zumchak, Reinagel, and Gullo had birthed the Sonic V, was part of a complex of dilapidated nineteenth-century buildings, originally built as a gelatin factory. James Chalmers, a Scottish immigrant, had established the Chalmers Gelatine company there in 1872, supplying gelatin for desserts and photographic film for almost a century. But behind Chalmers' appealing product claims—a 1902 ad touted "cooling jellies" to "tempt the languid summer appetite"—the brutal process of extracting gelatin from ground-up animal parts still permeated the psychic air hanging over the property. "These buildings have the feeling of a haunted castle," Bob wrote Florence. "You can practically see the ghosts of the laborers shoveling stinking hides in the vast unventilated spaces."[2]

The building where bones, skins, hooves, and tissues of pigs and cows had been cooked to release their gelatin essence stood abandoned—a spooky, dank cavern reverberating with the echoes of an occasional visitor's voice. Gullo called it "something out of the dark ages."[3] A honeycomb of concrete pits was coated with decades of white residue from the lime baths the animal hides had soaked in. Around the pits stood large cypress wood vats where the parts had been boiled to filter out the gelatin. Wooden risers ran between the pits so that workers could stir the chemical soups.

The collection of old buildings included one where remnants of sewing machines remained from the days when parachutes were stitched there during World War II. There was a warehouse, a building housing the boiler, and a man-made pond out front as a water source in case of fire. The property sat just beyond the end of Academy Street and an elementary school, where the pavement trailed off into a dirt road, down a hill to the company's gravel and mud parking lot. "It was just a horror show when it rained," Dave Van Koevering remembered. "You'd slide all the way down the hill; you couldn't get out. They had to get a John Deere tractor with big high wheels to tow your car out of the parking lot."[4] The road at that point wasn't even a legitimate street; the buildings had no address, only a post office box number.

The main company building had a separate staff entrance where all employees—including Bob—punched a time clock on their way to the production and test areas. The pungent smell of cigar smoke lingered in the air from boxfuls of A&C Grenadiers that Waytena puffed through the day, despite the spurts of air freshener women in the front office fought back with. Ironically, Bob found himself sidelined at his own company and subjected to the same petty scrutiny as the lowest-ranking employee—even made to sign in and out every time he left the building on his lunch break. He told Florence he was "accepting the role of spectator. It's not much different than being a bat boy at a baseball game."[5] Shirleigh despaired to Florence, "The big $ man is not exactly a dream of a human being but the line was only 1 deep for takers."[6]

A half-mile from the plant, in suburban Williamsville, Bob and Shirleigh's new home lay along a nondescript street with parallel cement driveways marking off tidy front lawns. A requisite tree poked up occasionally from a flat landscape. "This is your nephew, writing from the heart of American Dream Suburbia," Bob reported to Florence. "The people across the street keep track of us, right down to using binoculars!" The area was a half-hour's drive from Buffalo, but only about a mile from the airport. "When we first moved in," Bob told Florence, "people predicted that we wouldn't hear the planes after a while, - and they were right."[7]

The new family home, at 70 Melrose Road, was a small Cape Cod, slightly larger than Bob's childhood home in Flushing, on a shallow, one-third-acre property—a sobering adjustment from the 52-acre luxury of the Trumansburg farmhouse. But Bob and Shirleigh were indefatigable, squeezing in a bountiful vegetable garden at the far end of the backyard, lavishing on the cow manure. "Needless to say we're not happy to leave T'burg," Shirleigh lamented to Florence. Emotionally they remained tied to the Trumansburg home and the Arcadian life they relished, hoping to return one day. In the meantime, the elder Moogs had sold their Flushing home when George retired from Con Ed, and were renting the farmhouse. Bob saw his three-year contract with Waytena as a temporary sacrifice wagered on a secure future. "At best," Shirleigh told Florence, "a large giant super-duper will buy us out & we'll be rich and maybe free to come back & put in 52 acres of grapes. At worst we'll still be debtless and have 3 years of someone else worrying about where the dinero comes from."[8]

But Waytena was finding out how hard it was to keep the operation going. Ray Updike, the service manager, was the only Trumansburg employee to come to Williamsville, and the new assemblers were struggling to figure out how Minimoogs were built. On top of it, the company was still trying to unload its first run of 100 Sonic Vs that were coming back in droves for repairs. Waytena had had to back off his bluster with Van Koevering when he realized that salespeople like him were key to his success. With a green light from Waytena, Van Koevering and Trubey started up again as VAKO and convinced 22 retail stores nationally to stock Minimoogs, hoping to land 24 more dealers by year's end. But their efforts were stymied by the slow output at the factory.

Waytena was also realizing that scant name recognition of the Musonics brand was diluting the four letters that spelled "synthesizer" for most people. Bob never liked the coupling of "Moog" with "Musonics," and at NAMM he'd seen companies called Musiconics and Musitronics that all blended together in his mind. On September 7, Waytena dropped the Musonics tag altogether and registered, "Moog Music, Inc." with the New York Department of State as the new entity name.

Owning the brand was one thing, but competitors with lesser names were beginning to smell as sweet to buyers. A September *New York Times* article by an avant-garde composer, Larry Austin, revealed how jam-packed the synth field was getting. Austin's preferred synthesizer lineup led off with the ARP 2600, which he talked up as "a complete mini-studio . . . extremely reliable and easy to operate." He mentioned the Buchla, the Putney, and a new entry, the DIMI, a Finnish instrument that was "digitally operated" and "complete with computer core memory." The Moog was conspicuously absent, except for a dismissive quote from the exalted composer Igor Stravinsky, who used it, not as a brand reference, but as a snide generic substitute for the word "synthesizer": "The young musician takes his degree in computer technology now, and settles down to his Moog, or his mini-synthesizer as routinely as in my day he would have taken it in counterpoint and harmony and gone to work at the piano."[9]

Coming into 1972, Academy Street's production was just getting up to speed as its pack of competitors were sprinting out ahead. David Friend published an article in *Music Trades* magazine, "All You Ever Wanted To Know about Synthesizers," but the sprawling, three-page piece was really "everything you wanted to know about *ARP* synthesizers," with all five photos devoted to images of the company's synths.[10] ARP ads were adorned now with a smart new logo: a musical G-clef with a tail flourish of an electrical cord and plug, and they featured photos of the latest celebrity ARP users like the Who's Pete Townsend, and Stevie Wonder. Pretentious catchphrases attempted to turn the name into a verb: "ARP it up," and "No wonder Stevie ARPs."

EMS in England, along with its Putney, had added a large modular system, the Synthi 100, and the Synthi AKS, a small portable with a built-in digital sequencer—a complete system that fit into a little hinged suitcase and sold for £420 (about $1,050). Like ARP, EMS was rolling out an aggressive ad campaign with its own frolicsome slogans: *Every Nun Needs a Synthi*; *Every Picnic Needs a Synthi*; *Every School, Every Band, Every Dream, Everybody*, and so on. One unabashed ad popped a startling shot of a topless blonde into the corner to beckon the viewer in a speech balloon: *Psst! . . . Don't play M**G play SYNTHI*.

As the competition marched on, Waytena's iron-fisted control at Moog was coupled with his legendary miserliness. With each transaction he managed to skim off everything he could and cut every corner. His Venture Technology soaked Moog Music for an additional 100% surcharge over the landlord's rent, and he skimmed off $41,000 from the company for so-called improvements to the physical plant—though the "improvements" were apparently invisible to the naked eye.

Maintenance was handled by the janitor and night watchman, Frank, whom employees described as a codger who did odd jobs around Waytena's house and slept at Academy Street rent-free as an off-hours guard. When robbers entered in the middle of the night once, Gullo remembered, "Frank was an old guy and he went and hid. Poor old Frank is terrified." Waytena gave Frank a tongue-lashing the next day, not for the few items that were stolen, but, as Gullo recalled, "because Frank wasn't thinking! Why didn't he take all that equipment that was in the studio and go throw it in that pond that was out in front of the building so we could tell the insurance company we got robbed and get paid for it, 'cause who needs that crap anyway?"[11]

Waytena's penny-pinching knew no limits. The staff sweltered through summers with no air conditioning, and one employee recalled an intolerable dog day: "It literally turned into an oven inside and people couldn't stay in the building. Waytena had connections in town—under the table stuff—so he asked the Fire Department to come up with a fire truck and pump water from the pond beside the place onto the roof to cool the thing down."[12]

∿∿∿

In a world apart, Emerson, Lake, and Palmer's debut album had arrived on U.S. shores in early January 1971. Despite the group's mega-star reputation in Great Britain, ELP was still a new name across the Atlantic, where the band's classically tinged rock was an unfamiliar sound—even an acquired taste.

But the group's American fan base was growing through regular airplay of a targeted single. ELP had an ardent new advocate on New York City's airwaves: Scott Muni, the adventurous guru of progressive rock on the City's popular FM radio station, WNEW. During the band's first North American tour in the spring of '71, Keith recalled, "as we drove into Manhattan, we heard the tail-out Moog solo to 'Lucky Man' on WNEW and Scott's voice growling, 'That was the first single from the very new band, Emerson, Lake and Palmer.'"[13] By July, ELP's second album, *Tarkus*, was released in the U.S., sparking another North American tour starting that month. Bookings at huge venues like the Hollywood Bowl and New York's Madison Square Garden were signs of the group's ballooning superstar standing.

On September 1, Bob accepted Keith's invitation to witness a live ELP concert for the first time, held at a remote venue on the outskirts of New York City. Gaelic Park was a sandlot athletic field north of Manhattan in the Riverdale section of the Bronx. It sat two blocks from the end of the subway line where the elevated tracks of the 240th Street Rail Yard wrapped around one side of the field. The grounds were home to generations of Irish immigrants who fraternized there for hurling games, Gaelic football, and flirtations with potential spouses. On nearby Waldo Avenue, apartment dwellers hung out of top-floor windows or stood on rooftops on sticky summer nights to steal a view of shows in the Park.

For ELP's concert, Bob recalled, "Keith had invited me to come wherever backstage was. He and I piled into his mandatory limousine and we went through the mud, rocks, and broken glass—which is what you expect to find underneath the tracks of a New York City subway train—onto the soccer field. He got out with the rest of the group and they walked onto the field up to this wooden platform stage out by one goal."[14] Keith remembered the image of Bob standing behind the Marshall speakers during the sound check, "just laughing his head off."[15]

When the gates opened, a crowd of thousands swarmed across the grassy pitch. Blankets were laid over balding spots and mud holes, and latecomers scavenged for remaining places to squeeze in. Others streamed into low stands around the periphery or perched in tight formations on fences. The scent of vendors' beer hovered in the air.

The first blasts of sound over the field came from Keith's modular Moog, introducing the concert like a great cyborg emcee proclaiming that *this* band was going to be different. There were hypnotic whines like car alarm loops; a high-pitched bubbling gargle, a siren dipping and rising; the alarm again, and the whistle of a falling bomb slamming into the raw, distorted opening chords of "Barbarian"—a sampling of the group's trademark timbres to warm up the audience.

Chuck Pulin, a critic from *Sounds* magazine, described the scene: "Carl Palmer . . . drove the crowd to their feet. . . . His drumming at times sounded like sharp cracks of thunder and his gongs reverberated across the crowd into the streets surrounding Gaelic Park. . . . The climax of the evening's set was Keith Emerson flailing away at his organs, and manipulating his magic Moog. . . . He leaps from his Hammond and machine-guns the audience down with his Moog keyboard, a sadistic snarl on his boyish face . . . theatrically lowers his Hammond upon his prone body, and one gets caught up as he plunges his knife repeatedly into the organ keyboard; and as a grand finale sends the organ crashing to the stage floor, while the audience roars their approval."[16]

Bob watched the concert from the back of the field near a line of portajohns. "Everybody in the trains and the high rises were hanging out of their windows and digging it, along with the thousands of people on the field itself," he remembered. "Keith was electrifying the audience. . . . Shirts and hats were flying through the air. People all over the place were waving their arms and screaming."[17] At one point, Bob was startled to see Gershon Kingsley standing in the back. "I meet up with Gershon by the row of portajohns and he's completely disoriented and freaked out. In back of us, you can smell all the shit and piss and the doors to the johns are banging open and closed. And in front, here's this guy throwing an organ around, making keys go flying off, and making the instruments scream. All of a sudden, Gershon shrieks, 'This is the end of the world!' "[18]

For Bob, the spectacle of his instrument being played live in front of the huge crowd was thrilling—watching Keith grapple with a modular Moog before a massive audience, a feat no one else had attempted.[19] Keith recalled that at the end, "Bob came running up to me laughing and shaking his head in disbelief. 'That was the most incredible experience I've ever had,' he said."[20]

Around the same time, Stevie Wonder had discovered the modular Moog. When ARP's ad claimed, "Stevie ARPs," it neglected to mention that Stevie also "Mooged." On his latest album he used both brands in a synergistic musical partnership that belied the arch-rivalry between the two companies. In a market glutted with synthesizers now—all loaded with competing options—musicians no longer hewed to brand loyalty, but mixed and matched different manufacturers' models to suit their needs. The synths Stevie used, in fact, were built into a single hybrid "instrument," conceived by two producers who would keep stacking their system with equipment of various manufactures, like bricklayers, eventually assembling the largest combo synthesizer ever.

Bob Margouleff and Malcolm Cecil were an independent production and engineering duo, and their monolithic synthesizing setup burgeoned from modest beginnings. In 1968, Margouleff had rented a Moog to produce the debut album of Lothar and the Hand People at his Manhattan loft studio, Centaur Sound. Later, when he met Malcolm Cecil, a recently transplanted British jazz musician and classical bass player, the two pooled their talents on the Moog. In June 1971 they released *Zero Time*, a solo LP of original music made entirely on an expanded Moog IIIc. The album cover billed them as "Tonto's Expanding Head Band"—Tonto being the Moog, in the spirit of "Lothar" the theremin. When the combo synth grew to gargantuan proportions several years later, they recast its name as an acronym: TONTO, for "The Original New Timbral Orchestra."

When *Zero Time* came out, Stevie Wonder appeared on Cecil's doorstep clutching the album, thirsty for knowledge of the Moog, which he'd also heard on *Switched-On Bach*. His long-term contract with Motown Records had expired on his twenty-first birthday in May 1971, and he felt a restless artistic maturity blooming inside him. Part of his frustration at Motown was his lack of creative control over his recordings. Because of his blindness, he'd typically play his songs for an arranger who'd build arrangements, record them, and return with instructions on how and where to drop the vocals into the mix. But the results never really jibed with the conceptions in his head.

When Stevie sat at Cecil and Margouleff's Moog, everything came together: now he could link his songs organically to his own arrangements, with colors straight from his imagination, playing everything himself without a middleman. Songs he'd been stockpiling in his brain for years suddenly could be liberated. The Moog, he discovered, offered "a way to directly express what comes from your mind."[21]

With Cecil and Margouleff as associate producers, Stevie recorded a new album, aptly titled *Music of My Mind*, playing most of the traditional instruments himself, and an augmented system that now included Moog and ARP synths, and some custom-designed modules by Malcolm Cecil. A special-recipe Moog bass sound cooked up by Cecil and Margouleff added a piquant flavor to the mix that would remain a distinctive ingredient in Stevie's sonic palate.

Music of My Mind was released in March 1972 to a jubilant press and a swift ascent in the charts. It was the first of four albums lauded as Stevie's golden era—the blossoming of an original style crossing pop and R&B, legitimizing the synthesizer in soul, and igniting an electronic revolution in the genre that others would take up. Stirring together elements of jazz, funk, rock 'n' roll, gospel, and African and Latin rhythms with synth-laced textures—adding synthesizers for original sounds, never to imitate acoustic instruments—Stevie altered the course of soul forever, taking both Black and White audiences along for the ride.

The wave of Moog LP releases continued on. There was Stevie Wonder's next album, *Talking Book*; ELP's *Trilogy*; Tangerine Dream's *Zeit*; the Moody Blues' *Every Good Boy Deserves Favour*; Kingsley and his collaborator, Leonid Hambro, produced *Switched-On Gershwin*; and Alice Cooper's *Killer*, a top seller, logged $1 million in sales and earned Bob a Gold Record from Warner Bros.

At Disneyland, a 30-minute Moog soundtrack played every night for the California theme park's Main Street Electrical Parade, the spectacle of floats and Disney characters illuminated by half a million lights that reliably elicited tears and joy across generations. The Parade premiered in June 1972, marching to Paul Beaver's arrangement of "Baroque Hoedown" from the 1968 Perrey and Kingsley album, *Kaleidoscopic Vibrations*. Over loops of the original Moog-laced track, Beaver layered additional oscillator swoops, signature electronic splats, and synthetic instrumental licks.

Kingsley's tune "Pop Corn" became an international hit single in a 1972 version by Hot Butter, an instrumental cover band fronted by Stan Free, an original member of Kingsley's First Moog Quartet. Hot Butter's "Popcorn," showcasing the Moog, shot to No. 1 on the charts in several European countries and sold millions of copies worldwide. The tune became so ubiquitous that on his travels, Kingsley heard a bouzouki player strumming it on the

Greek island of Crete, and a hotel pianist in Rome tinkling through it. He remembered when he heard it on the sound system at a German store: "There was a girl there and I said, 'I'm the composer!' and she said 'Sie haben dieses Stück Scheiße geschrieben?' ('You wrote this piece of shit?')." In Hamburg's Reeperbahn red-light district he witnessed an adult sex show at a strip club with "Popcorn" as the soundtrack. Back home, an auto mechanic fixing Kingsley's car confronted him: "He came out with pliers and said, 'You wrote Popcorn? I'm going to kill you.'—'Why?'—'That's the only song my wife wanted, to make love to me.'"[22]

But even Kingsley, a devout Moog acolyte, could be tempted to convert to the competition. When he made noises about buying an ARP Soloist, an infuriated Bob wrote to Kohler, "We should get in touch with Kingsley to let him know that a) we will have presettable synthesizers, b) we want to work with him and will loan him equipment, but that c) we are not prepared to kiss his ass and will expect a certain amount of cooperation in the promotion of our products."[23]

Bob clung to the belief that the Moog brand still had its allure, and events like ELP's Gaelic Park spectacle confirmed that for him. Just months before that concert, he'd written to Kohler, "By now it should be obvious to all of us that there is a tremendous charisma surrounding the name 'Moog.' With the young people, it approaches reverent adoration. We MUST nurture this! I feel strongly that it is potentially our biggest asset."[24]

In what had suddenly become a volatile, fast-paced industry, though, the Moog name would still have to be stamped on a fresh line of products for the company to stay in the game. Gene Zumchak, who found himself in the awkward position of working alongside Bob again, floated a proposal for a guitar synthesizer. His intuitions had always run ahead of the curve—the Synthesizer 10 and the Sonic V—and now he thought he was on to something that could rescue the company. No one was selling synthesizers in the thousands, he argued, because the price tags were high and the monophonic instruments weren't always attractive for keyboard players. But the electric guitar was a favorite of young musicians, and he suggested the idea of plugging a guitar into a special type of synth to modify its sound.

Before his proposal could be considered, Zumchak was fired again. He recalled, "Waytena figured, 'I've got Moog now, I've got the big guy, and I don't need this guy anymore.'"[25] Eventually the Academy Street plant rolled out two new accessories: a Percussion Controller for triggering Moog synth modules by striking a small drum head, and a Guitar Interface—following up on Zumchak's guitar synthesizer idea when he wasn't around to take the credit. In further echoes of his work, his original Synthesizer 10 was upgraded to become the Synthesizer 12, with new improved "921 series" oscillators.

In the push for new models, Bob was charged with resuscitating Zumchak's Sonic V. Paltry sales and an epidemic of mechanical failures had put an end to the model after its original 100 units, but Waytena refused to give up on it. With misgivings, Bob tweaked and repackaged Zumchak's and Reinagel's design as a second-generation model called the Sonic Six, that would bear the Moog nameplate. Like its predecessor, it was aimed at the educational market. There were few systemic changes from the Sonic V, except for the addition of a pitch bend wheel and a new portable case.

Fittingly, as Bob's stepchild instrument, the Sonic Six contained no wood. Instead, it had a sturdy shell against heavy classroom handling—everything made with synthetic materials. The control panel—nearly identical to the Sonic V in layout—was a polyester laminate dashboard of friendly aquamarine rectangles marking off the various functions. It was housed in a hinged lid that folded down and latched over the keyboard to form a rectangular suitcase of tough gray plastic, similar to a gun case.

Bob and the Moog Company went from being the bellwether of the industry to suddenly being a whole turn behind in the leapfrogging game. It was hard to catch up, even with the spectacle of Keith's Monster Moog, or Kingsley's medicine show of spaghetti-cabled modules. Miniaturization and user-friendliness were now the order of the day. Consumers, and most performing musicians, wanted quick-and-dirty preset options to access on the fly and modify at the flick of a switch, or the twist of a dial. Van Koevering's nightclub keyboardists and kids in garage bands got their kicks by parroting a handful of familiar patches from popular rock albums, not from burrowing down rabbit holes after novel effects. It was all so easy now. The ARP Soloist had turned the notion of a synthesizer into a musical toy teetering atop an electric organ. With one hand on your Hammond or Wurlitzer, you could be an instant "synthesist" with the other.

Bob finally capitulated. His response to the newest generation ARP Soloist—the *Pro Soloist*—was the Moog Satellite, a stripped-down, no-frills instrument he pressed into service as a late entry in the race. Like the Pro Soloist, it was a lightweight, three-octave keyboard with a single oscillator and a colored pencil set of basic sounds and rudimentary modifiers.

The Satellite couldn't have been more un-Bob-like. Its 12 presets, selected with "Quick-Set tabs" were divided into five categories: Brass, Reed,

String, Bell, and Lunar. A flyer promised: *For the professional musician the SATELLITE can produce the sounds of the seventies at the lowest possible cost; For the amateur musician, the SATELLITE is the means of exploring exciting synthesizer sounds without an extensive technical knowledge of synthesizer programming.* In a toe-to-toe challenge to ARP, the flyer pledged: *One-hand operation permits the musician to play the SATELLITE and organ simultaneously.* Unlike the ARP Pro Soloist, the Satellite's case was made entirely of wood, a concession to Bob.

At the June 1972 NAMM show in Chicago, the Satellite drew a regular stream of excited gawkers, a flurry that didn't escape the notice of reps from the Thomas Organ Company at the next booth. The latest sonic fast food was an electric organ served with a side of synthesizer, and a few Wurlitzer models had the Orbit III, a small monophonic "synth," built right into the console. And with the ARP Pro Soloist as the classic add-on topping for organs now, the Satellite was designed with the same pairing in mind. It naturally caught the fancy of the Thomas Company. Eyeing an irresistible bargaining advantage, Waytena seized on the Thomas Company's hunger, and in August he brokered a deal—weighted heavily in Moog Music's favor—granting the California-based firm a license to manufacture the Satellite and integrate some of the units into its organs.

∿∿∿

Bob and Shirleigh needed a pressure release, and in the summer of 1972 they found a brief psychological escape hatch. George Kelischek, the builder of replica folk, Renaissance, and Baroque instruments, who'd encouraged Bob at the 1965 MTNA convention, now lived and worked on his own 40-acre property in Brasstown, North Carolina. Kelischek was planning a weeklong workshop out of his home for participants to build dulcimers from kits, and he invited Bob to do a tutorial on constructing a simple electronic instrument. Bob wouldn't be paid, but he and the family would be the Kelischek's guests for the week.

Brasstown was worlds away from the sterile infrastructure of suburban Buffalo. Tucked into the southwestern tip of North Carolina, only a few miles from the Georgia border, it was nestled in the southern Appalachians, a jewel of the Great Smoky Mountains. The surrounding terrain was a verdant haven of valleys, rivers, lakes, and whitewater river gorges—a lush and resplendent paradise that called out to Bob and Shirleigh. Brasstown was home to the famous Campbell Folk School, an internationally recognized center of Appalachian Mountain folk arts just a mile up the road from Kelischek's property.

When the Moogs arrived, Bob's emotional distress was evident. "He'd been reduced to manager of a factory," Kelischek recalled, "and he wasn't a scientist anymore. And it really bothered him. He was very envious of the independence that I had." Kelischek sensed that the approaching digital revolution would overrun Bob's analog work, and he counseled him to unload what he could of his business before it was too late. "I told him to come to North Carolina and buy himself a hundred acres of land and build himself a house and live happily ever after."[26]

In the July sessions at Kelischek's place—the *Switched On-And-Off* workshop—Bob coached a group of young locals through the construction of a one-octave synthesizer circuit he dubbed the "Brasstown Banger." In the evenings he gave a series of lecture-demonstrations on "The Sensation of Hearing" to 20 or 30 participants gathered in a large room of the house.

At week's end, attendees cleared out and Bob found himself in a luthier's haven. All around him stocks of raw wood waited to take shape as musical instruments, each about to be endowed with a musical voice in Kelischek's skilled hands. Bob's passion for wood was as potent as ever, and, scanning the workshop, he had a thought. "He confided in me," Kelischek remembered, "that his father always said Bob wasn't good with his hands! His father didn't think that much of having a doctorate degree and thinking with the head. Out of that notion, he said, 'I would like to make something that convinces my father that I can do something with my hands. Can you help me make a guitar?'"[27]

Hasty arrangements were made for the family to stay on another week, and with Kelischek's guidance, Bob would attempt to craft a classical guitar from scratch in five days. "I only showed him how to do it," Kelischek recalled, "but he did by far most of the work, and he got a few blisters and callouses on his hands—he worked really, very hard."[28] As Bob applied the finishing touches to the guitar, there was no time for multiple coats of varnish to dry and Kelischek sprayed the instrument with a quick-drying lacquer. By Friday night the instrument was strung with nylon strings and christened with Kelischek's blessings. On Saturday morning the Moogs piled into their Chevy Suburban and took off for New York City, the first stop en route to Trumansburg, where Bob would unveil the guitar for his father's approval. Then it would be on to Williamsville again.

The long drive to New York allowed time for reflection. "We had always wanted land with woods on it," Shirleigh recalled, "but we could never afford it. Well, *there* was George Kelischek with forty acres of largely wooded land, and the price of land down there was much, much less, so that sort of planted a seed. We went home and aimed our life in such a way as to get enough money to move to North Carolina."[29]

In Manhattan the family dropped in on Wendy Carlos, who was basking in two recent synthesizer triumphs: the soundtrack for Stanley Kubrick's violent, dystopian crime film, *A Clockwork Orange*, with Moog arrangements of Beethoven and other classical composers, plus a Carlos original, "Timesteps"; and *Sonic Seasonings*, a 2-LP meditation on the four seasons that mixed together ambient environmental sounds leavened by Carlos's own Moog compositions. Bob proudly showed off his guitar to Carlos, and brought it back to the Chevy that was parked on the street.

At the end of the visit, the family returned to their vehicle to find it had been broken into. Their suitcases were missing and the guitar was gone. "The police had absolutely no sympathy," Shirleigh recalled. "They said anyone who leaves more than a box of tissues in their car is a fool. So that was that."[30] Kelischek remembered Bob's distressed call the next day: "He was almost crying on the phone. I've never seen him as sad and as downtrodden as on that phone."[31] In Trumansburg now, George Moog would have to content himself with his son's account of building a guitar.

∿∿∿

Bob was humiliated in front of his aunt that fall when he gave a visiting lecture at her home base, Washington University in St. Louis. The *St. Louis Post-Dispatch* reported, "Washington University did not show its guest its own electronic-music lab in the attic of the Music Building, for it is full of recently purchased ARP equipment."[32] Bob's talk centered on the exponential rise of the synthesizer industry since his last visit to the campus three years earlier. Savvy students aimed pointed questions at him, flaunting synth vocabulary as second nature, and pressed him on recent computer applications of electronic musical instruments. It was a glaring reminder of how rapidly the industry was evolving.

To help hold off the competition, Dave Van Koevering moved up to Williamsville from Florida with his family to join the company as vice president of marketing. Stretching back into an office chair at his new marketing command central, he tracked a huge U.S. wall map dotted with push pins that marked conquered retail stores, like emblems of downed planes on the fuselage of some flying ace. As top sales honcho, he dispatched his own handpicked cadre of regional reps to scour assigned territories for new leads.

Attempting to spar in the advertising ring, Moog Music trotted out a feeble little mascot—Maestro Moog—a cartoon eighteenth-century elf musician with a ruffled shirt, buckle shoes, a Pinocchio nose, beady eyes, a tousled wig, and a gentle smile. Maestro appeared in the corners of flyers to personify the *Switched-On Bach* associations with the Moog synthesizer, capitalizing on the classical music gravitas only the Moog brand could invoke.

But the company knew who really buttered its bread, and it couldn't afford to alienate its base of pop musicians. Maestro did double duty, happily consorting with rockers. One brochure pictured him playing a Minimoog in a band with a hipster guitarist and a drummer, one of them working the Guitar Interface, the other the Percussion Controller. The ad copy strained to speak in hip code: TIL NOW . . . *you haven't been "wayout," you've only been "OUT"! NOW—Maestro Moog invites YOU to "MAKE THE SCENE". . . WITH MOOG'S SWINGIN' SYNTHESIZERS . . . . NOW, YOU TOO CAN JOIN THE 'IN'strument SOUND of the PROS!*[33] Another flyer, titled, *Moog makes the scene*, featured an imposing pen and ink portrait of Bob with the messianic aspect of an Eastern mystic staring transfixed into the distance, orbited by musicians like ELP, and a middle-aged Kingsley portrayed as a cool dude in sunglasses.[34]

But in truth, there *was* a freewheeling, hip side to the company, at least among the general staff. In the fall of 1972, a young married couple looking for work found a genial welcome and even managed to expose a chink of compassion in Waytena's heavy armor. After a 1,200-mile drive, Roger and Kathy Luther had shown up unannounced, asking for a job, and were told Moog wasn't hiring. But Roger persisted, promising they'd sweep floors—anything—just to work for the company. Waytena, on the spur of the moment, invited the Luthers to lunch at an upscale local restaurant with Gullo, Van Koevering, and Bob.

Roger was a recent graduate of the University of Southern Mississippi where he'd studied music theory and composition and worked with an abandoned Moog modular he'd discovered in a campus lab; he wound up having the instrument all to himself. Luther was smitten with synthesizer technology, and after graduation he solicited work from Paul Beaver, Tristram Cary, Eric Siday, Buchla, and ARP, all without success. He and Kathy decided to take a chance and show up on a lark at the Moog plant in their VW Microbus, their only real possession. "They were almost penniless," Van Koevering remembered. "They had enough gas and food to get to Williamsville."[35] Gullo recalled, "We didn't need musicians, we needed *engineers*, but Waytena said, 'Jeez, these kids just drove all the way across the country, just give 'em a job—something!' Bill had a soft heart in so many ways; he was a softie like that."[36] Van Koevering was disarmed: "I *did* see a heart in the man: Real kind, real gentle."[37] "We couldn't believe it," Kathy recalled. "He hired us! It was a dream come true."[38]

On their second day, the Luthers arrived to find everyone in costume—one woman dressed as a witch. It was Halloween. Despite Waytena's iron grip on the engineering and executive staff, lower-order employees enjoyed an unsupervised water cooler culture of camaraderie and chitchat. "It was just a big family atmosphere," Roger recalled. "One day we'd have Cowboy Day, so all the test technicians would come dressed in cowboy hats. We'd have hot jalapeno pepper eating contests." Luther initiated a new group pastime: launching model rockets in the empty fields out back at the end of the workday. Many of the hobbyist missiles were as tall as five feet and were set off with sticks of dynamite. "We'd have five stage rockets," he recalled. "They'd just go out of sight after the third stage."[39]

From the start, the Luthers had their own take on Waytena. "I felt like he really cared about us," Kathy recalled, "because every Thanksgiving he'd order Jaindl turkeys and give 'em out to everyone, and at Christmas he always gave out wine or cigars. He had a heart of gold. We just adored him. Bob Moog hated him, but I didn't have Bob's perspective."[40] Out of view of the rank-and-file employees, Waytena reserved his heavy-handed maneuvering for engineering and managerial staff. Shirleigh recalled, "A good day for him was if he could reduce everybody to tears, and he treated Robert like dog meat."[41] Gullo chalked it up to insecurity: "Waytena was scared to death of Bob Moog. As much as he wanted Moog and wanted everything about him, he was terrified of him."[42]

Nonetheless, Gullo could see that all along Waytena had only one goal in mind: "Waytena was an opportunist. His motivation for starting Moog was to sell it. Always. He wanted to start the company, make it into a great commercial success, and sell it."[43] The first step in that process was to look toward Japan, where Waytena saw a burgeoning love affair with the synthesizer. The composer and synthesist Isao Tomita had released his debut album there, *Electric Samurai: Switched On Rock*—Moog arrangements of hits by the

Beatles, Elvis Presley, and Simon & Garfunkel—and ELP had just wrapped their first Japanese tour in July with Keith's Monster Moog blasting out to throngs in Osaka and Tokyo.

Japanese companies had yet to throw their hat into the synth ring, but the market was fertile ground, with a well-established manufacturing infrastructure already tooled up and rolling out quality, high-volume consumer electronics. Two recent attempts at industrial espionage right under Bob's nose were a portent that synths were on Japanese radar: in 1970, Nippon Gakki (later to be called the Yamaha Corporation) had ordered modules from Trumansburg, and in late 1971, two Minimoogs were purchased by the Yamaha Music Center. At the moment, an entrepreneurial Japanese inventor, Ikutaro Kakehashi, also had his eyes on the synth prize.

Kakehashi had been working since the 1950s to devise low-cost, compact electronic instruments with simple intuitive interfaces for professional and amateur musicians. In 1960 he formed Ace Electronic Industries and rode the Japanese transistor tsunami with his own rhythm boxes and a drum machine that mimicked a menagerie of percussion instruments. The Hammond Company was captivated, and integrated the device into some of its organs, eventually licensing Ace as the Hammond importer in Japan. But there was a risk for the American company. Like many Japanese inventors, Kakehashi admitted, "In those early days the only way we could pursue our development efforts was by examining imported instruments and adapting their technology."[44]

In April 1972, Kakehashi started a new company that he dubbed Roland, a made-up name with two syllables he reckoned people could pronounce in any language. Roland's first product was an updated drum machine. But Kakehashi had bigger plans. Realizing he was squeezed out of Japan's acoustic piano industry by Yamaha and Kawai—the two giants that shared a lock on the market—he knew he had to produce another type of keyboard instrument that could generate its own consumer base. In the past he'd tinkered with electronic keyboard prototypes, and though none of them ever made it into production, he'd never let go of the idea.

One day Kakehashi suddenly appeared on the production floor at the Williamsville plant, pen and clipboard in hand, freely strolling the workstations and scrutinizing assemblers. Gullo remembered, "He came to learn from Bob Moog! He observed, talked with Bob, talked about building circuits, studied the engineering, and stuff like that." Kakehashi was there at Waytena's invitation, but, as Gullo recalled, no one on the staff was quite sure why: "I remember Waytena was saying Kakehashi had great contacts in Japan and great manufacturing. So the thought was that there was some collaboration, some good would come out of it. Maybe it was gonna be good for us."[45]

Bob was caught in the middle—forced to let the fox into the henhouse because Waytena had masterminded the visit—trapped into giving away the family jewels over some precarious gamble. The *St. Louis Post-Dispatch* had rightly observed, "Hardly anything about the synthesizer is patentable; it is a 'system' or organization of well-known electronic components rather than an invention."[46] Indeed, Bob's only patented component was his ladder filter, leaving the rest of his work perilously open to theft.

During Kakehashi's month-long stay, he had a front row seat on the Academy Street environment, observing the relaxed pace and casual conviviality among the workers—rocket meets, hot pepper contests, and the like—a staggering contrast to the sober workplace culture back in Japan, where employees were cogs in a regimented mechanism pointed solely toward maximum output. On the Japanese production floor, so-called waste, or non-value-added behavior—rest time, bathroom breaks, wiping away sweat, speaking to other workers—was anathema. Days of unrelenting 11- or 12-hour shifts—even 24-hour stints—aged employees prematurely and occasionally took the life of a worker stricken with a sudden heart attack or stroke, spurring a new Japanese term, *karoshi*, or "death from overwork."

Kakehashi had just rented a factory in Japan and ordered raw materials, anxious to leap into production. "Moog is braced for the inevitable Japanese entry into the synthesizer business," the *St. Louis Post-Dispatch* had reported.[47] Two years earlier, Gershon Kingsley, in an interview for the CBS radio show *The Reasoner Report*, had seen it coming: "Kingsley," Harry Reasoner explained, "says when the Japanese get wind of its possibilities we will undoubtedly find the marketplace filled with miniature moogs."[48]

Despite Waytena's hopes, however, the Japanese varieties would have no need to carry the Moog name.

22

Vexations

Moog was still "the first name in synthesizers," as the company liked to crow in its advertising. But the tagline was almost beside the point now. On the ground, in the plant, Waytena was more concerned with having a chief engineer who was a prodigious technical mind to lead the firm into the future and who could come across as a strong corporate ambassador. So he hired David Luce.

As a person, Dave Luce was in every way Bob's opposite. He projected an air of seriousness and propriety—an owl-like intensity with his black horn-rimmed glasses, bald head, and dark mutton chop sideburns. He'd studied nuclear physics at MIT but ended up doing his Ph.D. thesis on musical acoustics. When he graduated in 1963, he joined his physics professor, Melville Clark, Jr., to work on developing Clark's original polyphonic keyboard, an 88-note electronic device Clark was tinkering with in his garage. Several of their joint inventions for the instrument were patented and assigned to Clark.

Waytena was bent on rolling out the first polyphonic synthesizer—an industry game changer—and Luce was brought on to realize the project. Bob had actually recommended Luce as someone to assist with the effort, but he couldn't have anticipated the role Luce would come to play in the company.

In light of Luce's hiring in January 1973, Bob began to assess his own position in the company. In a letter to his lawyer, Don Runyon, he admitted that Waytena had made good on the original agreement: debts and loans were paid off, and he and Shirleigh owned stock in the company. But on a professional level, he complained that he had no authority or responsibility: "I have been . . . embarrassed at having to contend with the chasm between what the public thinks my responsibility is by virtue of my title, and what it actually is in practice. . . . I feel more and more like a fish out of water."[1]

Left on the sidelines, Bob retreated into a corner to tinker with a pet project: an experimental electronic violin designed by Max Mathews of Bell Labs. The "Maxolin" had a conventional violin body made of wood—right up

Bob's alley—with strings and a fingerboard. But it deflected the sound energy away from the box with electrical resonators set to duplicate the resonances of a fine violin. Bob hoped to equip Mathews' prototype with added synth technology and turn it into a commercial Moog product. In 1972, when the instrument was still in utero, he made an audaciously unrealistic boast to the *Chicago Reader*: "Our new Maxolin can and does produce the sounds of a Stradivarius. Electronically, it can be done. People can't do it . . . but electronics can."[2]

Luce was moving ahead with Waytena's mandate for the polyphonic synth. He'd been hoping to incorporate some of the advanced technology he'd developed with Melville Clark, but Clark bristled, refused to sign a contract, and initiated a suit to guard his work. Luce was forced to scratch his head and start over. The result was a polyphonic keyboard prototype called the "Apollo." As a companion device he invented a bass pedal instrument with Moog's engineering manager, Tony Marchese, a self-proclaimed born-again Christian whom the staff nicknamed "the Reverend" for his habit of moralizing and chiding coworkers. The 13-pedal five-octave bass synth, the "Taurus," got its name, Luce remembered, because "someone said, 'the thing's gotta be a *bull!*' "[3]

To complete a suite of three prototype instruments, Bob designed a monophonic, Minimoog-style touch-sensitive keyboard called the "Lyra." The three-instrument "synthesizer ensemble" was designed to function as a single console to be played like an organ: the Apollo on a stand, the small Lyra piggybacking on it, and the Taurus pedals sitting on the floor. The stacked ensemble was dubbed the "Constellation," a one-off trial run for a later, more sophisticated polyphonic concept the company would develop. Roger Luther remembered that Bob labeled the power switch on his Lyra, "juice," just to be mischievous.

But Bob was mainly preoccupied with the Maxolin, a project close to his heart and his roots: a symbol of the classical music world, and an invention of a scientist colleague. When he demonstrated it to Moog company personnel, though, Waytena put the kibosh on it. Too esoteric to manufacture, he contended. Bob was convinced now that his long-range research priorities were out of sync with the company's corporate mindset. He told Runyon he'd made up his mind: "I have no intention of considering extending my employment contract on any terms. . . . The company needs me like a hole in the head right now."[4] It meant weighing the unthinkable: rowing a lifeboat away from the ship he'd built and navigated since he was 19, watching another captain steer off with his priceless trademark while he heaved at the oars, nameless, through unknown waters.

On May 23—his thirty-ninth birthday—he sought his lawyers' advice about his legal options when his contract ran out in another year, knowing he'd still have a non-compete clause hanging around his neck. Their answers were devastating.

Could he develop the Maxolin? The answer was no: he'd already worked on it at the company and shown it around the production floor. Anything done at the plant was the property of the employer. Could he make custom electronic instruments? No: he'd be competing with the company's "professional products division." Could he create instruments like the ones R. A. Moog, Inc., made years earlier? No: because Waytena could claim his ownership rights extended to everything the company had ever produced. Could he sell kits? No.

The lawyers *did* throw Bob a few crumbs, though: he could lecture and write magazine articles.

But the most galling piece of news they gave him had nothing to do with his post-company life: if Waytena wanted to sell the company—which looked increasingly likely—Bob couldn't even quit. He was still the company's most valuable commodity, and if he bowed out, he could be accused of devaluing his boss's original investment. Waytena could insist that Bob's services were, as the lawyers termed it, "unique and extraordinary." As the founder of the industry, he was Moog Music's intellectual capital. He wasn't merely good at what he did, he was *extraordinary*. Perversely, that left him unprotected. His hallowed status was now his biggest liability.

Increasingly, Bob's disconnect from the job drifted into apathy. His mail was flooded with requests for information and equipment—letters demanding immediate attention—but he often let them molder on his desk until he forgot about them entirely. When Frank Zappa wrote him in 1973 asking for a frequency shifter for a Mothers of Invention concert at London's Wembley Stadium, in front of 100,000 people, he got around to answering eight months later, long after the concert had passed.

Yet Bob characteristically responded right away to letters from kooks and strangers—lonely teenagers obsessed with circuitry, or well-meaning hobbyists offering him secret advice on how to make the next big synth. The requests were nutty: *Mr. Moog, I would be very thankful if you would tell me how to convert a plain accordion into one of your marvels; Dear Mr. Moog: Since I can not afford to buy one of your units . . . could you send me some of your schematics*. Bob treated the writers like spiritual brethren, answering all of them with the respect afforded a CEO, thanking each for his letter and offering earnest advice and lists of resources.

While Bob was happily bantering with strangers, the competition was heating up. ARP's latest contender was the Odyssey, a rival to the Minimoog that was basically a hardwired 2600 wrapped in a compact, two-foot-wide case that gigging musicians could carry around easily.

When Moog engineers listened closely to its sound, they heard something fishy. The Odyssey's tone was eerily close to the classic "fat Moog sound" that resulted from Bob's patented ladder filter. The engineers also detected the same quality in ARP's Pro Soloist and its 2600. Dave Luce ordered a Moog engineer, Rich Walborn, to dissect a 2600 to see what he could uncover.

Walborn had started at the company as a summer intern in 1971, just before the Trumansburg plant was shuttered. He recalled his introduction to the boss: "Bob had a plaid shirt, green corduroy pants, sandals with black socks, and headphones on, listening to a Minimoog. I go, 'You're Bob Moog?' He goes, 'Yeah.' I go, 'I read a lot about you.' He goes, 'So has everybody else, so what?' and he walked away." Walborn stayed on that fall doing part-time engineering work at Williamsville while he finished his degree at the State University of New York (SUNY) at Buffalo, and became another of Bob's on-the-spot hires. "I was working on the Bode Frequency Shifter," he recalled, "and Bob was explaining to me how it works. And he goes, 'Can you understand that?' and I go, 'Yeah, Bob. You know, I'm a senior in electrical engineering.' He goes, 'You are? I thought you were a musician.' And he goes, 'Ever think of working here full time when you graduate?'—'Yeah, sure!'"[5]

Two years later, in 1973, Walborn was prying into the ARP 2600 when he discovered its filter was encapsulated in a hard epoxy block. To get to the circuitry he had to chisel away for several days with an ice pick, soaking the plastic cocoon in acetone and grinding it down to dig out the filter. When he unearthed the prize, it was just as everyone had suspected: "I saw the ladder of transistors there, and I go, 'Oh yeah—this is the R. A. Moog circuit. There's no question they copied it.'"[6] Alan Pearlman had failed to pull off his patent swap scheme back in 1970, but it hadn't stopped him from snatching Bob's filter design anyway. He'd just hidden it in a hard protective shell. It was a red-handed bust and litigation was sure to follow.

Bob remained in the dark over management decisions at the company, but he figured Waytena was still pacing around looking for an exit strategy with a hefty return on his investment. Only by "questioning third parties and by eavesdropping," he told Runyon, had he learned in May 1973 that Waytena was actively juggling several deals, intent on closing one within a few weeks.[7]

It turned out Waytena *was* on the verge of a deal. But as the company headed into the red once again, he was less concerned now with a lucrative buyout than simply a tossed lifeline. He'd learned how impossible the synthesizer business was, grappling with the same demons Bob had always faced.

After his windfall Thomas Organ contract at the 1972 NAMM show, Waytena managed to score again at the June 1973 event, snagging a potential buyer to take Moog Music off his hands: the Chicago Musical Instrument Company. CMI was founded in 1920 and became a top distributor of Gibson and Epiphone guitars, Lowrey organs, Selmer wind and brass instruments, Pearl drums, and other big-name brands. The firm was a subsidiary of a giant Panamanian holding company based in New York City—originally known as the Ecuadorian Corporation Limited (ECL)—a conglomerate dealing in the unlikely mix of beer, cement, and real estate. In 1969 ECL acquired CMI and renamed itself Norlin, a portmanteau of the names of ECL's president, Norton Stevens, and CMI's president, Arnold Berlin. For 1972, Norlin reported sales of $138 million. With a built-in distribution network, CMI looked like the answer Waytena had been hunting for. What he didn't know was that CMI had been slipping badly ever since it had become associated with Norlin.

Bob had no part in the negotiations. To the contrary, he remembered, Waytena brought Dave Luce along to the New York offices of Norlin and "introduced Dave Luce as a future leader of the company. . . . Went through the whole deal without anybody from Norlin ever talking to me as much as two sentences."[8]

Waytena talked up the generous royalty he'd suckered out of Thomas Organ for the license to build Satellites—a one-time-only deal, but his only true ace in the hole. "He told Norlin that all sorts of new exciting products were about to be put into production," Bob recalled. "And Norlin, much to their discredit, believed him without investigating. . . . They did not know anything more than Waytena told them . . . astronomical denominations of bullshit."[9] Tom Gullo was disgusted: "Waytena sold it to them as such a good deal. 'They don't have to pay for it—it would be paid for out of the profits of the company.' "[10]

Waytena made sure to look out for himself first. In the agreement, consummated on September 24, 1973, he arranged to sell his own shares for over half a million dollars. His stockholders, who owned the remaining shares, were left to gamble on selling their portion through the vagaries of company profits over the next four years. Waytena would stay on as boss until CMI acquired the remainder of the company. He'd collect a $35,000 salary, though he didn't have to be around full-time.

No sooner did Waytena have the Norlin contract sealed and in hand than he reverted to his skinflint ways and began searching for every ploy to make the new controlling firm cover the tab. His first order of business was to fire all his salespeople, telling the new owners they'd have to pick up the slack. But Norlin's salespeople were all MBAs with no previous experience in musical instruments, and they had no idea how to sell synthesizers. Gullo recalled, "Some of the young marketing guys they put on worked for guys like Ralston Purina before, and they would tell you they were experts at marketing 'cause they could sell cat food, and you couldn't talk to a cat. It was just a bunch of bullshit."[11]

Van Koevering, with his ear to the ground, had sensed trouble and quit before the contract was signed. "I didn't want to work for a big company like CMI," he recalled. "The guys over there didn't know how to market anything. They were running Gibson into the ground and they were running Pearl drums into the ground; they're making big mistakes and they're going to do that with the Moog company."[12]

Bob himself was in a bind. With less than a year left on his current contract, it was just as his lawyers had predicted: he wound up as part of the sale, saddled with the distinction of being "unique and extraordinary"—though apparently only "extraordinary" enough to merit a $28,500 salary. He was compelled to sign a new contract—a management agreement—committing him to four more years of full-time work at the company, though with the carrot of possible bonuses and the cashing out of his stock.

Bob couldn't catch a break. He lamented to Runyon, "it seems to me that I am laying myself open to Waytena's proven ability to screw people that he no longer needs."[13] The saddest part was the Maxolin; the company had no interest in developing it, yet he couldn't take it with him in the future. By October, the prototype was returned to Max Mathews.

The reluctance of Shirleigh and the kids to move to Buffalo in the first place—for what was supposed to be a three-year commitment, ending in June 1974—was intensified when the Norlin deal extended Bob's obligations through 1977. "Suffice it to say," he confided to an exec, "that I bought their resistance out with a crockful of rosy futures!"[14] For his part, he grumbled to top brass that under the new contract he was relegated to taking care of "piddling details that could be easily done by someone working at a small fraction of my present salary," and complained, "I feel very uncomfortable in a situation where my recommendations are being ignored and my talents are being wasted."[15]

In a bizarre sort of parallel universe, Bob's public image remained ascendant in the culture; no one on the outside would have suspected the sort of treatment he was subjected to at the Williamsville plant. All through the month of June 1973, thousands of airline passengers leafing through TWA's in-flight magazine, *Ambassador*, came upon a three-page feature capped by a caricature of Bob's head with tumbling eighteenth-century locks and earphones, attached to a tiny body. "Dr. Moog's Synthesizer; A New Music Form, or Just Switched-on Bosh?" covered Bob's rescue from Trumansburg by Waytena and painted a glowing picture of the new company.[16]

Bob even made it into a United States Information Agency film documentary released in the summer of 1973. In *The Visionaries*, he was profiled along with four other American science pioneers, including the co-inventor of lasers and the developer of the Learjet. The movie was screened around the world—except in the U.S.—as a plug for American ingenuity and free market capitalism.

Bob's segment was an odd assemblage of vignettes from his life that barely touched on the impact of his work. Rather than being interviewed, he was seen with his recent mutton chop sideburns passively observing musicians playing his instruments; in a lab drawing a bow across the Maxolin; working with students and listening to a Renaissance consort at the Kelischek house; and sledding with Chris Swansen's kids while Swansen soloed on the synth in a farmhouse near Ithaca. The film ended with a narrated pitch for democracy with a capital "D": "These men . . . are all in the tradition of the great American dreamers of the past: the Edisons, the Bells, the Wrights, the Fords. Their lives and work symbolize the idea that in a FREE society, new ideas will flourish."[17] In a USIA viewer survey the feature was generally well rated, though one group in Bogota, Colombia, called it "gringo propaganda."[18]

On October 1, Bob appeared as a celebrity contestant on the nationally syndicated TV game show *To Tell the Truth*. The episode opened with a special Moog arrangement of the show's theme music. In the program's classic format, a four-person panel of stars, guided by host Garry Moore, shot questions at Bob and two imposters claiming to be Robert Moog. Based on their answers, each panel member had to guess which of the three was really Bob. Each wrong vote meant an uptick in the cash award given to all three "challengers." Bob and the pretenders managed to stump the panel—no one voted for him—and on Moore's iconic cue, "Will the real Robert Moog please stand up, *sir!*" Bob shot out of his seat like a jack-in-the-box, flashing his poker face into a broad grin. He'd just won $500.

TV viewers had a recurring reminder of Bob's synthesizer that year in a one-minute Schaefer beer ad featuring television composer Edd Kalehoff. The spot was an echt 1970s morsel of commercialized grooviness, opening with a title screen—*Edd Kalehoff at the MOOG Synthesizer*—followed by the mop-haired, mustachioed Kalehoff in wire-rimmed glasses and flowered shirt, head-bopping at the Moog, with rapid-fire zooms and crossfades: close-ups of one hand dancing on the keyboard with the other hand twisting a knob, pans of patch cords, a VU meter, an oscilloscope, and Kalehoff pulling a pop-top to pour a beer into a mug, all to his full Moog arrangement of the Schaefer theme in swooping and gurgling synth clichés: *Schaefer—is the— one beer to have, when you're—having—more—than—one.*

~~~

In November, *Brain Salad Surgery*, ELP's fourth studio album, was released with Keith on the Constellation prototype, which he'd borrowed to use in the instrumental mix. When he brought the Constellation on the album tour, the flimsy one-off needed a Moog staffer to keep it functioning. Rich Walborn— the only unmarried engineer—was recruited as the instrument's chaperone. Joining the road crew on the first tour date in Miami, he rode on ELP's private jet, stayed in the band's hotels, and became Keith's drinking buddy. When Keith threatened to cancel a concert several times after radio frequency interference toyed with his Monster Moog, Walborn saved the day by wrapping the huge modular in aluminum foil, "like a Thanksgiving turkey."[19] Walborn recalled one mishap when Keith aimed his Moog ribbon controller from between his legs to fire a charge out over the crowd. Rocky Morley had loaded it up with too much flash powder. Keith pushed the button, and the explosion blew back and ripped off his thumbnail. "Twenty minutes into the gig," Walborn recalled, "his thumb is bleeding, and I'm going, 'Don't get blood on the Moog!' "[20]

Bob caught up with the *Brain Salad Surgery* tour at Buffalo's Rich Stadium on July 26, 1974. Shirleigh, Laura, and Renée came along, and Laura remembered her dad dropping off a case of Utica Club, his favorite beer, backstage before the concert, and hanging with Keith to polish off a few bottles. The tour had recently been immortalized in a live album, with its title taken from an ELP song lyric the emcee bellowed out to introduce the band to a cheering crowd: *Welcome back, my friends, to the Show that never ends ~ Ladies and Gentlemen, Emerson Lake & Palmer!* The Rich Stadium show was especially memorable for 13-year-old Laura, sitting in a crowd of 70,000, who recalled, "They began the intro to 'Lucky Man' and said, 'This number is dedicated to our Lucky Man, Robert Moog,' and then they swung the spotlight around, and we were sitting way far away in the stands—next to someone who was offering us pot."[21]

Out of the spotlight and back on Academy Street, the Lucky Man didn't feel very lucky. Wafting in the cigar smoke around Waytena's office, Bob sniffed an air of secrecy and intrigue. Knowing he'd be the last to hear about any decisions affecting his own status, he started a memo pad diary for his own protection to jot snippets of gossip:

Dec. 27: Gullo came in and ... mentioned that tattling is rampant. Arky and Frank can't be trusted; Monday, Jan 7, 1974: Gullo pointed out that he's not supposed to know where stuff is being shipped. November 27: Marge told Tom that Waytena was putting through a lot of phony expenses.[22]

Waytena was still looking out for himself first, even in the shambles the company was now in. His most outrageous skullduggery—which Bob noted in his diary after Waytena admitted it to him—was to trick a Norlin exec into signing a sham purchase order for instruments that hadn't actually been requested by Norlin, in order to boost the bonus he got paid for number of instruments sold. The Williamsville plant produced the units (523 Minimoogs, 236 Sonic Sixes, and a dozen System 15 modulars) and warehoused them at the Academy Street property, waiting for Norlin's payment of the invoice—almost half a million dollars.

"Waytena made an unbearable prick of himself," Bob recalled. "The Norlin people literally screamed for mercy."[23] Gullo remembered, "He became such a pain in the ass that they bought him out much earlier than they expected to."[24] Norlin arranged to pay Waytena for the remaining portion of stock he owned in the company and released him from his contract. Norlin would plan to acquire 100% ownership of Moog Music, eventually buying out the remaining shareholders, including Bob.

When Waytena took off in December of 1974, he left Moog holding the bag on the huge bogus instrument order with Norlin. Bob alerted his lawyer about the outstanding bill for it, and mentioned another discovery: "Norlin owes us about $60,000 in royalties that they never bothered to report," and "rumor has it," he divulged, that a Norlin exec "got Waytena to sweep it under the rug so it didn't 'queer the deal.'"[25]

With Waytena gone, CMI was no longer the intermediary and Moog Music employees worked directly for Norlin. Bob signed a new contract covering his three remaining years at the company. He was still chained to a 40-hour workweek and a two-year non-compete clause after he left. But he was granted a modest salary boost to $30,000 with scheduled annual buyouts of his stock each January for five years.

With his vexations boiling over in the fall of '74, Bob found solace snoozing under a grand piano at the local university, even with an audience watching him. It was a far remove from Waytena's world: he was basking in the psychic comfort of an avant-garde happening staged around a piece of classical music. The event, on November 6, was sponsored by SUNY Buffalo and was broadcast live on the campus radio station, WBFO. The evening was a sort of musical relay race—a succession of musicians taking half-hour turns at the piano to play the same minute-and-a-half-long composition again and again before surrendering the instrument to the next player for more of the same, until collectively they'd logged a total of 840 repetitions. The short piece was an 1890s trifle called *Vexations*, by the quirky French composer Erik Satie. The tradition of running a round-the-clock marathon of the piece, taking literally Satie's cryptic note in the score about playing it 840 times in a row, was started by—who else—John Cage.

At the University performance, part of the fun was seeing how long audience members could hold out. The first pianist began at 6 p.m., with the last projected to reach the finish line at repetition number 840 by 8 a.m. the following morning. The lineup of roughly 20 keyboard players tackling the slow, meditative, and harmonically dreary piece included graduate students, music faculty members, and musicians like Lejaren Hiller, and former Grateful Dead keyboardist Tom Constanten. "The internationally known inventor, Robert Moog," the *Buffalo Evening News* reported, "was asleep under the piano. He'd already taken his half-hour turn at the keyboard. But the hypnotic spell of the music had gotten to him, and he didn't want to go home."[26] Bob told Aunt Florence that the experience of playing the work was "almost visceral," something akin to the relaxed mind focus of transcendental meditation.[27]

Out in the material world, Bob's work remained under continued threat from competition. What he'd found in Japan when Norlin sent him over on assignment in the fall of 1973 was alarming. The company had chosen Yamaha as its Moog agent in Japan, tossing Bob into the belly of the beast. "I expect that this will be an 'initiation by fire' for me," he wrote Jacqueline Harvey.[28] Off the plane in Japan, he could see that was an understatement. "Already, two Japanese manufacturers are producing synthesizers," he alerted Walter Sear.[29] Kakehashi's Williamsville visit, it turned out, had borne fruit amazingly fast: Roland's SH-1000, the first Japanese synth, had just come out, bearing a striking resemblance—physically and functionally—to the Moog Satellite. The Korg company had followed with the miniKORG, an homage to the Minimoog. Unlike the SH-1000 with its preset sounds, the miniKORG was a true synth with interactive functions. Both instruments were selling in Japan for a quarter of the price of a Minimoog, and both were flying off the assembly line in greater numbers.

But the most disturbing news hadn't reached Bob's ears yet: Roland's just-released SH-2000, a simplified version of its SH-1000, concealed an unauthorized clone of his patented ladder filter.

It seemed so many of the elements of Bob's early success were slipping away—even one of his staunchest promoters. Out on the West Coast, an era ended abruptly on the morning of January 15, 1975. At the Morgan Park Community Center in Los Angeles, Paul Beaver had set up a Moog modular for a large high school audience in a talk called "Coming Next—2,000 A. D.," his take on the future of music. As he spoke, with no warning, he collapsed and tumbled unconscious to the stage floor. He was rushed to Cedars of Lebanon Hospital in East Hollywood with a ruptured brain aneurysm and lay in a coma. The following day, with his parents and sister present, it was determined his situation was inoperable and he was removed from life support. He was 49 years old.

According to his wishes there was no funeral, but a group of friends honored him at a private gathering. In the family home of Candi Carley, a talented blind girl he'd mentored and helped to acquire a Hammond B3 organ of her own, a small group of professionals from the southern California organ scene sat around and remembered him one evening. "It wasn't a tearful affair," one friend wrote in an appreciation, "just a chance to talk about Paul with his friends in surroundings which would have pleased him."[30] His kindness and generosity in helping other musicians were celebrated.

Bob, in fact, owed him the biggest debt of all. If it hadn't been for Paul's vision and initiative—beginning with the 1967 AES when Bob and Shirleigh were close to throwing in the towel—Bob's very career might not have materialized as it did. In a reference to an early organ LP Paul recorded, one writer mused, "Paul left his own requiem, the brooding, moody music in his *Perchance to Dream*."[31]

23

Genericide

The Norlin management figured they could put the Moog name on anything and have a hit. The classic trademark would carry the day. As for the man himself—he was no longer needed. He'd become incidental.

The company's reputation was coasting on the flagship Minimoog. The instrument was popping up more and more on albums under the fingers of rising superstars like Jan Hammer, keyboardist of the jazz-rock fusion band, the Mahavishnu Orchestra. Bob was especially taken with Hammer's playing, telling the *Los Angeles Times*, "He's done more to use a small keyboard synthesizer expressively than any other one musician. There are 10,000 keyboard players breaking their fingers trying to do what he did."[1]

Rick Wakeman, the English rocker whom critics were comparing to Keith Emerson for his manic fireworks across the keys, was also a Minimoog devotee. "To me that's the most important keyboard instrument that's ever been played," he told Bob. "It changed the face of music."[2] Wakeman gloated over the way the Minimoog shifted the balance of power in bands: keyboardists had always been "back-room boys," he told *Entertainment Weekly*. "When it came solo time, you were either drowned out completely or the band had to embarrassingly drop their volume in order for you to be heard. Guitarists would inevitably smirk to the bass player, as if to say, 'I don't even know why we have these people on stage.' Then the Moog hit the scene, and here was an instrument with a sound that would cut concrete. Guitarists fell to their knees in fear."[3] Wakeman amassed eight Minimoogs, keeping as many as four at a time on stage during his shows.

Anxious to build on the Minimoog legacy, Norlin badgered Moog Music to rush out new products. The latest models, released in 1975, would keep Bob's name in the suffix, but they'd be born without his input. Dave Luce was head of engineering now, and the first instrument to answer the call was a smaller, cheaper, simpler alternative to the Minimoog, called the Micromoog. Jim Scott—who'd joined the company again—devised it and had it done in two weeks. The company touted the 20-pound instrument as something the size of a ballpark vendor's tray, so you could carry it around the stage while you played. At under $800, it had many of the functions of the Minimoog, plus a winning new feature: a temperature-stable VCO circuit Scott developed to correct the infamous Moog pitch drift. A second new instrument also came to life without Bob's involvement, but still bore his name: the Minitmoog—an expanded spinoff of the Satellite.

Another instrument that wasn't Bob's progeny was becoming a delinquent in the company ranks. The Sonic Six, touted as the whiz kid educational model designed to get schoolchildren frolicking in a sandbox of sound, was temperamental and ill-behaved. With its top-heavy hinged lid open, it liked to flip backwards off a table. It didn't do well on trips: its case flexed, warping the keyboard and causing rivets to loosen up, circuits to come apart, and knobs to pop off. And it was stubborn about being serviced. Moog personnel nicknamed the Sonic Six the "Chronic Sick," and groaned that it had a 200% failure rate, meaning that instruments returned to owners after a repair usually boomeranged right back for a second fix. Schools hadn't grabbed it up in large numbers, and musicians preferred the sound of the Minimoog. "Nobody wanted the Sonic Six," Jim Scott recalled. "They built a lot of Sonics and it took a long time to get rid of the production run."[4]

Even with Waytena gone, Bob remained in a kind of purgatory at the company. In a letter to a Norlin exec, he blamed Waytena for biasing the new owners against him and painting him as "some kind of ivory-towered goof who walks around with a soldering stuck between his ears."[5] The higher-ups at Norlin were a demanding bunch, Bob recalled: "They had three patent attorneys full time and these guys would sit across the table . . . and they would say, 'What did you invent in two weeks?'"[6] But Bob refused to lay golden eggs on command. He just couldn't see eye to eye with the management: "The people involved were not in love with the musical instrument business. They operated it just to make money. Their view was always short range."[7]

With the Moog line becoming a drag on Norlin's profits, the company announced in June 1975 that it was handing off its Gibson, Epiphone, Cordovox, and Maestro brands to Academy Street to add to the plant's manufacturing schedule. Now, with the assembly line choked with amplifiers and Les Paul Deluxe Pickups, Bob was put to work designing amp circuits, Maestro foot pedals, and the electronics for the Gibson RD guitar. He was occasionally farmed out as a consultant for electronic accordions and Sennheiser microphones. "It's really ironic," he despaired to an interviewer, "that Luce wound up working on all the synthesizers and I wound up working on everything else."[8] On a phase shifter pedal he designed for Maestro, he added a wink of graffiti, labeling the functions for "speed" and "depth," "Speed" and "*Balls.*"

The yawning chasm between Bob's immense international reputation and the Norlin management's disdain for his presence at the factory was widening. *Rolling Stone*, in its February 1975 issue, had declared that Bob's synthesizers, "Bent the Course of Music Forever."[9] The article, "That Little Old Wavemaker MOOG," a double interview with Bob and Utopia band member Roger Powell, was the latest public nod to his enshrined status. But it came at an odd moment: he hadn't made any new "waves" for some time, and at Norlin he was unwelcome to remain on the course he'd allegedly "bent forever."

In October, Bob was subjected to a Norlin "Merit Review," a kind of report card evaluating his job performance. The form contained boxes checked off by a "Supervisor"—one of the many faceless suits at the Chicago office who'd likely never met Bob or even visited the factory. Under the column, "Clearly Outstanding," Bob didn't earn a single checkmark. Most of his ratings fell under "Exceeds Expectations" or "Met Expectations." But 11 items were graded under "Short of Expectations," including "cooperation with other departments," "understands, sets priorities," "budgets and uses time effectively," and "quantity of work."[10]

Outside the business, no one would have suspected Norlin was warehousing its synth pioneer. Publicly, the company made a show of showering Bob with hosannas and genuflecting before his graven image. The marketing department eagerly dressed him up in the cult persona he'd always been mantled in, as the high priest of electronic hipness. On the cover of the company's booklet, *IMOOGINATION,* his nearly life-sized likeness stared out in a Peter Max-style psychedelic pop portrait, his head doused in a whipped cream cloud of white hair laced with trippy cartoons of trains, planes, circus elephants, a rock band, and other hallucinogenic visions.

The 20-page newsprint pamphlet—a grab-and-go handout at Norlin's convention tables—was peppered with news stories on every corner of Moog history and the brand's latest instruments. Bob's constant presence on the pages cast him as the guiding light behind the company: "Dr. Moog says affectionately of some of his staff, 'They're all musicians, and one's crazier than the next.' . . . you'll have to admit, that's some incredible band Dr. Moog has put together."[11] The Norlin takeover was spun as a happy "merger" necessitated by unprecedented growth at Moog Music, and Bob was portrayed as a magnet for celebrities, and shown in photos with Keith Emerson and Roger Powell. Popping up everywhere were shots of famous Moog users like Rick Wakeman, Chick Corea, and Patrick Moraz.

But in the zeal of its chicanery, Norlin's Chicago office revealed how disconnected it was from the reality on the ground in Williamsville. Its staff apparently never bothered to learn the pronunciation of the brand name, leading off one article with a bad pun on the word "moon," "Phases of the Moog." A section titled, "We stand behind our records"—a list of Moog LPs—included albums by Elton John and Pink Floyd that used only competitors' synths.

Bob was revered in Japan, and Norlin had *IMOOGINATION* translated into Japanese. Despite the wholesale leeching of his technology in that country, his role as founder of the industry was held in great esteem there; lately he'd even been asked to pen an article for a Japanese music magazine. The Moog modular, in particular, had gained mythic status in Japan through Isao Tomita's four recent RCA Red Seal albums of Moog-dominated arrangements: classical favorites of Debussy, *Snowflakes Are Dancing* (the title track perilously close to Ruth White's more elegant Moog version on her 1971 album); and grandiose realizations of Mussorgsky's *Pictures at an Exhibition*, Stravinsky's *Firebird*, and Holst's *The Planets*. The cover of the Japanese *IMOOGINATION* booklet was a merry-go-round of cartoon images orbiting a caricature of Bob as a mad scientist with protruding eyeballs, a sweat-beaded brow, and maniacally parted lips spewing bolts of lightning. "Professor Moog's pathological obsession," the caption read in Japanese characters.[12]

Far from the Asian island nation, and the Norlin hype Bob was yoked to, his "pathological obsession" to invent was once again shoved aside in the quotidian machinations at Academy Street. The company needed to save itself now with a new product, and Dave Luce was put on the case. It was time to deliver on the long-delayed polyphonic synth project.

The original Constellation ensemble—the Apollo, Taurus, and Lyra— was broken up, with the Taurus pedals peeled off as a separate product, and the Apollo prototype set to evolve into a standalone instrument slated as the company's new crown jewel. It would be yet another model with the Moog suffix: the Polymoog. Bob's contribution to the Constellation prototype, the Lyra, was dumped in the process. The new polyphonic keyboard would be Moog Music's major thrust in 1975 and 1976. "I had nothing to do with the Polymoog. That instrument was the brainchild of David Luce,"[13]

Bob explained. "He never involved me in any of the design of it."[14] Norlin was wagering the entire future of Moog Music on the Polymoog, and Gullo, the new company general manager, warned his directors, "If the Polymoog doesn't sell, it could take Moog down with it."[15]

The Polymoog was analog—like all synths at the time—but Norlin was on a slippery slope as the digital revolution approached. In the twilight years of analog circuitry, Dave Luce and his team would be scrambling to keep up with a mercurial music market that shifted daily with warp speed advances in technology. The Polymoog made a small bow to the future with its digital switching circuitry that controlled analog components. And it stretched the existing technology as the first synth with full polyphony: it could sound all its keys at once—71 simultaneous tones. But Norlin took a risky gamble in hurrying the analog Polymoog into production. "I had a suspicion that digital synthesis was coming around the corner," Luce confessed. "The writing was on the wall."[16]

Crammed inside the Polymoog was a dizzying assemblage of miniature components. Each of its 71 keys had, in effect, its own tiny synthesizer—a custom integrated circuit chip the size of a penny with a VCF, two VCAs, and an envelope generator that together shaped the sound of that particular note. ICs at the time were fabulously expensive, and the supply of these proprietary "polycom" chips—made exclusively for Moog by National Semiconductor—set Norlin back $100,000. Before the project was done, Norlin bragged it had sunk half a million dollars into R & D and the instrument's integrated circuitry.

With all its high-tech features, the Polymoog still wasn't a synthesizer by Bob's definition. It was loaded with eight preset sounds called "modes" (String, Piano, Organ, Harpsi, Funk, Clav, Vibes, and Brass), that could be tapped in pure form, or morphed into original sounds through the "variation" mode.

At the June 1975 NAMM convention, Norlin unveiled the Micromoog and the Polymoog prototype. Riding on the history of Bob's name, the company trumpeted, "Moog . . . has broken the monophonic sound barrier with its revolutionary Polymoog."[17] The instrument's fall 1976 rollout befitted a new species of musical instrument. A California music store ad echoed the fanfare of Norlin's national campaign: "Polymoog is here! Come in and witness the greatest breakthrough in music since Moog invented the synthesizer."[18]

Anticipating the autumn release, musicians had flocked to the Polymoog earlier in the year in live performances and on records: Jan Hammer; Chick

Corea; Michael Urbaniak; and composer and synthesist Larry Fast. In coming years, the instrument would be taken up by bands from Blondie and Devo to the Electric Light Orchestra, and artists like Rick Wakeman. The Polymoog became a trademark sound for Gary Numan, who owned a whole collection of the instruments. At $4,000 it was a serious commitment, but it sold well in a limited market.

More units might have sold if it hadn't been for a host of glitches. As a gig instrument the Polymoog was bulky and cumbersome: at 82 pounds it took two roadies to move it. The complex network of tiny circuits in its guts made it fragile and mechanically unreliable. Tossed into the back of a truck on tours, the 71 individual "modulator cards" with polycom chips would rattle loose and pop out of their slots; contacts would corrode and fail. Tom Gullo cringed whenever he put a Polymoog on his vibration table for a final endurance test: "They would strap it into this thing and turn the thing on, and it would shake the shit out of it. The Minimoog could take a helluva lot of abuse and it would live, but the Polymoog was just prone to fall apart by the way it was designed."[19]

Dave Luce despaired that the Polymoog had been rushed into production before it was ready because Norlin was impatient to recoup its investment. "It was a problem, no question," he conceded. But he was quick to point out that scaling the peaks with the available technology was daunting: "That was true of the whole electronics industry; initially, ICs failed early. So it was almost just trying to climb a mountain that's ten times the height of Mt. Everest without oxygen."[20]

Bob was clearly unenthusiastic about the Polymoog: "The instrument has some interesting features, but I would have done a polyphonic instrument very differently. . . . Moog Music could have done it with a different engineering approach."[21] But no one at the company seemed to care about his input. "At one point," he recalled, "I took a completed Polymoog out, did a little market testing, offered some suggestions and the suggestions weren't implemented."[22] Michelle Moog remembered that her father thought the Polymoog was "designed poorly and he was embarrassed by it."[23]

Still, from Norlin's perspective, as long as Bob's name was blazoned across its instruments, the company insisted he brand every one of them with a hearty imprimatur. A Norlin flyer titled, "A blunt and totally biased viewpoint on electronic synthesizers from Bob Moog," gave him the floor to read obediently from the company script. With all the candor of a hostage in a videotaped confession, Bob made his official pronouncement: "Polymoog, our most recent development, is an example of 'musical engineering' at its finest. Here is the first polyphonic synthesizer. . . . With eight rich sounding preset modes to choose from, four independent output channels and many of the best Moog circuits and performance features, Polymoog is an instrument of almost limitless potential. No other keyboard even comes close."[24]

The one genuine element of Bob's legacy that did remain in the company's instruments—including the Polymoog—was his classic ladder filter. But even that was still under attack. In 1973, when Norlin lawyers threatened Alan Pearlman with a lawsuit over his pirated Moog filter, he admitted the thievery and the case appeared to be a slam dunk. A year later, in April 1974, Bob happily reported, "We received a letter from their patent attorney expressing an interest in a case settlement (to us)."[25]

But things dragged on as Pearlman rummaged for a way out. Fanning the old embers, he hoped to fire up another incendiary patent claim against Moog to force a swap instead of paying a licensing fee. Searching for any possible circuit overlap between the two companies, he decided that the Minimoog VCO infringed his Nexus-era patent, the "Temperature Compensated Logarithmic Amplifier," the trusty element behind ARP's fabled pitch stability. Pearlman began making noises about it and Bob complained to a friend, "The rumor mill has it that Arp is suing us for infringing on *their* patents. If you know where those rumors come from, please let us know so we can try to stop them."[26]

Nailing any violation on Moog's part would prove elusive for Pearlman. The implementation used in the Minimoog VCO was not listed in the original claims of the Nexus patent. And there was the simple technicality that the Nexus patent remained the property of that company. But the biggest deterrent emerged when ARP's own lawyer found many precedents for the configuration, and for other ARP patents, during the process of "discovery." "We decided to drop the patent stuff," David Friend admitted, because his company feared, "all these patents would be invalidated if they ever went to court, including the Nexus patent."[27]

ARP had no case against Moog, but its directors took comfort in the conviction that the Minimoog VCO wasn't really a threat after all. As Friend explained: "We'd developed a manufacturing technique that kept everything at exactly the same temperature—we're talking thousandths of a degree—and Moog didn't understand that. But these manufacturing processes were trade secrets, not part of the patent."[28]

On November 13, 1975, Dave Luce reported to Moog management, "Suit against ARP on filter patent—Settlement in progress. No suits against Moog."[29] In the end, the dispute was restricted to bickering between patent attorneys and no case was ever brought to court. ARP had to pay a modest sum to Moog for its use of the ladder filter in previous models, and after dragging its feet for almost four years, the company finally swapped out the Moog filter in its new instruments for its own filter design starting in 1977.

Reclaiming proprietary use of Bob's ladder filter didn't shift Moog's bottom line, though. Everything now rested on pumping out Polymoogs, the instrument the company's whole future was staked on. But production mandates for Norlin's other brands were straining resources and there was no space to start manufacturing the new instrument. And the project would be daunting in any case. The complexity of making synthesizers was still the head-spinning conundrum that always plagued Bob. Gullo reminded the managers, "Moog stocks over ten thousand different parts. Proper scheduling of materials, labor and time is our single biggest weakness."[30]

Compounding everything, the physical plant continued to subsist on Waytena's tightwad legacy, and it was collapsing at the seams. Water from natural springs crept through floor cracks and flooded the place, and pallets laid down for walkways just floated and bobbed. The muddy winter driveway mired tractor trailer trucks in a snow and ice quicksand until burly "snow crew" staffers pushed them back up the hill. The mayor of Williamsville threatened to block the company's access to Academy Street altogether, and Gullo reported, "We are being made to look like irresponsible profit lords that have no feelings for the safety of local school-children."[31] The company would clearly need to relocate.

Gullo and Luce found a spacious rental property four miles south of Williamsville, in the Buffalo suburb of Cheektowaga. The former department store at 2500 Walden Avenue was about a mile from the Buffalo airport, and compared to the Trumansburg shop and the Academy Street plant, it looked like a true mass-production workplace. Norlin paid industrial engineers to lay out fancy automatic equipment across its vast floor spaces so Moog could keep punching out Gibson and Maestro products; the synthesizers—even the Polymoog—would continue to ride the coattails of the other brands.

For Bob, the expansion offered an excuse to distance himself from the daily political theatrics and indignities he'd become accustomed to. In a special arrangement, he was allowed to work remotely from a home shop— one in a new house the Moogs moved to in the spring of 1976 following the company's migration to the Walden Avenue plant. The new address, 17 miles south of the factory, was in East Aurora at 405 Fillmore Avenue. The 1890 farmhouse had double the square footage of the Williamsville home and sat on nearly an acre of land along a picturesque suburban street.

Yet even at a distance, Bob's latest assignment from Norlin had little to do with synths: he was to work on a new amplifier for Gibson guitars called the Lab Series. His part in designing some of its sophisticated solid-state circuitry was folded in with every company engineer who contributed to it, all of them credited in ads for the amp under the name "Moog"—not the man, but the company.

Still, there were a few consolations. Through Gibson, Bob had a chance to meet and stage a "publicity stunt" at the plant with one of his heroes: the guitar legend Les Paul, whom he revered for his pioneering work in multitrack recording. And for the first time in years, he was relieved of debt, earning a decent salary, and able to cash in the company's time-release shares. A few years earlier, things were so tight Shirleigh had had to defer payment for Renée's ballet lessons, only to face the typical barb: 'Oh come on now,' the dance teacher objected, "my son told me that you people are rolling in money."[32]

Working from home and luxuriating in a buffer of financial security, Bob dallied in domestic pleasures—the requisite vegetable garden, and a new diversion: making maple sugar candy from trees he tapped in his yard, cooking the sap over a wood-fired stove he built himself. His cherished spot in the new home was a carriage house on the property where he located his workshop, a sanctuary to indulge the basement solitude of his early years. He poured a concrete surface over its dirt floor and erected a staircase to a second level with an office and a guest bedroom.

The workshop oasis didn't last long. A neighbor, annoyed at the procession of delivery trucks pulling up outside, ratted him out to local authorities. The Village of East Aurora cited him for a zoning violation—conducting business in a residential neighborhood—and slapped a padlock on the door of the carriage house. Forced to find a new refuge, he leased a former firehouse a mile away in town at 80 Elm Street—a small, two-story corner building abandoned after the East Aurora volunteer fire department relocated 20 years earlier.

Despite the calmer waters of these East Aurora years, the undercurrent of Shirleigh's frustrations could bolt to the surface at the slightest ripple. In the midst of a cheery domestic moment one night when Bob asked for family volunteers to help him assemble a ping-pong table, Shirleigh flexed her muscle to offer her help, and Bob pinched the flab under her arm, mocking her teasingly. The slight set off an explosive argument and Bob stalked off, Shirleigh hollering in pursuit, while the kids scrambled to clear the table and disperse to their rooms. Eventually Shirleigh retreated to her bedroom. When Laura went in to check on her mother, she found her clinging by a thread to consciousness, and marshaled the siblings. Michelle recalled, "Laura told us. 'She took a bunch of sleeping pills, she tried to kill herself!' An ambulance came, they got mom and carried her out. Dad went with her. They got her to the hospital and pumped her stomach."[33]

Shirleigh came home the same night, but eight-year-old Michelle struggled to reconcile the chilly pall of silence that hung over her parents, a void betraying guilt, denial, and embarrassment: "Dad wasn't the kind of person to come into my room and sit on my bed and talk to me about what just happened. He never asked her why she did it and never talked to her about it. That affected the rest of my life and how I treated my mother. I always felt like I was walking on eggshells and at any point she could do that again."[34] The incident, witnessed by the whole family, including six-year-old Matthew, was silently buried in the family dynamic, never to be exhumed.

∿∿∿

Bob had reached the point where the end of his Norlin contract couldn't come soon enough, and he was itching to turn his back on the Buffalo area. A psychological balm for everyone came in late summer with a three-week jaunt to North Carolina. Shirleigh and Bob finally fulfilled the promise they'd made to each other four years earlier: on August 30 they purchased 89 acres of wild land in Buncombe County for $46,150. In October they bought a second, adjoining 99-acre property for $60,000. Bob's Norlin contract had a year and a half to go, but with one foot in the tall grasses of North Carolina, the idyllic future felt closer.

It constantly seemed to be the case that the things Bob took the most pleasure in never bore any monetary fruit, and often wound up emptying his wallet as well. But a dose of his ready celebrity could always chase down the bitter pills he had to swallow from Norlin. One happy indulgence was the regular column he'd been invited to write for *Contemporary Keyboard* magazine. The first of his "On Synthesizers" series ran in the inaugural issue—September/October 1975—along with a laudatory profile on his life and

302 AN APOCALYPSE NOW

work by assistant editor Dominic Milano. For each 400- to 500-word article, Bob was paid $50.

In his last months in Buffalo in the fall of 1977, Bob ran out the clock on his contract by escaping into the world of his earliest professional success: the theremin, the only area of his work where he remained top dog and unchallenged by competitors. The project involved the venerated queen of the theremin, Clara Rockmore, who'd enjoyed a decades-long concert career following her Town Hall debut in 1934 when Bob was a baby. "This lady was my idol while I was working my way through college," he told a customer. "She was the only one who could honestly be called a theremin virtuoso."[35]

Bob had met Clara as a young engineering student when he appeared at her door one day, naively sporting his latest theremin with its tiny radio speaker. He left with a pat on the head, some patronizing encouragement, and Clara's reminder that she owned a handmade instrument built for her by Leon Theremin himself, with a robust amp and speaker that could dominate a whole symphony orchestra. Bob learned an essential lesson: any electronic instrument's tone is only as good as its amplifier and speaker. Clara, to her credit, followed Bob's career and turned up in the audience at the 1969 MoMA Jazz in the Garden Concert. The two stayed in touch over the years.

Surprisingly, Clara had never left a vinyl trail to immortalize her playing, and in 1975 Bob coaxed the 64-year-old virtuosa out of retirement to lay down tracks for a commercial recording. It was a labor of love that he underwrote with $1,800 of his own money, and hours of sweat equity, chasing down label after label for a commitment to press and distribute the LP. The project was particularly selfless because Clara wouldn't be using one of his instruments—she'd be sticking with her Leon Theremin original. Bob served as engineer and wrote the liner notes for the album. In an uncharacteristic gesture, he tossed Shirleigh a bone, adding her to the project as "producer." Her duties amounted to general gofer and wardrobe mistress for Clara during the recording sessions, but she wound up with a credit on the album cover: *Shirleigh and Robert MOOG present CLARA ROCKMORE . . . "premiere artiste of the electronic music medium."*

The LP was released on the Delos label and debuted at a press party at Clara's New York apartment on November 3, 1977. Its 12 cuts—greatest hits of the adopted theremin repertoire by romantic and early twentieth-century classical composers—soared through melodic updrafts into over-the-top emotionalism in Clara's hands, accompanied at the piano by her sister, the pianist Nadia Reisenberg. Bob had managed to encase Clara's best performances in amber for all time.[36]

While Bob was busy with Clara's recording, his modular had just notched another first in the world: it sired the genre of electronic dance music. "I Feel Love," a hypnotic, seductive single by Donna Summer, the "Queen of Disco," had cast the Moog in a central role. Soon after the song's release in July 1977 it went to No. 1 in the UK, climbing to No. 6 in the U.S., and then perched atop charts internationally, eventually making the "top songs of all time" lists of magazines and critics worldwide. Donna Summer and her collaborator, composer Giorgio Moroder, had pushed the boundaries of disco permanently into the electronic sphere with this single song.

"I Feel Love" came from Summer's LP, *I Remember Yesterday*, a concept album traveling through styles from the 1940s to the 1970s. Moroder wanted the album to conclude with a song that sounded futuristic, and decided it had to be done with a synthesizer. He recalled, "This was the first song I did with a synthesizer, with the big Moog."[37]

The trademark sound of disco was typically erected on lush orchestrations of acoustic instruments, but for the album's futuristic cut, Moroder abandoned the orchestra for a mechanistic machine music. The mix of "I Feel Love" was spare, with only three ingredients: Summer's voice, the Moog modular IIIp, and an acoustic kick drum. The Moog even stood in for the sound of a hi-hat cymbal with clipped bursts of white noise. For the bass line, Moroder added a deep-in-the-gut fluttering effect by setting its left and right channels out of synch by a split-second.

"I Feel Love" caught fire on dance floors around the globe with an infectious, robotic beat that marched along relentlessly—a head-bopping metallic groove beneath intermittent episodes of Summer's breathy voice intoning snippets of melody and subtle vocal swoops. Its motoric rhythm was compared with Kraftwerk's recent "Trans-Europe Express," but this was real *dance* music; "I Feel Love" turned the thumping, automated pulse into a new trance drug for the disco crowd. Soon after its release, David Bowie was in a studio in Berlin recording his *Heroes* album when his collaborator, Brian Eno, rushed in wielding a copy of "I Feel Love," and panting, "I have heard the sound of the future. . . . This is it, look no further. This single is going to change the sound of club music for the next fifteen years."[38] Eno was right. "I Feel Love" would spawn EDM genres like electro, house, techno, and trance, and influence other pop styles from new wave to post-punk and synth-pop.

Most people who heard the synthesizer in "I Feel Love" might've assumed it was a Moog. The name "Moog" was, as *Rolling Stone* declared in 1975, "synonymous with synthesizer." The *New York Daily News* called the name "almost generic." Bob himself had admitted in his 1969 *New York Times* interview with Donal Henahan, "I like the idea of my name becoming a generic term for the synthesizer."[39] By 1974 his wish had come true, and he could smugly remind a Norlin exec, "The name is so powerful that our competition is beating their brains out and spending millions to stop the public from calling their products 'moogs.' "[40]

It was true. Bob's competitors were caught up in the vortex of the Moog name again and again. In the middle of a Buchla demo once, puzzled spectators interrupted to ask, "Isn't that what is called the Moog Synthesizer?"[41] A Minneapolis newspaper covering a school show by musician, Herb Pilhofer—under the tired out headline, ". . . In The Moog for Music"—explained that Pilhofer's synthesizer was "a space-age instrument linked most with Robert Moog, its chief creator."[42] Pilhofer had actually used an ARP 2600, but a photo of it bore the caption: *MUSICIAN HERB PILHOFER . . . BROUGHT HIS "MOOG."* *Rolling Stone* reported that a *Playboy* music poll "listed six men as being 'moog' players when in fact they all played ARP equipment."[43] David Friend at ARP went ballistic when he got an inquiry from a university professor asking for a price quote on a Moog. Friend fired off a seven-page screed setting the customer straight and skewering Bob's instruments while he was at it.

In the halcyon era of Moog renown, the name crept into the most unlikely places. A John Updike short story, "Love Song, for a Moog Synthesizer," showed up in *The New Yorker* in 1976, though it made no reference to a synthesizer.[44] A full-page *New York Times* fashion ad for B. Altman & Co. in 1975 pitched a "2002 A.D. dress" and a "Flash Gordon jumpsuit," promising, "The excitement will begin the second you zip in. . . . Looking for all the planet as though you'd just stepped off the set of Star Trek. (A little **moog music**, please)."[45]

But there was a downside to having a name approach the level of a generic. Many companies had suffered what became known as "genericide"—the death of a trademark caused by popular usage that turned it into a common noun. Xerox, Jello, Band-aid, Kleenex, Cellophane, and Linoleum all became standard monikers. This "generification" was a mixed blessing. On the surface it looked like free advertising, but it could also drain the original brand, weakening its uniqueness, siphoning off sales to competitors, and threatening the protection of the trademark. Bob's distinctive name lent itself naturally to genericide: it appeared frequently in the press in lowercase, as "moog"; practitioners were referred to as "moogists"; it was used as a verb, "to moog"; and it was sometimes applied in the plural: not "Moog synthesizers," but "moogs."

The name could also be used to the advantage of Bob's competitors. By 1973 ARP had apparently found it was easier to embrace the misnomer and steal away unwitting customers. Bob noted an alarming wording on an ARP brochure and alerted a patent attorney: "It seems that ARP is pushing hard to make MOOG a generic term. What plan of action should we follow?"[46] He jotted the lawyer's advice in his memo pad: report "if bad usage occurs. Bad usage is when 'Moog' is used as a noun, or when it is not capitalized."[47]

Nonetheless, the name "Moog"—now, the *word* moog—had truly come to mean *any* synthesizer, a phenomenon glaringly apparent on albums. The cover illustration for the 1973 *Moog at the Movies: Synthesonic Sounds*, showed an ARP 2600 inset into a theater organ, with the name MOOG incongruously labeled above it. The 1974 *Alamooga Esinlenmeler,* by Turkish musician Metin Alatli, pictured an ARP 2600 on the cover and listed that instrument in the credits. If any title screamed "Moog," it was *Switched-On Switzerland*, but the 1976 album was recorded on an EMS 100. The same year, Robin Workman's release, *Moog & Guitars Play ABBA*, had a meticulously detailed instrument list on the jacket that included four different ARP models and a Roland SH-5. No Moogs. The synths on the 1976 LP from the French musician Roger Roger, with the loopy title, *Chatta MOOGA Choo Choo*, were credited as an ARP, a Putney VCS3, and "special custom," whatever that was.

The ultimate signal that genericide had eroded Bob's brand was evident in a *Pasadena Star-News* article from 1974. "How to Make Your Own Moog Music" described an adult evening course purporting to teach students how to build a synthesizer "for $50 and $100 . . . by buying pieces of junked machines."[48] The technology had been relegated to a collection of hobbyists' circuits in the public domain.

As Bob prepared to turn his back on the corporate world and wander into the unknown of the Appalachian Mountains, he was leaving his name behind. But the vividness of the supposedly indelible trademark itself was fading like the colors of a flag that had waved for too long in the brilliant sun.

24
Yankee Go Home

Shirleigh's euphoria spilled over in a letter to Florence as the family headed south to their new home in the summer of 1978. "I'm feeling as giddy as the day we were married—free—& doing our thing."[1]

On June 26, rumbling along the last three unpaved miles of South Turkey Creek Road, they turned off at the "dead end" sign onto their own one-third-mile driveway. The dirt path led up to a broken-down 100-year-old cabin on the rambling property of hills, creeks, and tree varieties of wild cherry, apple, chestnut, sassafras, locust, poplar, pine, oak, hickory, and black gum. The family would camp out in the old cabin for the summer, living within eyeshot of an adjacent hill where the groundbreaking and construction of their new home was about to begin.

The Moogs' new habitat lay in the Blue Ridge Mountains of western North Carolina, part of the southern Appalachian range near the eastern gateway to Great Smoky Mountains National Park. Of the two properties they owned, they'd chosen to settle on the 89-acre stretch of virgin land in Leicester Township, Buncombe County, sitting at an elevation of 2,700 feet. The nearest city was Asheville, 12 miles to the southeast.

The little cabin where the family would hunker down for the summer was barely a shelter, open to the air, with no glass or screens in the windows and gaps between the logs where the chinking had deteriorated. An exterior fireplace was littered with snakeskins. The structure was perilously close to nature, but the dormant Boy Scout in Bob was roused, and he reported to Florence, the biologist, "Mud-dauber wasps are laboriously building mud Quonset huts on our ceiling, and the spiders are getting grotesquely fat on the bugs that are attracted to our gasoline lantern."[2] Matthew and Michelle were taught the difference between poisonous and non-poisonous snakes, and the family cooked on a propane stove, bathed in a babbling stream down the hill behind the cabin, and used a port-a-john planted in the meadow.

In early July a construction crew arrived, swarming over the hill and bouncing around in heavy machinery to dig the footings for the house foundation. This would be no ordinary home. Bob and Shirleigh had opted for a round house, a 15-sided cylinder, 40 feet in diameter, made by the Asheville-based Deltec Company. The two-story, 3,000-square-foot "Polyrama 1200" was a prefab model that would be assembled on site from pre-constructed units. The finished house would have a redwood exterior, a deck wrapping halfway around the circumference, 360-degree windows, and a view out to Tennessee. The interior walls would be non-load-bearing so they could be installed later as dividers for any number of room configurations. The open-ended design appealed to the Moogs, who planned to finish most of the inside themselves, personalizing it to their taste.

In the fall, the family moved into the shell of the house. There was barely any plumbing or electricity, and the water supply came from a mountain spring on the property, diverted down the hill. Bob felled trees to rack and stow cords of firewood for stoking Shirleigh's log-fueled stove and the wood-burning furnace. Shirleigh drooled over her root cellar, where she would can a cornucopia of fruits and vegetables from a garden she daydreamed about. Bob roared around on his Ford tractor with the blithe abandon of a boy on his first bike, towing a rotary mower to "bush hog" acres of tall grass. Shirleigh swooned to Florence, "Very few get to go to heaven <u>before</u> they die. We keep pinching ourselves & smiling like fools."[3]

When word got out in the community, the *Asheville Citizen-Times* showed up to welcome its celebrity gentleman farmer. "We want to spend as much time out with our hands in the dirt as possible," Shirleigh explained. "Right now we just want to be known as the Moogs at the end of the road."[4] But the remove from Buffalo was measured in more than just mileage. Bob let on to Florence, "One of our neighbors told me that the only way to get woodchucks is with a rifle, and the best time to do that is around sundown, 'when a man's work is done and he has the patience to set and watch the garden for an hour or so.'"[5]

Bob and Shirleigh had wound up in God's Country once again. It wasn't a matter of whether you would join a church, but only which one you would join. "In that community," Michelle found out, "it was, like, what's your name and what church do you go to? I never knew what to say to that—like, 'I don't know—the Jewish church?' Because if I identified with anything, it would have been that. But it was more a question of heritage, not a question of conviction."[6]

The Moog children were aware that their parents had grown up in Jewish households, but the faith and the traditions were foreign to them. Food was the main connection. "My exposure to Judaism was matzo ball soup," Michelle recalled. "We got pickled herring and bagels." But Christianity wasn't in their life experience either. "Christmas was just a holiday," she confessed. "It was a Pagan thing. My mom carried the Christmas torch more than my father. I think it's just because she liked the fun of it. Dad was never a person who liked days when you had to give gifts. He didn't like it on birthdays; he just didn't like it."[7]

For Matthew and Michelle, the hour-long school bus ride each morning to Leicester Elementary, a mid-sized country school, was a stomach-clenching ordeal. With each new arrival on board, the cultural noise separating them from the local children intensified. "These kids grew up together," Michelle recalled, "They went to the same church. And we weren't blonde-haired and blue-eyed and didn't have the typical southern look. It wasn't long before they told us, 'Damn Yankees, go home.' We were like heathens."[8] Every day Michelle's class would stand to recite the Lord's Prayer, and one by one, the children read from the Bible. When her turn came, Michelle froze: "I remember being completely unfamiliar with the type of language, fumbling and being very uncomfortable, and there were 20 southern Baptist faces staring at me, and Ms. Brookshire with her very stern affect. Nothing like that had ever happened in New York."[9]

Bob and Shirleigh were livid and felt it was unconstitutional, but neighbors warned them not to say anything. Michelle recalled, "When you're northerners living on a hundred acres of land at the end of a road with a bunch of closely-knit, gun-wielding, right-winged, southern Baptists, you either better mind your manners or fear for your life. So we minded our manners."[10]

At home, Bob and Shirleigh were clear about what they taught their kids: "In place of a conventional personal God," he explained to Florence, "we talk about an impersonal Great Spirit that ties the universe together. In place of traditional Christian morals, we discuss the rights of others to enjoy good lives, and how respecting these rights will be our greatest rewards.... We have decided against public association with any organized religion at this time, simply because we don't believe in it and it would be hypocritical of us to subject our children to it for the sake of social expediency."[11]

But Bob discovered that the Asheville region did have its diversity of cultures. "Many of the people we know," he assured Florence, "don't set foot in a church from one end of the year to the other, while others have chosen 'alternate' religions like Sufi, Reform Judaism, and (don't laugh)

Scientology.... People who live at the ends of dirt roads around here tend to have non-conformist streaks."[12]

The Moogs gradually adapted. "It was character building," Michelle realized. "It was important to understand, we *did* move in among these people who have been here for generations." From her friend Tammy, Michelle picked up a typical southern retort that Bob loved: "golly bum," an expression of surprise that stood in for the harsher, "well, God *damn!*"[13] And the Moogs found parts of the southern culture they could really get into. Shirleigh reported to Florence, "One of our friends had a Pig Roast & Hoe Down for 150 which also blew the kids away."[14]

Bob only checked in with Norlin through a secretary he was using as a mole. "I may be out of the company, but I still like to gossip!" he wrote her. "Haven't designed a circuit or touched a soldering iron in months.... We're having a great time with the plastic pipe, 2 x 4's, and sheet rock."[15] He was on a mental holiday from his old life, but he also needed to tread water until his non-compete clause with Norlin expired at the end of 1979, when he'd be free to pursue original work again.

For all Norlin's efforts to capitalize on Bob's legacy and trademark, though, its incompetent captains were navigating the Moog ship through rough waters and were in serious danger of running aground. Van Koevering's predictions were coming true. Bob told Florence smugly, "Norlin, of course, is losing money ... because the higher-ups don't know diddly-squat about music or musical instruments."[16]

In a strategy to stay afloat, the Walden Avenue plant began rolling out a line of smaller synths, beginning in 1978. The first model had Bob's name on it as a suffix—something the company insisted on—but like the Polymoog, he'd had no part in it. The Multimoog was the creation of Jim Scott, who recalled, "They came up with this terrible name—Multimoog—sounds like it's polyphonic when it's not."[17] The next year, Rich Walborn and Tony Marchese dreamed up a bare-bones Minimoog-style instrument called the Prodigy that sold for $500. "We just dumped it on them and said, 'What do you think of this?'" Walborn recalled.[18] Management woke up, and the Prodigy was rushed into production. "The Norlin guys were all a bunch of screwballs," Gullo recalled. "They were never in control. They were all politicians fighting with each other."[19]

Another Walborn and Marchese creation debuted in 1980: the Liberation, a synth keyboard on a guitar-shaped body. The instrument strapped on over the shoulder so the player could move around the stage like a guitarist. With its long neck sprouting from a cluster of vertical keys, it resembled a giant toothbrush cradled in a musician's arms. The Liberation was polyphonic, but it could be switched over to a solo monophonic lead.

That same year, Herb Deutsch became the inspiration behind another small synth. On temporary leave from his Hofstra professorship since January, he commuted from his home on Long Island for a four-day workweek to serve as Moog's marketing director. For the new instrument, he mapped out the functionality and drew the front panel layout; Dave Luce then designed all the electronics in two weeks. Because the polyphonic keyboard had string, organ, and brass sounds, Herb wanted to call it the S.O.B.— "Bob would have loved that," he recalled.[20] But Norlin flinched, and Herb opted for something more traditional: the Opus 3.

Because the Moog name and trademark remained under lock and key at Norlin, Bob was forced to come up with entirely new branding if he wanted to hang out his shingle again. Back on June 2, 1978, in Buffalo, he'd registered Articles of Incorporation for a new company—a modest setup that would be housed now in a prefab 1,500-square-foot steel building erected at the end of the driveway, across from the new house. The firm would be called Big Briar, Inc. It was a logical choice because the Moog property was known as Big Briar Cove on the topographic map of the Leicester region. This "cove" terrain was a valley surrounded by Jones Mountain to the east, Rockyface Mountain to the south, and Big Butt Mountain to the west. The Moogs, in fact, referred to their property as "the Cove."

By January 1980, Bob had broken free of his suffocating non-compete clause with Norlin and he could start building products under the Big Briar name. But his workshop in the steel building wasn't ready, and in the urge to get going with anything he could attach his name to, he wrote the Heathkit company, proposing a "Heathkit-Robert Moog synthesizer kit." He told the firm confidently that he estimated the market would be "hundreds of thousands, perhaps millions, of high school students and young adults," wanting to assemble the classic name-brand synthesizer as a hobby project.[21] Heathkit shrugged at Bob like he was just another person off the street, and responded with a form letter and an application for unsolicited proposals. After a perfunctory back and forth, it was clear the company had no interest.

Several months later, Bob was on top again as Robert Moog, the man who needs no introduction, with an honor that, as usual, came with no financial reward, but great prestige. *Eureka!* was a Washington, D.C., exhibit that opened in May, recognizing, "America's 12 most innovative inventions of the past 200 years."[22] The Moog synthesizer took its place in the pantheon alongside the telephone, phonograph, artificial heart valve, ice cream cone, and zipper. The inventions were chosen by the Association of Science-Technology Centers of Washington, D.C., and the exhibit was sponsored by the Office of Advocacy of the U.S. Small Business Administration.

President Jimmy Carter's official statement on the exhibit rang poignantly true of Bob, lauding the inventors for a willingness "to risk money and reputation on untried products and ideas that have made our economy prosper."[23] Western New York congressman Jack Kemp, in his own panegyric on the floor of the U.S. House of Representatives, a statement entered into the Congressional Record, remarked, "Playing to over 2½ million enthusiasts, the Moog synthesizer is easily the most popular component of the Eureka exhibit."[24] Following its D.C. opening, the show was slated to go on tour to 11 major science museums around the U.S. At the hands-on displays, visitors could zip a 5-foot-long zipper with wooden teeth, pump fluid through an artificial heart valve, make their own ice cream, or play a tune on a Minimoog.

A major film premiere in August 1979 was further evidence that Bob's synth remained a vital force in the culture, even if its creator was quite literally out to pasture. Francis Ford Coppola's two-and-a-half-hour epic war drama, *Apocalypse Now*, inspired by Joseph Conrad's novella, *Heart of Darkness*, followed a grueling odyssey of violence and terror amid the American presence in Vietnam. Coppola wanted a fresh approach for the soundtrack, and placed the Moog in a central role to illuminate the horrific realities faced by the hallucinating, disoriented Captain Willard (Martin Sheen) and his crew, in their nightmare journey traversing the jungles of Southeast Asia.

Coppola had been impressed by Tomita's all-Moog album, *Snowflakes Are Dancing*, and hoped for a collaboration with the Japanese synthesist. Tomita was unavailable, it turned out, but the *Snowflakes* album remained Coppola's inspiration—"By then, I had the sound of it in my ear," he recalled. Coppola turned to his father, the composer Carmine Coppola, who'd written music for the *Godfather* films, and suggested he compose a score as a template for a final synthesizer realization that would "transliterate it into a sound somewhat like the Tomita." Francis explained that his father wrote "an actual orchestral score, note by note. Everything was scored. So it had a kind of symphonic basis to it." Francis saw the instruments as the actual elements of nature and the war, and suggested synthesized sounds to replace the original acoustic instruments: "I had laid out what the music was trying to express; I went through it and said, 'I want this to sound like wind, and I want this to sound like cicadas.' So I was more like a creative producer/co-composer."[25] In the iconic opening tableau of the film, the thumping of synthesized helicopter blades sets the tone for the score's unique ambient atmosphere.

When *Apocalypse Now* was released, Bob penned an enthusiastic article for the January 1980 issue of *Contemporary Keyboard*. The five-page feature, with photos, detailed the synthesizer phase of the production. "The commander was Francis Ford Coppola," he wrote, echoing the movie's military theme. "The mission was the realization of the film's synthesizer score, a unique multistage effort."[26]

The method of forging the soundtrack was a first: Carmine's full orchestral score was reduced to a piano version that Francis conducted, indicating the tempo at different points to a pianist who was recording it in sync with the film's footage. Then a team of synthesists synchronized their arrangements of the music to this piano "guide track" across the remaining tracks of a 24-track tape. "The synthesists were instructed to adhere to the melodic and harmonic relationships of the score," Bob explained in his article, "but were encouraged to experiment with tone colors."[27] Don Preston, former keyboardist for Frank Zappa's Mothers of Invention, and Bernie Krause each worked with Moog modulars. Patrick Gleeson used E-mu Systems equipment, and Nyle Steiner employed his EVI (electronic valve instrument)—a woodwind-controlled synthesizer he'd invented. Carmine, steeped in the old school tradition of orchestral film scores, was pleasantly surprised: "We were able to get colors that an orchestra simply does not have."[28]

By refracting a symphonic palette through the synthesizers' lens, the film's final scene, in particular, projects a chilling, surreal affect. Dissonant, otherworldly music from a synthetic orchestra—how an acoustic orchestra might sound to a disturbed or drugged mind—underscores Captain Willard's emergence on the steps of the temple compound. Thin, high-string-like melodies, wavering and eerie, are underlaid with menacing bass tones that advance in growling waves, joined by a searing synthesized trumpet in strange clarion calls, building to a flesh-tingling climax.

For the music of *Apocalypse Now*, Carmine and Francis Coppola shared a Golden Globe Award for "Best Original Score."

At the Cove, Bob and Shirleigh were basking in their homesteading life. Two years in, they continued building and outfitting their dream house from the inside out while they lived in it. They'd tiled the bathrooms themselves, and Bob had installed all the plumbing and electricity by earning licenses in both fields. The vegetable garden was expanded to farming dimensions to harvest everything from broccoli, zucchini, and corn, to rhubarb, blackberries, and strawberries. Bob dug in a small vineyard and cleared land for an orchard; bushels of wild apples were sauced, baked, and pied, and Shirleigh packed away jams, jellies, pickles, and sauerkraut in her root cellar. Bob found himself dispatching intruding copperheads in the kitchen with a shovel, but hiking the gorge and creek on the property was a cathartic communion with nature. In a letter to Wendy Carlos, he marveled, "I get what I think is a hint of what the early pioneers must of thought and felt as they asserted control over a very small piece of wilderness. For us, it has been a joyous and sensual exercise."[29]

Just before the move to North Carolina, Shirleigh had emerged briefly from Bob's shadow, into her own spotlight. With the publication in April 1978 of *Moog's Musical Eatery: A Cookbook For Carefree Entertaining*, her culinary talents were put on display. The 209-page paperback, dedicated to Bob, was a diary of the dishes she'd regaled his V.I.P. dinner guests with over the years—everything from Chicken in Lemon Caper Butter, served to John Cage and David Tudor, to the vein-clogging Roasted Game Hens With Cheese & Sausage Stuffing she'd made for Keith Emerson. The pages were peppered with stories of celebrity dinners she'd hosted, and filled with soup-to-nuts recipes covering breads, dips, desserts, and drinks. The book was published by Crossing Press, a small outfit run by friends who'd suggested the idea to her. "I got sick and tired of people putting Moog on stuff and selling it," she recalled, "and I thought, 'Well, *I'll* write a *cookbook*.'"[30]

The book was well publicized and half the first printing of 7,500 sold in a year. But it barely moved the meter for Shirleigh in her role as an appendage to Bob's fame. He told friends that when a reporter described her as "Bob Moog's quiet, homespun wife," she went through the roof and snapped, "I should have told that sonofabitch to go fuck himself. Then he wouldn't think I was so quiet and homespun!"[31]

It was the end of the line for the Minimoog—literally—when Walden Avenue announced it had ceased production of the classic synth in July 1981. The final 25 instruments rolled off the production line encased in select hand-finished walnut and fitted with brass plaques. When the last unit was on the test bench, Roger Luther walked over and played, "The Party's Over." The *very* last instrument was destined for Bob as a gift. After one short decade, the Minimoog was already being characterized in the *Buffalo Courier-Express* as "The Model T Ford of synthesizers."[32] In a little more than 10 years, only about 12,000 Minimoogs had been made, but the company was ready to move on.

Jogging to keep up with the tech market, the Walden Avenue plant quickly moved past the Minimoog with what the company called the "offspring of Mini"—two new analog models with microprocessors.[33] The Source was Moog's first instrument offering programmable patches that could be stored in memory and called up instantly; it featured digitally recorded preset sounds from Jan Hammer, Gary Wright, and Devo's Mothersbaugh, that could be loaded from cassette tapes.

The Memorymoog was another brainchild of Rich Walborn, a pet project he claimed was inspired by the Minimoog, so much so that he spent months deconstructing the Minimoog's sound with a spectrum analyzer. The Memorymoog could store up to 100 patches in computer memory and had sophisticated digital control of its analog functions. Walborn likened the six-voice polyphonic instrument to having six Minimoogs in a box.

Despite the blip from the Source and the Memorymoog, the company was losing steam. Out in the hinterlands, Bob got all the latest dope from the mole secretary at Moog Music: "Boy, do we miss you! . . . Sales have been brutal. . . . People here are losing their 'moogitis.'"[34] Bob couldn't hide his schadenfreude in a reply to a stranger's inquiry: "As a business, Moog Music is in the shithouse," he reported, passing on a rumor that despite six or seven million dollars in sales, Norlin had nosedived, with losses in the seven-figure range the past year, and the once-thriving CMI was being driven into the ground.[35]

At the Walden Avenue plant, Roger Luther—who'd since ascended through the ranks to become general manager—saw the handwriting on the wall in a spreadsheet he compiled comparing Moog products with the competition. The tally wasn't pretty: Moog was losing the market to Japanese manufacturers, and it was lagging behind technologically.

Desperate to supplement synth production, Moog managers like Tom Gullo began prowling for odd jobs just to keep the lights on. And the jobs were decidedly odd for the company. The first gadget off the line was a Fisher-Price toy: the Alpha Probe space shuttle with a Rich Walborn–designed circuit board that made push-button space sounds. The toy was a hit: 360,000 were made. Another item manufactured in astronomical numbers—beyond anything Moog could have hoped for with synths—was commissioned by Lockheed Martin Aerospace. The Prayer Times Clock was a timepiece that sounded an alarm alerting Muslim travelers to the six daily prayer times, and had a built-in compass that pointed in the direction of Mecca. Walborn recalled, "Lockheed Martin did $300 million a year in business with Saudi Arabia in spare parts for military aircraft. They financed this whole thing as a PR thing to keep Saudi Arabia happy. We made like 100,000 of them. We actually made one with a solid gold case, given to the king."[36]

Even with the boost of these contract manufacturing jobs, Gullo was ready to throw in the towel at Moog. In eight years he'd had seven different bosses, courtesy of Norlin. Luce remembered one president who showed up to take the helm at 9 a.m., only to be fired over the phone 30 minutes later. When the latest president quit in December 1980, Norlin tapped its go-to source for hires: the huge management consulting firm, McKinsey. "Norlin was just full of McKinsey guys," Gullo recalled. "Norlin didn't make any decision without McKinsey tellin' them it was ok."[37] The firm's advice this time: bring in an industrial psychologist to vet the contenders.

Four candidates were drafted and made to undergo a battery of tests to determine the last man standing: Luce, Gullo, Herb Deutsch, and a sales executive from the Chicago office. The four nominees spent two days taking odd exams. "I remember some of the questions they asked us," Gullo eye-rolled, "like, 'If you could be an animal, which one would you be?'"[38] Perhaps not realizing how this one would be weighted, Luce took a chance: "I said, 'a cockroach.' Cockroaches have survived for 230 millions . . . they've survived under the worst possible conditions ever."[39] A month later Norlin sent out a press release: "Norton Stevens, Chairman, announced that David A. Luce has been named President of Moog Music effective January 15, 1981."

Well practiced now in high-volume manufacturing, the new Moog management set out to make a cheap, mass-market synth. But to move merchandise in colossal numbers required the heft of a giant corporation like Fisher-Price, or something on the order of a Radio Shack, with its chain of 7,000-plus stores across the U.S. Bob's informer wrote him in March 1980, "The 'boys' went to Radio Shack this week and it looks like they can strike up a deal with them for 'Prodigy' type instruments. Thank God."[40]

Herb, Walborn, and Gullo arrived at Radio Shack's corporate offices in Texas for a scheduled show-and-tell of a Prodigy, anxious to make their case.

They'd have an audition in front of the company's no-nonsense senior vice president, Bernie Appel, who'd flash a thumbs up or a thumbs down. Appel snapped that he had 40 of these demos that day, and the Moog guys had five minutes to make their pitch.

It was a thumbs up, but Walborn could see that for Appel, the bottom line was the bottom line. Moog would need to sell each unit to Radio Shack for $200 so Radio Shack could turn around and charge $500 in stores. That way, if the product failed, they could slash the price by 50% and still make money. Bells and whistles weren't important. "Radio Shack guys would tell you," Walborn recalled, "that if you can take out 50% of the functionality, and reduce the cost by 5%, *do it*. Luce and Moog would've said, 'I can add this, and it only adds a little bit of cost—look what it does!' "[41] But Appel, Gullo recalled, told them bluntly: "You guys don't understand. The customer's gonna use this thing for three months and then it's gonna go in the closet with the rest of the junk we sell them. Then we gotta find somethin' else to sell them."[42]

Walborn took the challenge. He and Marchese had just finished another small synth, the Rogue—"an even smaller, stripped down version of the Prodigy,"[43] as Walborn called it—which debuted at the June 1981 NAMM and was priced "low enough to be a perfect first instrument for beginners." By adding polyphonic capability to what was essentially a Rogue, Walborn came up with something that met Radio Shack's requirements. Like the Liberation, the new synth was both monophonic and polyphonic (Walborn's design incorporated his own U.S. patent, "Electronic Musical Instrument Simultaneously Operable in Monophonic and Polyphonic Modes"), and it had Bob's genuine patented ladder filter that the company continued to put in its synths. The instrument was dubbed the 'Concertmate MG-1, and was marketed under Radio Shack's "Realistic" brand as the "Realistic MG-1 Synthesizer by Moog."

The MG-1 and the Rogue hit stores at the same time in the fall of 1981. In its ads, Radio Shack landed a celebrity endorsement with a captioned photo: "Elton John with the Realistic MG-1 Synthesizer."[44] The company's 1982 and 1983 catalogs advertised the MG-1 with Elton John's picture, and carried a headline to ambush the reader's eye: *Now—The Ultimate Musical Instrument!... Puts a Universe of Sound at Your Fingertips.*[45] The pop legend was happy enough to pose with the keyboard—Gullo, the unofficial company photographer, had taken the shot—but the MG-1 and other Moog-branded synths were never credited on any Elton John albums, except for a Moog on one song from his eponymous 1970 LP. His go-to instruments were mostly ARPs.

Herb remembered gingerly carrying back a $2 million royalty check by hand to Walden Avenue for the initial sale of MG-1s. Estimates of final sales varied, but Walborn guessed: "They ended up selling, like, 23,000 of 'em . . . a $12 million product line—not too shabby for something I put together in a couple months."[46]

Ironically, the MG-1 boasted the highest sales of any Moog-labeled synth to date—a thorn in Bob's side. When it appeared in stores, Herb remembered, "I got a call from Bob, and he was really upset. He said, 'I really don't understand why I have to see my name on an instrument at Radio Shack!' So I said, 'Well Bob, it's not *your* name. It's the name of our *company*."[47]

The wide exposure had Bob's phone ringing. When the designer of the *Eureka!* exhibit invited him to demonstrate the MG-1 at a science museum, Bob bristled: "The Radio Shack Moog synthesizer was designed, built, and distributed well after I left the company. While it will probably make money for Moog Music . . . it is not an instrument that I am anxious to associate myself with. It is a poorly-made gadget with little in the way of redeeming musical value."[48]

Bob's indignation was on full display in an August 1982 *Newsweek* feature: "Moog admits to feeling a twinge of resentment when he sees Radio Shack ads featuring a $499 'Moog' synthesizer which brings him not a penny in royalties."[49] The writers ended the column with Bob's kiss off: "But he is also relieved to be rid of the invention that people often refer to as his baby. Comments Moog: 'That baby had grown up to be an ugly bastard.'"

25

The Briar Patch

Bob strode across his driveway and flung open the steel doors of the metal building. Big Briar, Inc., was officially open for business. It was February 1982. "I'm not interested in having it grow to be a major entity," he explained to *Newsweek*. "At my point in life, I'm happy to have a minuscule niche in the music business and do it right."[1] He told the *Charlotte Observer*, "All you need is a work bench, a soldering iron and a pair of pliers."[2]

A garage operation seemed a safe bet after the latest cataclysm to rock the synth world. Just the year before, Bob's once formidable rival, the mighty ARP, had collapsed into bankruptcy. As recently as 1977, the ARP 2500 had had a pivotal role in Steven Spielberg's classic, *Close Encounters of the Third Kind*. ARP engineer, Philip Dodds, in his 15 minutes of fame, had played it on screen to intone the now-legendary five-note sequence used to communicate with outer space aliens. That same year, the 2600 had given voice to the robot R2-D2 in the first *Star Wars* film. But the firm's latest products wound up tanking the company: a guitar synth had proved a commercial flop; an electronic piano debuted, but it was wracked with defects; and a last-ditch polyphonic synth deployed to bail out the company came too late. ARP's creditors sued, and its assets were liquidated. Stockholders forfeited millions and Pearlman lost his shirt. CBS Musical Instruments picked over the spoils and acquired ARP's remaining inventory. It was a precipitous tumble for a brand that had ascended to such heady peaks.

For Bob now, even a cottage business would be risky. He and Shirleigh had come to North Carolina with a fat purse from selling the East Aurora and Trumansburg properties and cashing in their Norlin stocks, but their endless indulgences in the round house had turned it into a sinkhole that quickly devoured their savings. No expense had been spared. They'd even hired a team of three carpenters at $300 a week for two years to turn the whole interior into an extravaganza of wood, with handmade paneling, doors, and furniture. "Those guys were like uncles to us by the end," Michelle joked.[3] And itching for more land, the Moogs took out a small mortgage in March 1982 to annex another 29 acres to their second property in Sandy Mush Township.

All this came on top of two bank loans in the past year totaling $110,000, with the Cove as collateral. Now they faced tuition payments for Laura and Renée, each off in college, with Michelle and Mathew following soon behind.

But Bob boldly went ahead and launched the Big Briar operation, hiring his first full-time employee: a technician, Dale Ong. Ong was thrilled with his first assignment: to restore the original modular prototype Herb had owned since the days Bob had gifted it to him. Herb had managed to extract a letter from Bob certifying its authenticity, and he planned to put the system up for auction.

At Sotheby's New York Galleries on June 9, 1982, the prototype sat in a lot with the iconic "Rosebud" sled from Orson Welles' screen classic, *Citizen Kane*, and a set of erotic lithographs by John Lennon. Herb told the *Buffalo News* he considered the prototype as important to music as the very first piano (invented by Cristofori around 1700), and the Stradivarius violin. The paper disclosed, "the Moog synthesizer that transformed the musical world" was estimated to haul in up to $20,000, the same as the Rosebud sled.[4]

Unfortunately, the modules didn't even generate the minimum starting bid and were returned to Herb. Undaunted, he called the Smithsonian, pitching the instrument as a must for the national museum, but the Institution wasn't willing to pay. Eventually he managed to find the modules a permanent home at the Henry Ford Museum in Dearborn, Michigan, but the system had to be donated.

Increasingly, Bob could see he had a legacy to curate, and he was anxious to set the record straight. In a letter to the director of the *Eureka!* exhibit, he protested: "I have seen one newspaper account . . . that referred to Mr. Deutsch as the co-inventor of the Moog Synthesizer. Although Mr. Deutsch's role in initiating the development is certainly important, I believe it is incorrect to consider him a co-inventor, or to give any other musician with whom I collaborated such a credit."[5] In an attached statement Bob pointed out—as he had numerous times over the years—that several musicians had contributed along the way to the evolution of the mature system that he was finally ready to call a "synthesizer" by 1967: Siday had asked for the oscillator bank, Ussachevsky the ADSR envelope generator, Ciamaga the voltage controlled filter, and Carlos the fixed filter bank. But that didn't qualify any of them as co-inventors. For good measure, Bob forwarded a copy of his *Eureka!* statement to Herb.[6]

Big Briar's first real outing was a commission from the Italian firm Crumar, to design a small analog synth called the Spirit, to be manufactured at the company's plant in Italy. A year into the project, Bob was reaching into his own pocket to pay a subcontracted team: Jim Scott, Tom Rhea (the esteemed electronic music historian, industry expert, and former marketing VP at Moog), along with Dale Ong and a part-time secretary. By 1983, after hundreds of hours of sweat, two trips to Italy to iron out technicalities, and little remaining profit for Big Briar, Crumar ended up manufacturing fewer than 100 units of the Spirit, and discontinued production the following year.

The freelance jobs weren't cutting it financially, or even creatively. Bob's heart, as always, was in original designs, and he wrote to a friend that Big Briar's purpose was to make custom electronic musical instruments and accessories, "for those who want absolutely the best and are willing to pay for it."[7] The operative phrase was "willing to pay for it." To produce "absolutely the best," Bob would have to pour untold amounts of his own money into R&D, parts, labor, and marketing, and *he'd* have to be "willing to pay for it."

Hoping to repeat his groundbreaking achievement and take the world of electronic music to the next level, Bob threw his weight behind an idea no one else seemed much interested in: electronic controllers—what engineers call the "interface" or "control surfaces" that make electronic instruments go. He'd worked with ribbon and percussion controllers, joysticks, and modulation wheels, but he thought there might be more ways for musicians to interact with instruments. The "control surfaces" of acoustic instruments—like the fingerboard of a violin or the mouthpiece of a trumpet—respond so naturally to the most minute gestures of a player's hands or lips. Bob's goal was to give that same kind of flexibility to electronic musicians. But his quest for the perfect controllers would morph into an obsession that would overshadow Big Briar and insinuate itself into the family dynamic for the next decade.

In the spring of 1982, Bob unveiled Big Briar's inaugural products in a flyer with the company's brand-new logo: a G-clef wrapped in a prickly blackberry briar vine. *BIG BRIAR CONTROLLERS: NEW Dimensions in Hands-on Control* featured three interface devices: a touch plate to let a player control functions on an external synth with the tap or swipe of a finger; a theremin-like antenna controller; and a keyboard interface. The touch plate was Bob's clear favorite—the "Greatest Invention Since the Wheel!" he called it in a Big Briar ad. But none of the devices pictured in the flyer were more than prototypes; if anyone wanted one, Bob would make up a custom unit on order.

Bob had first toyed with the controller idea back in 1972 in discussions with Indiana University composer and professor John Eaton. The two had put their heads together to hypothesize a super-responsive tactile keyboard instrument, and Bob had begun tinkering with the idea on and off in his spare time. The concept originated with Eaton's experience in the early 1960s at the electronic music studio of the American Academy in Rome.

A sound engineer at the Academy, Paolo Ketoff, with no knowledge of what Bob and Herb were doing around the same time, had invented a system in 1964 that featured many of the same functions as Bob's first prototype. Ketoff called his tabletop instrument the "Synket" (for "Synthesizer Ketoff"), and Eaton debuted it, playing it live at a concert on June 16, 1965, at the Academy. Eaton had spent hours learning the elaborate sequence of body motions required to operate the Synket's foot pedal and dial interfaces, and to make a vibrato by wiggling its toy-piano-sized keys from side to side. The instrument's vacuum tube and transistor circuitry could generate and modify a wide variety of sounds in real time, and Eaton loved touring with it, especially as a soloist in his own *Concert Piece for Synket and Symphony Orchestra*. Ketoff built several one-off versions of his instrument, but it was never manufactured. When Bob learned of Ketoff's work, he invited the Italian engineer to join his Trumansburg staff in 1967, but the salary wasn't enough to entice Ketoff to relocate to the United States.

After John Eaton met Bob, he added the Moog modular to his Synket concerts, and sensing there was more expressive potential lurking in his digits than Ketoff's instrument could handle, he talked to Bob about making a more refined keyboard.

Bob wasn't modest about the proposed instrument. Writing to Eaton's University Dean to ask for funding to complete the project, after years spent working on it as an unpaid labor of love, he claimed it represented "perhaps the single most important piece of electronic musical instrument development work of this decade," and called it a keyboard "of far greater sophistication and musical potential than any keyboard that has ever been made."[8]

The instrument was projected to have standard synth circuitry, but the wizardry would be in the keys. Each one would digitally register finger motion in three dimensions—up/down, left/right, and front to back—and the performer's hand motions would be updated every few milliseconds by an interfaced computer. Bob and Eaton called the instrument the MTS, for "Multiply-Touch-Sensitive Keyboard."

Besides John Eaton, it was never clear who would want or need the MTS. But Bob was convinced that Eaton would take it on tour and whip up a frenzy of enthusiasm, stimulating orders from universities and experimental musicians. Shirleigh got her hopes up, telling Florence, "This one instrument . . . will be the spring board for our new business . . . the beginning of a positive cash flow."[9] For an instrument with an unorthodox, finicky interface, Bob's expectations seemed wholly unrealistic. He estimated a "basic starter system" MTS would sell for $15,000—a figure based on a projected output of at least several hundred a year.

Yet to crank out just one prototype was evacuating the cash flow. By October of 1982, Indiana University's allotted funding for the project was exhausted, and Bob was on his own. But he pushed ahead anyway. The complexity of the computer interface for the MTS necessitated hiring software programmers who lived at the Cove for weeks at a time. Bob and Shirleigh were so confident of success that they took out a bank loan for $100,000, again with the Cove as collateral. By January of 1983, facing a bill from the software developer, Bob pled poverty: "The Eaton project has drained all of our available resources, and then some." A "fiasco" with one of the programmers, he explained, "cost us well into five figures, as well as a year of our time."[10]

In March 1983, Bob confessed to Florence that he and Shirleigh had put their 128-acre second property in Sandy Mush Township up for sale—land they'd set aside as a retirement nest egg. They'd maxed out their bank loans, and appealed now to Florence's largesse for a $10,000 loan to get them through the next three months. If she could manage it, Bob hinted, an additional $20,000 would allow him to devote full-time to finishing the Eaton instrument. Florence produced the $10,000, and after three months Bob returned, hat in hand, asking for the $20,000. The MTS keyboard, he promised her, was sure to generate more work if he could only finish it. Her reply was unusually laconic: "It's good news that Eaton's alleged instrument has generated some useful publicity. Accordingly my check is enclosed."[11]

The June 1983 NAMM show was the do-or-die moment for Norlin, and for Moog Music. NAMM shows were always nail-biters, particularly for American firms. As Tom Rhea put it, "You're living from one NAMM show to the next. If you don't have a hit at one show, you'd better at the next, or you're dead."[12] Everything now was riding on Rich Walborn's latest, a less pricey follow up to the Memorymoog. The new synth was dubbed the SL-8 (for Split/Layer 8-voice), because its keyboard could be split into two timbral regions, a single key could have two notes layered on it, and up to eight notes could be sounded simultaneously across the keyboard. The instrument was analog, but it boasted some digital functions.

The SL-8 also sported a feature that was starting to appear on newer synths—a game-changing advance in music technology. The concept was a "universal interface standard" that allowed synthesizers, computers, and electronic studio devices of different manufacturers to connect and communicate with each other—a sort of United Nations of gear. Bob had announced the breakthrough in his October 1982 "On Synthesizers" column in *Keyboard*, and by early 1983 the standard was christened MIDI, for Musical Instrument Digital Interface. Bob was elected to the MIDI Evolutionary Committee, a panel of industry heavies from the U.S. and Japan selected to huddle and discuss norms for its implementation. Moog's new SL-8 was MIDI-equipped—ready to shake hands with other manufacturers' equipment—and it also boasted an advanced 16-bit microprocessor.

The SL-8 might have had a fighting chance if it weren't for the fact that it wasn't finished. The instrument arrived at NAMM as a work-in-progress prototype sequestered in a hotel suite across the street from the convention center. Its microprocessor and software guts were still hanging out and had to be concealed behind a curtain and tethered to the instrument through hidden cables. Dealers were ushered over for private demos. They watched a makeshift presentation of 10 sounds with interest and even a little excitement. The SL-8, they were told, would go into production soon and be ready for delivery by October.

Out on the convention floor, though, another synthesizer was finished, and passersby were devouring it. Crowds were congregating around the Yamaha booth, ogling a sleek black synth with no knobs or sliders, driven by a revolutionary technology. It was a jet aircraft among propeller planes. Everything about the all-digital DX7 shouted computerized sound in a box: a liquid crystal display with complex menus and submenus for users to access 128 presets, or program their own sophisticated patches to store in memory with an original filename; a velocity- and pressure-sensitive five-octave keyboard; MIDI compatibility; and 16-voice polyphony.

But the most precedent-shattering feature of the DX7 was the way it generated sounds, unlike anything in analog synthesis. Frequency Modulation synthesis, or FM synthesis, was the discovery of a Stanford University composer and professor, John Chowning, in 1967. Chowning had used one oscillator to modulate the tone of a second oscillator and he found that many of the sounds he produced resembled acoustic instruments. Stanford patented the method and sold an exclusive license to Yamaha.

The DX7's FM synthesis sounds had a crisper, glassier quality than the mellower, fuzzier tones of analog instruments, a change many musicians seemed to like. Its preset sounds would soon turn up as common ingredients in '80s pop, and the instrument would become the first commercially successful digital synth. The DX7 was the result of nearly 10 years of FM synthesis experimentation by Yamaha; the company, like other gargantuan Japanese firms, had the resources to survive multiple product failures as it pursued long-range planning and years of R&D to eventually land a major success.

At the Moog booth, a "Memorymoog Plus," retrofitted with MIDI ports, sat next to Keith Emerson's Monster Moog—a monument to past glories and a reminder to attendees of where it all began. But NAMM wasn't a museum, and flaunting illustrious forbears didn't cut it anymore.

Moog personnel were devastated. After wandering back stunned from the Yamaha display, they could see that the Japanese titan had done everything right. The DX7, with its supersonic powers and a $1,995.00 price tag, was $500 cheaper than the SL-8, and Yamaha was turning out units in numbers beyond what any synthesizer model had ever achieved—figures no American company could hope to compete with. In its first year, the DX7 would sell 150,000 units, and reach 200,000 after three years, compared to the Minimoog with a lifetime total of 12,000 over 10 years. The royalties on Yamaha's FM synthesis license would earn Stanford University $20 million.

The SL-8, the last synth the Walden Avenue Moog engineers would ever conceive—and Norlin's last shot at staying in the game—was stillborn, its lone prototype body with its microprocessor organs spilling out, laid to rest in the mausoleum of drawing board contenders.

Predictably, Norlin continued its free fall. In its latest hare-brained scheme, the company put all its muscle behind its Lowrey Organs, hoping to place an organ in every living room. Never mind that digital synthesizers and personal computers were coming for the home organ. Norlin recklessly committed to 25-year leases on stores in 175 malls around the U.S., subleasing the spaces to mom-and-pop instrument retailers. Predictably, the stores tumbled like dominoes, leaving Norlin holding a pile of 25-year commitments on empty mall storefronts. The company had already sold off its Ecuadoran cement and beer holdings to offset a $145 million loss in its music business since 1975. Now it would have to divest itself of music as well.

On Walden Avenue, with the music operation reduced to a side business, Dave Luce and his executive vice president, F. Scott Chapman, looked at the thriving contract manufacturing business keeping Moog afloat, and made Norlin an offer. With financing from several sources, they bought Moog for $1.3 million on December 29, 1983. Moog Music would now be relegated to a division of the partners' new holding company, "Moog Electronics." The Music division would only handle repairs, and continue to manufacture the last surviving instruments: the Taurus II pedals, the Source, the Rogue, and the Memorymoog. The last music product the plant rolled out bearing the Moog trademark came in 1984: the Song Producer, a MIDI hardware/software interface for a Commodore 64 home computer that allowed users to record, edit, and mix tracks on the computer.

In a sad vestige of its synthesizer legacy, Moog Electronics' big seller now was the sound-generating circuitry for the Chexx tabletop hockey game that played crowd noises, the National Anthem, and the "charge" fanfare from a miniature scoreboard that prominently displayed the Moog logo—the classic trademark that Luce and Chapman now owned. Under the banner of *Moog Telecommunications*, the company even started making telephone devices. Luce was reminded of just how far the business had strayed from its musical roots during a contract lawsuit negotiation: "The guy opened the meeting and pulled a machine gun out from underneath the table. He said, 'If I don't get what I want from this thing here we're gonna have some troubles.'"[13]

But Luce and Chapman had rushed the remnants of the Moog company to safety just in time. In January 1984, Norlin became the target of a hostile takeover by a brokerage and private investment bank. In October, Lowrey organ was sold off, followed by Gibson in early 1986 when the Norlin logo ceased to exist. In a bizarre series of events, the controlling brokerage firm was closed down and one of its two partners was convicted of income tax fraud and evasion and sentenced to jail in 1988. With everything dried up, Norlin evaporated into history.

<hr />

"We are happy to inform you that we liquified our nest egg, and are therefore able to repay your loan," Bob announced to Florence in December 1983.[14] Cashing in their Sandy Mush property—the safety net intended for their retirement—was a bittersweet exchange for a quick $140,000 to shore up debts. And they still weren't out of the woods: they owed the bank another $50,000. Bob had been forced to come clean with Florence months earlier: "It seemed that all of our efforts to generate income vanished like Aladdin's genie, back into the lamp."[15] There were "encouraging inquiries" he assured her: he'd had an offer to appear in a special music program with Miss Piggy, Jim Henson's Muppet; and he'd floated the idea of writing a book on electronic music. But none of these ideas promised more than incidental income. He admitted to Florence, "We finally . . . arrived at the tack of selling my body as a consultant."[16] In a chance encounter at the June 1983 NAMM show where Yamaha dominated with the DX7, Bob landed his first client: a professional liaison who would alter the course of his career.

The inventor Ray Kurzweil had founded Kurzweil Music Systems in 1982, in partnership with Stevie Wonder as musical advisor. Stevie had originally bought the inventor's groundbreaking print-to-speech reading machine for the blind and asked if a keyboard instrument that could play realistic clones of acoustic instruments was a feasible invention. At the NAMM show, Ray Kurzweil debuted his prototype Kurzweil 250, an intricate, refined keyboard with a unique computerized architecture. The instrument used "sampling" technology—digitally recorded sound snapshots of individual notes taken from acoustic instruments that could be played back on an electronic keyboard to mimic the original acoustic sounds.

Ray Kurzweil was particularly proud of his instrument's piano samples, insisting that they sounded more like an acoustic piano than anything except the real thing. But his bluster didn't convince everyone, and his engineers were stumped. Bob was tapped for his finely tuned analog ears, perfect for troubleshooting this kind of problem, and his solutions made their way into the K250, which went into production in early 1984. After this "save," he was hired as an ongoing consultant to the company.

But he was still gluing together shards of work to make a whole piggybank. He could always earn the occasional fee as a guest speaker at events like the 1982 US Festival in California, sponsored by Apple Computer cofounder Steve Wozniak, where he'd joined a celebrity roster that included author Ray Bradbury, comedian and civil rights activist Dick Gregory, and astronaut Rusty Schweikert. But subsisting as a freelancer remained a struggle, and the hardscrabble reality had become an open secret in the family. Michelle recalled, "Mom was just hanging on with him, just waiting for some kind of security. They thought they had that with the buyout of the shares from

Moog Music, but that quickly dissipated and it was obvious that this whole Big Briar scenario—the custom musical instruments and the writing and the public speaking—it was not going to generate what they needed."[17] Bob's consulting work for Kurzweil from his southern backwater, as it turned out, didn't make the difference either.

Bob's biggest asset remained his untarnished status as the doyen of the industry, and in the summer of 1984 he had to cash in on it. On June 12, the *Boston Globe* carried a brief announcement: "Robert A. Moog, a pioneer in electronic music, has joined Kurzweil Music Systems Inc. of Waltham.... Kurzweil manufactures the $10,500 Kurzweil 250."[18] The family would continue their peripatetic tradition, moving yet again just as they were settling into the finished Cove house. The decision was hard to process as anything but a defeat.

A brief summer holiday to take the heat off only turned up the psychological temperature. In late July, the Moogs rented a house for a week in Ocean Isle, North Carolina, with their good friends, Richard and Renee Brandt— the children's godparents—and the Brandt's kids. Bob had been burning the candle late into the night to finish work in order to join the family on the trip, but he was in no mood for an enforced getaway. "We had an argument before we went," Shirleigh recalled, "and the car was silent-as-death going there."[19] At the beach, Bob stewed, and exploded again, grabbing the work briefcase he'd taken along, fleeing home on the bus, and leaving Shirleigh to drive the brood back at the end of an uncomfortable week.

Back at the Cove, Shirleigh recalled, "The way Robert greeted us was, 'Well, it's obvious to me that we're going to get a divorce.' No apology. No 'I'd like to sit down and talk.'"[20] She and Bob went out on the deck, and Michelle recalled, "You could hear them yelling and disagreeing. Mom was drinking brandy and I went out there and she had puked all over herself. And she was totally drunk. So I went cleaning her up and getting her to bed."[21]

Amazingly, after these outbursts, things always managed to piece themselves together. By October 2 the Moogs were back to the status quo, taking out another bank loan for $50,000, betting the Cove property as collateral for the third time. Shirleigh readied the Cove for rental as they prepared to leave for Boston. This time they were eyeing a home they hoped to buy in Natick, Massachusetts, 10 miles west of Boston, and 13 miles southwest of Bob's new job at Kurzweil Systems in Waltham. But no bank would extend them a mortgage without a large down payment. They came again to Florence, who dutifully got out her checkbook and loaned them $50,000 with a 10-year payback schedule and interest. On November 30, Bob and Shirleigh signed a mortgage for the Natick house. On December 20 they left for Massachusetts. Bob would start at Kurzweil the day after Christmas.

At least one member of the family was happy to be leaving the Cove. "Matthew is already at the starting line," Bob told Florence. "The prospect of . . . not having to go on the school bus with boys who chew tobacco, is definitely improving the quality of Matt's life."[22] Matthew seconded the opinion, telling Florence in a letter that he was "looking forward to being close to a big city and not being classified as a 'Yankee.'"[23]

PART VI
THE GRAND POOBAH

26

Genius for Hire

"Dead I'd be worth a lot to you."

Aunt Florence was never one to mince words.[1] Even in her steadfast benevolence, she felt the need to assure Bob she'd keep the spigot flowing from the other side. And there'd be no repayment schedule or interest, then.

But warm, she was still "worth a lot." The family's new home at 2 Indian Ridge Road in Natick was another voilà courtesy of Florence. The 20-year-old split-level on a densely wooded suburban lot was a bourgeois sequel to the quirky luxury of the Cove house. But even for the pleasure of this woodsy setting, Bob would have a half-hour daily drive each way to his new 9-to-5 position.

For a $47,000 annual salary, Kurzweil had purchased the designer label synthesizer king. But the company hadn't really decided what to do with him. Bob wasn't entirely sure what his purpose was either. He was handed the title of 'Chief Scientist,' but he told the *Computer Music Journal*. "It doesn't really describe what I've been doing. I exist partly in marketing and partly in engineering."[2] Much of the job seemed to be wheel-spinning and make-work—sitting around in two-day brainstorming roundtables to imagine what the hot products might be in five years.

Bob was essentially leveraging his name to endorse Kurzweil's products. He'd already been forced to rave in print about the Polymoog—another engineer's child—and much of his new job was to talk up the K250. It was an odd bargain, pledging fidelity to a keyboard that could mimic 30 acoustic instruments and stand in for live players—a conundrum that threatened to land him back in the old minefield of out-of-work union musicians. He told the *Computer Music Journal*, "My boss Ray Kurzweil has made the outrageous statement that he's going to bury the acoustic piano, and I think he just might pull it off."[3] A bewildering rationalization revealed how beholden he was to the company agenda. Pushing Kurzweil's sampling instruments with the *Philadelphia Inquirer*, he set aside his luthier's soul to declare, "There is a real need for high-quality home keyboard instruments.... That's a need that's hard to meet with acoustic pianos. The world is running out of wood and craftsmen."[4]

Beyond the company hype, Bob was rattled by the clubby atmosphere of the mostly MIT-trained engineers at Kurzweil. In a letter to Gene Zumchak, whom he'd recently reconnected with, he grumbled about the cheerless brain trust at the company: "There must be special courses at MIT where you learn to do things in the most complicated, roundabout, convoluted ways, and where you learn to tuck your chin in, furrow your brow, and come on like a professor."[5] On a casual visit to Kurzweil, David Borden realized he'd suddenly rekindled Bob's natural levity that had been snuffed out. Ribbing with the old, "Well it sounded like you were having a very deep shit conversation," he sent Bob into a giggling jag. A Kurzweil PR man quizzed Borden: How did he get Bob to laugh? He'd never seen that before. Borden was true to form: "I said, 'Just use a few four-letter words—just say anything that comes to mind that you can end with 'fuck' or 'shit' or 'balls' or something.' And the guy looked at me like I was insane."[6]

Even the corporate dress code at Kurzweil was stifling to Bob. At the Cove, Michelle recalled, "dad would put on his carpenter jeans and worn out flannel shirt, stick his pens in his pocket, put on his old shoes, and walk across the driveway. All of a sudden he was in suits. That was weird."[7] "Six months into Boston," Shirleigh remembered, "he wanted to burn all his suits and leave. But we couldn't afford to go home after six months."[8]

In high school one day, Michelle heard everyone buzzing about her dad being on the radio, but she had no idea what they were talking about. He'd apparently gotten a RockWalk award in Hollywood. She called the radio station and someone confirmed the rumor. Poking around Bob's home office, she unearthed the evidence: "Sure enough," she recalled, "lying on top of his filing cabinet, with a couple papers on top and the first layer of dust, was a plaque."[9] On November 13, 1985, Bob had been inducted into the newly opened RockWalk, a concrete entrance court in front of Hollywood's Guitar Center on Sunset Boulevard. The celebrity forecourt was styled after the grid of movie stars' hands, feet, and signatures at Grauman's Chinese Theatre. Bob joined an inaugural group with Les Paul and other luminaries, and the cement square immortalizing his handprints and signature lay next to the squares of Stevie Wonder and Emerson, Lake, and Palmer. The Walk was dedicated to rock legends and innovators who made rock 'n' roll "a universally accepted art form."

"He would never tell us about any of that stuff," Michelle explained. "And it was so typical. He used to say, 'Michelle, it's all just a crock of shit.' Honestly, if the outside world hadn't told me, I wouldn't have known my dad invented the Moog synthesizer."[10] It was partly Bob's frustration over the stream of symbolic accolades that never translated into monetary success—people assumed he had all that already; part of it was simple discomfort at being in the limelight. Out in public when his renown stalked him, it usually upset his equilibrium. Michelle remembered an encounter at a NAMM show: "We're walking along and this guy says, 'Oh-My-God, are you Bob Moog?' And Dad got very uncomfortable immediately. And he said 'yes,' and the guy dropped to his knees, and said, 'Oh my God, you're my idol.' Blah-blah-blah. Dad was so uncomfortable. He had his hands in his pockets and he was shifting his weight."[11]

Idolatry aside, Bob was now reduced to the role of genius-for-hire, and it was equally frustrating. His Kurzweil contract forbade him from carrying on side jobs as Big Briar, and that business remained dormant. To keep the creative juices flowing, he pressed on with the MTS project, which still beckoned. He converted the furnace room of the Natick house into a tiny shop to spend off-hours hammering out the remaining elements of a prototype. Reaching into his own pocket again in early 1986, he hired a local piano technician, Larry Fine, to help him fabricate keytop sensors for the MTS. He assured Fine the job would take about three months of Saturdays to complete.

Fine often stayed on well into the evenings, and Shirleigh saw her weekends melting away. Occasionally she angled in and grabbed Bob for a night at the ballet or a dinner out, but the boredom and loneliness drove her back to selling real estate, a pastime she'd started in North Carolina. "Robert was very happy that I was out making money," she recalled, "because when I sold a house in Boston I used to bring home three-, four-, five-thousand-dollar checks. And he thought that was dandy."[12]

Shirleigh shoveled even more into the family chest when her father died in 1986. Ben had left her a $100,000 inheritance on top of a $10,000 trust from her mother, who'd passed away in 1980. But these windfalls still couldn't keep the bank account satiated. Not long after the Boston move, Florence forgave the payback obligations on her $50,000 loan, fretting that with Michelle and Matthew about to start college the family couldn't swing it. Her hunch turned out to be right: in March 1987, only three months after Shirleigh came into her parents' money, she and Bob had to remortgage the Natick house for a $200,000 loan.

∽∽∽

The managers at Moog Electronics in Buffalo were scratching their heads over what to do with the remaining inventory of instruments. The Memorymoog, in particular, was virtually forgotten in the ballyhoo over the DX7, and it was also plagued with technical malfunctions that eroded its reputation. At a hefty $4,795, units were collecting dust in the warehouse.

It took Dave Van Koevering to find a special use for leftover Memorymoogs. At church services he sometimes played on one, together with the Taurus pedals, dazzling parishioners with a sort of multicolored organ effect. In 1985 he'd heard Moog Electronics was sitting on a stockpile of the last 100 units, and he sniffed an opportunity. He proposed to buy the Memorymoogs at cost, load them up with "church-related Moog sounds," and place them in the religious market. The only alternative he could see, he told the Moog managers flatly, was to burn them—it was their choice.

Moog Electronics bit, swallowed the loss, and Van Koevering found a group of undertakers—impressed with his church performances—to buy the entire lot with money from their casket corporation. He'd plan to go on the road and sell the instruments on commission, removing batches from the fireproof warehouse in Alma, Michigan, where they lay next to the coffins. To transport them, he bought a 1970 Cadillac hearse with all its original trimmings: a glass partition behind the front seat, window curtains, and fancy interior lights. He and Becky burned scented candles to disperse the odor of dead bodies and flowers, and set out on the road.

This time it wasn't the music store circuit, but Christian workshops. Van Koevering would arrange six Memorymoogs behind him and show how they could be used for worship and praise. But the inveterate salesman knew everything was in a name: he was careful never to let on that they were called Memorymoogs. "'Memorymoog' said nothing to the church," he explained. "I wanted the word 'sanctuary' because the sounds were specific to *them*. So it was a 'Sanctuary Synthesizer.'"[13] Walden Avenue hastily swapped out the Memorymoog nameplates for ones that said Sanctuary Synthesizer, and with Van Koevering's sleight-of-hand, it was likely none of his customers ever caught on to the ruse. In a small brochure, he assured buyers, "The Sanctuary Synthesizer by Moog is the world's first synthesizer designed for the Church. Moog Music made a commitment to the church musician . . . with the development of the Sanctuary Synthesizer."[14]

Dave and Becky traveled with about 20 Sanctuary Synthesizers at a time, towing a black trailer behind the hearse to fit the rest of their musical gear.

Becky remembered that there was never a problem with anyone trying to steal from the hearse—no one would ever come near it.

Dave loved running the hearse at full tilt. "We're leaving Colorado at night," he remembered, "and the Cadillac is rolling, and it was a big, powerful engine, and it's towing a trailer and it's heavy, and I just let it go. And we're probably rolling 95, approaching 100 mph, comin' down this mountain, and I see two semis ahead of me. And I had a CB radio with an antenna comin' out of the roof, and I can see these two trucks and I can hear them talkin' to each other. And I said to the first driver when I come up to him, 'Breaker, breaker, this is the Coffin Hauler!'—that was my handle—I said, 'This is the Coffin Hauler!'—*whoosh*—I passed the guy. And I interrupted him talkin' to the other guy. And he says to the other guy, 'By God you'll never believe what just passed me! I think it's a widow foolin' around with the undertaker'—Becky had her head against my shoulder. He said, 'I heard you can't take it with you when you go, but this guy figured out how to do it, cause he's haulin' a trailer and he's runnin' a hundred miles an hour!' "[15]

∽∽∽

At Washington University in St. Louis, Aunt Florence was suddenly having balance problems while teaching. Diagnosed with a tumor of the brainstem, she kept up a full-time classroom load, hoping to hold the cancer in check for as long as possible. By the spring of 1986 she'd made it through a year, just as Renée was graduating from the school with her bachelor's degree in French and International Development. In honor of Renée, Florence was determined to lead the commencement procession as Grand Marshal. Ambling along with a cane, she struggled over the cobblestone paths, but she insisted on doing it.

As her condition worsened, Florence was hospitalized. She couldn't walk and needed a feeding tube inserted into her stomach. By the fall of 1987 she required emergency surgery. With her doctor away on Labor Day, the operation was performed by a substitute surgeon. A relative recalled her last words to Bob: "Don't ever have an operation on Labor Day weekend."[16] Coming out of the procedure the surgeon had nicked the nerve center controlling salivation, causing her to aspirate. After a long period of unconsciousness, she succumbed on December 12, 1987. She was 72.

Laura recalled her shock at cleaning out Florence's apartment. The bare-bones modesty spoke volumes about her Aunt's no-nonsense frugality. A thin cotton ribcord bedspread was tucked pristinely around the bed, and Laura remembered that a big oriental rug was "the nicest thing in her apartment. She had a very simple stereo system, even though she loved opera."[17]

Years of scrimping had left behind a bank account in seven figures—a king's ransom liberally handed out in her will to a roster of pet institutions: civil rights organizations, Planned Parenthood; the St. Louis City Museum, Zoological Park, Opera Theater, and Botanical Garden; Washington University, and her alma maters Columbia and NYU. George and Shirley Moog got a modest slice. But Florence reduced by half the portion of her estate originally intended for Bob and Shirleigh, leaving them $300,000 and dividing the other half among the four Moog children. "She was very clear about it," Michelle recalled. "She didn't trust my Dad. If she gave him the money he'd spend it all on his business. She wasn't going to trust my parents to leave money for us, so *she* did it."[18] But Bob and Shirleigh also received Florence's Teacher's Annuity—$40,000 a year for five years.

When there was no more left to give, Florence gave of herself, literally. She donated her body to the Washington University Medical School.

∿∿∿

Bob's role at Kurzweil was diminishing by the day. For all his engineering prowess, the firm valued him mostly as a celebrity endorser of its products. The company was keeping him busy, Larry Fine recalled, by "sending him on speaking gigs of ever dwindling importance, and it was getting him down."[19] And despite its outer trappings of success, Kurzweil was stumbling. The company had run annual losses of between $2 million and $5 million for the past several years, and Bob soon realized he'd been rescued by a sinking ship.

But the stars were aligning in his favor, and a return path to North Carolina had opened up. Florence's final endowment meant they could pay off their debts and return to Leicester. Shirleigh and Bob made a pact: they'd live on the first fifth of Florence's annuity—$40,000—for one year, long enough to get Big Briar up and running again. After that, the company would sustain them and they'd save the remaining $160,000 for retirement.

In May 1988, Bob resigned from Kurzweil to devote himself full-time to the MTS project. By the time the moving vans arrived in mid-August, he and Fine had managed to squeak out the completed keytops. As usual, a project Bob thought would take three months had stretched over years.

As luck had it, Bob darted out of Boston just in time. In 1990 Kurzweil Music Systems, outpaced by foreign competition, filed for Chapter 11 bankruptcy protection. The company was acquired by the South Korean musical instrument distributor Young Chang, which assumed manufacture and distribution of its products, still under the Kurzweil name.

"My four years at Kurzweil came to nothing," Bob wrote a friend when he got back to the Cove.[20] The path forward would be a tough one now because he found himself at a crossroads. Digital technology had left his analog expertise in the dust, and the Asian synth market had thrown up roadblocks for everyone in the business. In a devastatingly confessional article for *Keyboard* magazine's May 1988 issue, he tramped through his whole career, from the early amplifier fiasco to the end of the Norlin years. The magazine tagged the feature, "Candid reflections on the rise and fall of Moog Music from the man who launched the synthesizer revolution."[21]

Bob continued writing for *Keyboard* from a position as the founding authority in the field. But he could see his eminence was a part of history now. In January 1989 the Stearns Collection of Musical Instruments at the University of Michigan acquired Alwin Nikolais' 1965 synth as a permanent exhibit—a glass-case relic. The museum's director told the campus newspaper, "The Model One Moog . . . is to the music world what the Wright brothers' airplane is to aviation."[22] Donal Henahan marked the occasion with a *New York Times* article, "And in This Gallery, We See the Ancient Moog," pondering, "the Moog in a museum? Wasn't it only last week that the most famous of synthesizers was at the cutting edge of modern art? . . . And now . . . . the first commercially produced model has gone to its reward."[23]

Hobbling along with Big Briar a year after returning to the Cove, Bob was still running a loss, and Shirleigh was running out of patience. By the summer of 1989, with no reliable income in sight, she pushed Bob to find a teaching position. Even at the local Asheville branch of the University of North Carolina, these jobs were tight, and Bob strained to impress with an application stuffed with his resume, copies of recent interviews he'd given, and one of his own articles.

The University wasn't able to offer him a full-time position, and Wayne Kirby, the music department chair, remembered "pushing and pushing" just to get him a three-quarter-time appointment with health and retirement benefits. On August 9, 1989, the *Charlotte Observer* announced, "Robert Moog, the man whose name is virtually synonymous with electronic music, has been named research professor of music at UNC-Asheville."[24] "He did it for the money,"[25] Shirleigh admitted flatly. But at least UNCA's dress code was looser than Kurzweil's. Kirby remembered Bob pressing him over whether or not he had to wear a tie: "I said, 'Don't wear a tie.' And he went, 'Oh, thank God!'"[26]

It was a brief halcyon period. Bob and Shirleigh luxuriated in the quiet of all four children being off in college, and the UNCA job was pulling in a regular income. Shirleigh managed to steal Bob away from his work for a few moments each day, luring him with suppers served up on elegant tablecloths adorned with flowers from her garden, and a bottle of wine. "Every meal is a sacrament," she remembered him saying after these dinners. "I knew that if he liked the meal he'd be tempted to stay and savor the wine," she recalled, "so I'd see more of him. It was almost like a courtship, a seduction. We'd sit out on the deck—it was like a planetarium because you could see all the stars. And it gave us 10 or 15 minutes together."[27] As soon as he could, Bob would dash across the driveway for his evening's work—not to study a spider building a web, but sometimes to stretch out on the rug in his office and chat for hours on the phone with Tom Rhea. Like Carlos, Rhea traveled on Bob's wavelength, speaking the same language; the two could shop-talk endlessly.

With his creative engine idling, Bob began volunteering in the community. When the family first arrived in North Carolina he'd given time to a pro-solar activist alliance against nuclear power, and now, in 1991, he joined the local American Civil Liberties Union chapter to rally for gay and lesbian rights, abolishment of the death penalty, separation of church and state, and free speech. At ACLU meetings, he scribbled topics on a pad: "Older Klan leaders reaching out to young skinheads; Big Problem: Get *most* people to think that white supremacy is *bad*; Need to crack down re: weapons in the school."[28] As publicity chair, Bob started a chapter newsletter, *Western North Carolina Civil Liberties Herald*. The inaugural issue began with an admonition: "Several local and state CLU activities in 1991 have again reminded us that eternal vigilance is the price of liberty."[29]

Before long, the UNCA teaching job got to Bob. He struggled with pacing the material and wrestled with the wide knowledge gaps among the students. Steve Dunnington, a student who excelled in the program, remembered, "This one guy couldn't get fractions. Bob couldn't get into the mindset that somebody didn't understand what a simple fraction was. But this was a local guy from Asheville who was in music because he wanted to 'get chicks,' and here he was in a classroom with *Bob Moog*. And it was like, 'I don't know what a fraction is. I don't know what a ratio is.' Bob couldn't get into the mindset of a beginner. He was just too far advanced."[30]

Bob's patience ran out in February 1992—the spring term of his third year at UNCA—when he wrote Zumchak: "I spent the last 2-1/2 class hours trying to get them to understand how to keep track of powers of ten. It's like pulling a cart with square wheels through the mud. So fuck it, I'm going back into the theremin business. Really! It's what I was doing before the synthesizer shit hit the fan, and it's the only time in my professional career that I ever made money.... I've given them my notice, - I'm through in May. It's too much like work.... I really like being able to roll across the driveway after breakfast, and roll back during the afternoon for a nap."[31]

Bob and Shirleigh were blowing through the fourth of five time-release allotments of Florence's annuity. With the teaching gig gone, it was unclear if a new line of theremins would offset the loss of his salary. But Bob was inspired. In 1989 he'd realized a lifelong dream when he came face to face with Leon Theremin at the International Festival of Experimental Music in Bourges, France, a royal summit of the founding fathers of electronic music where Bob had been a featured speaker. Theremin was making his first appearance outside the Soviet Union in 51 years and was held on a short leash by his KGB handlers, but the thrill of the encounter made Bob weak in the knees.

Now, after a 10-year hiatus from producing anything new, Bob introduced the Big Briar Series 91 theremins in 1992. The models used analog and digital circuitry to recreate the sound of Leon Theremin's original waveforms. Even the body styles of the Series 91's were an homage to Leon Theremin's models. The Option A cabinet was a dead ringer for the vintage 1929 RCA; the Option B model looked just like Theremin's 1980s-era U-shaped instrument that the inventor had sawed and screwed together in Soviet Russia from makeshift wooden scraps. Option C was a strikingly original futuristic design that Bob commissioned from sculptor David McCornack, with a cherry veneer.

Bob was also occupied with the MTS keyboard, which was finally finished and ready for an unveiling by John Eaton. Word that Bob Moog was releasing a new synth for the first time in years was catnip for the press. The *Orange County Register* reported, "Moog, 58, sees the new keyboard as the crowning achievement of his career in electronic instrument design."[32] Eaton promised the *Chicago Sun-Times* that the MTS was "the world's most sensitive instrument, next to the human voice"; in his hyper-enthusiasm he called it his "Can't Resistisizer."[33]

Eaton debuted the MTS at a concert on May 29, 1992, at the University of Chicago, where he now served on the faculty. The finished instrument was a monster: three 49-note polyphonic keyboards, each communicating with a dedicated computer and equipped with a large touch-sensitive plate, eight swell pedals, and four separate foot switches. On "A Concert of Premieres," Eaton played on all three keyboards at the same time in his new work, *Genesis*.

Larry Fine was in the audience, curious to see how the keys he'd helped fashion four years earlier would produce music. "To be honest," he admitted, "I can't remember much about the piece . . . but to call it 'atonal' would be an understatement. I tried to keep in mind that the keyboards themselves had no intrinsic sound and could just as well play Mozart as Eaton, but it was little consolation at the time."[34]

After the premiere, Bob was finally ready to wash his hands of the project. "I am at the end of my own involvement with it," he told *Piano & Keyboard* magazine. "I've given them to Eaton and to one other artist, Gregory Kramer, an experimental composer in upstate New York. Now it's my turn to take a breath and see what they do with them."[35]

The MTS had been Bob's white whale, and a money pit that further sunk his marriage. The *Piano & Keyboard* article finally exposed the *real* cost of the project that swallowed up Florence's money, bank loans, and the Sandy Mush nest egg, leaving the family in near penury. "Only five of these new keyboards yet exist," the column reported, "each one handmade by Moog and representing $100,000 per unit in development costs. 'If you asked my wife, she'd say it's much, much more,' says Moog."[36] When Bob was asked if these keyboards might be produced in any quantity, Larry fine recalled, "Shirleigh Moog chimed in, 'Not if I have anything to say about it. . . . Once in a person's lifetime is enough to go through that.'"[37]

For her part, Shirleigh was burying herself in another cookbook project, but it set off one of the worst domestic conflagrations in the marriage. Her second effort for Crossing Press, *A Guide to the Food Pyramid*, was a full-course compendium to aid readers in unraveling the new U.S. Department of Agriculture guidelines on fat and calories. Appearances on Asheville Public Radio and signings at local bookstores were planned.

A galley proof of the book arrived at the Cove in January 1993 on the eve of a trip to Puerto Rico that Shirleigh, Bob, and Michelle had been looking forward to. Preening over the look of her new book, Shirleigh waited for a congratulations from Bob, but it never came. In shades of the 1984 Brandt vacation debacle, Michelle recalled, "They got into a *huge* fight, and Dad decided he wasn't going to go with us the next morning. He dragged a mattress out to the shop and he slept out there so he didn't have to sleep inside with mom—even though there were four bedrooms downstairs."[38]

Shirleigh and Michelle were left to navigate the island vacation by themselves, casting a pall over the whole trip. Michelle remembered sitting on the beach at Culebra indulging hours of her mother's railing over Bob: "Everything he had ever done wrong to her, what a monster he was, how selfish he was, how dad had no idea how to run a business, how awful Grandma Shirley was, on and on." When they returned to the Cove, Shirleigh cloistered herself in her bedroom, brooding, and Michelle ran out to the shop to hear her father's side of the story. "He'd grown a week's worth of stubble," she remembered. "He looked like absolute hell. I doubt he'd slept well; I don't think he'd eaten well. I'd never seen him looking so bad. And I could tell he was deeply disturbed. He took me into his office and he sat at his desk, ranting about my mom."[39] Bob continued to spend nights out in the shop, and Michelle became an intermediary between her parents for the next few weeks until Bob moved back into the house.

That spring Bob and Shirleigh went through counseling. The outcome was a reaffirmation ceremony on the deck of the Cove house, to renew their wedding vows, officiated by the minister of the Unitarian Universalist Church they'd been attending for a few years. "It felt like a very joyous occasion," Renée recalled. "They were both in on it."[40]

∿∿∿

Bob's former company continued to be tossed around from owner to owner like a hot potato. After Luce and Chapman were dragged into technical default and the bank was ready to shut them down, Luce managed to unload the Moog operation on the EJE Research Corporation, a firm that scooped up dying companies for cents on the dollar. The new owners—three business partners from Jamestown, New York—used the company to manufacture products like subway door mechanisms and climate control systems. Only a small niche was reserved as a service department for old Moog equipment. A few engineers were kept on to function as "Moog Custom Engineering," filling sporadic orders for modulars assembled from leftover parts.

For years, Bob's old company had been lucky, slapping his name on new products and taking for granted the consumer trust, even the love, bound up with the Moog brand. The three EJE investors who owned the Moog trademark now—they'd bought it from Luce and Chapman as part of the deal—seemed to have little appreciation for its worth. When Young Chang bought Kurzweil, the company at least had the foresight to see the value of the Kurzweil name and the time it took to establish a brand's reputation and customer loyalty; they knew a name was often more valuable than the product itself. But under EJE, the potency of the Moog name was further diluted when the owners formed an umbrella holding company, Electronic Technology Group (ETG), to make items like guitar amps for other companies, under the name "Moog Music Manufacturing." Finally, in June 1993, the investors sold ETG, and by August, the small corner that handled Moog synthesizers was shut down for good. The firm Bob and his dad had set in motion in 1954 as the R. A. Moog Company had run its course.

Bob only learned of its demise when the Jamestown partners wrote to him to offer the remaining inventory of Moog parts. Their asking price: $185,000. Thrown into the bargain would be the Moog name and trademark. Bob didn't have that kind of cash, and it seemed like pure exploitation to try to sell him back his own name at that price. He countered with an offer of $50,000, then cut his bid to $25,000. When negotiations broke down, he passed altogether. If the three investors had no appreciation for what they owned, Bob seemed to have even less. Letting go of the chance to reclaim his name and trademark was a decision he'd come to regret.

∿∿∿

Like every other truce Bob and Shirleigh had called in their marriage, the reaffirmation ceremony didn't hold. With two of their daughters about to be married, the nuptial rituals that traditionally cement family bonds would prove a brief distraction from the combustible tensions heating up in their own relationship.

Michelle and her fiancé, Joseph Koussa, had announced their engagement in 1992. They'd met in Senegal, West Africa—Joseph's native country—while Michelle was visiting Renée, who was on assignment there with the Peace Corps. Their wedding, on November 13, 1993, was held at the Unitarian Universalist Church in Asheville. Shirleigh threw herself into the preparations for the formal event involving bridesmaids and groomsmen. At the ceremony, no one would have suspected the growing estrangement between her and Bob. She remembered a friend commenting, "The way you two dance, there's such electricity."[41] On December 18, Laura Moog married Tom Lanier in a more casual New Age–style ceremony at Asheville Jubilee Faith Community. Bob and Shirleigh, in a "Liturgy of Friendship," read from *The Prophet* by Kahlil Gibran.

Practically the minute they saw their daughters into marriage, the thin threads binding their own quickly began unraveling. Shirleigh had started a diary to vent to herself: "He is <u>NOT</u> MAKING $ & never has made more $ than he spends. . . . I said end of next year $ runs out—let's sell the house, buy something small & live on funds & have '<u>TIME TOGETHER</u>.' Wouldn't talk about it—wait & see . . ." On a page labeled, "<u>Irreconcilable Differences</u>," she scribbled, "For 30+ years I've been used . . . as a '<u>work</u>-horse.'"[42] Her diary pages were imprinted with words of celebrated feminists—every page had a quote from a famous woman. On one, a Virginia Woolf epigram read: "Women have served all these centuries as looking glasses possessing the magic and delicious power of reflecting the figure of man at twice its natural size."

On New Year's Eve, Shirleigh rained her soul onto the pages: "At 3:30 in afternoon we had a discussion about Social Security—(Could I get ½ of his amount if we're divorced? And my work & sweat equity in business—discussed an income from $500–2000 a month depending on business income) (he said <u>he'd consider</u> it). At the end of the discussion I felt very melancholy. . . I cried for 3 hours in the bedroom. . . . I was feeling very <u>very</u> ALONE. I hoped that maybe since R knew how miserable I was he would <u>do</u> something warm for New Year's eve—come in & sit with me—watch some Fred Astaire movies on T.V.—He did 0—at 12:05 when the movies ended I went down & told him I thought he was the coldest person I knew. . . .

"He really is missing emotional patch cords—WHOLE MODULES—He is an <u>ENGINEER.</u> . . . It's him & his machines. If you don't plug it in the wall it's not worth a damn!"[43]

27

Comes Now the Defendant

"As Mom will gleefully point out to anyone, my business has not produced any income in recent years," Bob wrote Michelle in January 1994. Michelle and Joseph were living in Senegal at a safe remove from the fallout, but Bob brought them up to speed: "For me, being near to Mom now is like walking through a mine field. Sometimes she's cool and civil; other times she dumps a load of incredibly vicious, nasty shit on me."[1]

A formal separation was in the works. The Cove property would be put up for sale, and Bob and Shirleigh would each look for their own homes. "With our assets being divided," he confessed, "it will be more necessary for me to produce a profit now. I hope I can do it. On the other hand, I've been put down so hard and for so long that I forget that I do have a lot of experience, and a reputation that I should be able to take advantage of. So the coming year or three are going to be a serious challenge. Say some prayers for me!"[2]

Shirleigh was smoldering over their eviscerated bank account. On a lined sheet she scrawled, "Joint monies used to keep Robert's 'hobby' Big Briar alive."[3] She tallied every asset the business had consumed over the past decade, starting with $110,000 from her parents' inheritance, $140,000 for the sale of the Sandy Mush property, $300,000 from Florence's will, and the additional $200,000 annuity. With other items, the total came to $780,000—all of it gone. She'd been patient and supportive, but in the end, she'd seen no returns for the marriage: "I really loved Robert, and the problem was, so did Robert—there was nothing there for me."[4]

She and Bob hired their own lawyers and the scrapping began. A "Separation Agreement," drafted on February 22, divvied up their joint belongings with the petty exactitude of two kids trading candy, specifying every household item from a waffle iron to a beanbag, a poster, and "the large beach towel from Puerto Rico with the brown border."[5] To keep each other at a distance, they agreed to take turns living at the Cove in alternating one-month periods over the spring.

Bob found emotional sanctuary at the home of his neighbors, Khatia and Rick Krebs—recent transplants from California who lived down the road on

42 acres, at Peepeye Cove. The Krebs hosted regular parties for a coterie of their rural mountain neighbors, with potlucks and themed gatherings like grape stompings. Khatia studied the practices of indigenous world tribes, especially Native American traditions, and she and Rick kept a sweat lodge on their property. Bob found himself easily absorbed into the New Age atmosphere the Krebs had erected around themselves.

At the Krebs' home, Bob met Frankie Moore, an artist who lived nearby in the valley. "Frankie was a young lady from the south from a very affluent family," Khatia recalled. "She lived a life of serenity—she was calm, and graceful, and quite deeply spiritual. She had a challenge with her legs—she had polio when she was younger." With Frankie, Bob began reading the Egyptian *Book of the Dead*, with its spells to guide the deceased through the underworld. "Bob had a budding relationship with Frankie," Khatia recalled. "She was a lovely person. They came up to the house and we'd be in the Jacuzzi or whatever. I know that he and Frankie had a very beautiful relationship. He was quite new at being single."[6]

∿∿∿

On March 22, Ileana Grams, a philosophy professor at UNCA, answered the phone in her office. "A voice at the other end said, 'My name is Bob Moog,'" she recalled. "You don't know me, but my assistant is renting an apartment from you.'"[7] It was Bob's turn to vacate the Cove and he needed temporary lodging. One of his former UNCA students, Houston Haynes, who was helping him build Series 91 theremins, lived in a small apartment Ileana rented out next to her home, and he figured she might have another space to let.

Ileana did have an extra bedroom upstairs, but she wondered who Bob needed it for. She remembered him from a lecture he'd given 10 years earlier at UNCA that she and her ex-husband had enjoyed. Shirleigh had been there selling her cookbook and Ileana purchased a copy that Shirleigh autographed. Ileana remembered thinking, "Well, *they* look like a solid married couple."[8] Bob explained that he and Shirleigh had separated. Ileana agreed to show him the room, but first she wanted to get a feeling for who he was, and invited him to dinner.

Ileana's home, at 332 Barnard Avenue, sat in the semi-rural outskirts of Asheville, five minutes from downtown, and close to the UNCA campus. The 1925 three-bedroom frame house had a musty, antique charm about it.

A bench swing was suspended from chains on the long porch which opened through a screen door into a dark interior of wide wooden floorboards, and a small living room with muted oriental rugs, dark wood furniture, traditional table lamps, and a potbelly stove. The cozy kitchen and dining room had a homespun, "sit-down-for-tea" feel. Behind the kitchen, a bright conservatory with deck flooring was cluttered with potted plants. An old carpeted staircase with heavy bannisters led upstairs to the bedroom Bob would be looking at. Bookcases short and tall, crammed to capacity with books, were tucked into every possible corner, upstairs and down, in bedrooms and hallways. From the back windows, the misty curves of the Blue Ridge Mountains peeked through the brush and trees of the surrounding wooded terrain. The two-acre property had a large backyard that sloped down and away from the house.

Ileana, twice divorced, lived with her 12-year-old daughter, Miranda, from her second marriage—a 10-year union with Bob Richmond, a doctor now remarried and living in Knoxville, Tennessee. Miranda was being raised in the Jewish tradition—Ileana was born in Switzerland just after World War II to Eastern European Jewish refugees, and came to the United States at the age of 11. She remained observant, lighting candles every week, celebrating the Jewish holidays, and attending the conservative synagogue in town with Miranda.

The night Bob came to dinner, he asked if, as a boarder, he'd be allowed to cook. Ileana cautioned that Passover was coming, and with its strict dietary conventions, it might not be the best time to share the kitchen. "So I started explaining what Passover was," she recalled, "at which point he said, 'Well I'm not observant, but I did have a bar mitzvah.' And I thought, '*What?* He's *Jewish?* Well *that's* convenient.' So we all had dinner, and it felt very homey."[9] Bob liked the room and startled Ileana when he asked to move in that night—his suitcase was waiting out in the car.

Bob soon made himself at home in Ileana's kitchen, whipping up tasty fare for his hosts: roasted root vegetables with Japanese dipping sauce, and pizza Margherita with dough he made from scratch. "From the beginning," Ileana reflected, "cooking was a real factor in our feeling comfortable with each other."[10] Miranda, in fact, had only recognized Bob's name at first from seeing Shirleigh's cookbook at home since she was little.

Ileana was startled again when her mother visited and mumbled, "You should marry that man. He's the kind of man that needs to be married. If *you* don't marry him, some mean woman will marry him." Soon after, Miranda took her mother aside in the kitchen and whispered, "You know mom, he'd make a really good stepdad!" When Ileana took Bob to her synagogue for a Passover Seder—he confessed he'd never been to a Seder before—the gossip wheels began turning. She recalled, "Apparently somebody said, 'Did *you know* about Ileana and Bob Moog?' And our rabbi told me he'd said, 'Oh yes, I knew right away. I knew when I saw them walk in together.' And at that point neither of *us* had a clue, certainly, but apparently Shmuel saw *something*."[11]

Bob's newfound domesticity was a comfort in the midst of his separation from Shirleigh, but it was soon shattered by the onset of a hernia. In a long confessional letter to friends he wondered, "I wasn't doing anything very physical . . .what I was doing most was sitting around thinking and feeling sorry for myself." He asked Frankie—who remained a good friend, though they'd ended any deeper involvement—what might have caused it. In a self-help book, she discovered that a frequent cause of hernia was a "ruptured relationship." "As soon as she told me that, a bright light went on in my head," Bob told his friends. "*Of course that's what happened.*"[12]

At the hospital before the operation, Frankie dropped off cassette tapes of New Age lectures and a book on Tibetan spiritual philosophy. "I still have the strong feeling that the material that Frankie loaned me helped me have a speedy recovery," he recalled. But there were still other, non-corporeal demons that lurked inside of him. "Shortly after my operation," he confessed to his friends, "I went with Khatia to a workshop of a spiritual practice called 'Awareness Release.' In this practice, you are guided to visualize your stresses as physical entities within your body, and then to confront them and deal with them. . . . in the second session I sensed something very black inside of me. I started to sob, and could not stop for half an hour."[13]

Bob's turn to move back to the Cove came up on April 23. His belongings were gone from Ileana's house, but over the next weeks she found a hanging basket of nasturtiums sitting outside her front door, and regular anonymous deliveries of spring water. She knew the water could have come from only one source: the Cove.

∿∿∿

Bob's mother had been critically ill since the fall and had been confined to a Los Angeles hospital. On May 30, Bob was alone at the Cove, out on the porch at night, stargazing. "He saw this shooting star," Michelle recalled, "and he said, 'I knew something had changed.' Then the phone rang and it was his mother's nurse saying she'd just died."[14] Shirley was 86, and had outlived George, who'd passed away two years earlier.

The couple had spent their final years in a double-wide at the San Vicente Mobile Home Park in Santa Barbara, California, a gated senior retirement community. Shirley had busied herself with courses in calligraphy and Chinese painting, and played bingo with friends. But George, socially adrift, had puttered around the garden, washed dishes, and tidied up, with little motivation and few friends. When his health deteriorated, Shirley had to put him in a nursing home. He passed away on July 31, 1992, at the age of 87.

Bob's mother had willed him a substantial sum. The day following her death, he wrote to Shirleigh, promising to split the inheritance: "I estimate that, after all taxes and expenses are paid, we will each have between $300,000 and $320,000."[15]

By mid-April, Shirleigh had moved into her own house. She'd managed to scrape together $42,000 to buy a three-bedroom home at 35 Crestmont Avenue in West Asheville. The 1926 house had plenty of space for a single person to stretch out.

In the separation tussle, Shirleigh had already gathered that Bob was planning to withhold, or cut down on, the majority of her expected settlement, and she was skeptical of his promise about his mother's estate. Desperate for a fair settlement, she left him a string of exasperated answering machine recordings which he transcribed, hoping to use them as evidence of harassment. Her phone machine monologues were a bitter audio diary of the root frustrations that had festered during her years with Bob:

I loved you. I supported you, I went through good times and bad times with you. . . . I gave our children the extra time that they needed, because there was only one parent home most of the time . . . . Worked at your business, did payroll, entertained your guests. . . . rubbed your back. . . . What does the checklist on your yellow pad look like, Robert? Is it, first lie . . . screw her out of alimony, make sure she gets no recognition of her part in the business, cut her out of the will. . . . You know, Robert, in all of 35 years that we were married . . . I never had any idea that you could be this cruel, this heartless, this vindictive. I just didn't know it was in you.[16]

In one message, she tapped her college psychology minor, deconstructing his psychic lineage:

It's an interesting family syndrome, that your mother acted out on your father the resentment she felt toward her father . . . and you took YOUR resentment of YOUR mother and what she did to your father. And whether you realize it or not, you decided to punish me for it. And it's no coincidence . . . that I happen to have the same name as your mother. And then you decided to make my life miserable. And to demean me. The way your mother demeaned your father. And work out your anger for your mother on me. . . . I don't think you really want to know—who you are—why you act the way you do.[17]

As a couple, Shirleigh and Bob had been friends with the Krebs, and through Khatia's network, Shirleigh heard about Bob's New Age therapies and psychological balms, and in another message she taunted him:

And YOU, you who want to be spiritual . . . maybe you just want to put a band-aid on the hurt that you're feeling. . . . The hurt will never go away no matter how much music you listen to, no matter how many prisms you stare at, no matter how many hikes in the woods you take or mushrooms you collect, because the hurt is the meanness that lives inside of you, that you are denying but it's there.[18]

There was no question Bob was turning the screws on Shirleigh. She was a reminder, in spite of his fame, of a life strewn with financial failures, workplace indignities, suffocating foreign competition, and professional miscues of his own making. She was the voice of his conscience, shouting from the back of his brain about every ego-deflating failure and humiliation. In one of her letters she shot off a strident litany: "My life with you has been a mine field—Rob's under stress at school, Rob's depressed because it's the holidays, Rob's behind <ALWAYS TRUE> Rob has $ worries, there are bugs in the machines, there are no orders, people are cancelling orders. For all these reasons you were—snappy, withdrawn, uncommunicative and of course had no time for aught but 'the business.'"[19]

Bob simply wanted to turn the volume down on her, and he sought the company of people who knew little of his history—the Krebs, Frankie, Ileana—those who saw only his exterior distress, and rushed to apply every salve.

Shirleigh, as the owner of record of the Cove property, began billing Bob for rent on the metal building, and on July 1 he was forced to relocate Big Briar to an industrial site at 554-C Riverside Drive in Asheville, a

2,500-square-foot space on the French Broad River. He signed a two-year lease, another cart-before-the-horse risk, eerily reminiscent of his precipitous move to the Main Street property in Trumansburg 31 years earlier. Now, as then, he hired a skeleton staff to build his only product: theremins.

On August 14, Bob staged an opening ceremony to christen his new headquarters. As a celebrant he enlisted Marylee DiLorenzo, a neighbor of the Krebs who lived on 30 acres at the top of the mountain and regularly practiced full moon ceremonies and indigenous rites. Before a small gathering of friends and new Big Briar employees, Bob faced DiLorenzo, who wielded an eagle wing and a seashell of burning herbs in a smudging ritual, waving the smoke into the air with prayers to bless him, the staff, and the new factory.

Bob was gambling on a large commercial space and three full-time, salaried employees, two of them former students from his UNCA classes. So far, all he was building was theremins, but each staff member was honored with a title worthy of an established operation: Houston Haynes, Bob's Series 91 technician, was "sales manager"; Dave Perkins was "production manager"; and Gail Arendell was "office manager." On his company business card, Bob chose a unique title for himself: *Bob Moog, Grand Poobah*.

With things as lean as they were, Bob nevertheless took on a fourth employee in one of his gut-instinct hires. Steve Dunnington, his former UNCA pupil, was kicking around Asheville after completing a degree in music and recording arts, working as a caterer and playing in a band. His skill set didn't exactly seem like a fit for Big Briar. "It was crazy," Dunnington recalled. "I was a music nerd and I also took calculus and physics classes and stuff, so I guess I was the kind of person Bob wanted around. He asked me, 'Have you ever used a table saw?' And I was thinking back to junior high school shop class. . . . 'Sure! Yeah, I've used a table saw!' 'Have you ever used a drill press?'. . . *(junior high school shop class)*. . . 'Yeah, sure.'" Bob was satisfied, and assured Dunnington, "You know, we'll pay you."[20]

Bob and the skeleton staff were flying by the seat of their pants. Dunnington was given the job of machinist, but when the production manager quit, he recalled, "Bob was like, 'Do *you* want to be the production manager?' And I was like, 'Okay!'" Dunnington got the title, but he was now doing double duty as the machinist as well. "I was machining these little ABS washers for the Series 91 theremins. It was this insane amount of labor—this little detail that goes on the outside of the instrument. It was pretty nuts. We had probably 50 or 60 orders for the Series 91's, and I think at the end of it we sold 125 of them, total. It was kind of a tough one; Bob was losing money on that."[21]

On the side, Bob had to bolster his income with any consulting work he could find. In the fall of 1994, Casio hired him as an expert witness in its challenge to the U.S. government. Import duties would be higher if the company's synths were counted as musical *instruments*, lower if they were simply considered machines. Bob had to testify in court that synthesizers weren't musical instruments at all, just machines. As the iconic synthesizer pioneer and a luthier of hand-built instruments, Bob was an unlikely hired gun. But his motivation, he admitted, was, "a thousand dollars a day. You know, where do you get a thousand dollars a day?"[22]

In an odd coincidence, Herb Deutsch turned out to be the expert witness for the U.S. He remembered, "Bob and I, sitting on either side of the court, just looking at each other, trying not to *laugh!*"[23] Herb wowed the judge with a majestic performance on a Casio keyboard, and, Bob recalled, "Casio lost, most of it. And the judge singled me out as being the most full of shit. The whole thing was a big joke."[24] But the joke was ultimately on Casio. If its lawyers had done their homework, they'd have known that Bob told *Polyphony* magazine in 1982, "When you look at something like Casio's VL-1, or all these new keyboard instruments . . . they're just a lot of fun."[25] In the same *Polyphony* article, Bob joked about the times he'd escaped import duty himself by distracting customs agents who just had to tell him about their own Moog synthesizers and their garage bands.

If nothing else, Herb recalled that their day in court helped reconcile their friendship after years of ups and downs. "Bob and I all of a sudden warmed our relationship right then and there. We never had any sense of saying apologies or anything, but we knew right away that we were really friends."[26]

Ileana sent Miranda to spend the night at a friend's house one evening and invited Bob over for dinner. "Something just really clicked," she recalled. Four days later Miranda had another sleepover when Bob returned for an encore repast. "At some point during the second dinner," Ileana remembered, "he said, 'Well I know I could never be Miranda's father because she *has* a father, but . . .' I thought, 'Oh my God, we're talking about spending our lives together.' It felt, on the one hand, completely astonishing, and on the other hand, completely natural."[27]

Ileana had to tiptoe around the situation with 12-year old Miranda, who recalled, "We were coming into the driveway and my mom said, 'You know,

Bob came over this weekend and we were talking about our retirement plans and we realized that they were together. So he's going to move in.'"[28]

On July 24, 1994, Bob changed his address to 332 Barnard Avenue. When he relocated to Ileana's bedroom, the arrangement came clear to Miranda. Ileana worried over the sudden change for Bob, who was climbing out of a 35-year marriage, but he reassured her: "He said that he'd known for about ten years that the day was going to come when he just couldn't do it anymore. It was like holding a wet paper bag; you knew it was going to burst at some point."[29]

Bob and Shirleigh were both present at Matthew's wedding to Lucy Morton Herman in Chicago that September, but Shirleigh sequestered herself in her own hotel room, smoking and drinking with the blinds drawn, while Bob went off to a bar, backslapping with Matt's friends. Afterward he wrote his lawyer, "My wife stayed so clear of me at our son's wedding that we didn't make eye contact *even once* during the entire weekend."[30]

That fall Bob wrote his lawyer about "the ongoing food fight with Shirleigh," a tit for tat that seemed to have no end in sight. He warned her she'd be treated as a trespasser if she came to the Riverside shop to claim possessions. She threatened to show up with a sheriff. He refused to pay storage on the metal building and she locked him out. He changed the locks and told his lawyer he'd close the gate and lock *her* out of the grounds altogether. The Cove was on the market and he accused her of overpricing it and impeding its sale. She worried that its appeal to buyers was undermined because he wasn't keeping it clean. "The grapes can be mowed down," she wrote him. "My enthusiasm for this land is gone."[31]

∿∿∿

Living with Ileana, Bob was unearthing bits and pieces of his Jewish upbringing and he told her he'd be happy to practice conservative Judaism with her. Miranda's thirteenth birthday was approaching in December, and she was preparing for her bat mitzvah in January, something Bob wanted to be involved in. After he began driving her to her Hebrew school sessions, he decided he wanted to perform a blessing at the ceremony. "It was clear that we were all doing this together," Ileana recalled. "So that was a really, really big shifting point." Miranda began calling Bob, Abba (Hebrew for "father"), and Bob's emotional bonds were deepening. He also enjoyed a new moniker Ileana was using for him that Michelle's husband Joseph had come up with—"Babu"—a variant of Bob's name that was a reference to the companion and advisor of the Islamic Prophet Muhammad, Abu Bakr, called "Babu" in Joseph's native Senegal, used there as a sign of respect for an older man.

At 49, Ileana was the antithesis of Shirleigh in nearly every way. Thin and petite, with a frail-looking frame, delicate fine features, no makeup, and long dark hair that complemented her straight, ankle-length dresses and skirts, she exuded a quiet naturalness. Her speech had the soft, measured cadence of a professor gently unfolding a subject for a class. She hailed from an intellectual tradition—her mother was a psychiatrist and her father a simultaneous interpreter for the United Nations. She spoke four languages, including Hebrew. Her academic specialties were the philosophy of religion, the philosophy of law, and environmental philosophy.

"Ileana and I are very happy together," Bob wrote friends. "If there's one word that characterizes Ileana more than any other, it is 'thoughtful.' She takes pride in understanding *exactly* what your point of view is, as well as carefully explaining what her point of view is. . . . Being with her is a comfort and a joy for me. Her mind is like a beautiful landscape, . . . with no fences, no barbed wire, and no land mines."[32]

For Ileana it was mutual: "Being with Bob is just like a lovely warm bath." The idea of marriage ran silently in the background, but one day Ileana blurted out her private assumptions and inadvertently landed the topic squarely on the table: "Bob was talking about getting medical insurance for himself," she recalled. "I said to him, 'But if you're married to *me*, you'll *have* medical insurance, because I'm covered.' I realized Bob hadn't yet gotten to the point of thinking we were going to be married. And Bob said, "Oh *yes*, right, that's the perfect *solution!*" And I thought, 'Oh my God, I just proposed to him!' " Still, she recalled, "Both of us, without ever saying a word about it to each other, had the same desire: to be an old married couple as soon as possible."[33]

In January 1995 Shirleigh served Bob with a civil summons; he filed a counterclaim in February. In March she followed with a "motion to dismiss" the counterclaim. She was "not acting rationally," Bob told his lawyer. If she'd be "reasonable," he promised, "then I <u>might</u> be willing to arrange for her to have some of her money."[34] Whatever she was owed in the settlement, he was still holding the purse strings, and he looked for any loophole to stall or whittle away her final share. He claimed that the terms of the separation agreement he'd signed off on were vague and unenforceable, and by May he'd managed to shrink her share of his mother's estate by almost two-thirds. Realizing the tug-of-war was far from over, he managed to sever the connection between the divorce judgment and the final distribution of assets. On July 11 an "absolute divorce" was conferred by the court.

~~~

Temporarily rid of one albatross, Bob's business anxieties were about to multiply. After he balked at buying EJE's leftover inventory of Moog parts for $185,000, the Jamestown owners held a public auction, surrendering the lot, as Roger Luther recalled, for $7,000, to a merchandising firm that turned around and put everything up for auction again. Bob was in the dark. The valuable cache of parts slipped through his fingers when two former EJE employees, Jim Suchora and Mike Bucki, bid successfully and walked away with the stockpile at the February 1995 auction.

Suchora and Bucki had a good use for the parts. They'd both worked in the Moog Custom Engineering corner of EJE and had assembled many one-off modules using hundreds of leftover parts to reconstitute classic Moog equipment whenever customers wanted a discontinued model. With EJE gone, Moog synthesizer owners were stuck when they needed repairs, and Suchora and Bucki were running interference around the world as Moog handymen, keeping modular systems going. Suchora, in fact, had taken over Rich Walborn's role as Keith Emerson's personal engineer. He kept the Monster Moog in line on tour, and wired up ribbon controller flares for Keith to shoot out over the audience, aim at the crowd backward through his legs, over his shoulder like a mirror trick shot, or over his band mates' heads.

But grabbing up the inventory was only a first step for Suchora and Bucki. The two had their eyes on a bigger prize. When the final Moog outpost closed down in 1993 in Jamestown, and Bob passed up the chance to buy back his trademark, the mark was soon abandoned. Bob was unaware it had expired on February 6, 1995. Now it was simply a freebie up for grabs by any first taker who knew it was available.

On March 24, Bucki filed for the trademark with the United States Patent and Trademark Office, and a feeding frenzy began. A Cincinnati, Ohio, man, Don Martin—a former employee of Manny's Music store in New York—filed for the trademark and incorporation as "Moog Music, Inc." Jim Suchora filed for "Moog Music Technology, Inc." Eugene DeWitt, the man who'd purchased ETG, threw his hat in the ring. And there would be others.

~~~

Back at the Riverside shop, it was clear that the Series 91 theremins alone couldn't sustain Big Briar. With their high-class designer cabinets and a price tag ranging from $2,500 to $2,900, they appealed mainly to serious collectors. In the fall of 1995, Bob convened an emergency visioning meeting with his staff to brainstorm: What could they do to keep the doors open? To find a product that Bob's glorified garage operation could easily assemble and sell in reasonable numbers—sidestepping digital technology and complex synthesizer manufacture with its now impossibly competitive market—Bob, as usual, circled back to the theremin. But this time he'd attempt a Melodia redux—a small unit perched on a microphone stand like its top-selling ancestor.

The timing was ideal. The theremin and its mystique were breaking through to the general public in Steven M. Martin's new documentary, *Theremin: An Electronic Odyssey*, released in September. Originally the film previewed on BBC television in November 1993, one day before the death of its subject, Leon Theremin, who was never to see the finished cut. In vignettes that ran through the footage, Bob was seen demonstrating a Vanguard model and waxing lyrical about the theremin.

On cue, in early 1996, Big Briar began production of the "Etherwave" theremin, a buyer-friendly instrument offered at $369, or $269 in kit form—the classic hobbyist formula that always got Bob's pulse racing. Among his new Big Briar merchandise, he couldn't resist offering two bumper stickers that read: *Theremin players do it with High Frequency*, and *Theremin players do it without touching*.

～～～

Bob and Shirleigh continued their legal skirmishes, endlessly trading roles as plaintiff and defendant. The latest court motion stated, "COMES NOW the defendant, ROBERT A. MOOG ... for an ORDER extending the time in which to file an Answer to the Plaintiff's REQUEST FOR PRODUCTION OF DOCUMENTS."[35] But Bob was clearly the victor in the end. In July, Shirleigh received $38,826.00 as her share of Bob's mother's $600,000 estate. And over a year later, Bob bought out her half of the Cove house for $126,000. After 35 years of marriage, these sums were her final payoff.

When it was all over, Bob turned on his lawyer, disputing nearly $60,000 in legal fees on top of the $8,000 he'd already spent.

～～～

"Bob said to me," Ileana recalled, "'What do you want most in a partner?' And the answer I gave was, 'I want a grownup.' And he said, 'I want to be loved unconditionally.' And I think we each got both of those things from each other. For each of us, the other person loved us just as we were. Doing anything, including, quite literally, walking to the mailbox—we would hold hands to get the mail—was just a treat with him."[36] Laura recalled, "Ileana loved him enough to allow him to like himself again."[37]

Preparations for Bob and Ileana's wedding began in the spring of 1996. In an odd reversal of fate, Bob flung himself with zeal into the very sort of Jewish wedding his former father-in-law had so yearned for 38 years earlier. "We wanted to be married under a chuppah," Ileana recalled.[38] Bob surprised Ileana with a hand-lettered *ketubah*, the Jewish marriage contract signed by the couple and the rabbi under the chuppah. Ileana brought Bob to a local jeweler where she'd picked out her ring, without revealing which one it was. When she asked him to choose one for himself, she was astounded when he picked out the identical design.

Their wedding, on May 19, 1996, was held before 200 guests at the Congregation Beth Israel in Asheville. At different points, the bride and groom paused to translate from the Hebrew for their guests. Ileana was decked in an elegant kimono under her prayer shawl and Bob wore a yarmulke. He'd chosen a text from Micah that was embroidered on his *atarah* (the neckpiece of his prayer shawl): "It has been shown you O man, what is good and what the Lord requires of you, to do justice, to love mercy, and to walk humbly with your God."

28

The Desperate Voyager

"Moog Music back in business," a headline on a European website proclaimed.[1] Moogmusic.com was listing a full range of newly manufactured gear for sale: the Minimoog, complete modular systems, the Source, Rogue, Prodigy, Liberation, and even the Polymoog. It was news to set the music world on fire.

The only problem was, the website belonged to an imposter, Don Martin, one of the vultures picking over the remains of the Moog name and trademark. By late 1996 he'd wasted no time in putting them to good use. For Bob, the worst part was the way he found out. Houston Haynes, who'd just left Big Briar, surfaced in Ohio and phoned Bob to announce proudly that he and Martin were building Minimoogs there. Martin, in fact, had already filed for the name "Minimoog," and, loading up his arms with everything he could carry away, he'd also applied for the name "ARP."

Martin's temptation to revive the classic Minimoog was irresistible: it hadn't been made in 15 years and people were clamoring for a rerun. But the very thought of a pirated Minimoog, and Houston's part in it, roused Bob's anger. *He* was Bob Moog. *He* should be the one to birth a new Minimoog. He knew about Bucki and Suchora, but with Martin in the game, too, he determined to put his flag back in the sand. On September 19, 1996, he hastily applied to the United States Patent and Trademark Office, the USPTO.

But now he'd have to get in line behind the others, and the field of pretenders was getting more crowded. In the UK, a man named Alexander Winter had registered the Moog name and trademark; Eugene DeWitt's application was still active; even Van Koevering was thinking of acquiring the Moog rights with the idea of sharing them with Bob. And the earliest grave robbers were now engaged in a tug-of-war over the spoils: Bucki was pressing on against the threat of lawsuits from Martin and DeWitt—trouble that had already frightened Suchora away. One way or the other, Bob was now the monkey in the middle, left to flail at his name as it was about to be tossed back and forth over his head many times.

With few legal remedies, Bob fought back the only way he could. Signaling that he was the authentic Moog, he changed his email address to realmoog@bigbriar.com. On his attorney's advice, he began offering autographed theremins—the "MOOG Signature Series Etherwave"—merely to brand his name on products in some way.

The period of the late 1990s was an unfortunate time to have his name stolen; the Moog was in vogue again, but he couldn't take advantage of the trend. The analog synths he'd founded the industry with were suddenly commanding hefty prices. "Moogs are back," *US News & World Report* announced, adding that mint condition models once unloaded in pawn shops for $50 could now fetch $12,000.[2] Some Moog modulars had changed hands for $20,000, according to Canada's *Globe and Mail*—a "bull market" for the retro models, the paper estimated.[3] In Bob's own backyard, the *Charlotte Observer* noted, "Moogs are once again hot."[4] The fact was driven home painfully when Jean-Jacques Perrey suggested to Bob, "If you'd manufacture some 'limited edition' of the old MOOG SYNTH, you'd make a fortune. So many people asked me 'where could I find THE same MOOG system you used in your records?'"[5]

The sounds of Perrey's and Kingsley's '60s-era albums were also making a comeback. A new two-man band, Moog Cookbook, named in honor of Shirleigh's *Moog's Musical Eatery*, was formed to celebrate—and spoof—the quirky, kitschy pop records that showcased the first generation of analog synths. Brian Kehew, a studio engineer and producer, and Roger Manning, a former member of the band Jellyfish, took advantage of the fact that the synth industry was emerging from a dormant period in the late '80s and early '90s when keyboards and synths weren't cool with bands anymore, and groups had returned to pure guitar rock. The two scooped up a warehouse worth of old analog gear at fire sale prices, and set out to reseed the cultural landscape with a flowering of synth sounds.

The duo produced two albums intended as both an homage to, and an irreverent parody of, 1969-era Moog pop LPs—the cheesy, electro-fluff covers of Beatles songs, or Bacharach hits. On their first, eponymously titled LP, *The Moog Cookbook*, released in May 1996, Kehew and Manning piloted a roomful of 41 analog devices—Moogs, ARPS, Rolands, Oberheims, EML synths, racks of drum machines, processors, and several acoustic instruments. The album was a playful jab at the grunge and alternative bands of the early '90s that eschewed synths, covering their hits with in-your-face onslaughts of electronic whipped cream. Songs of bands like Green Day,

Pearl Jam, and Nirvana were marched through a forest of silly lead sounds—squawks, wah-wahs, and slides, laced with robotic vocoder voices, whistling bombs, and thunder static, over traditional background harmonies and standard pop beats driven by acoustic drums. The Cookbook's second and last album, *Ye Olde Space Bande*, released in October 1997, gave similar treatment to FM radio rock classics like Lynyrd Skynyrd's "Sweet Home Alabama" and the Eagles' "Hotel California."

In live shows, Kehew and Manning took the stage in silver space suits with astronaut helmets, using the aliases, "Meco Eno" for Manning, and "Uli Nomi" for Kehew. The idea wasn't just the revival of synths, but *analog* instruments in particular. Musicians were turning away from the sanitized digital sound that had once put analog in the shadows. There was a nostalgia now for the warmth of analog. Bob, of course, was always a pure analog guy. Clean digital tone, he thought, was tiring on the ears; and he also disliked the pushbutton interface of digital synths. In 1997 he told *EQ*, "Musicians have been temporarily distracted by a bunch of fancy digital whizbangs for the past 15 years or so. Now they're understanding that nice round knobs and truly continuously changing waveforms are *good*."[6] Thanks to Kehew, Manning, and others, synths were back in force by the late '90s.

∿∿∿

In its November 1997 issue, *Music Merchandising Review* announced, "Moog Reissues the Minimoog." A photo pictured an immaculately built copy of the instrument with a blurb that declared, "Over 25 years after its introduction, Moog has decided to bring back its Minimoog model. . . . manufactured exactly to the original specifications."[7]

That came as news to Bob.

Martin, as it turned out, had managed to make a working Minimoog clone and he was openly advertising it. Bob finally blew a gasket. In February 1998 he filed a federal lawsuit against Martin and Moog Music, Inc. A Big Briar press release announced, "Robert Moog's action is for unfair competition, false advertising, and violation of Mr. Moog's right of publicity."[8] Bob also filed a Notice of Opposition with the USPTO to block Martin's registration of the Moog Music and Minimoog trademarks. On top of it, Bob discovered that Mike Bucki had just put up his own website displaying the Moog trademark, operating now as Moog Music Custom Engineering.

Coming off the legal entanglements with Shirleigh and the astronomical lawyers' fees, Bob had cold feet over committing to yet another protracted battle. He wasn't sure it was worth it, Michelle recalled. But he'd already set the ball in motion and there was no turning back.

In May, Bob and Ileana remortgaged the Cove property for $250,000, anticipating the cost of the legal brawling ahead. Bob was a plaintiff once again, and his lawyers rolled up their sleeves and began digging. And charging. There were meetings, memos, briefs, document research, expert witnesses, case law reviews, subpoenas, discovery requests, defendants' exhibits, and email investigations. By August, the attorneys had clocked in over $94,000 in hours. And they were battling on another front at the same time: in Wales, Alex Winter was making Minimoogs as "Moog Music Ltd." and selling T-shirts and merchandise with the Moog logo. Winter had discovered that the trademark was abandoned in the UK, and jumped on it, arguing that Moogs were essentially generic equipment now, and he was respectfully building on their fabled quality.

When the pressures got to Bob and he needed a release, he'd down another dose of New Age narcotic. One spring, on Marylee DiLorenzo's property, Moon Song, he spent three days at a male bonding retreat, *Spirit in Flight: A Spring Gathering of Men*. Participants donned new identities with "Spirit Names" like "Wandering Laughter," "Rainbow Man," and "Lightning Wings." Bob was "Living Seeker," and was designated as the "elder" for the assembly of 32 men during the weekend of Native American rituals. The group was encouraged to share poems and stories about manhood, and gathered for drumming ceremonies and a talking circle where any man holding the talking stick could speak for as long he liked. There was a sweat lodge, and each man was asked to make a prayer rattle—Bob filled his with pebbles that he brought along. The organizer, "Wind River," wrote Bob afterward "in brotherhood," addressing him, "Aho Living Seeker!" concluding that the group had "found our wings and have taken flight." He told Bob, "Stay well and always in the Light!"[9]

In the fall of 1998, Bob was thrown into more legal runarounds as Martin tried to find a way out. A proposal to cut a deal offered Bob the chance to buy out all Martin's assets—inventory, tools, customer databases, and the like. Then the lawyers hatched an alternative: Bob could get his name and trademark back, but he'd *license* them to Martin, who'd continue to manufacture instruments as Moog Music, Inc.

By January 1999 it was all a moot point. Martin had filed for bankruptcy and the curtain was pulled back: it turned out he'd erected a façade of a company all along, with nothing behind it. The boastful lists of Moog equipment on his website were nothing more than that; creditors were stalking him for payment of supplies, and other than a few employees, he had no real manufacturing capability. He *had* managed to produce two functioning Minimoogs—later dubbed "Donnimoogs"—but there was little evidence he'd made any serious transactions. Wresting the name and trademark from him, though, would take time, and more of Bob's resources. And Alex Winter in the UK, and Bucki and DeWitt in the U.S. still had to be dealt with. Bob groused to Roger Luther, "Who will come out ahead? The lawyers, for sure!"[10]

Beyond his legal expenses, Bob was supporting a staff of eight at Big Briar. In 1996 the company had reported a loss of $81,000. The 1997 news wasn't as bad: a loss of only $17,000. Bob hoped 1998 would be a better year, if he could make a splash with a new product.

The Ethervox MIDI theremin was a high-tech deluxe model that functioned like a conventional theremin. But with its MIDI interface, a player—through the wave of a hand near its antennas—could magically control and shape sounds on any connected synth or electronic device. One of its operational modes allowed the continuous siren sound to be sliced into discrete steps, so the sweep of a hand in the air sounded like the slow stroking of strings on a harp, with 16 selectable scales. The eight-octave instrument had a handmade mahogany cabinet that sat on a pedestal with four slender legs. "Bob had envisioned making about 250 of them," Dunnington recalled, "but they were too expensive and quirky. We ended up selling only about fifty."[11] At $3,500 a unit, it was the Series 91 conundrum all over again.

Bob decided that a line of foot pedals would be a cheaper item to generate real income. "Musicians buy those things like candy bars," he told Michelle.[12] The idea was to miniaturize a few of his classic voltage controlled modules into stomp boxes so musicians could trigger the sounds with the tap of a foot. Players could process a guitar, bass, keyboard, or vocals through the boxes for synthesizer effects.

Bob gave the device a name nobody would ever forget. A Big Briar postcard teased: *What do you get when you cross an analog synth module with an effects pedal? moogerfooger.* Bob borrowed the name from a sticker he'd spied on a New York client's recording console years earlier. The first two models, with "real hardwood sides," were the MF 101 Lowpass Filter, and the MF 102 Ring Modulator.

The moogerfoogers boosted income, but still couldn't do the trick. Big Briar logged $392,000 in sales in 1998, but came in with a loss of $110,000. By

1999 income had grown to nearly $1 million, but the company posted a loss again. In April 2000, as a last resort, Bob took out a bank loan for $150,000 to keep Big Briar afloat, using the remaining 29-acre tract of the Cove property for collateral.

Bob knew he needed another industry touchstone like the Minimoog for Big Briar to really make its mark. He'd been dangling the idea of an updated model in front of the press since 1997. But in true form, his promised delivery dates came and went before there was even a prototype. A 1997 AES article announced that a "souped-up" version was on its way. The next year, Bob told *Sound on Sound* it would be ready by the end of 1998. In April 2000 the *Washington Post* reported that a new model would be rolled out later in *that* year. By January 2001, a prototype still wasn't ready for a planned showing at NAMM. Now it was nearly futile. The Riverside shop was in a race against time to get the instrument into production before Big Briar would be forced to shut its doors for good.

A momentary rescue for the company came from an unlikely source: the king of Sweden. In May, Bob received the Polar Music Prize—a top international honor, presented to him in Stockholm by His Majesty King Carl XVI Gustaf of Sweden. Past honorees included Paul McCartney, Stevie Wonder, Elton John, Joni Mitchell, Ravi Shankar, and classical musicians like cellist Mstislav Rostropovitch. Along with Bob, the other 2001 recipients were Karlheinz Stockhausen and Burt Bacharach. Each awardee received one million Swedish Crowns—about $115,000 in U.S. currency.

Bob and Ileana were feted at a reception in Stockholm at the American Ambassador's residence, and had cocktails with Their Majesties The King and Queen. Bob's official citation read: *Robert Moog is being awarded the Polar Music Prize for 2001 for his design of the MiniMoog, the first compact, easy-to-use synthesizer, which paved the way to the realm of electronic sounds that has revolutionized all genres of music during the past half-century.* Accepting his prize, Bob remarked: "For the past fifty years or so I've been designing and building electronic musical instruments, and I've had the great pleasure of working with hundreds of talented and creative musicians. These are the same people who have literally composed our contemporary musical culture, who have created, from scratch, the world of music that brings us all together. And for that, I am humbly grateful."[13] There was no mention of Hemsath, Hunt, or Scott.

Ileana remembered what happened to Bob's Polar Prize money: "With the exchange rate, it was a little less than $100,000. By that time Bob was in a very scary period. Talk about stress and insomnia. It was clear that the re-engineered Minimoog was not going to be ready before he ran out of money. The Polar Music Prize disappeared without a trace, instantly, into the business."[14]

The working name for the new Minimoog was simply "the New Performance Synth," but Bob wanted something catchier. He decided to run a naming contest, soliciting suggestions from customers, with one of the new instruments as the prize for the winning submission. Nearly two thousand entries poured in from around the world. Many were simply goofy—"Bob's Big Boy," or "the Cardinal Synth." Steve Dunnington remembered the worst of them: "The Smack My Bitch Up" Moog.[15]

Bob vetted the entries, forwarding his favorites to a panel of judges that included Brian Kehew, Wayne Kirby, and Dave Van Koevering. "A lot of names," he wrote them, "had suggestions of violence, war, and similar 'masculine attributes.' I axed the worst of them. I KNOW that most of the customers will be guys, but I think it would be hip as well as culturally correct to soft-pedal the macho business and go for something poetic, lyrical, or just plain musical."[16]

The winning entry, announced on the company's website on July 16, was "Voyager." The new keyboard would be the "MiniMoog Voyager."

The Voyager's planned debut at the July 2001 Summer NAMM show in Nashville was a scramble. "They put together a prototype," Michelle recalled, "but apparently it didn't really play. Dad got it as far along as he could—he pulled an all-nighter, trying to get it ready, and he had to stay behind." The Riverside crew went on ahead, and Bob got a ride to the show with a Big Briar employee, Dave Hamilton. "Dave is driving," Michelle remembered, "and he starts telling dad what an honor it is for him to be driving him to NAMM; what an honor it was to have worked for him; how proud he is to be part of this launch of the Voyager; how much he respects dad. And Dave said, 'I'm just going on and on, and I look over and your dad's fast asleep.'"[17]

The *Financial Times* had already leaked news of the Voyager in June, calling it "the launch of the decade."[18] The Big Briar website promised customers two versions: a limited run, "Signature Edition," with a hand-finished cabinet in a choice of fine woods, bearing a gold-plated nameplate and Bob's signature, for $3,495; and a standard, "Performer Edition" encased in hardwood, priced at $2,995. The website welcomed orders "for delivery this coming fall."

Over fifty orders came in the first day, Dunnington recalled. But with no real instrument in sight, it became his job to appease customers and keep them from jumping ship after they'd put money down. "It was all speculative," he recalled. "We had a non-working prototype that we'd shown. It was a very stressful time. I was like, 'This is really nuts, are we going to pull this off?' I'd stuck with it because I wanted to see how it ended. It was either going to be a glorious story or a great tragedy."[19]

When one piece of good news came in, there was no time or energy to celebrate it: Bob finally got the Moog Music trademark back from Don Martin. Van Koevering was on hand—Bob had just brought him in as a provisional sales manager for the Voyager—and he paraded the official notice around the factory, exhorting the staff to rejoice: "*This is a big moment!*" But Dunnington remembered it was hard to digest: "We hadn't delivered the Voyager. It was all like, *We can start calling ourselves 'Moog,' yay! This is great . . . we're totally screwed.*"[20]

Van Koevering had actually been working with Big Briar for several years, tapping Bob's expertise and throwing him a bone to help keep the company from starving. In 1995 he'd begun a new venture: the Van Koevering Interactive Piano, a state-of-the-art digital keyboard. He'd assembled a design team and enlisted Bob to create a virtual synthesizer for the system based on sound samples, and to develop its audio scheme. Bob was paid as a consultant, and Big Briar was granted a small royalty on each instrument sold. With classic fanfare, Van Koevering told the *Chicago Tribune*, "We are the grand piano of the 21st Century."[21] This time, though, he wasn't exaggerating.

The Van Koevering Interactive Piano had every feature under the sun. It looked like a standard piano, but it had no strings or soundboard; its case disguised an amplifier and multiple speakers connected to an onboard network of devices. It had an interactive touch screen monitor to display sheet music, a library of 128 digitally mastered instrument presets that could be loaded from the hard drive, a virtual multitrack studio, an integrated CD burner, MIDI links to drum machines and synthesizers, a modem for a Windows 95 operating system to download updates, and a built-in CD-ROM that offered videotaped piano lessons. Four models ranged in price from $7,000 to $17,000. The instrument's piano sounds, taken from samples of world class acoustic pianos, strove to match the fidelity of the originals, although the subtlety of the analog vibrations set off by real strings and the thousands of variants in a player's touch still remained out of reach.

The Van Koevering Interactive Piano debuted at NAMM in 1997 and sold a good number of units. In 1999, Van Koevering kicked off his "New Century

Tour," showing off the piano with Bob at a press conference at New York's Plaza Hotel, and on *Good Morning America*.

Sales were strong until things took a sudden, unexpected turn. On September 10, 2001, Van Koevering's principal investor, a venture capitalist whose support the whole enterprise rested on, had signed $125 million in bearer bonds—securities that exist only as paper documents, like cash—and deposited them in a safe at a brokerage firm in the North Tower of the World Trade Center, several stories down from the top floor. "The next morning," Van Koevering recalled, "when those people came to work, they're upstairs, and their courier was going to show up that morning to fly the bonds to Europe, and the courier hadn't gotten there yet. When the towers fell, my investor lost over $125 million."[22] The backer was forced to shut the company down, but despite his loss, he nursed Van Koevering's operation through a final payroll. After only 4,700 pianos were manufactured, the project was over. Bob lost $10,000 worth of shares that he and Ileana had invested in the company.

Bob got another surprise on 9/11: the name "Minimoog" had legally reverted to his ownership that day. But like his reclaiming of "Moog Music, Inc.," it was a victory in name only. At a meeting with the Big Briar staff on October 30, the status report was sobering: Van Koevering was out of the picture now; sales were down and virtually no marketing or advertising plans were in place; the projection for a fall rollout of the Voyager had been premature because its development was behind schedule; and late January was the next estimate of an unveiling. Even to make that deadline, though, extra personnel would be needed, and the company was already losing an average of $20,000 to $30,000 a month. By December, the worst news arrived: the balance sheet put Big Briar's loss for 2001 at $244,320.

"I was worried about Bob," Ileana recalled. "I had that feeling, something is gonna happen. It's just too much." Fearing for his mental health, she reached out to her friend Mary Ellen, who conducted therapy sessions to "read" disturbances in people's energy fields. "She'd been a social worker most of her life," Ileana recalled. "She was a very normal, suburban housewife, upper middle class, who was a medical intuitive."[23] In a private appointment with Mary Ellen in December, Bob nervously recorded notes on a yellow lined pad, jotting his spontaneous thoughts as they emerged during the session:

LOWER AREA OF BODY: "Bright white energy." Turmoil and confusion—
"What have I done? Can I start over, or is it too late? Cerebral Cortex: Can't

fight, won't flee—so I'm immobilized. Second Chakra: Anger. *I'm in a financial mess. Livid about debt that's being incurred. I have to sort this out.* Third Chakra: "The will." *Need to get this product out now. Urgency.* Throat Chakra (5th): Awareness that I've lost my voice. *I may have grown up in a household where there was shaming. A shamed child. "There's something wrong with you." There's nothing wrong with you. Feeling wounded, like I'm a defective burden.*[24]

With the negative thoughts discharged, the session pivoted:

Affirmation for me: "My heart knows the way. I have boundless inner wisdom." 7th Chakra: Something wonderful: "God, Flow through my mind and my heart, and show me the way." *It will come to me. I don't have to do this alone.*[25]

29

Patron Saint of Electrogeeks

Two hundred thirty thousand dollars. It was a stiff price, drawn from his own pocket, to get his name and trademarks back. But by February 2002, Bob could finally sign over his hard-won intellectual property—"Moog Music, Inc." and "Mini Moog,"—to Big Briar. It had taken five years of legal squabbling. It was a victory, but literally in name only. It didn't help the bottom line. By this point he'd lost an additional $364,000 of his personal money pumped into the business over the years, and he'd have to rationalize that now as a "loan" to be cancelled in exchange for additional "capital" in the company—a company with *no* capital at all, running heavily into minus numbers. Plus, he'd just brought on another engineer to help rush the Voyager to the finish line: August Worley.

Worley was a veteran of the Walden Avenue plant from the early '80s, after Bob had left, and he later joined Bucki and Suchora as a roadie for Keith Emerson on ELP tours in the late '90s. Until now, Bob had been the only engineer on the Voyager; now, he and Worley would be redesigning much of it, while Dunnington continued placating restless customers.

The stress over the Voyager was getting to Bob, and in another therapy session with Mary Ellen in January, he scribbled his anxieties:

> Have to think through how to present the Voyager. Thighs: Red Alert - Get it done - also some panic - frozen fear. Solar Plexus 3rd: Debts are building. Have diminishing hopes. Root 1st: Element of "Not being a good boy" - Crying and being by myself. Mother is "imposing." Never enough. A little bit of "unworthiness." Self doubt getting in the way. Thighs: Mantra: "I take the helm. My company survives and thrives." I'll do it my way.[1]

But for the company to survive, much less thrive, Bob had to take a drastic step: all his salaried employees were asked to go on half salary. It was a risky gamble of staff loyalty—especially for Worley, who'd just moved to Asheville and jumped wholeheartedly into working for his hero. But the newcomer remained sanguine: "Ok, this is like, we got a *mission*. We gotta do this thing because it's going to literally save the company. There's no pressure!"[2]

Bob continued tapping his energy fields with Mary Ellen:

First Chakra - <u>Right foot</u>: Not completely sure of myself in the banking world. Hope for the best; prepare for the worst. . . . I could let a lot of people down. Need to affirm: The earth yields to my request. I am confident that this product uplifts mankind and brings joy to the world of music. <u>Left side</u>: Affirm: "As I succeed, I bring others along with me." "And as I support others, money comes to me immediately." Third Chakra - "I feel my power coming back." "I have a renewed interest in life."[3]

Once again, Bob was suddenly jerked from the reality of his life as a floundering small businessman and thrust onto the international stage as the industry standard-bearer. On February 26 in Los Angeles, he received a Technical Grammy Award from the National Academy of Recording Arts & Sciences, recognizing him for outstanding contributions to technology in the recording industry. The other 2002 Technical Grammy awardee was Apple Computer, cited for hardware and software that advanced music production.

Bob was up there with Apple—renown that again reinforced his company's image as a big-league player. But on Riverside Drive it was the same old makeshift story. The computer Worley was using—an old CRT—whined and whistled with high frequencies until he slapped it repeatedly, shoving it once so hard that it punched a hole in the drywall. To ask for a replacement, he went to see the bookkeeper, Michelle's husband, Joseph Koussa. "It was hand to mouth," Worley recalled. "Joseph gets out this stack of credit cards, fans 'em out—he's got, like, six of 'em. So I pull one and it doesn't come. I pull another one and it doesn't come. I pull a third one, and that one comes out. So this is the one that's got room on it. This is not a good sign." One afternoon while the boss was out, Worley had to retrieve a drawing from Bob's desk and his eye fell on a stack of papers. "There's the bill for the American Express card," he recalled. "It had, like, $98,000 on it. It's like, 'wow, I really didn't want to see that.' *We owe American Express almost a hundred grand?*"[4]

On March 1 the staff learned that Big Briar was changing its name to Moog Music, Inc. But the company by any other name was still hobbling along, subsisting on theremins and moogerfoogers—low-dollar, low-volume items that didn't turn a profit. The so-called Engineering Department, responsible for the Voyager's gestation, was just Bob, Worley, and a technician, Tom Dudley. Things were moving slowly. Eight months after the first orders had been taken, Worley recalled, "A lot of the circuits hadn't been completed yet. The overall concept was somewhat fleshed out but there was just a butt-load of work to be done." And he could tell that no one was thinking ahead to how the Voyager would be tested or produced once the prototype was finished: "We'll burn that bridge when we come to it—*if* we happen to still be in business." And with a manufacturing history of only theremins and moogerfoogers, he fretted, "This would be like a company going from doing scooters to suddenly doing dump trucks!"[5]

It was "déjà vu all over again"—an uncanny sequel to the Minimoog marathon 32 years earlier with a staff trying to save their skins, racing to beat the clock before the money ran out. Now it was just a different Minimoog everyone's hopes were pinned on. Hemsath, Scott, and Hunt had become Worley, Dudley, and Dunnington. The $250,000 debt incurred in 1970 was echoed by Big Briar's recent loss of over $244,000 in 2001. And just like the first time around, only an outside investor could save the day.

The call was out for a white knight on a shining steed, the staff was told. "Suddenly the 'dog and pony show' is comin' through," Worley recalled. "We gotta kind of dress more respectably. I've got an office in the back of the warehouse; it's Asheville, North Carolina, so I'm sittin' in 80 degree weather, trying to do my thing, and this cavalcade of Japanese investors are comin' through—guys in suits and stuff—and I gotta paste this smile on my face."[6]

It so happened that an Asheville resident, Mike Adams, was looking for a new entrepreneurial opportunity. Adams had a mechanical engineering degree from North Carolina State University and a 25-year track record with electrical equipment companies. He'd implemented entire factory automation systems, and had been a sales engineer, a marketing director, and recently, the plant manager for a 350,000-square-foot facility of the Square D company branch in Asheville, where he'd supervised 750 employees in molding and stamping operations. He wasn't in a particular hurry to find something new, but the Moog company intrigued him.

Through a mutual friend, Adams met Bob and came to the Riverside shop on May 1 to scope out the situation. Like Waytena, he was impressed by the stellar Moog name and the potential of a new portable keyboard instrument. "I knew I could get that Minimoog into production," he recalled. "I'd put way more complicated products into production than that thing." Adams had no background in music or playing a musical instrument, and growing up he hadn't really been aware of Bob's work. But he shook on the deal: "It seemed like everything I ever did prior to this job was in preparation for this job."[7]

At 47, Adams was "the right age," Bob felt.[8] With decades of experience behind him, he still had years ahead to build something new. And he wasn't a venture capitalist like Waytena, looking to make a quick buck and get out; he was in it for the long run, committed to erecting a substantial company edifice around the armature of Bob's work. He agreed to begin as an unsalaried consultant/president for several months to make sure it was the right fit.

Adams came on board on May 8. With a background in sleek, automated production lines and precision inventory management, he spotted the bloat right away: "There were too many people there. Bob had about 18 people and about 17 of them didn't have anything to do. There was nothin' to build. There were two people in shipping—they were like, 'we didn't ship anything.' There were no procedures in place. There were no policies."[9]

Adams conducted one-on-one interviews with staff members and let 10 people go. It was a blow to Bob's abiding loyalty to his flock. "He never really wanted to make the hard decisions you have to make as a business person," Adams recalled. "He was really good at thinking through the strategic part of it. He just didn't like telling people, 'you're fired.' I don't look forward to ever having to do that. But you got to be willing to make those hard decisions. As a person who is way more conservative than liberal, I think Bob tried to run the company in a very compassionate, democratic, and liberal fashion. And that doesn't work in business, in my view. The way I was going to do it, it was going to be successful."[10] For Bob it was a conundrum: it would take someone from the opposite political camp to make his company profitable.

Adams marched the seven survivors of his thinned-out staff, including Bob, into the shipping area. A surplus inventory of moogerfoogers had been made just to keep people busy and employed, but he warned that the company couldn't do business that way. Dunnington remembered Adams' message: "You see all this stuff? That's your paycheck. It's just sitting there. Until it moves we can't pay you.'"[11]

With Adams cracking the whip, the Voyager moved forward. But the rush to production took a toll. "Mike was a tough taskmaster," Worley recalled. "He drove Bob hard. Bob started to get more and more stressed—very short-tempered, kinda flaky." Bob was forced to give up his daily lunch hour nap, a ritual Worley saw as essential to Bob's creative inspiration: "That problem we were workin' on in the morning, we were pounding our heads over—he lays down for the nap, sets the intention of figuring it out, wakes up, and he would have it! And he'd get out his pencil and paper and start sketching: 'Here's what we're gonna do.' And that worked really, really well. Then that stopped."[12]

By July, four Voyager prototypes were finally complete. The new instrument resembled its classic forebear, with a slope-up control panel hinged above the keyboard, and modulation wheels on the left. Like the original, it was a three-oscillator monophonic analog synth. But it had a host of contemporary features, many that Bob had wanted to offer for years: a velocity- and aftertouch-sensitive keyboard, MIDI capability, an LCD screen for displaying functions, and a "Touch Surface Controller" on the front panel adapted from Bob's 1982 Touch-Sensitive Plate: a pad to touch, tap, or move a finger around, to "impart complex gestures to the sound of the Voyager."[13] The instrument had software-driven program memory to store as many as 128 knob and switch settings, and Bob commissioned Brian Kehew to devise preset sounds for 64 of the settings that could also be user-modified. The instrument's software was designed by Bob's colleague in Germany, Rudi Linhard.[14]

After the prototypes were completed, things accelerated nearly out of control. Orders for 600 limited edition Signature models were already spoken for, and the Guitar Center had ordered 700 Performer Edition instruments. Now it was merely the small matter of producing the 1,300 units. As always, part of the problem came down to capital: having the money to purchase the materials to build the pre-ordered instruments, sell them, and bring in the money to keep going and continue the process. Just to get production started, all the maxed-out credit cards had to be paid off first.

In the ignominious company tradition, Moog Music took out a $275,000 Deed of Trust Loan on July 23. This time it wasn't just Bob's Cove properties on the line. Adams threw in his own property for collateral as well. He'd signed on now as company president, agreeing to purchase the whole operation over a 10-year period. For the first time, Bob had a business partner with a long-range vision and a personal stake in the company. "The great thing about our relationship," Adams recalled, "was Bob was back there engineering Minimoogs and he had the pocket protector, and I was responsible for the sales and marketing and the manufacturing and the financing. He told me, 'Just give me a paycheck every two weeks and I'll be pretty happy.'"[15]

The other hurdle in producing Voyagers was setting up an efficient assembly line. Bob's staff was accustomed to leisurely construction routines peppered with smoking breaks. Over a weekend, Adams came in and set up a no-nonsense "Demand Flow Technology" system—something he'd learned at Square D—to jolt workers into high gear. On Monday morning they got their marching orders: "I showed them five units already in each stage. It's like a cafeteria line. 'Here's what Station 1 looks like completed. Here's what Station 2 looks like completed.... Station 3.... Here's what a completed unit looks like.' They said, 'Oh, I got it—we do this here and this here and this here,

and just keep rotating it like that.' And I said, 'There you go! Start doin' it.'"
The assembly process accelerated and Adams recalled, "I was sleeping maybe 3 to 4 hours a night, just trying to get everything completed. And I could tell Bob was just as stressed as I was."[16]

When Voyagers finally began rolling off the line, Adams peeled one off as a present for Herbie Hancock, who debuted it on stage at the Asheville Civic Center on November 12. "It was the first time I realized the power of the Moog synthesizer," Adams recalled. The crowd had been rather low key, but when Hancock put his hands to the instrument, Adams remembered, "Literally within 30 seconds his audience was up dancing. It just completely transformed the feel of it. It was amazing to watch."[17]

Two weeks before Hancock's Voyager premiere, awareness of Bob's legacy got a significant boost with the release of a new book: *Analog Days: The Invention and Impact of the Moog Synthesizer*.[18] Authors Trevor Pinch and Frank Trocco chronicled for the first time the history of Bob's work during the formative stages of his career, and its enormous influence on music and culture. For Bob, with the energy flowing back into his company under Adams' direction, and a dynamic new instrument on the market, the timing was perfect.

Keyboard's MOOG MANIA issue in May 2003 plastered Bob's smiling image across the cover, framed by an old Minimoog and a new Voyager. With his first commercially available synth in over 30 years, Bob had reclaimed his analog primacy. The new instrument channeled the coveted Minimoog sound and added contemporary bells and whistles. "There's a lot of shit in this thing!" he told the *Keyboard* staff, boasting that the Voyager analog circuit board alone had over 800 parts.[19]

Bob's commitment to advancing ever more complex hardware was a precarious bet in the changing dynamics of technology. On the same *Keyboard* cover, just below his picture, a caption revealed a new existential threat to his work. Reviewed inside the issue was the Arturia company's Moog Modular V ("V" for "virtual"), a computer software emulation of Bob's original modular with updated features including 64-voice polyphony. The "soft synth" had Bob's blessing, but at $329, and installable on any Windows or Mac home computer, it gave the Voyager—retailing for nearly 10 times as much—a serious run for its money.

Virtual synth software pointed up yet another financial downside to manufacturing hands-on instruments. Bob admitted in *Sound On Sound* that a software company could have a higher profit margin: "Once you design a piece of software, the actual manufacturing . . . is peanuts. So the more you sell, the more profit you make and the curve is very steep. With us the curve is not that steep. We put a lot of engineering in, but now we're putting a lot of manufacturing expertise into it too and a lot of high-quality materials. We don't have a lot left over to do media blitzes."[20]

The Voyager hit the international retail market, but there was a problem in the UK. Alex Winter's Moog Music, Ltd., was keeping a tight legal grip on the Moog name, and a judge in England ruled against Bob. Any Voyager sold in the UK had to be labeled, "Voyager by Bob Moog," with every other mention of the Moog name removed from the instrument, down to its circuit boards, chassis, user's manual, and even the shipping carton. It was the last branding barrier standing in the way. Even Bucki had relented, changing his Moog Music Custom Engineering name to "Modusonics." But in the U.S., Europe, and Japan, the Voyager was selling well.

Bob was proud of the Voyager. But with all his creations, there was always something intangible for him in the way they were conceived. Kirby remembered, "He truly believed that he wasn't responsible for any of the stuff he did. That he was just channeling the universal consciousness."[21] Ileana recalled that Bob always insisted, "You don't come up with ideas. The ideas are somehow there and you connect to them. He would say, 'You get it off the network.'"[22] Bob told *XLR8R* magazine, "There's something I refer to as the cosmic network, from which creativity is derived, and I have the ability to tap into that information to do what I do."[23]

Ileana explained, "He grew to have more confidence in his feelings that there *is* this whole intuitive realm. That it's real. That it *isn't* all accounted for by our current scientific paradigm. I spent years crossing out 'I feel' in student essays and substituting 'I think,' because I was teaching philosophy and trying to get them to start with these premises and what follows from them—a rational process. So I would occasionally say, 'I think . . .'" and Bob would say, "You don't *think*. You *feel*." Which is one of the things that made him a wonderful balance of the rational deductive part and the intuitive, creative part."[24]

More and more Bob was attracted to the paranormal. Along with pondering the channels of inspiration, he was interested in psychic communication among beings, especially the ideas of author and scientist Rupert Sheldrake. He and Ileana attended a book-signing at Asheville's celebrated Malaprop's bookstore for Sheldrake's latest release, *Dogs That Know When Their Owners Are Coming Home—And Other Unexplained Powers of Animals*.

Bob found his beliefs were further cemented during dinner with Sheldrake afterward.[25] They discussed the author's theories about "morphic fields"—telepathic channels connecting animals and humans over long distances—a phenomenon Sheldrake used to explain his many well-researched examples of dogs' and other animals' thought transference abilities with each other, with humans, and even with machines. Kirby recalled, "Bob saw that as proof that we're all one, and we're all connected through universal consciousness."[26]

Bob went public with his thoughts at the Icograda World Congress in Nagoya, Japan, in October 2003. Addressing an audience of 3,000, he spoke about "The Man-Machine Interface," confessing before the delegation, "I've spent a lifetime working with electronic instruments, and I know that I am able to connect,- to communicate,- with electronic circuitry. I just don't know how I do it." Referring to Sheldrake, he explained, "He has presented significant evidence . . . that people and chickens alike are able to influence the supposedly-random operation of a complex digital system without there being any physical interactions that we're aware of. Can such interactions also exist between musicians and electronic instruments? I can't imagine why not! . . . . Please take this seriously. It's real, even though I certainly never learned about it when I was in engineering school."[27]

Van Koevering remembered that Bob had even applied his technology to plants, once building a custom oscillator for Eric Siday to stimulate hydroponically growing fruits and vegetables.

Bob had a strong conviction, Ileana recalled, that "a musician is joined into a single being with the instrument—a single system. That's why he was interested in touch-sensitive keyboards. I think that's why he loved the theremin so much. And that's why he was so interested in expressivity. He always said, 'I'm not a musician. I'm a toolmaker for musicians.' So the more perfect an instrument can be at expressing what the musician is thinking and feeling . . . he wanted to facilitate that kind of union between the two. He wanted to make that close-to-perfect tool."[28]

Yet despite Bob's beliefs about the psychic resonance between musicians and their electronic circuitry, he recognized the phenomenon as a kind of closed system, turning the musician inward and away from contact with other humans. At times he descended into somber introspection and elegiac ruminations over what his own work had wrought in that regard. At the University of the Arts in Philadelphia on May 22, 2003, as he was awarded an Honorary Doctor of Fine Arts degree, his commencement talk took a sharp turn toward the unexpected. He began with a bow to recent electronic miracles any musician could exploit to make music, "with a modern laptop computer that's smaller than a Philadelphia phone book." And he added, "I guess that I could stop here, on a note of undiluted optimism that Music Technology is going to provide only good things for musicians and artists. But I would like to say a little bit more."[29]

Reflecting on "the times before electronics," he mused, "music-making back then was always an opportunity for people to gather together.... Those of you who've taken your axes out into the street and played for the people walking by know what I'm talking about." He cautioned, "We're letting technology separate us and alienate us from each other, and thereby to take away the joyful experience of being a real community."[30] Ileana recalled, "I think he regretted deeply that his technology made it possible to bypass that whole social function. I think he was sad, because electronic musical instruments *could* be used in a way that continues the social function of music—but they so often aren't."[31]

Bob ended his speech with a soul-searching moment of contrition: "You talented, fortunate artists who are graduating today already know first-hand about the magic of creating a community by picking up your instruments and playing together. Please cherish what you can now do so well. We're going to need you to hose down the psychic dust that technology is likely to create in the future. We're depending on you to remind us what life is all about."[32]

For better or worse, though, the lifeblood of the Moog factory remained electronic gear, and with the Voyager in full swing, new products followed. The PianoBar was an ingenious creation of Don Buchla who'd sold a few units and then passed the design to the Riverside shop to adapt and market as a Moog device. The PianoBar allowed pianists to play synthesized sounds from the familiar touch and comfort of their own instrument. A scanning bar positioned across the length of an acoustic piano keyboard, away from the hands, used sensors to track the motion of the keys, and a scanner pad on the floor registered pedal motions. The key and pedal information was converted to MIDI data that triggered synthesized sounds that played along with the piano. The MIDI data could also be played back later on any electronic instrument, removing the acoustic piano sound from a final recording. The Moog PianoBar went on sale in the summer of 2003, but the response was tepid.

Once again, Dave Van Koevering rushed to the rescue. In a sequel to the Sanctuary Synthesizer, he relabeled the units, the Moog PianoBar "Kingdom Edition," hitting the church market with everything he had. In a 30-minute televangelist-style infomercial, he preached the glory of the 100 Moog sounds specially tailored for the church. A beaming Van Koevering turned to the camera: "God has birthed inside of you *a song*. A sound. And *your sound has to be found*. Moog has been in the business of helping people *find their sound* for 50 years. I hope you'll give us a chance to let him help you find the sound that God has birthed in you." Then he added, "If you call that number today, we have a very limited number of these that are available for trial in the churches. And *your* church could qualify. All you have to do is give us a call, and we'll qualify your church."[33]

At Mike Adams' prompting, another new product, the Moog Etherwave Pro theremin, debuted in 2004. Adams wanted a physically arresting theremin body for stage performances, and the Pro was a work of sculptural beauty: a slender vertical torso rising from its tripod pole, sheathed in a curved, light wood breastplate of birds-eye maple. With wooden pitch and volume knobs like two eyes, and a horizontal wooden arm holding up the pitch antenna, it resembled a retro modern robot. Bob considered it his finest theremin design ever.

∿∿∿

At the factory, the biggest news of 2004 was the fiftieth anniversary of the R. A. Moog Company, celebrated worldwide. To commemorate the occasion, Adams and the Riverside operation commissioned a souvenir Bob Moog doll, a six-inch-high superhero toy in colorful soft vinyl. The smiling, large-head figurine, topped with a molded plastic puff of Bob's trademark white hair, had a movable neck and arms, a red bowtie, and a gray cloth sports jacket with lettering on the back proclaiming, *50 YEARS OF ELECTRONIC GENIUS!* Eyeglasses and a miniature Minimoog on a stand were included as accessories. The toy and its decorative box, with a caricature of Bob at his modular, were the work of rocker and cartoonist Archer Prewitt, creator of the *Sof' Boy and Friends* comic book series.

With fiftieth anniversary paeans swelling to a resonant climax, 2004 became Bob's banner year. Invitations for lectures and appearances poured in. At Scotland's Triptych festival he spoke about "How 'Moog Synthesizer' Got to Be a Household Name." In Japan he gave lectures in Hamamatsu and Kyoto and greeted lines of autograph hounds at a Tokyo Moog dealer. In Spain, at Barcelona's trendy Moog Club, patrons thrashing around to techno and house caught a peek at the man himself; Bob sat for in-depth press interviews in Madrid and signed Moog instruments for star-struck devotees at a Copenhagen music retailer. There were talks at conferences and music festivals, national radio and TV spots, VIP tours of research labs, museums, and Moog distributors, and in-store demos and clinics. Thereminists serenaded him, and everywhere capacity crowds jammed into venues to hear him speak, vying for photo ops and autographs. The gifted thereminist Pamelia Kurstin, who'd been Bob's design consultant for the Etherwave Pro, told the *Washington Post*: "He's viewed like a god. Everybody knows who he is, especially in Europe. He's a superstar."[34]

"This Man Rocks," *Entertainment Weekly* proclaimed, calling Bob "one of the most influential innovators in the history of rock & roll."[35] At the first annual Moogfest, hosted by the B.B. King Blues Club & Grill on West 42nd Street in New York, the magazine reported, "One of the world's greatest living music legends is in a New York club tonight."[36] The May 18, 2004, event, "To honor Robert Moog and commemorate his groundbreaking achievements," was a sold-out four-hour gala with Keith Emerson, Rick Wakeman, and a roster of more than 22 guest artists doing the performing honors. "Hundreds of worshippers, "*Entertainment Weekly* observed, "wearing T-shirts emblazoned with his name, wildly undulate to the wacky, spaced-out sounds he unleashed on the world some 40 years ago. Others crowd near the entrance, waiting anxiously for the briefest glimpse of their beloved cult hero."[37] Ever himself, Bob managed to blend into the crowd: "The 70-year-old object of all this adoration is currently perched in a specially reserved booth, taking a nap." Still, the magazine explained, "Thanks to a full-fledged Moog renaissance, he's finally feeling the love."[38]

Back at the Riverside plant, the *Entertainment* reporter added a postscript: " 'Wanna see something wild?' Moog asks, plucking up a picture sent in by an overeager fan. It shows a half-naked woman with the word 'MOOG' tattooed on her back. 'I just can't . . . it's baffling to me,' he stammers, shuffling the photo under some other papers."[39]

Pulled into the vortex of Bob's fame, Ileana saw how easy it was to become an accessory to his presence. "I really came to have some understanding of what it must have been like for Shirleigh being married to Bob," she recalled, "because I was a well-liked professor, with a very strong identity of my own, and I'd never been at a social event where I was essentially invisible. Bob was visible and that was great. But I remember thinking, 'Well, this is what it's going to be like, and it's going to be an interesting experience.' "[40] Shirleigh, in fact, had found her own niche after the divorce. The *Asheville Citizen-Times* had recently showcased her as the organizer of a district conference on anti-racism, quoting her position: "This community has had a lot of racism for a long time. Out of this have come very innovative, successful and long-term solutions to many past hurts and injustices."[41]

For Bob, the 2004 celebrations climaxed when his image and persona were magnified to many times life size. "Forty years after he invented the synthesizer that bears his name, Bob Moog is back for an encore," the *New York Times* reported. "The patron saint of electrogeeks is the subject of 'Moog,' a documentary opening this month."[42] Director Hans Fjellestad's 70-minute film premiered at theaters in New York and Seattle on September 24. The improvisational trip through Bob's thoughts and inspirations eschewed the typical A to Z historical-biographical format for a patchwork quilt of moments from his life. With no narration, and cinema vérité pacing, Fjellestad's camera got out of the way to let Bob reminisce casually with old colleagues—Deutsch, Kingsley, and Sear—and chat with musician fans like Rick Wakeman, Bernie Worell, and younger artists like DJ Spooky. Performance clips alternated with Voyager assembly-line sequences and show-and-tell moments of Bob talking about his circuits. Domestic moments zoomed in on a cooking session at home with Ileana and Miranda, and Bob plucking vegetables in a tour of their organic garden out back.

At the end, Fjellestad offered Bob a platform to expound on his pet fascination. Reaching into the metaphysical, Bob explained, "The more you get into material, into matter, the more you realize that all there is in matter is energy. There's a blur between energy and consciousness. All material is conscious to some extent or another. All material can respond, to some extent or another, to the vibrations of energy that is different from the energy you learn about in physics.... There *is* a level of reality where there is no time and there is no space, there's just energy. And we have contact with that through the intermediate layers. So if the right channels—if the right connections—are established, I don't see why a piece of matter, a piece of broken glass or an old record, can't make contact through this very high level of reality that has access to everything past and future." He added, "I suppose my instruments do retain some sort of memory of me."[43]

When the film opened in Portland, Oregon, where Renée was living, a merchant recognized her name with excitement: "Oh, Moog!" the woman told her. "I'm going to go see the Moog film tomorrow night." Renée was perplexed: "'The Moog film?'—'Oh yeah, there's this film in town and it's all about the inventor of the Moog synthesizer.'—And I'm like, 'Really?' And of course I looked it up and sure enough. So of course, I call him up and I'm like, 'Dad! Guess what! There's a film about you—did you know that? Why didn't you say anything?'... He just didn't want the attention."[44]

Through the chorus of international alleluias and the Fjellestad film, nothing went to Bob's head. At home in Asheville, he slipped comfortably back into the role of local citizen, if a quirky one. Fjellestad's documentary had flashed a brief clip of Bob tooling around town in his only car, a 20-year-old Toyota Tercel wagon with a hole in the floor—a jalopy he affectionately called the "*shanda*-mobile" (a Yiddish-ism for "disgrace car"). But it stood out for more than just its rusty fenders. Its one-of-a-kind appearance happened on an impulse, and always turned heads.

In 1997 Bob had noticed Miranda's best friend, Erin, wearing a pair of Birkenstock shoes she'd whimsically marked up with colored patterns, and he asked to have the same treatment on his Toyota. Handing 15-year-old Miranda and her friend a box of metal enamel paints from the auto supply store, he told them to "have at it." He talked about snail images, or just "the letter S on the hubcaps so people would say, "look at that S car go!"—a pun on escargot. But the girls lavished the body with flowers, a theremin, a rainbow, a goldfish, a butterfly, stars, a mountain landscape on the hood, creeping vines up the window pillars, and a giant snail on the driver's door.

"It became an icon in Asheville," Miranda recalled. "People called it the Crayola car, the Rainbow Car. The youth thought it was really cool that Bob Moog drove that car."[45] Ileana remembered, "He loved the fact that it made people smile."[46] A plant image on the fuel door was captioned, "FEED ME," a reference to the human-eating plant in Bob's favorite musical, *Little Shop of Horrors*, a show he'd eagerly volunteered for as the keyboardist in an Asheville Community Theatre production, just before he and Ileana were married.

For social recreation, Bob began hanging out in a mock secret society. Wayne Kirby and a group of friends, fed up with state politics, formed their own political party in jest. Kirby was the "political director and campaign manager," and called all the party meetings, held at the Jack of the Wood pub. Their "Party Down Party" (PDP) had one agenda: beer and jokes. No political talk allowed. Members had goofy aliases worn on buttons. Kirby was "Chairman Nao." Minutes for meetings were scrawled on coasters. Dozens of people in town eventually joined, but early on, Kirby recalled, "I mentioned it to Bob and he said, 'I want in!' He was a founding member of the PDP." For his Party identity, Bob told Kirby, "My name is Drizzlepuss."[47] Bob remembered it as a slight a homeless man in New York once shouted at him.

The sacrosanct rule at PDP meetings was that everyone had to tell a joke. "Bob had two jokes that he would tell at every meeting," Kirby recalled. His well-worn favorite, which everyone called his "parrot joke," was recalled by Dunnington, who knew if from work: "It's this story about this parrot who's got it in for this one guy who keeps walking past him on the street. And the owner of the parrot threatens him, saying, 'If you say 'fuck you' one more time I'm going to strangle you.' So the guy walks past and the parrot looks at him and goes, '*You* know.' And Bob would just erupt in laughter. What made it so funny is that he'd just be completely guffawing and laughing at his own joke." Another recurring PDP Bob favorite was a recipe he'd seen for a cake in the shape of a kitty litter box. "He thought it was the funniest thing," Kirby remembered. "You put Tootsie-Rolls around it like it was poop."[48]

In November 2004, Mike Adams took stock of Moog Music's financial health, and brought Bob up to speed: orders were coming in and equipment was shipping out; the company was making a profit and might even be able to absorb all its debt. Adams never forgot Bob's reaction: "He paused, and he had tears in his eyes. He said, 'Mike, I want you to know how happy I am to finally be part of a successful company. I've been working at this for a long time and we were never really successful. I'm proud to be able to provide a salary, a living wage for the people who work here—proud of everything you've done.'" Adams admitted, "I was a complete basket case. But what struck me was, I never thought it was that important for him to be successful in business. But it was really evident that it was critically important. That his *business* was a success. That's what made me the proudest, personally."[49]

Bob was once again the sole engineer—Worley was gone—and he was taking a hard look down the road. He told Adams he hoped to retire in the next few years, bringing in a protégé to train, and cutting back his own hours—eventually to 50%—and then bowing out altogether. "We'd planned to do that in three to four years' time," Adams recalled.[50] Bob wasn't searching actively for candidates, but through some mysterious divine providence, an email out of the blue would prove decisive to the future of Moog Music.

30
The Show That Never Ends

In Chapel Hill, North Carolina, 200 miles east of Asheville, a guitarist named Cyril Lance was considering a midlife career change. In 2002 he'd released a CD, *Stranger in My House*, with covers and seven original tunes. Johnny Neel of the Allman Brothers Band was on the album, and *Billboard* magazine raved, "Lance has masterminded one of the best contemporary blues albums of the year. His virtuosity on guitar and lap steel is undeniable, and his songwriting makes him an instant item in bluesville."[1]

But Lance had other talents. After earning a bachelor's degree in engineering physics from Cornell, he worked in Boston designing original circuitry for research instruments in atmospheric physics. All the while he kept up with his music, gigging with his band and working in a recording studio. In 1994 he moved to North Carolina, toured the U.S. with his band, and continued his engineering jobs until they dried up in 2004. With a family now, he needed to find a new source of income.

A family friend In Asheville, it turned out, caroused every Monday night at PDP meetings with Bob, and told Lance about the Moog company. Cyril had heard of Bob and was aware of his work, but he had no idea the firm was local. In an email he introduced himself to Bob, sent his resumé, and got an invitation to visit the factory.

Lance drove up in a snowstorm in January 2005, and Bob showed him around the Riverside shop. Their Cornell engineering physics backgrounds were a common bond, and Lance's experience in recording studios, live performance, and his circuitry work were a plus. But he confessed a weakness: "I said, 'Bob, I have this very shameful admission to tell you . . . . I've only ever had experience with one synthesizer, and it was back in the '80s, when Casio came out with this teeny little synthesizer for $99 with these teeny keys. But it was so cool because you could adjust the sounds and stuff.' And I said, 'That's the only synthesizer that I ever liked.'" Amazingly, Lance recalled, it wasn't a deal breaker: Bob told him, "Hey, I had the same synthesizer!"[2]

Lance's takeaway was hopeful: "It was a real eye-opener for me that there was this sweet guy and he was still this kind of craftsman-toolmaker. And

Switched On. Albert Glinsky, Oxford University Press. © Albert Glinsky 2022.
DOI: 10.1093/oso/9780197642078.003.0030

I think he really enjoyed the fact that I was doing physics and there was kind of this sympatico of ideas and technology." When the session ended, he recalled, "it was just, 'Really good meeting you. We'll stay in touch.'"[3] Bob asked Adams about bringing Lance on board, but the budget couldn't support it yet. A couple weeks later, Adams called Lance, suggesting there might be a project in the fall that they could use him on.

In the meantime, the business had outgrown 554C, and Bob and Adams signed a lease for a facility four miles up the river at 2004 Riverside Drive. The unfinished space needed to be renovated first, so the plan was to move the operation on the weekend before Labor Day.

~~~

At the January 2005 NAMM show in Anaheim, fans stood in line for 40 minutes to get Bob's autograph. He was sharing a hotel room with Steve Dunnington at the convention, and in the downtime they tossed around ideas for a sequel to the successful Voyager. Dunnington recalled, "He was like, 'You've got to define what it is and I'll make it. Tell me what people want.' So, we had the basic idea, we did some back-of-the napkin stuff and said, 'This is how much it's going to cost. We'll give it a go.'"[4] The concept was for a stripped-down, price-friendly alternative to the Voyager that preserved the classic Moog sound—especially the celebrated "fat" sound that journalists punned on endlessly. In a 1996 issue of the Beastie Boys' *Grand Royal* magazine, a feature heralding the analog revival—and all things Moog—had the title, "The Survival of the Fattest." Dunnington, who'd come up with the names Etherwave and Ethervox, suggested they call the new synth the "Little Phatty." The spelling, with a "PH," had ribald overtones and also referred to a marijuana joint. "Bob liked it," Dunnington recalled. The Little Phatty it would be.

For Dunnington, the trip was also memorable for an unsettling moment in the hotel room that would later seem like a foreshadowing: "Bob woke me up in the middle of the night with night terrors—he was screaming in his sleep. It was like, *holy crap, is he okay?* I just kind of brushed it off. Maybe it was nothing. Just a bad dream."[5] It might have been an isolated incident, but other peculiar episodes were surfacing. In March, Ileana recalled, "Bob came in from using the chain saw to cut wood and showed me his left hand and said that he couldn't quite control it. There was no tingling, nothing that tells you that you have nerve irritation."[6] Later in the spring, on their way to Alaska,

Bob lost the ability to tie his shoes because his left hand wasn't working well enough, and he was starting to have trouble putting on a shirt or jacket. At a stop-off in Portland, Renée noticed that he couldn't buckle his own seatbelt.

Bob's cousin Ron Spatz—Aunt Estelle's son—was an English professor and dean at the University of Alaska at Anchorage. He'd invited Bob to give the inaugural lecture of the new Graduate Research & Discovery Symposium series at the University. Bob titled his speech, "Where Do Ideas Come From?" "He wasn't really quite sure what he was reaching to say," Ileana recalled. "That was the talk that extended him farthest into territory he'd never been in before."[7]

At the April 14 keynote address, a standing-room-only audience was rapt as Bob cracked the door to his transpersonal realm, exhorting his listeners to open themselves up to new ideas, and the ideas will come. He suggested, "You'd be amazed at how much you can learn just watching ants build a nest. But you have to watch them in a focused, directed way."[8] He talked about Copernicus, Newton, and Einstein, and rhapsodized over Edison, describing the inventor's habit of holding weights in his hands during an afternoon nap and jolting awake when they dropped, seizing the images of his dreams as the basis for his next invention. Bob played recorded examples and demonstrated a theremin and the Voyager. Spatz recalled, "I noticed that he was really sweating—it seemed like he was having some difficulty, and it wasn't clear why."[9]

At a restaurant, Spatz noticed Bob struggling with his arm and suggested he might've moved a disc in his neck. It wasn't that, Bob averred—no numbness—and Spatz recalled, "Like an engineer, he said, 'It isn't following the signals that I send it.' This scared me. I just knew when he told me this that it was really bad. And man, that was like a lightning bolt."[10]

Michelle was alarmed at a lunch with her dad when she saw him lurch his whole body around in order to swing an arm into his jacket. Dunnington recalled, "I knew something was really wrong, and I'd hoped it was just a minor stroke or something and he'd just do physical therapy and get back. It was weird to watch him have to lift his arm up with his other working arm. He was still trying to do stuff. We were going to design another synthesizer. We were growing the business."[11]

A CAT scan turned up nothing, but right after an MRI on April 29, Michelle got an uncharacteristic 11 a.m. call from her father while she was at Amore, the Asheville gift shop she owned. The doctor had confirmed it wasn't a pinched nerve, and Michelle remembered, "I said, 'Oh! Whatya have?' He said, 'I have a brain tumor.' And at that moment, the whole world shifted underneath my feet."[12] A neurologist, Bob explained, advised surgery within two weeks, but Michelle and Matthew thought he should get a second opinion.

On the 30th, Bob and Ileana came into Riverside to inform Adams and the staff. "It was just like getting punched in the face," Dunnington recalled.[13] On May 18, Adams phoned Cyril Lance. "Just from the very first sentence," Lance remembered, "I knew something was wrong."[14] Adams asked Lance to stand in for Bob during what he imagined would be a period of treatment and recovery. Lance began work the next day, as Bob was at Duke University having a biopsy—the result of a second opinion from the head of neurosurgery there. Ileana came along—it was their ninth wedding anniversary. They were cautioned that there was a 10% chance the procedure could trigger a brain bleed.

On Bob's birthday, May 23, he and Ileana got the diagnosis. The doctor at Duke explained that it was a glioblastoma multiforme—a brain tumor with a 2% survival rate. The median survival time, he explained, was about 3½ months. He thought the tumor was growing aggressively and was inoperable. Operating, he said, would only accelerate metastasis and diminish Bob's quality of life faster. He recommended a new low-dose chemotherapy drug, Temodar, and radiation treatments. In desperation, Ileana looked into an alternative treatment through the Burzynski Clinic in Houston, Texas, known for its benign cancer therapies using urea. She'd read the Clinic's claims of a 50% survival rate, even for glioblastoma. The one requirement was that the patient had to be ambulatory to come to Houston for the treatments. Bob said he'd consider it.

On his very sobering seventy-first birthday, Bob showed up at Riverside before a numb staff wearing its most stoic face. "It was very poignant," Lance recalled. "This incredible love and concern for this man and the level of sweetness in the room as they brought in the cake and the candle. And I remember him saying as he looked at the candle, 'You guys probably all know what I'm wishing for.'"[15]

Miranda was in France with her father, Bob Richmond, and his wife, when she got a call from her mother. Richmond was a pathologist, and Miranda remembered, "I got off the phone and he said, 'He'll be dead in 3 or 4 months.' And my whole world fell apart."[16] She left for Asheville the next day.

On the 26th it became clear Bob was in the unlucky 10% to suffer brain bleeds after a biopsy: the bleed had shut down his ability to walk. He was moved to a hospital bed in the living room, and because he was no longer ambulatory, the Burzynski Clinic was out now. Frantically, Ileana consulted a nutritional specialist and put him on a vitamin D regimen and a vegetarian diet. Sugar, and chocolate—his favorite—were banned. Renée came for the month of June to help out, and within 24 hours after her arrival, Bob lost complete use of his left side. An occupational therapist was brought in to teach him to move from his bed to a chair. When the course of chemo and radiation began, Renée took him to the sessions in a wheelchair that staff volunteers from Riverside helped lift down the front porch to the waiting van, until Ileana had a ramp built that ran across the steps and the side of the garden.

Once or twice a week, Mary Ellen came over to do energy healings. "I wouldn't say it accomplished any miracles," Ileana recalled, "but Bob would feel slightly stronger and be able to move a little bit more easily."[17] Matthew set up a CaringBridge website for Bob and Ileana to communicate with friends and family.

At the company, Lance recalled, "Bob wasn't coming around and I think everybody was just holding their breath and praying for a miracle. His desk was there, his books; it was like he could just come in and start working. And we were very busy because we were desperately trying to keep the company surviving."[18] In 2001 Bob had told the *Financial Times* that he hoped his company would continue as a viable business "over the next three to five years," with "an engineering department into which I will have dumped the contents of my head."[19] Chillingly, he'd told *EQ* in 1997 when asked what his long-term plans were, "Just to keep at it until my brain shuts down."[20] Over the 4th of July weekend, Bob's energy was waning after the radiation had been bumped up, and it was clear he couldn't meet with Lance, whom he'd hired but never had a chance to speak with formally.

The family kept nurturing their optimism. "He was such a good patient," Michelle recalled. "We all had this hope, that with the radiation and the nutrition and his positive attitude, he was going to get better."[21] But Ileana saw Bob's perspective, perhaps all too well. His diagnosis had resurrected thoughts of Aunt Florence's final illness—also from a brain tumor, at the same age—and it amplified the fatalist in him. "Bob's father," Ileana recalled, "had a very unhappy retirement. It became clear to me that Bob had neither the expectation nor the desire to live to be very old."[22] Miranda saw it as well: "I had this strong intuitive sense that he thought, 'this is it,' from the moment he got the diagnosis. I think he was undergoing all the treatment and doing all the things, seeing all the specialists, for the kids and for mom, and not for himself. And so there was that moment of pulling back and sort of observing him, very patiently accepting."[23]

In early August, the Ether Music 2005 Conference, a theremin celebration drawing musicians from around the world, was going on at the Orange Peel, a trendy music venue on Biltmore Avenue in Asheville. The festival was co-sponsored by Moog Music and featured workshops, master classes, speakers, performances, and a tour of the Riverside shop. Among the participants was the Russian thereminist Lydia Kavina, a relative of Leon Theremin, who was the teacher on Bob's instructional video for the Etherwave theremin. Bob was scheduled to give a keynote speech at the Conference and he would have been in his element. But Ileana had to appear in his place to communicate his regrets. On May 31, he'd also had to miss the second annual Moogfest in New York.

When Bob's chemo and radiation treatments ended, a second MRI on August 9 showed that the tumor had grown by 30%. "Up until that point," Michelle recalled, "we were so convinced that things could be turned around. And after that point I knew they couldn't. All he said was, 'bummer.' He knew. And things went downhill pretty quickly after that. He was already sleeping a lot during the day and sort of out of it here and there, emaciated, and his eating was really minimal."[24]

∿∿∿

Barging in on the somber stillness of family and caregivers, a stranger shattered the quietude in a dreamlike episode that left everyone shell-shocked. A young woman named Daniela who'd met Bob in Copenhagen in 2004—Ileana guessed she was in her thirties—learned of his illness and emailed with an offer to deliver a miracle elixir and administer it to him personally. She'd fly over on her own dime with a tea made from a poisonous plant, Purple Hellebore—a brew she claimed Romanian researchers had found effective in shrinking brain tumors. Ileana did some research and thought it couldn't hurt; perhaps it could even help. "It was a decision born out of desperation," she recalled.[25] Miranda admitted, "When you're on a sinking ship, you do grasp at straws."[26]

Miranda and her French boyfriend, Julien Mouillot—soon to become her husband—picked Daniela up at the Charlotte airport. They were crestfallen the minute they saw her: a short woman with hennaed red hair, heavy dark makeup, dressed in tight leather pants and top, with a cigarette in one hand and a diet coke in the other. What sort of healer smokes a cigarette and drinks a diet coke?, they wondered.

Daniela stayed in a bedroom in the house. The next morning the family was startled to find her lying on a blanket on the front lawn, sunbathing in nothing but hot pants and a bandana tied around as a crop top, sipping another diet coke. The tea she'd brought had a brownish-green color and was sealed in unmarked clear plastic soda bottles. Daniela insisted on doling out the doses herself. Bob claimed the first dose tasted bitter. The tea was supposed to be taken with food, but Bob was losing the ability to swallow or eat. "She was convinced that she knew what to do," Miranda recalled. "She kept saying, 'He has to eat, he has to eat. You have to give him big meals; you have to cook what he likes.'"[27]

In a moment of stillness, after family members had retreated to separate corners of the house, Miranda recalled, "It was out of that quiet that we heard my dad yell. I ran downstairs, and smack into Daniela, her hair pulled into straggly pigtails and shoved under a blue and white trucker cap, an oversized sweatshirt nearly covering her short shorts . . . heavy eyeliner and circles of bright rouge on her cheeks. . . . She glared up at me with big dark eyes. 'He has to laugh. . . . You are all so serious. He needs jokes, and snuggles. I made faces at him, like this, and he liked it.'" Miranda heard Bob moaning and ran into his room to find his caretaker, Kathleen, stroking his forehead. "That was the damndest thing," Kathleen gasped. "I left the room for five minutes and she was up on the bed with him when I came back."[28]

Ileana thought it was a "father-crush."[29] Miranda figured it was "that weird fan thing: she was drawn to his fame and her perception of his genius more than anything else. And in that attraction was a conviction that she somehow knew a more pure, more real version of him than his family did."[30]

Miranda remembered, "When my mother told her she would have to leave, Daniela started to cry." She complained that "we didn't understand how to administer the treatment. It wasn't the treatment, even, it was that we didn't understand my father. . . . She didn't have the money to go home. We were doing everything wrong. We were being closed-minded and selfish and ungrateful to someone who'd come all this way with the one thing that could save him."[31] With a promise from Ileana to cover some of her airfare, Daniela flew back to Copenhagen.

Several days later, a musician and thereminist friend of Bob's and the family's, Nicoletta Stephanz, showed up. Around 11 p.m., Nicoletta was sitting in the living room with Ileana, Miranda, and Julien, listening to the crickets, when they heard a commotion on the front porch. Suddenly Daniela bolted through the front door, down the hall, and into Bob's room. "Was that Daniela?" Ileana asked the others. "I wondered if I was hallucinating."[32] Miranda recalled that Julien "stalked into the room and took her by the arm and marched her out of the house. And we heard her shouting and we heard him shushing her.

"She'd flown all the way back to Denmark. Then she came back. When we wouldn't take her calls she started calling Moog Music and talked them into picking her up at the airport and driving her here. They were waiting up by the road, so when Julien took her up to the road he in no uncertain terms made it clear that she needed to leave, and they drove her away."[33] Miranda rushed in to check on Bob, finding him "terribly agitated, panicked, even, his eyes wide and his back arched and tense. I stood in the hall while my mother stroked his forehead, promising him that it was all over, that Daniela was gone, that there would be no more tea."[34] Julien plucked a rose from the garden and tucked it under Bob's oxygen tube. He and Miranda sat on opposite sides of the bed, each holding one of his hands.

~~~

Bob was having difficulty sleeping at night and began filling the hours listening to CDs of music people had sent him over the years. A good friend, two-time Grammy-winning producer Steven Heller, had brought over a CD of his son Drew's band, Toubab Krewe. The Asheville-based American group filtered a rock sensibility through West African influences, playing guitar, organ, and bass, mixed with South Asian and West African instruments in rousing instrumental tracks. In the Senegalese language of Wolof, "Toubab" means "white person," and "Krewe," denotes a group of people. Bob was smitten with the band's music. "They're such damn good musicians," he told Laura, who'd arrived and was staying in a bedroom upstairs.[35] He told her how he envisioned himself dancing with Ileana to their music.

Laura remembered how her dad had been offered marijuana to ease his pain, but it was hard for him to inhale: "So he moved into this 'ahh ahh ahh ahh,' which everyone called his marijuana song. 'MAIR-uh-WAH-nuh.' 'Ahh ahh ahh ahh.' And it went on for hours sometimes." During one of those episodes, it suddenly became 1974 at Rich Stadium in Buffalo with ELP all over again. Laura recalled: "I could tell his tone was sounding agitated. So

I just said 'shh.' And he turned to me and said, 'Laura ... don't ... shush me.' And he hadn't spoken in days. And I said, 'Welcome back my friend.' 'Cause it was like, he hadn't been with us. And he said, *to the show that never ends.* ... And I said, *Ladies and Gentlemen, it's* ... and he said, *Emerson* ... and I went, *Lake and* ... and he said, *Palmer.*"[36] Then, she recalled, her father finished with a sustained, dramatic exhale suggesting a crowd's applause. She remembered their exchange as the last words he uttered to anyone.

"At the end he couldn't speak," Miranda recalled. "So we didn't have conversations. I sat with him and I remember telling him, 'I need nothing more. You were the best thing that ever happened to me.'" Ileana realized the circles were contracting more tightly around him: "He didn't want to see most people. He really had made up his mind. He was acting like somebody who was going to die, certainly from the time he could no longer get up from bed. He understood that people were concerned about him, but he just couldn't muster up the energy, and it was very clear that he didn't want to see anyone."[37]

There were occasional exceptions. "Ileana gave me a call," Dunnington remembered, "and said, 'If you want to say goodbye to him, you had better come. It's not going to be much longer.' He recognized me still. He couldn't talk at that point, but he lit up, and I just thanked him and said, 'It's been an honor to work with you and be your colleague and your friend.'"[38]

Bob was often anxious. Hospice was called in to administer Haldol and morphine. On August 18, Laura was downtown buying bagels and glanced at the headline in the *Asheville Citizen-Times*: "Moog suffers brain tumor—Musician's ailment may be inoperable."[39] The family had tried to keep Bob's condition under wraps, but news had leaked out through the CaringBridge site. "Miranda and I took a walk," Ileana recalled, "and that was when I really faced that he was going to die. And at our turnaround point I looked down and there were some four-leaf clovers. I'd gone through a very long period of not being able to find them."[40]

On the 20th, Renée and her husband, Paul Sylvester, whom she'd married in 2003, showed up to join the family. At that moment, a paralysis fell over the group, as though time were suspended. There was no way backward, but there was no path forward either. Emotionally spent, Michelle planned to take a hiatus for a while; Matthew was preparing to leave the next morning, and Laura planned to depart in the afternoon.

∿∿∿

Sunday, August 21.

Most everyone was out of the house. Michelle was hosting a brunch at her home for Laura, Renée, and Paul. Matthew was traveling back to Chicago. Julien had gone to see *Million Dollar Baby* at the movie theater. Miranda was working as a last-minute stand-in fortune teller at a New Age bookstore for the afternoon. Ileana and the nurse were the only ones home with Bob.

In a strange karma, the Sunday *New York Times* that morning ran an article about a record label devoted to cross-cultural currents in Jewish music, with plans to reissue Gershon Kingsley's *Shabbat for Today*. "The Moog is a quizzical, at times mournful instrument," the writer opined, "and the religious compositions Mr. Kingsley wrote on it are invariably strange: in places ominous, elsewhere blissful. The compositions turn religious reverence on its ear; the Moog sound, with its infinite modulations, invites and suggests questioning."[41]

At about two o'clock in the afternoon, the nurse came in to tell Ileana that Bob's breathing had changed and was shallower. "I went in and sat with him and she left," Ileana recalled. "I was telling him that it was ok to go, that I loved him, and that he should move toward the light. And then the phone rang, and he was very sensitive to noise. So I went over and picked it up and it was Erin. And I told her Miranda wasn't home and that I needed to get off the phone. When I came back, he didn't look any different, and I wondered if he was still alive . . . and he wasn't. I think he may have chosen that moment when I was out of the room. I've always wondered whether he couldn't actually let go while I was in the room, because in spite of the fact that I had said it was ok, he knew I didn't want him to die."[42]

Laura was the first to hear. She'd stopped off at the house on her way back to Greensboro to say a last goodbye. One by one the family was alerted. Matthew, midway to Chicago, turned around.

∿∿∿

Ileana and Miranda suggested a traditional Jewish burial, a ritual the rest of the family supported. The funeral would be on Tuesday, and for two days Bob's body would remain in the house as family and friends paid their respects and carried out the rites of transition to the next world. People from the Buddhist temple in town came over to install two air conditioners in the room and help the family perform a ceremonial washing and powdering of the body.

The *Shemira*, the Jewish custom of visitors coming to sit with the body in two-hour shifts—because a body cannot be left alone—began at 10 p.m. Sunday and continued around the clock until noon on Tuesday. Seventeen friends and family members, some volunteering for two shifts, took turns watching over Bob in private vigils from a seat in the frigid, air-conditioned room. Miranda scrawled a note that was taped to the porch door:

> *If you are coming to sit with Bob, come on in—he's at the end of the hall on the left (2nd door), and the person sitting will let you know what to do. It is a way of showing respect for the deceased by keeping their body company between the deathbed and the grave. It is traditional to sit quietly, reflecting or reading spiritual texts (traditionally the psalms), which are on the dresser by the big blue chair. If you get hungry or thirsty, help yourself to whatever you like in the refrigerator. If you see that candle beneath the oil diffuser has burnt out, please replace & relight it.*[43]

At 12:30 p.m. on Tuesday, Ileana, Miranda, Michelle, Renée, Laura, and Matthew began the ritual preparation of the body, the *Chevra Kadisha*. Bob's good friend from the synagogue, Wolff Alterman, led them through the tasks. Bob's body was laid on the back porch. "We all had wash cloths," Michelle recalled, "and it was very quiet and we all set about cleaning. It kinda felt sweet and tender, like we were taking care of him—something very pure and peaceful. We were all outside and dad loved to be outside."[44]

Bucketfuls of water were poured over the body and flowed down through the deck boards into the ground. Then a white shroud was put on: "Very loose white pants," Michelle recalled, "a loose button-down white shirt with the collar up, little booties to put over his feet and little mitts to put over his hands. And then Wolff put a hood over his head . . . and I just lost it."[45] "It's devastatingly final," Miranda explained. "It's very helpful in the grieving process, because it's clear there's no sanitizing within the framework of this thousands-of-years-old ritual."[46] Laura, Matthew, and Wolff carried Bob's body down the stairs and into the coffin that was waiting on an elevated platform. "We're all out there in the beating sun," Michelle recalled, "and Ileana put his prayer shawl around him and slipped his wedding ring back on his finger."[47] "It was sort of like getting married all over again," Ileana remembered.[48]

At the 4 p.m. funeral at Beth Israel Synagogue, a standing-room-only crush of mourners heard remembrances of family members and impromptu comments by anyone wishing to stand up and speak from their seat. One of the scheduled speakers was Jennifer Lapidus, a professional bread baker and friend of Bob's and Ileana's. Lapidus spoke of the conviction she and Bob shared over their psychic connection to their work—he with his circuits, and she with her bread. She confessed that she'd known Bob for some time simply as a friend who loved good bread because he'd never bothered to tell her what he did. Having no previous familiarity with his professional name or work, she introduced him once as "my friend Bob," and was taken aback when the man asked with great excitement, "Aren't you Bob *Moog*?" Only then did she learn that there was more to the story.

After the funeral, family members formed a police-escorted caravan for the ride out to a private family burial. Ileana and Miranda followed behind the hearse in Bob's painted Toyota. Ileana, Michelle, and Miranda had chosen a plot at the Lou Pollack Memorial Park, a gated Jewish cemetery in Asheville not open to the public. "We picked the spot because it was close to a tree," Ileana recalled.[49] Laura saw it as a reflection of Bob's favorite childhood book about Ferdinand the Bull, who loved sitting under a cork tree to smell the flowers.

After the casket was lowered, each person cast a shovel of dirt into the grave. In the Jewish tradition, a headstone would be erected one year after the date of death—an unveiling on the *Yahrzeit*. Rather than a traditional tombstone, the family decided on a granite bench. "I thought, Bob would really love that," Ileana mused. "He's so hospitable—he would really enjoy having someone sit down and be comfortable."[50] Along with his name and dates, the epitaph carved into the bench—suggested by Renée—would simply read, "Good Vibrations."

∽∼∽

On Wednesday, a public memorial celebration was held at the Orange Peel. People poured in from the East and West Coasts and from abroad, on hours' notice, in time for the noon kickoff. The mood was mostly upbeat—a sort of improbable homecoming mix of friends, colleagues, Moog luminaries, synth geeks, and hip local music lovers—a party Bob would've reveled in. Matthew emceed from behind a podium on stage. Among the crowd of 500, he spied a few who appeared a bit formal, and he immediately set down the ground rules: "I think my dad would appreciate it if you would take off your ties." Spotting a group of standees at the rear of the club, Laura took the mic to quip, "I am especially grateful for those of you who are in the back and leaning against the bar. 'Cause that's where he would be . . . with a cold beer and a piece of chocolate."[51] A table along the side was crowded with oversize baskets heaped with hundreds of brownies from Bob's favorite Asheville bakery.

There were brief remarks from the family, and 16 scheduled speakers who came forward to share endearing moments, and life lessons they'd learned from Bob. Herb Deutsch, David Borden, Wendy Carlos, and Mike Adams spoke. Wayne Kirby told Bob's parrot joke and read the kitty litter cake recipe. Dave Van Koevering marshaled his wavering preacher's cadence to rhapsodize over Bob's legacy, choking up as he proclaimed, "He *is*, in the potential of every instrument that bears his name . . . the songs that are not yet written." Steve Dunnington played "Amazing Grace," a Bob favorite, on the Etherwave Pro theremin. Cyril Lance picked and strummed an original instrumental on his acoustic guitar, then piped a soulful cover of Bob Dylan's "You're Gonna Make Me Lonesome When You Go." Nicoletta Stephanz conjured a sound improvisation with her voice and an Etherwave theremin, looping phrases with a delay pedal, building, layering, and overlapping sounds, climaxing with a legerdemain of sitar-like licks hammered out invisibly in the air with Buchla's hand-held "Lightning" wands, finishing with a throbbing chorus of haunting vocal "ahhs" morphing into a high, sustained electronic yowl, into fadeout.[52]

Keichi Goto, a synth programmer and professor, and Bob's good friend, came all the way from Japan with his wife and daughter to speak before the Orange Peel crowd. At Keichi's 1990 wedding, Bob and Shirleigh had been honored guests, seated behind the bride and groom in kimonos, and had traveled with the couple for the first three days of their honeymoon.

Matthew had estimated the celebration would last about two hours. After 4½ he called the show. Toubab Krewe was onstage as the featured band to play as the audience came in, and between some of the speakers. They'd been asked to perform by special request, and had hightailed it back to Asheville in the middle of a New England tour. As they began the exit music, the crowd stayed glued to their seats, transfixed by the infectious rhythms. Suddenly Renée pulled Michelle up to the front and the two began dancing. Gradually, the energy spread as audience members wandered up to join in. After a few minutes, the floor was rocking with a sea of bopping limbs, dancing to Toubab Krewe as Bob had dreamed of doing with Ileana. The afternoon ended on a note of high energy.

Back at the house afterward, Ileana hosted a small gathering for the out-of-towners, with food and quiet conversation. A shy Japanese man standing by himself wandered into the kitchen to pick over the plates of food. He didn't know anyone there, and he had no particular connection to the Moog legacy. He was just an ordinary citizen who'd traveled from Japan to pay his respects.

As evening fell, the house cleared out. With it came that stinging realization that there was one less person there now. Michelle stayed for a while to help Ileana clean up, then got in her car to head for home.

As she drove up Riverside Drive in the dark, past the scrap metal yards and abandoned railway tracks, skirting the French Broad River lined with its industrial waste plants, auto parts stores, and the shuttered 554C factory, something happened that hadn't occurred in Asheville in almost 90 years. At 11:09 p.m., a 3.8 magnitude earthquake rattled the city. It was enough to send Joseph clattering down to their basement to check whether the water heater had exploded. The temblor shook homes as far away as Athens, Georgia.

A coincidence? Perhaps.

But somewhere—in that realm—beyond the stars, and above the speed of light, where there is no time and no space, only energy—where we might make contact with a piece of broken glass or an old record—out past the morphic Elysian Fields—Robert Arthur Moog may have stumbled upon his network, that place where ideas come from. And he may have made contact, through his deepest, fattest bass, to let us know he'd joined that network that we can always access, if only we open ourselves up to it, and remember—his eternal... Good Vibrations.

Postlude

Whenever I think of Bob, an image flashes through my mind of the time he walked into our house, reached into the pocket of his sports jacket, and tossed a few garlic bulbs onto our kitchen table, the dirt still clinging to them. "Do you like garlic?" he asked. A gift from his organic garden.

Anyone who knew him remembers these typical "Bob moments"—spontaneous and genuine. At work, Steve Dunnington remembered, "He was this legendary guy, but he didn't really have a big ego about it. He just did this stuff because it was interesting. He liked physics and music and put the two together and had this incredible career. But when you were dealing with him one-on-one from day to day, he was just Bob. He was just a really cool guy, funny and fun to be around."[1]

Bob disdained easy labels, once joshing with the *Philadelphia Daily News*, "If I'm the 'father' of electronic music—as I'm often called—then who's the mother?" He told the paper frankly, "I'm the first guy who ever made money selling synthesizers. I took them out of the laboratory environment, but I'm hardly the inventor."[2] He once told an interviewer, "I happened to be there at the time that the culture needed me. It's just a fluke—it could have been somebody else.... or if the culture had gone a different way, I might have become a scientist at Bell Labs."[3]

Bob's attitude aside, many of the people I interviewed for this book began with the usual rhapsody of plaudits: what an amazing, brilliant, creative inventor he was; he altered the course of music. But I always made sure to ask for any favorite "Bob moments," a question that typically netted me a story or two, usually with a great punch line. It was in those offhanded recollections—some of them central to the main story—that the real Bob emerged in all his endearing complexity.

In piecing together so many of these inside glimpses, a fresh take on Bob's fabled money failures emerged. There were, of course, many interviewees who thought he was simply a bad businessman, period. He himself usually perpetuated that idea. "From the point of view of competence," he once said of his Trumansburg years, "we were never a business. Never. We got some of the elements in place, but none of the controls or forecasting, or planning that go with a well-run business. We just never had it."[4]

But there were many of his former associates I talked to who thought he was a *good* businessman, seeing his stumbles as more a matter of things that were beyond his control.

Setting aside the question of why a person trained in engineering should be expected to command equal facility in business, it's only fair to point out that manufacturing techniques like "Just in Time," and "Demand Flow Technology" weren't widely known in the U.S. when Bob was starting out. He was the lonely pioneer, feeling his way as he went, and trying to figure out if anyone at all could make money with this new technology. Dave Luce remembered Bob's oft-repeated line, "The guy out in front is the guy with all the arrows in his back."[5]

There's no question that Bob legitimized the synthesizer as a musical instrument, founded an industry around it, raised public awareness, fueled demand, and plowed the path his competitors would follow. But he ran his business in an unorthodox way. Graduates of management training programs would probably cringe at most of his decisions, and today's students of Business 101 probably know more about scheduling than he ever did. Still, the many remarkable things he got *right* are often overlooked, and no easy formulas can fully explain his achievements.

While Norlin, with its McKinsey-driven methodology for hiring, cycled through a roster of failed managers and clueless MBAs who drove the company into the ground, Bob's gut-level hires were invariably on the mark. Engineers like Bill Hemsath, Jim Scott, and Rich Walborn became long-term, dedicated innovators who birthed many of the company's classic instruments. Bob's habit of casting aside degrees and credentials, and zeroing in on the potential of the human being standing in front of him, was certainly nothing you learned in business school. And if he hadn't fostered an atmosphere of experimental tinkering among his engineering staff—projects with no particular ends in mind—Hemsath might never have thrown together the Minimoog prototype that made the whole future of the company possible.

Bob also understood the power of his workers' pride in the business, nurturing a loyal coterie of employees whose happiness in their work, and the knowledge that they wouldn't be dumped at the next downsizing, kept the business humming and productive. In light of the tendency of companies to view their workers as inanimate pawns to move around, manipulate, and toss off the board at will in the profit-maximizing game, Bob's workplace philosophy was admirable. And customer loyalty was another major dividend from the personal touch of his small operation. Musicians developed an uncommon affection for Bob's synths, largely because his designs reflected an uncommon attentiveness to *them*. Moog synths had to look beautiful, sound great, and be ergonomically natural. Dave Luce said that Bob's motto, reiterated at least once a day, was, "an instrument needs to feeeeeeel good."[6]

None of these successful outcomes could possibly have been quantified, or predicted by rubrics, algorithms, or data. And business experts could sometimes miss the forest for the trees: when the SBA named Bob the New York State Small Businessman of the Year in 1970, the honor was calculated on his company's sales growth. The fact that Bob was near bankruptcy, and actually surviving on an SBA loan when he accepted the award, apparently slipped past the Association's notice.

When I first raised the question of Bob's business acumen with the consummate professional Mike Adams, I half expected him to roll his eyes and snicker. Instead, he cited Jacqueline Harvey's early publicity work, arguing, "Bob was an excellent business person. Let me give you an example. Back in the '60s, he spent $25,000 on a public relations person to basically get the concept of the Moog name associated with synthesizers. And to this day, the *New York Times* crossword puzzle says, 'A four letter word for Synthesizer,' and it's *Moog*. I don't think a person who's just a geek would have spent $25,000 in the '60s—that's probably a quarter million dollars' worth of PR today—unless he was a good business person."[7]

In the immediate aftermath of Bob's death, the question on everyone's mind was whether the company could survive without him. The factory's move to larger headquarters in late August 2005 had been planned for months, but it seemed totally eerie now, coinciding as it did with Bob's death. Cyril Lance remembered those agonizing days:

"There's just international press going on all over the world and descending on the town, and everything on the Internet. So, the 'moment' is—I remember this very clearly—Mike and I closed up 554 Riverside. We were all alone and Mike closes the door, locks it, and he looks at me and he goes, 'Cyril, we have to make a decision. By the end of today, we have to make a public announcement as to what your role is in the company. I need to be able to announce that you are Bob's hand-picked successor.'" Lance was nearly paralyzed. "I looked at Mike and said, 'I don't know if I can do what needs to be done.' I felt very uncomfortable with the idea of jumping onto this ship and grabbing the helm." Adams knew that Bob had already given his nod to Lance, and, channeling Bob and his spirit of spontaneous hires, Lance recalled, "Mike looked at me and said, 'I have 100% confidence that you can learn what you need to do.'"[8]

Lance agreed to the announcement and signed on, but he continued to have doubts: "Sometimes I'd say, 'What am I thinking? Why don't they just get some guy who's designed synths his whole life?' But then there was this other part of me that said that for some reason I met Bob on that snowy night and this is the way things happen. I've had this put in my lap and for some reason that I can't explain, I'm going to have to figure out how to make it work."[9]

In the days, weeks, and months that followed, the employees at Moog were holding their breath. The most urgent order of business was to put out a new product to signal that the company was able to continue on. The Little Phatty—the last instrument Bob had conceived—had begun development in July while he was undergoing radiation and chemo. Now that Lance was in charge, work began on it in earnest. "I started designing the circuits and studying the Voyager," he recalled. "Everybody chipped in on that thing and put in their heart and soul. It was like everybody's tribute to their love for Bob's industrial design. I think that design is so beautiful and so unique. The user interface was a real combination of everybody's ideas—mine, Steve's, Mike's, artists', and it was kind of new and it solved a lot of problems that were happening at the time. It was a real team effort and I really feel like that instrument is a real expression of Bob."[10]

Like the Minimoog, the Little Phatty was rushed into being with some of its warts left in place—warts that lent it its distinctive character. "It's got limitations," Lance admitted, "because we ran out of time or I didn't anticipate a circuit working because of inexperience, or because I didn't have time to analyze it enough. But that's what makes these instruments lovely and beautiful and coveted." The Little Phatty shipped in June 2006, and Lance and the crew were ecstatic: "That was the instrument that people said, 'Okay, Moog will continue on.'"[11]

During the final week of Bob's life, the family had started thinking about how best to honor his memory. Matthew suggested they start a foundation of some sort, and the family had discussions about what its focus should be. After considering various causes, from organic gardening to brain tumor research, Michelle suggested electronic music, the solution that was staring them in the face. On the first anniversary of Bob's death, August 21, 2006, the Bob Moog Foundation was launched, with Michelle at the helm as executive director.

BMF was founded as "a reflection of Bob Moog's legacy: To educate and inspire people through the power and possibilities of electronic music, and through the intersection of music and science." The Foundation conducts several signature projects, including the curating of its archival collection, and administering *Dr. Bob's Sound School*, an outreach program designed to "teach children about the science of sound through music and technology." In the spring of 2019, Michelle opened the Moogseum, a mini museum of all-things-Bob, located in the heart of downtown Asheville.

On June 11, 2015, the *New York Times* ran a story announcing that Moog Music was now an employee-owned company. Mike Adams had sold 49 percent of Moog Music to his staff, echoing Bob's employee-centric philosophy. The *Times* hailed the move as "a victory for the small company, whose financial success has not always matched its cultural impact," observing that "Mr. Adams has worked to maintain the open, collaborative atmosphere that Bob . . . instituted."[12] There was a photo of a radiant Ileana on the factory floor; she told the newspaper that employee-ownership was the fulfillment of one of Bob's dreams. The article noted that Moog Music had added dozens of employees and had maintained its reputation as an artisanal, all-local workplace. Earnings had risen an average of 18% per year, and the company had gone "from selling six products to more than 100, with the instruments ranging in price from a few thousand dollars to $35,000 for one top model." Under Adams' leadership, the operation burgeoned into a multimillion-dollar company.

Cyril Lance grew comfortably into Bob's shoes to lead Moog Music's technical advancements as chief engineer. "I really wish Bob could see what happened over the last 10 years," he reflected, "because this has been just a remarkable celebration of his legacy. There's not a day we don't think about him, and don't think about it from his perspective. These basic ideas and values are as strong and inexhaustible today as they were 30 years ago."[13]

Bob may not have been trained in business, but he knew the old maxim, "It takes money to make money." Getting a huge infusion of capital from an angel investor was one goal that had eluded him from the earliest days in Trumansburg: "We were always in the red. We had no capital. None. Zero!"[14] When a friend wrote him in 1992, asking for tips on how to fundraise, Bob answered with typical candor: "I feel more than a little stupid giving you advice.... In all of my career I've never been able to raise a dime for anything. Nothing. Gar nichts!!!"[15]

In July 2004, Adams and Bob took out life insurance policies on each other to ensure the future stability of the company. Thirteen months later, after Bob was laid to rest, aftershocks of the earthquake were felt at Moog Music, too. Bob's life insurance policy had paid the company a million dollars.

Call it a gift from the ultimate angel investor.

Acknowledgments

This book began with a phone call. In late 2009, Michelle Moog-Koussa contacted me to discuss the idea of a biography of her father. She and Bob's widow, Ileana Grams-Moog, had agreed that a major portrait of Bob's life—particularly Bob *the man*—was long overdue. Bob, they told me, had a particular fondness for my biography of Leon Theremin—for which he'd written the foreword—and he'd kept extra copies around to give as presents to friends, scrawling notes in the margins of his favorite passages. Given his deep connection to the theremin, and his approval of my portrait of its inventor, Michelle and Ileana wondered if, in that spirit, I might give the same treatment to Bob. In a flash, I accepted the challenge happily, and with gusto. I'd just slipped backwards on a banana peel.

I'm deeply grateful to Michelle and Ileana for entrusting me with this great undertaking, and for placing at my disposal a huge body of resources to carry out the mission. Michelle opened the Bob Moog Foundation's storehouse of archival treasures all the way, shared her family's personal archives, pointed me toward a list of interviewees, and tossed any informational tidbits my way that she thought might add glints of jeweled detail to the story. Ileana offered me unrestricted access to the Aladdin's cave of archival riches in her home—a portion of which later wound up at Cornell University.

As I rolled up my sleeves for the archaeological dig through the worldly remains of Bob's legacy, my brilliant and insightful wife, Linda Kobler, became my partner in the field for the entire project (and she doesn't even like synthesizers!). Without her constant support and assistance in researching, cataloging, transcribing, and acting as a daily sounding board for ideas about Bob's philosophies and cultural impact, there would have been no book at all. Together, we traveled coast to coast for interviews, made multiple research jaunts to Asheville for weeks at a time, harvested enough photocopies to circle the world—8,000 sheets from one trip alone—filled a room in our house with over 40 large ring binders covering the sweep of Bob's life and career, and photographed and scanned documents everywhere we went.

Only with Linda's help in sorting through the dozens of boxes of undocumented, randomly stashed papers in Ileana's home, Linda's transcriptions of scores of interviews, her detailed spreadsheets and 100-plus-page summaries of thousands of articles, corporate documents, and letters covering each era in the binders, could I have synthesized such a mind-numbing mass of resources into a coherent and readable text. As the chapters materialized, she acted as constant reader to judge the road-worthiness of each one. And while I wrote, she did double duty with tasks I had no time for. I often joked that it takes a village to write a Bob Moog biography, and it often felt as though the two of us were the whole village. The 12-year span of this saga, I figured, could easily be doubled: between us, 24 years of work went into this book. No words can express the depth of my appreciation for Linda's collaborative role, all the way to the finish line.

No shower of thanks could sufficiently acknowledge Brian Kehew—synthesizer guru, Moog maven, and music technology expert—for lending his support to this book by offering me invaluable insights and documentation that helped crack some of the more stubborn myths in the Moog world, and for ultimately reading through and vetting the manuscript with his eagle eye for any errant historical or technical details that might have slipped under the radar.

Trevor Pinch's enthusiasm for synthesizer lore pervades *Analog Days* and has infused conversations and emails we've exchanged. I'm grateful to him for his support of this book, and particularly for his insightful comments when he reviewed the manuscript in its last stages. I am also profoundly grateful to Trevor, and to Frank Trocco, for gracing posterity with what must be the longest and most in-depth interviews ever conducted with Bob Moog—sessions they held in 1996 and 1997 in preparation for writing *Analog Days*. Access to those many hours of Bob's frank and intimate reflections on his life and career were invaluable to me as an adjunct to Bob's other interviews.

Special thanks must go to Dr. Phillip Belfiore of Mercyhurst University, who, in his position as Vice President for Academic Affairs, appointed me as a Research Fellow, allowing me to work with six student research assistants on projects for the book. Carolyn Carlins did related literature searches and developed databases of databases, eventually mining hundreds of journal and newspaper articles as a foundation for my research. Andrea Flores, from the business department, spent months analyzing reams of Bob's financial documents—spreadsheets, reports, and capital projections—uncovering the fiscal land mines hiding in the numbers, and translating them for me. Jessica Hillburn, from the history department, took on a study of Japanese industrial labor practices that assisted me in understanding the competitive manufacturing climate Bob operated within. Kayleigh Ferguson, Rachel Masters, and Christy Moore did their share of interview transcriptions and dug up occasional buried gems.

Hearty thanks go to Lori Krasnesky, the Interlibrary Loan Specialist at Mercyhurst University. "St. Lori of Mercyhurst," as she's known in our household, never complained when bombarded with my constant requests for books and articles, and she even dispatched some while she was away on vacation. A nod also goes to Darci Jones, Mercyhurst Director of University Libraries, for invaluable tutorials on database research, and to staff members Jennifer Harris, Karen Niemla, and Angela Okey.

Supplementing the storehouse of documentary resources—print and virtual—interviews conducted with major and minor players in the Moog story formed a core element of my research. At the top of the list, of course, is Bob Moog himself, and the 1997 interview I did with him. Shirleigh Moog sat for long interviews on our multiple trips to Asheville, and opened up her scrapbooks. Michelle Moog added flesh-and-blood poignancy to the story by opening her personal vault, granting me multiple interviews—one lasting 13 hours over four days—plus several in the car on the fly during research trips, others over meals, and some during our extended stays with her family. The depth and nuance of these tellings were enough to make a biographer giddy. Ileana Grams-Moog granted me hours of interview time in multiple sessions over repeated trips to Asheville, unpacking her unique perspective on Bob's later years, and deconstructing, in her philosopher's manner, so many of Bob's profound reflections on musicians, technology, and the cosmos.

I'm deeply thankful to others who generously granted me interviews, some who welcomed us into their home for several days, and many who allowed us free reign to sift through their personal archives, or followed up with encores of documents and photos:

Mike Adams, David Borden, Don Buchla, Irwin Chusid, Suzanne Ciani, Francis Ford Coppola, Herb Deutsch, Steve Dunnington, Larry Fast, David Friend, Tom Gullo, Bill Hemsath, Marilyn Herman, Ray Herman, Greg Hockman, Jac Holzman, Dick Hyman, Brian Kehew, George Kelischek, Gershon Kingsley, Wayne Kirby, Gregory Koussa, Joseph Koussa, Bernie Krause, Khatia Krebs, Rick Krebs, Cyril Lance, Rudi Linhard, Ken Lopez, David Luce, Kathy Luther, Roger Luther, Peter Mauzey, Doug McKechnie, Dominic Milano, Laura Moog, Renée Moog, Mike Nesmith, Ray Newman, Nathaniel Nord, Erik Norlander, Dina Pearlman, Cora Portnoff, Miranda Richmond Mouillot, Maxine Ringelheim, Andrew Rudin, Lee Santa, Jim

Scott, Shana Sear Gaskill, Walter Sear, Ronald Spatz, Jim Suchora, Meg Swansen, Becky Van Koevering, Dave Van Koevering, Rich Walborn, Jon Weiss, Georgeanna Whistler, August Worley, and Gene Zumchak. I'm indebted to Anne-Marie Bonnel and Suzanne Ciani for generously facilitating what was to be the last interview Don Buchla ever granted.

Much gratitude to Roger Luther for graciously allowing me the run of his own personal Moog archive—an extensive collection he began assembling as the original keeper of the flame during Bob's lifetime. Special thanks to Thom Holmes for letting me pick his formidable historian's brain on occasion, and for referring me to valuable contacts.

Bob's multidimensional story often strayed into technical regions where I needed guidance: Friedrich Fahnert and Marisol Fahnert steered me through patent issues; Mike Wagner and Patrick Phelps traced through the mazes in Moog and ARP circuit diagrams; psychology professors Gerard Barron, Robert Hoff, and Marilyn Livosky helped me fathom Bob's Rothenberg project and aspects of psychological testing; Jim Voss helped me follow the trail of Bob's different corporate identities; Keiko Miller translated Japanese documents. Others who uncovered fresh information, decoded mysteries, or offered expert opinions include Jeni Dahmus, Marc Doty, Jane Gottlieb, Michael Griffin, Arthur Kobler, Dr. Michael Latzer, Nelson Muniz, Luigino Pizzaleo, and Dr. Daniel Wyman.

Many organizations provided valuable archival materials, including the Rockefeller Foundation, and the Music Division of the New York Public Library for the Performing Arts at Lincoln Center. I also owe a special debt to the archivists, researchers, and hunter-scholars at various institutions who helped me nail down details: John K. Blanchard, Manhattan School of Music; Seth Cluett, Sound Art Program, Columbia University; Dan Del Fiorentino, NAMM; Cathy Dorin-Black, NC State University Libraries; Dorie Gilbride, guest researcher, Ohio University Libraries; Catherine Heitz, American Academy in Rome (New York City); Sebastian Hierl, American Academy in Rome (Rome); Elisa Ho, The Jacob Rader Marcus Center of the American Jewish Archives; Stacey Lavender, Ohio University Libraries; Bill Levay, New York Philharmonic Leon Levy Digital Archives; Laura Maidens, Rock & Roll Hall of Fame Library & Archives; William McQuaide, Journal of the Audio Engineering Society; Anahid Nazarian, American Zoetrope; Jeffrey T. O'Donald, Small Business Administration; Jenn Parent, The Museum of Flight; Nick Patterson, Music & Arts Library, Columbia University; Amy Reytar, National Archives and Records Administration; Anne Rhodes,

Yale University Library; Dr. Lauren Rosati, Museum of Modern Art, New York; Eddie Silva, St. Louis Symphony; Souksavat Soukhaseum, The Free Synagogue of Flushing; and Josie Walters-Johnston, Moving Image Section, Library of Congress.

Particular thanks are extended to those who facilitated contacts, offered advice or technical assistance, gave permissions, or provided images for the book: Fred Arellano, Dr. Juan Argaez, Dana Arvig, Sidney Ashen-Brenner Jr., David Bailey, Judith Bass, Esq., Vicki Berndt, The Leonard Bernstein Office; Aaron Bremner, Robert Carl, Deborah Chalcroft, Rachel Cooper, Day Darmet, Joyce Sydnee Dollinger, Esq., Connie Finnerty, Shana Sear Gaskill, Olivia Harrison, Michelle Harvey, Caitlin Holton, Sara Juday, David Kean, Gene Lee, Laura M. Linke, Dr. Scott Meier, Matthew Moog, Renée Moog, Dr. John Olszowka, Tom Parker, Trevor Pinch, Richard Radford, Katherine Reagan, Gino Robair, Peter Scheer, Elliott Sears, Taral Shah, Steve J. Sherman, Jim Siergey, Wendy Sievert, Stephen Smith, Dan Sullivan, and John Waterhouse.

Deepest gratitude to my editor, Norm Hirschy, for his foresight and enthusiasm about this project from the beginning, for meticulously walking the manuscript through the final stages of vetting to tighten some screws, and for deftly shepherding it into the pipeline for production. Thanks also to my peerless Project Editor, Zara Cannon-Mohammed, and the whole team at Oxford, including Linda Roppolo, Anna-Lise Santella, and Henry Wilkinson, and heartfelt appreciation to my outstanding Project Manager, Vinothini Thiruvannamalai at Newgen Knowledge Works, and her colleagues who assisted in preparing the manuscript for publication. A note of thanks also to my Copy Editor, Dorothy Bauhoff for her immaculate eye.

Francis Ford Coppola's contribution to Moog history is remarkable. I'm profoundly grateful to him for sharing his reflections on this legacy in the Foreword to this book.

A special shout out to Dr. Randall Wong, Retinal Specialist extraordinaire, for giving me the clear vision to finish writing this book.

I'm grateful to my daughter, Allegra, and my son, Luka, for their support and encouragement over 12 years, and for their valuable read-throughs, offering (mostly) unbiased comments and suggestions. Your love and sensibilities are in these pages, too!

Lastly, I want to thank Bob Moog for bequeathing to us a life, and a legacy, that are a biographer's dream—so much richness to tell, and to revel in, in the telling. Bob: perhaps a few things in these chapters were taken down from your network. In any case, I hope you approve....

Notes

KEY TO MAJOR MANUSCRIPT COLLECTIONS

CIGM = Collection of Ileana Grams-Moog
CBK = Collection of Brian Kehew
BMF = Bob Moog Foundation
MFA = Moog Family Archives

NOTE: Several years after the author's perusal and documentation of the CIGM collection at the original site where it had been housed after Bob Moog's death—the home of Ileana Grams-Moog—a portion of the collection was transferred to Cornell University to establish the Robert Moog Papers at the Division of Rare and Manuscript Collections, Cornell University Library.

Prelude

1. In this book, the term "electronic musical instruments," as it's now generally used, refers only to instruments where the sound originates in electrical circuits and is amplified. The electric guitar, for example, is not an electronic musical instrument—it's electro-mechanical—because its sound originates from the strings that a musician sets in motion, which are then amplified through a pickup.
2. Al Padorr memo to Moog Music, Inc., staff, December 23, 1969. CIGM.
3. Renée Moog interview with Albert Glinsky, June 10, 2018 (hereafter, "Glinsky, Renée Moog, 2018").
4. Walter Sear interview with Albert Glinsky, August 29, 1997 (hereafter, "Glinsky, Sear, 1997").

Chapter 1

1. From Court Order, as reported in Wenkbach [Germany] civil records, page 164, transcribed by Robert L. Moog in a genealogical typescript statement, "Georg Conrad Moog," included in Robert L. Moog letter to Florence Moog, August 28, 1985. CIGM.
2. Ileana Grams-Moog interview with Albert Glinsky, July 26–27, 2012 (hereafter, "Glinsky, Grams-Moog, 2012").
3. Glinsky, Grams-Moog, 2012.
4. Shirleigh Moog interview with Albert Glinsky, October 29, 2011 (hereafter, "Glinsky, Shirleigh Moog, 2011").

5. Glinsky, Grams-Moog, 2012.
6. Glinsky, Shirleigh Moog, 2011; Shirleigh Moog interview with Albert Glinsky, July 24, 27, 2012 (hereafter, "Glinsky, Shirleigh Moog, 2012"); Glinsky, Grams-Moog, 2012; Michelle Moog-Koussa interview with Albert Glinsky, October 31–November 3, 2015 (hereafter, "Glinsky, Moog-Koussa, 2015").
7. Glinsky, Moog-Koussa, 2015.
8. 1939 New York World's Fair, opening program, https://archive.org/stream/newyorkworldsfai00newy/newyorkworldsfai00newy_djvu.txt.
9. "Here Is the Fair," *New York Times*, special section, "The Fair and the City" (April 30, 1939), Section 8:3.
10. "Here Is the Fair," 3.
11. "The City of Light; on the Plaza of Light at the New York World's Fair, 1939," descriptive brochure, Consolidated Edison Company of New York, Inc., 1939.
12. Arnold Lesti, "The Radio Organ of a Trillion Tones," *Radio-Craft* (January 1931), 402, 403, 430.
13. F. M. Sammis, "The 'Polytone,'" *Radio-Craft* (May 1934), 657.
14. Edward E. Kassel, "A 'Syntronic' Organ," *Radio-Craft* (August 1934), 77.
15. Robert L. Doerschuk, "12 Who Count: Bob Moog," *Keyboard Magazine* (February 1995), 96.
16. Bob Moog, February 2, 1979, interviewed by Joan Thomson. OHV 213 d–f. Major Figures in American Music, Oral History of American Music, in the Music Library of Yale University (hereafter, "Moog, Yale interview, 1979").
17. Typescript for a review, "Syntauri's Metatrak, A Recording Studio for Electronic Sound," January 26, 1983. CIGM.
18. Moog, Yale interview, 1979.
19. Mr. Bonzai, "Bonzai Beat: Bob Moog," *EQ* (April 1997), 50.
20. Frank Houston, "Brilliant Careers: Bob Moog," *Salon.com* (April 25, 2000), https://www.salon.com/2000/04/25/moog/
21. Bob Moog letter to Nathaniel Nord, September 30, 1972. CIGM.
22. Mr. Bonzai, "Robert Moog," 46.
23. Terry Gross, *Fresh Air*, WHYY/National Public Radio, November 3, 2000.
24. Bob Moog interview with Trevor Pinch and Frank Trocco, June 5–6, 1996 (hereafter, "Pinch, Trocco, Moog interview, 1996").
25. Moog, Yale interview, 1979.
26. Nathaniel Nord interview with Albert Glinsky, March 9, 2018 (hereafter, "Glinsky, Nord, 2018").
27. Glinsky, Grams-Moog, 2012.
28. Robert Moog, Report Card, P.S. 24, Queens; Board of Education, City of New York, June 1945. MFA.
29. Glinsky, Nord, 2018.
30. Glinsky, Nord, 2018.
31. R. Moog, handwritten college application essay draft, October 10, 1951. MFA.
32. Moog, Yale interview, 1979.
33. Glinsky, Grams-Moog, 2012.
34. Glinsky, Grams-Moog, 2012.
35. Glinsky, Shirleigh Moog, 2011.

36. Glinsky, Shirleigh Moog, 2011.
37. Bob Moog letter to Nathaniel Nord, September 30, 1972. CIGM.
38. Steve Knezevich and Jamie Fraser, "Bob Moog: Scientific Method Man," *Grand Royal* (Spring/Summer 1996), 57.
39. Bob Moog letter to Nathaniel Nord, September 30, 1972.
40. Bob Moog letter to Nathaniel Nord, September 30, 1972.

Chapter 2

1. Glinsky, Grams-Moog, 2012.
2. Moog, Yale interview, 1979.
3. Glinsky, Shirleigh Moog, 2011.
4. Doerschuk, "12 Who Count: Bob Moog," 96.
5. Robert Moog, "Guidance Card," The Bronx High School of Science, September, 1948. MFA.
6. Glinsky, Shirleigh Moog, 2011.
7. Robert A. Moog, text of address delivered at The Florence Moog Memorial service, Graham Chapel, Washington University, February 17, 1988, memorial booklet for Florence Moog, 15. CIGM.
8. Robert A. Moog, Memorial booklet for Florence Moog, 15. CIGM.
9. Glinsky, Grams-Moog, 2012.
10. Bob Moog, interview with Albert Glinsky, August 17, 1997 (hereafter, "Glinsky, Bob Moog, 1997").
11. Ernest J. Schultz, "A Simple Electronic Musical Instrument; The THEREMIN," *Radio & Television News* (October 1949), 66–67.
12. Leonard Liebling, "Theremin Concert by Clara Rockmore Has Novel Effect," *New York American* (October 31, 1934), n.p.; "Theremin Takes Forward Step," *New York World-Telegram* (October 31, 1934), n.p.
13. Ernest Newman, "Melody from the Air," *Sunday Times* (London), (December 11, 1927), 17.
14. Schultz, "A Simple Electronic Musical Instrument; The THEREMIN," 66.
15. Moog, Yale interview, 1979.
16. "'Tone Synthesizer' Amazes Scientists," *New York Times* (January 26, 1946), 28.
17. "'Tone Synthesizer' Amazes Scientists," 28.
18. Bob Moog, foreword to Albert Glinsky, *Theremin: Ether Music and Espionage* (Urbana and Chicago: University of Illinois Press, 2000), ix.
19. "Character and Personality Report to be Submitted to Colleges," Bronx High School of Science Guidance Committee, ca. 1951. MFA.
20. Jerome Karabel, *The Chosen: The Hidden History of Admission and Exclusion at Harvard, Yale, and Princeton* (Boston: Houghton Mifflin, 2005).
21. "Character and Personality Report to be Submitted to Colleges," Bronx High School of Science Guidance Committee, ca. 1951. MFA.
22. R. Moog, handwritten college application essay draft, October 10, 1951. MFA.
23. Bob Moog, letter to Nathaniel Nord, September 30, 1972. CIGM.

Chapter 3

1. Robert K. Fullinwider and Judith Lichtenberg, *Leveling the Playing Field: Justice, Politics, and College Admissions* (Lanham, MD: Rowman & Littlefield, 2004), 61.
2. Moog, Yale interview, 1979.
3. George Moog, interview on *The Late Show*, WPIX Television, Channel 11, New York, NY, December 2, 1953. 78 r.p.m. acetate record. CIGM.
4. Bob Moog statement to Roger Luther about the 201 Theremin Pictorial schematic, November 2003. moogarchives.com.
5. Robert Moog, "The Theremin," *Radio & Television* (January 1954), 37.
6. *RCA Theremin Musical Instrument: Instructions*, Part II—Operation, page 3. Radio-Victor Corporation of America, 1929.
7. Pinch, Trocco, Moog interview, 1996.
8. "Theremin Coils & Kits," ad in *Radio & Television News*, January 1954.
9. Moog, Yale interview, 1979.
10. *The R. A. Moog Theremin*, product catalog, 1954. CIGM.
11. *The R. A. Moog Theremin*, product catalog, 1954. CIGM.
12. *The R. A. Moog Theremin*, product catalog, 1954. CIGM.
13. *The R. A. Moog Theremin*, product catalog, 1954. CIGM.
14. "Prices and Terms of Sale," R. A. Moog Company, November 1, 1954. Typescript. BMF.
15. Glinsky, Bob Moog, 1997.
16. Glinsky, Bob Moog, 1997.
17. Glinsky, Shirleigh Moog, 2011.
18. Moog, Yale interview, 1979.
19. Glinsky, Shirleigh Moog, 2011.
20. Glinsky, Shirleigh Moog, 2011.
21. Robert Moog, "Music from Electrons," *Audio Craft* (June 1956), 16–19, 33.
22. Bob Moog letter to Florence Moog, June 1, 1956. CIGM.
23. Jorge Munnshe, "Interview with Robert Moog," *Amazing Sounds* (1998), http://www.amazings.com/articles/article0036.html.
24. Irwin Chusid, phone interview with Robert Moog, May 19, 1993. Transcript, https://www.raymondscott.net/features/bob-moog/.
25. Bob Moog, "Memories of Raymond Scott," www.raymondscott.net.
26. Bob Moog, "Bob Moog's memories of his friend and colleague Raymond Scott," https://raymondscott.blogspot.com/2012/05/bob-moogs-memories-of-raymond-scott.html.
27. Glinsky, Shirleigh Moog, 2011.
28. Glinsky, Shirleigh Moog, 2011.
29. Glinsky, Grams-Moog, 2012.
30. Glinsky, Shirleigh Moog, 2011.
31. Bob Moog letter to Shirley Leigh, December 7, 1956. CIGM.
32. Glinsky, Shirleigh Moog, 2011.
33. Bob Moog letter to Florence Moog, April 1, 1957, MFA.
34. Glinsky, Shirleigh Moog, 2012.

35. Glinsky, Shirleigh Moog, 2011.
36. Glinsky, Shirleigh Moog, 2011.

Chapter 4

1. Bob Moog letters to Florence Moog, October 21, 1957; January 8, 1958. MFA.
2. Florence Moog letter to Robert Moog, October 13, 1957. CIGM.
3. Bob Moog letter to Florence Moog, June 6, 1958. CIGM.
4. Florence Moog letter to Bob Moog, December 12, 1957. CIGM.
5. Enclosed in Shirley Leigh's letter to Bob Moog, February 3, 1957. CIGM.
6. Bob Moog letter to Shirley Leigh, December 5, 1957. CIGM.
7. Glinsky, Shirleigh Moog, 2011.
8. Bob Moog letter to Florence Moog, October 21, 1957. MFA.
9. Bob Moog letter to Florence Moog, October 21, 1957. MFA.
10. Florence Moog letter to Bob Moog, ca. December 2, 1957. CIGM.
11. Bob Moog letter to Florence Moog, January 8, 1958. MFA.
12. Bob Moog letter to Florence Moog, October 21, 1957. MFA.
13. Bob Moog letter to Shirley Leigh, October 6, 1957. CIGM.
14. Florence Moog letter to Bob Moog, October 13, 1957. CIGM.
15. Bob Moog letter to Florence Moog, January 8, 1958. MFA.
16. Lillian Leigh letter to Bob Moog, October 7, 1957. CIGM.
17. Bob Moog letter to Shirley Leigh, January 13, 1958. CIGM.
18. Bob Moog letter to Shirley Leigh, February 19, 1958. CIGM.
19. Bob Moog letter to Shirley Leigh, February 1, 1958. CIGM.
20. Bob Moog letter to Shirley Leigh, ca. March 10, 1958. CIGM.
21. Bob Moog letter to Shirley Leigh, April 26, 1958. CIGM.
22. Shirley Leigh letter to Bob Moog, February 1, 1958. CIGM.
23. Bob Moog letter to Shirley Leigh, November 20, 1957. CIGM.
24. Bob Moog letter to Florence Moog, June 6, 1958. CIGM.
25. Shirley Leigh letter to Bob Moog, June 1, 1958. CIGM.
26. Cora Portnoff interview with Albert Glinsky, June 29, 2016 (hereafter, "Glinsky, Portnoff, 2016").
27. Glinsky, Shirleigh Moog, 2011.
28. Glinsky, Shirleigh Moog, 2011.

Chapter 5

1. Glinsky, Portnoff, 2016.
2. Glinsky, Shirleigh Moog, 2012.
3. Glinsky, Shirleigh Moog, 2011.
4. Bob Moog letter to Shirley Leigh, January 11, 1958. CIGM.

5. Glinsky, Shirleigh Moog, 2011.
6. Bob Moog letters to Florence Moog, February 8, 1959; April 20, 1959. CIGM.
7. "The R. A. Moog Theremins; music's most modern instrument," product catalog, 1959. CIGM.
8. Bob Moog letter to Florence Moog, November 8, 1959. CIGM.
9. Francis Bellow, "The Year of the Transistor," *Fortune* (March 1953), quoted in Jon Gertner, *The Idea Factory: Bells Labs and the Great Age of American Innovation* (New York: Penguin, 2012), 163–164.
10. Bob Moog letter to Florence Moog, July 18, 1956. MFA.
11. The R. A. Moog Theremins; music's most modern instrument," product catalog, 1959. CIGM.
12. The R. A. Moog Theremins; music's most modern instrument," product catalog, 1959. CIGM.
13. Glinsky, Bob Moog, 1997.
14. "On Program At Zoar Methodist Church," *The Herald*, Jaspar, IN (January 28, 1958), 3.
15. Joan Thomas letter to Bob Moog, September 10, 1981. CIGM.
16. Bob Moog letter to Florence Moog, August 25, 1960. MFA.
17. Robert A. Moog, "A Transistorized Theremin," *Electronics World* (January 1961), 30–32, 125.
18. Moog, "A Transistorized Theremin," 30–32, 125.
19. "Music," *Time* (1947), no date; n.p.
20. Bob Moog letter to Florence Moog, January 19, 1961. MFA.
21. Bob Moog letter to Florence Moog, May 5, 1961. CIGM.
22. Bob Moog letter to Florence Moog, June 24, 1961. CIGM.
23. Moog, Yale interview, 1979.

Chapter 6

1. Larry Fine, "In the Shop with Bob Moog: A Personal Account," *Acoustic and Digital Piano Buyer*, 1993, http://www.pianobuyer.com/article/in-the-shop-with-bob-moog-a-personal-account/.
2. *Moog Music* (Fall–Winter 1962). Collection of Howard Mossman.
3. Bob Moog letter to Florence and Emma Moog, September 25, 1962. CIGM.
4. Bob Moog, "Use of Electronics in the Production of Music Expands as New Techniques Are Developed," *Moog Music* (Fall–Winter 1962), 2, 7. Collection of Howard Mossman.
5. Moog, "Use of Electronics in the Production of Music Expands as New Techniques Are Developed," 2.
6. "Music of the Future," *Time* (July 2, 1956), 36.
7. "Music: The Tapesichordists," *Time* (November 10, 1952), n.p.
8. Jay S. Harrison, "Music and the Machine," *New York Herald Tribune* (October 28, 1952), n.p.

9. Harold G. Schonberg, "Nothing But Us Speakers," *New York Times* (May 21, 1961), 9.
10. Vladimir Ussachevsky, interviewed by Joan Thomson, April 14, 1977. OHV 201 h-l. Major Figures in American Music, Oral History of American Music, in the Music Library of Yale University.
11. Bob Moog letter to Florence Moog, September 25, 1962. CIGM.
12. Bob Moog letter to Florence Moog, January 24, 1963. CIGM.
13. Shirleigh Moog letter to Florence Moog, June 10, 1963. CIGM.
14. Trevor Pinch and Frank Trocco, *Analog Days: The Invention and Impact of the Moog Synthesizer* (Cambridge: MA: Harvard University Press, 2002), 19.
15. Bob Moog letter to Florence Moog, October 21, 1963. CIGM.
16. Bob Moog letter to Florence Moog, October 21, 1963. CIGM.
17. Bob Moog letter to Florence Moog, January 24, 1963. CIGM.
18. Bob Moog, Leave of Absence or Withdrawal Form, October 2, 1963, Cornell University. MFA.
19. Glinsky, Bob Moog, 1997.
20. Herb Deutsch interview with Albert Glinsky, October 15–16, 2011 (hereafter, "Glinsky, Deutsch, 2011").
21. Carter Thomas, "Interview with Bob Moog," *Synapse* (May/June 1977), 27.
22. Glinsky, Deutsch, 2011.
23. Bob Moog letter to Herb Deutsch, December 17, 1963. CIGM.
24. "Gets Music Out of Sculptured Junk," *New York Daily News*, Queens-Long Island Section (January 26, 1964), Q12.
25. "Talk of the Town," *The New Yorker* (January 25, 1964), 22.
26. "Far-Out Art, Music Event," *New York Daily News*, Kings Section (January 5, 1964), 13K.
27. "Talk of the Town," 22.
28. Moog, Yale interview, 1979.
29. Glinsky, Deutsch, 2011.

Chapter 7

1. "Trumansburg Newest Industry Explained," *Ithaca Journal* (April 9, 1964), n.p..
2. Bob Moog letter to Herb Deutsch, February 11, 1964. Collection of Herb Deutsch.
3. Moog, Yale interview, 1979.
4. Vladimir Ussachevsky, interviewed by Joan Thomson, April 10, 1978. OHV 201 m-p. Major Figures in American Music, Oral History of American Music, in the Music Library of Yale University.
5. Moog, Yale interview, 1979. Bob wrote to Ussachevsky from Ithaca, NY, in 1959 (Robert A. Moog to Vladimir Ussachevsky, September 16, 1959, Music & Arts Library, Columbia University, courtesy Nick Patterson). Bob had graduated from Columbia two years earlier, and in his letter, in which he introduces himself to Ussachevsky, he expresses curiosity about the newly formed Columbia-Princeton Electronic Music Center and its financial support from the Rockefeller Foundation. During Bob's time

at Columbia, as he explained to the interviewer at Yale, he'd never met Ussachevsky or visited the electronic music studio. Peter Mauzey, Bob's Columbia lab instructor at the time, confirmed in an interview with the author (June 8, 2018) that he remembered Bob only as an engineering student at Columbia, not as someone who'd ever visited, or participated in, the campus electronic music studio where Mauzey was serving as Ussachevsky's technical advisor.

6. Bob Moog interview with Trevor Pinch and Frank Trocco, November 16, 1997 (hereafter, "Pinch, Trocco, Moog interview, 1997").
7. Peter Mauzey interview with Albert Glinsky, June 8, 2018.
8. Thaddeus Cahill, "Art of and Apparatus for Generating and Distributing Music Electrically," U.S. Patent 580,035, April 6, 1897.
9. In the 1920s, the dawn of radio broadcasting ushered in the age of vacuum tube oscillators that powered monophonic instruments like the theremin and the *ondes martenot*, but these instruments had limited tone colors and required unorthodox playing techniques. In the 1930s, polyphonic instruments—that allowed the playing of two or more notes simultaneously—offered a range of tonal colors with inventions like the Polytone, the Syntronic Organ, and the Novachord, but their spectrum of timbral variants was still narrow. The Hammond organ borrowed the technology of the Telharmonium in miniaturized form, replacing the mammoth rotors with small tone wheels that operated now courtesy of vacuum tube amplification, but the instrument hardly had an unlimited spectrum of sounds. In the 1940s, Hugh Le Caine invented his Electronic Sackbut, a monophonic keyboard instrument that allowed some sophisticated methods of manipulating sound.

All these instruments—and myriad other attempts—were geared toward live performance. But some inventors created instruments specifically for composers—devices to offer a plethora of raw material sounds that could be manipulated and used in compositions that the machine could play back. At the 1929 Paris Exposition, the Coupleaux-Givelet "Automatically Operating Instrument of the Electric Oscillation Type" was a prototype organ-like device that could play up to four tones at once, and was fed by a player-piano-like paper roll that composers could encode with holes specifying different parameters of sound, like pitch, tone color, and articulation. After the Exposition, little more was heard of it.

The convoluted lengths some inventors went to was typified in the Hanert Electrical Orchestra, developed in 1945 for the Hammond Organ Company. The device involved a 60-foot-long table where composers could place cards marked with graphite pencil notations that conducted electricity. A scanner moving along the table read the cards and sent the data to a roomful of machinery that converted the scribblings into sounds. Complex control over sound was possible, and changes could be made by simply erasing and rewriting the pencil marks. The device was intended to allow composers to hear their work instantly and not have to wait months for a live orchestra to perform it.

The 1946 "Tone Synthesizer" from Bell Labs was yet another entry in the race, though its purpose was directed more toward theoretical analysis of sounds. The Composer-Tron, invented in the early 1950s, was an apparatus that "read" patterns drawn with a grease pencil on the surface of a television-like cathode ray tube and translated them into sound. One method was developed by the British electronic composer and cofounder of the BBC Radiophonic Workshop, Daphne Oram, in 1957. Her Oramics composition machine involved drawing shapes on 35 mm film that were read by photocells, translating the marks into sound.

Likely the strangest way of creating new electronic sounds was immortalized in the 1956 film *Forbidden Planet*. The soundtrack composers, husband and wife, Louis and Bebe Barron, were experimenters who made abstract sound fragments for the movie in their living room with three tape recorders, and circuits Louis had built himself. The couple treated their circuits like a menagerie of living creatures, allowing each to voice its individual sounds as it lived out a kind of biological life cycle, without interference, through cybernetic entropy. The Barrons recorded each unique circuit in its long death throes, and Louis explained, "these circuits are as if a living thing were crying out, expressing itself" (Ted Greenwald, "The Self-Destructing Modules Behind Revolutionary 1956 Soundtrack of Forbidden Planet," *effectrode thermionic*, Effectrode.com). Bebe recalled, "They would shriek and coo. . . . They would start out and reach a kind of climax, and then they would die and you could never resurrect them" (Bebe Barron, "Making Music for Forbidden Planet," in *Projections 7: Filmmakers on Film-making* ed. John Boorman and Walter Donohue [London: Faber and Faber, 1997], 256). The Barrons' soundtrack, groundbreaking as the first completely electronic score for a feature film, fit perfectly with the realm of rockets, alien planets, and robots that the movie portrayed, but the sounds had been created in a random, undirected way, so none of them could be recreated.

Time magazine rallied its readers to the new sonic experience, declaring, "American listeners have a chance to feast their ears on their native brand of electronic composition on the sound track of M-G-M's science-fiction extravaganza, *Forbidden Planet*" ("Music of the Future," *Time*, July 2, 1956, p. 36). For the broader public in 1956, this was the most "popular" any electronic music would get.

Bob himself liked to talk about many of these earlier attempts at making electronic music. His extensive knowledge of these inventors and their methods surfaced in interviews he gave, and he delighted in offering his standard slide lecture on these pioneering instruments and their creators.

10. Robert K. Plume, "Electronic Device Can Duplicate Every Sound," *New York Times* (February 1, 1955), 1.
11. Howard Taubman, "Synthesized Piano Music Found to Have Tone Matching Grand's," *New York Times* (February 1, 1955), 35.
12. Robert K. Plume, "Science in Review: Electronic Synthesizer Produces Good Music and May Later Imitate Human Speech," *New York Times* (February 6, 1955), E9.
13. Moog, Yale interview, 1979.
14. Joel Chadabe, *Electric Sound; The Past and Promise of Electronic Music* (Upper Saddle River, NJ: Prentice Hall, 1997), 141.
15. Pinch, Trocco, Moog interview, 1996.

16. An example of an exponential relationship in music is the octave. Taking the 440 vibrations per second that produce the note "A" (440 Herz), and doubling the vibrations to 880 per second, results in the "A" one octave higher. Doubling the vibrations again to 1,760 per second produces the "A" an octave above that, and so on.
17. Pinch, Trocco, Moog interview, 1996.
18. Terry Gross, *Fresh Air*, 2000.
19. Moog, Yale interview, 1979.
20. Robert Moog, "Music from Electrons," *Audiocraft* (June 1956), 16–19, 33.
21. Bob Moog, "The Development of Moog Synthesizers," typescript for speech delivered at the International Festival of Experimental Music, Bourges, France, June 1989. CIGM; Pinch, Trocco, Moog interview, 1996; Pinch, Trocco, Moog interview, 1997.
22. Alan Korwin, "Music Synthesis: Moog," *Musicians Classified* (November 1975), 21.
23. Moog, Yale interview, 1979.
24. *Moog: A Documentary Film by Hans Fjellestad*, directed by Hans Fjellestad (Los Angeles, 2004: ZU33), DVD.
25. Glinsky, Deutsch, 2011.
26. At this point in the development of Bob's prototype, he hadn't built a separate envelope generator module, but used the keyboard in conjunction with the VCA module to shape a sound. He explained, "The first keyboard we built used an organ keyboard mechanism, along with some circuitry that would open and close the voltage control amplifier every time you pressed a key, which made an envelope on the sound. You could adjust how fast the sound built up by holding the attack, and how fast the sound would decay by manipulating the decay. The envelope generator inside the keyboard opened up the voltage-controlled amplifier every time you pressed a key, and that is how the sound was shaped" (Ben Kettlewell, *Electronic Music Pioneers* (Vallejo, CA: ProMusic Press, 2002), 115).
27. Pinch, Trocco, Moog interview, 1996.
28. Fjellestad, *Moog*.
29. Doerschuk, "12 Who Count: Bob Moog," 99.
30. Fjellestad, *Moog*.
31. Glinsky, Deutsch, 2011.
32. Glinsky, Deutsch, 2011.
33. Moog Yale interview, 1979.
34. John Norton, "Moog Analyzes the Evolution of the Synthesizer," *PTM-World of Music* (November 1978), 22.
35. Glinsky, Shirleigh Moog, 2011.
36. Glinsky, Deutsch, 2011.
37. Chadabe, *Electric Sound*, 141-142.
38. Bob Moog, "The Abominatron," tape recorded verbal letter and demonstration, August 1964, issued as a digital track on *From Moog to Mac: A Retrospective; Electronic Music by Herbert Deutsch*, audio CD, 2007.
39. Pinch, Trocco, Moog interview, 1996.
40. Moog, "The Abominatron."

Chapter 8

1. Shirleigh Moog letter to Florence Moog, October 1, 1964. CIGM.
2. Shirleigh Moog letter to Florence Moog, October 1, 1964. CIGM.
3. Thomas, "Interview with Bob Moog," 28.
4. Connor Freff Cochran and Bob Moog, "The Rise and Fall of Moog Music; Shuffle Off to Buffalo," in *Vintage Synthesizers*, ed. Mark Vail (San Francisco: Miller Freeman, 2000), 39.
5. Thomas, "Interview with Bob Moog," 28.
6. On his prototype Bob did not label his modules VCO or VCA. The two VCOs were each labeled "Generator Module," and the two VCAs were each labeled "Amplifier Module."
7. Moog, Yale interview, 1979.
8. Jay Lee, "Interview: Robert Moog," *Polyphony* (January–February 1982), n.p.
9. Glinsky, Shirleigh Moog, 2011; Bob Moog, "The Development of Moog Synthesizers," 1989. CIGM.
10. "Day at Night interview with Alwin Nikolais," (November 29, 1974), https://www.youtube.com/watch?v=atmek4ra-UU.
11. Moog, Yale interview, 1979.
12. Thomas, "Interview with Bob Moog," 28.
13. Moog, Yale interview, 1979.
14. Bob Moog letter to Eric Siday, November 12, 1964. Eric Siday papers, JPB 00-4. Music Division, The New York Public Library for the Performing Arts.
15. Shirleigh Moog letter to Florence Moog, December 11, 1964. CIGM.
16. *Moog Music, 10th Anniversary Issue*, R. A. Moog Company (Fall–Winter 1964). CIGM.
17. *Moog Music, 10th Anniversary Issue*, R. A. Moog Company (Fall–Winter 1964). CIGM; *Moog Electronic Music Equipment,* product brochure, R. A. Moog Company, 1964. CIGM.
18. *Moog Music, 10th Anniversary Issue*, R. A. Moog Company (Fall–Winter 1964). CIGM.
19. *Moog Electronic Music Equipment,* product brochure, R. A. Moog Company, 1964. CIGM.
20. Glinsky, Shirleigh Moog, 2011.
21. Moog, Yale interview, 1979.
22. Glinsky, Moog interview, 1997.
23. Moog, Yale interview, 1979.
24. Shirleigh Moog letter to Florence Moog, December 23, 1964. CIGM.
25. Florence Moog letter to Bob Moog, December 30, 1964. CIGM.
26. Bob Moog letter to Florence Moog, January 5, 1965. MFA.
27. Moog, Yale interview, 1979.
28. Moog, Yale interview, 1979.
29. Shirleigh Moog letter to Florence Moog, March 15, 1965. CIGM.
30. Winston Grant Gray, *The Dance Theatre of Alwin Nikolais*, doctoral thesis, University of Utah (1967), 117.
31. Allen Hughes, "Work by Nikolais Introduced Here," *New York Times* (March 21, 1965), 85.

418   NOTES

32. Bob Moog letter to Shirleigh Moog, April 1, 1965. CIGM.
33. George Kelischek interview with Albert Glinsky, August 12, 2015 (hereafter, "Glinsky, Kelischek, 2015").
34. Bob Moog letter to Shirleigh Moog, April 1, 1965. CIGM.

Chapter 9

1. Shirleigh Moog letter to Florence Moog, December 17, 1965. CIGM.
2. Pinch, Trocco, Moog interview, 1997.
3. Glinsky, Sear, 1997.
4. Walter Sear letter to Bob Moog, October 21, 1965. CBK.
5. Walter Sear letters to Bob Moog: September 17, 1965, CIGM; November 2, 1965, CIGM; November 13, 1965, CBK; December 2, 1965, CIGM; Bob Moog letters to Walter Sear: September 21, 1965, CBK; October 21, 1965, CIGM; October 28, 1965, CIGM; December 6, 1965, CBK.
6. *Electronic Music Composition-Performance Equipment; Short Form Catalog—1967*, R. A. Moog Co., 20.
7. Moog, Yale interview, 1979.
8. Glinsky, Shirleigh Moog, 2011.
9. Glinsky, Shirleigh Moog, 2011.
10. Bob Moog letter to Florence Moog, July 19, 1965. CIGM.
11. Glinsky, Bob Moog, 1997.
12. Allen Hughes, "Leaps and Cadenzas," *New York Times* (August 1, 1965), X10.
13. Bob Moog letter to Florence Moog, July 19, 1965. CIGM.
14. George Moog letter to Florence Moog, July 25, 1965. CIGM.
15. Shirleigh Moog letter to Florence Moog, June 6, 1965. CIGM.
16. Glinsky, Shirleigh Moog, 2011.
17. Glinsky, Deutsch, 2011.
18. Transcript of a review of the New York Improvisation Quartet by Paul Price, for the WNCN News and Public Affairs Department, September 27, 1965, broadcast over WNCN radio, September 28, 1965. Typescript. CIGM.
19. Fjellestad, *Moog*.
20. Moog, Yale interview, 1979.
21. Bob Moog letter to David Rothenberg, December 6, 1965. CIGM.
22. Shirleigh Moog letters to Florence Moog, November 22, 1965; December 17, 1965. CIGM.
23. Betty Friedan, *The Feminine Mystique* (New York: W. W. Norton, 1963, 50th anniversary edition, 2013).
24. Friedan, *The Feminine Mystique*, 5.
25. Friedan, *The Feminine Mystique*, 2.
26. Friedan, *The Feminine Mystique*, 9.
27. Shirleigh Moog, 2011; Shirleigh Moog letter to Florence Moog, December 17, 1965. CIGM.
28. Shirleigh Moog letters to Florence Moog, November 22, 1965; December 17, 1965. CIGM.

Chapter 10

1. David W. Bernstein, ed., *The San Francisco Tape Music Center: 1960s Counterculture and the Avant-Garde* (Berkeley: University of California Press, 2008), 62.
2. Appendix I, "Tape Music Center Studio Equipment," from San Francisco Tape Music Center application letter to the Rockefeller Foundation, May 20, 1965. Rockefeller Foundation records, projects, RG 1.2 (FA387), Box 413, Folder 3566, 1965.
3. "Grant in Aid to the San Francisco Tape Music Center, Incorporated," typescript letter, June 11, 1965, the Rockefeller Foundation. Rockefeller Foundation records, projects, RG 1.2 (FA387), Box 413, Folder 3566, 1965.
4. Chadabe, *Electric Sound*, 147.
5. Bernstein, *The San Francisco Tape Music Center*, 166, 114.
6. "Voltage-Controlled Electronic Music Modules," *Journal of the Audio Engineering Society* 13, no. 3 (July 1965), 200–206.
7. Bob Moog, "Memories of Raymond Scott," April 8, 2000. Archived in wayback machine at: Raymondscott.com/moog.html.
8. Raymond Scott had constructed a prototype sequencer as early as the spring of 1960, according to Irwin Chusid in an article on Scott's work. Chusid mentioned that Scott also built a second sequencer around 1961–62 that used uni-junction transistors. Herb Deutsch recalled seeing that device during a visit to Scott's laboratory in 1965. Speaking of Scott's sequencer, Bob told Chusid, "Scott was definitely in the forefront of developing the technology and in the forefront of using it commercially as a musician." (Irwin Chusid, "Raymond Scott's Push-Button Musical Universe," *Mix* (October 1993), 127, 129). In a written statement, Scott revealed that after Bob had seen the sequencer, he [Scott] had implored Bob not to compete with him by developing a sequencer of his own: "Bob Moog, who visited me occasionally at my lab on Long Island, was among the first to see and witness the performance of my UJT-Relay sequencer.... I was so secretive about my development activities—perhaps neurotically so—that I was always reminding Bob that he mustn't copy or reveal my sequencer work to anyone. I understand, now, my personal need for secrecy at that time. Electronic music for commercials and films was my living then—and I thought I had this great advantage—because it was my sequencer. Word naturally got around about the nature of what my device accomplished, but Bob Moog continued to be loyal. I must say Bob Moog is a most honorable person. He steadfastly refrained from embodying my sequencer in his equipment line until the sheer pressure of so many manufacturers using the sequencer forced him to compete. Yet, he used the simplest version, though he knew about my most advanced sequencer. Quite a gentleman, and a super talent besides" (Raymond Scott, ca. late 1970s, in an unaddressed letter found in his personal papers, quoted in Irwin Chusid and Jeff Winner, "Circle Machines and Sequencers: The Untold History of Raymond Scott's Electronica," www.raymondscott.net/em-article-2001).
9. Pinch and Trocco, *Analog Days*, 40.
10. Bernstein, *The San Francisco Tape Music Center*, 204.

11. "Trips Festival 1966 Documentary," The Rock Poster Society, posted on January 22, 2016, https//:trps.org/2016/01/22/trips-festival-1966-documentary/.
12. Glinsky, Sear, 1997.
13. Walter Sear letter to Bob Moog, December 14, 1967. CBK.
14. Bob Moog letter to Walter Sear, December 17, 1966. CIGM.
15. "Swurpledeewurpleddeezeech!," *Time* (November 4, 1966), 68.
16. Florence Moog letter to Shirleigh Moog, June 25, 1966. CIGM.
17. Bob Moog letter to Walter Sear, February 10, 1967. CIGM.
18. Bernstein, *The San Francisco Tape Music Center*, 173.
19. Paul Hertelendy, "Sound of Future at Mills Tape Center," *Oakland Tribune* (September 30, 1966), 22.
20. Pinch and Trocco, *Analog Days*, 50.
21. *Electronic Music Composition-Performance Equipment; Short Form Catalog—1967*, R. A. Moog Co., 20. CIGM.
22. Bob Moog typescript prepared for Dallas Arbiter Ltd., November 9, 1973. CIGM.
23. Moog, Yale interview, 1979; Terry Gross, *Fresh Air*, 2000.
24. Pinch, Trocco, Moog interview, 1996; Pinch, Trocco, Moog interview, 1997.
25. Chadabe, *Electric Sound*, 143.
26. Pinch, Trocco, Moog interview, 1996; Moog, Yale interview, 1979.
27. Pinch, Trocco, Moog interview, 1996; Moog, Yale interview, 1979; Steve Knezevich & Jamie Fraser, "Bob Moog: Scientific Method Man," Grand Royal (Spring/Summer 1996), 56.
28. Paul Beaver, resume of performance experience, ca. 1955. Typescript. Collection of the author.
29. Paul Beaver, biographical statement, ca. 1972. Typescript on Warner Bros. Records Inc. letterhead. Collection of the author.
30. Mick Houghton, *Becoming Elektra: The True Story of Jac Holzman's Visionary Record Label* (London: Jawbone Press, 2010), 10.
31. Jac Holzman interview with Albert Glinsky, February 17, 2015 (hereafter, "Glinsky, Holzman, 2015").
32. Moog, Yale interview, 1979.
33. Terry Gross, *Fresh Air*, 2000; Moog, Yale interview, 1979.
34. Pinch, Trocco, Moog interview, 1996; Pinch, Trocco, Moog interview, 1997.
35. Moog, Yale interview, 1979.
36. Pinch, Trocco, Moog interview, 1996.
37. Harvey Kubernik and Henry Kubernik, *A Perfect Haze: The Illustrated History of the Monterey International Pop Festival* (Santa Monica, CA: Santa Monica Press, 2011), 51.
38. Ken Lopez interview with Albert Glinsky, April 6, 2018 (hereafter, "Glinsky, Lopez, 2018").
39. Glinsky, Lopez, 2018.
40. Glinsky, Lopez, 2018.
41. Joe Fitzpatrick, "Monterey International Pop Festival," *Monterey Herald* (June 17, 1967), n.p.
42. Kubernik and Kubernik, *A Perfect Haze*, 211.
43. Kubernik and Kubernik, *A Perfect Haze*, 211.

Chapter 11

1. Walter Sear invoice to Bob Moog, February 2, 1968, CIGM; Walter Sear letter to Bob Moog, July 30, 1968. CBK.
2. Chadabe, *Electric Sound*, 148.
3. Sylvie Reice, "Swinging Set: Electric Circus!" *The Press Democrat*, Santa Rosa, CA (July 16, 1967), 29.
4. Martina Seeber, "Interview mit Alvin Curran," (November 2007), www.geraeuschen.de/3.html.
5. Bob Moog letter to Theodore Prounis, October 12, 1967. CIGM.
6. Bob Moog letter to Walter Sear, December 18, 1967. CBK.
7. Glinsky, Shirleigh Moog, 2011.
8. Quincy Jones, video interview, "Ironside," Television Academy Foundation, Archive of American Television, The Interviews, http://interviews.televisionacademy.com/shows/ironside#.
9. Ray Manzarek, *Light My Fire: My Life with the Doors* (New York: Berkeley, 1998), 256–257.
10. Richard Buskin, "Classic Tracks: The Doors 'Strange Days,'" *Sound on Sound* (December 2003), n.p.
11. Jerry Hopkins, "The Rolling Stone Interview: Jim Morrison," *Rolling Stone* (July 26, 1969), n.p.
12. Gerry Goffin and Carole King, "Star Collector," 1967, recorded by the Monkees on their album *Pisces, Aquarius, Capricorn, & Jones Ltd.*, 1967.
13. Michael Nesmith, "Daily Nightly," recorded by the Monkees on their album *Pisces, Aquarius, Capricorn, & Jones Ltd.*, 1967.
14. N.A., "A Long Time Comin'," *Billboard* (March 30, 1968), 69.
15. Shirleigh Moog letter to Florence Moog, May 5, 1968. CIGM.
16. "Consumer Electronics: Moog Music," *Electronics Review* (March 4, 1968), 42.
17. Walter Sear letter to Bob Moog, March 5, 1968. CBK.
18. Merle Goldberg, "Robert A. Moog," *Eye* magazine (March 1968), 24.
19. J. Kirk Sale and Ben Apfelbaum, "Report from Teeny-Boppersville; They've Got the Generation Gap Blues," *New York Times* (May 28, 1967), 81.
20. Harold C. Schonberg, "The New Age Is Coming," *New York Times* (January 14, 1968), D15.
21. Shirleigh Moog letter to Florence Moog, December 8, 1967. CIGM.
22. "Moog Music," *Electronics* (March 4, 1968), 41–42.
23. Howard Junker, "Electronic Music—Wiggy," *Newsweek* (May 22, 1967), 98–99.
24. Pinch, Trocco, Moog interview, 1996
25. Alan Korwin, "Music Synthesis: Moog," 25.
26. Glinsky, Shirleigh Moog, 2011.

Chapter 12

1. Donal Henahan, "Noel Plugged in at Carnegie Hall," *New York Times* (December 27, 1967), 44.

2. Harold C. Schonberg, "The New Age Is Coming," *New York Times* (January 14, 1968), D15.
3. Donal Henahan, "The Avant-Groove: We're All in It," *New York Times* (July 7, 1968), D11.
4. Theodore Strongin, "Contemporary Classical Disks Rising," *New York Times* (December 20, 1967), 50.
5. Andrew Rudin interview with Albert Glinsky, December 23, 2018 (hereafter, "Glinsky, Rudin, 2018").
6. Freff Cochran and Moog, "The Rise and Fall of Moog Music," 39.
7. Susan Reed, "After a Sex Change and Several Eclipses, Wendy Carlos Treads a New Digital Moonscape," *People* (July 1, 1985), 83.
8. Wendy Carlos, "Looking Back on Synthesized Bach," liner notes, *Switched-On Boxed Set; Book One: New Notes*, 16–17.
9. Reed, "After a Sex Change and Several Eclipses," 83.
10. Carlos, *Switched-On Boxed Set, Book One*, 84–85.
11. Carlos, *Switched-On Boxed Set, Book One*, 84–85.
12. Benjamin Folkman, liner notes, *Switched-On Bach*, vinyl recording, 1968.
13. Bob Moog letter to Shirley Moog, January 25, 1958. CIGM.
14. Andy Blinx, "Wendy Carlos: From Bach to the Future," *Grand Royal* (Spring–Summer 1996), 60.
15. Walter Sear letter to Bob Moog, August 1968. CBK.
16. Walter Sear letter to Ray Hemming, August 26, 1969. CBK.
17. Glinsky, Sear, 1997.
18. While Bernie Krause has made a unique contribution to the history of the Moog synthesizer, the point at which he entered the Moog timeline needs to be amended. To set the record straight, it's helpful to start with Krause's own testimony. In his Preface to *The Nonesuch Guide to Electronic Music*, published in 1968, Krause writes, "In late 1967, while I was studying with Paul Beaver in Los Angeles, California, the thought occurred to me to spell out, for a larger audience, a short introduction to electronic music based upon his seminars." This statement appears to date Krause's early exposure to the Moog to late 1967, at which point he was still "studying with Paul Beaver." Many published accounts, however, have him as a participant in such projects earlier that year as *The Zodiac Cosmic Sounds* recording session, the Moog sales booth at the Monterey Pop Festival, and the recording session for the Doors' *Strange Days* album, among others. None of the interviews conducted for this book—or any of the contemporaneous documents—substantiates any of those claims. Krause has described a period of a year leading up to Monterey Pop in June 1967, during which he and Paul Beaver allegedly had little luck in convincing Hollywood film and recording producers to use the Moog. But the first appearance of the Moog on the West Coast was at the AES conference in April 1967, when Paul alone (according to Bob Moog's account, and many others) first encountered the instrument. The Moog was instantly embraced by the Hollywood music and film industries, and a mere seven weeks later Paul was taking orders for Moog modulars at Monterey Pop. In other words, the discouraging year Bernie described—which would have culminated at Monterey Pop—does not fit within the historical timeline. Krause has also said that he and Paul Beaver first saw the Moog on a trip to Trumansburg. In his article, "Paul Beaver: Analog Synthesist Extraordinare," published in the journal *Film Music 2* (2004),

Warren M. Sherk, in footnote 31, states, "Bernie Krause recalls traveling with Beaver to Trumansburg, New York, around 1966 to Robert Moog's 'lab barn' where Moog pushed the instrument off a table to demonstrate its durability (Bernie Krause, personal communication, September 2, 1997). Moog does not remember meeting Beaver prior to the 1967 AES convention (Robert Moog, personal communication, September 3, 1997)." (Warren M. Sherk, "Paul Beaver: Analog Synthesist Extraordinaire," in Claudia Gorbma and Warren M. Sherk, eds., *Film Music 2: History, Theory, Practice* (Sherman Oaks, CA: Film Music Society, 2004), 140.) Krause has also declared that after he and Paul visited Trumansburg, they combined their savings to purchase their own Moog for $15,000. Besides the fact that the most expensive Moog at the time would have cost less than half that figure, sales records only indicate a purchase of an instrument in early 1968, by Paul Beaver alone. Oral testimony is certainly a starting point for reconstructing chronology, but it is notoriously slippery—memories fade, facts become blurred—and must always be evaluated against other records. In this case, further corroborating evidence from sales records, correspondence, interviews, and contemporaneous newspaper accounts—too voluminous to include here—requires a correction of these stories, which have continued to circulate in otherwise reputable publications and books.

19. Glinsky, Holzman, 2015.
20. Glinsky, Holzman, 2015.
21. Paul Beaver and Bernard L. Krause, *The Nonesuch Guide to Electronic Music*, Nonesuch, HC-73018, 1968.
22. Glinsky, Holzman, 2015.
23. Warren M. Sherk, "Paul Beaver: Analog Synthesist Extraordinaire," in Claudia Gorbma and Warren M. Sherk eds., *Film Music 2: History, Theory, Practice* (Sherman Oaks, CA: Film Music Society, 2004), 135.
24. Freff Cochran and Moog, "The Rise and Fall of Moog Music," 41.
25. Freff Cochran and Moog, "The Rise and Fall of Moog Music," 41.
26. Freff Cochran and Moog, "The Rise and Fall of Moog Music," 41.
27. "Columbia Switches On At Party for Three New LPs," *Record World* (December 21, 1968), 6.
28. Freff Cochran and Moog, "The Rise and Fall of Moog Music," 41.
29. John McClure, "It's Not a Synthetic Anything, It's a Real Moog," news release, Columbia Records, ca. 1969.
30. Donal Henahan, "Switching On to Mock Bach," *New York Times* (November 3, 1968), 26D.
31. Carlos, *Switched-On Boxed Set, Book Two*, 25.
32. Gene Lees, "The Electronic Bach: Johann Sebastian in a Wild, Wild Breakthrough," *Hi Fidelity* (December 1968), n.p.
33. Donal Henahan, "Mark II is Dead, Long Live the Moog!" *New York Times* (December 11, 1968), 56.

Chapter 13

1. Harold C. Schonberg, "A Merry Time with the Moog?" *New York Times* (February 16, 1969), D17.
2. Pinch, Trocco, Moog interview, 1996.

3. "Electronic Synthesizer: Produces Unlimited Sounds," *Syracuse Herald-American* (December 8, 1968), 40.
4. "Electronic Synthesizer: Produces Unlimited Sounds," 40.
5. Herbert Kupferberg, "Symphony by Synthesizer: Mr. Moog and His Monster Synthesizer," *National Observer* (July 21, 1969), 16.
6. Jon Weiss interview with Albert Glinsky, December 5, 2016 (hereafter, "Glinsky, Weiss, 2016").
7. Pinch and Trocco, *Analog Days*, 61.
8. Andy Davis, liner notes for Jackie Lomax album, *Is This What You Want?*, Apple Records, 1969.
9. Bernie Krause, *Into a Wild Sanctuary* (Berkeley: Heyday Books, 1998), 62.
10. Krause, *Into a Wild Sanctuary*, 65.
11. Krause, *Into a Wild Sanctuary*, 66.
12. Krause, *Into a Wild Sanctuary*, 67.
13. Krause, *Into a Wild Sanctuary*, 67.
14. Marc Shapiro, *Behind Sad Eyes: The Life of George Harrison* (New York: St. Martin's Press, 2002), 92.
15. George Harrison, *Electronic Sound* (1968). Remastered, 2014. Quoted in 2014 liner notes by Dhani Harrison, n.p.
16. Arthur Bell, "Playboy Interview: Wendy/Walter Carlos," *Playboy* (May 1979), 100.
17. Master telecast report, *Today Show*, NBC television network, February 5, 1969. Typescript. Moving Image Section, Library of Congress.
18. Leonard Bernstein, New York Philharmonic Young People's Concert, "Bach Transmogrified." Video of April 27, 1969, broadcast over the CBS television network. https://www.youtube.com/watch?v=cPjva0C5_Cc%t=1239s.
19. Robert T. Jones, "Children Served Bach a la Moog," *New York Times* (February 10, 1969), 43.
20. *The Electric Eclectics of Dick Hyman*, liner notes, Command Records, 1969.
21. Walter Sear letter to Bob Moog, May 15, 1968. CBK.
22. Gershon Kingsley interview with Albert Glinsky, August 20, 2011 (hereafter, "Glinsky, Kingsley, 2011").
23. "Religioso Rock Scores in Special Service at Temple Rodeph Sholom," *Variety* (April 16, 1969), n.p.
24. "'Shabbat-Now' Service to Be Performed at Sharey Tefilo," *The Jewish News*, Newark, NJ (April 25, 1969), n.p.
25. Glinsky, Kingsley, 2011.
26. Gene Zumchak interview with Albert Glinsky, February 28, 2012 (hereafter, "Glinsky, Zumchak, 2012").
27. Glinsky, Zumchak, 2012.
28. Bill Hemsath interview with Albert Glinsky, March 19, 2016 (hereafter, "Glinsky, Hemsath, 2016").
29. Elva Holman, "Despite Disabilities, Employees Performed Useful Work," *Ithaca Journal* (August 9, 1969), 7.
30. David Borden interview with Albert Glinsky, March 28–29, 2015 (hereafter, "Glinsky, Borden, 2015").

31. Glinsky, Borden, 2015.
32. Glinsky, Borden, 2015.
33. Glinsky, Hemsath, 2016; Glinsky, Borden, 2015.
34. Glinsky, Borden, 2015.
35. Glinsky, Borden, 2015.
36. Glinsky, Hemsath, 2016.

Chapter 14

1. Featurette: *The Music Man: Mort Garson*. From DVD of film, *Do Not Disturb, 1965*. Cinema Classics Collection, 20th Century Fox, 2007.
2. Karen Monson, "Mort Garson Becomes the First Space-Age Composer," *Los Angeles Times* (July 16, 1969), Part IV: 1, 18.
3. Transcript of communication between Apollo 11 crew and Mission Control, Day 7, Apollo 11 mission, https://www.history.nasa.gov/afj/ap11fj/23day7-tv-food-prep.html.
4. Patricia Nordheimer, "Moog Concert Is Enjoyed," *Ithaca Journal* (August 7, 1969), 12.
5. Hilda Murphy, "Robert Moog Has Arrived," *Free Press*, Trumansburg (March 13, 1969), 3.
6. Glinsky, Borden, 2015.
7. Meg Swansen interview with Albert Glinsky, September 22, 2016 (hereafter, "Glinsky, Swansen, 2016").
8. Glinsky, Swansen, 2016.
9. Shirleigh Moog letter to Florence Moog, August 21, 1969. CIGM.
10. David Borden, "Technique, Good Taste, and Hard Work." Unpublished written recollection (April 4, 2019). Courtesy David Borden (hereafter, "Borden, 'Technique, Good Taste'").
11. Nordheimer, "Moog Concert Is Enjoyed," 12.
12. Borden, "Technique, Good Taste."
13. Bill Landis, *Anger: The Unauthorized Biography of Kenneth Anger* (New York: Harper Perennial, 1995), 170.
14. Mark Lewisohn, *The Complete Beatles Recording Sessions: The Official Story of the Abbey Road Years: 1962–1970* (New York: Sterling, 2000), 185.
15. Randy Lewis, "The Monkees' Moog Synth: From John Lennon to Bobby Sherman," *Pop & Hiss, the L.A. Times Music Blog*, September 25, 2009, latimesblog.latimes.com/music_blog/2009/09/micky-dolenz-moog-synth-from-john-lennon-to-bobby-sherman.html.
16. George Harrison, John Lennon, Paul McCartney, Ringo Starr, *The Beatles Anthology* (San Francisco: Chronicle Books, 2000), 340.
17. Harrison, Lennon, McCartney, Starr, *The Beatles Anthology*, 340.
18. Harrison, Lennon, McCartney, Starr, *The Beatles Anthology*, 340.
19. Geoff Emerick and Howard Massey, *Here, There and Everywhere: My Life Recording the Music of THE BEATLES* (New York: Gotham Books, 2006), 300.
20. Harrison, Lennon, McCartney, Starr, *The Beatles Anthology*, 340.

21. George Martin, liner notes for *Ragnarök; Electronic Funk by Paul Beaver and Bernie L. Krause*, vinyl recording, Limelight, 1969.
22. Kupferberg, "Symphony by Synthesizer," 16.
23. Pinch and Trocco, *Analog Days*, 152.
24. "Moog España," *Record World* (August 2, 1969), 12.
25. "Special Merit Picks," *Billboard* (July 12, 1969), 63-a.
26. "Plugged in Pop," *Record World* (August 30, 1969), 16.
27. "Special Merit Picks," *Billboard* (August 30, 1969), 52.
28. Bob Moog letter to Florence Moog, June 5, 1969. CIGM.
29. Donal Henahan, "Is Everybody Going to the Moog?" *New York Times* (August 24, 1969), D 28, D 15.
30. Henahan, "Is Everybody Going to the Moog?" D15.
31. Henahan, "Is Everybody Going to the Moog?" D15.
32. Walter Sear letter to Ray Hemming, August 26, 1969. CIGM.
33. Bob Moog letter to Walter Sear, April 4, 1969. CBK.
34. Walter Sear memo to Bob Moog, ca. January 17, 1969. CBK.
35. "An AFM Ban on the Moog Synthesizer?" *Rolling Stone* (April 19, 1969), 10.
36. Bob Moog lecture, Hofstra University, February 1, 1979. OHV 213 a-c. Major Figures in American Music, Oral History of American Music, in the Music Library of Yale University.
37. "An AFM Ban on the Moog Synthesizer?" 10.
38. Richard Freedman, "Synthesizing Johann S. Bach," *Life Magazine* (January 24, 1969), n.p.
39. "Electronic Marvel Called Moog Produces Sounds of a Symphony," *UPI/Springfield Union* (August 25, 1969), n.p.
40. Kupferberg, "Symphony by Synthesizer," 16.
41. Henahan, "Is Everybody Going to the Moog?" D15.
42. Henahan, "Is Everybody Going to the Moog?" D28.
43. Walter Sear letter to Ray Hemming, August 27, 1969. CBK.
44. Don Fleming, "Don Fleming on the Prolific Career of Walter Sear," *Grand Royal* (Spring–Summer 1996), 67.
45. Steve Guttenberg, "Walter Sear's Analog Rules," *Stereophile.com* (March 27, 2005), http://www.stereophile.com/interviews/305sears/index.html.

Chapter 15

1. Glinsky, Moog interview, 1997.
2. Pinch, Trocco, Moog interview, 1997.
3. Glinsky, Shirleigh Moog, 2011.
4. Glinsky, Deutsch, 2011.
5. Edward Bland letter to Robert Moog, August 7, 1969. The Museum of Modern Art archives.

6. Glinsky, Sear, 1997.
7. Don Heckman, "Four Moogs in a Garden," *Downbeat* (October 16, 1969), n.p.
8. Pinch, Trocco, Moog interview, 1996; Pinch, Trocco, Moog interview, 1997.
9. Allen Hughes, "Moog Approves of Moog-Made Jazz," *New York Times* (August 29, 1969), 24.
10. Pinch, Trocco, Moog interview, 1997.
11. "'Socket to Me, Baby' Is Theme of Moog's Synthesizer Concert," *Variety* (September 3, 1969), n.p.
12. Bertram Stanleigh, "Moog Jazz in the Garden," *Audio* (November 1969), 98.
13. "'Socket to Me, Baby' Is Theme of Moog's Synthesizer Concert," n.p.
14. Pinch, Trocco, Moog interview, 1997.
15. Glinsky, Deutsch, 2011.
16. Hughes, "Moog Approves of Moog-Made Jazz," 24.
17. Ron Dobrin, "Moog Music Blows Fuses At Museum," *New York Post* (August 29, 1969), n.p.
18. "'Socket to Me, Baby' Is Theme of Moog's Synthesizer Concert," n.p.
19. Dobrin, "Moog Music Blows Fuses At Museum," n.p.
20. Stanleigh, "Moog Jazz in the Garden," 98.
21. Hughes, "Moog Approves of Moog-Made Jazz," 24.
22. Herb Deutsch interview with Albert Glinsky, August 25, 1997 (hereafter, "Glinsky, Deutsch, 1997").
23. Heckman, "Four Moogs in a Garden," n.p.
24. Edmund O. Ward, "Records," *Rolling Stone* (May 3, 1969), 27.
25. Mike Gross, "Moog the Medium as Cos. Get Electronic Message," *Billboard* (July 26, 1969), 1.
26. "Electronic Marvel Called Moog Produces Sounds of a Symphony," n.p.
27. Frank Peters, "Moog Music Is Here to Stay," *St. Louis Post-Dispatch* (September 7, 1969), 5C.
28. Stewart Brand, *Whole Earth Catalog: Access to Tools* (Menlo Park, CA: Portola Institute, 1970), 79.
29. Nicholas von Hoffman, "A Book to Build Your World With," *San Francisco Examiner* (July 20, 1969), 5.
30. R. A. Moog, Inc., product brochure, October 1969.
31. John Peck, "Moog Plans to Build Manufacturing Plant," *Ithaca Journal* (September 18, 1969), 19.
32. John S. Wilson, "Two Concert Novelties: Moog and Topless," *New York Times* (November 10, 1969), 53.
33. Walter Sear memo to Al Padorr, November 10, 1969. CIGM.
34. Bell, "Playboy Interview: Wendy/Walter Carlos," 100.
35. Donal Henahan, "A Tale of a Man and a Moog," *New York Times* (October 5, 1969), 14.
36. Mark Voger, *Groovy: When Flower Power Bloomed in Pop Culture* (Raleigh, NC: TwoMorrows, 2017), 146.
37. Doug McKechnie interview with Albert Glinsky, January 27, 2015 (hereafter, "Glinsky, McKechnie, 2015").

38. John Burks, "In the Aftermath of Altamont," *Rolling Stone* (February 7, 1970), n.p.
39. Harrison E. Salisbury, ed., "Arts in the 60's: Coming to Terms With Society and Its Woes," *New York Times* (December 30, 1969), 20.

Chapter 16

1. Walter Sear letter to Paul Beaver, November 26, 1969. CBK.
2. Edmund O. Ward, "Records," *Rolling Stone* (May 3, 1969), 27.
3. Bob Moog letter to Walter Sear, April 4, 1969. CBK.
4. Walter Sear letter to Bob Moog, September 2, 1969. CBK.
5. Al Padorr memo to R. A. Moog distributors and representatives, November 5, 1969. CIGM.
6. Paul Beaver letter to Bob Moog, November 20, 1969. CBK.
7. Jim Scott interview with Albert Glinsky, June 15, 2016 (hereafter, "Glinsky, Scott, 2016").
8. Glinsky, Scott, 2016.
9. Glinsky, Scott, 2016.
10. Glinsky, Scott, 2016.
11. Glinsky, Hemsath, 2016.
12. Glinsky, Scott, 2016.
13. Glinsky, Scott, 2016.
14. Mary Campbell, "It's Called a Moog It Plays Music," *AP Newswire* (September 27, 1969), n.p.
15. Featurette: *The Music Man: Mort Garson*.
16. "A Man and His Moog Make The New Sounds of Music," *Long Island Press* (November 29, 1970), n.p.
17. "Moog Moves Market Film," *Sunday Standard-Times*, New Bedford, MA (April 5, 1970), n.p.
18. Glinsky, Zumchak, 2012.
19. Glinsky, Hemsath, 2016.
20. Glinsky, Hemsath, 2016.
21. Glinsky, Hemsath, 2016.
22. Bill Hemsath email to Michelle Moog-Kousa, forwarded to the author by Michelle Moog-Kousa, January 29, 2016.
23. Glinsky, Hemsath, 2016.
24. Pinch, Trocco, Moog interview, 1997.
25. Glinsky, Hemsath, 2016.
26. Glinsky, Hemsath, 2016.
27. Jim Scott, "The Development of the Minimoog," unpublished manuscript (May 1999). Courtesy Jim Scott (hereafter, "Scott, The Development of the Minimoog").
28. Ian Dove, "Mini-Moog to Be Unveiled," *Billboard* (January 24, 1970), 1, 98.
29. Bob Moog letter to Tom Montgomery, February 19, 1970. CIGM.

30. Glinsky, Shirleigh Moog, 2011.
31. Glinsky, Shirleigh Moog, 2011.
32. Glinsky, Shirleigh Moog, 2011.
33. Glinsky, Shirleigh Moog, 2011.
34. Rebecca Kluchin, *Fit to Be Tied: Sterilization and Reproductive Rights in America, 1950–1980* (New Brunswick, NJ: Rutgers University Press, 2010), 50.
35. Glinsky, Shirleigh Moog, 2011.
36. Bob Moog letter to Florence Moog, March 22, 1971. CIGM.
37. Florence Moog letter to Bob Moog, April 4, 1971. CIGM.
38. Florence Moog letter to Bob Moog, April 4, 1971. CIGM.
39. Pinch, Trocco, Moog interview, 1996.
40. Moog, Yale interview, 1979.

Chapter 17

1. Dave Luce interview with Albert Glinsky, June 26, 2016 (hereafter, "Glinsky, Luce, 2016").
2. David and Becky Van Koevering interview with Albert Glinsky, July 28–29, 2012 (hereafter, "Glinsky, Van Koevering, 2012").
3. "An Open Invitation to Music Educators, Composers, and Performers," R. A. Moog ad, *Music Educators Journal* (1969), 26.
4. Glinsky, Van Koevering, 2012.
5. Glinsky, Van Koevering, 2012.
6. Glinsky, Kingsley, 2011.
7. Glinsky, Van Koevering, 2012.
8. Glinsky, Van Koevering, 2012.
9. Gershon Kingsley's "First Moog Quartet," program booklet, Carnegie Hall, January 30, 1970. Collection of Gershon Kingsley.
10. "Cool Hands at Composing for the Moog," *The Daily Freeman*, Kingston, NY (January 24, 1970), 16.
11. Harriet Johnson, "Words and Music: Four Moogs Make Carnegie Debut," *New York Post* (January 31, 1970), n.p.
12. Glinsky, Van Koevering, 2012.
13. Winthrop Sargeant, "Musical Events," *The New Yorker* (February 7, 1970), 80.
14. Peter G. Davis, "Moogists Try On Bach and Beatles," *New York Times* (January 31, 1970), 36.
15. Glinsky, Van Koevering, 2012.
16. Glinsky, Van Koevering, 2012.
17. Glinsky, Van Koevering, 2012.
18. Keith Emerson, *Pictures of an Exhibitionist* (London: John Blake, 2004), 166.
19. Emerson, *Pictures of an Exhibitionist*, 167.
20. Mike Vickers gave British television viewers their first introduction to the Moog synthesizer when he presented a five-minute demonstration of the modular system with

explanatory narration by Derek Cooper, on the BBC 1 program *Tomorrow's World*, on September 30, 1969.
21. Emerson, *Pictures of an Exhibitionist*, 176.
22. Ray Hammond, "Emerson/Moog," *Instrumental Musician and Recording World* (June 1975), 7.
23. Emerson, *Pictures of an Exhibitionist*, 167.
24. Emerson, *Pictures of an Exhibitionist*, 167.
25. Martyn Hanson, *Hang On to a Dream: The Story of the Nice* (London: Forule Classics, 2014), 145.
26. Richard Green, "Nice Versatility Is Limitless," *New Musical Express* (February 14, 1970), n.p.
27. Emerson, *Pictures of an Exhibitionist*, 168.
28. Emerson, *Pictures of an Exhibitionist*, 180.
29. Emerson, *Pictures of an Exhibitionist*, 180.
30. Emerson, *Pictures of an Exhibitionist*, 180.
31. Carl Wiser, "Greg Lake of Emerson, Lake & Palmer," Songfacts.com. May 2, 2013. https://www.songfacts.com/blog/interviews/greg-lake-of-emerson-lake-palmer.
32. Emerson, *Pictures of an Exhibitionist*, 180–181.
33. George Forrester, Martyn Hanson, and Frank Askew, *Emerson, Lake & Palme: The Show That Never Ends . . .* (London: Foruli, 2013), 63.
34. "ELP Album: Track-by-Track Comment by Bass-Player Greg Lake," *Melody Maker* (November 28, 1970), 35.
35. Emerson, *Pictures of an Exhibitionist*, 181; Simon Barrett, "An Interview with Keith Emerson," *Blogger News Network*, August 26, 2007, http://www.bloggernews.net/an-interview-with-keith-emerson/.
36. Emerson, *Pictures of an Exhibitionist*, 185.
37. Emerson, *Pictures of an Exhibitionist*, 186.
38. Mark Beaumont, "'They Booed Joni Mitchell and Threw S*** at Jimi Hendrix': The Amazing Story of the 1970 Isle of Wight Festival," *Independent* (August 13, 2020), https://www.independent.co.uk/arts-entertainment/music/features/isle-of-wight-festival-history-1970-lineup-bob-dylan-jimi-hendrix-leonard-cohen-joni-mitchell-a9681921.html.
39. Emerson, *Pictures of an Exhibitionist*, 186–187.
40. Emerson, *Pictures of an Exhibitionist*, 187.
41. Edward Macan, *Endless Enigma: A Musical Biography of Emerson, Lake & Palmer* (Chicago: Open Court, 2006), 109.
42. Emerson, *Pictures of an Exhibitionist*, 188.
43. Fred J. Solowey, "Berrigan Appears at Fest: Continues to Elude the FBI," *Cornell Daily Sun* (April 20, 1970), 1.
44. Joseph Masci, "Festival Offers Speeches and Music to Capacity Crowd in Barton," *Cornell Daily Sun* (April 20, 1970), 16.
45. Patricia Nordheimer, "Just What Did Happen at Berrigan Weekend?," *Ithaca Journal* (April 20, 1970), 10.
46. Judith Horstman, "Electronic Music. . . ." *Ithaca Journal* (April 20, 1970), 8.
47. Nordheimer, "Just What Did Happen at Berrigan Weekend?," 10.

NOTES 431

48. John Hinds, "Robert Moog Conversation with John Hinds—September 9, 1991—Stanford, CA," *Sun Ra Research* (Millbrae, CA: Omnipress, 1998), 42–43.
49. John F. Szwed, *Space Is the Place: The Lives and Times of Sun Ra* (New York: Pantheon Books, 1998), 274.
50. Tam Fiofori, "Moog Modulations: A Symposium, *Downbeat* (July 23, 1970), 34.
51. Trevor Pinch and Frank Trocco, "The Social Construction of the Early Electronic Music Synthesizer," in Hans-Joachim Braun ed., *Music and Technology in the 20th Century* (Frankfurt: Wolke Verlag, 2000), 77–79.
52. Lee Santa interview with Albert Glinsky, March 25, 2018.
53. "Mini-Moog to Be Unveiled at Museum Concert," *Billboard* (July 11, 1970), 8.
54. Walter Sear letter to Al Padorr, July 7, 1970. CBK.
55. Dick Hyman interview with Albert Glinsky, August 17, 2016.
56. John S. Wilson, "Hyman, at Museum, Gives Moog Synthesizer Concert," *New York Times* (August 20, 1970), 21.
57. Wilson, "Hyman, at Museum, Gives Moog Synthesizer Concert," 21.

Chapter 18

1. *Tomorrow's World*, BBC 1, London, March 6, 1968.
2. Suzanne Ciani, interview with Albert Glinsky, July 12, 2016 (hereafter, "Glinsky, Ciani, 2016").
3. Chadabe, *Electric Sound*, 286.
4. Chadabe, *Electric Sound*, 287.
5. Tod Dockstader, "The Wild Bull: a Composition for Electronic-Music Synthesizer by Morton Subotnick," *The Musical Quarterly* 55, no. 1 (January 1969), 136.
6. Thomas Willis, "Critic Meets Putney, Makes a Friend, Takes Him to Church," *Chicago Tribune* (June 14, 1970), Section 5: 2.
7. Glinsky, Hemsath, 2016.
8. Jim Scott email to author, November 20, 2016.
9. Glinsky, Hemsath, 2016.
10. Scott, "The Development of the Minimoog."
11. Notes on Staff Meeting, September 10, 1970. Bob Moog Desk Notebook (July 2, 1969–December, 1971). CIGM.
12. Jim Scott unpublished manuscript of annotated Minimoog information, emailed to author, November 10, 2016. Courtesy Jim Scott.
13. Bob Moog, "Minimoog; The Ultimate in Antique Analog?," in *Vintage Synthesizers*, 159.
14. Glinsky, Hemsath, 2016.
15. Glinsky, Hemsath, 2016.
16. Jim Scott email to author, April 30, 2019.
17. Program, "Thirty-Ninth Convention . . . Exhibition of Professional Products . . . Audio Engineering Society, October 12–15, 1970," Session B: Electronic Music. Courtesy William McQuaide, Audio Engineering Society.

18. Program, AES, October 12–15, 1970.
19. Bob Moog letter to Verne Siegel, March 6, 1970. CIGM.
20. "Tonus Develops ARP Unit," *Billboard* (April 11, 1970), 4.
21. Carol Off interview with David Friend, *As It Happens*, CBC Radio (January 17, 2019), transcript. https://www.cbc.ca/radio/asithappens/as-it-happens-thursday-edition-1.4981984/how-alan-r-pearlman-revolutionized-the-music-industry-with-his-arp-synthesizers-1.4981944.

    Interestingly, in a talk at the 1989 Bourges Festival, Bob maintained that his original oscillators, designed for Herb's first prototype, happened to be triggered by a traditional musical keyboard, but that the intent was never to perfect them for stable intonation because traditional tonal music was not the goal of their collaborative work: "The notion that the oscillators would be accurate and stable enough for a keyboard to be used to play equally-tempered scales never really occurred to us. For Herb's purpose, we were building a system for the systematic manipulation of timbre, not a system to build melodic or harmonic structures" (Bob Moog, transcript of speech delivered on June 15, 1989, at the International Festival of Experimental Music, Bourges, France. Typescript, p. 4). This remark, of course, begs the question of why Bob framed his breakthrough realization of 1964 in terms of the musical interval ratios that form the basis for the melodic and harmonic structures of Western music: "I'm not sure at which point I saw this clearly but musical parameters are exponentials. Pitch, you know—one octave is a factor of two. All musical intervals are ratios" (Pinch, Trocco, Moog interview, 1996). The implication that Bob designed a system based on the exponential ratios of Western music seems to contradict his later assertion that his first system for Herb was not intended for such purposes.

    In addition, in his first published description of his modular system, "Voltage-Controlled Electronic Music Modules," published in the July 1965 issue of the *AES Journal*, Bob states: "In order to be musically valuable, a voltage-controlled oscillator (VCO) should generate a fixed frequency ratio for a given control voltage change. . . . An equally tempered scale is produced by scanning the voltages of a series of equally spaced taps on a potentiometer divider." (Voltage-Controlled Electronic Music Modules," *Journal of the Audio Engineering Society* 13, no. 3 (July 1965), 200–201).

22. "Close Enounters of the ARP Kind: ARP 2500 Modular Analogue Synthesis System," *Sound on Sound* (August 1996), archived on the wayback machine, www.soundonsound.com/sos/1996_articles/aug96/arp2500.html.
23. Ernest Leogrande, "The $155-an-Hour Ego Trip," *New York Daily News* (September 4, 1970), 6.
24. Ad for ARP Synthesizer, *Journal of the Audio Engineering Society* 18, no. 2 (April 1970), 187. Courtesy William McQuaide, Audio Engineering Society.
25. A.T., "Moog—Man and Machine," *Beat Instrumental* (December 1970), n.p.
26. Bob Moog letter to Shirleigh Moog, October 20, 1970. CIGM.
27. Bob Moog Desk Notebook, 1970. CIGM.
28. "MM Pollwinners Rock the Party of 1970," *Melody Maker* (September 26, 1970), 29.
29. Scott, "The Development of the Minimoog."
30. Glinsky, Hemsath, 2016.

31. Glinsky, Hemsath, 2016.
32. Glinsky, Hemsath, 2016.
33. Glinsky, Shirleigh Moog, 2011.
34. Pinch, Trocco, Moog interview, 1996.
35. Bob Moog Desk Notebook notation, October 26, 1970, from Desk Notebook (July 2, 1969–December 1971).
36. Pinch, Trocco, Moog interview, 1996.
37. Glinsky, Scott, 2016; Jim Scott, "The Mini D VCO Evolution; A Saga of Many Blunders, 1970–1977," unpublished manuscript, September 2019. Courtesy Jim Scott (hereafter, "Scott, 'The Mini D VCO Evolution'"); Glinsky, Hemsath, 2016.

Chapter 19

1. Bob Moog letter to Florence Moog, March 22, 1971. CIGM.
2. Glinsky, Hemsath, 2016.
3. Pinch, Trocco, Moog interview, 1997.
4. Glinsky, Scott, 2016.
5. Scott, "The Development of the Minimoog."
6. Peter Kirn, "The Minimoog at 40 from the Dawn of the Synth Age to New Voyages," *Keyboard, Super Special Moog Collector's Issue!* (October 2010), 34.
7. Glinsky, Borden, 2015.
8. Glinsky, Zumchak, 2012.
9. Tom Gullo interview with Albert Glinsky, July 15, 2016 (hereafter, "Glinsky, Gullo, 2016").
10. Glinsky, Zumchak, 2012.
11. Glinsky, Gullo, 2016.
12. Leah Carpenter letter to Eric Siday, October 29, 1970. Eric Siday papers, JPB 00-4. Music Division, The New York Public Library for the Performing Arts.
13. Walter Sear letter to Stan Goldstein, August 14, 1970. CBK.
14. "Synthesizers Tour Europe," *Billboard* (November 21, 1970), 84.
15. "Synthesizers in New Offices," *Billboard* (December 5, 1970), 3.
16. Bob Moog letter to Herb Deutsch, September 24,1970. CIGM.
17. Herb Deutsch letter to Bob Moog and John Huzar, January 18, 1971. CIGM.
18. Jason Wallace, "Dr. Moog's Synthesizer; A New Music Form, or Just Switched-on Bosh?" *TWA Ambassador* (June 1973), 13.
19. Robert Arthur Moog, Employment Resume, "current areas of capability and interest," (January 28, 1971), 3.
20. Jay Lee, "Interview: Robert Moog," n.p.
21. Glinsky, Zumchak, 2012.
22. Glinsky, Gullo, 2016.
23. Pinch, Trocco, Moog interview, 1997.
24. Mary Nic Shenk, "'Just Another Ding-A-Ling,'" *St. Petersburg Times* (October 15, 1970), 2-D.

25. Glinsky, Van Koevering, 2012.
26. Glinsky, Van Koevering, 2012.
27. Glinsky, VanKoevering, 2012.
28. Glinsky, Van Koevering, 2012.
29. Pinch and Trocco, *Analog Days,* 241-242.
30. Peggy Peterman, "In the Mood with Moog," *St. Petersburg Times* (March 1, 1971), 6-D; Pinch and Trocco, *Analog Days,* 242.
31. "The Island of Electronicus," *Grand Royal* (Spring–Summer, 1996), 64; Glinsky, Van Koevering, 2012.
32. "The Island of Electronicus," 64; Glinsky, Van Koevering, 2012.
33. Glinsky, Van Koevering, 2012.
34. Glinsky, Van Koevering, 2012.
35. Glinsky, Van Koevering, 2012.
36. Peterman, "In the Mood with Moog," 6-D.
37. Bill Burrell letter to Bob Moog, June 3–4, 1971. CIGM.

Chapter 20

1. Lee Winfrey, "Getting Your Kicks in the 70s: Sex, The Moog, and The Tube," *Detroit Free Press* (January 11, 1970), 4E.
2. Pinch, Trocco, Moog interview, 1997.
3. Bob Moog Employment Agreement, Exhibit F, February 21, 1971. CIGM.
4. John Peck, "Moog Company Is Sold," *Ithaca Journal* (June 17, 1971), 8.
5. Glinsky, Ciani, 2016.
6. Glinsky, Ciani, 2016.
7. Glinsky, Ciani, 2016.
8. Pinch, Trocco, Moog interview, 1997.
9. *Dave Fredericks plays the amazing ARP SOLOIST; It's a one hand band!* Liner notes for ARP Soloist demo record, 1971.
10. Pinch, Trocco, Moog interview, 1997.
11. Kirn, "The Minimoog at 40," 33.
12. Doerschuk, "12 Who Count: Bob Moog," 96. Bob was committed to using knobs on his instruments, as opposed to sliders—a major difference from ARP models. He found that the ergonomic finesse of knobs was more suited to human motor skills, allowing for more subtle control of functions. Jim Scott explained one example: "ARP instruments totally lacked octave switching, leaving the musician no option but to change pitch ranges by manipulating a slide pot several inches long. This was a cumbersome adjustment, as the short and rather awkward hand and finger movements resulted in coarse pitch changes, making fine tuning rather difficult over the wide pitch range of the instrument. The Mini Moog octave clicker in contrast got the musician very close instantly when making a range change, and afforded recourse to a much more easily operated knob to fine tune the oscillator. This rotary control, operated by using opposed thumb and forefinger, coupled with wrist rotation, is also ever so much easier to manipulate

compared to having to move the entire forearm—as is required to tweak the ARP pitch linear controller. The human hand and brain evolved to achieve the former sort of precision manipulation, not the latter" (Scott, "The Mini D VCO Evolution.")

13. Pinch, Trocco, Moog interview, 1997.
14. "The Island of Electronicus," 64; Glinsky, Van Koevering, 2012.
15. "The Island of Electronicus," 64.
16. Glinsky, Van Koevering, 2012.
17. Glinsky, Van Koevering, 2012.
18. Glinsky, Van Koevering, 2012.
19. Glinsky, Van Koevering, 2012.
20. Glinsky, Van Koevering, 2012.
21. Glinsky, Van Koevering, 2012.
22. John Peck, "Moog Plant Is Moving to Buffalo Area," *Ithaca Journal* (August 31, 1971), n.p.
23. Glinsky, Van Koevering, 2012.
24. Glinsky, Van Koevering, 2012.
25. Bob Moog memo to Bill Kohler, July 31, 1971. CIGM.
26. Glinsky, Hemsath, 2016.
27. Glinsky, Borden, 2015.
28. Pinch, Trocco, Moog interview, 1997.

Chapter 21

1. Glinsky, Scott, 2016.
2. Bob Moog letter to Florence Moog, November 17, 1971. CIGM.
3. Glinsky, Gullo, 2016.
4. Glinsky, Van Koevering, 2012.
5. Bob Moog letter to Florence Moog, November 17, 1971. CIGM.
6. Shirleigh Moog letter to Florence Moog, undated—*terminus ante quem*, September 18, 1971. CIGM.
7. Bob Moog letter to Florence Moog, November 17, 1971. CIGM.
8. Shirleigh Moog letter to Florence Moog, undated—*terminus ante quem*, September 18, 1971. CIGM.
9. Larry Austin, "Can Electronic Music Be Romantic?" *New York Times* (September 19, 1971), D15, 18.
10. David Friend, "All You Ever Wanted to Know about Synthesizers," *The Music Trades* (April 1972), 56, 61, 90.
11. Glinsky, Gullo, 2016.
12. Glinsky, Luce, 2016.
13. Emerson, *Pictures of an Exhibitionist*, 207.
14. Mark Vail, "Keith Emerson's Moog: The World's Most Dangerous Synth," in *Vintage Synthesizers*, 116.
15. Pinch and Trocco, *Analog Days*, 211.

16. Chuck Pulin, "U.S. Live Sounds: ELP," *Sounds* (September 25, 1971), 28.
17. Liv G. Whetmore and Jim Podraza, "Dr. Bob Moog the man behind the Moog synthesizer," *Impressions* (November 1999), n.p.
18. Whetmore and Podraza, "Dr. Bob Moog the man behind the Moog synthesizer," n.p.
19. Exactly eight weeks after the Gaelic Park concert, on October 27, 1971, Keith's new Minimoog (Serial # 1203) shipped from Buffalo. Keith would continue to perform live on his trademark "Monster Moog," but he would increasingly use the Minimoog as well as a more compact, easier-to-handle alternative. (Minimoog Model D sales records, R. A. Moog Company, transcribed on moogarchives.com).
20. Emerson, *Pictures of an Exhibitionist*, 215.
21. "D.U.U. Major Attraction: Stevie Wonder," *Duke University CALENDAR* (September 28, 1972), 5.
22. Glinsky, Kingsley, 2011.
23. Bob Moog memo to Bill Kohler, July 1, 1971. CIGM.
24. Bob Moog memo to Bill Kohler, July 1, 1971. CIGM.
25. Glinsky, Zumchak, 2012.
26. Glinsky, Kelischek, 2015.
27. Glinsky, Kelischek, 2015.
28. Glinsky, Kelischek, 2015.
29. Glinsky, Shirleigh Moog, 2011.
30. Glinsky, Shirleigh Moog, 2011.
31. Glinsky, Kelischek, 2015.
32. Frank Peters, "The Synthesizer Wants YOU," *St. Louis Post-Dispatch* (October 1, 1972), n.p.
33. Product flyer, Moog Music, Inc., 1972.
34. "Moog makes the scene," flyer, Moog Music, Inc., 1972. The "eastern mystic" portrait of Bob was adapted from a formal black-and-white studio photo of Bob.
35. Glinsky, Van Koevering, 2012.
36. Glinsky, Gullo, 2016.
37. Glinsky, Van Koevering, 2012.
38. Roger and Kathy Luther interview with Albert Glinsky, March 29–30, 2015 (hereafter, "Glinsky, Luther, 2015").
39. Glinsky, Luther, 2015.
40. Glinsky, Luther, 2015.
41. Glinsky, Shirleigh Moog, 2011.
42. Glinsky, Gullo, 2016.
43. Glinsky, Gullo, 2016.
44. Ikutaro Kakehashi, *I Believe in Music: Life Experiences and Thoughts on the Future of Electronic Music by the Founder of the Roland Corporation* (Milwaukee: Hal Leonard, 2002), 160.
45. Glinsky, Gullo, 2016.
46. Peters, "The Synthesizer Wants YOU," n.p.
47. Peters, "The Synthesizer Wants YOU," n.p.
48. Harry Reasoner, *The Reasoner Report*, CBS Radio Network (May 29, 1970). Transcript of radio broadcast. Courtesy Gershon Kingsley.

Chapter 22

1. Bob Moog letter to Don Runyon, May 23, 1973. CIGM.
2. "Moog Muses: An interview with the father of the synthesizer," *Chicago Reader* (June 30, 1972), 4.
3. Glinsky, Luce, 2016.
4. Bob Moog letter to Don Runyon, May 23, 1973. CIGM.
5. Rich Walborn interview with Albert Glinsky, June 25, 2016 (hereafter, "Glinsky, Walborn, 2016").
6. Glinsky, Walborn, 2016.
7. Bob Moog letter to Don Runyon, May 23, 1973. CIGM.
8. Moog, Yale interview, 1979.
9. Moog, Yale interview, 1979.
10. Glinsky, Gullo, 2016.
11. Glinsky, Gullo, 2016.
12. Glinsky, Van Koevering, 2012.
13. Bob Moog letter to Don Runyon, May 23, 1973. CIGM.
14. Bob Moog letter to Pete LaPlaca, September 7, 1974. CIGM.
15. Bob Moog memo to R. S. Rubin, September 5, 1974. CIGM.
16. Wallace, "Dr. Moog's Synthesizer," 12–14.
17. *The Visionaries*, United States Information Agency film, 1973. National Archives at College Park—Motion Pictures.
18. "Audience Reaction to the IMV Film, 'The Visionaries,'" United States Information Agency, Office of Research and Assessment (January 22, 1974), 7.
19. Glinsky, Walborn, 2016.
20. Glinsky, Walborn, 2016.
21. Laura Moog interview with Albert Glinsky, August 2, 2012 (hereafter, "Glinsky, Laura Moog, 2012").
22. Bob Moog Log Book (November 7, 1973–November 27, 1974). CIGM.
23. Bob Moog letter to James Potthast, February 15, 1980. CIGM.
24. Glinsky, Gullo, 2016. In the agreement between CMI and Moog Music, Inc. (September 11, 1973), CMI arranged to pay Waytena for his share in the company (40.5% of the company stock, valued at $508,000) in two installments: a cash payment of $122,000 at closing, and the balance of $386,000 to be paid over a period of four years in equal installments, with an interest rate of 5% per annum on the unpaid balance. When Norlin released Waytena from his contract in December 1974, earlier than expected, the company bought out his stock for the outstanding balance he was owed, which was paid in installments over the following years. He did not receive any additional incentive payment to leave, beyond what he was owed from his original contract.
25. Bob Moog letter to Ed Bloomberg, December 28, 1974. CIGM.
26. John Dwyer, "Musical Marathon With a Flock of Pianists Leaves Some Sated With Satie Composition," *Buffalo Evening News* (November 7, 1974), 43.
27. Florence Moog letter to Bob Moog, January 1, 1975. CIGM.
28. Bob Moog letter to Jacqueline Harvey, September 25, 1973. CIGM.

29. Bob Moog letter to Walter Sear, October 18, 1973. CIGM.
30. Stu Green, "Closing Chord," *Theatre Organ* 17, no. 2 (April 1975), 46. Collection of the author.
31. Green, "Closing Chord," 46.

Chapter 23

1. Don Snowden, "Moog on the State of the Synthesizer," *Los Angeles Times*, Calendar (June 7, 1981), 60.
2. Fjellestad, *Moog*.
3. Nancy Miller, "This Man Rocks," *Entertainment Weekly* (September 17, 2004), 36.
4. Glinsky, Scott, 2016.
5. Bob Moog letter to Pete LaPlaca, September 7, 1974. CIGM.
6. Pinch, Trocco, Moog interview, 1996.
7. Pinch, Trocco, Moog interview, 1996.
8. Moog, Yale interview, 1979.
9. Ben Sidran, "That Little Old Wavemaker, MOOG," *Rolling Stone* (February 13, 1975), 28.
10. Bob Moog, Merit Review, Norlin Music, Inc., October 1975. CIGM.
11. "Is There Liver in Reality? The Story of Moog," *Imoogination*, Norlin brochure (1976), 6.
12. Cover of Japanese *Imoogination*, 1976. Translation, Keiko Miller.
13. Gary Flanagan and C. S. Graves, "Robert Moog: The Father of Modern Synthesis," *Nightwaves* (July 2001), Issue 4. n.p.
14. Moog, Yale interview, 1979.
15. Tom Gullo, General Manager's Report, Moog Music, Inc., Director's Meeting, November 13, 1975. CIGM.
16. Glinsky, Luce, 2016.
17. Norlin promotional material for NAMM, June 21–24, 1975. CIGM.
18. Coleman Music Co. ad for the Polymoog, *The Bakersfield Californian* (December 21, 1976), 16.
19. Glinsky, Gullo, 2016.
20. Glinsky, Luce, 2016.
21. Flanagan and Graves, "Robert Moog: The Father of Modern Synthesis," n.p.
22. Moog, Yale interview, 1979.
23. Glinsky, Moog-Koussa, 2015.
24. Norlin promotional ad, "A blunt and totally biased viewpoint on electronic synthesizers from Bob Moog," ca. 1976.
25. Bob Moog letter to Bill Hoskins, April 30, 1974. CIGM.
26. Bob Moog letter to Bill Hoskins, April 30, 1974. CIGM.
27. David Friend email to author, June 12, 2020.
28. David Friend emails to author, June 12 and 15, 2020.
29. D. A. Luce, Moog Engineering Report, November 1975. CIGM.

30. Tom Gullo, General Manager's Report, Moog Music, Inc., Director's Meeting, November 13, 1975. CIGM.
31. Tom Gullo, General Manager's Report, Moog Music, Inc., Director's Meeting, November 13, 1975. CIGM.
32. Glinsky, Shirleigh Moog, 2012.
33. Glinsky, Moog-Koussa, 2015.
34. Glinsky, Moog-Koussa, 2015.
35. Bob Moog letter to Ed Taylor, November 23, 1977. CIGM.
36. Delos reissued the recording on CD in 1987 under the title, *The Art of the Theremin: Clara Rockmore*. In 1998, through Big Briar, Inc., Bob published a videocassette titled, *Clara Rockmore: The Greatest Theremin Virtuosa*. The one-hour film had been videotaped in Clara's New York apartment on 57th Street in 1976, and featured Clara demonstrating theremin technique and performing selections from the 1977 album. The video included a roundtable discussion with Clara, her sister (pianist, Nadia Reisenberg), Reisenberg's son (radio host and music critic Robert Sherman), electronic music historian Tom Rhea, and Bob.
37. Torsten Schmidt, Interview with Giorgio Moroder, *Red Bull Music Academy*, 2013, http://www.redbullmusicacademy.com/lectures/giorgio-moroder.
38. Rob Sheffield, "Dim All the Lights for Donna Summer," *Rolling Stone* (May 17, 2012), https://www.rollingstone.com/music/music-news/dim-all-the-lights-for-donna-summer-242108/
39. Henahan, "Is Everybody Going to the Moog?" D15.
40. Bob Moog letter to Peter LaPlaca, September 7, 1974. CIGM.
41. Al Padoor memo to staff, R. A. Moog, Inc., December 23, 1969. CIGM.
42. "That's Him . . . In The Moog for Music," *The North Minneapolis Post* (February 24, 1972), n.p.
43. Sidran, "That Little Old Wavemaker, MOOG," 28.
44. John Updike, "Love Song, for a Moog Synthesizer," *The New Yorker* (June 14, 1976), 29.
45. Ad for B. Altman & Co., *New York Times* (November 18, 1975), 7.
46. Bob Moog letter to Leonard Stoll, June 22, 1973. CIGM.
47. Bob Moog Desk Notebook (January 1972- October 14, 1974). CIGM.
48. Harold N. Hubbard, "How to Make Your Own Moog Music," *Pasadena Star-News* (September 18, 1974), n.p.

Chapter 24

1. Shirleigh Moog letter to Florence Moog, June 24, 1978. CIGM.
2. Bob Moog letter to Florence Moog, July 26, 1978. CIGM.
3. Shirleigh Moog letter to Florence Moog, September 28, 1978. CIGM.
4. David Brown, "Switched-On Music," *Asheville Citizen-Times* (October 15, 1978), D1.
5. Bob Moog letter to Florence Moog, May 28, 1979. CIGM.
6. Glinsky, Moog-Koussa, 2015.
7. Glinsky, Moog-Koussa, 2015.

440 NOTES

8. Glinsky, Moog-Koussa, 2015.
9. Glinsky, Moog-Koussa, 2015.
10. Glinsky, Moog-Koussa, 2015.
11. Bob Moog letter to Florence Moog, May 28, 1979. CIGM.
12. Bob Moog letter to Florence Moog, May 28, 1979. CIGM.
13. Glinsky, Moog-Koussa, 2015.
14. Shirleigh Moog letter to Florence Moog, September 20, 1978. CIGM.
15. Bob Moog letter to Linda Tower, October 26, 1978. CIGM.
16. Bob Moog letter to Florence Moog, January 24, 1979. CIGM.
17. Glinsky, Scott, 2016.
18. Glinsky, Walborn, 2016.
19. Glinsky, Gullo, 2016.
20. Glinsky, Deutsch, 2011
21. Robert Moog letter to Heath Company, January 10, 1980. CIGM.
22. Congressional Record, Vol. 127, No. 142 (October 6, 1981), 1.
23. Statement by President Jimmy Carter, Eureka exhibit brochure, May 1980. CIGM.
24. Congressional Record, Vol. 127, No. 142 (October 6, 1981), 1.
25. Francis Ford Coppola interview with Albert Glinsky, November 22, 2011.
26. Bob Moog, "Apocalypse Now: The Synthesizer Soundtrack," *Contemporary Keyboard* (January 1980), 47.
27. Moog, "Apocalypse Now: The Synthesizer Soundtrack," 49.
28. Moog, "Apocalypse Now: The Synthesizer Scoundtrack," 49.
29. Bob Moog letter to Wendy Carlos, July 9, 1979. CIGM.
30. Glinsky, Shirleigh Moog, 2011.
31. Bob Moog letter to Michael and Nancy Iseberg, April 15, 1980. CIGM.
32. Dale Anderson, "New Synthesizer Returns Moog to State of the Art," *Buffalo Courier Express* (August 8, 1982), F-4.
33. *INTERFACE, The Moog Newslette*r, Vol. III (June 1982), 1. Courtesy of Roger Luther.
34. Linda Tower letter to Bob Moog, March 21, 1980. CIGM.
35. Bob Moog letter to Jim Wilde, February 22, 1980. CIGM.
36. Glinsky, Walborn, 2016.
37. Glinsky, Gullo, 2016.
38. Glinsky, Gullo, 2016.
39. Glinsky, Luce, 2016.
40. Linda Tower letter to Bob Moog, March 21, 1980. CIGM.
41. Glinsky, Walborn, 2016.
42. Glinsky, Gullo, 2016.
43. Glinsky, Walborn, 2016.
44. MG-1 ad, Radio Shack, *The Spokesman-Review*, Spokane, WA (October 11, 1981), 5.
45. Radio Shack Catalog, 1982: 23; Radio Shack Catalog, 1983: 55.
46. Glinsky, Walborn, 2016.
47. Glinsky, Deutsch, 2011.
48. Bob Moog letter to Shab Levy, November 5, 1981. CIGM.

49. Jean Seligmann with Eleanor Clift, "A Musical Inventor Tunes Up His Life," *Newsweek* (August 2, 1982), 10.

Chapter 25

1. Seligmann and Clift, "A Musical Inventor Tunes Up His Life," 10.
2. Mona Gault, "A Musical Moog: Inventor Who Changed Rock Lives in a Lower Key Now," *The Charlotte Observer* (July 8, 1979), 6F.
3. Glinsky, Moog-Koussa, 2015.
4. John Dwyer, "Interview: Composer Deutsch Gets Sentimental about an 18-Year Old 'Antique' Synthesizer," *Buffalo News* (June 4, 1982), n.p.
5. Bob Moog letter to Sheila Grinell, January 16, 1980. CIGM.
6. Herb originally asked Bob if the instrument that emerged from their work together in 1964 could be named "The Moog-Deutsch Synthesizer." Herb recalled: "There was really only one discussion about the instrument being named for both of us, and it was after the finished prototype was made and Bob was looking for customers. So it was the late fall of 1964. The design had been made and he was already starting to assemble modular instruments. And I did ask him. And Bob simply said, 'No.' And the reason he said no was that, 'I'm the designer. I'm the engineer. I'm basically the person who has built this instrument.' At the time I was distraught, but I got what he was saying. A number of people asked me in the first five years and my response was, 'I was the musician who met him at that time, and talked to him about my musical ideas, and gave him the insight about what a musical instrument like that should be.' If he hadn't met me, he would have met someone else. I know there is a lot of me in the basic Moog synthesizer. And I'm happy to say that." (Glinsky, Deutsch, 2011).
7. Bob Moog letter to Buck Munger, July 9, 1979. CIGM.
8. Bob Moog letter to William Christ, October 17, 1978. CIGM.
9. Shirleigh Moog letter to Florence Moog, January 16, 1982. CIGM.
10. Bob Moog letter to Dave DeLauter, January 4, 1983. CIGM.
11. Florence Moog letter to Bob Moog, July 5, 1983. CIGM.
12. Tom Rhea, as quoted in Dominic Milano, "American Synthesizer Builders; Triumphs & Crises for an Industry in Transition," in *Vintage Synthesizers*, 27.
13. Glinsky, Luce, 2016.
14. Bob Moog letter to Florence Moog, December 5, 1983. CIGM.
15. Bob Moog letter to Florence Moog, March 16, 1983. CIGM.
16. Bob Moog letter to Florence Moog, March 16, 1983. CIGM.
17. Glinsky, Moog-Koussa, 2015.
18. "Who's What, Where: Electronic Music Pioneer Joins Waltham Firm," *Boston Globe* (June 12, 1984), 41.
19. Glinsky, Shirleigh Moog, 2012.
20. Glinsky, Shirleigh Moog, 2012.
21. Glinsky, Moog-Koussa, 2015.

22. Bob Moog letter to Florence Moog, October 16, 1984. CIGM.
23. Matthew Moog letter to Florence Moog, November 6, 1984. CIGM.

Chapter 26

1. As quoted in Bob Moog's letter to Florence Moog, November 27, 1978. CIGM.
2. Henning Lohner, "Interview with Robert Moog," *Computer Music Journal* 9, no. 4 (Winter 1985), 62.
3. Lohner, "Interview with Robert Moog," 65.
4. Ken Franckling, "Synthesizer: More than a novelty," *Philadelphia Inquirer* (June 15, 1986), 13-H.
5. Bob Moog letter to Gene Zumchak, February 15, 1992. Courtesy Gene Zumchak.
6. Glinsky, Borden, 2015.
7. Glinsky, Moog-Koussa, 2015.
8. Shirleigh Moog interview with Albert Glinsky, February 28, 2010 (hereafter "Glinsky, Shirleigh Moog, 2010").
9. Glinsky, Moog-Koussa, 2015.
10. Glinsky, Moog-Koussa, 2015.
11. Glinsky, Moog-Koussa, 2015.
12. Glinsky, Shirleigh Moog, 2012.
13. Glinsky, Van Koevering, 2012.
14. David Van Koevering, "Sanctuary Synthesizer by Moog," promotional flyer, 1985. Courtesy Roger Luther.
15. Glinsky, Van Koevering, 2012.
16. Glinsky, Grams-Moog, 2012.
17. Glinsky, Laura Moog, 2012.
18. Glinsky, Moog-Koussa, 2015.
19. Larry Fine, "In the Shop with Bob Moog: A Personal Account."
20. Bob Moog letter to Gene Zumchak, February 15, 1992. Courtesy Gene Zumchak.
21. Bob Moog, "Shuffle Off to Buffalo; The Rise and Fall of Moog Music," *Keyboard* (May 1988), 44, 54–56, 61, 65.
22. Rhett Stuart, "Stearns Collection Home to First Commercial Moog," *The University Record*, University of Michigan 44, no. 16 (January 9, 1989), n.p.
23. Donal Henahan, "And in This Gallery, We See the Ancient Moog," *New York Times* (February 5, 1989), 23.
24. "Elsewhere In North Carolina," *The Charlotte Observer* (August 9, 1989), 2B.
25. Glinsky, Shirleigh Moog, 2011.
26. Wayne Kirby interview with Albert Glinsky, August 8, 2016 (hereafter, "Glinsky, Kirby, 2016").
27. Glinsky, Shirleigh Moog, 2011.
28. Bob Moog, personal notes Western North Carolina ACLU meeting, March 9, 1992. CIGM.

29. Western North Carolina Chapter, North Carolina Civil Liberties Union, *Civil Liberties Herald* 1 (January 1992), 1. CIGM.
30. Steve Dunnington interview with Albert Glinsky, August 14, 2015 (hereafter, "Glinsky, Dunnington, 2015").
31. Bob Moog letter to Gene Zumchak, February 15, 1992. Courtesy Gene Zumchak.
32. John von Rhein, "TECHNOLOGY: Moog's Newest Keyboard Puts the World at Musicians' Fingertips," *Orange County Register* (May 30, 1992), f10.
33. Nancy Malitz, "And Moog Created 'Genesis': The Master Remakes the Keyboard," *Piano and Keyboard* (March/April 1993), 20.
34. Fine, "In the Shop with Bob Moog: A Personal Account."
35. Malitz, "And Moog Created 'Genesis': the Master Remakes the Keyboard," 22.
36. Malitz, "And Moog Created 'Genesis': the Master Remakes the Keyboard," 21.
37. Fine, "In the Shop with Bob Moog: A Personal Account."
38. Glinsky, Moog-Koussa, 2015.
39. Glinsky, Moog-Koussa, 2015.
40. Glinsky, Renée Moog, 2018.
41. Glinsky, Shirleigh Moog, 2012.
42. Shirleigh Moog diary, March 3, 1993. MFA.
43. Shirleigh Moog diary, March 3, 1993. MFA.

Chapter 27

1. Bob Moog letter to Michelle Moog-Koussa, January 8, 1994. CIGM
2. Bob Moog letter to Michelle Moog-Koussa, January 8, 1994. CIGM.
3. Shirleigh Moog diary, n.d. MFA.
4. Glinsky, Shirleigh Moog, 2011.
5. Shirley and Robert Moog Separation Agreement (February 22, 1994), Exhibit "A," "Distribution of Household Effects" (January 23, 1994). CIGM.
6. Khatia and Rick Krebs interview with Albert Glinsky, March 22, 2018 (hereafter, "Glinsky, Krebs, 2018").
7. Glinsky, Grams-Moog, 2012.
8. Glinsky, Grams-Moog, 2012.
9. Glinsky, Grams-Moog, 2012.
10. Glinsky, Grams-Moog, 2012.
11. Glinsky, Grams-Moog, 2012.
12. Bob Moog letter to Rose Marie and Dave Ederer, February 22, 1995. CIGM.
13. Bob Moog letter to Rose Marie and Dave Ederer, February 22, 1995. CIGM.
14. Glinsky, Moog-Koussa, 2015.
15. Bob Moog typed note to Shirleigh Moog, May 31, 1994. CIGM.
16. Shirleigh Moog phone message, May 12, 1994 (transcript). CIGM.
17. Shirleigh Moog phone message, May 12, 1994 (transcript). CIGM.
18. Shirleigh Moog phone message, May 9, 1994 (transcript). CIGM.

19. Shirleigh Moog letter to Bob Moog, April 24, 1994. CIGM.
20. Glinsky, Dunnington, 2015.
21. Glinsky, Dunnington, 2015.
22. Pinch, Trocco, Moog interview, 1997.
23. Glinsky, Deutsch, 2011.
24. Pinch, Trocco, Moog interview, 1997.
25. Lee, "Interview with Bob Moog," n.p.
26. Glinsky, Deutsch, 2011.
27. Glinsky, Grams-Moog, 2012.
28. Miranda Richmond Mouillot interview with Albert Glinsky, August 10, 2015 (hereafter, "Glinsky, Richmond Mouillot, 2015").
29. Glinsky, Grams-Moog, 2012.
30. Bob Moog letter to Roger Smith, September 21, 1994. CIGM.
31. Shirleigh Moog letter to Bob Moog, April 24, 1994. CIGM.
32. Bob Moog letter to Rose Marie and Dave Ederer, February 22, 1995. CIGM.
33. Glinsky, Grams-Moog, 2012.
34. Bob Moog fax to Roger Smith, January 20, 1995. CIGM.
35. Motion for Extension of Time; District Court Division 95 CVD 217, December 5, 1995. CIGM.
36. Ileana Grams-Moog interview with Albert Glinsky, August 10, 2015 (hereafter, "Grams-Moog, 2015").
37. Glinsky, Laura Moog, 2012.
38. Glinsky, Grams-Moog, 2012.

Chapter 28

1. Archived in wayback machine at: https://web.archive.org/web/19980208211024/http://www.workshop.ch/news/1996/moogmusic.html.
2. Brendan I. Koener, "Back to Music's Future," *U.S. News & World Report* (March 3, 1997), 18.
3. Robert Everett-Green, "Good, Good, Good, Good Vibrations," *Globe & Mail*, Canada (December 5, 2000), R1.
4. Kenneth Johnson, "Moog Music," *Charlotte Observer* (November 16, 1997), F1.
5. Jean-Jacques Perrey letter to Bob Moog, January 2, 1998. CIGM.
6. Mr. Bonzai, "Bonzai Beat: Bob Moog," 48.
7. "Moog Reissues the Minimoog," *Music Merchandising Review* (November 1997), 102.
8. "Robert Moog Institutes Lawsuit Against Don Martin and Moog Music, Inc.," press release, Big Briar, Incorporated, February 16, 1998.
9. John Waterhouse letter to Bob Moog, May 21, 1997. CIGM.
10. Bob Moog email to Roger Luther, October 10, 1999. Courtesy Roger Luther.
11. Glinsky, Dunnington, 2015.
12. Glinsky, Moog-Koussa, 2015.

13. "Robert Moog gratitude speech—Polar Music Prize, 2001," https://www.youtube.com/watch?v=zOGLVKL3ygI.
14. Glinsky, Grams-Moog, 2015.
15. Gordon Reid, "Voyager by Bob Moog," *Sound on Sound* (June 2003), https://www.soundonsound.com/reviews/voyager-by-bob-moog; Glinsky, Dunnington, 2015.
16. Bob Moog letter to "Naming Contest Judges," May 7, 2001. CIGM.
17. Glinsky, Moog-Koussa, 2015.
18. Alan Cane, "Moog Back in Vogue," *Financial Times* (June 12, 2001), 6.
19. Glinsky, Dunnington, 2015.
20. Glinsky, Dunnington, 2015.
21. Lou Carlozo, "The Computerized Piano," *Chicago Tribune* (December 16, 1997), Section 5, 1.
22. Glinsky, Van Koevering, 2012.
23. Glinsky, Grams-Moog, 2015.
24. Bob Moog handwritten notes from session with Mary Ellen Rifkin, December 13, 2001. CIGM.
25. Bob Moog handwritten notes from session with Mary Ellen Rifkin, December 13, 2001. CIGM.

Chapter 29

1. Bob Moog handwritten notes from session with Mary Ellen Rifkin, January 4, 2002. CIGM.
2. August Worley interview with Albert Glinsky, August 10, 2016 (hereafter, "Glinsky, Worley, 2016").
3. Bob Moog handwritten notes from session with Mary Ellen Rifkin, January 29, 2002. CIGM.
4. Glinsky, Worley, 2016.
5. Glinsky, Worley, 2016.
6. Glinsky, Worley, 2016.
7. Mike Adams interview with Albert Glinsky, July 30, 2012 (hereafter, "Glinsky, Adams, 2012").
8. Glinsky, Adams, 2012.
9. Glinsky, Adams, 2012.
10. Glinsky, Adams, 2012.
11. Glinsky, Dunnington, 2015.
12. Glinsky, Worley, 2016.
13. *Minimoog Voyager User's Manual*, Moog Music, (2008), 38.
14. Linhard had been bartering with Bob for 10 years—European distribution of Big Briar theremins in exchange for Bob's help in pushing Linhard's upgraded Memorymoogs in the U.S. No money had ever changed hands between them. Bob didn't have much knowledge of the Memorymoog, but he'd agreed to retrofit some old models at Big

Briar with Linhard's newly designed software and hardware fixes for the synth. Named after Linhard's small company, Lintronics, the renovated models were known as LAMM systems, for "Lintronics Advanced Memorymoog." The LAMM upgrade jobs were yet another project the small Riverside staff juggled along with everything else. For the Voyager software, Bob had worked out a per-unit royalty payment so Linhard could finally be compensated for one of their collaborations.

15. Glinsky, Adams, 2012.
16. Glinsky, Adams, 2012.
17. Glinsky, Adams, 2012.
18. Trevor Pinch and Frank Trocco, *Analog Days: The Invention and Impact of the Moog Synthesizer* (Cambridge, MA: Harvard University Press, 2002). Pinch, a Cornell professor, had also provided testimony on Bob's behalf for the court case involving the dispute over the Moog name and trademark. Speaking as an expert on the history of the Moog synthesizer, he attested that Bob invented the Moog modular synthesizer in 1964, and the Minimoog in 1970, a statement which was used in court (Trevor Pinch, email to the author, September 20, 2021).
19. Ernie Rideout, "Fantastic Voyager: The making of a Minimoog for the millennium," *Keyboard* (May 2003), 33.
20. Joe Silva, "Bob Moog: Voyage of Discovery," *Sound on Sound*, March 2003, http:www.soundonsound.com/sos/mar03/articles/bobmoog.asp.
21. Glinsky, Kirby, 2016.
22. Glinsky, Grams-Moog, 2015.
23. Martin Turenne, "Bob Moog: America's Rogue Synthesizer Guru Talks about the Birth of His Glorious Machine," *XLR8R Magazine* (April 2004), 34–35.
24. Ileana Grams-Moog interview with Albert Glinsky, August 11, 2016 (hereafter, "Glinsky, Grams-Moog, 2016").
25. Rupert Sheldrake, *Dogs That Know When Their Owners Are Coming Home—And Other Unexplained Powers of Animals* (New York: Three Rivers Press, 1999).
26. Glinsky, Kirby, 2016.
27. Bob Moog, "The Man-Machine Interface of Musical Instruments," October 3, 2003, typescript of lecture delivered to the 2003 Icograda Congress, Nagoya, Japan, October 10, 2003. CIGM.
28. Glinsky, Grams-Moog, 2015.
29. Bob Moog commencement speech, the University of the Arts, Philadelphia, May 22, 2003. Typescript. CIGM.
30. Bob Moog commencement speech, the University of the Arts, Philadelphia, May 22, 2003. Typescript. CIGM.
31. Glinsky, Grams-Moog, 2015.
32. Bob Moog commencement speech, the University of the Arts, Philadelphia, May 22, 2003. Typescript. CIGM.
33. Moog PianoBar KINGDOM EDITION, sales film with David Van Koevering, https://www.youtube.com/watch?v=FtngB164R1M&t=1207s.
34. Richard Leiby, "Starting to Make Synths," *Washington Post* (April 15, 2000), C1.
35. Miller, "This Man Rocks," 34.

36. Miller, "This Man Rocks," 33.
37. Miller, "This Man Rocks," 33.
38. Miller, "This Man Rocks," 34.
39. Miller, "This Man Rocks," 36.
40. Glinsky, Grams-Moog, 2016.
41. Eden Foster, "Anti-Racism Conference to Seek Solutions," *Asheville Citizen-Times* (March 10, 2002), B2.
42. Steffie Nelson, "The Remix: Moog Music," *New York Times* (September 19, 2004), Section 6: 70.
43. Fjellestad, *Moog*.
44. Glinsky, Renée Moog, 2018.
45. Glinsky, Richmond Mouillot, 2015.
46. Glinsky, Grams-Moog, 2015.
47. Glinsky, Kirby, 2016.
48. Glinsky, Kirby, 2016.
49. Glinsky, Adams, 2012.
50. Glinsky, Adams, 2012.

Chapter 30

1. "Blues," *Billboard*, (January 12, 2002), L 21.
2. Bob Moog Tribute, the Orange Peel, Asheville, NC, August 24, 2005. Moog Music, Inc., 2006. DVD.
3. Cyril Lance interview with Albert Glinsky, August 13, 2015 (hereafter, "Glinsky, Lance, 2015").
4. Glinsky, Dunnington, 2015.
5. Glinsky, Dunnington, 2015.
6. Glinsky, Grams-Moog, 2015.
7. Glinsky, Grams-Moog, 2015.
8. Paul Bryner, "Synthesizer Inventor Discusses Where Ideas Come From at U. Alaska-Anchorage," *The Northern Light*, University of Alaska-Anchorage (May 10, 2005), n.p.
9. Ron Spatz interview with Albert Glinsky, February 6, 2016 (hereafter, "Glinsky, Spatz, 2016").
10. Glinsky, Spatz, 2016.
11. Glinsky, Dunnington, 2015.
12. Glinsky, Moog-Koussa, 2015.
13. Glinsky, Dunnington, 2015.
14. Glinsky, Lance, 2015.
15. Glinsky, Lance, 2015.
16. Glinsky, Richmond Mouillot, 2015.
17. Glinsky, Grams-Moog, 2015.
18. Glinsky, Lance, 2015.
19. Cane, "Moog Back in Vogue," 7.

20. Mr. Bonzai, "Bonzai Beat: Bob Moog," 48.
21. Glinsky, Moog-Koussa, 2015.
22. Glinsky, Grams-Moog, 2015.
23. Glinsky, Richmond Mouillot, 2015.
24. Glinsky, Moog-Koussa, 2015.
25. Glinsky, Grams-Moog, 2015.
26. Glinsky, Richmond Mouillot, 2015.
27. Glinsky, Richmond Mouillot, 2015.
28. Miranda Richmond Mouillot, "Daniela," unpublished written recollection, 2015. Courtesy Miranda Richmond Mouillot.
29. Glinsky, Grams-Moog, 2015.
30. Glinsky, Richmond Mouillot, 2015
31. Miranda Richmond Mouillot, "Daniela," unpublished written recollection, 2015. Courtesy Miranda Richmond Mouillot.
32. Glinsky, Grams-Moog, 2015.
33. Glinsky, Richmond Mouillot, 2015.
34. Miranda Richmond Mouillot, "Daniela," unpublished written recollection, 2015. Courtesy Miranda Richmond Mouillot.
35. Glinsky, Moog-Koussa, 2015.
36. Glinsky, Laura Moog, 2012.
37. Glinsky, Richmond Mouillot, 2015.
38. Glinsky, Dunnington, 2015.
39. Paul Clark, "Moog Suffers Brains Tumor," *Asheville Citizen-Times* (August 18, 2005), 1, 3.
40. Glinsky, Grams-Moog, 2015.
41. Jon Caramanica, "Funny, It Doesn't Sound Jewish," *New York Times* (August 21, 2005), 23.
42. Glinsky, Grams-Moog, 2015.
43. Miranda Richmond Mouillot, written note, August 22, 2005. CIGM.
44. Glinsky, Moog-Koussa, 2015.
45. Glinsky, Moog-Koussa, 2015.
46. Glinsky, Richmond Mouillot, 2015.
47. Glinsky, Moog-Koussa, 2015.
48. Glinsky, Grams-Moog, 2012.
49. Glinsky, Grams-Moog, 2015.
50. Glinsky, Grams-Moog, 2015.
51. Bob Moog Tribute, the Orange Peel, DVD.
52. Bob Moog Tribute, the Orange Peel, DVD.

Postlude

1. Glinsky, Dunnington, 2015.
2. Jonathan Takoff, "Moog Music Has Fan and Foe: He Popularized the Synthesizer," *Philadelphia Daily News* (April 26, 1988), 40.
3. Pinch, Trocco, Moog interview, 1997.

4. Freff Cochran and Moog, "The Rise and Fall of Moog Music," 39.
5. Glinsky, Luce, 2016.
6. Glinsky, Luce, 2016.
7. Glinsky, Adams, 2012.
8. Glinsky, Lance, 2015.
9. Glinsky, Lance, 2015.
10. Glinsky, Lance, 2015.
11. Glinsky, Lance, 2015.
12. Joe Coscarelli, "Moog Music Gives Employees More Control," *New York Times* (June 11, 2015), Section C: 1.
13. Glinsky, Lance, 2015.
14. Freff Cochran and Moog, "The Rise and Fall of Moog Music," 39.
15. Bob Moog letter to Otto Luening, April 3, 1992. CIGM.

Index

A&M records, 180
Abbey Road, 168–70, 180, 189
ABC television, 193
Acoustical Society of America, 131–32
Adams, Mike, 371–72, 376, 380, 381–82, 384, 393, 397–98, 399, 400; assumes leadership of Moog Music, 369–70; background, 369
additive synthesis, 67–68
Advision Studios (London), 208
Affenstunde, 221
Age of Electronicus, The, 170, 180
Alamooga Esinlenmeler, 305
Albert, Dorothy Jacobs (Aunt), 203, 204
Altamont Speedway Free Festival, 184–86, 210
Alterman, Wolff, 391
Amazing New Electronic Pop Sound of Jean Jacques Perrey, The, 156
Ambassador (TWA magazine), 286
American Academy in Rome, 321
American Civil Liberties Union (ACLU), 338
American Telephone & Telegraph (AT&T), 8, 157, 193
Analog Days, xvi–xvii, 372
Andover Academy, 23
Anger, Kenneth, 167
Apocalypse Now, ix–x, xii, 311–12; *Apocalypse Now Redux*, x; *The Music of Apocalypse Now*, x. *See also* Coppola, Francis Ford
Apollo 11 moon landing, xii, 163–64, 165–66, 217
Apple Computer, 326–27, 368
Apple Records, 149, 150, 151–52
Arendell, Gail, 350
Armstrong, Neil, 163–64
ARP Synthesizers, 228–30, 236, 238–39, 257–58, 265–66, 269, 276–77, 304–5, 317, 357, 434–35n.12; ARP 2500, 229–30, 249–50, 318, 358–59; ARP 2600, 249–50, 257, 265, 283, 304, 305, 318; ARP Odyssey, 283; ARP Pro Soloist, 272–73, 283; ARP Soloist, 251–53, 257–58, 271, 272; bankruptcy, 318; *Close Encounters of the Third Kind*, 318; *Star Wars*, 318; theft of Moog filter, 283, 298–99; Tonus, 228. *See also* Pearlman, Alan Robert
Arturia, 372
Asheville Citizen-Times, 307, 377–78, 389
Asheville Jubilee Faith Community, 342–43
Aspinall, Neil, 151–52
Atomic Energy Commission, 92
Audio, 178, 179
Audio Engineering Society (AES), 79, 80–82, 86, 95, 96, 104, 111–12, 113–14, 121, 123, 129, 136, 142, 181, 191, 224, 225–26, 227–28, 230–31, 249–50, 362, 422–23n.18
Audio Fidelity (record company), 203
Audiocraft, 30–31, 32, 72–73
Austin, Larry, 265

Babbitt, Milton, 70
Bach, Johann Sebastian, 21, 62, 70, 72, 74, 75, 77, 134–35, 136, 137, 138–39, 142–43, 144–45, 153–55, 195, 204, 206
Bacharach, Burt, 358–59, 362
Baez, Joan, 210, 211–12
Baldwin Organ, 22
Baroque Beatles Book, The, 134–35, 142
Barrie, George, 233–34
Barron, Bebe and Louis, 414–15n.9
Barry, John, 174
Bartók, Béla, 208
BBC (Radio and Television), 213, 222, 355, 414–15n.9, 429–30n.20

Beach Boys, the, 107–8, 131, 164; "Good Vibrations," 107–8; "I Just Wasn't Made for These Times," 107–8; *Pet Sounds*, 107–8
Beat Instrumental, 231
Beatles, the, xii, 66, 89, 115, 127, 131, 133, 134–35, 149, 170–71, 204, 206, 245–46, 277–78, 358–59; *Abbey Road* album, 168–70, 180, 189; *Sgt. Pepper's Lonely Hearts Club Band*, 126–27, 128, 134, 183
Beausoleil, Bobby, 167–69, 185–86
Beaver, Paul, 111–12, 139–40, 148–49, 150, 189, 221, 248–49, 276–77; at 1967 Monterey Pop Festival, 117, 118, 125, 127, 128, 422–23n.18; background, 112–13; death of, 290–91; and Disneyland Main Street Electrical Parade, 270; and *Nonesuch Guide to Electronic Music*, 140–42, 150, 422–23n.18; *Perchance to Dream*, 291; on recordings, 113–14, 116, 120, 123–27, 128, 170; as west coast Moog rep, 116, 117, 125, 173–74, 190
Becker, Juliane, 3
Beethoven, Ludwig van, 11, 66
Belar, Herbert, 82
Bell, Glen, 241–42, 243
Bell Labs, 23, 48, 92–93, 280–81, 414–15n.9
Berg, John, 139
Berlin, Arnold, 284
Bernstein, Leonard, 59, 154–55, 207
Berrigan, Daniel, 214–15
Beth Israel Synagogue (Asheville), 356, 391–92
Big Band Moog, 221
Big Brother and the Holding Company, 102, 106–7
Billboard, 126, 128, 141–42, 144, 153, 155, 170–71, 172, 180–81, 189, 193, 196, 219, 226, 229, 238–39, 248, 381
Birds, The (film), 122
Black Mass Lucifer, 248–49
Black Panther Party, 168, 215
Blaine, Hal, 114, 116

Bley, Paul, 182, 238–39
Blondie, 296–97
Bloomfield, Mike, 124–25
Bob Moog Foundation (BMF), 398–99; *Dr. Bob's Sound School*, 399; Moogseum, 399
Bode, Harald, 70–71, 78, 82, 108–9, 112
Bonnie and Clyde, 4
Borden, David, 159–62, 164–66, 168, 236, 258–59, 332, 393; background, 159; *Easter*, 214–15, 216; and Min A, 214; Mother Mallard's Portable Masterpiece Company, 214
Boston Globe, 327
Boston Pops Orchestra, 213
Boston Symphony Orchestra, 138
Botnick, Bruce, 126
Bourges festival (France), 339, 432n.21
Boy Scouts of America, 13–14. *See also* Moog, Bob: Early Years: scouting
Brain Salad Surgery. See Emerson, Lake and Palmer
Brand, Max, 122
Brandeis University Electronic Music Studio, 82
Brandt, Renee and Richard, 60, 327, 340–41
Bronx High School of Science. *See* Moog, Bob: Education
Brown University, 135–36, 228
Buchla, Donald, 110–11, 116, 250–51, 276–77; background, 103; development of modular system, 103–6; and Electric Circus, 120–21; Lightning wand, 393; and live performance, 106–7, 109–10; PianoBar, 375–76; sales of instruments, 110, 119, 222, 250–51; at San Francisco Tape Music Center, 103–6; and *Silver Apples of the Moon*, 119–21
Buchla instruments, 173, 222–23, 224, 228, 238, 250, 265, 304; Buchla 100 (MEMS, Buchla Box), 104–6, 110, 119–20, 140, 144, 145, 222, 228, 250, 265; Buchla 200, 222–23

Bucki, Mike, 354, 357, 360–61, 367; Modusonics, 373; Moog Music Custom Engineering, 359, 373
Buffalo Courier-Express, 313–14
Buffalo Evening News, 289–90
Buffalo News, 319
Byrds, The, xii, 117, 128, 130; "Moog Raga," 128; *Notorious Byrd Brothers, The*, 128

Cage, John, 90–92, 94, 101, 102, 105, 166, 215, 289, 313; *Variations V*, 91–94, 129, 133, 154
Cahill, Thaddeus, xiii, 67–69. *See also* Telharmonium
Canby, Vincent, 186
Cannon, Geoffrey, 213
Captain Kangaroo, 63
CaringBridge, xvii, 385, 389
Carley, Candi, 290–91
Carlos, Wendy, 139–40, 154, 155, 183–84, 312–13, 319, 393; background, 135–36, 338; *Clockwork Orange, A*, 275; Grammy Awards, 189; and *Moog 900 Series Electronic Music Systems* demo recording, 136; *Sonic Seasonings*, 275; and St. Louis Symphony, 182–83, 184; *Switched-On Bach*, xii, 136–39, 142–43, 144–45, 146, 153, 155, 164, 170, 172, 173, 180, 182–83, 189, 202, 206, 248, 269, 276; on *Today Show*, 153; *Well-Tempered Synthesizer, The*, 182–83
Carnegie Hall, 59, 133, 135, 140, 202–5, 213
Carpenter, Leah, 160, 161, 238, 256, 258
Carter, Jimmy, 311
Cary, Tristram, 224, 276–77
Casio company, 351, 381; VL-1, 351
CBS (musical instruments/equipment), 79, 96, 222, 250, 318
CBS radio/television, 59, 63, 155, 163, 193, 279
CBS Records, 136, 139, 143–44; Columbia Masterworks, 134, 143, 183; Columbia Records, 136, 139, 143–44, 170, 180, 182–83, 248

Cecil, Malcolm, 269–70
CEMS (Coordinated Electronic Music Studio), 223
Chadabe, Joel, 223
Chapman, F. Scott, 325, 341–42
Charlotte Observer, 318, 337–38, 358
Chatta MOOGA Choo Choo, 305
Chicago Musical Instrument Co., (CMI), 285, 289, 314, 437n.24; background, 284. *See also* Moog, Bob: Moog Companies: 1971–1973, Moog Music, Inc.
Chicago Reader, 280–81
Chicago Sun-Times, 339
Chicago Tribune, The, 225, 364
Chopin, Frederic, 9, 11, 15
Chopin Á La Moog, 221
Chowning, John, 318
Christmas Becomes Electric, 180
Ciamaga, Gustav, 77, 79, 108–9, 319
Ciani, Suzanne, 223, 250–51
Cinemoog, 221
Circus Maximus, 133
City Scale, 102
Clapton, Eric, 149, 151–52
Clark, Melville, Jr., 280, 281
clavinet, 156, 217
Clayton, Merry, 148
Clockwork Orange, A, xii, 275
Cockerell, David, 224
Cold War, 31, 39–40
Collins, Judy, 114, 143–44
Columbia-Princeton Electronic Music Center, 70, 81, 91, 94, 104, 110, 119, 133, 135–36, 413–14n.5
Columbia Records. *See* CBS Records: Columbia Records
Columbia University, 18, 23, 336. *See also* Moog, Bob: Education
Columbia University electronic music studio, 58–59, 65, 67, 413–14n.5
Command Records, 155–56, 170–72
Commodore 64 computer, 325
Composer-Tron, 414–15n.9
Computer Music Journal, 331–32
Congressional Record, 311
Conly, Paul, 230

Consolidated Edison Company of New York (Con Ed), 5–6, 8, 11, 25–26, 264–65
Constanten, Tom, 289–90
Constellation. *See* Luce, David; Moog, Bob: Moog Instruments/Equipment Designed By/With Bob Moog
Contemporary Keyboard (*Keyboard*), 301–2, 312, 323, 337, 372
Cooder, Ry, 148
Cooper, Alice, 270
Copper Plated Integrated Circuit, The, 170–71, 172
Coppola, Carmine, ix–x, 311–12
Coppola, Francis Ford, 311–12
Corea, Chick, 294–95, 296–97
Corman, Roger, 124
Cornell University, 23, 160, 214–16, 446n.18. *See also* Moog, Bob: Education
Coupleaux-Givelet instrument, 414–15n.9
CRI (record label), 134
Crosby, Stills, Nash & Young, 185
Crumar, 320
Cunningham, Merce, 92–94, 123
Curran, Alvin, 121–22

Dark Side of the Moon, 209–10
David Sarnoff Research Center, 69–70
Davis, Clive, 144
Davis, Richard, 220
Davis, Sammy, Jr., 153
Day, Doris, 114
Day The Earth Stood Still, The, 53
Debussy, Claude, ix, 102, 295
Dellinger, David, 215
Delos Records, 302–3, 439n.36
Dern, Bruce, 124
Detroit Free Press, 248
Deutsch, Herbert, 63–65, 108–9, 210, 310, 315, 378, 393, 419n.8; *A Little Night Music-1965*, 95; and Casio court case, 351; *Contours and Improvisations*, 65; disposition of original modular prototype, 319; *Jazz Images: A Worksong and Blues*, 74; and Jazz in the Garden, 175–76, 178–80; and MG-1, 315–17; and New York Improvisation Quartet, 96, 104; and Opus 3, 310; and Project Pulse, 239; role in invention of Moog synthesizer prototype, 65, 66, 70, 71–77, 78–79, 319, 432n.21, 441n.6; and Summer 1965 Workshop and Seminar, 94–96
Devo, 296–97, 314
DeWitt, Eugene, 354, 357, 360–61
DiLorenzo, Marylee, 350, 360
DIMI synthesizer, 265
disco, xii, 303
Disneyland, 270
DJ Spooky, 378
Dockstader, Tod, 223–24
Dolby surround sound, x
Dolenz, Micky, 118, 127–28, 163
Donovan, Tom, 244
Doolittle, Artie, 178
Doors, the, xii, 114, 125–26, 210, 422–23n.18; "Spanish Caravan," 126; *Strange Days*, 125–26, 128, 422–23n.18
DownBeat, 177, 179–80, 182, 217, 238–39
Downs, Hugh, 153
"downtown" music, 91, 101
Drews, Steve, 214, 258–59
Dr. Zhivago, 113
Dudley, Tom, 368–69
Duke University, 384
Dunnington, Steve, 338–39, 350, 361, 363–64, 367, 369, 370, 380, 382–83, 384, 389, 393, 395, 398
Dylan, Bob, 153, 207, 393

Eastman, Linda, 143–44
Eastman School of Music, 63, 159, 219
Easy Rider, 124
Eaton, John, 321–22, 339–40
Ed Sullivan Show, The, 66
EDM (electronic dance music), electro, xii; house, xii, 303–4; techno, 303; trance, 303
Einstein, Albert, 7
Electric Christmas, An (Carnegie Hall concert), 133, 204

Electric Circus, The, 120–21, 133–34
Electric Ear Series, 120–21, 133–34
Electric Flag, 124–25; *A Long Time Comin'*, 128; *The Trip* (soundtrack album), 125
Electric Hair, 221
Electric Light Orchestra, 296–97
Electric Love, 180
Electric Lucifer, 221
Electric Samurai: Switched On Rock, 277–78
Electric Symphony, The, 221
Electric Zodiac, The, 180
ElectroComp synthesizer. *See* EML (Electronic Music Laboratories, Inc.)
Electronic Hair Pieces, 180
Electronic Music from Razor Blades to Moog, 221
Electronic Sackbut, 77, 414–15n.9
Electronic Sound. See Harrison, George
Electronics, 70–71
Electronics Review, 129, 131
Electronics World, 52–53, 109, 224
Elektra Records, 114, 116, 119, 134–35, 140–41
Elektronische Musik, 57–58
Elkind, Rachel, 136, 137, 145, 183
Emelin, John, 130
Emerson, Keith, xv, 207, 213, 221–22, 230, 294–95, 367, 377; "Lucky Man," 208–10, 267; meets Bob Moog, 231; and Minimoog, 436n.19; and Modular Moog ("Monster Moog," "The Beast"), xvi, 206, 210, 268–69, 272, 277–78, 287–88, 324, 354, 436n.19; with the Nice, 135, 206–8; and ribbon controller, 287–88
Emerson, Lake and Palmer (ELP), 210, 276, 277–78, 313, 332, 367, 388–89; *Brain Salad Surgery* (album and tour), 287–88; debut album, 208–10, 231, 267; Gaelic Park concert, 267–69, 271, 436n.19; Isle of Wight Festival (1970), xvi, 210–13; "Lucky Man," 208–10, 288; *Pictures at an Exhibition*, 208, 210–11, 212, 248–49; *Tarkus*, 267; *Trilogy*, 270; *Welcome back, my friends*, 288, 388–89
E.M.I. Studios (London), 149, 168–70
EML (Electronic Music Laboratories, Inc.), 227–28, 236, 239, 358–59
Emmons, Rev. Curt, 50
EMS (Electronic Music Studios, Ltd.), 231; EMS 100, 305; Synthi 100, 266; Synthi AKS, 266; VCS3 ("Putney"), 222, 224–25, 227, 236, 257, 265, 266, 305. *See also* Zinovieff, Peter
Eno, Brian, 303
Entertainment Weekly, 292, 377
EQ, 359, 385
Erb, Donald, 158
Esquire, 217
Ether Music 2005, 386
Evans, Mal, 151–52
Every Good Boy Deserves Favour, 270
Everything You Always Wanted to Hear on the Moog, 248
Exotic Moog, 170
Experimental Music Studios, University of Illinois, 82, 104
Eye Magazine, 130

Faryar, Cyrus, 114
Fast, Larry, 296–97
Fellner, Dag, 231
Feminine Mystique, The, 97
Ferdinand the Bull, 10, 392
Fiedler, Arthur, 213
Fillmore East, 153
Financial Times, The, 363, 385
Fine, Larry, 333, 336, 340
Firebird, The, 295
Fisher, Linda, 214
Fjellestad, Hans, 378–79. *See also* Moog, Bob: Awards and Honors
Flushing Queens (New York), 4, 6, 7, 13–14, 17–18, 34–35, 38
Flying Burrito Brothers, the, 185
FM synthesis, 323–24
Folkman, Benjamin, 137, 138, 145
Fonda, Peter, 124
Forbidden Planet, 414–15n.9
Ford Motor Company, 8–9

Fornoff, Erin, 379, 390
Fortune, 48
Free Press, The (Trumansburg), 164
Free Synagogue of Flushing, 14, 17–18
Fricke, Florian, 221
Friedan, Betty, 97
Friend, David, 229, 257, 265–66, 298, 304

Galper, Hal, 178
Gandharva, 248–49
Garson, Mort, xvi, 114, 155, 156, 163, 180, 193, 248–49
General Electric Company, 8
Genuine Electric Latin Love Machine, 170, 172
Gibson guitars, 284, 285, 293–94, 299, 300, 325
Gleeson, Patrick, ix–x, 312
Globe and Mail, 358
Gnazzo, Anthony, 77
Goffin, Gerry, 127
Golden Globe Award, 312–13
Goldsmith, Jerry, 113
Good Morning America, 364–65
Gorewitz, Rubin, 123, 125
Goto, Keichi, 393
Grammy Awards, 135, 189, 368
Grams-Moog, Ileana, 349, 353, 362–63, 365, 382–83, 384–86, 387–88, 389, 390, 391–92, 393–94, 399; background, 345–46; courtship and marriage, 351–52, 356; and Judaism, 346–47, 390–92; meeting Bob, 345, 346
Grand Royal, 382
Grateful Dead, the, 102, 106–7, 109–10, 115, 117, 118, 120–21, 130, 185–86, 289–90
Great Depression, The, 4, 5–6, 9, 27, 34
Gregory, Charles, 62
Guardian, The, 213
Guitar Center, 332, 371
Gullo, Tom, 237, 263, 276–79, 284–85, 288–89, 295–96, 297, 299, 309, 314–15; background, 237; and MG-1, 315–16; and Sonic V, 237–38, 240, 263

Hair (musical), 155, 180
Hambro, Leonid, 270
Hamilton, Dave, 363
Hammer, Jan, 292, 296–97, 314
Hammond, Laurens, 22
Hammond Novachord, 8–9, 113, 414–15n.9
Hammond organ, 8–9, 22, 113, 150, 172–73, 207, 268, 272, 278, 414–15n.9
Hancock, Herbie, 372
Handel, George Frideric, 134–35, 182–83
Hanert Electrical Orchestra, 414–15n.9
Happy Moog, The, 180
Harrison, George: *Electronic Sound*, 149–52, 168, 169–70; *Wonderwall Music*, 149. *See also* Beatles, the
Harvard University, 159, 230
Harvey, Jacqueline, 79, 129–30, 143, 189, 290, 397
Hatch, Bruce, 184
Haynes, Houston, 345, 350, 357
Heathkit company, 56, 310
Heber-Percy, Victoria, 222, 224
Heckman, Don, 179–80, 182
Hell's Angels, 106–7, 109–10, 166–67, 184–85, 186, 211–12
Hemming, Ray, 158, 171–72, 173–74, 190–91
Hemsath, William, 158, 161–62, 176, 258, 362, 369, 396; and 1CA preset boxes, 176, 191–92, 205, 210; and 959 X-Y Controller, 232; and Min A, 194–96, 214, 225, 396; and Mini B, 195–96, 216; and Minimoog C, 225–27; and Minimoog D, 232–33, 234, 235, 236; and pitch and modulation wheel, 232–33
Henahan, Donal, 133–34, 144–45, 171, 173, 183–84, 304, 337
Hendrix, Jimi, 117, 118, 153, 181, 210, 211–12, 230
Henry Ford Museum, 319
Henson, Jim, 189, 325–26
Herman, Lucy Morton (daughter-in-law), 352
Herman, Ray (cousin), 41–42
High Fidelity, 121, 145
Hiller, Lejaren, 82, 120–21, 289–90

Hitchcock, Alfred, 53, 122
Hitler, Adolf, 122, 207
Hoffman, Samuel, 53–54, 163–64
Hofstra University, 63, 64, 72
Holst, Gustav, 295
Holzman, Jac, 114, 119, 134, 140–42
Hopper, Dennis, 124
Hughes, Allen, 93–94
Hunt, Chad, 191, 225–26, 362, 369
Hurok, Saul, 202–3
Huzar, John, 190–91, 196, 249
Hyman, Dick, 155–56, 170, 180; and Mini B, 219–20; "Minotaur," 172, 219, 220; *MOOG: The Electric Eclectics of Dick Hyman*, 155–56, 172, 220

"I Feel Love," xii, 303–4
I Remember Yesterday, 303
In a Wild Sanctuary, 221
In den Gärten Pharaos, 248–49
In Sound From Way Out, The, 156
Indiana University, 321, 322
Invocation of My Demon Brother, 167
Ironside, 125
Island of Electronicus. *See* Van Koevering, David
Isle of Wight Festival (1970). *See* Emerson, Lake and Palmer
Ithaca Journal, 66–67, 89, 95, 159, 164, 166, 181–82, 215–16, 249, 256

Jacobs, Max [Szymanski] (grandfather), 5, 9
Jacobs, Rebecca [Szymanski] (grandmother), 5
Jagger, Mick, 147–48, 166–67, 184, 185–86
Japan, 51–52, 323, 369, 373, 376–77; as competitor to Moog instruments, xiv, 278–79, 290, 295, 314, 323–24, 337; and electronic music technology, 89, 278; Icograda World Congress (Nagoya), 374; *karoshi*, 279; respect for Bob in, 295; and transistor technology, 50–51, 278
Jarre, Maurice, 113
Jefferson Airplane, 102, 117, 185

Jewish News, The, 157
John, Elton, 295, 316, 362
Johnny Carson Show, The, 53–54
Johnson, J. J., 164
Jones, Brian, 118, 148, 166–67
Jones, Hank, 178, 179–80
Jones, Quincy, 125
Joplin, Janis, 102, 117, 153

Kakehashi, Ikutaro, 278–79, 290
Kalehoff, Edd, 287
Kaleidoscopic Vibrations, 156, 270
Kavina, Lydia, 386
Kawai Musical Instruments Manufacturing Company, 278
Kaye, Carol, 114
Kehew, Brian, 358–59, 363, 370–71
Kelischek, George, 87–88, 286; and Bob's acoustic guitar, 274–75
 Brasstown workshop, 273–74
Kemp, Jack, 311
Kennedy, Robert F., 120
Kennedy, Ted, 165–66
Kesey, Ken, 106–7
Ketoff, Paolo, 321
Killer, 270
King, Carole, 127
King Crimson, 208
Kingsley, Gershon, 156, 171, 180–81, 193, 213–14, 217, 221, 268, 270, 271, 272, 276, 279, 358, 378, 390; background, 156–57; and "First Moog Quartet" Carnegie Hall concert, 202–5, 213, 229; *Kaleidoscopic Vibrations*, 156, 270; *Music to Moog By*, 157, 171; "Pop Corn" ("Popcorn"), 157, 204, 270–71; *Shabbat ' 69 (Shabbat for Today, Shabbat Now)*, 157, 175, 390
Kirby, Wayne, 337–38, 363, 373–74, 379–80, 393
Klein, Allen, 147, 152
Kock, Winston, 22
Kohler, Bill, 249, 257–58, 271
Kooper, Al, 118
Korean War, 25, 63
Korg, Inc., 290

Koussa, Joseph (son-in-law), 342–43, 344, 352–53, 368, 394
Kraftwerk, xii, 303
Kramer, Gregory, 340
Krause, Bernie, ix–x, 148–51, 155, 170, 172–73, 175, 221, 248–49, 312; background, 140, 422–23n.18; and George Harrison's *Electronic Sound*, 149–51, 152, 168; and *Nonesuch Guide to Electronic Music*, 140–42, 150, 422–23n.18
krautrock, xii, 221
Krebs, Khatia, 344–45, 347, 349, 350
Krebs, Rick, 344–45, 349, 350
Kurstin, Pamelia, 376–77
Kurzweil Music Systems, 326, 327–28, 336–37, 341–42; Kurzweil 250 (K250), 326, 327, 331–32
Kurzweil, Ray, 326, 331–32

Lake, Greg, 208–10, 212–13
Lance, Cyril, 381–82, 384, 385, 393; background, 381; assumes Chief Engineer position at company, 397–98, 399
Lanier, Tom (son-in-law), 342–43
Lapidus, Jennifer, 391–92
Lawrence, Arnie, 220
Lebzelter, Shipen, 143–44
Le Caine, Hugh, 77, 82, 414–15n.9
Lees, Gene, 145
Leigh, Ben (father-in-law), 34, 38, 41, 42, 333
Leigh, Lillian (mother-in-law), 34, 40, 333
Leigh, Matthew, 34, 198
Lennon, John, 152, 157, 168, 169, 319. *See also* Beatles, the
Life, 173
Ligeti, György, 207
Lincoln Center, 90, 92–93, 154–55, 175, 238–39
Linhard, Rudi, 370–71, 445–46n.14
Lomax, Jackie, 149, 150
Long Island Press, 193
Lopez, Ken, 117–18
Los Angeles Times, 163, 292
Lothar and the Hand People, 130, 175, 193, 230, 269

Louisville Orchestra, 59
Love, Mike, 108
Lowrey organ, 155–56, 284, 324–25
LSD, 106–7, 109–10, 115, 120, 124, 134
Lucas, George, ix
Luce, David, 82, 283, 284, 292–94, 299, 316, 325, 396–97; and Apollo (polyphonic synthesizer), 280, 281, 295–96; background, 280; and Constellation, 281, 287–88, 295–96; and Polymoog, 295–96, 297; as President of Moog Music, 315; purchase of Moog Music, 325; sale of company to EJE Research Corporation, 341–42; and Taurus pedals, 281, 295–96
Luening, Otto, 58–59, 66, 67, 69, 70, 134, 135–36
Luther, Kathy, 276–77
Luther, Roger, 276–77, 281, 313–14, 354, 360–61; background, 276–77

MacDowell, Edward, 15
Maestro brand, 220, 293–94, 299
Maginnis, Bill, 105–6
Magnetic Monster, The, 113
Mahavishnu Orchestra, 178, 292
Mamas & the Papas, the, 117
Mandel, Johnny, 113, 125
Manhattan Project, 31
Manhattan School of Music. *See* Moog, Bob: Education
Manning, Roger, 358–59
Manny's Music, 257, 354
Manson, Charles, 168
Manzarek, Ray, 114, 125–26
Marchese, Tony, 281, 309–10, 316
Margouleff, Bob, 269–70
Marks, J., 143–44
Martin, Don, 354, 357, 359, 360–61, 364
Martin, George, 170
Martin, Steven M., 355
Massachusetts Institute of Technology (MIT), 23, 280, 332
Mathews, Max, 92–93, 280–81, 285
Mauzey, Peter, 67, 81, 413–14n.5

McCartney, Paul, 143–44, 147, 149, 157, 168–69, 170, 362. *See also* Beatles, the
McClure, John, 143–44, 170
McCornack, David, 339
McGuinn, Roger, 118, 128, 152
McKechnie, Doug, 184, 185
McKinsey & Company, 315, 396
McLaughlin, John, 178
Melody Maker, 231
Melvoin, Mike, 114
Merry Pranksters, The, 106–7
Mickey Mouse Club, The, 53–54
MIDI (Musical Instrument Digital Interface), 323, 324, 325, 364, 370–71, 375
Midnight Cowboy, 174
Mike Douglas Show, 183
Milano, Dominic, 301–2
Mills College, 110, 140
minimalism, 143, 221
Minimoog. *See* Moog, Bob: Moog Instruments/Equipment Designed By/With Bob Moog
Mitchell, Joni, 211–12, 362
Mixtur-Trautonium, 122. *See also* Sala, Oskar; Trautonium
Monkees, the, xii, 118, 126–28, 131; "Daily Nightly," 127–28; *The Monkees* (TV show), 127, 128; *Pisces, Aquarius, Capricorn, & Jones, Ltd.*, 127–28; "Star Collector," 127–28
Monterey Herald, 118
Monterey International Pop Music Festival (1967), 117–18, 422–23n.18
Monteverdi, Claudio, 182–83
Moody Blues, the, 224, 270
MOOG, BOB (ROBERT ARTHUR)
—AUDIO ENGINEERING SOCIETY (AES), 422–23n.18; 1964 AES (introduction of original prototype synthesizer), 79, 80–82; 1967 AES (Los Angeles), 111–12, 291; 1968 AES (presentation of *Switched-On Bach*), 142; 1970 AES (introduction of Minimoog C), 227; AES Fellow, 181
—AWARDS AND HONORS, 1970 Grammy (NARAS Trustees Award), 189; 2002 Technical Grammy Award, 368; AES Fellow, 181; Billboard Trendsetter Award, 189; Bob Moog doll, 376; *Eureka!* exhibit, 310–11, 317, 319; *Moog* (documentary film), 378–79; Moogfest, 377, 386; Polar Music Prize, 362; RockWalk, 332–33; SBA, 200, 397; University of the Arts, 374–75; *The Visionaries* (film), 286; Warner Bros. Gold Record, 270
—CHILDREN, 54–55, 60, 123, 197–99, 258, 286, 288, 300–1, 306
—EARLY YEARS, birth, 4; electronic measuring device, 13–14; electronic organ, 20; family heritage, 3–5; geiger counter, 20; ham radio, 19, 27; Moogatrons, 23; Parsons Avenue home, 6; piano lessons and playing, 9–10, 11, 12, 15, 17; RAMCO, 26; scouting, 13–14, 17–18, 25; theremins, 20, 22, 23
—EDUCATION, Air Force ROTC, 25; Alpha Phi Omega (APO), 25, 30; Bronx High School of Science, 17, 22, 23–24; Columbia University, 25, 35, 48, 67, 70, 413–14n.5; Cornell University, 35–36, 37, 38, 39, 45–47, 52, 54, 55, 59–60, 62, 70, 92, 138, 205, 381; Manhattan School of Music, 11, 15, 17; P.S. 24, 10–11, 12–13, 15–16; Queens College, 25, 28, 30, 42
—FINAL ILLNESS AND DEATH, xvii, 382–94, 397
—FINANCIAL DIFFICULTIES, 29, 61, 66, 76, 80, 82–83, 84–85, 86, 87, 89–90, 97, 108, 111, 123, 171, 191, 192–93, 196–97, 200, 221–22, 225, 233–34, 235, 238–41, 256–57, 291, 300, 318–19, 322, 325–26, 327–28, 332, 333, 336, 337, 339, 340, 343, 344, 350–51, 360, 361–62, 365, 367–69, 371, 395–96, 397, 399–400

MOOG, BOB (ROBERT ARTHUR) (cont.)
—FINE WOOD AND INSTRUMENT CRAFTSMANSHIP, xv, 26, 29, 47, 52, 76, 81, 85–86, 88, 108, 190, 192–93, 195, 196–97, 226–27, 272–73, 274, 280–81, 313–14, 332, 339, 351, 361, 363, 376
—GARDENING AND NATURE, 17–18, 45, 60, 62, 83, 129, 264–65, 273–74, 275, 300, 301, 307, 312–13, 368
—AND HIRING, 158–59, 191, 283, 350, 396–97
—AND ILEANA GRAMS, 349, 373–74, 375, 377–78, 382–83; background, 345–46, 353 courtship and marriage, 351–53, 356; and Judaism, 346–47; meeting, 345, 346
—LECTURES AND WORKSHOPS, 66, 142, 339, 376–77; 1964 AES ("Voltage-Controlled Electronic Music Modules,"), 82; 1967 AES (Los Angeles), 112; 1968 AES (presentation of *Switched-On Bach*), 142; 1970 AES (introduction of Minimoog C), 227; Acoustical Society of America, 131–32; Bourges Festival, 432n.21; Bourges Festival (meets Leon Theremin), 339; Brasstown workshop, 273–74; Icograda World Congress (Nagoya), 374; Summer 1965 Workshop and Seminar, 94–95, 98, 221; University of Alaska, Anchorage, 383; Washington University in St. Louis, 275; Young Presidents' Organization, 241
—MOOG COMPANIES:
—1954–1963 R. A. MOOG CO. (Queens Ithaca), 27–30, 33, 46–48, 49, 50, 51–53, 54, 55, 56, 57, 341–42; established as legal entity, 28
—1963–1971, R. A. MOOG CO. (Main St., Trumansburg), 60–63, 66, 76, 80, 89–90, 96, 108, 110–11, 123, 125, 129–30, 136, 146–47, 158–59, 175–76, 181–82, 190–96, 198, 200, 201, 202, 213, 221–22, 225–27, 230, 231, 235, 238–41, 248–49, 256–59, 278, 282, 283, 321, 395–96, 422–23n.18; atmosphere, 61, 74, 89–90, 94, 158, 160, 190, 191–92, 194, 225, 258–59, 349–50; Challenge Industries, 159; *Electronic Music Review*, 108–9, 133, 160–62; First Synthesizer Catalog (1967), 110–11, 121; incorporation, 139; Independent Electronic Music Center (shop studio back-room studio), 111, 146, 158, 159, 160–62, 166, 217; *Moog Music* (newsletter), 56, 57–58, 59, 83–84; takeover by William Waytena, 196–97, 200, 240–41, 249–50, 256–57, 286
—1971–1973, MOOG MUSIC, INC. (Academy St., Williamsville), 249, 256, 258, 263–64, 265–67, 271–73, 275–79, 280–86, 299; atmosphere, 263–64, 266–67, 277, 279, 299; Bob's difficulties at company, 252–53, 264, 274, 277, 278–79, 280, 281–82, 284, 285–86, 288–89, 292–94, 295–96, 297–98, 301–2; Maestro Moog, 276; Moog Musonics, Inc., 249, 265; sale of company to Norlin/CMI, 284–85
—1973–1976, MOOG MUSIC, INC. (Academy St., Williamsville, under Norlin), 288–89, 290, 292–95, 437n.24
—1976–1977, MOOG MUSIC, INC. (Walden Ave., Cheektowaga, under Norlin), 295–98, 337; Bob's difficulties at company, 300, 301; move to Walden Ave., 299–300
—1978–1993, BIG BRIAR, INC. (Big Briar Cove), 318, 319, 320, 332, 333, 336, 337, 339; controllers, 320; establishment of, 310, 318; Heathkit, 306; Kurzweil consultancy, 326–27; logo, 320; Multiply-Touch-Sensitive Keyboard (MTS), 321–22, 336, 339–40; restoration of modular prototype, 319; Series

91 theremins, 339, 345, 355; Spirit (Crumar), 320
—1978–1983, MOOG MUSIC, INC. (Walden Ave., Cheektowaga, under Norlin), 309–10, 313–14, 324–25, 367; contract manufacturing, 314–15; Lowrey organ fiasco, 324–25; SL-8, 322–24
—1984–1987, MOOG ELECTRONICS (Walden Ave., Cheektowaga, under Luce and Chapman), 325; company purchase by Luce and Chapman, 325; *Moog Telecommunications*, 325; sale to EJE Research Corporation, 341–42; Sanctuary Synthesizer (Memorymoog), 334–35; subsidiary: Moog Music, 325
—1987–1993, EJE RESEARCH CORPORATION/ELECTRONIC TECHNOLOGY GROUP (ETG) (Walden Ave., Cheektowaga and Jamestown), 341–42; liquidation of Moog inventory, name, and trademark, 341–42, 354; Moog Custom Engineering, 341, 354; Moog Music Manufacturing (Jamestown, under ETG), 342; purchase of Moog Electronics, 341
—1994–2002, BIG BRIAR, INC. (554-C Riverside Drive, Asheville), 355, 359, 361–64, 365, 368–69, 439n.36, 445–46n.14; establishment of facility, 349–50; Series 91 theremins, 350, 355, 357; Voyager, 367
—2002–2005, MOOG MUSIC, INC. (554-C Riverside Drive, Asheville), 368–69, 370–73, 375; Adams assumes leadership, 369–70; Voyager, 368–69, 70–73, 375–76, 377, 380, 381–82, 383, 384, 385, 386, 388, 394, 397–98, 399–400
—2005–2011, MOOG MUSIC, INC. (2004 Riverside Drive, Asheville), 382, 397–98
—2011–present, MOOG MUSIC, INC. (160 Broadway St., Asheville), 399; as employee-owned company, 399

—MOOG INSTRUMENTS/ EQUIPMENT DESIGNED BY/ WITH BOB MOOG:
—acoustic guitar, 274
—Big Briar Controllers: 100 Series Keyboard Controller, 320; 300 Series Touch-Sensitive Plate, 320, 370–71; 500 Series Theremin-type Controller, 320
—Constellation, 281, 287–88, 295–96
—Guitar Interface, 271–72, 276
—high-gain differential amplifier, 121–22
—interactive antennas (for John Cage), 90, 91–94, 129, 156
—"junk" amplifiers, 89–90, 94, 108, 109
—Lab Series amplifier, 300
—Little Phatty, 382, 398
—Lyra, 281, 295–96
—Maestro phase shifter pedal, 293–94
—Maxolin, 280–82, 285
—microtonal polyphonic performance instrument, 90
—Min A, 194–96, 214–16, 220, 283, 396; Bob's reaction to, 195, 290; and David Borden, 214
—Mini B, 195–96, 216, 225–26, 238; Bob's reaction to, 196; and Dick Hyman, 219–20; and Sun Ra, 217–19
—Minimoog C, 225–27, 231, 232
—Minimoog D (development of production model), 232–33, 234, 235–36
—Minimoog, xvi, 221, 225, 236, 238, 242–43, 244–46, 249–50, 251–52, 253–58, 265, 288, 292–93, 297, 311, 314, 324, 357, 362, 365, 367, 369, 398, 434–35n.12, 436n.19, 446n.18; end of production, 313–14; Martin copies of ("Donnimoogs"), 359, 360–61; popularity with musicians, 292–93; Winter copies of, 360
—Model 400 amplifier, 29
—Modular Synthesizers, xiv, 129, 204–5, 213, 221, 225, 249, 295, 303, 321, 357, 430n.21, 446n.18; 901

MOOG, BOB (ROBERT ARTHUR) (cont.)
  Voltage-Controlled Oscillator, 96, 194–95; 902 Voltage-Controlled Amplifier, 96; 905 Reverberation Unit, 192; 921 series oscillator, 271–72; 951 keyboard, 194; Arturia Moog Modular V, 372; frequency shifter, 282, 283; ladder filter, 181, 190, 224, 229, 279, 290, 316; ladder filter dispute with ARP, 283, 298–99; modular prototype ("Abominatron"), xiii, 65, 66, 70–79, 129, 416n.26, 432n.21, 441n.6; polyphonic generator for Wendy Carlos, 138; polyphonic synthesizer for Peter Nero, 122; ribbon controller (stringer, slide-wire, linear controller, Melsinar), 85–86, 108, 128, 287–88, 354; sequencers, 152, 154–55, 158, 223–24, 236, 419n.8; Synthesizer I, 111; Synthesizer II, 111; Synthesizer III, 111, 112, 114, 117, 127, 143–44, 147–48, 149, 152, 154, 269; Synthesizer 10, 193–94, 202, 205, 214, 241, 244, 271–72; Synthesizer 12, 271–72; Synthesizer 15, 288
—Moog-MRS, 191
—moogerfooger, 361–62, 370; MF 101 Lowpass Filter, 361; MF 102 Ring Modulator, 361
—Moogtonium, 122–23
—Multiply-Touch-Sensitive Keyboard (MTS), 321–22, 333, 339–40
—Percussion Controller, 271–72, 276
—PianoBar, 375–76
—PMS-15 portable hi-fi amp kit, 61, 62, 66, 83–84, 337
—Satellite, 272–73, 290, 292–93
—Sonic Six, 272, 288, 293
—Spirit (Crumar), 320
—Theremins, 339; Ethervox, 361, 382; Etherwave, 355, 382, 386; Etherwave Pro, 376, 393; Melodia (and kit), 51–53, 54, 55, 56, 60–61, 62, 63, 80, 84, 202, 355; Model 201, 26–28, 86; Model 305, 28–29, 32–33; Model 351, 28–29, 30–31; Professional, 46, 48–49, 51–52; Series 91 theremins, 339, 345, 350, 355, 361; Troubador, 61, 130; Vanguard, 46, 47, 48–49, 63, 355
—Van Koevering Interactive Piano, 364–65
—vocoder, 191
—Voyager, 363–64, 367–69, 370–73, 375, 378, 382, 383, 398
—MOOG INSTRUMENTS/ EQUIPMENT/PRODUCTS NOT DESIGNED BY/WITH BOB MOOG:
—1CA preset boxes, 176, 191–92, 205, 210, 276–77
—Alpha Probe, 314–15
—Apollo, 281, 295–96
—Chexx tabletop hockey game, 325
—Concertmate MG-1 (Radio Shack Realistic MG-1), 315–17; Bob's reaction to, 317
—Liberation, 309–10, 357
—Memorymoog, 314, 322–23, 325, 334; LAMM upgrade (Lintronics), 445–46n.14; Memorymoog Plus, 324; Sanctuary Synthesizer, 334–35
—Micromoog, 292–93, 296
—Minitmoog, 292–93
—Multimoog, 309
—Opus 3, 310
—Polymoog, 295–98, 299, 309, 357; Bob's reaction to, 297–98
—Prayer Times Clock, 314–15
—Prodigy, 309, 315–16, 357
—Rogue, 316, 325, 357
—Sanctuary Synthesizer (see Memorymoog)
—SL-8, 322–24
—Song Producer, 325
—Sonic V, 237–38, 249, 257, 265, 271
—Source, 314, 325, 357
—Taurus pedals, 281, 295–96, 334; Taurus II pedals, 325
—MOOG NAME, as brand name, xii, 95–96, 240, 249, 265, 271, 279, 280, 292, 297–98, 305, 309, 310,

317, 441n.6; as generic, 171, 204, 231, 304–5, 360, 397; logo, 84; pronunciation of, 4, 15, 26, 46, 170, 221, 255, 295
—MOOG TRADEMARK BATTLE, 357–58, 359–60, 364, 365, 367, 368–69, 446n.18; liquidation of Moog inventory, name, and trademark, 341–42, 354, 360–61
—MUSICIANS' UNION ISSUES, 132, 170–74, 242, 331–32
—PERSONAL QUALITIES, xii, 10–11, 12–13, 17–18, 23–24, 25, 29–30, 40, 46, 57, 62, 63, 85, 89, 90, 92, 97, 115, 122–23, 130, 131, 132, 138, 144, 146, 171, 195, 199, 233, 235, 258–59, 282–83, 301, 332–33, 337–39, 343, 346, 349, 370, 376, 377, 378–80, 381–82, 385–86, 391–92, 395, 396–97, 419n.8
—POLITICS, 18–19, 39–40, 308, 370; volunteer work for ACLU, 338
—PUBLICITY AND APPEARANCES, 55, 129–30, 143, 144, 145, 146, 171, 231, 253, 286, 287, 288, 289–90, 294, 364–65, 374–75, 376–77, 397; 2004 Moogfest, 377, 386; *Imoogination*, 294–95; *Imoogination* (Japan), 295; Jazz in the Garden, 1, 175–80, 302; performance in *Little Shop of Horrors*, 379; *To Tell the Truth*, 287; *Today Show*, 153; US Festival, 326–27
—RELATIONSHIP TO AUNT FLORENCE, 18–19, 37, 38–39, 46–47, 52, 55, 57, 59–60, 62, 109, 199
—RELATIONSHIP TO FATHER, 11–12, 18–20, 25–26, 274–75, 349
—RELATIONSHIP TO MOTHER, 4, 6–7, 9–10, 12–13, 17, 18, 29–30, 33, 35–36, 45–46, 349, 365–66, 367
—RELIGIOUS LIFE, 38–39, 307–9; Ethical Culture, 38–39, 41, 42, 45; Judaism, 13–15, 17–18, 23–24, 38, 307–8, 346–47, 352–53, 356, 379
—RESIDENCES, Barnard Avenue (Asheville), 345–46, 352; Bethel Grove apartment, 45; Big Briar Cove house, 306–7, 310, 322, 327–28, 331, 332, 337, 338, 340–41, 344, 347–48, 349–50, 355, 360, 361–62; Cayuga St., Trumansburg, 83; East Aurora house, 299–301; King St., Trumansburg, 62; Natick house, 327–28, 331; North Carolina land purchases and sales, 301, 318–19, 322, 325–26, 340, 344; Trumansburg farmhouse, 129, 258, 264–65; Williamsville house, 264–65
—AND REVIVAL OF ANALOG SYNTHESIZERS, 358–59
—ROCKMORE ALBUM, 302–3
—AND SHIRLEIGH (SHIRLEY MAY LEIGH), 286, 338, 353, 393; conflicts with, 198–99, 300–1, 327, 340–41, 342–43, 344, 377–78; courtship and marriage, 30, 33, 35–36, 37–38, 39, 40–42; separation and divorce, 344, 345, 347, 348–50, 352, 353–54, 355, 360
—SPIRITUAL AND EMOTIONAL LIFE, 205, 274–75, 289–90, 344–45, 347, 349, 352–53, 360, 365–66, 370, 371–72, 373–75, 378, 380, 383, 391–92
—TEACHING, 52; Cornell, 240; UNCA, 337–39
—VIEWS ON MOOG RECORDINGS AND ARTISTS, 115, 142, 146–47, 165, 170, 171–72, 221, 248, 268–69, 292
—WORK FOR KURZWEIL MUSIC SYSTEMS, 327–28, 331–32, 333, 336–38
—WRITINGS, 27–28, 30–31, 92, 108–9; announces MIDI, 323; on *Apocalypse Now*, 312; *Contemporary Keyboard* (*Keyboard*), 301–2, 312, 323, 337, 372; "Electronic Music—Its Composition & Performance," 109, 224; "On Synthesizers" series, 301–2; "Voltage-Controlled Electronic Music Modules," 104, 432n.21

Moog, Florence (aunt), 4, 18–19, 35, 37, 38–39, 41, 46–47, 52, 55, 57, 59–60, 62, 80, 89, 92, 94, 95, 97, 109, 130–31, 235, 264, 275, 289–90, 306, 307, 308–9, 322, 325–26, 328; background, 18–19, 171, 199; financial support of Bob, 47, 84–85, 86, 322, 327–28, 331, 333, 336, 339, 340, 344; final illness and death, 335–36, 385–86; religious views, 38–39

Moog, Freda Ott (grandmother), 4, 18, 84–85

Moog, Georg Conrad (great-grandfather), 4

Moog, George Alfred (grandfather), 4

Moog, George Conrad (father), 4–5, 42, 94, 139, 264–65, 336, 349, 385–86; basement workshop, 6–7, 14–15, 20, 26, 177, 274, 275; death of, 347–48; engineering work, 6, 25–26; marriage to Shirley Jacobs, 5

Moog, Jacob (great-great-grandfather), 3

Moog, Laura (daughter), 54–55, 60, 98, 288, 300–1, 318–19, 335, 342–43, 356, 388–89, 390, 391, 392–93

Moog, Matthew (son), 197–98, 199, 301, 306, 308, 318–19, 328, 352, 383–84, 385, 389, 390, 391, 392–93, 398–99

Moog, Michelle [Michelle Moog-Koussa] (daughter), xii, 129, 300–1, 306, 307–8, 309, 318–19, 326–27, 336, 340–41, 342–43, 344, 352–53, 361, 383–84, 385–86, 389, 390, 391, 392, 393, 394, 398–99

Moog, Renée (daughter), 60, 288, 300, 318–19, 335, 341, 342–43, 378–79, 382–83, 384–85, 389, 390, 391, 392, 393

Moog, Shirleigh [Shirley May Leigh] (wife), 30, 45–46, 49, 50, 54, 55, 60, 65, 80, 84–85, 89, 92, 97–98, 109, 129, 130–31, 161, 176, 225, 231, 233, 264–65, 277, 288, 300, 302, 306, 318–19, 322, 332, 333, 336, 337–38, 340–41; *A Guide to the Food Pyramid*, 340–41; background, 34; and children, 52, 54–55, 56, 60, 123, 129, 197–99, 258, 348; conflicts with Bob, 76, 98, 198–99, 327, 340–41, 342–43; and cooking, 45, 83, 84, 95, 97, 98, 307–8, 312–13, 338; courtship and marriage, 33–36, 37–38, 39; Crestmont Ave. home (Asheville), 348; experiences with anti-Semitism, 34, 38, 301; *Moog's Musical Eatery*, 313, 345, 358; nature and gardening, 45, 60, 62, 83, 129, 264–65, 273–74, 275, 300, 301, 306, 307, 312–13, 338; Queens College, 30, 33, 34, 41; as real estate salesperson, 333; separation and divorce, 344, 348–50, 352, 353–54, 355; suicide attempt, 300–1; teaching, 45, 50, 52, 54, 60, 98; work for company, 54, 61, 76, 83, 95, 97, 98, 198, 249, 343, 348

Moog, Shirley Jacobs (mother), 5–7, 42, 94, 177, 264–65, 336, 341, 349; bequest to Bob, 348, 355; death of, 347–48; Judaism, 5, 13, 14–15, 356; marriage to George Moog, 5; relationship to Shirleigh (Shirley), 33, 35

Moog!, 221

Moog and Guitars Play ABBA, 305

Moog at the Movies, 305

Moog Cookbook, 358–59; *Moog Cookbook, The*, 358–59; *Ye Olde Space Band*, 358–59

Moog España, 170, 221

Moog Groove, 170, 189

Moog Indigo, 221

Moog Mass, A, 221

Moog modular synthesizers. *See* Moog, Bob: Moog Instruments/Equipment Designed By/With Bob Moog

Moog Music, Inc. *See* Moog, Bob: Moog Companies

Moog Musonics, Inc. *See* Moog, Bob: Moog

Companies: 1971–1973, Moog Music, Inc.; Waytena, William
Moog Plays the Beatles, 170–71
Moog Power, 170
Moog Rock, 170
Moog Strikes Bach, 180
MOOG: The Electric Eclectics of Dick Hyman. *See* Hyman, Dick
Moogfest (2004, 2005), 377, 386
Moogie Woogie, 221
Moogseum, 399
Moore, Frankie, 345, 347, 349
Moraz, Patrick, 294–95
More Switched On Bacharach, 221
Morita, Akio, 51
Morley, Rocky, 211, 212, 287–88
Moroder, Giogio, 303–4
Morrison, Jim, 126, 210
Moses, Bob, 178
Mother Mallard's Portable Masterpiece Company. *See* Borden, David
Mothersbaugh, Mark, 314
Motown Records, 130–31, 140, 269
Mouillot, Julien, 386–88, 390
Mozart, Wolfgang, 66
Murch, Walter, ix, x
Museum of Modern Art, New York (MoMA), 205; 1969 Jazz in the Garden, xi, 175–80, 203, 210, 219–20, 302
Music Educators National Conference (MENC), 221–22, 225
Music for Sensuous Lovers, By "Z," 248
Music Merchandising Review, 359
Music of My Mind. See Wonder, Stevie
Music Out of the Moon, 53–54
Music Teachers National Association (MTNA), 87–88, 273
Music to Moog By, 157, 171
Music Trades, 265–66
Musica Elettronica Viva, 121–22
Musical Quarterly, The, 223–24
musicians' union, xi, 153, 172–74. *See also* Moog, Bob: Musicians' Union Issues
musique concrète, 57–58, 65, 77, 81, 91–92, 93, 95, 102–3, 221, 222

Musonics, Inc. *See* Waytena, William
Mussorgsky, Modest, 208, 213, 295
My Brother the Wind. See Sun Ra

NASA, 103, 163–64
Nashville Gold—Switched On Moog, 221
National Association of Music Merchandisers (NAMM), 130, 251–53, 257, 265, 273, 284, 296, 316, 322–24, 325–26, 333, 362, 363, 364–65, 382
National Observer, 146–47, 170, 173
NBC television, 32, 153
Nero, Peter, 122, 147
Nesmith, Mike, 127
New Musical Express, 207, 208
New Sound Element: "Stones," 116
New York Daily News, The, 64, 65, 230, 304
New York Herald Tribune, The, 58–59
New York Philharmonic, 59, 93, 144
New York Post, 179
New York Pro Musica, 133
New York Research Group, 90, 96, 122–23, 200
New York State School Music Association (NYSSMA), 63–64, 240
New York Times, The, 59, 69, 86–87, 93–94, 123, 130–31, 133, 144–45, 146, 153, 155, 171–72, 173–74, 177, 179, 182, 183–84, 186, 205, 220, 265, 304, 337, 378, 390, 397, 399
New York University (NYU), 336
New York World's Fair (1939–40), 7–9, 34
New Yorker, The, 64, 65, 204–5, 304
Newsweek, 131, 317, 318
Nice, the, 135, 206; *Ars Longa Vita Brevis*, 206; Royal Festival Hall concert, 207; with Royal Philharmonic Orchestra, 207–8
Nikolais, Alwin, 81, 85, 86–87, 89, 95, 104, 108, 121, 337
Nitzsche, Jack, 148
No Exit, 41
Nonesuch Guide to Electronic Music, The, 140–42, 150, 422–23n.18
Nonesuch Records, 119, 121, 134–35, 140–41, 422–23n.18

Nord, Nathaniel, 12–14, 15
Norlin Corporation, 304, 396, 437n.24;
    background, 284; demise, 324–25;
    Lowrey organ fiasco, 324–25.
    See also Moog, Bob: Moog
    Companies: Moog Music, Inc.,
    [1971–1973; 1973–1976; 1976–
    1977; 1978–1983]
Numan, Gary, 296–97

Oakland Tribune, 110
Ochs, Phil, 215
Offord, Eddie, 208
Ohio University, 228
Oliveros, Pauline, 101–2, 105–6, 110, 120–
    21, 140, 143
Olson, Harry F., 82
ondes martenot, 414–15n.9
ondioline, 156
Ong, Dale, 319, 320
Ono, Yoko, 152
Oram, Daphne, 414–15n.9
Oramics composition machine, 414–15n.9
Orange County Register, 339
Orange Peel, The, 386, 392–93
oscillator, 8, 48, 58, 64, 69–70, 71, 72–73
Ott, Emma (great aunt), 41, 47
Owsley (Augustus Owsley Stanley III),
    106–18, 185

Paderewski, Ignace, 9
Padorr, Al, 182, 190
Paik, Nam June, 92–93
Pakkala, Don, 233
Pallenberg, Anita, 148
Palmer, Carl, 208–9, 268
Pasadena Star-News, 305
Paul, Les, 293–94, 300, 332
PDP-8. *See* Zinovieff, Peter
P.D.Q. Bach (Peter Schickele), 135, 142
Peacock, Annette, 182, 238–39
Pearl drums, 284, 285
Pearlman, Alan Robert, 251, 283, 298, 318;
    background, 228–29; development
    of ARP 2500, 229–30. *See also* ARP
    Synthesizers
Peel, John, 213
Performance (film), 148

Perkins, Dave, 350
Perrey, Jean Jacques, 156, 221, 358;
    Kaleidoscopic Vibrations, 156, 270
Philadelphia Daily News, 395
Philadelphia Inquirer, 331–32
Philadelphia Orchestra, 144
Piano & Keyboard, 340
Pictures at an Exhibition. See Emerson,
    Lake and Palmer; Mussorgsky,
    Modest; Tomita, Isao
Pilhofer, Herb, 304
Pinch, Trevor, xvi–xvii, 372, 446n.18
Pink Floyd, 209–10, 213, 295
Pirone, Jim, 178
Planets, The, 295
Plastic Cow Goes Moooooog, The, 170
Playboy, 153, 304
Plimpton, George, 120
Point Blank, 125
Polyphony, 351
Polytechnic Institute of Brooklyn, 5–6
Polytone, 8–9, 414–15n.9
"Pop Corn," 157, 204, 270–71
"Popcorn," (Hot Butter), 270–71
Popul Vuh, 221, 248–49
Popular Electronics, 20, 197
Portnoff, Cora, 41–42, 45
Powell, Roger, 294–95
Presley, Elvis, 278
Preston, Billy, 168
Preston, Don, ix–x, 312
Princeton University, 23, 70
Progressive, The, 18–19
Psychedelic Percussion, 116
Pulin, Chuck, 268

Queens College, 25. *See also* Moog,
    Bob: Education; Moog, Shirleigh

Rachmaninoff, Sergei, 11, 15, 21
Radio and Television News, 20, 27, 52
Radio City Music Hall, 63
Radio Cologne, 58, 65
Radio Corporation of America (RCA),
    8–9, 69–70
Radio News, 20
Radio Row, 19–20
Radio Shack, 315–17

Radio-Craft, 8–9
Radiodiffusion Francaise (Paris), 58, 65
Ragnarök, 170
RCA Mark I synthesizer, xiii, 69, 82
RCA Mark II synthesizer, xiii, 69–70, 75, 81, 82, 110–11, 145, 173
RCA Records, 130–31, 134, 180, 295
RCA theremin, 27, 29, 31, 62, 113, 201–2, 204–5, 339
Reasoner Report, The, 279
Record World, 144, 170–71
Redding, Otis, 117
Reinagel, Fred, 238, 263, 272
Reisenberg, Nadia, 302–3, 439n.36
Revenge: "The Bigger The Love The Greater The Hate," 238–39
Rhea, Tom, 322–23, 338, 439n.36; and Spirit (Crumar), 320
ribbon controller. *See* Moog, Bob: Moog Instruments/Equipment Designed By/With Bob Moog: Modular Synthesizers
Rich Stadium (Buffalo), 288, 388–89
Richards, Emil, 112, 114, 116
Richards, Keith, 147–48
Richmond, Bob, 346, 384
Richmond-Mouillot, Miranda (stepdaughter), 346–47, 351–52, 384, 385–88, 389, 390–92
Rifkin, Joshua, 134–35
Rifkin, Mary Ellen, 365, 367, 368, 385
Riley, Terry, 143, 144; *In C*, 143, 144
Ritter, Dick, 158, 190
Robb, John Donald, 221
Rock and other Four Letter Words, 143–44
Rockefeller Foundation, 70, 103–4, 110, 413–14n.5
Rockmore, Clara, 22, 31; debut on theremin, 21–22, 52–53; *Clara Rockmore: The Greatest Theremin Virtuosa* (videocassette), 439n.36; *Shirleigh and Robert Moog present Clara Rockmore* (LP), 302–3; *The Art of the Theremin* (CD), 439n.36
Roland Corporation, 278, 358–59; SH-5, 305; SH-1000, 290; SH-2000, 290
Rolling Stone, 126, 152, 172–73, 180–81, 186, 190, 217, 294, 304

Rolling Stones, the, 89, 118, 147–48, 166–67, 184–86, 206
Roosevelt, Franklin, 6, 7
Rossini, Gioachino, 68, 204
Rothchild, Paul, 126
Rothenberg, David, 90, 96, 122–23, 200
Royal Festival Hall, 207, 221–22
Royal Philharmonic Orchestra, 207–8
Rozsa, Miklos, 53
Rudin, Andrew, 134, 193
Runyon, Don, 280, 281–82, 284, 285
Rzewski, Frederic, 121

Sack, Henri, 92
Sainte-Marie, Buffy, 148
Sala, Oskar, 122
Sam Ash music store, 257–58
San Francisco Conservatory of Music, 101
San Francisco Examiner, 181
San Francisco Tape Music Center, 101–7, 110, 143
Santa, Lee, 218
Satie, Erik, 289–90
Saturday Review, 153
Satyricon, 193
Scarlatti, Domenico, 182–83
Schaeffer, Myron, 77
Schaeffer, Pierre, 58, 64
Schlesinger, Arthur, Jr., 120
Schonberg, Harold, 59, 130–31, 133, 146, 153, 186
Schultz, Ernest J., 20, 22, 27
Scientific American, 18
Scott, Jim, 191–92, 202, 258, 263, 293, 362, 369, 396, 434–35n.12; and Micromoog, 292–93, 296; and Minimoog C, 225–26, 227; and Minimoog D, 232–33, 234, 235; and Multimoog, 309; and Spirit (Crumar), 320
Scott, Raymond, 32–33; Clavivox, 32–33, 105, 164; sequencer, 419n.8
Sear, Walter, xv, 90, 108, 130, 154–56, 170–71, 176–77, 180, 182, 189, 206, 219, 236, 378; background, 63; and 'junk' amplifiers, 89–90, 108, 109; as sales rep for R. A. Moog, 63, 109, 119, 123, 139–40, 171–74, 190, 238–39

Seawright, James, 81
Segovia, Andrés, 108
Seley, Jason, 64–65
Sender, Ramon, 101–5, 106–7, 110
Sequencer, 105. *See also* Moog, Bob: Moog Instruments/Equipment Designed By/With Bob Moog: Modular Synthesizers
Sesame Street, 189
Shank, Bud, 114
Shankar, Ravi, 117, 149, 362
Shapiro, Gerald, 228, 230
Shaughnessy, Ed, 220
Sheldrake, Rupert, 373–74
Sherk, Warren M., 422–23n.18
Sherman, Robert, 439n.36
Short Circuits, 248–49
Sibelius, Jean, 207
Siday, Eric, 82–83, 85–86, 89, 94, 104, 108, 112, 140, 147, 157, 238, 276–77, 319, 374
Siegel, Vernon, 196–97, 200, 229
Silver Apples of the Moon. See Subotnick, Morton
Simon, John, 132
Simon, Paul, 118, 204
Simon & Garfunkel, 117, 181, 278; "Save The Life Of My Child," 132
Slick, Grace, 102
Small Business Administration (SBA), 76, 198, 200, 310–11, 397
Solar-Myth Approach, The. See Sun Ra
Sonic V. *See* Moog, Bob: Moog Instruments/Equipment/Products Not Designed By/With Bob Moog
Sony Corporation, 51
Sound on Sound, 362, 372–73
Sound Recorder Studios, 149
Sounds, 268
Spacecraft, 121–22
Spaced Out, 170–71
Spatz, Estelle (aunt), 28, 49, 383
Spatz, Ronald (cousin), 383
Spellbound, 53
Sperry-Rand Corporation, 48
Stanford University, 323–24
Starr, Ringo, 149, 169. *See also* Beatles, the

State University of New York at Albany (SUNY), 223
State University of New York at Buffalo (SUNY), 191, 283, 289–90
Stearns Collection of Musical Instruments, 337
Steiner, Nyle, ix–x, 312
Stephanz, Nicoletta, 387–88, 393
Stevens, Norton, 284
St. Louis Post-Dispatch, 155, 180–81, 275, 279
St. Louis Symphony, 182–83
Stockhausen, Karlheinz, 58, 59, 66, 108–9, 121, 126, 134, 135, 143–44, 146–47, 258, 362
Stone, Sly, 211–12
Storytone electric piano, 8–9
St. Petersburg Times, 242, 246
Strassberg, Susan, 124
Stratton-Smith, Tony, 206
Stravinsky, Igor, 265, 295
Subotnick, Morton, 101, 110, 133, 143, 144; and Electric Circus, 120–21; and San Francisco Tape Music Center, 101–5; *Silver Apples of the Moon*, 119–21, 134; *The Wild Bull*, 223–24
Suchora, Jim, 354, 357, 367; Moog Music Technology, Inc., 354
Summer, Donna, 303–4
Summer of Love, 116–17, 124
Sun Ra, 216, 248–49; background, 216–17; and Mini B, 217–19, 258; *My Brother the Wind*, 217, 218; *Nuits de la Fondation Maeght*, 219; *Solar-Myth Approach, The*, 248–49; *Space Is the Place*, 218–19
Swansen, Chris, 165, 166, 173, 191, 202, 210, 215–16, 286; background, 165; and Jazz in the Garden, 175–76, 178–79
Swansen, Meg, 165
Swickard, Ralph, 111–12, 113–14
Swingle Singers, The, 135
Switched-On Bach. See Carlos, Wendy: *Switched-On Bach*
Switched-On Bacharach, 170
Switched On Blues, 221

Switched-On Buck, 248–49
Switched-On-Country, 221
Switched-On Gershwin, 221, 270
Switched-On Nashville, 180
Switched-On Rock, 170
Switched On Santa!, 180
Switched-On Switzerland, 305
Sylvester, Paul (son-in-law), 389, 390
Synket, 321
Syntronic Organ, 8–9, 414–15n.9
Syracuse Herald-American, 146

Taco Bell, 241–42
Talking Book, 270
Tangerine Dream, xii, 270
Tanner, Paul O. W., 107–8
Tarkus, 267
Taylor, Derek, 151–52
Tchaikovsky, Pyotr Ilyich, 21
Teitelbaum, Richard, 121, 175
Telharmonium, xiii, 67–69, 414–15n.9
Ten Years After, 210
theremin (musical instrument), xiii, 20–22, 51–54, 376–77. *See also* Moog, Bob: early years: theremin projects; Moog, Bob: Moog Instruments/Equipment Designed By/With Bob Moog: theremins; RCA theremin
Theremin, Leon (Lev Sergeyevich Termen), 28, 302, 339, 355, 386, 414–15n.9; Bourges Festival, meets Bob Moog, 339; espionage work, 22, 31; invention of theremin musical instrument, 21
Theremin: An Electronic Odyssey, 355
Thomas Organ Company, 273, 284–85
Time, 58, 108, 140, 155, 414–15n.9
To Our Children's Children, 224
To Tell the Truth, 287
Today Show, The, 153
Tomita, Isao, *Electric Samurai*, 277–78; *Pictures at an Exhibition*, 295; *Snowflakes are Dancing*, ix, 277–78, 295, 311–12
Tone Synthesizer (Bell Labs), 22–23, 414–15n.9
TONTO synthesizer, 269, 270

Tork, Peter, 128
Tormé, Mel, 114
Toubab Krewe, 388, 393
Town Hall (New York City), 21, 96, 104, 135, 182, 238–39
Townsend, Pete, 265–66
transistor technology, 48–49, 50–52, 71
Trautonium, 122
Trautwein, Friedrich, 122
Trident Studios (London), 149
Trilogy, 270
Trinity Church, 214
Trip, The (film), 124–25
Trip, The (soundtrack album), 125
Trips Festival, 106–7, 109–10, 116, 244, 246
Trocco, Frank, xvi–xvii, 372
Trubey, Les, 242–43, 253, 265
Trumansburg, New York, 61, 95, 131, 164–65, 181–82, 191, 216; Rotary Club, 66
Truth or Consequences, 53–54
Tudor, David, 92–93, 94, 313
Tureck, Rosalyn, 175
Twain, Mark, 68
2001: A Space Odyssey, 144, 154, 207

Unitarian Universalist Church (Asheville), 341, 342–43
United States Information Agency (USIA). *See Visionaries, The*
University of Alaska Anchorage, 383
University of California at Berkeley (UC Berkeley), 103–4, 191, 223, 250
University of Chicago, 340
University of North Carolina Asheville (UNCA), 337–39, 345–46, 350
University of Pennsylvania, 134, 198
University of the Arts, 374–75
University of Toronto Electronic Music Studio (UTEMS), 76–78, 79
Updike, John, 304
Updike, Ray, 265
UPI, 173, 180–81
"uptown" music, 91, 101, 104, 143
Urbaniak, Michael, 296–97
US News & World Report, 358
Usher, Gary, 128

Ussachevsky, Vladimir, 58–59, 64, 66, 67, 69, 70, 75, 81, 94, 119, 131, 134, 135–36, 145, 173, 319, 413–14n.5

vacuum tube, xiii, 48, 414–15n.9
Van Koevering, Becky, 201–2, 334–35
Van Koevering, David, 202, 203, 204, 309, 357, 363–64, 365, 374, 375–76, 393; background, 201–2, 374; Island of Electronicus (Tierra Verde), 243–47, 249, 253; and Moog PianoBar "Kingdom Edition," 375–76; as sales rep for Moog instruments, 242–46, 253–58, 265, 272, 275–76, 285; and Sanctuary Synthesizer, 334–35; school shows, 203, 205–6, 213, 221–22, 224; and Taco Bell, 241–42; Van Koevering Interactive Piano, 364–65; and Williamsville plant (Academy St.), 263–64, 276–77
Variety, 178, 179
VCS3 ("Putney"). *See* EMS (Electronic Music Studios, Ltd.)
Verdi, Giuseppe, 138
Very Merry Electric Christmas To You!, A, 180
Vexations, 289–90
Vickers, Mike, 168, 206–7, 208, 210, 429–30n.20
Vietnam war, ix–x, 95, 158, 198, 211, 311–73
Visionaries, The, 286
Voder, 8
Vogue, 189
voltage control, 71–72

Wagner, Richard, 138
Wakeman, Rick, 292, 294–95, 296–97, 377, 378
Walborn, Rich, 314–15, 396; and ARP 2600 filter, 283; background, 283; and Liberation, 309–10; and Memorymoog, 314; and MG-1, 315–17; and Prodigy, 309; as roadie for ELP, 287–88, 354; and Rogue, 316; and SL-8, 322–24
Warner Bros., 148, 270

Washington Post, 376–77
Washington University in St. Louis, 18, 275, 335, 336
Way Out, 63
Waytena, William, 196–97, 200, 251, 271–72, 273, 276–79, 293, 369–70; background, 197; departure from Moog Music, 288–89, 437n.24; Moog Electronic Music, Inc., 237; Moog Musonics, Inc., 249, 265; Musonics, Inc., 237; sale of Moog Music to Norlin/CMI, 284–85; and Sonic V, 237–38, 240; takeover of R. A. Moog, 196–97, 200, 240–41, 249–50, 256–57, 286; Venture Technology, 236–38, 266; and Williamsville plant (Academy St.), 263, 264, 266–67, 271–72, 280, 281–82
Weidenaar, Reynold, 108–9
Weir, Bob, 118
Weiss, Jon, 146–48, 159, 166, 167, 178, 216, 217, 218
Welcome back, my friends. See Emerson, Lake and Palmer
Well-Tempered Synthesizer, The. e Carlos, Wendy
Westphal, Arnold Carl, 49–50
White, Joshua, 153
White, Ruth, 248–49, 295
Who, the, 117, 210, 213
Whole Earth Catalog, 181
Wild Bull, The. See Subotnick, Morton
Wilson, Jacques, 114, 155
Wilson, John S., 220
Winter, Alexander, 357, 360–61, 373
WNCN Radio, 96
Wolfe, Tom, 120
Wonder, Stevie, xii, 265–66, 326, 332, 362; discovery of Moog synthesizer, 269; *Music of My Mind*, 270
Woodstock Festival, 184, 186, 210
Worell, Bernie, 378
World War II, 9, 34, 50–51, 112–13, 263–64
Worley, August, 367, 368–69, 370, 380
Wozard of Iz, The, 155, 156

Wright, Gary, 314
Wurlitzer organs, 242–43, 272; Orbit III, 273
Wurman, Hans, 180, 221

XLR8R (magazine), 373

Yale University, 23, 229, 413–14n.5
Yamaha Corporation, xvi, 278, 290; DX-7, xvi, 323–24, 325–26, 334
You Asked for It, 53–54
Young Chang, 337, 341–42
Young Presidents' Organization (YPO), 241
Your Hit Parade, 32

Zappa, Frank, xv, 213, 282, 312
Zapple Records, 150, 151–52
Zeit, 270
Zero Time, 269
Zinovieff, Peter, 231; background, 222, 224; and PDP-8, 222, 224, 231; and VCS3 ("Putney"), 222, 224–25
Zodiac Cosmic Sounds, The, 113–16, 119, 155, 180, 422–23n.18
Zumchak, Eugene, 158, 197, 236–37, 240, 271–72, 332, 339; and sequencer, 158, 236; and Sonic V, 237–38, 263, 271–72; and Synthesizer 10, 193–94, 202, 236, 271–72